Teaching in the Middle and Secondary Schools

TENTH EDITION

Jioanna Carjuzaa

Montana State University, Bozeman

Richard D. Kellough

California State University, Sacramento

PEARSON

Boston   Columbus   Indianapolis   New York   San Francisco   Upper Saddle River
Amsterdam   Cape Town   Dubai   London   Madrid   Milan   Munich   Paris   Montréal   Toronto
Delhi   Mexico City   São Paulo   Sydney   Hong Kong   Seoul   Singapore   Taipei   Tokyo

Acquisition Editors: Kelly Villella Canton
Editorial Assistant: Annalea Manalili
Associate Editor: Anne Whittaker
Project Manager: Karen Mason
Production Coordination: Element LLC
Photo Coordinators: Annie Fuller and Mike Lackey
Cover Design Coordinator: Diane C. Lorenzo
Cover Design: Jennifer Hart
Cover Image: Images.com
Director of Marketing: Darcy Betts Prybella

For related titles and support materials, visit our online catalog at www.pearsonhighered.com.

Between the time Web site information is gathered and then published, it is not unusual for some sites to have closed. Also, the transcription of URLs can result in typographical errors. The publisher would appreciate notification where these errors occur so that they may be corrected in subsequent editions.

Library of Congress Cataloging-in-Publication Data
Carjuzaa, Jioanna.
  Teaching in the middle and secondary schools / Jioanna Carjuzaa,
Richard D. Kellough. – 10th ed.
    p. cm.
  Richard D. Kellough listed as first author on 8th and 9th editions.
  Includes bibliographical references and index.
  ISBN-13: 978-0-13-269620-3 (alk. paper)
  ISBN-10: 0-13-269620-7 (alk. paper)
 1. High school teaching–United States. 2. Middle schools--United
States. I. Kellough, Richard D. (Richard Dean) II. Title.
  LB1737.U6C27 2012
  373.1102--dc23
                                              2012006602

Printed in the United States of America
10 9 8 7 6 5 4

ISBN-13: 978-0-13-269620-3
ISBN-10: 0-13-269620-7

Brief Contents

Contents

PART 4 Assessment of Teaching and Learning 293

CHAPTER 11 Assessing and Reporting Student Achievement 293

Preface

As its primary purpose, this textbook provides a practical, concise, criterion-referenced, performance-based, mastery learning model for college or university students who are in a general secondary or middle school methodology course or in the field component of teacher education. The chapter and part organization of this textbook shows instructors of methods courses how to provide enough basic instruction that they can individualize their instruction and devote their time and attention to specific learning activities. Others who will find this textbook useful are experienced middle and secondary teachers who desire to continue developing their teaching skills and curriculum specialists and school administrators who desire to have a current, practical, and concise book of methods about teaching for reference. In fact, many educators have added this textbook to their professional libraries.

New to This Edition

- Chapter Two, **Middle and Secondary Schools Today and Tomorrow: Reform Efforts, Challenges and Issues, and Trends and Practices,** is new to this edition and examines the changing nature of school reform, fundamental characteristics of exemplary education including 21st-Century Skills, Response to Intervention, and Differentiated Instruction, and the challenges, problems, and issues that face schools today.

- Chapter Seven, **Designing Lesson and Unit Plans to Engage All Students,** is new to this edition and emphasizes the importance of learning how to design lesson and unit plans that respond to the needs of all students.

- In keeping with the book's title, an improved balance of content between middle and secondary schools emphasizes the middle school as uniquely different from both the high school and the traditional junior high school.

- A multicultural education philosophy is infused throughout the book with an emphasis on meeting the needs of diverse learners and promoting educational equity and social justice.

- New technologies appear in chapters and chapter features.

- New features, including Teaching Scenarios, Activities, and Lesson Plans, were added.

- New contributions from pre-service and in-service middle and secondary school teachers, teacher educators, and educational scholars and researchers have been added to strengthen the tie between theory and practice.

- Updated Internet references and resources appear in every chapter.

- Lesson and unit plans from a variety of disciplines have been included. Updates from former contributors have also been added, as have descriptions of the contributors' educational journeys and extensions to their lesson and unit plans.

- New activities allow students to expand their knowledge on relevant topics and issues.

- New exercises are provided for students to complete outside of the classroom.

Throughout the book, we consistently provide information useful for teachers and the numerous decisions they must make on a daily basis. How best to integrate technology is infused throughout the book. Meaningful Teaching Scenarios highlight challenges that middle and secondary school classroom teachers face. We also provide frequent exercises and in-class activities for practice in handling concepts in ways that facilitate metacognitive thinking. All exercises and activities require the user to deal in some descriptive, analytical, or self-reflective manner with text concepts and actual practice. Most exercises and in-class activities are adaptable for cooperative or collaborative group processing.

The book is organized around four developmental components: *why*, *what*, *how*, and *how well*. The developmental components can be described in the following manner: *why*—the rationale to support the components that follow; *what*—what you will be teaching; *how*—how you will teach it; and *how well*—how well you are teaching it. These components are represented by the four parts of the book. The four parts and the chapters that make up each one are described in the following paragraphs.

Part 1, "Introduction to Teaching and Learning in Middle and Secondary Schools," contains three chapters that were written to reflect the reality and challenge of teaching today—to provide the rationale, or the *why*, to support the organization and details of the components that follow. Chapter 1 presents an important overview of the historical evolution of secondary education and introduces the purpose, organization, and structure of our schools, Chapter 2 covers a variety of current trends and practices in our schools and the problems, challenges, and issues facing educators and plaguing the education system today; it also looks at projected trends. Chapter 3 addresses developments in cognitive science and constructivism that enhance and celebrate the differences among students and their learning styles and capacities. It provides specific guidelines for meeting the challenge with specific groups of learners.

Part 2, "Planning for Instruction," is made up of four chapters designed to reflect the *what* component. Because teachers must have students' attention before they can effectively implement any instructional plan, guidelines for establishing and maintaining a psychologically and intellectually safe and supportive learning environment are presented in Chapter 4. Along with providing important rationale and guidelines for selecting and using content and textbooks and preparing instructional objectives, Chapter 5 focuses on what you are going to teach by reviewing information about the national standards for subject areas across the curriculum. It also introduces the planning process by focusing on preparing instructional objectives. Chapter 6 provides information on the design of syllabi and disclosure documents along with the use and preparation of various types of units and guidelines for writing cognitive, affective, and psychomotor instructional objectives. Chapter 7 provides a model lesson plan and goes into the details of how to create engaging lesson plans that integrate technology and meet the needs of diverse learners. It contains numerous examples of lesson and unit plans for middle and high school students in a variety of subject areas. The lesson and unit plans were contributed by middle and high school pre-service teachers, novice and veteran in-service teachers, teacher educators, and others.

Part 3, "Selecting and Implementing Instructional Strategies," addresses the *how* component and consists of three chapters. Chapter 8 on student-centered instructional strategies, focuses attention on grouping students for learning, using assignments, ensuring equality in the classroom, using project-centered teaching, and writing across the curriculum. Chapter 9, which focuses on teacher-centered instructional strategies, provides guidelines for using teacher talk, demonstrations, thinking, inquiry, and games.

Intricately interwoven with teaching and learning is the teacher's use of fundamental classroom tools (e.g., writing board, overhead projector, and bulletin boards) and the selection and use of printed materials and visual displays, resources, networks and educational technology, media tools, and computer-based instructional tools. The use of all these tools and aids to create engaging lesson and unit plans to meet the needs of diverse learners is the focus of Chapter 10, the final chapter of Part 3.

Part 4, "Assessment of Teaching and Learning," includes two chapters and focuses on the fourth component of competent teaching—*how well* the students are learning and how well the teacher is doing. Chapter 11 examines the assessment of what students know or think they know before, during, and after the instruction. The chapter also provides practical guidelines for parent-teacher collaboration and for grading and reporting student achievement. Chapter 12, an important chapter for student users and sometimes studied first, provides an emphasis on how well the teacher is doing—the assessment of teaching effectiveness as well as guidelines and resources for ongoing professional development. Chapter 12 also provides guidelines and resources for student teaching and for finding a teaching position. These guidelines—and this book in general—have proven to be useful as references for years beyond the current methods course.

Features of the Text

- Teaching Scenarios provide an assortment of meaningful examples from middle and secondary school.
- Sample Lesson and Unit Plans demonstrate educators' creativity in using a multitude of tools and technology to diversify instruction to meet the needs of all students.
- In-class Activities support key concepts and highlight supplemental material.
- Revised Exercises for active learning are found at the end of each chapter. The exercises are designed to have the student continually assess his or her progress in the understanding and skill development of teaching and involve the candidates in active and collaborative learning. (*Note:* Because some exercises necessitate a visit to a school to have dialogue with students and staff, exercises should be reviewed early so that you can plan your visits and work schedule. In fact, because certain exercises build on previous ones or suggest that help be obtained from teachers in the field, we advise that all exercises be reviewed at the beginning of the course. Because it is unlikely that all exercises could [or should] be completed in a one-semester course, you will have to decide which exercises will be done.)
- Performance assessment rather than paper-and-pencil testing of teaching skills development is encouraged by the micro peer-teaching exercises found in Chapters 2, 7, and 12. Indeed, Exercise 12.2 is a useful performance assessment to use at the conclusion of this course.
- The Short-Explanation and Essay Questions at the end of each chapter have been revised and can serve as an assessment of the chapter and as springboards for further discussion.
- Answers to Self-Check Exercises 5.7, 5.8, 5.9, 5.10, 9.2B, and 9.3 have been grouped together and can be found at the end of the book in the Answer Key.

- To promote mastery learning, we employ a competency-based chapter format. Each chapter contains (a) an opening list of specific learning objectives (or learning targets) for that chapter, (b) a presentation of content as related to those objectives, (c) an integration of practice and reinforcement in each chapter, and (d), at the completion of the chapter, a posttest assessment of how well the opening targets have been achieved.

New! CourseSmart eTextbook Available

CourseSmart is an exciting new choice for students looking to save money. As an alternative to purchasing the printed textbook, students can purchase an electronic version of the same content. With a CourseSmart eTextbook, students can search the text, make notes online, print out reading assignments that incorporate lecture notes, and bookmark important passages for later review. For more information, or to purchase access to the CourseSmart eTextbook, visit www.coursesmart.com.

Supplements

Instructor's Manual/Test Bank and PowerPoint Slides

An Instructor's Manual to accompany this book has been provided by the authors to assist teacher educators with using this book for their courses. This manual includes the following for each chapter: key terms, chapter outline, list of exercises, and supplemental classroom activities. The Instructor's Manual also includes a **Glossary** of terms, additional Suggested **Readings** for each chapter, **Posttest Questions** and their corresponding answers, and additional **Short-Explanation and Essay Questions.** PowerPoint slides are also available for every chapter.

The Instructor's Manual/Test Bank and PowerPoint Slides may be downloaded from the Instructor Resource Center at the Pearson Higher Education website (http://www.pearsonhighered.com). Your local Pearson representative can help you set up a password for the Instructor Resource Center.

Acknowledgments

Although teaching and learning in middle and secondary schools has become increasingly complex—with many new and exciting things happening as schools continue to restructure their efforts to provide the best learning for today's youth—we strive to keep the text at a reasonable length and to keep it user friendly. We thank all the persons who helped in its development. We thank those who contributed and who are acknowledged at appropriate places throughout, as well as our friends, colleagues, preservice and in-service teachers, undergraduate and graduate students, and the highly competent professionals at Pearson who have maintained their belief in and support for this textbook.

In our preparation of this 10th edition, we carefully heeded the recommendations made by users and reviewers of the previous edition. We acknowledge and offer a sincere thank-you for the cogent reviews and recommendations made by Ruth Ference, Berry College; Meryl Greer Domina, Northern Illinois University; W. Dean Marple, St. Ambrose University; and Kristi Planck Johnson, Marymount University.

Although this edition is the result of the contributions of many professionals, we, as always, assume full responsibility for its shortcomings. Our aspiration for this 10th edition is that it will spark reflective thinking about your teaching and that you will find it stimulating and professionally rewarding

A special thanks goes out to a remarkably dedicated teacher, Anastasia Sunday, for her contributions to this textbook. We would also like to thank the following educators who contributed syllabi, disclosure documents, teaching scenarios, lesson plans, rubrics, and other work. Their names are listed here in the order in which they appear in the textbook: Dorothea M. Susag, Dr. Holly Hunts, Dr. Xaé Alicia Reyes, Jim Bryngelson, Daniel Blanchard, Scott E. Taylor, Paul Andersen, Joyce Jarosz Hannula, Paula Maguire, Ryan Hannahoe, Peter Detterline, Kathy Klipstein, Dr. Stephanie Standerfer, Colby Carruthers, Leslie Jackson, Dan Burfeind, Hillary Stacey, Megan Hamilton, Roger Aguirre Lopez, Mike Jetty, Dr. James Loewen, Dr. Nivea Lisandra Torres, Dr. Melanie A. Reap, Jennifer Norton, Jordanne Nevin, Erin Pleiman, Chantal Gee, Heather Tyler, Tony Coppola, Rob Baither, Adam Rudolph, Abderrahman Ouarab, Dr. Lynn Kelting-Gibson, Jennifer Devine Pfeifer, Dennis Devine, Eileen Kugler, and Tina Storer.

CHAPTER ONE

Courtesy of the Library of Congress

Middle and Secondary Schools in the Past:
Purpose, Organization, Structure, and Reform

If we value independence, if we are disturbed by the growing conformity of knowledge, of values, of attitudes, which our present system induces, then we may wish to set up conditions of learning which make for uniqueness, for self-direction, and for self-initiated learning.[1]

—**CARL ROGERS**

Specific Objectives

At the completion of this chapter, you will be able to:

▸ Define and differentiate middle schools and secondary schools.

▸ Describe the purpose, organization, and structure of the various schools at the middle and secondary school levels.

▸ Describe similarities and differences between the exemplary middle school and the traditional junior high school.

▸ Explain the educational opportunities of various subgroups in the past.

Chapter 1 Overview

In this chapter we will define secondary schools and discuss the development of high schools, junior high schools, and middle schools. Our reasons for reviewing the milestones in the secondary school movement and the many variables that affect the teaching-learning process today are simple: to be a competent teacher, you must not only know *how* schools are designed to facilitate student learning but also understand *why* an eclectic teaching style is the best way for you to meet the varied needs of *all* your students. To accomplish this goal, you need to have an understanding of the historical context of our pluralistic society. The material in Part 1 provides a foundation of middle and secondary schools and students that will help you select the appropriate instructional strategies and techniques presented in subsequent chapters.

Introduction

Because schools are microcosms representative of the complexity of the larger society, the rapid and dramatic demographic changes occurring in the United States today are reflected in our middle and secondary schools. In addition, recent discoveries about the teaching and learning process influence our pedagogy. Consequently, the school in which you soon will be teaching most likely will differ dramatically from the secondary school from which you graduated—in its curriculum, its student body, its methods of instruction, and even its physical appearance. Before we go any further, let us define what is meant by the term **secondary school**. Then we will briefly review the inception and growth of secondary and middle schools in the U.S. We will also highlight the key issues driving the recent middle and secondary education reform movements.

Middle and Secondary Schools

A *secondary school* is any school that houses students in some combination of what traditionally have been known as grades 7 through 12. However, because **middle schools**, which may begin with students in the sixth and even fifth grades, as discussed later in the chapter, usually house students through the eighth-grade level, we use both terms—*middle school* and *secondary school*—in this book's title and throughout the text. Although the evolution of these schools is covered in detail in foundations courses, we will take a quick look at when and how secondary schools came to be. We will also describe transitional schools by highlighting how junior highs and middle schools differ.

Colonial Education: The First Schools

This brief evolution of the history of education in the U.S. differs from the historical perspective presented in foundations courses or other methodology textbooks in that a multicultural approach addressing issues of equality is infused throughout. That being said, we felt compelled to highlight how inequities based on race, ethnicity, socioeconomic status, religion, gender, and linguistic ability have plagued our educational system from its inception. It is important to point out that before Columbus arrived in the New World and "discovered" America, many Indigenous peoples already populated this continent. Little was known about the pre-Columbian Americas until recent findings in a variety of research fields confirmed that the early inhabitants were, in fact, culturally advanced. Still, little is shared about their early teachings in our history books or in descriptions of the evolution of education in the U.S.

Even if we start our discussion with colonial education, it becomes evident that many of the same issues we currently face in our schools were controversial from the beginning. Even though the separation of church and state in schools is protected by law today, religion played a key role in education in colonial New England. The Puritans, having been persecuted for their religious beliefs in England, were determined to secure the power of their church by providing their children with an education grounded in their Protestant beliefs.

Education started in the home where parents were responsible for overseeing their children's moral development and teaching them how to read the Bible. As the vocational and other skills young people needed became more specialized, **dame schools** formed.[2] Women dedicated to teaching reading, writing, and basic math skills started these schools in their homes where they prepared youngsters for a fee.

After finishing one to three years of study, boys would complete an apprenticeship to master a trade. From the beginning, everyone did not benefit from the same educational opportunities—a reality that many argue persists today. Socioeconomic status determined opportunity; the wealthier the family, the more desirable the apprenticeship the boys could choose. Some efforts to educate the disadvantaged did take place but were minimal. Gender differences also existed. After one or two years of reading and writing basics, girls focused on homemaking skills. Race and religion dictated educational opportunity as well. African Americans and American Indians were prohibited from seeking an education. As more religiously diverse settlers came to the New World, several religious schools were founded so that parents could exercise control over their children's religious instruction.

Colonial education varied tremendously. In an effort to standardize the education students received, legislators in Massachusetts checked in on masters training apprentices and parents who were homeschooling their children. Once towns grew to more than 50 households, the inhabitants were required by law to hire a teacher. When the town doubled in size, they had to establish a secondary school. Local control determined the curriculum, and property taxes funded the schools.

The Advent of Secondary Education: The Forerunners of Today's High Schools

The early secondary schools fell into one of three categories: **Latin grammar schools**, **academies**, and **English classical schools**.[3] The first secondary school was established in Massachusetts. Boys of poorer families, females, and nonwhite children had limited educational opportunities. However, for the children of the privileged class who were expected to pursue a university education, attending elementary school was considered inadequate preparation. To meet the needs of these wealthier students, the first secondary schools were founded.

Latin Grammar Schools

In 1635, only 15 years after the Puritans arrived in America, the Boston Latin Grammar School opened. In the Latin grammar schools, young boys between 7 and 14 years of age received an education focused on the classics. During the seven to eight years students spent in these secondary schools, they mastered Latin. After they graduated from one of these prep schools, the students were expected to attend college to pursue a career in politics or the ministry. One year after the Boston Latin Grammar School was founded, Harvard College was established to prepare ministers.[4] As colonies were established along the eastern seaboard and more individuals completed an elementary education, more secondary schools and colleges were established.

Academies

More than 100 years after the first Latin grammar school was established, a new kind of private secondary school, the academy, opened. The first of its kind, the Franklin

Academy, bears the name of its founder, Benjamin Franklin. Established in Philadelphia in 1751, this school's curriculum was free of religious influence and much more practical in its offerings than what the standard Latin grammar school curriculum included. The academies prepared students for a number of fields. Students could select from a variety of courses including such electives as "mathematics, astronomy, athletics, navigation, dramatics, and bookkeeping."[5] These schools charged tuition like the Latin grammar schools, but the majority of these private academies welcomed both girls and boys. The academies became very popular, and over 6,000 were established. Still there were limited options for children of middle- or working-class families.

Horace Mann is credited with reforming education and leading the effort to establish formal, free public education for *all* students. He attempted to promote moral development and encourage tolerance by educating the masses, which were representative of tremendous socioeconomic, religious, and ethnic diversity. Although initially it impacted only elementary education, the concept of a free public education spread to **normal schools** (schools designed to prepare teachers for the public elementary schools) and then to secondary schools. Mann believed in a humane, practical education that would better prepare individuals to enter the workforce and participate in a democratic society. The spread of the Common School Movement went hand in hand with westward expansion.[6]

English Classical Schools: The First American Public High Schools

A third secondary school model, the English grammar school, provided a free public education for all students. The English Classical School, later renamed the English High School, first opened in Boston in 1821. These high schools offered a practical curriculum including courses in everything from navigation to foreign languages. In fact, boys enrolled in the English grammar schools often studied to become mechanics and merchants. Five years after the boys' school was founded, a public high school for female students was established in the same city, but the girls' high school remained open for only two years; students were eager to attend, but taxpayers were reluctant to foot the bill. See Table 1.1 for the evolution of middle and secondary schools.

Funding for Public Secondary Education

Most of the other secondary schools that were established throughout the nation in the early 1800s charged tuition and fees and shared little resemblance to the public secondary schools of this century. Just as the Deluder Satan Act required Massachusetts residents to financially support elementary education as early as 1647, new legislation in 1827 required that communities with more than 500

families establish publicly funded high schools.[7] With some local financial support, public high schools spread, although slowly at first. By 1860, there were approximately 40 public high schools in the U.S. Then, in 1874, the Kalamazoo, MI, case[8] provided state governments with the ability to levy taxes to support high schools; by 1900, there were over 6,000. Public high schools continued to open; in the 1930s, there were approximately 4 million high school students. By the 1960s, that number increased to over 10 million students. By 2005, there were more than 14 million students in America's high schools.[9]

The Creation of Junior High Schools

Even with an expanded education, all students' needs were not being met by the elementary-secondary school configuration. Although intermediate schools were established on the East Coast at the beginning of the 20th century, the first notable junior high school was founded in Berkeley, CA, in 1909.[10] Its curriculum resembled the discipline organization of the traditional high schools. In fact, junior highs were established to help prepare students for the academic rigor demanded of them as high school students. Junior high schools, initially housing students in grades 7, 8, and 9, sprang up throughout the country. These in-between schools caught on; by 1930 there were over 2,000 junior

Table 1.1	The Evolution of Middle and Secondary Schools in the United States
1620	Puritans arrive in America Colonial education—homeschooling and dame schools Secondary education
1635	Boston Latin Grammar School opened
1636	Harvard University established
1751	Franklin Academy opened in Philadelphia
1821	The English Classical School opened in Boston
1826–1828	The English High School for Girls opened for two years
1860	Forty public high schools in the United States
1900	Over 6,000 high schools in the United States
1905	Intermediate schools including seventh and eighth grades were established in New York City
1909	First junior high school opens in Berkeley, CA
1915	Ninth grade added to intermediate schools
1930s	4 million high school students in the United States; over 2,000 junior highs established
1940s–1950s	Comprehensive high schools gain popularity
1950s	Middle school movement begins
1960s	10 million high school students in the United States
1970s	8,000 junior highs
2003–2004	16,500 public high schools
2005	Over 14 million high school students in the United States
2006–2007	26.1 million secondary students in the United States
2010	Total P–12 students public and private: 55,350,000 Total P–8 students in public schools: 34,730,000 Total 9–12 students in public schools: 14,657,000

Table 1.2	Summary of Differences Between Junior High Schools and Middle Schools	
	Junior High School	**Middle School**
Most common grade span	7–8 or 7–9	6–8
Scheduling	Traditional	Flexible, usually block
Subject organization	Departmentalized	Integrated and thematic; interdisciplinary; usually language arts, math, science, and social studies
Guidance/counseling	Separate advising by full-time counselor on individual or "as-needed" basis	Adviser-advisee relationship between teacher and student within a home base or homeroom
Exploratory curriculum	Electives by individual choice	Common "wheel" of experiences for all students
Teachers	Subject centered; grades 7–12 certification	Interdisciplinary teams; student centered; grades K–8 or 6–8 certification
Instruction	Traditional; lecture; skills and repetition	Thematic units; discovery techniques; "learning how to learn" study skills
Athletics	Interscholastic sports emphasizing competition	Intramural programs emphasizing participation

highs, and in the 1970s there were over 8,000.[11] Some felt the junior highs were the answer to bridging elementary and high school education and making the transition of the students "caught in the middle" easier (see Table 1.2).

The Creation of Middle Schools

Forty years after the first junior high schools were established, middle schools, created to better meet the unique academic and psychosocial needs of pre- and early adolescents, gained popularity. Schools at the middle level have a specialized mission, structure, and organization. Middle schools expanded the seventh- to ninth-grade span of the junior high schools to include fifth and sixth graders. When the awarding of Carnegie Units became a popular way to determine credit earned toward graduation from high school, the ninth-grade link to grades 10 to 12 was emphasized.[12]

Some combination of grades 5 through 8, interdisciplinary teaching teams, integrated curriculum, age-appropriate student-centered instructional strategies, block scheduling, and teacher advisory programs are the foundation of the middle school philosophy and characterize today's middle schools. Middle schools were designed to nurture students' developmental needs by providing a community atmosphere and helping students to make a smooth transition between elementary and secondary school. Debates continue as to whether middle-grade schooling should focus on the students' academic or affective development. While many agree that we need to nurture adolescent well-being, raising the level of academic performance remains the key focus.[13]

The Changing Purpose of Education

The primary role of high schools has been disputed for years. Although today as a nation we aspire to provide all children with equal educational opportunities so they can reach their social and academic potential, this egalitarian philosophy has not always been embraced by everyone. The changing social milieu, cultural context, political climate,

and economic reality of the U.S. impacted the secondary school movement. The nature and aims of education have evolved, as have our ideas about the best way to organize and structure schools.

Schooling in the colonial era sought to support moral development and encourage adherence to religious doctrine while securing social stability.[14] From the beginning, the reality of differentiated educational opportunities prevailed. The inception of public secondary schools addressed the needs of a very diverse student body—students from a variety of ethnic heritages, religious backgrounds, and socioeconomic realities.

In the 1800s, schooling focused on preparing students for the changing economy. Educating only the elite and focusing exclusively on religious instruction was replaced with a more equitable approach and practical application. As we shifted from an agrarian nation to an industrialized economy, our young nation needed better-trained workers. To meet the needs of a diverse student body, **comprehensive high schools** offered college preparatory, general, vocational, and agricultural tracks. The high schools of the 20th century, by promoting social harmony and emphasizing citizenry, sought to Americanize the great waves of immigrants by preparing them to participate in our democracy and helping them to assimilate into the dominant culture (see Activity 1.1).

Some see the key purpose of secondary education today as preparing students for work. They believe contemporary high schools should prepare students for a knowledge-driven interdependent global economy.[15] Others believe that a high school curriculum should prepare students for postsecondary education. Although the purpose of school is still debated today, there is agreement that serious challenges face our educational system. The growing number of students who are unsuccessful in our schools is of great concern; the high illiteracy and dropout rates are alarming. The achievement gap between wealthy and poor students and white and nonwhite students appears to be ever widening. The disparity in academic performance cannot be ignored.[16]

Activity
1.1

Indian Boarding Schools

There are many federal policies that have had and continue to have devastating effects on American Indians. As future teachers, it is important to review the history and foundation of American Indian education policy, in particular, the Boarding School Era. This experiment in forced assimilation was orchestrated by the U.S. government and led by Captain Richard E. Pratt. In 1879, Pratt opened the first **Indian Boarding School** in Carlisle, PA. His motto was, "Kill the Indian and save the man." He attempted to accomplish this by removing Indian children from their homes, transporting them across the country, stripping them of their identity, requiring them to learn English, and forcing them to become "civilized." In reality, Indian children were isolated from their communities, brutalized, and "imprisoned" in boarding schools.

To learn more about the legacy of Indian Boarding Schools, complete this activity. You can work alone, with a partner, or in a small group. You will be using the **K-W-L technique** developed by Donna Ogle (1986). This will help you organize your knowledge about Indian Boarding Schools. Start the activity by brainstorming and recording your responses to the first two categories, K and W. K stands for what you KNOW about Indian Boarding Schools; W stands for what you WANT to learn about Indian Boarding Schools.

After you have recorded what you already know about Indian Boarding Schools, do not worry if you have minimal background knowledge; come up with questions you would like to know the answers to that you think will help you to better understand American Indian students, their families, and their communities. Then select a few of the websites listed below to peruse to begin to answer your questions.

American Indian Boarding Schools Haunt Many
http://www.npr.org/templates/story/story
.php?storyId=16516865

The Reservation Boarding School System in the United States, 1870–1928
http://www.twofrog.com/rezsch.html

Remembering Our Indian School Days: The Boarding School Experience
http://www.heard.org/currentexhibits/hmm/
BoardingSchoolExperience.html

Assimilation through Education: Indian Boarding Schools in the Pacific Northwest
http://content.lib.washington.edu/aipnw/marr.html

Boarding School Native American Indian Student richheape.com
http://www.youtube.com/watch?v=0Q48PlBr70c

Our Spirits Don't Speak English
http://www.richheape.com/boarding-school.htm

Apply Your Knowledge

Next, complete the L category on your K-W-L chart. L stands for what you LEARN from your "intervention" by thinking about your answers to the following questions.

1. What factual information did you uncover about Indian Boarding Schools that you did not previously know?
2. What stood out to you the most when you heard survivors retell the horrors they experienced while attending boarding schools? Why?
3. Many educators believe that it is important to learn about Indian Boarding Schools because it is our shared history and we cannot change what we do not acknowledge. Do you agree with this approach? Why or why not?
4. What did you learn about healing and confronting generational trauma?

Elliot W. Eisner believes that for schools to address this key issue, we have to question several assumptions regarding the education system. Because we are products of our education system and our secondary schools are steeped in tradition, transforming high schools is very challenging. Eisner asserts, "Schools have a special difficulty in changing their nature. Part of this difficulty comes from the fact that all of us have served an apprenticeship in them—and from an early age. Indeed, teaching is the only profession I know in which professional socialization begins at age 5 or 6. Students, even those of so tender an age, learn what it takes to 'do school.'"[17]

Still, many believe that democratic equality can be realized through educational opportunity and support a free and appropriate education for all children in this nation. Education is seen as the great equalizer; for many, obtaining an education is equated with changing one's economic reality.[18] Next we will highlight some of the more meaningful secondary school reform efforts designed to promote educational equity.

Early Reform Efforts

From their inception, secondary schools varied greatly. To address this inconsistency, in 1892 the *National Education Association (NEA)* presented the *Committee of Ten* with the task of establishing a uniform policy for high schools that could be implemented nationally. The college presidents and professors that served on the Committee of Ten sought to standardize the secondary curriculum. Committee consensus identified the purpose of high school as preparation of gifted students (wealthy white males for the most part) for university study. Therefore, the committee's recommendations promoted a traditional curriculum focusing on the classics; electives were to be kept to a minimum.

In almost every decade since the Committee of Ten published its report back in the late 1800s, several task forces have been formed to evaluate the current state of affairs in public school education and propose recommendations. In 1918, the NEA established a more diverse committee including education professors, high school administrators,

Activity
1.2
Brown v. Board of Education

Racial segregation was practiced and enforced throughout the U.S. in the early 1950s in all domains, including public schools. Although all the schools in a given district were supposed to be equal, most black schools were far inferior to white schools. In Topeka, KS, a black third grader named Linda Brown had to walk one mile through a railroad switchyard to get to her black elementary school, even though a white elementary school was only seven blocks from her home. Linda's father, Oliver Brown, tried to enroll her in the local white elementary school, but the principal refused to let her in. In 1951, Brown, along with other parents, filed a class-action lawsuit on behalf of their children against the Board of Education of the City of Topeka.

The precedent of *Plessy v. Ferguson*, the 1896 U.S. Supreme Court decision that upheld the constitutionality of "separate but equal" school systems for blacks and whites, had not been overturned yet. Consequently, the court felt "compelled to rule in favor of the Board of Education." After losing the case in the state courts, Brown and the National Association for the Advancement of Colored People (NAACP) decided to take the case all the way to the U.S. Supreme Court. They appealed to the Supreme Court on October 1, 1951; their case was combined with other cases that challenged school segregation in South Carolina, Virginia, and Delaware.

The Supreme Court struck down the "separate but equal" doctrine of *Plessy* for public education, ruled in favor of the plaintiffs, and required the desegregation of schools across America.

The landmark decision was read by Chief Justice Earl Warren on May 17, 1954. Peruse the websites listed here to learn more about the *Brown* decision and answer the questions that follow.

"With an Even Hand," *Brown v. Board at Fifty,* Library of Congress
http://www.loc.gov/exhibits/brown

Brown v. Board of Education
http://www.youtube.com/watch?v=D2XHob_nVbw

Separate Is Not Equal, Smithsonian National Museum of American History
http://americanhistory.si.edu/brown

Apply Your Knowledge

1. Explain what impact this landmark case has had on the education system and the students in this country.
2. Some people claim that schools are more segregated today than they were in the past. Do you agree with them? Why or why not?
3. In May 2004, during a celebration commemorating the fiftieth anniversary of the *Brown* ruling, then President George W. Bush described the ruling as "a decision that changed America for the better, and forever." Do you agree with Bush's claim? Why or why not?

and classroom teachers to evaluate the high schools. Unlike the Committee of Ten, which focused on the elite few destined to earn a university degree, these evaluators focused on the needs of the majority of students who most likely would be ending their academic pursuits after high school. They proposed a curriculum that would help high school graduates become self-sufficient, happy, moral citizens in an industrialized economy.

The *comprehensive high school* resulted from the NEA's Commission Report in 1918. Because there was great debate over whether high schools should offer a college preparatory curriculum or a vocational track, the commission recommended offering both under the umbrella term *comprehensive high school*. This focus on offering a varied curriculum to meet students' differing needs remains popular today. Comprehensive high schools became popular in the 1940s and 1950s when the curriculum was expanded to include a variety of electives and vocational programs. Despite the growing popularity of the progressive education movement, most high schools remained unchanged in the decade following World War II except for the expansion of the vocational and general curriculum offerings. This focus was redirected when the 1983 National Commission on Educational Excellence published its report. It claimed we were lagging behind other nations in science, math, technology, and business. The push to raise our students' level of performance in these disciplines continues today (see Activity 1.2).

Recent Reform Efforts

Goals 2000

Since the 1980s, education reform efforts have been national in scope. In 1989, then President George H.W. Bush convened all the governors to discuss the state of education. They developed educational standards and proposed six national education goals known as Education 2000. Under President Bill Clinton, these goals were modified and became **Goals 2000**. According to the expectations, all of America's students were to meet each of the six goals by the beginning of the 21st century. Although 2000 came and went and we were unsuccessful in meeting the guidelines laid out in Goals 2000, this reform effort initiated a critical analysis of the education system. As a result, national and state content standards have been developed for the core curricular areas as well as for all the other disciplines. For a summary of the National Education Goals outlined in Goals 2000: Educate America Act (P.L. 103-277), see Table 1.3.

No Child Left Behind

On January 8, 2002, the **No Child Left Behind (NCLB)** Act became law. This landmark legislation promised to improve student achievement and change the culture of America's schools while providing educational opportunity for all students. President George W. Bush's education reform was built on four common pillars: accountability,

Table 1.3	Summary of Goals 2000: Educate America Act

"By the Year 2000—

1. All children in America will start school ready to learn.

2. The high school graduation rate will increase to at least 90 percent.

3. All students will leave grades 4, 8, and 12 having demonstrated competency over challenging subject matter including English, mathematics, science, foreign languages, civics and government, economics, the arts, history, and geography, and every school in America will ensure that all students learn to use their minds well, so they may be prepared for responsible citizenship, further learning, and productive employment in our nation's modern economy.

4. United States students will be first in the world in mathematics and science achievement.

5. Every adult American will be literate and will possess the knowledge and skills necessary to compete in a global economy and exercise the rights and responsibilities of citizenship.

6. Every school in the United States will be free of drugs, violence, and the unauthorized presence of firearms and alcohol and will offer a disciplined environment conducive to learning.

7. The nation's teaching force will have access to programs for the continued improvement of their professional skills and the opportunity to acquire the knowledge and skills needed to instruct and prepare all American students for the next century.

8. Every school will promote partnerships that will increase parental involvement and participation in promoting the social, emotional, and academic growth of children."

NOTE: President Clinton signed the original six goals of Goals 2000: Educate America Act into law on March 31, 1994. The last two goals were added later.

SOURCE: U.S. Department of Education. See http://www.ncrel.org/sdrs/areas/issues/envrnmnt/stw/sw0goals.htm.

scientific research, parental options, and local control and flexibility. This reform effort focused on performance standards and was intended to measure how well students meet the content standards laid out in previous reform efforts.

In 2007, Congress was supposed to decide whether to reauthorize the legislation signed into law on January 8, 2002, by President George W. Bush, the No Child Left Behind Act of 2001 (Public Law 107-110), or let it die. This legislation reauthorized a number of federal programs aiming to improve the performance of students in elementary and secondary schools across the country. The premise was that states have failed to meet the academic needs of many students and that federal intervention is the remedy. Therefore, with NCLB, the states, local school districts, and individual schools are being held accountable. This is enacted by federally mandating standardized testing of all students at several grade levels in a variety of content areas. The policy also claims to provide parents with a greater variety of school choice. It has also reauthorized the Elementary and Secondary Education Act of 1965 and emphasized the importance of reading proficiency through the Reading First initiative (see Activity 1.3).

Reforming Middle Schools

One of the national goals laid out in the NCLB of 2001 mandates increasing student performance. The legislation requires that by 2014, all students completing eighth

Activity 1.3	No Child Left Behind (NCLB)

The effectiveness of NCLB is highly debated. Those that support the legislation claim that it encourages accountability, offers choice, and narrows the achievement gap. The critics of NCLB have several objections. The most frequent criticisms can be organized into the following broad categories: (a) inadequate funding from the federal government to fully implement the act places financial strain on local school districts; (b) corruption is suspected because schools feel pressure to demonstrate adequate yearly progress (AYP) to earn incentives and avoid penalties; (c) overreliance on standardized test scores has created a "teaching to the test" mentality; (d) unconstitutional violation of states' rights and a limitation on local control; (e) violation of the separation of church and state; (f) a division of resources that is not equitable, causing schools to set lower expectations; (g) state education budget cuts; (h) a curricular focus on reading, writing, and math at the expense of other content and extracurricular areas; and (i) provides military recruiters the same access to secondary school facilities as higher education recruiters.

Apply Your Knowledge

As highlighted here, there is a lot of debate over the effectiveness of NCLB. To explore answers to the following questions, visit the websites listed here.

U.S. Department of Education: No Child Left Behind Reauthorization
http://www.ed.gov/nclb/overview/intro/reauth/index.html

The White House
http://www.whitehouse.gov/news/reports/
no-child-left-behind.html

Krashen on NCLB and Testing
http://fislanguage.blogspot.com/2007/03/
krashen-on-nclb-and-testing.html

17 Reasons Why No Child Left Behind Must Go
http://nochildleft.com/2006/sept06killing.html

1. Has achievement increased under NCLB?

2. Do you think NCLB is doing more good than harm for the following students: racial minorities, special education students, and English Language Learners?

3. Do you believe one of the unintended consequences of NCLB has been the narrowing of the curriculum at the expense of subjects like social studies, science, and physical education? Explain your position.

grade achieve academic proficiency.[19] In the past decade, the founders of the National Forum to Accelerate Middle School Reform and other supporters have advocated substantive systemic reform and recommend increased academic achievement of middle school students. In order to realize this goal, we continue to modify the organization and structure of our middle and secondary schools.

Organizing Education to Meet Students' Needs

Organization

The organization of schools varies greatly throughout the U.S. In an attempt to best meet the needs of their youth, communities have organized their schools in a variety of ways. Some districts adhere to an elementary and secondary 6+6 (six years of elementary school and six years of secondary school) organizational plan. Others follow an elementary, middle, and high school 6+3+3 (six years of elementary school, three years of middle school, and three years of secondary school) or a 5+3+4 or 6+2+4 configuration. Next, we will discuss how different communities choose to organize schools and the impact the organization has on its students.

The Middle School Concept and Philosophy

Exemplary middle schools, as shown in Table 1.2, are quite different from traditional junior high schools. To understand the significance of what has become known as the middle school concept, certain background information may prove helpful. As mentioned earlier, reasons for the reorganization away from the concept of junior high school and the adoption of a middle school education included to provide a program specifically designed for children in this age-group, to set up a better transition between the elementary school and the high school, and to move grade 9 to the high school or, as has happened in some school districts in recent years, to a location designed solely for ninth graders, known as a *ninth-grade center*.[20]

Although any combination of grades 5 through 9 may be included in a middle school, the most common configuration is grades 6 through 8. The trend of including sixth graders and excluding ninth graders is a reflection of the recommendation of the National Middle School Association in its official position paper ***This We Believe***,[21] which we will address in more detail in Chapter 2. The trend continues. For example, in California, grades 6 to 8 are now the most common grade span included in middle schools in that state.

The term *middle-level education* identifies school organizations based on a philosophy that incorporates curricula and instructional practices specifically designed to meet the needs of youngsters between the ages of 10 and 14. This philosophy is often referred to as the *middle school concept*. The notion that greater and more specific attention should be given to the special needs of young adolescents became known as the *middle school movement*. Basic to the

movement is the belief that middle school teachers need specialized training to work most effectively with young adolescents.

Middle Schools and Junior High Schools

When you receive your state teaching credentials, you may or may not be certified to teach at the middle school level. In some states, a secondary school credential certifies a person to teach a particular subject at any grade level, K-12. In other states, such a credential qualifies a person to teach only grades 7 through 12. At least 33 states provide a middle school teaching credential to candidates who have successfully completed a program specifically designed to prepare teachers for that level.

Curriculum Tracks and Homogeneous Grouping

Some school systems, especially large urban systems, provide different schools for youths planning for different vocations. In most school systems, though, offering a variety of curricula in comprehensive high schools accommodates these differences. With a judicious selection of courses, students can prepare themselves for entrance to a four-year college or university or for a specific vocation that may include a continuing postsecondary education vocational program. Such a choice of curricula is probably the most common administrative or organizational means of providing for individual differences at the high school level. Although a student's choice of a curriculum may begin in middle school or junior high school, it usually becomes apparent at the high school level.

Traditionally, and still today, many high schools are organized on the basis of the demonstrated ability of students. For instance, a school may provide one sequence for honors students, a second sequence for college-preparatory students, a third sequence for general students, and a fourth sequence for academically challenged or seemingly unmotivated students. These different sequences—sometimes called *tracks*—may differ from one another in difficulty and complexity of subject content, rate of student progress, and methods of instruction.

As traditionally practiced, ability grouping, or **tracking**, is the assignment of students to curriculum and class groups based on evidence of academic ability. Grouping and tracking do not seem to increase overall achievement of learning, but they do promote inequity. Although many research studies conclude that tracking should be discontinued because of its discriminatory and damaging effects on students, many schools continue using it either directly by counseling students into classes according to evidence of ability and the degree of academic rigor of the program or indirectly by designating certain classes and programs as *college prep* and others as *noncollege prep* and allowing students some degree of latitude to choose.

Tracks are, in effect, a type of homogeneous grouping. Homogeneous groups are formed by dividing students into class sections according to some criterion or a combination of criteria. Usually the criteria include a combination of motivation and prior academic success. Other criteria are educational-vocational goals (e.g., business English or college-preparatory English) or just interest. In any case, the reasons for forming homogeneous groups are to provide for the differences in students and to make teaching more efficient and perhaps easier. Theoretically, when classes are grouped homogeneously, teachers can more easily select content and methods that are suitable for all students in that group.

In some instances and to some degree, tracking according to proven ability and interests works. For example, when all the students in an advanced mathematics class are interested, motivated, and self-confident (and have similar learning capacities, styles of learning, and modality preferences), teaching them is no doubt easier. And finding content, textbooks, and methods suitable for everyone in a class is also easier if the group is homogeneous in these respects. In some cases, tracking is used to afford opportunities to certain students while denying others those opportunities. Nevertheless, homogeneous grouping as discussed here is not necessarily the answer to the challenge of addressing individual student differences.

In the first place, homogeneous groups are not truly homogeneous; they are merely attempts to make groups similar, according to certain criteria. All that homogeneous grouping does is to reduce the heterogeneity of classes, making certain aspects of providing for individual differences in students a bit more manageable.

Whatever the advantages of homogeneous grouping, this organizational scheme also has several built-in problems. One occurs when the teacher assumes that all class members are the same. In classes grouped according to demonstrated ability and interest, the range of proven academic ability may be reduced, but the range of interest, ambitions, motivations, and goals is probably just as wide as in any other class. No matter how much a school attempts to homogenize classes—and no matter what plan of grouping is used—you as the teacher will always face the necessity of attending to and providing for individual student differences.

Another very real problem of traditional ability grouping is that students of the less academically rigorous courses may get shortchanged, with little expected of them and with little for them to do. Furthermore, these students have little opportunity to interact with and to learn from their more motivated or more educationally advantaged peers. Students can learn a great deal from one another. When this opportunity for interaction is not provided, classes for the less motivated and educationally disadvantaged students become educational ghettos. If there is anything that has been learned in recent years, it is that there is no student in a public school who cannot learn when given the proper learning environment, opportunity, and encouragement.

Structuring Schools to Meet Students' Needs

The Structure of Middle Schools and High Schools

We begin our quest for understanding how schools are structured by presenting some of the more significant characteristics of today's middle and secondary schools. First, we will describe the school calendar year. Next, we will look at a typical school day, school start times, teaching teams, and scheduling variations.

The School Calendar Year

Conventional and **year-round school** years vary from state to state, from district to district, and from school to school. Most school years begin in mid- to late August or early September and continue through late May or mid-June. However, to accommodate more students without a significant increase in capital costs and to better sustain student learning, an increasing number of schools are eliminating the traditional long summer break by switching to *year-round education*, which, by the way, has been around for more than half a century.[22] Whether or not the school follows a year-round schedule, the school year still approximates 180 days for teachers and students in the U.S.

Although experts are not in agreement as to how negatively a shortened school year impacts achievement, it is interesting to note that the United States has a shorter school year than many other nations. The following is a list of approximate school days per year in several countries: Japan, 243; West Germany, 240; South Korea, 220; Luxembourg and Israel, 216; Russia, 211; Netherlands, Scotland, and Thailand, 200; Hong Kong, 195; England/Wales and Hungary, 192; Switzerland, 191; Nigeria and Finland, 190; France, 185; Ireland, 184; Spain and the United States, 180; French Belgium, 175; and Flemish Belgium, 160.[23] If you compare the number of days students in Japan and students in the United States spend in school, you see a dramatic difference. Over a 12-year period, Japanese students will spend 756 more days in school (63 days per year $\times$ 12 years); that equates to approximately four years, 36 days, longer in school by the time a student graduates from high school.

In a school with year-round education, a teacher might teach for three-quarters of the year and be off for one-quarter or teach in a 45/15 program, which means nine weeks of school (45 days) "on track" followed by three weeks of school (15 days) "off track" throughout the year. Nearly 70% of schools with year-round education use the 45/15 plan.[24] In 45/15 arrangements, teachers and students are on tracks, referred to as A track, B track, and so on, with starting and ending times that vary depending on the track and time of year. At any one time, there is always at least one track on vacation. "Intersession" programs may be held during off-track time, at which time students might participate in short classes specifically planned for remediation or enrichment.

The School Day

The regular school day begins about 8:00 A.M. and lasts until about 3:00 P.M. In addition to this regular school day, there may be special earlier starting and later ending classes and co-curricular activities. District and state laws vary, but generally teachers are expected to be in the classroom no less than 15 minutes prior to the start of school and to remain in their classrooms no less than 15 minutes after final dismissal of students. Many teachers engage in a variety of other activities or have other commitments, responsibilities, or duties that require them to spend several additional hours per week on the school campus.

Nonstandard Daily Starting Times

Some schools are experimenting with modified starting times, drawing on studies of adolescent sleep patterns as well as the need to find ways to deal with crowded schools or to cut transportation expenses by reducing the number of buses and drivers needed.[25] For example, a school might not even begin classes until around 9:30 A.M. or mid-morning. Or a school might schedule activities or classes such as the visual and performing arts and physical education first, in early morning, to be followed by classes dealing with the core curriculum subjects. Or to allow for adolescent sleep patterns and work schedules, a school may give students the option of attending early day classes or late afternoon and evening classes. Some schools offer a *zero period* in which classes meet before the standard bell schedule, sometimes as early as 6:30 A.M.

Teaching Teams

Traditionally, junior and senior high school teachers have taught their subjects five or six times each day in their own classrooms and fairly isolated from other teachers and school activities. In many schools, that is still the case. Increasingly, however, both middle school and secondary school teachers are finding themselves members of a collaborative **teaching team** in which several teachers from different discipline areas work together to plan the curriculum for a common group of students.

A distinction must be made between *teaching teams* and **team teaching**. Team teaching refers to two or more teachers simultaneously providing instruction to students in the same classroom. Members of a teaching team may participate in team teaching. There are several variations on team teaching. Two or more teachers may choose to split the instructional time in many ways. Maybe they share the class time and each instructor is responsible for part of the instruction, maybe they alternate days and/or meetings, or maybe both teachers are present for all class meetings and provide their unique discipline perspective on everything.

The teaching team may comprise only a few teachers, such as high school teachers who teach the same group of 11th-grade students in English and in world history; they may meet periodically to plan a curriculum and learning activities around a common theme, such as the Elizabethan era. Often, especially in middle schools, teaching teams comprise one teacher each from English/language arts, mathematics, science, and history/social studies. These four subject areas are known as the **core curriculum**. In addition to the core-subject teachers, specialty-area teachers may be part of the teaching team, including teachers of physical education, visual and performing arts teachers, and even special education teachers and at-risk specialty personnel or school counselors. In addition, some teams may invite a community-resource person to be a member. Because the core and specialty subjects cross different disciplines of study, these teams are commonly called **interdisciplinary teaching teams** or simply **interdisciplinary teams**.

The School-Within-a-School (SWAS) Concept

As mentioned earlier, the current trend is to personalize schools. There are several strategies for making large schools feel more welcoming. Separate and autonomous units known as **schools within a school** have proven effective in diminishing the isolation students often experience in bigger schools. The Adams Ninth Grade Campus at McMinnville High School in Oregon is an example of a small group functioning within a larger school. Ninth graders spend their mornings taking core curriculum courses and eating lunch in their separate food court before joining the other high school students on the main campus in the afternoon.

An interdisciplinary teaching team and its common group of students can be thought of as a school within a school (also referred to as a *village*, *pod*, *learning family*, *academy*, or *house*) where each team of teachers is assigned each day to the same cohort of students for a common block of time. Within this block of time, teachers on the team are responsible for the many professional decisions necessary, such as how the school can be made *developmentally responsive*, or most meaningful, to students' lives; what specific responsibilities each teacher has each day; what guidance activities need to be implemented; which accommodations should be made to meet the special needs of students; and how students will be grouped for instruction. Members of such a team get to know their students well and thereby build the curriculum and instruction around their students' interests, perspectives, and perceptions. Because they "turn on" learning, the school and its classrooms become exciting places to be in and to learn in. (In contrast, "symptoms of turned-off learning include students' seeming inabilities to grasp concepts, to exert effort, or to display enthusiasm; repeated lateness or absence; boredom; and work that is sloppy or of poor quality."[26])

The school-within-a-school concept helps students make important and meaningful connections among disciplines. It also provides them with both peer and adult group identification, creating an important sense of belonging. In some schools, such as Quest High School (Humble, TX), Gnarly High School (Norfolk, VA), and Celebration School (Celebration, FL), using an arrangement called **looping**, the cohort of students and teachers remain together as a group for several or for all the years a student is at that school.[27]

The advantages of being a member of a teaching team in a school-within-a-school environment are numerous. This year at Estes Park Middle School in Estes Park, CO, the sixth-grade team has added two new members. The novice mathematics and language arts teachers are joining their senior social studies and science colleagues. The new members will benefit from the experience and support of their team members. Moreover, the combined thinking of several teachers creates an expanded pool of ideas, enhances individual capacities for handling complex problems, and provides intellectual stimulation and emotional support. The synergism of talents produces an energy that has a positive impact on the instructional program. A beginning teacher who joins a team has the benefit of support from more experienced teammates. More and better planning for students occurs as teachers discuss, argue, and reach agreement on behavioral expectations, curriculum emphasis, instructional approaches, and materials.

Teachers' Daily Schedules

For many middle school and secondary school teachers, the school day consists of the traditional seven or eight periods; each period lasts about 40 to 50 minutes. This traditional schedule includes teaching three or four classes before lunch and three or four following lunch. One period each day is reserved as a *preparation* or *prep period*, referred to sometimes as the *conference* or *planning period*. When a teacher's preparation period falls during either the first or the final period of the day—or just before or after lunch—the teacher is still expected to be present on the campus during that time to be available for conferences with students, parents, guardians, counselors, other teachers, or administrators. Most teachers are quite busy during their preparation periods, reading and grading student papers, preparing class materials, meeting in conferences, or preparing for use of media equipment. Sometimes, this is a period when the teacher may prefer to sit and relax over a cup of tea or coffee, perhaps in the pleasant surroundings of the faculty lounge.

Common Planning Time for Interdisciplinary Teams

For an interdisciplinary teaching team to plan most effectively and efficiently, members must meet together frequently. This is best accomplished when they share a *common planning time*, preferably no fewer than four hours each week. This means that in addition to each member's preparation period, members of a team share a common planning time to plan the curriculum and to discuss the progress and needs of the students within their cohort.[28]

Each teaching team assigns a member to be a *team facilitator* or lead teacher. The lead teacher organizes the

meetings and facilitates discussions during the common planning time. Usually, this person also acts as a liaison with the administration in order to ensure that the team has the necessary resources to put its plans into action. A team's lead teacher (or another member designated by the team) may also serve on the *school leadership team*, a group of teachers and administrators (and sometimes students) designated by the principal or elected by the faculty (and student body) to assist in the leadership of the school. Sometimes, in lieu of a traditional site principal, the school leadership team is the leadership for the school.[29]

Nontraditional Scheduling

To maximize the learning time, to allow for more instructional flexibility, and to accommodate common planning time for teachers, many schools are using some form of **block scheduling**. Block scheduling means that, for at least part of the school day or part of the week, blocks of time ranging from 70 to 140 or more minutes replace the traditional structure of the seven- or eight-period day with 40- to 50-minute-long class periods. The possible variations are nearly limitless.

For example, the school year in some schools consists of three 12-week trimesters, and each school day is divided into five 70-minute-long class periods. Such a schedule is referred to as a 5×7 *block plan*. Some schools use a 4×4 *block plan*, whereby students take four 85- to 90-minute-long *macroperiods* (or *macroclasses*) each day, each semester.[30] Other schools use an A-B, or *alternating day*, block plan, in which classes meet every other day for the entire school year for 90-minute blocks.[31]

Using *macroperiods* lengthens the time each day that students are in a course, thereby simultaneously reducing the number of courses taken at one time. The macroperiod allows the teacher to supervise and assist students with assignments and project work and with their reading, writing, thinking, and study skills. Macroperiods provide more time for interactive and interdisciplinary thematic instruction that might otherwise be difficult or impossible to accomplish in shorter class periods.

Block Scheduling: Advantages and Disadvantages

Reported advantages of schools using block scheduling include (a) greater satisfaction among teachers and administrators and (b) improvement in both the behavior and the learning of all students (regardless of ability level), attitude toward school, and degree of school success. Teachers get to know the students better and are therefore able to respond to a student's needs with greater care. Consequently, students do more writing, pursue issues in greater depth, enjoy classes more, feel more challenged, and gain deeper understandings.

In evaluating schools using block scheduling, researchers have found more course credits completed, equal or better mastery and retention of content, and a significant reduction in discipline problems and dropout rates. Other reported benefits of the block plans are that (a) in one school year, the total hours of instruction are significantly greater; (b) each teacher teaches and is responsible for fewer courses during a semester and is responsible for fewer students; (c) student-teacher interaction is more productive, and the school climate is positive, with fewer discipline problems; (d) because planning periods are longer, there is more time for teachers to plan and to interact with parents; and (e) more students can take advanced placement classes.[32]

There are also benefits to taxpayers. During one school year, teachers teach more courses and potentially more students, thereby decreasing the number of faculty needed. In addition, fewer textbooks are needed. For example, instead of all sophomores taking history for an entire year, half of them take it the first semester and half the second, thereby reducing the number of textbooks needed by one-half.

The reduction of bells ringing from as many as eight times a day to perhaps only two or three times a day or not at all creates less disturbance. Because students are not roaming halls for three to five minutes five or six times a day, teachers can more easily supervise unstructured time and thereby have better control over portions of the unplanned and subtle message systems within schools, referred to as the *hidden curriculum*. The messages of the hidden curriculum are the school climate, the feelings projected from the teacher and other adults to students and from the students to one another, not only in classrooms but also before and after school, at social events, and in the halls, restrooms, and other areas of the school that are not monitored as closely as the individual classrooms.

Nontraditional school schedules are not without their problems. Problems that sometimes arise from block scheduling are that (a) content coverage in a course may be less than that which was traditionally covered; (b) there may be a mismatch between content coverage and that expected by state-mandated tests and the dates those tests are given to students; (c) when absent a day from school, a student will miss more in a subject area; and (d) community relations problems may occur, such as when students are out of school and off campus at nontraditional times.

Some schools have successfully used *modified block schedules*, thus satisfying teachers who prefer block scheduling and those who prefer a traditional schedule. A modified block schedule can provide both traditional 40-minute periods (sometimes called *split-block periods*) that meet daily (sometimes preferred, especially by teachers of mathematics[33] and foreign languages) and longer blocks. A modified block schedule centers on a seven or eight 45- or 40-minutes-per-period day along with alternate longer blocks. In a modified block schedule, all students might start the day with a 30- or 40-minute-long first period, which serves as a homeroom or adviser-advisee time. From there, some students continue the morning attending traditional-length periods, while others may move into a morning block class. Throughout the day, teachers and students may pass from block classes to those of traditional length or vice versa.

Some schools use a *flexible block schedule*; check out the block scheduling used at Lexington High School in

Table 1.4 Lexington High School, Lexington, MA   Sample Class Block Schedule

Monday	Tuesday	Wednesday	Thursday	Friday
A_1 7:45–8:30	D_2 7:45–8:40	X 7:45–8:30	C_3 7:45–8:40	B_4 7:45–8:30
B_1 8:35–9:25	B_2 8:45–9:40	A_3 8:35–9:25	B_3 8:45–9:40	C_4 8:35–9:25
C_1 9:30–10:20	homeroom 9:45–9:55	C_2 9:30–10:20	homeroom 9:45–9:55	D_4 9:30–10:20
	A_2 10:00–10:55		A_4 10:00–10:55	
E_1 10:25–11:15 or 10:55–11:45		E_3 10:25–11:15 or 10:50–11:40		E_4 10:25–11:15 or 10:55–11:45
	G_2 11:00–11:55 or 11:30–12:25		G_3 11:00–11:55 or 11:30–12:25	
F_1 11:20–12:10 or 11:50–12:40		F_2 11:20–12:10 or 11:45–12:35		F_4 11:20–12:10 or 11:50–12:40
D_1 12:45–1:35	H_1 12:00–12:55 or 12:30–1:25	H_2 12:40–1:30	H_3 12:00–12:55 or 12:30–1:25	G_4 12:45–1:35
G_1 1:40–2:25	E_2 1:30–2:25	D_3 1:35–2:25	F_3 1:30–2:25	H_4 1:40–2:25
Z 2:30–3:00 Daily				
No Scheduled Activities.				
Lunch Periods				
Monday	Tuesday	Wednesday	Thursday	Friday
10:20–10:50	10:55–11:25	10:20–10:45	10:55–11:25	10:20–10:50
11:15–11:45	11:55–12:25	11:15–11:40	11:55–12:25	11:15–11:45
12:10–12:40	12:55–1:25	12:10–12:35	12:55–1:25	12:10–12:40

SOURCE: Lexington High School scheduling information from http://lps.lexingtonma.org/domain/251. Used with permission.

Lexington, MA, at **http://lps.lexingtonma.org/domain/251**. Their daily schedule consists of a seven-period day with all seven classes meeting on Monday. Periods 1 through 4 meet for 75 minutes, while periods 5 through 7 meet for 30 minutes. On Tuesdays and Thursdays, periods 1 through 4 meet for 105 minutes each, and on Wednesdays and Fridays, periods 5 through 7 meet for 120 minutes each. A 30-minute period after lunch allows students to attend club meetings or pep rallies, to make up tests, or to receive guidance and counseling or tutorial help. In short, there is little doubt that longer blocks of instructional time with students are a positive factor contributing to students' meaningful learning, especially when combined with some form of year-round education, the use of interdisciplinary thematic instruction, and the elimination of curriculum tracking (see Table 1.4).

Modifying the Curriculum to Facilitate Student Learning

Striving to Provide Quality Education for All Students

Nontraditional scheduling is part of the effort to restructure schools to deliver quality learning opportunities to all students. The students of a *quality education school* see the relevancy in what they are learning to their lives. A quality school provides a stimulating learning environment.

Sometimes it may appear that more energy is devoted to organizational change (*how* the curriculum is delivered) than to school curriculum (what is taught). School organization has a direct effect on what students learn; if it didn't, educators wouldn't be spending so much valuable time trying to restructure their schools to effect the most productive (and cost-effective) delivery of the curriculum.

School restructuring has been defined as "activities that change fundamental assumptions, practices, and relationships, both within the organization and between the organization and the outside world, in ways leading to improved learning outcomes."[34] Exemplified by efforts mentioned in the preceding discussions, the movement to year-round education and the redesigning of schools into "houses" represent a movement that is becoming increasingly common across the country. With this redesign, the intention is that schools will better address the needs and capabilities of each unique student. To that end, a number of specific trends are discussed later in this chapter and in Chapter 2.

Providing Challenging Curriculum Options

Consequently, the trend in public schools is to replace what traditionally were known as the general curriculum and the low-level curriculum tracks with more challenging, rigorous, and meaningful curriculum options (see Figure 1.1).[35] For example, dedicated to the premise that all students can learn, Souderton Area High School (Souderton, PA) eliminated its general curriculum track, raised standards for graduation from 17 to 23 credits, and required all students to take four years of mathematics, science, language arts, and

Figure 1.1 **Multiple Pathways to Success: Productive Ways of Attending to Student Differences, of Providing a More Challenging Learning Environment, and of Stimulating the Talents and Motivation of Each Student**

- Advisory programs and adult advocacy relationships for every student
- Allowing a student to attend a high school class while still in middle school or to attend college classes while still in high school
- Allowing a student to skip a traditional grade level
- Community service learning
- Cooperative learning in the classroom
- Curriculum compacting
- High expectations for all students
- Integrating new technologies into the curriculum
- Interdisciplinary teaming and thematic instruction
- Mid-year promotions
- Multiage grouping
- Peer and cross-age teaching
- Problem-centered learning
- Second-opportunity recovery strategies
- Specialized schools and flexible block scheduling
- Student-centered projects within-class and across disciplines

social studies. Just five years after making those changes, students' failure rate had dropped from 10% to 3%, suspensions from school declined by 60%, and average daily attendance of students increased from 87% to 93%.[36] With its commitment to higher expectations for all students, Lee County High School (Beattyville, KY) replaced its general track with an integrated curriculum that emphasizes active learning, includes continuous reinforcement of academic content with vocational application, and offers ongoing career planning and preparation with an advisory system to guide students to high achievement.[37] And, at Colonial High School (Orlando, FL), *all* ninth graders start their portfolios that include career assessments and programs of study that lead to enrollment in a postsecondary education program[38] (see Figure 1.1 and Activity 1.4).

Embracing Student Diversity to Meet Students' Needs

At-Risk Students

The term *at risk* is used to identify students who have a high probability of not finishing school. Researchers have identified five categories of factors that cause a young person to be at risk of dropping out of school. These categories are personal pain (exemplified by drugs, physical and psychological abuse, suspension from school), academic failure (exemplified by low grades, failure, absences, low self-esteem), family tragedy (exemplified by parent illness or death, health problems), family socioeconomic situation

Activity
1.4

Walkout: Mexican American Students Protest

In March 1968, thousands of Mexican American students, led by student activist Paula Crisostomo, staged a protest and walked out of their high schools in East Los Angeles. The students staged the peaceful protest because they were fed up with the poor conditions and the anti-Mexican bias they endured. Their story of courage was told in the 2006 HBO film *Walkout*, which is based on the true story of a young Mexican American high school teacher, Sal Castro, and the students he mentored. The film is set against the backdrop of the civil rights movement and depicts the fight for justice and empowerment by 10,000 Mexican American students who protested against the discrimination they faced in the public school system. *Walkout* is considered a breakthrough film of sorts because of its portrayal of racism in the schools.

Apply Your Knowledge

Peruse the websites listed here and answer the questions that follow.

Shame of a Nation, Jonathan Kozol
http://www.youtube.com/watch?v=5pB-niRGNms&feature=related

A Tale of Two Schools
http://www.youtube.com/watch?v=5xdfVAPvv9A&feature=related

Disparity in Public Education
http://www.youtube.com/watch?v=FU1woTRYxcs&feature=related

Inequality in Schools—2009 Oprah—School Switch Experiment in Chicago
http://www.youtube.com/watch?v=MgvpRoAn-ro&feature=related

A Tale of Two Schools—New York 2008—libertynjustice4all
http://www.youtube.com/watch?v=nd6OwPkxYAw&feature=fvwrel

1. Uncover what some of the inequities the Mexican American students protested about were. Do the inequities persist today?
2. What does Jonathan Kozol have to say about the inequities in our schools today?
3. What other student protests are you familiar with?

(exemplified by low income, negativism, lack of education), and family instability (exemplified by moving, separation, divorce).[39] Many students experience risk factors from more than one of these categories. A modified school schedule alone, without quality individualized attention, may not be enough to address the needs of students who are at risk of not completing school. It has been estimated that by 2020, the majority of students in American public schools will be at risk.[40] We address dropout trends in Chapter 2.

Responsive Practices for Helping All Students Succeed in School

Because of the enormous diversity of students, using a combination of practices concurrently is the best way to help all students succeed in school. The reorganization of schools and the restructuring of school schedules, then, represent only two aspects of efforts to help all students make successful transitions.[41]

Other important responsive practices (including attitudes) are (a) a perception, shared by all teachers and staff, that all students can learn when they are given adequate support, although not all students need the same amount of time to learn the same thing; (b) high, although not necessarily identical, expectations for all students; (c) personalized and individualized attention, adult advocacy, scheduling, and learning plans to help students learn in a manner by which they best learn—research clearly points out that achievement increases, students learn more, and students enjoy learning and remember more of what they have learned when individual learning styles and capacities are identified and accommodated; (d) engagement of parents and guardians as partners in their child's education; (e) extra time and guided attention to basic skills—such

as those of thinking, writing, and reading—rather than on rote memory; (f) specialist teachers and smaller classes; (g) peer tutoring and cross-age coaching; and (h) attention and guidance in the development of coping skills.

Preparing Teachers to Teach in a Diverse Classroom

The Fundamental Characteristic of Exemplary Education

Wherever and however the students are housed and regardless of other responsive practices, in the end it is the dedication, commitment, and nature of the understanding of the involved adults—the teachers, administrators, bus drivers, cooks, grounds crew, security staff, custodial staff, and support personnel—that remain the decisive element. That, in our opinion, is the fundamental characteristic of exemplary public education: to celebrate and build on the diverse characteristics and needs of students. That is the essence of the content of Chapter 3.

Committed Teachers

Public school teachers are unique individuals. Let us imagine that a teaching colleague mentions that Lou Compton, in room 17, is a "fantastic teacher," "one of the best teachers in the district," "super," and "magnificent." What might be some of the characteristics you would expect to see in Lou's teaching behaviors?

We can expect Lou to (a) be understanding of and committed to the school's statement of philosophy or mission (see Figure 1.2); (b) know the curriculum and how best to teach it; (c) be enthusiastic, motivated, and well organized;

Figure 1.2 Sample Exemplary Mission Statements

A. Middle School Mission Statements

Riverside Middle School
Riverside Middle School, Billings, MT
http://www.billingsschools.org/riverside.htm

Freeport Middle School Mission Statement
Freeport Middle School, Freeport, ME
http://fms.freeportpublicschools.org/Pages/FMS_Admin/about

Thomas J. Pappas School for the Homeless
Thomas J. Pappas Schools for the Homeless, Mesa, AZ
http://www.tjpappasschool.org/

Chimacum Middle School
Chimacum Middle School, Chimacum, WA
http://csd49.org/cms/middle/mission.htm

South Sevier Middle School: Belief Statements
South Sevier Middle School, Monroe, UT
http://web.archive.org/web/20040423225336/
   www.ssm.sevier.k12.ut.us/belief.html

Eugenio Maria De Hostos Charter School
Eugenio Maria De Hostos Charter School, Philadelphia, PA
http://www.phila.k12.pa.us/charter_schools/mission.html#dehostos

B. High School Mission Statements

Paseo Academy of Fine and Performing Arts
Paseo Academy of Fine and Performing Arts,
Kansas City Missouri School District, Kansas City, MO
http://www.kcmsd.k12.mo.us/schools/
   home3.asp?schoolid=46&t=1&s=373

Taunton High School
Taunton High School, Taunton, MA
http://www.tauntonschools.org:16080/ths/
   ths_mission_statement.htm

Cape Elizabeth High School
Cape Elizabeth High School, Cape Elizabeth, ME
http://www.cape.k12.me.us/sHigh.html

Lexington High School
Lexington High School, Lexington, MA
http://lhs.lexingtonma.org/lhsmission.html

Poplar Public School District 9 and 9B
Poplar School District, Poplar, MT
http://www.poplar.k12.mt.us/19181081317210647

(d) show effective communication and interpersonal skills; (e) be willing to listen to the students and to risk trying their ideas; and (f) be warm, caring, accepting, and nurturing of all students.

Students need teachers who are well organized and who know how to establish and manage an active and supportive learning environment (the topic of Chapter 4), even with its multiple instructional demands. Students respond best to teachers who provide leadership and who enjoy their function as role models, advisers, mentors, and reflective decision makers. Students also need teachers who hold high expectations for each and all of them; teachers who are culturally competent, that is, teachers who have the knowledge, skills, and dispositions to work with students who are different from them; teachers who understand the key role that cultural heritage and life experiences play in the teaching/learning process; and teachers who see the strength in diversity and celebrate students' differing gifts (see Activity 1.5).

Reflective Decision Making and the Locus of Control

During any school day, a teacher makes hundreds of decisions, many of them instantaneously. In addition, in preparation for the day, the teacher will already have made many decisions. Thus, during one school year, a teacher makes literally thousands of decisions, many of which can and will affect the lives of students for years to come. For you, this should seem an awesome responsibility—which it is. In the nearly poetic words of Brown and Moffett, "We [teachers]

influence students in myriad, unperceived ways that affect them and the lives of people with whom they interact like the widening circles extending from a stone tossed into a tranquil pond."[42]

To be an effectively and positively influential teacher, you must become adept at decision making. You must make decisions developed through careful thinking over time as well as decisions on the spot that arise from unforeseen circumstances. To make decisions that affect the students in the most positive kinds of ways, you need common sense, intelligence, a background of theory in curriculum and instruction with extended practical experience in working with young people, and the willingness to think about and reflect on your teaching and to continue learning all that is necessary to become an exemplary classroom teacher.

Initially, of course, you will make errors in judgment, but you will also learn that teenagers are fairly resilient. You will find experts to guide you and help you so you can learn from your errors. Keep in mind that the sheer number of decisions you make each day will mean that not all of them will be the best ones that could have been made if you had more time to think and if you had better resources for planning.

Although effective teaching is based on scientific principles, good classroom teaching is as much an art as it is a science. In fact, the selection of content, instructional objectives, materials for instruction, teaching strategies, responses to inappropriate student behavior, and techniques for assessment are all the result of subjective judgments. Although many decisions may be made unhurried, such as when you plan the instruction, many others must be made on the spur of the moment. At your best, you will base

Examining the Impact of *Lau v. Nichols*

If you take people who are the same and treat them differently, it results in one form of discrimination, but if you take people who are different and treat them the same, it is equally discriminating, even if it is a subtler form of discrimination.

In 1970, Kinney Timmon Lau and 1,800 Chinese American students filed a class-action lawsuit against the San Francisco Unified School District, alleging that they were being discriminated against on the basis of their national origin and, therefore, were not being afforded their Fourteenth Amendment rights. The students claimed that they were denied a meaningful education even though they were exposed to the same instruction as their classmates since English was the language of instruction and they were not proficient in English.

Even though the school district countered that its policies were not discriminatory because all students, regardless of their national origin, were offered the same instruction, in 1974 the U.S. Supreme Court ruled unanimously in favor of the plaintiffs in this landmark civil rights case. The Court found that by offering instruction in English only, the school district had not made the necessary linguistically appropriate accommodations for their Chinese-speaking students; the students were effectively denied equal educational opportunities. This case, consequently, expanded the rights of Limited English Proficient students nationwide. The Supreme Court stated that these students should be treated with equality among the schools. As a result, *Lau* promotes the now widely accepted view that a person's language is so closely intertwined with his or her national origin.

Apply Your Knowledge

Peruse the websites listed here and answer the questions that follow.

Developing Programs for English Language Learners: *Lau v. Nichols*
http://www2.ed.gov/about/offices/list/ocr/ell/lau.html

Lau v. Nichols (1974) and Asian Americans 30th Anniversary
http://aajc.schipul.net/files/lau_backgrounder.pdf

Lau v. Nichols
http://www.youtube.com/watch?v=jb3juqzHoig

1. What impact has the *Lau v. Nichols* decision had on bilingual education policies today?
2. Do you agree with the view that a person's language is closely intertwined with his or her national origin? Why or why not?
3. What linguistically appropriate accommodations are made for English Language Learners in your local K–12 school district?
4. What coursework and practical experiences are offered in your teacher preparation program to prepare you to work with culturally and linguistically diverse students?

---

decisions on your knowledge of school policies and your teaching style as well as on pedagogical research, the curriculum, and the nature of the students in your classroom. You will also base your decisions on instinct, common sense, and reflective judgment.

The better your understanding and experience are with schools, the content of the curriculum, and the students—and the more time you spend on thinking and careful reflection—the more likely it will be that your decisions will result in the student learning that you had planned. You will reflect on concepts developed from one teaching experience and apply them to the next. As your classroom experiences accumulate, your teaching will become more routinized, predictable, and refined.

Decision-Making and Thought-Processing Phases of Instruction

Instruction can be divided into four decision-making and thought-processing phases: (1) the planning or *preactive phase*, (2) the teaching or *interactive phase*, (3) the analyzing and evaluating or *reflective phase*, and (4) the application or *projective phase*.[43]

The preactive phase consists of all those intellectual functions and decisions you will make prior to actual instruction. The interactive phase includes all the decisions made during the actual teaching. As mentioned before, decisions made during this phase are likely to be more intuitive, unconscious, and routine than those made during the planning phase. The reflective phase is the time you will take to reflect on, analyze, and judge the decisions and behaviors that occurred during the interactive phase. As a result of this reflection, decisions are made to use what was learned in subsequent teaching situations. At this point, you are in the projective phase, abstracting from your reflection and projecting your analysis into subsequent teaching actions.

Reflection and the Decision-Making Process

During the reflective phase, teachers have a choice of whether to assume responsibility for the positive instructional outcomes of the planned instruction while placing the blame for the negative outcomes on outside forces (e.g., parents and guardians or society in general, students, other teachers, administrators, textbooks). Where the responsibility for outcomes is placed is referred to as *locus of control*. Just because a teacher thinks that he or she is a competent teacher doesn't mean it is so. If many of a teacher's students are not learning, then that teacher is not competent. In the words of the late Madeline Hunter, "To say that I am an effective teacher, and acknowledge that my students may not be learning is the same as saying I am a great surgeon, but most of my patients die."[44] Competent teachers tend to assume full responsibility for the instructional outcomes regardless of whether the outcomes are as intended from the planning phase.

Developing a Teaching Style

Every teacher develops a personal style of teaching with which he or she feels most comfortable. A teaching style can be defined as the way a teacher teaches, including the teacher's distinctive mannerisms complemented by his or her choices of teaching behaviors and strategies. This style develops both from the teacher's personal traits and from the knowledge and skills the teacher has in methodology, subject matter, and pedagogical theory. The most effective teachers can vary their styles; that is, their styles are flexible enough to encompass many and various strategies. Those teachers, therefore, are prepared to address the students' preferred learning styles.

The most effective teachers can modify their styles by selecting the strategy that is most appropriate for the situation, thus securing active student involvement and the greatest amount of student achievement. Highly effective teaching of this sort requires expertise in a wide variety of methods.[45] It also requires a command of the subject matter and an understanding of the students being taught. Thus, to be an effective teacher, you must accomplish three things: (1) learn as much about your students as you can, including their learning capacities, styles, preferred modalities, and interests; (2) develop an eclectic teaching style accompanied by a large repertoire of strategies and techniques; and (3) develop your knowledge and skills in using instructional media and resources.

A Model for Teaching

You should incorporate the following five-step model into your teaching style: (1) diagnosis or preassessment, (2) planning and preparation, (3) guidance of student learning, (4) continual assessment of student learning, and (5) follow-up. The diagnosis is an initial assessment of the students' present knowledge as well as their needs and desires. Through such preassessment, you (and the students) can determine what should be accomplished and how it might best be done.

Next, you plan and prepare for the instruction. This step includes planning the units and lessons and the corresponding motivational strategies, preparing instructional activities, gathering materials and equipment, and arranging the environmental setting for instruction. Often these things are done in collaboration with the students.

Although steps (1) and (2) are within the preactive phase of the thought-processing and decision-making phases of instruction, step (3), guidance of student learning, is within the teaching or interactive phase. It includes implementation of the learning activities, that is, the instruction—showing students how, making information available to students, and providing opportunity for dialogue and constructive feedback to students about their work.

In step (4), assessment, you and the students reflect on and assess the ongoing progress of their learning and, in so doing, the success of the instruction. Assessment provides information to both you and your students about where progress has been made and where it has not. As part of the reflective phase of instructional decision making, those data provide a basis for determining the follow-up, the projective phase. On the basis of assessment data, you follow up the instruction by helping students fill in what they have missed and by building on what they have learned.

As is true for the four decision-making and thought-processing phases of instruction, these five steps of the model for instruction tend to merge. For example, the assessment and follow-up for one unit or lesson may become the diagnosis, preparation, and guidance phases for the next one. But even when truncated, this five-step model is evident in exemplary teaching.

Accessing Community Resources to Meet Students' Needs: Telecommunications Networks, Members of the Community, and Parent Organizations

Vehicles for Obtaining and Sharing Ideas and Information

Exemplary educators make focused efforts to enhance the connections among the home, school, and local and global communities to promote the success of all students.

Home and School Connections

It is well known that parents' involvement in their child's education can have a positive impact on their child's achievement at school. For example, when parents of an at-risk student get involved, the student benefits with more consistent attendance at school, more positive attitudes and actions, better grades, and higher test scores. In recognition of the positive effect that parent and family involvement has on student achievement and success, the National PTA published *National Standards for Parent/Family Involvement Programs* in 1997.[46]

Many schools have adopted formal policies about home and community connections. These policies usually emphasize that parents should be included as partners in the educational program—that teachers and administrators will inform parents about their child's progress, about the school's family involvement policy, and about any programs in which family members can participate. Some schools are members of the *National Network of Partnership 2000 Schools*. Efforts to foster parent and community involvement are as varied as the people who participate and include (a) student-teacher-parent contracts and assignment calendars, sometimes available via the school's Web page on the Internet; (b) home visitor programs; (c) involvement of community leaders in the classroom as mentors, aides, and role models;[47] (d) newsletters, workshops,[48] and electronic hardware and software for parents to help their children; (e) homework hotlines; (f) regular phone calls[49] and personal notes home about a student's progress; and (g) involvement of students in community service learning.[50]

Figure 1.3 **Internet Sources on Community Service Learning**

- **Big Dummy's Guide to Service-Learning**
  http://www.fiu.edu/~time4chg/Library/bigdummy.html
- **Campus Compact Service Learning Links**
  http://www.compact.org/links/service.html
- **Service Learning Project**
  http://www.aahe.org/service/srv-links.htm
- **UCLA Service Learning Clearinghouse**
  http://www.servicelearning.org/library/items/
  ucla_clearinghouse_web_site_archive/index.php

Community Service Learning

Via service learning, students can learn and develop through active participation in thoughtfully organized and curriculum-connected experiences that meet community needs[51] (for Internet sources of additional information and descriptions of community service projects, see Figure 1.3).

Community members, geographic features, buildings, monuments, historic sites, and other places in a school's geographic area constitute some of the richest instructional laboratories that can be imagined. In order to take advantage of this accumulated wealth of resources, as well as to build school-community partnerships, you should start a file of community resources once you have been hired by a school. It is a good idea to start your professional resources file immediately and maintain it throughout your professional career; for that, see Figure 1.4.

Telecommunications Networks

Teachers looking to guide their students toward becoming autonomous thinkers, effective decision makers, and lifelong learners and to make their classrooms more student centered, collaborative, interdisciplinary, and interactive are increasingly turning to telecommunications networks and the global community. Webs of connected computers allow teachers and students around the world to reach one another directly and gain access to information previously unimaginable. Students using networks learn and develop new inquiry and analytical skills in a stimulating environment and gain an increased appreciation of their role as world citizens. Sample websites and addresses are shown in Figure 1.5. See others elsewhere in this book, especially Figures 8.2 and 8.3 in Chapter 8.

The Emergent Overall Picture

Certainly, no facet of education receives more attention from the media or causes more concern among parents and teachers than students' achievement in the public schools. Reports are issued, polls taken, debates organized, and blue-ribbon commissions formed. Community members write letters to local editors about it, news editors devote editorial space to it, television anchors comment about it, and documentaries and specials focus on it in full color. What initiated this attention that began about half a century ago and continues today? We are not sure, but it has never been matched in its political interest and participation, and it has affected and continues to affect both the public schools and programs in higher education that are directly or indirectly related to teacher preparation and certification.[52]

In response to the reports, educators, corporations, local businesspersons, and politicians acted. Around the nation, their actions resulted in the following:

■ Changes in standards for teacher certification. For example, model standards describing what prospective teachers should know and be able to do in order to receive a teaching license were published by the Interstate New Teacher Assessment and Support Consortium (INTASC), a project of the Council of Chief State School Officers (CCSSO), in a document titled *Model Standards for Beginning*

Figure 1.4 **Beginning a Professional Resources File**

A professional resources file is a project that you could begin now and maintain throughout your professional career. Begin your resources file on a computer database program and list (a) name of the resource, (b) how and where to obtain the resource, (c) description of how to use the resource, and (d) evaluative comments about the resource.

Organize the file in a way that makes the most sense to you now. Cross-reference your system to accommodate the following categories of instructional aids and resources.

- Articles from print sources
- Compact disc titles
- Computer software titles
- Games
- Guest speakers and other community resources
- Internet resources
- Media catalogs
- Motivational ideas
- Pictures, posters, graphs, cartoons, quotes

- Resources to order
- Sources of free and inexpensive materials
- Student worksheets
- Test items
- Thematic units and ideas
- Unit and lesson plans and ideas
- Videocassette titles
- DVD titles
- Miscellaneous

Figure 1.5 **Sample Internet Sites for Teachers and Students**

- **Beginning Teacher's Tool Box**
  http://www.inspiringteachers.com/
- **Classroom Connect** http://corporate.classroom.com/
- **ClubMid** http://www.phschool.com/ Middle grades network
- **Community Learning Network** http://www.cln.org/
- **Council of the Great City Schools** http://www.cgcs.org/
- **EdIndex** http://www.pitt.edu/~poole K–12 education links
- **Education World** http://www.education-world.com
  Electronic version of *Education Week*
- **EduServe / GlobaLearn** http://www.eduserveinc.com/GLN7.htm
- **Eisenhower National Clearinghouse for Mathematics and Science (ENC)** http://www.goenc.com/
- **FedWorld** http://www.fedworld.gov Access to information from government agencies
- **GEM, the Gateway to Educational Materials**
  http://www.thegateway.org/index.html
  National government's effort to provide access to Internet-based educational materials
- **Global Schoolnet Foundation** http://www.gsn.org/
  Global resources and links
- **GLOBE (Global Learning and Observations to Benefit the Environment) Program** http://www.globe.gov
  An international environmental science and education partnership
- **Homeschool Internet Resource Center** http://www.rsts.net/
- **HomeworkCentral** http://www.homeworkcentral.com/
  For lesson plans and subject research
- **Kathy Schrock Guide** http://kathyschrock.net/
- **Kathy Schrock's Guide for Educators**
  http://school.discoveryeducation.com/schrockguide/
  for resources and information on education
- **Library of Congress** http://lcweb.loc.gov/homepage/lchp.html
  National Digital Library life history manuscripts from the WPA Federal Writers' Folklore Project, Civil War photographs, early motion pictures, legal information, and research sources
- **I Love that Teaching Idea**
  http://www.ilovethatteachingidea.com/
- **Microsoft Lesson Connection** http://www.k12.msn.com
  Lesson plan resources and more
- **MiddleWeb** http://www.middleweb.com/ Middle school focus
- **National Consortium for School Networking** http://cosn.org
- **PedagoNet** http://www.pedagonet.com Learning Resources Center for exchange of educational resources
- **Study Web** http://www.studyweb.com Place for students and teachers to research topics
- **Teachers First** http://www.teachersfirst.com
  Resources provided by the Network for Instructional TV (NiTV)
- **Teachers Helping Teachers**
  http://www.pacificnet.net/~mandel
- **United Nations CyberSchool Bus**
  http://www.un.org/Pubs/CyberSchoolBus/
  Curriculum units and projects, databases on U.N. member states, and global trends
- **United States Department of Education**
  http://www.ed.gov/index.html
- **Virtual Reference Desk** http://www.vrd.org/
- **Yahoo Education Index** http://dir.yahoo.com/Education/

Teacher Licensing and Development. Representatives of at least 36 states and professional associations make up the group, including the NEA, the *American Federation of Teachers*, the *American Association of Colleges for Teacher Education*, and the *National Council for the Accreditation of Teacher Education*. The standards are performance based and revolve around a common core of principles of knowledge and skills that cut across disciplines. The INTASC standards were developed to be compatible with the *National Board for Professional Teaching Standards (NBPTS)*.[53] Specifically addressing middle-level instruction, the NBPTS in 1997 released 11 categories of standards for certification as a middle childhood/generalist. These 11 categories are knowledge of students, knowledge of content and curriculum, learning environment, respect for diversity, instructional resources, meaningful applications of knowledge, multiple paths of knowledge, assessment, family involvement, reflection, and contributions to the profession.[54] The categories include the following:

- Emphasis on education for cultural diversity and ways of teaching culturally and linguistically diverse students.

- Emphasis on helping students make effective transitions from one level of schooling to the next and from school to life, with an increased focus on helping students make connections between what is being learned and real life as well as connections between subjects in the curriculum and between academics and vocations.

- Emphasis on raising test scores, reducing dropout rates (i.e., the rate of students who do not complete high school or receive the equivalent degree), increasing instructional time, and changing curricula.

- Federally enacted Goals 2000: Educate America Act and the development of national education standards for all major subject areas (see Chapter 6).

- Formation of school-home-community connections.

- New "basics" required for high school graduation.

- School restructuring to provide more meaningful curriculum options.

Your Emerging Teaching Style

It is indeed a challenge to teach middle and secondary school students. To help you meet the challenge, there is a wealth of information and resources available. As you build broader frameworks of understanding of teaching and learning, as you practice the development of your instructional skills, and as you reflect on that experience, you will be well on your way to becoming the most effective teacher you can be by developing your own personal style of teaching. As mentioned earlier, this teaching style will develop from a combination of personal traits; from expertise you have in methodology, subject matter, and pedagogical theory; and from your knowledge about your particular group of students.

The most effective teachers are those who can vary their instructional styles. Effective teachers can select and use the strategy that is most appropriate, thus promoting active student involvement and the greatest amount of student achievement. Highly effective teaching of this sort requires both expertise in a wide variety of methods and a feeling for the appropriate situation in which to use each method. Such teaching also demands a good command of the subject matter and an understanding of the students being taught.

To be an effective teacher, you should (a) develop a large repertoire of techniques in order to be prepared for the many possible contingencies; (b) learn as much about your students as you can; (c) develop an eclectic style of

teaching, one that is flexible and adaptable; and (d) build into your teaching use of the five-step model of diagnosis, preparation, guidance of student learning, continual assessment of the learning, and follow-up.

In deciding which methods to use, you will be influenced by a number of factors, each of which is explored further in subsequent chapters. To continue your learning about methods available and a teacher's decision-making process, now do Exercises 1.1, 1.2, and 1.3.

Summary

In this chapter, we have reviewed the chronological development of secondary schools. We have covered colonial education, homeschooling, and dame schools. We have also talked about Latin grammar schools, academies, English classical schools, and comprehensive high schools. We have distinguished between middle and junior high schools while discussing the changing purpose, organization, and structure of our schools. We have highlighted educational opportunities afforded to some students while denied to others. We have also included key past and current reform

---

Exercise 1.1

Methods of Instruction

Instructions: The purpose of this exercise is for you to reflect on how you have been taught (throughout your schooling) and share those reflections with your classmates, looking for differences as well as commonalities.

1. The following is a list of methods of instruction and a variety of tools. Rate each according to your familiarity and experiences with it, using this rating scale: **A** = very familiar and with good learning experiences, **B** = somewhat familiar, **C** = never experienced, **D** = familiar but with bad learning experiences.

_____ Assignment	_____ Drama	_____ Lecture	_____ Self-instructional module
_____ Audiovisual equipment	_____ Drill	_____ Library/resource center	_____ Simulation
_____ Autotutorial	_____ Expository	_____ Metacognition	_____ Study guide
_____ CD/DVD	_____ Field trip	_____ Mock-up	_____ Symposium
_____ Coaching	_____ Game	_____ Multimedia	_____ Telecommunication
_____ Collaborative learning	_____ Group work	_____ Panel discussion	_____ Term paper
_____ Computer-assisted learning	_____ Guest speaker	_____ Periodicals	_____ Textbook
_____ Cooperative learning	_____ Homework	_____ Problem solving	_____ Think-pair-share/ think-write-pair-share
_____ Debate	_____ Individualized instruction	_____ Project	_____ Tutorial
_____ Demonstration	_____ Inquiry	_____ Questioning	_____ Visual tools
_____ Discovery	_____ Laboratory investigation	_____ Review and practice	
	_____ Laser videodisc	_____ Role-play	

2. Now list the methods in four columns according to the rating you gave to each.
   A Methods   B Methods   C Methods   D Methods

3. In small groups (three or four per group), share the responses in your columns with your classmates. Do some methods show up consistently in certain columns? If so, try to analyze why. Questions that you might discuss in your groups are the following:
   - Were certain methods more consistently used at any one level of your education, such as college, high school, junior high, and so forth?
   - In what ways have your teachers' teaching styles differed?
   - Which have appealed to you most? Why?
   - What qualities did your teacher have that you would most like to emulate? Avoid?

efforts. We have discussed the role teachers, students, parents, administrators, and community members play in a quality education school. We have advocated for an eclectic teaching style as the best approach to meeting the varied needs of our diverse students. In Chapter 2, we will address many of the current issues facing educators. In Chapter 3, we will talk about the many ways students are different while pointing out commonalities. We will also explore ways to leverage the diversity you are likely to find in your classrooms.

Exercise 1.2   The Teacher as Reflective Decision Maker

Instructions: The purpose of this exercise is to learn more about the nature of the decisions and the decision-making process used by teachers. To accomplish this, you are to talk with and observe one middle school or secondary school teacher for one class period. Tabulate as accurately as possible the number of decisions the teacher makes during that time period and then share the results with your classmates. Obtain permission from a cooperating teacher by explaining the purpose of your observations. You will need to have a follow-up discussion with the cooperating teacher regarding your tabulations. A follow-up thank-you letter is appropriate.

School, teacher, and class observed: _____

1. Use the following format for your tabulations. You may first want to make your tabulations on a separate blank sheet of paper and then organize and transfer those tabulations to this page. Tabulate and identify each decision. To tabulate the decisions made before and after instruction, confer with the teacher after class.

Decisions Made Before Instruction	Decisions Made During Instruction	Decisions Made After Instruction
Examples:	Examples:	Examples:
• Objectives of lesson	• Called on Roberta to answer a question	• To review a particular concept tomorrow
• Amount of time to be devoted to particular activities	• Teacher remained silent until students in back corner got quiet	• To arrange a conference with Sean to talk with him about his hostility in class
• Classroom management procedures	• Talked with tardy student	• To make a revision in Friday's homework assignment

2. What was the total number of decisions made by this teacher

   before instruction? _____   **during instruction?** _____   **after instruction?** _____ Compare your results with those of others in your class.

3. Did you observe any evidence that this teacher assumed full responsibility for the learning outcomes of this class session? Describe the evidence.

4. What percentage of all decisions by this teacher

   were planned? _____   **were spontaneous?** _____

5. Did you share your results from this exercise with the cooperating teacher? What was his or her reaction?

6. What are your conclusions from this exercise?

Exercise 1.3   Reflecting on My Own School Experiences

Instructions: The purpose of this exercise is to share with others in your class your reflections on your own middle school and secondary school experiences. We suggest that you do this first in small groups, perhaps no larger than four people, and then share highlights or commonalities of the small-group discussion with the whole group.

1. What school(s) did you attend, where, and when? Were they public or private?

2. Describe the school(s)—for example, urban or rural, large or small. How many classmates were in your school; your graduating class?

3. What do you remember most from your middle and secondary school experiences?

4. What do you remember most about your teachers?

5. What do you remember most about the other students?

6. What do you remember most about your overall school life?

7. What grade (or class or teachers) do you specifically recall with fondness? Why?

8. What grade (or class or teacher) would you just like to forget? Why?

9. What do you recall about peer and parental pressures?

10. What do you recall about your feelings during those years?

11. Is there any other aspect of your life as a middle school or secondary school student you wish to share with others?

Chapter 1   POSTTEST

Short Explanation

1. Clearly distinguish these types of schools: middle school, junior high school, high school, secondary school.
2. Describe the house concept and its advantages and disadvantages from an educational standpoint.
3. Define school restructuring, describe its purpose, and give examples of some of the results of efforts to restructure schools.
4. Describe the philosophy that drives the middle school movement.
5. Describe the meaning of the term *quality education*.

Essay

1. It has been predicted that by 2020, 20% to 30% of the U.S. public schools will be run by for-profit corporations (see page 67 of the February 7, 2000, issue of *BusinessWeek* magazine). Are for-profit public schools actually increasing in number from the approximately 200 such schools in 2000? Why or why not, do you suppose, is the for-profit public school alternative growing in popularity?

2. From what you now know about middle and secondary schools, at which do you believe you would most like to teach? Explain why.

3. From your current observations and fieldwork (related to your teacher preparation program), clearly identify one specific example of an educational practice that seems contradictory to exemplary practice or theory as presented in this chapter. Present your explanation for the discrepancy.

4. Describe any prior concepts you held that changed as a result of your experiences with this chapter. Describe the changes.

Todd Yarrington/Merrill

Middle and Secondary Schools Today and Tomorrow:
Reform Efforts, Challenges and Issues, and Trends and Practices

The illiterate of the 21st Century will not be those who cannot read and write, but those who cannot learn, unlearn or relearn, as stated by Alvin Toffler in the foreword to a work by Gibson. These words come from Herbert Gerjuoy, whom Toffler cites in full as follows: The new education must teach the individual how to classify and reclassify information, how to evaluate its veracity, how to change categories when necessary, how to move from the concrete to the abstract and back, how to look at problems from a new direction—how to teach himself. Tomorrow's illiterate will not be the man who can't read; he will be the man who has not learned how to learn.

—ALVIN TOFFLER[1] and HERBERT GERJUOY[2]

Specific Objectives

At the completion of this chapter, you will be able to:

▶ Describe the Common Core State Standards Initiative.

▶ Describe recent and current middle and secondary school reform efforts and their goals.

▶ Identify current challenges and issues that plague the nation's schools.

▶ Describe current trends and practices in middle and secondary public school education in the U.S.

▶ Describe efforts to enhance the connections among the home, school, local, and global communities to promote the success of all students.

Chapter 2 Overview

In this chapter, we expand on current school reform and describe alternatives for organizing middle and secondary schools. We then highlight several of the challenges and issues that plague the nation's schools, test our educators, and impact our students, including adolescent illiteracy, high dropout rates, the ever-widening achievement gaps, and exit exams and other high-stakes testing. We also address current trends and practices in our middle and secondary schools, including meaningful curriculum options to meet the needs of all learners, such as differentiated instruction, Response to Intervention and tiered assignments, Understanding by Design, and backwards design. We end the chapter by describing key trends designed to prepare our students for the future including 21st Century Skills, data-driven decision making, and service learning.

Introduction

In order to talk about current challenges and issues as well as key trends and practices affecting the educational system, it is important to briefly describe our schools. During the 2001–2002 academic year, there were a total of 94,112 public elementary and secondary schools in operation across the United States. According to the National Center for Education Statistics, in the fall of 2001, the K–12 public and private schools served a record 54 million students. That marked a 19% increase from 1988 to 2001. Between 2001 and 2013, enrollment in grades 9 through 12 is projected to increase by 4%. Migration within the country, immigration, and high birthrates are cited as the key factors affecting the increase.[3] In tandem with the increase in the number of students in middle and secondary schools is an increase in student diversity. Whether we are talking about race, ethnicity, religion, language, exceptionality, or other cultural aspects, we must consider the best ways to prepare our teachers to meet the needs of the individual students who make up our diverse K–12 student population. According to U.S. Secretary of Education Arne Duncan, "Achieving a quality education for all children is the civil rights issue of our generation."[4]

Middle and Secondary School Reform

We reviewed Goals 2000 and introduced the No Child Left Behind Act (NCLB) in Chapter 1. Here we will summarize the impact of recent federal legislation and discuss what the proposed reforms to NCLB through the reauthorization of the Elementary and Secondary Education Act (ESEA) are. Even though many complain that NCLB was grossly underfunded, the federal government poured more than $100 billion into the public education system under this reform initiative. Still, its effectiveness is constantly debated. Going forward, it is important that we critically examine preceding reform initiatives and embrace the opportunity and need to transform American education.

With NCLB, a new era of accountability was put in place in this country, and many subgroups that were formerly "invisible" in our schools, such as English Language Learners, were thrust into the spotlight. The intent of the law was to ensure that *all* students receive a high-quality education, regardless of race, ability, or socioeconomic status. Schools have been required to show student improvement in all student subgroups. Critics complain that NCLB set unrealistic, unobtainable goals, such as the goal to graduate all students from high school by 2014. They also claim that NCLB has done a lot of negative labeling of schools as failures since several schools have been unable to successfully meet Adequate Yearly Progress (AYP). Critics also claim that the NCLB requirement that all students receive proficient or higher scores on assessments across the curriculum by 2014 has had an adverse effect on the education system and made failing schools targets of negative consequences, including serious sanction or public embarrassment (to review the pros and cons of NCLB in more detail, see Chapter 1).

As highlighted in Chapter 1, there have been and continue to be different views on the main purpose of secondary education and the best ways to meet students' needs. Some feel that secondary education should prepare students

for postsecondary education. Others believe that contemporary high schools should prepare young adults to enter the workforce; they believe that students should be prepared for the knowledge-driven interdependent global economy.[5] Still others do not see the goals as mutually exclusive and promote their synthesis.

Although everyone is not in agreement as to the purpose of secondary schooling, most individuals feel a sense of urgency and would agree that our education system could benefit from critical examination and thoughtful reform efforts. The growing number of students who are unsuccessful in our schools is of great concern. The high **illiteracy** and dropout rates are alarming, as are the ever-widening achievement gaps between wealthy and poor students, white and nonwhite students, and our students and their international counterparts. Furthermore, the disparity in academic performance cannot be ignored.[6]

Current Reform Efforts

Currently, there are several reform initiatives in place in America's middle and secondary schools. Some focus on a *policy-oriented approach*, while others promote a *student-centered approach*. Both approaches have their strengths and weaknesses. Aligning *content standards* with the curricula and utilizing *high-stakes testing* are variables associated with the policy-oriented approach. Those advocating a student-centered approach suggest, as a starting point, downsizing schools in order to cultivate learning environments where students can be nurtured and as a result thrive.[7] Recent reform has focused on the dismantling of large high schools and the creation of smaller, more intimate learning environments. The Bill and Melinda Gates Foundation, Carnegie, Brode, Annenberg, and other philanthropic organizations have been supporting smaller high schools.[8] Small secondary schools that combat the feelings of anonymity that permeate our larger schools have made a big difference in narrowing the achievement gap. One of the nation's largest school districts in New York City is phasing out its lowest-performing high schools and replacing them with smaller schools.[9]

There are two kinds of reform: *systemic reform* and *superficial change*. The former focuses on the most comprehensive school reform and seeks to positively impact all aspects of a school's culture. Systemic local reform efforts usually involve the teachers, administrators, staff, students, parents, and even the greater community in the decision-making process.[10] Involving all the key players results in greater buy-in, and, as a result, systemic reform programs are usually successful, significant, and long lasting. However, reform efforts generated from a top-down management initiative rarely produce meaningful, sustainable change.

The 40 national organizations that make up the *National High School Alliance* reported that there are many challenges to realizing school reform.[11] The recent formation of the *National Forum to Accelerate Middle-Grades Reform*

Table 2.1	Secretaries of Education and Important Legislation

Secretary	Term	President(s) in Office	Legislation/Reports
Arne Duncan	2009–present	Barack Obama	Race to the Top
Margaret Spellings	2005–2009	George W. Bush	NCLB
Roderick Paige	2001–2005	George W. Bush	NCLB
Richard Riley	1993–2001	Bill Clinton	Goals 2000
Lamar Alexander	1991–1993	George H. W. Bush	Education 2000
Lauro Cavazos	1988–1990	Ronald Reagan, George H. W. Bush	America 2000
William J. Bennett	1985–1988	Ronald Reagan	
Terrell Bell	1981–1985	Ronald Reagan	A Nation at Risk
Shirley Hufstedler	1979–1981	Jimmy Carter	Department of Education established in 1979

SOURCE: U.S. Department of Education, http://www.ed.gov/index.jhtml, and United States Secretary of Education, http://en.wikipedia.org/wiki/United_States_Secretary_of_Education

has brought a variety of these issues to the forefront.[12] The effort of trying to reform and restructure schools has been compared to trying to rebuild a jetliner while it's in flight.[13] The challenges have multiplied through the years, but the goal remains consistent: reforming schools to benefit students and ensure their academic and future success.

In March 2010, President Barack Obama sent his revised proposal of the reauthorization of ESEA to overhaul NCLB to Congress. It focused on raising standards and rewarding successful educators and students. In fact, President Obama and Secretary of Education Arne Duncan have pledged money to support four central reform efforts designed to improve educators and prepare students for postsecondary education and the workplace. The reform efforts include (a) the adoption of internationally benchmarked standards and assessments; (b) the recruitment, development, retention, and rewarding of effective educators; (c) the creation and implementation of data-driven systems to measure student success and inform teachers and principals of what is working and what they need to improve on; and (d) the turnaround of low-performing schools so that they are effective in meeting students' needs.[14]

The headline "Many Nations Passing U.S. in Education" highlights the president's major concern for the state of our education system and the future of our nation's economy. President Obama emphasized that we have lost ground. "Not only does that risk our leadership as a nation, it consigns millions of Americans to a lesser future. For we know that the level of education a person attains is increasingly a prerequisite for success and a predictor of the income that person will earn throughout his or her life. Beyond the economic statistics is a less tangible but no less painful reality: unless we take action—unless we step up—there are countless children who will never realize their full potential."[15] President Obama made the following suggestions: "investing in better schools, supporting teachers, and committing to clear standards that will produce graduates with more skills. Our competitors understand that the nation that out-educates us today will out-compete us tomorrow."[16]

To address the concerns the president raised, his administration launched **Race to the Top**, a plan that requires states to prove their commitment to reform and the raising of standards by writing grant proposals and competing for funding. Race to the Top builds in flexibility and charges the states and local school districts with setting the bar high and figuring out the best way to turn low-performing schools around. Of course, there are critics of this initiative whose main goal is that every student should graduate from high school ready to pursue higher education and enter into a career (see Table 2.1).

Middle School Reform

Middle school reform is vitally important since research in recent years has highlighted the link between academic outcomes in middle school and high school success. Students ages 10 to 15 represent a special, critical period of adolescent development. Referred to as both the "wonder" and the "worry" years, preadolescence and early adolescence are a time of great change and turmoil. We have concentrated on early childhood programs and high school programs in previous education reforms, but recent research has highlighted the significant role middle school education can play in boosting academic achievement and reducing dropout rates.

High-quality middle school programs adopt practices and policies that improve the school environment by creating respectful, inclusive learning communities and put early warning systems in place to identify and help struggling students. By doing so, middle school educators can help students to be successful during their middle grades and better prepare students for the challenges they will face in high school, college, and the workplace. Early intervention is key to retaining students. Former First Lady Laura Bush pointed out, "We know now from research that a lot of kids that drop out in high school really drop out in middle school."[17]

Middle schools have been described as the weak link in the public education chain. One of the national goals laid out in NCLB mandated increasing student performance.

The legislation required that by 2014, all students completing eighth grade would achieve academic proficiency.[18] In recent years the founders of the *National Forum to Accelerate Middle-Grades Reform* and other middle school supporters have advocated substantive systemic reform and recommend increased academic achievement of middle school students. In order to realize this goal, we continue to examine and modify the organization and structure of our middle schools.

The Association for Middle Level Education developed 16 characteristics of successful middle schools. Those characteristics are described in detail in their well-respected position paper released in 2010 titled "This We Believe: Keys to Educating Young Adolescents." In the report, the 16 characteristics of successful schools capture the essence of the middle school philosophy we described in Chapter 1. They are covered within a framework of four essential attributes that suggest that an education aimed at young adolescents must be developmentally responsive, challenging, empowering, and equitable. Furthermore, the 16 research-based characteristics are organized into three areas: (1) curriculum, instruction, and assessment; (2) leadership and organization; and (3) culture and community. See Figure 2.1 for a detailed description of the characteristics that fall under the previously mentioned three areas.

Secondary School Reform

High schools across the country are receiving a lot of attention from state and federal policymakers, businesses, and communities interested in investigating how best to reform our high schools and prepare our graduates to be competitive in the global economy. Most high school reform efforts focus on the following core principles: increasing student attendance, promoting student achievement, reducing dropout rates, and improving graduation rates. Designing comprehensive reforms, implementing those reform initiatives, and monitoring progress toward goals are key.

Some students have a difficult time making the transition from middle school to high school. Because of the changes in structure and functioning of large high schools, many ninth graders often miss the family-like environment they experienced in middle school and feel anonymous and lost in high school. High school reform initiatives have worked on how best to help students avoid the impersonal feeling that characterizes many large high schools. One solution, the school-within-a-school concept addressed in Chapter 1, seems to be very effective. Several schools have created separate Freshman Academies to help students during their first year of high school since it is a critical transitional year for students. By creating small learning communities within larger schools, students get a chance to better know their teachers and appreciate that their teachers care about them and their academic success. These programs create an atmosphere conducive to learning in an effort to prepare students for success in high school and a productive life once they graduate.

An example of a large school district that has embraced a reform strategy known as Secondary School Reform is Miami-Dade County Public Schools. Secondary School Reform addresses the core principles mentioned here and organizes students in a ninth-grade academy to help them transition into high school and choose a theme-based career academy: a smaller community to belong to in high school. In career academies, where students take classes together for two or more years, students follow a college-preparatory curriculum based on a career theme to help them see relationships and connections between academic subjects and their application in the real world of work. The following six goals of Secondary School Reform provide high schools with a framework meeting the previously listed high school reform goals: "(1) personalize the learning environment; (2) increase academic engagement of all students; (3) empower educators; (4) develop accountable leaders; (5) engage community and youth; and (6) integrate a system of high standards, curriculum, instruction, and assessment."[19] Career academies are successful because they develop partnerships with employers, the community, and colleges and share resources and provide internship and other work opportunities for students.

In 2006–2007, the Association for Supervision and Curriculum Development (ASCD), an educational leadership organization, made high school reform its priority. ASCD's reform proposal focuses on the following five components: (1) multiple assessments, (2) personalized learning, (3) flexible use of time and structure, (4) professional development for teachers and school leaders, and (5) business and community partnerships. Instead of the single assessments that NCLB usually focuses on, ASCD promotes multiple assessments to determine what students can do, including portfolio assessments, demonstrations, oral presentations, and applied projects. ASCD also believes that student learning needs to be personalized since students are at higher risk of dropping out if they do not see their schoolwork as relevant. ASCD believes too many schools are inflexible when it comes to time and structure and suggests attendance requirements are too strict. Some students could be encouraged to finish high school sooner, and some may need more time and finish later instead of focusing on the outdated Carnegie Unit attendance requirements that have been in place for over 100 years. If we support teachers by providing practical, researched-based professional development, then they can help students be more academically successful. Business and community engagement provides students with opportunities for experiences inside and outside of school. ASCD's High School Reform Proposal is new legislation that offers an alternative to NCLB to those schools that choose to embrace it. Schools that choose to participate in this reform effort must demonstrate transparency and accountability and focus on high academic achievement.[20]

There are also other reform efforts in place in our high schools. MDRC, a nonprofit, nonpartisan education and

Figure 2.1 This We Believe: Essential Attributes and Characteristics of Successful Schools

The Association for Middle Level Education, formerly National Middle School Association, position paper, *This We Believe: Keys to Educating Young Adolescents* (2010), has an overarching framework of four essential attributes that connect with the 16 characteristics of successful middle schools.

Essential Attributes—An education for young adolescents must be:

Developmentally responsive—Using the distinctive nature of young adolescents as the foundation upon which all decisions about school organization, policies, curriculum, instruction, and assessment are made.

Challenging—Ensuring that every student learns and every member of the learning community is held to high expectations.

Empowering—Providing all students with the knowledge and skills they need to take responsibility for their lives, to address life's challenges, to function successfully at all levels of society, and to be creators of knowledge.

Equitable—Advocating for and ensuring every student's right to learn and providing appropriately challenging and relevant learning opportunities for every student.

Characteristics of Successful Schools

This We Believe: Keys to Educating Young Adolescents (2010) organizes the 16 research-based characteristics of effective middle grades education into three areas: Curriculum, Instruction, and Assessment; Leadership and Organization; and Culture and Community.

I. Curriculum, Instruction, and Assessment

* Educators value young adolescents and are prepared to teach them.
(*Value Young Adolescents*)
Effective middle grades educators make a conscious choice to work with young adolescents and advocate for them. They understand the developmental uniqueness of this age group, the appropriate curriculum, effective learning and assessment strategies, and their importance as models.

* Students and teachers are engaged in active, purposeful learning.
(*Active Learning*)
Instructional practices place students at the center of the learning process. As they develop the ability to hypothesize, to organize information into useful and meaningful constructs, and to grasp long-term cause and effect relationships, students are ready and able to play a major role in their own learning and education.

* Curriculum is challenging, exploratory, integrative, and relevant.
(*Challenging Curriculum*)
Curriculum embraces every planned aspect of a school's educational program. An effective middle level curriculum is distinguished by learning activities that appeal to young adolescents, is exploratory and challenging, and incorporates student-generated questions and concerns.

* Educators use multiple learning and teaching approaches.
(*Multiple Learning Approaches*)
Teaching and learning approaches should accommodate the diverse skills, abilities, and prior knowledge of young adolescents, cultivate multiple intelligences, draw on students' individual learning styles, and utilize digital tools. When learning experiences capitalize on students' cultural, experiential, and personal backgrounds, new concepts are built on knowledge students already possess.

* Varied and ongoing assessments advance learning as well as measure it.
(*Varied Assessments*)
Continuous, authentic, and appropriate assessment measures, including both formative and summative ones, provide evidence about every student's learning progress. Such information helps students, teachers, and family members select immediate learning goals and plan further education.

II. Leadership and Organization

* A shared vision developed by all stakeholders guides every decision.
(*Shared Vision*)
When a shared vision and mission statement become operational, middle level educators pursue appropriate practices in developing a challenging academic program; they develop criteria to guide decisions and a process to make needed changes.

Figure 2.1 **This We Believe: Essential Attributes and Characteristics of Successful Schools** *continued*

* **Leaders are committed to and knowledgeable about this age group, educational research, and best practices.**
(*Committed Leaders*)
Courageous, collaborative middle level leaders understand young adolescents, the society in which they live, and the theory of middle level education. Such leaders understand the nuances of teaming, student advocacy, exploration, and assessment as components of a larger middle level program.

* **Leaders demonstrate courage and collaboration.**
(*Courageous and Collaborative Leaders*)
Leaders understand that successful schools committed to the long-term implementation of the middle school concept must be collaborative enterprises. The principal, working collaboratively with a leadership team, focuses on building a learning community that involves all teachers and places top priority on the education and healthy development of every student, teacher, and staff member.

* **Ongoing professional development reflects best educational practices.**
(*Professional Development*)
Professional development is a continuing activity in middle level schools where teachers take advantage of every opportunity to work with colleagues to improve the learning experiences for their students.

* **Organizational structures foster purposeful learning and meaningful relationships.**
(*Organizational Structures*)
The ways schools organize teachers and group and schedule students have a significant impact on the learning environment. Interdisciplinary teams' common planning time, block scheduling, and elimination of tracking are related conditions that contribute to improved achievement.

III. Culture and Community

* **The school environment is inviting, safe, inclusive, and supportive of all.**
(*School Environment*)
A successful school for young adolescents is an inviting, supportive, and safe place, a joyful community that promotes in-depth learning and enhances students' physical and emotional well-being.

* **Every student's academic and personal development is guided by an adult advocate.**
(*Adult Advocate*)
Academic success and personal growth increase markedly when young adolescents' affective needs are met. Each student must have one adult to support that student's academic and personal development.

* **Comprehensive guidance and support services meet the needs of young adolescents.**
(*Guidance Services*)
Both teachers and specialized professionals are readily available to offer the assistance many students need in negotiating their lives in and out of school.

* **Health and wellness are supported in curricula, school-wide programs, and related policies.**
(*Health & Wellness*)
Abundant opportunities are available for students to develop and maintain healthy minds and bodies and to understand their personal growth through health-related programs, policies, and curricula.

* **The school actively involves families in the education of their children.**
(*Family Involvement*)
Schools and families must work together to provide the best possible learning for every young adolescent. Schools take the initiative in involving and educating families.

* **The school includes community and business partners.**
(*Community & Business*)
Genuine community involvement is a fundamental component of successful schools for young adolescents. Such schools seek appropriate partnerships with businesses, social service agencies, and other organizations whose purposes are consistent with the school's mission.

http://www.amle.org/AboutAMLE/ThisWeBelieve/The16Characteristics/tabid/1274/Default.aspx

SOURCE: Association for Middle Level Education *formerly National Middle School Association*, 4151 Executive Parkway, Suite 300, Westerville, OH 43081. Phone: 614-895-4730 or 800-528-6672. Fax: 614-895-4750. Used with permission.

social policy research organization, searches for ways to improve programs and policies that affect students in poverty. With funding from the Bill and Melinda Gates Foundation and the James Irvine Foundation, MDRC evaluated three comprehensive initiatives currently being implemented in more than 2,500 high schools in the U.S. Various components of the programs are also being used in thousands of other high schools across the country. The programs include Career Academies, First Things First, and Talent Development. MDRC identified five major challenges that were associated with low-performing high schools: (1) creating a personalized and orderly learning environment, (2) assisting students who enter high school with poor academic skills, (3) improving instructional content practice, (4) preparing students for the world beyond high school, and (5) stimulating change. Like other initiatives presented here, MDRC found that creating a positive school climate is really key to improving adolescents' academic success.

The Common Core State Standards Initiative

The development, adoption, and implementation of content standards at the national, state, and local levels across a variety of disciplines are described in detail in Chapter 5. Here we will discuss briefly what standards are and when they were adopted in addition to highlighting the key points in the recent discussion surrounding the adoption of **Common Core State Standards.**

Curriculum standards define what students should know and what they should be able to do. At the national level, standards did not exist until they were developed and released for mathematics education in 1989. Shortly thereafter, several national organizations articulated national standards for their respective disciplines. In 1994, Goals 2000 was released (see Chapter 1). That act was amended two years later, and states were encouraged to set state standards across the curriculum. The national and subsequent state standards were developed by expert panels charged with identifying the essential elements of a basic core of subject knowledge that all students should acquire. The national standards were designed to serve not as national mandates but rather as voluntary guidelines to encourage curriculum development and to help teachers provide clear goals for student learning to ensure that their students acquire the skills and knowledge they should. At this point, nearly all states have completed state standards in all disciplines.

Many critics of the standards movement believe that standards were developed to tell teachers how and what to teach, but supporters argue that standards were created to help teachers figure out the knowledge and skills their students should have so that they can design the best lessons and create the most supportive learning environments for their students. Supporters also believe that standards are helpful in aiding students and parents by setting clear and realistic goals for success. Whether you support the development, adoption, and implementation of standards or not,

it appears that they are here to stay. Of course, standards are not the answer to what ails our education system, but they do provide teachers with benchmarks for skills and knowledge that students should acquire in a particular time frame and are seen as a crucial first step.

In an effort to define the skills and knowledge all students should obtain during their K–12 education regardless of where they live and attend school and to guarantee that students are ready for college courses or entry into the job market when they graduate high school, a draft of the Common Core State Standards was released for public comment in March 2010. Proponents believe that Common Core State Standards will strengthen our public school education system and help ensure that all students, across all states and in all schools, are prepared to be successful in their postsecondary academic and career pursuits. It is believed that consistency will ensure that all of our students are well prepared with the skills and knowledge necessary to compete with their peers here at home as well as with their counterparts from around the world. Some educators are concerned that Common Core State Standards are the first step toward nationalizing education in this country, but the federal government has not been involved in the development of the Common Core State Standards, and the federal government claims that it will not have a role in their implementation. Rather, the Common Core State Standards are a state-led initiative.

Still there are many critics of this initiative. Nevertheless, efforts have been made to ensure that the process was open, inclusive, and rigorous. Professional education organizations, including the National Education Association, the American Federation of Teachers, the National Council of Teachers of Mathematics, and the National Council of Teachers of English, among other organizations, have been instrumental in bringing together teachers to provide feedback on the standards. Teachers, parents, school administrators, and other experts from across the nation also collaborated with members of the Council of Chief State School Officers (CCSSO) and the National Governors Association Center for Best Practices (NGA Center) to develop the standards. Both of these organizations have provided opportunities for public comment and have encouraged constituents to submit feedback on the draft of the standards documents so that their comments could be incorporated into the final copy of the standards.

English-language arts and mathematics K–12 standards were the first subjects chosen for the common core because it is believed that literacy and numeracy skills, which are emphasized in these two subject areas, are the skills on which skill sets in other disciplines are built. They also happen to be the two areas that are most frequently assessed for accountability purposes. Of course, other subject areas are critical to students' academic success, and once the implementation of English-language arts and math standards is completed, common core standards in additional subject areas will likely follow. Moreover, the standards were designed to incorporate both rigorous content and application of knowledge through higher-order thinking skills.

As a result, the standards have been informed by the best available evidence and the best standards across the country and around the globe and designed by a diverse group of teachers, experts, parents, and school administrators. The standards are benchmarked to international standards to guarantee that our students are competitive in the emerging global marketplace. It is believed that if high standards are consistent across states, they will provide teachers, parents, and students with a set of shared goals and clear expectations that everyone can work toward.

All but six states have decided to adopt the standards. The voluntary adoption process varies, depending on the laws of each state. Some states have adopted the standards through their state boards of education, and other states have adopted the standards through their state legislatures. In each state, teachers, principals, superintendents, and others will decide how the standards are to be met. The states that choose to adopt the Common Core State Standards will be able to share resources to develop high-quality tests to better evaluate student progress. You can find out more about the Common Core State Standards at **http://www. corestandards.org**.

Alternatives for Reorganizing Middle and Secondary Schools

In Chapter 1, we started the discussion on student diversity. In Chapter 3, we define microcultures and highlight the cultural differences your future students are likely to reflect. Here, we highlight different ways to organize schools to best meet students' needs. We start with a discussion about a variety of different types of schools and then discuss the K–8 configuration.

Organizational Provisions for Student Differences

Today, there continues to be an attempt to provide different types of schools for students with different needs or aspirations. The secondary level includes comprehensive high schools, ninth-grade centers, middle schools, and junior high schools, which were discussed in Chapter 1. Other types of middle and secondary schools listed here include magnet schools, fundamental schools, charter schools, for-profit schools, tech-prep high schools, International Baccalaureate schools, and transitional high schools.

A school might be called a **magnet school**, that is, a school that specializes in a particular academic area. For example, Austin High School for Teaching Professions (Houston, TX) specializes in preparing students for the teaching professions, Murry Bergtraum High School (New York, NY) for business careers, and Chicago High School (Chicago, IL) for the Agricultural Sciences, and Renaissance High School (Detroit, MI) emphasizes college admissions for all its graduates. Still other magnet schools

may specialize in the visual and performing arts, science, mathematics, and technology or in language and international studies. For example, in Norwalk, CT, the Center for Japanese Study Abroad is a magnet program that allows students in a house program for grades 9 through 12 at Brien McMahon High School to become proficient in the Japanese language through an interdisciplinary Japanese studies curriculum that includes economics, literature, arts, and music and to obtain firsthand knowledge of the Japanese culture through a two-week experience in Japan.[21]

A school might also be a *comprehensive college-preparatory high school* (see Chapter 1). Other options are (a) a **fundamental school**, a school that specializes in teaching basic skills; (b) a **charter school**, a school that is "an autonomous educational entity operating under a charter, or contract, that has been negotiated between the organizers, who create and operate the school, and a sponsor who oversees the provisions of the charter";[22] (c) a **for-profit school**, a public school that is operated by a for-profit company; (d) a **partnership school**, a school that has entered into a partnership agreement with community business and industry to link school studies with the workplace;[23] (e) a **tech prep high school**, one that has a 4–2 coordinated curriculum that is articulated from grades 9 through 12 to the first two years of college, leading to an associate of applied science degree;[24] (f) a **full-service school**, a school that serves as a hub for quality education and comprehensive social services, all under one roof;[25] (g) an **International Baccalaureate school** with a curriculum approved by the International Baccalaureate Organization (IBO), a worldwide nonprofit educational foundation founded in the 1960s and based in Switzerland[26] (the prestigious International Baccalaureate Diploma Programme is now offered in 2,000 public and private schools around the world; in fact, over 130 countries offer this rigorous two-year high school program); and (h) a **special transitional school**, such as New York City's Liberty High School, a one-year school designed to help recent immigrant students feel welcome and self-assured and to succeed in learning to read and write in English.[27] It might also be a *private school*, a *church-affiliated school*, or a *continuation* or *alternative high school*.[28] Or perhaps it might be another type or a combination of these, such as a *for-profit charter school* or a *charter-magnet-fundamental school*. Although in different ways and with various terminology, the historical practice of providing different routes for students with different needs and different vocational and academic aspirations continues (see Table 2.2).

Charter Schools

In recent years, charter schools have gotten a lot of coverage in the press and were featured as the panacea to the problems in public education in the 2010 documentary by Davis Guggenheim, *Waiting for "Superman."* The gripping film follows five families forced to rely on a lottery to get their children into charter schools and on the road to success. It even suggests that their neighborhood public schools across the

Table 2.2	Different Types of Middle and Secondary Schools
Charter Schools	ARISE High School, Oakland, CA **http://www.arisehighschool.org/school** Granada Hills Charter High School, Granada Hills, CA **http://www.ghchs.com/s/379/index_2col.aspx** The Villages Charter Middle School, Orlando, FL **http://www.thevillagescharterschool.org/middleSchool/ middleSchool.asp** Sheridan Japanese Charter School, Grades 4–12, Sheridan, OR **http://www.sjsfoundation.com** Boulder Preparatory High School, Boulder, CO **http://www.boulderprep.org**
Alternative Schools	Technology High School, Rohnert Park, CA **http://www.orpusd.org./tech.html** September School High School, Boulder, CO **http://www.septemberschool.org** Franklin Alternative Middle School, Columbus, OH **http://www.columbus.k12.oh.us/franklinalt/index.html**
Tech Prep Schools	Wayne High School, Ontario Center, NY **http://wayne.k12.ny.us/High.cfm?subpage=83209** Englewood Tech Prep Academy, Chicago, IL **http://www.englewood.cps.k12.il.us/administration/ index.htm**
Magnet Schools	East Millbrook Magnet Middle School, Raleigh, NC **http://eastmillbrookms.wcpss.net/modules/news** Roskruge Bilingual Magnet Middle School, Tucson, AZ **http://www.ade.az.gov/srcs/ReportCards/57552003.pdf** Thomas Edison Middle School: A Science, Mathematics and Technology Magnet, Meriden, CT **http://www.aces.k12.ct.us/tedison** Leroy Martin: A Gifted and Talented Middle School, Raleigh, NC **http://martinms.wcpss.net**
College-Preparatory Schools	Florida Air Academy: College Preparatory Day and Boarding School, Grades 6–12, Melbourne, FL **http://www.flair.com/pages/academy/index.htm** Chaminade College Preparatory School, Grades 6–12, St. Louis, MO **http://portal.chaminade-stl.com** KIPP: LEAD College Prep Charter School, Middle School, Gary, IN **http://www.kipplead.org/06**

U.S. are so bad that their only hope is to get into a charter school. Although the film has been praised for shining the spotlight on the desperate need for educational reform, many critics feel that the film was much too simplistic and that it painted an unfair comparison between privately well-funded charter schools and the public school system. No doubt there are "dropout factories" and low-performing schools that are unacceptable, but critics claim that the film ignores that there are excellent traditional public schools as well.

Today, the charter school model has gained popularity, and the Obama administration is making charter schools important in the education reform agenda. Still other critics complain that the charter schools' "success" rate is exaggerated in *Waiting for "Superman"* and point out that the

model is not replicable in a large enough scale to have a meaningful impact on our public school system. Still, charter schools are gaining popularity.

By 2010, there were over 4,700 charter schools across 39 states and the District of Columbia serving more than 1.5 million students. Although several charter schools have closed in the past decade, many others have opened, and the overall number of charter schools has increased by 5%. In addition to the increase in the number of charter schools, the enrollment in individual charter schools has grown over time. Even though there has been an increase in school enrollments since 1999–2000, they still tend to serve fewer students than traditional public schools. In fact, over 30% of charter schools had fewer than 300 students in 2008–2009. To find out more about charter schools, complete Activity 2.1 and Activity 2.2.

K–8 Schools

Many grade configurations have been considered in order to better meet the needs of young adolescents. In the past 30 years, school districts across the U.S. have placed "tweens" in middle schools and junior highs; that is, they have separated young adolescents from younger children and older adolescents. As mentioned in Chapter 1, the dominant middle school configuration houses students in grades 5 through 8 or 6 through 8 and was designed to serve as the "bridge" to high school. These new middle schools became quite popular and displaced both traditional **K–8 schools** and junior high schools during the 1960s and 1970s. Many schools switched to the new grade configuration; between 1970 and 2000, the number of middle schools dramatically increased from 1,500 to 11,500[29] but failed to adopt the middle school philosophy. Rather, their policies and practices remained practically unchanged, and they continued to run their middle schools just as they had before the reorganization. Of course, these superficial changes did not prove to be effective.

Although the current research on grade configuration is not definitive, one proposed reorganization alternative, the K–8 schools, has gained popularity. Recently, several large urban school districts across the country in Cincinnati, Cleveland, Milwaukee, New York City, Philadelphia, and Portland, as well as in other cities, have converted their middle schools to K–8 schools. In an effort to better address the developmental needs of their preadolescents and early adolescents, many educators have embraced the return to the K–8 school and have focused on three essential elements: striving for academic excellence, meeting adolescents' unique needs, and promoting social equity.[30] In fact, high-quality middle-grade schooling is critical, and research has shown that the middle grades do matter.[31] Middle grades should prepare young adolescents for the demands of high school, college, and careers while boosting academic achievement and reducing dropout rates. Complete Activity 2.3 to weigh the pros and cons of the K–8 school configuration.

Activity
2.1   **Charter Schools**

The number of charter schools in the U.S. is on the rise. It follows, then, that the student enrollment in charter schools has also increased. In fact, in the decade spanning from 1999–2000 to 2008–2009, the number of students enrolled in public charter schools more than tripled from 340,000 to 1.4 million students. Although a significant overall increase, only a small percentage of the approximately 54 million K–12 students in this nation attend charter schools.

In 2008–2009, over half the charter schools, approximately 54%, were elementary schools, while secondary schools accounted for 27% and combined schools 19% of all charter schools. Public charter schools are now found across the U.S., although the prevalence of charter schools definitely varies by state. There are many high-profile charter schools, such as the Promise Academy Charter Schools of Harlem Children's Zone, Inc.; the KIPP: Knowledge Is Power Program, America's largest network of charter schools; and the SEED School of Washington, D.C., a public charter school, as well as the nation's first college-preparatory, tuition-free boarding school. Charter schools are now found in 40 states and the District of Columbia, but a charter school law has not yet passed in the following 10 states: Alabama, Kentucky, Maine, Montana, Nebraska, North Dakota, South Dakota, Vermont, Washington, and West Virginia.

Charter schools are publicly funded schools that enter into an agreement with a group or organization under a legislative contract or charter with their respective state. They often receive additional funding from private donors. By agreeing to the stipulations of their charter, the school is then exempted from certain state or local rules and regulations. In return for receiving funding and exercising its autonomy, the charter school must meet the accountability standards specified in its charter. Every three to five years, the schools are reviewed to make sure they meet the guidelines laid out in their charters.

Apply Your Knowledge

Peruse the websites about charter schools listed here and answer the questions that follow.

U.S. Department of Education, National Center for Education Statistics
http://nces.ed.gov/fastfacts/display.asp?id=30

U.S. Department of Education, National Center for Education Statistics: Numbers and Types of Public Elementary and Secondary Schools from the Common Core of Data: School Year 2009–10
http://nces.ed.gov/pubs2011/pesschools09/tables/table_02.asp

Colorado League of Charter Schools: Focus on Achievement
http://www.coloradoleague.org/colorado-charter-schools/
  charter-schools-fact-sheet.php

Charter School Performance in Pennsylvania
http://credo.stanford.edu/reports/
  PA%20State%20Report_20110404_FINAL.pdf

Studies That Grade Charter Schools Rely on Imperfect Math
http://online.wsj.com/article/
  SB10001424052748704170404575624562978485450.html

KIPP: Knowledge Is Power Programs
http://www.kipp.org

KIPP Schools: A Reform Triumph or Disappointment?
http://www.time.com/time/nation/article/0,8599,2067941,00.html

SEED Foundation
http://www.seedfoundation.com

SEED Foundation: Washington, D.C.
http://www.seedfoundation.com/index.php/seed-schools/
  washington-dc

How the SEED School Is Changing Lives
http://www.cbsnews.com/stories/2010/05/21/60minutes/
  main6506911.shtml

1. What information did you uncover about charter schools? What do critics of charter schools question? What do supporters of charter schools claim?
2. Although there is debate, there is some consensus among various studies to support that charter schools have been effective with certain student populations. Researchers generally have found that charter schools in low-income, urban areas boost test scores, while suburban charter schools in wealthier areas do not. What evidence did you find to support or refute this statement?
3. What similarities and differences did you uncover between the philosophies of KIPP and the SEED Foundation?

Activity
2.2   **Geoffrey Canada and the Harlem Children's Zone**

Geoffrey Canada is known as a passionate advocate for educational reform. Since 1990, Canada has served as the president and chief executive officer for Harlem Children's Zone. He is committed to a block-by-block approach to ending poverty and ensuring educational opportunity for disadvantaged inner-city children. Canada's vision includes an integrated, comprehensive range of social, medical, and educational services for his students, their families, and the community. As a matter of fact, he promises to follow his students along the educational pipeline from the time they enter his schools until they graduate from college. The *New York Times Magazine* referred to Canada's efforts as "one of the most ambitious social experiments of our time." Moreover, it has been reported that his rigorous,

high-quality, well-rounded academic program has moved in on closing the achievement gap between black and white students.

A graduate of the Harvard Graduate School of Education, Canada is a true visionary who has led the new renaissance in Harlem and attained superhero status. In 2005, he was named one of "America's Best Leaders" by *U.S. News and World Report*. In the 2010 documentary *Waiting for "Superman,"* his accomplishments were praised, and once again, in 2011, his efforts were recognized when he made *Time* magazine's "2011 TIME 100" list. In addition, he has appeared on many television programs, including *60 Minutes*, *Oprah Winfrey*, *Today*, *Good Morning America*, and *Nightline*, among others.

A c t i v i t y 2.2   *continued*

In its inception, Canada's pilot program reached out to children in a one-block area in central Harlem. Today, the Zone Project targets an area covering 100 city blocks and provides services to some 10,000 children. In addition to providing a good education, the Harlem Children's Zone also offers early childhood programs, after-school services, and parenting programs as well as other assistance.

The Promise Academy Charter Schools were created in partnership with Harlem Children's Zone, Inc., to provide safety, structure, cultural enrichment activities, and much more for their students. The Promise Academy Charter Schools boast a dedicated staff, a one-to-six teacher-to-student ratio, a first-class gym, state-of-the-art science labs, and other amenities. With an annual operating budget of $36 million and a $42 million new school building; unlimited medical, dental, and mental health services; and an impressive "A" rating on the New York City Department of Education's progress report, parents are anxious to enroll their children in the Promise Academy Charter Schools. Unfortunately, admission is by lottery, and many disappointed students and their families are turned away.

Apply Your Knowledge

Peruse the websites focusing on Canada and the Harlem Children's Zone and the Promise Academy Charter Schools listed here and answer the questions that follow.

About Geoffrey Canada: Leading HCZ in Its Work with Inner-City Children
http://www.hcz.org/about-us/about-geoffrey-canada

Harlem Children's Zone: Doing Whatever It Takes to Educate Children and Strengthen the Community
http://www.hcz.org

Promise Academy Charter Schools
http://www.hcz.org/programs/promise-academy-charter-schools

The 2011 TIME 100: Geoffrey Canada: School Reformer
http://www.time.com/time/specials/packages/
    article/0,28804,2066367_2066369_2066100,00.html

New York Times **Articles about Geoffrey Canada**
http://topics.nytimes.com/topics/reference/timestopics/
    people/c/geoffrey_canada/index.html

1. What criticisms could people possibly have about schools like the Promise Academy Charter Schools, which are designed to help the neediest of children?
2. What are the keys to Geoffrey Canada's success?
3. What are the challenges to replicating the Harlem School Zone model across the U.S.?

A c t i v i t y 2.3   **K–8 Schools**

In January 2007, half the schools in New York City that did not meet Adequate Yearly Progress under the NCLB guidelines were middle schools, and more than 70% of the eighth graders in the city failed to meet the state standards in reading and math.[32] To combat the poor academic performance of middle schoolers, educators in major school districts across the country have converted from the traditional middle schools to a K–8 configuration in hopes of improving teaching and learning. Because of middle school students' unique cognitive and emotional needs, teaching them is considered to be challenging. This predicament leaves stakeholders asking the question of how best to configure our K–12 schools to meet the needs of seventh and eighth graders. In the 1960s, middle schools were considered the answer. Recently, there has been a trend to reexamine the K–8 concept to best meet the needs of "elemiddles," that is, 12- to 13-year-old students. By creating a community atmosphere and stability for the young adolescents, the hopes are that seventh and eighth graders will thrive in K–8 schools.

Apply Your Knowledge

Read about the advantages and challenges associated with the K–8 configuration by perusing the websites listed here and then answer the questions that follow.

K–8 Schools: An Idea for the New Millennium?
http://www.educationworld.com/a_admin/admin/
    admin115.shtml

The Middle School Crisis: The Challenge of Engaging Adolescents
http://pdarea.teachingmatters.org/node/918

What the Research Says (or Doesn't Say) About K–8 v. Middle School Grade Configurations
http://www.nwrel.org/nwedu/11-03/research

Education May Get Old School K–8 Look
http://www.courierpress.com/news/2007/jan/22/
    education-may-get-old-school-k-8-look

Boston Shifts to K–8 Schools to Help Students in Middle
http://www.boston.com/news/education/k_12/articles/2004/
    12/04/boston_shifts_to_k_8_schools_ to_help_students_
    in_middle

1. What are the most interesting pros and cons you uncovered for the K–8 configuration?
2. What do you think is the best configuration for addressing the developmental needs of preadolescents and young adolescents? Why?
3. How can K–8 schools promote academic achievement and still foster self-exploration, socialization, and group learning?

Challenges and Issues That Plague the Nation's Middle and Secondary Schools

Major problems and issues plague our nation's schools, some of which are listed in Figure 2.2. Some of these are discussed in subsequent chapters (see index for topic locations). Perhaps you and members of your class can identify other issues and problems faced by our nation's schools.[33]

Adolescent Illiteracy

It has been said that reading is the cornerstone of academic achievement. In fact, students who are not reading at grade level by third grade are very likely to experience increasing academic failure throughout their education. There is no question that reading is an important building block not only in language arts but also in all other core and extracurricular areas, including subjects such as science and mathematics. Yet national data show that 69 % of all eighth graders are not proficient in comprehending the meaning of their grade-appropriate texts and that 26 % of students read below the basic level. In middle and high school, the literacy demands increase because the structural complexity increases (sentences are longer and more complex, and the vocabulary is more sophisticated), the importance of graphic representations increases (illustrations become more complex, their meaning becomes more difficult to interpret, and the conceptual challenge increases), (the concepts become increasingly more abstract and rely more on previous knowledge and the application of that

knowledge).[34] The research shows that adolescent students are often unable to synthesize from one task to another and from one set of concepts to the next set of concepts. In middle and secondary school, not only does the reliance on texts increase, but the texts used across a variety of content areas differ greatly as well. This makes reading compression and writing demands more challenging. Moreover, studies also reveal that even those high school students who have average reading ability and read at grade level are unprepared for the literacy demands they will face in college and the workplace.[35]

Adolescent illiteracy is a national crisis; adolescent illiteracy is as high as 50 % among certain minority and special needs groups in our middle and secondary schools. Even among more heterogeneous school populations, 15 % to 20 % of high school students are likely to read significantly below their grade level. Every day in the U.S., more than 7,000 students drop out of school; that means that 1.2 million adolescents per year do not graduate with their peers.[36] Poor reading achievement has been identified as one of the key factors influencing a student's decision to quit school. Adolescent literacy proficiency is tallied yearly and reported in "The Nation's Report Card" compiled by the National Assessment of Educational Progress, which recently reported that more than two-thirds of our eighth graders nationwide (68 %) read below the proficient level and that as many as one-quarter are unable to read at even the most basic level.[37]

Many of the dropouts have low literacy skills, which means they cannot read well and often are unable to

Figure 2.2 **Problems and Issues That Plague the Nation's Schools**

- A demand for test scores and statistics that can be used to judge schools and their principals
- Buildings badly in need of repair and upgrading
- Bullying of students by other students
- Continued controversy over traditional ability grouping or tracking
- Continuing controversy over books and their content
- Continuing, long-running controversy over values, morality, and sexuality education
- Controversy created by the concept of teaching less content but teaching it better
- Controversy over concept of a national curriculum with national assessments
- Identification and development of programs that recognize, develop, and nurture talents in all our youths at all levels of education
- Retention in grade versus social promotion
- Scarcity of teachers of color to serve as role models for minority youth
- School security and the related problem of weapons, crime, violence, and drugs on school campuses and in school neighborhoods
- Schools that are too large
- Sexual harassment of students, mostly from other students but sometimes from school employees
- Shortage of qualified teachers, especially in special education, bilingual education, science, and mathematics, and in schools located in poverty-stricken areas
- Teaching and assessing for higher-order thinking skills
- The education of teachers to work effectively with students who may be too overwhelmed by personal problems to focus on learning and to succeed in school

Activity
2.4
Addressing Adolescent Illiteracy

Excellent, well-prepared teachers possess more than factual knowledge in their subject areas; they also acquire a deep understanding of how to teach their content to students. Along the same lines, all middle and secondary school teachers are reading teachers regardless of the subject area they teach. Therefore, teachers should know about the literacy demands their students face and how to recognize and address specific literacy difficulties. In fact, teachers who are the most effective in meeting the needs of middle and secondary school students understand their respective content areas well and the specific literacy challenges the texts they assign to their students present.

No doubt, teachers will have students who read on grade level as well as students who read above grade level in their classes. They also will have students who struggle with reading and are in need of reading interventions in order to access and grasp the same content as their classmates. Since students may have basic literacy skills and still struggle with the more sophisticated demands reading in the content areas presents, teachers need to differentiate instruction, that is, address student differences, to meet the literacy needs of all of their students.

Students at Shiprock High School on the Navajo Reservation in New Mexico are involved in a program designed to improve reading achievement. In Mr. Espinoza's freshman science class, he groups students according to their reading levels and has students working on a variety of tasks simultaneously. Espinoza has students engaged in the following: "a group of students follows the directions to conduct an experiment on soil analysis; another group works at a bank of computers in the back of the room preparing PowerPoint presentations on sections of the textbook

chapter; a few students cluster around a computer looking up information on the Internet; and others read scientific materials silently."[39]

Apply Your Knowledge

Check out the websites listed here to learn about efforts to address adolescent illiteracy and answer the questions that follow.

Motivating Reluctant Adolescent Readers
http://www.nwrel.org/learns/tutor/win2000/index.html

Leadership for Literacy: High School Principals and the Reading Challenge
http://principalspartnership.com/feature302.html

Adolescent Literacy: A National Reading Crisis
http://teacher.scholastic.com/products/read180/pdfs/
   612_Profl_Paper_Fleishman.pdf

Carnegie Corporation's Advancing Literacy Initiative
http://www.carnegie.org/literacy/why.html

New York Times: "In Cities, a Battle to Improve Teenage Literacy"
http://query.nytimes.com/gst/fullpage.html?res=9F04E7DB163BF
   937A25757C0A9629C8B63&sec=&spon=&pagewanted=print

1. What can you do as a future (your subject area) _____ classroom teacher to promote reading across the curriculum?
2. What services were available in your middle and/or secondary school to help struggling readers?

comprehend what is written in their textbooks. In fact, students with below-grade-level reading skills are twice as likely to drop out of school. For middle and secondary school students, the social and economic ramifications of being a poor reader are often cumulative and profound. If an adolescent fails to earn a high school diploma, he or she may be barred from pursuing a higher education, which may result in lifelong underemployment or unemployment. Poor readers may also suffer from poor self-esteem if they experience school failure and have trouble relating to others.[38] Complete Activity 2.4.

In addition to developing basic literacy skills, students can benefit by learning how to read critically. **Critical literacy** was developed by followers of Paulo Freire's critical pedagogy philosophy and is designed to examine the relationship among power, inequality, and social injustice in the education context. Critical literacy is an instructional approach that provides students with strategies to actively analyze the texts they are assigned to read and increase their comprehension. In critical literacy, students decode words, examine syntax, interpret messages, and uncover hidden meanings. They actively analyze the content of textbooks and other materials to look for various forms of bias. Students learn to look for selective removal

of certain topics or issues. Critical literacy is compatible with **21st Century Skills,** which are discussed later in this chapter. Complete Activity 2.5 now to examine perspective and stereotypes in texts.

Struggling Students/High School Dropouts

Even though graduation rates can be viewed as the ultimate indicator of school performance, only in recent years have dropouts been tracked and graduation rates reported accurately. As a result, the public has been made aware of the gravity of the dropout crisis, and high schools have come under scrutiny. Every school day, approximately 7,200 students drop out of school. That translates to a young person dropping out every 26 seconds. In fact, on average, only 70% of students graduate from high school on time with a diploma.[40] If we break down the graduation rates according to race, we see that minority students are the least likely to graduate. On average, the graduation rates for minority students, except for Asians, have been alarmingly low. The graduation rates for African Americans (54.7%), Hispanics (50.8%), and American Indian and Alaska Natives (46.6%) reflect that reality. On the other hand, the graduation rate

A c t i v i t y
2.5
Activity for Critical Literacy

Working in pairs, students will examine a set of two to four excerpts from published literature by or about American Indians. The excerpts share a common motif, theme, or setting, but they differ in other ways, including perspective.

To discuss PERSPECTIVE, students may ask the following:

• How do word choice, imagery, and details or ideas help to communicate the author's perspective in each excerpt?
• What *is* the author's perspective?
• What may have contributed to that perspective? Culture, personal experience, historical and geographical context? Anything else?
• Is the perspective a point of view, or is it bias? How can you tell?
• How might the perspective influence or affect meaning?

To discuss STEREOTYPES, students may ask the following:

• How might the selections support or contradict any popular stereotypes of American Indians in particular?

Or

• What stereotypes might this excerpt perpetuate?

To COMPARE and CONTRAST, students may ask the following:

• How might they compare or contrast with each other? (perspective, imagery [both visual and verbal], motif, theme, setting, and so on)
• How might different audiences respond to these texts, depending on their age or culture or ethnic background or historical time period?

Examples:

Set A

1. Smith, John. 1894. "General History of Virginia." In *American Literature, Yellow Level,* 14–19. Evanston, IL: McDougal, Littell. A page describing one of Smith's first encounters with Indians.
2. Washburn, Wilcomb E., ed. 1964. Document 5 of "Personal Relations: Captain John Smith." *The Indian and the White Man.* Documents in American History Series. Garden City, NY: Anchor. Two of Smith's men, Walter Russell and Anas Todkill, include remarks of Wahunsonacoch (Powhatan) regarding John Smith.
3. Banks, Lynne Reid. *Return of the Indian in the Cupboard.* New York: Doubleday, 1986. pp. 34–35.

4. Catlin, George (circa 1832). "Journals of Exploration." In *The Last Best Place,* ed. William Kittredge and Annick Smith (Helena: Montana Historical Society Press), pp. 181–82.

Set B

1. Fleischer, Jane. *Sitting Bull.* Mahwah, NJ: Troll Associates. pp. 30–31.
2. Mcleese, Don. *Sitting Bull.* Native American Legends Series. Vero Beach, FL: Rourke Publishing, 2004. pp. 4, 11.
3. Sneve, Virginia Driving Hawk (Lakota). "Tatanka Yotanka, Sitting Bull: 1831 or 38–1890, Hunkpapa Teton." *They Led a Nation: The Sioux Chiefs—Biographical & Pictorial Essays of 20 Dakota Leaders.* Sioux Falls, SD: Brevet Press, Inc., 1992. p. 28.

Set C

1. Highwater, Jamake. *Anpao: An American Odyssey.* Philadelphia: Lippincott, 1977. p. 20.
2. Medicine Crow, Joseph (Crow). *Counting Coup: Becoming a Crow Chief on the Reservation and Beyond.* Washington, DC: National Geographic, 2006. p. 103.
3. Wallis, Velma (Athabascan). *Bird Girl and the Man Who Followed the Sun.* New York: HarperCollins, 1997. p. 200.

Set D

1. Jones, David E. *Sanapia, Commanche Medicine Woman.* Prospect Heights, IL: Waveland Press, 1972. pp. 18–19.
2. Ancona, George. *Powwow.* New York: Harcourt Brace & Co., 1993.

Set E

1. Wilder, Laura Ingalls. *Little House on the Prairie.* New York: Harper & Row, 1971. pp. 32–33.
2. Medicine Crow, Joseph (Crow). *Counting Coup.* Washington, DC: National Geographic, 2006. pp. 39–40.

Set F

1. Eurbank, Patricia Reeder. *Seaman's Journal.* 2002. page—"Off Teton River, September 1804."
2. Sneve, Virginia Driving Hawk. *Bad River Boys: A Meeting of the Lakota Sioux with Lewis and Clark.* New York: Holiday House, Inc., 2005. Sicangu Chiefs honoring American chiefs and "Historical Note."

SOURCE: Contributed by Dorothea M. Susag, author of *Roots and Branches: A Resource of Native American Literature Themes, Lessons, and Bibliographies.* Urbana, IL: National Council of Teachers of English, 1998.

for Asians is the highest at 77.9% and for whites it is 69.8%.[41] Approximately 2,000 chronically underperforming high schools, referred to as "dropout factories," make up only 12% of the high schools across the country but account for more than half the nation's dropouts.

Although there is no one reason why students drop out of high school, all too often the choice to drop out is made in the middle school grades. Unfortunately, high schools inherit the accumulated effects of previous failures. That means that more than half the ninth graders at urban high schools begin their high school experience with academic skills several years below grade level. Consequently, they struggle in high school, and more than 1 million of ninth graders who start high school each fall fail to graduate with

their classmates four years later. In reality, one-third of all dropouts leave school in ninth grade. Since academic success in ninth grade is predictive of a student's likely graduation from high school, schools are designing programs to help ninth graders reach their academic and social potentials. Current reform efforts, many of which are discussed here, are aimed at identifying at-risk students earlier and providing them with the support they need to be successful, stay in school, and graduate.

High school dropout rates are related to several negative outcomes, including incarceration, reliance on public programs and social services, lack of health care, and diminished occupational opportunities. Dropouts often pay a steep economic price in terms of wages, unemployment

Teaching Scenario	**Drop Out or Push Out?**

Mark was a happy, well-adjusted, curious child until the spring of second grade. The youngest of four siblings, he attended a Montessori school from the age of three until he started kindergarten at Potter Elementary School. He loved school. He loved his classmates, his teachers, and his lessons. Right before spring break of his second-grade year, Mark's father was laid off from his well-paying job as a petroleum engineer. He applied for several positions in the months following his dismissal, but all he could find was a temporary job as a truck driver. The route was grueling; it took him away from his family for long stretches of time. When his contract expired, he found himself unemployed once again. At the end of that summer, Mark's dad left for Alaska in search of work, leaving the family behind in Montana. He called weekly and visited occasionally, but the contact Mark had with his dad over the next several months was minimal. The jobs Mark's dad found were short lived. He moved from Alaska to Kansas to Texas. It was a difficult time for everyone, but Mark missed his dad the most.

Eight months after he left, the family received a message that his dad had dropped dead unexpectedly at his warehouse job in his home state of Texas. Mark was only nine years old. He was devastated. Mark's grandmother buried her only son before his family was able to reach Houston. Consequently, Mark did not have the opportunity to say good-bye.

In addition to the emotional loss, the family suffered financially. Their home went into foreclosure, and they were forced to move to a small apartment. Mark's third-grade year was difficult. He was moody and depressed. Mark was obviously grieving the loss of his father. Unfortunately, his teacher seemed insensitive to his pain. She flunked Mark on a seed project, and his mother was called to the school. The teacher was openly hostile and blurted out in front of Mark that she thought he should be held back. Mark was very hurt by the comment; his mother was incensed. She shared her outrage with the principal, who assured her that this would not happen again, but things between Mark and his teacher escalated.

In the teacher's opinion, Mark was unfocused and inattentive. This teacher was frustrated and sent Mark to the school counselor, who diagnosed him as having attention deficit disorder. Mark's mother disagreed with the diagnosis and fought to keep Mark off Ritalin. Mark's mother consulted another therapist, who suggested trying an alternative prescription, Adderall. It didn't work. The diagnosis changed from attention deficit disorder to depression, and Mark started taking an antidepressant medication, Paxil.

Mark's mother kept him at Potter Elementary School, thinking he needed the stability, even though she didn't have a car and had to call taxis to transport her son to and from school. In addition, Mark's mother, who had always been a stay-at-home mom, was forced to get a full-time job, leaving Mark with friends and family between 3:00 P.M. and 6:00 P.M. during the school week. Mark's mom tried to console her son. She had this to say about what she told Mark: "This was all so sad; we were changed irrevocably, but we needed to move on. We had to honor the things about Dad that were good, but we couldn't stay in mourning forever."

Mark remained at Potter through sixth grade. He did not do well. He just limped through. Comments on his report cards often included statements like this: "Not living up to his potential" or "Angry and passive aggressive." Things at Chief Plenty Coup Middle School only exacerbated Mark's isolation. The first week of school his guidance counselor said, "I remember your brother; you're not getting away with anything here!" When his mother heard about the comment, she asked that Mark be switched to another counselor. Mark still wore a long face and appeared withdrawn. His inappropriate behavior, negative demeanor, and academic failures were excused by many of his teachers at his new school, who felt sorry for his circumstances. "We can't expect too much," was the attitude. Mark's mom was dismayed to find that three years after her husband's death, Mark's teachers were still letting him slide.

Mark squeaked through middle school, although it was a very rough road. Mark ended up hanging with the "stoners," and his mother suspected that pot was not the only drug her son was using. At the end of the first semester at East High, it was obvious that Mark's frequent absences and numerous tardies had resulted in failing grades in all his subjects. At the end of his freshman year, the disciplinarian, Mr. Keruthers, suggested that Mark transfer to the alternative high school. Mark had not earned any credits as a ninth grader.

Mark's mother did not know what to do. She tried creative bribery. She gave Mark $5.00 for lunch if he promised to go to school and tempted him with another $5.00 if he stuck out the day. Often, he would leave for school in the morning but walk off campus when he felt like it. The principal at the alternative school suggested that Mark drop out. She encouraged him to lay low until his 16th birthday and then quit. She stopped reporting his absences. Mark did not share his circumstances with his mother, nor did the school. In fact, it was six weeks after he officially dropped out of school before his mother heard about his situation. She was shocked to find out that no parental approval was necessary for her son to drop out of school. She felt that 16 was just too young to be making such a life-altering decision.

rates, and career mobility. Not every dropout faces a bleak future, but the lack of a high school diploma can close many doors. The costs of high dropout rates to individuals, communities, and the nation are significant. In fact, the Alliance of Excellent Education claims that if, by 2020, high schools and colleges in this country could raise the graduation rates of African American, Hispanic, and American Indian/Alaska Native students to 70%, the same level as white students, the increased personal income would add more than $310 billion to the U.S. economy.[42]

Meaningful Curriculum Options

Decision makers rely on evidence-based data to make sound curricular decisions. Here we describe a few of the most popular curriculum options that are data-driven, align with the standards, and provide students with individualized instruction designed to meet their needs. The curriculum options covered here include differentiated instruction and **tiered assignments,** Response to Intervention, and **Understanding by Design and backwards design.**

Differentiated Instruction

Since students are not all alike, it stands to reason that they take in and process information differently. One of the best approaches for providing opportunities for students to rely on their strengths and work on their weaknesses is differentiated instruction, which requires teachers to be flexible and to tailor their instruction. The differentiated instruction philosophy supports adjusting the curriculum instead of having the students adjust; that is, it promotes adapting instructional strategies to students instead of expecting students to change themselves for the curriculum. Carol Ann Tomlinson defines differentiated instruction as the process of "ensuring that what a student learns, how he/she learns it, and how the student demonstrates what he/she has learned is a match for that student's readiness level, interests, and preferred mode of learning."[43] It is a student-centered approach that addresses student differences by incorporating multiple options for taking in information and making sense of ideas. Differentiated instruction is based on the premise that instructional approaches should vary and be adapted in relation to individual and diverse students in classrooms.[44]

Differentiated instruction is viewed as a proactive approach to instruction and a philosophy that has as many faces as practitioners. Teachers who are committed to this approach spend time getting to know their students because they believe that who they teach shapes how they teach since who the students are as individuals shapes how they learn. In differentiated instruction, teachers use an eclectic approach to lesson planning and vary instructional strategies. Since all students are different, a one-size-fits-all approach is inadequate. To be effective, teachers have to keep each student's interests, preferences, readiness, and needs in mind when they are planning instruction.

There are several different elements that instructors can differentiate on the basis of students' learning profiles, readiness, and interests. The most common ones include content (what the student needs to learn), process (the activities the students engage in), products (the culminating projects that demonstrate what the student has learned), and the learning environment (what the classroom environment is like). As a classroom teacher, to differentiate content, you could provide students with supplemental materials to reach all the learning modalities (auditory, visual, tactile, and kinesthetic) and provide opportunities for small groups to review concepts or opportunities for advanced students to extend their skills. Examples of process differentiation include using tiered instruction to address students' needs, varying the time students spend on tasks and activities depending on their needs, allowing students to explore lesson extensions according to their interests, and supplying hands-on activities for those who need them. Product differentiation can include providing students with multiple ways to demonstrate their learning and using rubrics that correspond to their various individual skill levels. Differentiating the learning environment includes setting up different spaces within the classroom for individual and group work and laying out guidelines for independent work that matches students' individual needs.[45] Creating a classroom climate conducive to learning where students feel both comfortable and challenged is key. Complete Activity 2.6.

Response to Intervention: A Tiered Approach to Instructing All Students

Response to Intervention is a framework that allows educators to make critical educational decisions in order to improve educational outcomes. It is a tiered, multilevel approach to instruction designed to ensure that the needs of all students are met. In fact, **Response to Intervention (RTI)** can be adopted as a schoolwide strategy to instruct all students. Instead of just waiting for students to fail academically before intervening, educators implementing RTI models address students' learning difficulties with early intervention strategies. They do this by frequently monitoring all students' academic progress in hopes of identifying students who are struggling so that modifications to the instruction can be made that match the students' needs.[46]

Interest in RTI is growing, and almost every state has adopted an RTI model. RTI models use assessment data to design instruction on a tiered, gradually intensifying basis.[47] The tiered RTI framework requires a research-based core curriculum and instruction program designed to meet the needs of most students supplemented with a variety of increasingly intensive interventions for students having difficulty. With RTI, teachers and administrators focus on making changes in the environment of struggling students instead of just identifying deficiencies in those students. Consequently, RTI puts the burden on educators to demonstrate that they have done everything possible to help each student be successful.

Most commonly, RTI is used for instruction in reading, writing, and math. There are different models of RTI, several of which incorporate a three-tiered model that is often depicted as a triangle. At each tier in a three-tiered model, students receive effective, differentiated instruction. The intensity of instruction at each tier varies, depending on the students' needs. In a tiered framework, all students participate in tier 1 instruction, where they receive effective differentiated instruction delivered by their regular classroom teacher. It is estimated that instruction at tier 1 can be expected to meet the learning needs of approximately 80% to 85% of the students. Students whose needs are not met by tier 1 instruction will require more intensive interventions. Tier 2 interventions are offered to the 15% of students who need additional help; it builds on the instruction provided at tier 1 and offers more intensive, systematic, evidence-based instruction designed to help students so that they can catch up with their classmates. Tier 2 interventions are usually delivered by the classroom teacher or another educator who is trained in the implementation of RTI. The students who receive the intensive additional

The Blueberry Story

In his infamous speech, one that has become known as the "Blueberry Story," Jamie Vollmer angered his audience of educators when he boasted, "If I ran my business the way you people operate your schools, I wouldn't be in business very long."

Vollmer, former chief executive officer of the Great Midwestern Ice Cream Company, was thrown into a media frenzy when *People* magazine chose his company's blueberry ice cream as the "Best Ice Cream in America" in 1984. His accolades resulted in numerous speaking invitations on various topics, including education, but it was the Blueberry Story that captured the nation's attention. Like many other business leaders, Vollmer thought he had the answer to what plagued the education system and decided to share it with a crowd of teachers, principals, bus drivers, classroom aides, custodians, and support staff. In fact, Vollmer explained his assumptions about the education system: (a) public schools were archaic and profoundly flawed, (b) teachers were reticent to change, and (c) schools should be run like businesses.

The fateful day of the Blueberry Story, a high school English teacher taught an important lesson when she challenged Vollmer's claims. She pointed out that unlike chief executive officers, teachers cannot send back inferior blueberries. She explained that teachers do not control the quality of their raw material, nor do they have unlimited revenue streams. She also noted that educators are under constant scrutiny from various and often opposing groups.

Vollmer's Blueberry Story was a life-changing occasion. He listened to what teachers, students, parents, and community members had to say, and he visited lots of schools. Once a harsh critic of our education system, Vollmer is now an advocate for school improvement. Since his transformation, he promotes strong community-school partnerships and solicits support for America's schools. Even though Vollmer's candid confession of his memorable speech highlights, "the speech was perfectly balanced—equal parts ignorance and arrogance," he still argues for change. He insists that America must change if we expect the education system to change and insists that educators cannot

do it alone. He insists that change must be systemic; it must encompass what, when, and how we teach to provide all students with equal educational opportunities if we want them to thrive in a postindustrial society.

Today, Vollmer works as a consultant and motivational speaker. He is the author of *Schools Cannot Do It Alone: Building Public Support for America's Public Schools*, and he has produced the following highly acclaimed videos: *Why Our Schools Need to Change*, *Building Support for America's Schools*, and *Praise for America's Teachers*. Vollmer has also compiled a decade-by-decade list of all the academic, social, and health responsibilities that have been added to the curriculum in the past 100 years. He first called his compilation the "Increasing Burden on America's Schools," but it is now known across the country simply as "Vollmer's List."

Apply Your Knowledge

The Blueberry Story first appeared in print in the March 6, 2002, issue of *Education Week* and has been recounted and reprinted in numerous venues. If you are unfamiliar with the Blueberry Story or would like to refresh your memory, check out the first website listed below. To learn more about Mr. Vollmer, see the other sites listed.

The Blueberry Story: The Teacher Gives the Businessman a Lesson
http://teachers.net/gazette/JUN02/vollmer.html

Jamie Vollmer
http://www.jamievollmer.com/about.html

Vollmer's List: The Increasing Burden Placed on America's Public Schools
http://www.jamievollmer.com/list.html

Bill Cirone: Story about Blueberries Shares Important Message about Teaching
http://www.noozhawk.com/article/
  060111_bill_cirone_blueberries_and_teaching

---

targeted tier 2 instruction still continue to receive the general tier 1 instruction with their classmates. In other words, tier 2 interventions do not replace the core curriculum but are designed to supplement it by offering extended learning opportunities based on data that have been collected about students' individual challenges.[48]

In tier 3, the most intensive interventions are offered for the small percentage, approximately 5% of students, for whom tier 2 interventions were not enough. Tier 3 instruction is delivered to individual students or small groups of students by a specialist or by a special education teacher. The intensity of the intervention is increased, as are the opportunities for direct instruction and catching up with classmates. Like tier 2 interventions, the interventions at tier 3 are also designed to supplement the instruction at tier 1. For the small percentage of students for whom tier 3 interventions are not adequate, special education services may be recommended.[49]

One advantage of the tiered assignments is that students do not have to be labeled as disabled in order to receive these interventions. RTI is a student-centered approach, and decisions on what interventions to implement are made on the basis of data and ongoing formative and summative assessments. Although there has been a lot of research done on the implementation of RTI in the elementary grades, less is known about how effective RTI strategies are with middle and high school students. In fact, some educators feel that RTI is an elementary model being imposed at the secondary level. Dr. William Bender has studied the implementation of RTI at the middle and secondary levels and points out that even though there are commonalities, there are some differences between implementing RTI in primary and secondary schools. He suggests that RTI might work best during key transition periods, that is, when students move between elementary and middle school and again between middle school and high school. He points out that by the time a student enters middle school, educators have a more comprehensive picture of a student's academic achievement since there are several assessments in the student's file. He also mentions the fact that middle and high schools often have programmatic differences and that instead of using learning centers and stations as a means to organize instruction, tier 2 interventions are usually not done by the general classroom teachers in high school; rather, students may seek help during a planned intervention period, for example, in a math or writing lab. Another challenge is time since high school schedules may not be conducive to team meetings. Above all, Bender points out the importance of looking at schools that have model RTI programs in place in order to differentiate and improve instruction for all students.[50]

Understanding by Design and Backwards Design

Understanding by Design is a widely used framework designed to guide curricular improvement and increase student achievement. It was developed by Drs. Grant Wiggins and Jay McTighe and published by the ASCD in 1998. It is focused on "teaching for understanding." Understanding by Design emphasizes the critical role teachers play in student learning. Wiggins and McTighe's framework is based on what they describe as the "six facets of understanding." These include students being able to do the following: "explain, interpret, apply, have perspective, empathize, and have self-knowledge about a given topic."[51]

Backwards Design is the central premise of Wiggins and McTighe's larger Understanding by Design framework. It focuses on outcomes and addresses the question, "What deep and enduring understandings do I want my students to come away with from the content I teach?" Simply, it has educators start with the outcomes in mind and then work backward. When using Backwards Design, teachers focus on the desired outcomes in order to plan and design their curriculum, instruction, and assessments.

According to proponents of Understanding by Design, the typical approach to designing curriculum is flawed. Traditionally, teachers start curriculum planning by focusing on the activities they would like to do and the textbooks they want to cover instead of thinking about the big picture and identifying classroom learning goals and planning towards those goals. Backwards Design, on the other hand, encourages teachers to start the process by identifying outcomes before planning the curriculum and choosing activities and materials. They believe that this outcomes-based approach helps teachers better determine their students' abilities and foster their learning.

Backwards Design includes three stages: goal setting, designing assessments, and planning instruction. In Backwards Design, teachers ask themselves, "At the conclusion of my instruction, what should the students know or be able to do as a result of the instruction that they did not know or were unable to do before?" Teachers who apply Backwards Design effectively should design coherent curriculum, clearly articulate their goals by sharing the big ideas and essential questions with their students, lay out the performance requirements and the criteria that will be used to evaluate the students' work, and set high expectations for all students. Teachers should assess their students regularly, review the results of achievement data, and seek constructive feedback from their students and their peers in order to tweak their curriculum design and instructional strategies.

There is a comprehensive training package available for Understanding by Design that is designed to help teachers clarify learning goals and design, edit, critique, share, and improve their lessons and assessments. Teachers, schools, and districts benefit by collaborating on Understanding by Design because their work is more focused, engaging, coherent, and effective.

Key Trends Designed to Prepare Our Students for the Future

There are a variety of key trends and practices today, many of which are addressed throughout this text. In this section, we focus on three areas designed to engage students and promote college and career readiness for future global demands. We briefly cover 21st Century Skills, data-driven decision making, and **service learning**. To view a list of additional key trends and practices in today's middle and secondary schools, see Figure 2.3.

21st Century Skills

In order to be college and workplace ready and to be globally competitive, our middle and secondary school students need to develop new skills. Teachers today are preparing students for jobs that do not exist now and an environment that is unknown. This is a daunting task. How do we know what our students will need? Although we cannot predict the specifics surrounding the knowledge, skills, and abilities the future will demand, what educators do know is that our students will need a synthesis of "specific skills, content knowledge, and expertise and literacies."[52]

Twenty-first Century Skills is one of the most ubiquitous terms used in current debates on education. There are multiple descriptions of 21st Century Skills, but most definitions include a combination of these skill sets: life skills, workforce skills, interpersonal skills, applied skills, and noncognitive skills. Technology literacy is also often included. In actuality, the 21st-century label can be misleading since knowing how to think critically, analytically, and creatively are not skills specific or unique to this century; they have been around from ancient times with Socrates to the 20th century with John Dewey. Yes, philosophers and educators have argued for centuries that students need to develop these skills; these are not new skills, just newly important ones.[53] The framework for 21st-century learning describes a holistic view of student outcomes. It

Figure 2.3 **Key Trends and Practices in Today's Middle and Secondary Schools**

- Dividing the student body and faculty into smaller cohort groups and using nontraditional scheduling and interdisciplinary teaching teams
- Encouraging self-control and problem solving
- Facilitating students' social skills as they interact, relate to one another, and develop relationships and peaceful friendships
- Facilitating the developing of students' values as related to families, the community, and schools
- Holding high expectations, although not necessarily the same expectations, for all students by establishing goals and assessing results against those goals
- Integrating the curriculum, and introducing reading, thinking, and writing across the curriculum
- Involving communities in the schools and involving parents and guardians in school decision making
- Involving students in self-assessment
- Making multicultural education work for all students
- Providing meaningful curriculum options with multiple pathways for academic success
- Providing students with the time and the opportunity to think and to be creative, rather than simply memorizing and repeating information
- Redefining giftedness to include nonacademic as well as traditional academic abilities
- Using heterogeneous grouping and cooperative learning, peer coaching, and cross-age tutoring as instructional strategies
- Using the Internet as a communication tool and learning resource
- Using occupations to contextualize learning and instruction to vitalize the transition from school to work

summarizes the key elements of 21st-century learning by the four Cs: (1) critical thinking and problem solving, (2) communication, (3) collaboration, and (4) creativity and innovation.[54]

There are both proponents and critics of 21st-century learning. One of the greatest critics of the 21st Century Skills is the Core Knowledge Foundation, whose supporters argue that students need a core foundation of knowledge and opportunities to develop critical thinking and problem solving before they can learn for themselves. They believe that the focus on 21st Century Skills detracts from teaching the core curriculum. On the other hand, supporters of 21st Century Skills think that for students to be employed in the future or to attend college, workers and students need to be "independent thinkers, problem solvers, and decision makers." Therefore, many believe the focus should be on what high school graduates can do with knowledge instead of what knowledge they have acquired. Perhaps it is best to have a focus on both content and skills. Complete Activity 2.7 now.

Activity 2.7

Ken Robinson Says Schools Kill Creativity

British-born author and educator, Sir Ken Robinson is a creativity expert. He serves as an international adviser on education in the arts to a variety of organizations including various governments, nonprofits, education systems, and art groups. He was the director of the Arts in Schools Project from 1985 to 1989 and from 1989 until 2001 was a professor of arts education at the University of Warwick in Coventry. Originally from a working-class Liverpool family, Robinson was knighted in 2003 for his service to the field of arts education.

Sir Ken Robinson challenges the way we are educating our children. He champions a radical rethink of our school systems. He emphasizes the importance of cultivating creativity and acknowledging multiple types of intelligence. He says that schools kill creativity. In his riveting, humorous, widely distributed TEDTalk, Robinson highlights how our school systems squelch students' creativity.

Apply Your Knowledge

Listen to Robinson's illuminating TEDTalk on creativity (the first website listed) and peruse the other websites about his ideas on creativity. Then answer the questions that follow.

Ken Robinson Says Schools Kill Creativity
http://www.ted.com/talks/
    ken_robinson_says_schools_kill_creativity.html

TED Ideas Worth Spreading: Ken Robinson: Author Educator
http://www.ted.com/speakers/sir_ken_robinson.html

Ken Robinson: Changing Education Paradigms
http://www.ted.com/talks/
    ken_robinson_changing_educationdigms.html

Sir Ken Robinson: Bring on the Learning Revolution
http://www.ted.com/talks/
    sir_ken_robinson_bring_on_the_revolution.html

1. What do you think of Sir Ken Robinson's views on creativity?
2. What can be done to promote student creativity in your subject area?

Exit Exams

States want to improve the academic achievement of their students. In order to accomplish that goal, many of them are requiring high school students to pass exit exams in order to obtain their diplomas. However, these exit exams often harm students who fail to pass them and at the same time do not really benefit students who pass them successfully.[55] Students once earned their high school diplomas by attending classes and earning passing grades. The Carnegie Unit, based on "seat time," granted credits to students who satisfactorily passed their courses. If students obtained the required minimum number of credits toward graduation, they graduated from high school and earned a high school diploma. This accountability system has been in place for over 100 years even though critics believe it is outdated. In the late 1970s, states started requiring that students pass exit exams to receive their diplomas. Exit exams are comprehensive standardized tests designed to assess students' core knowledge in a number of subject areas and basic skills. To date, 23 states have added "exit exams" to their graduation requirements. In fact, in 2009, it was estimated that two out of three high school students in the U.S. were required to pass an exit exam in order to obtain a high school diploma.

We have all heard the tragic story of a high school graduate unable to read his or her own diploma. No one is saying this scenario is acceptable. Since so many students were lacking basic literacy and numeracy skills upon graduation, requiring students to pass exit exams has become popular. Unfortunately, exit exams deny diplomas to some and may even cause others to drop out. In fact, many researchers concluded that state exit exams negatively impact graduation rates and force teachers "to teach to the test." Although some employers may think that students who have passed an exit exam demonstrate tenacity and follow-through, the research here does not support their implementation.

Teaching Scenario | **Data-Driven Decision Making**

Dr. Holly Hunts is a teacher-educator at Montana State University in Bozeman. In addition to supervising secondary student teachers, she teaches courses in methods of teaching family and consumer sciences, curriculum development in family and consumer sciences, research methods in health and human development, and lifespan: human development and personal and family finance. She has provided a rationale for knowing how to access, interpret, and analyze statistics to make informed, data-driven decisions.

Keeping up with the latest in educational trends and research empowers teachers to be the following:

- Prepared for discussions with administrators and school boards about policy decisions
- Able to design curriculum that is current in addressing national/ state strengths and deficiencies
- Ready to write strong grant proposals by being able to include the current research in support of the grant
- Include current data in lesson plans
- Understand national reports on the state of education, including dropout rates, diversity issues, achievement levels, teacher performance, and a host of other topics

While in college, be sure to take advantage of your university's library. Reference librarians specialize in helping college students and faculty learn how to successfully search for valid and reliable research. The research skills learned in college can last a lifetime.

To find local and state education statistics, visit the state's department of education. A "top six" list of national and international education statistics websites follows.

1. **National Center for Education Statistics**
   http://nces.ed.gov
   This is a very comprehensive website for finding education statistics.

2. **ChildStats**
   http://childstats.gov/americaschildren
   This is a collection of statistic reports about children and families from 22 government agencies.

3. **Secretary's Annual Report on Teacher Quality**
   http://www2.ed.gov/about/reports/annual/teachprep/t2r6.pdf
   This is a good source for finding statistics about the state and quality of teachers at all levels.

4. **U.S. Census Bureau**
   http://www.census.gov
   The census reports on a wide variety of topics, including population information about households, families, race, age, education level, income, and poverty.

5. **Research and Statistics: U.S. Department of Education**
   http://www2.ed.gov/rschstat/landing.jhtml
   This site focuses on national-level school and student assessments, especially as they pertain to the ESEA.

6. **United Nations Educational, Scientific and Cultural Organization (UNESCO)**
   http://www.uis.unesco.org/Pages/default.aspx
   This is a reliable source for worldwide educational statistics.

Think About It

1. Challenge yourself to visit each of the websites listed and your state's department of education website. Record a statistic from each site, making sure to include the corresponding URL.
2. Choose at least two of the statistics from item 1. Describe how you could use each statistic in either a lesson plan, a school board presentation, a grant proposal, in curriculum development, at a faculty meeting, or in some other school-related way.

SOURCE: Dr. Holly Hunts, Montana State University, Department of Health and Human Development, Bozeman, Montana. Used with Permission.

Teaching Scenario — ROC (Reach Out & Care) Wheels Service Learning Project

Spring break 2011 holds a special meaning for a team of 24 students, adults, and physical therapists from Montana who traveled to Montego Bay, Jamaica, with the goal of improving the lives of children with disabilities by distributing 100 custom ROC Chairs that were made locally by students and youth group volunteers. By participating in this amazing service learning project, students used their gifts, talents, and hard work to change lives.

According to the World Health Organization, there are more than 20 million people around the globe who do not have the wheelchairs they need to be mobile and independent. Approximately one-third of those individuals are children. Even if an individual is fortunate enough to have a wheelchair, it is unlikely that he or she has one that fits his or her specific needs. ROC Wheels has focused on designing, building, and custom-fitting wheelchairs for children up to age 15 with a variety of disabilities.

Wayne and Lee Ann Hanson are the founders of ROC Wheels, a nonprofit based in Bozeman, Montana, that provides specialty wheelchairs for people with disabilities in developing countries where rocky, unpaved surfaces present a great challenge. ROC Wheels, through YEWTHS (Youth Empowered With The Helper Spirit) ROC Program, empowers young people to make a positive impact globally and locally by providing opportunities to participate in service learning and social entrepreneurship.

To date, ROC Wheels has distributed more than 8,000 custom-fit wheelchairs worldwide. Of those, over 4,500 were the therapeutic pediatric ROC Chair, which was designed by ROC Wheels's cofounder Wayne Hanson. These unique wheelchairs are durable, sturdy, virtually maintenance free, convenient to transport, and adjustable in size. In fact, the chairs are designed to grow with their users and have an expected life of five to six years.

Belgrade Middle School (BMS) students in Belgrade, Montana, embraced the ROC Wheels mission and built 40 ROC Chairs in their industrial manufacturing class under the guidance of their teacher, Mr. Travis Volkman. BMS is the first school where the wheelchairs have been assembled. Volkman serves as ROC's school wheelchair manufacturing consultant and is developing a nationwide curriculum that would allow schools across the U.S. to involve their students. "This will allow us to transfer [the program] from school to school," Volkman said, adding that the curriculum could also be used by other youth organizations, including Boys and Girls Clubs, 4-H clubs, and church youth groups.

Eighth graders at BMS learned to read blueprints and instruction manuals, learned manufacturing principles and helped improve the lives of people in developing countries by building wheelchairs. The chairs arrived at school as kits of about 320 parts each. A completed chair represents a total of eight hours of work by each two-person student team. The eighth graders assembled the wheelchairs during six-week sessions in Volkman's class. He says the students learned four key lessons during the process: teamwork, responsibility, accountability, and the manufacturing process and industrial manufacturing while making the wheelchairs.

The middle school students at BMS also created 100 beautifully hand-painted wooden rocking horses in their wood shop and art classes to give to the wheelchair recipients. Fund-raising was also done to purchase the wheelchair kits, which cost $350 each. Students in the home economics classes pitched in and made ROC Doll magnets to raise donations for sponsoring ROC Chairs. To support the ROC Wheels service learning project, during the fall 2010 semester, the Belgrade High School ceramics art class students composed wearable masterpieces using ceramic beads, string, glaze, and ribbon and sold their innovative jewelry designs. Sunday school children from nearby Amsterdam Church designed and printed colorful gift cards to raise awareness and sponsorship for ROC Chairs. Other local schools (Monforton in the Four Corners area, Sourdough Montessori, Heritage Christian, Manhattan Christian, Pass Creek, Belgrade High, Ridgeview Elementary in Belgrade, and Emily Dickinson in Bozeman) also helped ROC Wheels by raising funds through the sale of necklaces and dolls that they created in their art classes. Students at a neighboring middle school, Chief Joseph in Bozeman jumped in and also built wheelchairs, sewed wheelchair bags, and assembled gift bags filled with toiletries and toys.

To learn more about ROC Wheels and yewthsroc.org, consult the following websites.

Reach Out & Care Wheels
http://www.rocwheels.org

Building New Opportunities: Local Youth Are Making a Global Impact
http://www.rocwheels.com/Summer2010/summer_2010.pdf

Reach Out & Care Wheels Blog 2010
http://roc-wheels.blogspot.com/2010/07/jamaica-mon.html

Reach Out & Care Wheels Blog 2011
http://roc-wheels.blogspot.com

Middle Schoolers Learn Manufacturing Basics, Help Disabled Children Abroad
http://belgradebeacon.com/2010/03/03/
middle-schoolers-learn-manufacturing

Data-Driven Decision Making

In recent years, data-driven decision making has gained popularity in education. In fact, NCLB has presented new opportunities and incentives for educators to use data by providing schools and districts with additional data for analysis as well as increasing the pressure on them to improve student test scores. All too often, school leaders and classroom teachers have relied on gut feelings, intuition, anecdotes, or personal experiences to make decisions. People believe that looking at data can be too time intensive and too difficult, but instead of being overwhelmed by focusing on lots of data, what is more important is to collect, analyze, and interpret meaningful data. Schools already have numerous data sources involving leadership, professional development, instructional practices, school climate, and parental involvement.

The concept of data-driven decision making in education is not new and can be traced to the debates about measurement-driven instruction in the 1980s. Data-driven decision making in education is modeled on successful practices from industry and manufacturing that emphasize using various types of data to promote organizational improvement. Administrators and teachers are using several types of data to guide their decisions, including process or input data and other types of outcome data, such as student work, and achievement tests and state summative tests designed to test students' knowledge skills. Given the high stakes attached to student achievement tests and the fact that there is a federal mandate that states distribute these results in aggregate and disaggregated forms, it is not surprising that many superintendents, principals, and teachers view test scores as useful for guiding decision making. Flowers and Carpenter lay out five steps to help schools use data to make decisions that will lead to student successes: (1) review your school improvement plan, (2) determine how the data will be used, (3) identify relevant data, (4) examine and discuss the data and set goals, and (5) evaluate progress.[56] One of the greatest benefits of relying on data to inform decisions is that better decisions can be made because they are based on informed reflection. Another benefit of the data-driven decision-making process is that it can be used to back up and support decisions if you are faced with opposition.[57]

Service Learning with Global Impact

Service learning was first mentioned in Chapter 1, where we defined the concept. Here we will expand on our discussion of service learning and highlight how it helps with academic, civic, personal, social, ethical, and vocational development.[58] There are numerous studies praising the positive impact on students who choose to participate in service learning projects, but not all students have the opportunity to participate in service learning in their local communities, and even fewer have the chance to make a global impact. Although service learning has existed in K–12 education for over 30 years, it is found in less than 30% of primary and secondary schools.

It has been found that participation in service learning can have positive effects on students' performance on academic-content examinations. Supporters believe this is a direct result of an increased motivation toward school and more positive attitudes toward learning in general. By participating in service learning, students develop an enhanced civic responsibility and citizenship along with enhanced personal and social skills.[59] By nurturing adolescents' civic actions, motivations, and skills, learning benefits for both youth and society can be realized. This dynamic of mutual individual and societal benefit is the cornerstone of service learning.[60] To read about how middle school students in Montana who participated in a service learning project changed lives, read the Teaching Scenario on ROC Wheels.

Summary

There is an opportunity and a need to transform the education system in the U.S. New global demands require that students be ready for postsecondary education and the workplace when they graduate from high school. We must meet our students' individual and collective needs while blending essential skills and content knowledge in our curriculum and instruction. We must tackle the growing achievement gaps between wealthy and poor students, between white and nonwhite students, and between students here in this country and their international peers. We must hold high expectations for all students and identify struggling students early on in order to attack the dismal dropout rates.

Many educators envision a shift from the traditional education where textbooks, physical classrooms, lectures, worksheets, standardized tests, and everything else that characterized education in the 20th century are replaced. One thing is for sure: we need to provide our students with opportunities to be engaged, learn at their own pace, foster virtual relationships, rely on technology, and expand their creativity. Examples of how best to help students to be successful academically were presented in this chapter. In Chapter 3, we will discuss who the students of our middle and secondary schools are today and provide guidelines for how best to meet their needs.

Exercise 2.1   **My First Micro Peer-Teaching Demonstration—MPT I**

Instructions: Prepare a five-minute micro peer-teaching (MPT) demonstration and present it to your classmates. You may choose any topic and strategy, but the MPT should be video-recorded so that you can later compare this first MPT with Exercise 12.2.

Chapter 2   POSTTEST

Short Explanation

1. Describe recent reform efforts and their impact on middle and secondary schools and their students.

2. Describe the pros and cons of the adoption of Common Core State Standards.

3. Define 21st Century Skills and how they can help students to be prepared for college and the workplace.

4. Describe how differentiated instruction can meet the needs of diverse learners.

5. Describe how tiered assignments help students to be academically successful.

Essay

1. The Association for Middle Level Education describes the Essential Attributes and Characteristics of Successful Schools. Describe why you think several of the 16 characteristics included in their report promote effective middle-grades education.

2. Watch *Waiting for "Superman"* and share your thoughts on the best ways to turn around low-performing schools and eliminate "dropout factories."

3. How do you explain the phenomenal growth in the number of charter schools since the first charter school opened its doors in Minnesota about two decades ago? What do you see as the future for the charter school movement?

4. From your current observations and fieldwork (related to your teacher preparation program), clearly identify one specific example of an educational practice that seems contradictory to exemplary practice or theory as presented here. Present your explanation for the discrepancy.

Photo Fotolia

Middle and Secondary School Students:
Addressing Cultural Diversity

It is time for the preachers, the rabbis, the priests and pundits, and the professors to believe in the awesome wonder of diversity so that they can teach those who follow them. It is time for parents to teach young people early on that in diversity there is beauty and there is strength. We all should know that diversity makes for a rich tapestry, and we must understand that all the threads of the tapestry are equal in value no matter their color; equal in importance no matter their texture.[1]

—MAYA ANGELOU

Specific Objectives

At the completion of this chapter, you will be able to:

▸ Define the terms *cultural competence* and *multicultural education* and identify skills in recognizing, celebrating, and building on student diversity.

▸ Explain the five caveats and five domains used to describe adolescent development.

▸ Demonstrate an understanding of the significance of the concepts of learning modalities, learning styles, and learning capacities and of their implications for appropriate educational practice.

▸ Describe appropriate curriculum options and instructional practices for specific groups of learners.

▸ Apply your developing knowledge of practical ways of recognizing and attending to students' individual differences while working with a cohort of students.

Chapter 3 Overview

The ways in which individuals differ are innumerable. Not only are there differences in physical appearance and in personality traits, but there are also differences in life experiences and cultural backgrounds. Some students have academic talents that are readily identified, whereas others' gifts are not so apparent; some students seem well adjusted, whereas others do not appear as resilient; some students are from socioeconomic, religious, or ethnic backgrounds similar to yours, whereas others have drastically different identities. Some of these differences may be of no consequence as far as school is concerned; however, other differences are extremely important for teaching because what passes as sound educational practice for one person may not be as effective for another. Thus, in this chapter we cover some of the common characteristics and individual differences in students that you will need to consider when planning for instruction, and we provide guidelines for leveraging classroom diversity. While considering what to teach and how to teach it, you will need to focus on your students and the best way to be responsive to their developmental and individual needs. There is no one best method of teaching. Rather, there are numerous methods that may or may not be effective in a particular situation with particular students.

Introduction

Not only is there variation in the purpose, organization, and structure of our middle and secondary schools across America (as discussed in Chapter 1), but the students of today represent tremendous diversity as well. Although there are many commonalities among adolescents, each student is a unique individual. In fact, adolescent students differ in many ways. In order to teach preadolescents, early adolescents, and late adolescents successfully, you need to understand how they think, what motivates them, and where their interests lie. You also need to know their personal values and beliefs. This information, in addition to knowledge of what is developmentally appropriate at their age, will help you to make sound instructional decisions and create a classroom climate conducive to learning. This chapter is designed to help you gather this information and gain this understanding.

Adolescence

Characteristics of Middle and Secondary School Students

Middle and secondary school students embark on the journey from childhood to adulthood. In a dramatic growth spurt during the early years of middle school, children begin changing from little boys and girls to awkward adolescents with new secondary sex characteristics and all the problems that come with changing life roles. This growing up continues until the adolescent becomes a young adult—a process often not complete until the postsecondary years.

During the middle school years (ages 10 through 14) and throughout late adolescence (ages 15 through 19), individual differences in physical, intellectual, social, and emotional growth are striking. Individuals seem to change markedly from day to day, for this is not only a period of growth but also a period of instability and insecurity.

Although adolescents desire and need opportunities to act independently, they also need and want security and support. Because of these contrasting needs for dependence on and escape from adult domination, young people tend to band together for mutual support as they experiment with new sociosexual roles. To find comfort, they often become conformists and are extremely susceptible to peer pressure.

Nevertheless, adolescents normally are self-motivated, active, and interested in novelty. Their intellectual growth causes them to be interested in ideas and eventually allows them to cope with formal intellectual operations and abstract ideas. These desires compel some adolescents to adopt idealistic causes and others to try adventures and roles that get them into trouble.

Adolescence, undoubtedly one of the most trying times in life, is a period marked by change and uncertainty (see Figure 3.1). As discussed in Chapter 1, middle school educators generally have recognized that students in those early adolescent years need a nurturing educational experience to guide them through this unstable period. Educators have learned that to be most effective, school organization and instructional techniques must be quite different from those of the past.

Teaching Adolescents

The bell rings, and the students enter your classroom, a kaleidoscope of personalities, each a bundle of eccentricities,

different concentrations, different life experiences, and different dispositions and capacities. What a challenge this is—to understand and to teach 30 or so unique individuals in a class, all at once, and to do it for six hours a day, five days a week, 180 days a year!

So, how do you help each of your students reach his or her academic and social potential? Because adolescence is an important stage of identity development in which the rite of passage from childhood to adulthood remains unpredictable even if it may be typified, schools and teachers need to provide numerous opportunities for adolescents to explore and experiment in a stable and supportive environment. Adolescents share certain commonalities with their peers, so we can generalize what you need to know about what occurs during adolescence.

As educators, we want to make sure that adolescent learning needs are addressed in their school experiences. Learning is enhanced for adolescents when it is developmentally appropriate. In fact, integrating a combination of developmentally and personally appropriate accommodations is the best way to meet your students' needs. Complete Activity 3.1.

Also, to better understand how to support adolescent academic and social success, check out the comprehensive list of external and internal assets that the Search Institute compiled after conducting extensive research on students in grades 6 through 12. Their list appears in Figure 3.1 and highlights external and internal assets that help adolescents to grow up into productive, well-adjusted young adults Also, be sure to peruse their website (**http://www.search-institute.org/assets/forty.html**) to learn more about the 40 Developmental Assets for Adolescents and the available resources and support for communities, educators, and families.

Adolescent Development

In *Teaching Ten to Fourteen Year Olds*, Chris Stevenson highlights five "givens" concerning the passage from childhood to adulthood and then expands on what to expect in the five key domains that capture the changes that young adolescents go through.[2] The five caveats Stevenson outlines hold true universally for the adolescent experience. He explains them in the following manner:

> 1. Early adolescence is a growth period characterized by enormous change and variability among children.
> 2. Individual schedules of change are idiosyncratic.
> 3. Home, neighborhood, prevailing gender roles, and racial and ethnic identity influence development. 4. The influences and effects of early adolescent experiences are long-lasting. 5. Young adolescents thrive when their needs are being met.[3]

Summarized, these five truths suggest that even though all individuals go through tremendous changes during adolescence, they do so at their own pace. In addition, the home and school cultures influence the changes that usually result in profound effects. Stevenson's framework for understanding adolescent behavior considers these five

Figure 3.1 40 Developmental Assets for Adolescents

40 Developmental Assets® for Adolescents (ages 12–18)

Search Institute® has identified the following building blocks of healthy development—known as **Developmental Assets®**—that help young people grow up healthy, caring, and responsible.

External Assets

Support
1. **Family support**—Family life provides high levels of love and support.
2. **Positive family communication**—Young person and her or his parent(s) communicate positively, and young person is willing to seek advice and counsel from parents.
3. **Other adult relationships**—Young person receives support from three or more nonparent adults.
4. **Caring neighborhood**—Young person experiences caring neighbors.
5. **Caring school climate**—School provides a caring, encouraging environment.
6. **Parent involvement in schooling**—Parent(s) are actively involved in helping young person succeed in school.

Empowerment
7. **Community values youth**—Young person perceives that adults in the community value youth.
8. **Youth as resources**—Young people are given useful roles in the community.
9. **Service to others**—Young person serves in the community one hour or more per week.
10. **Safety**—Young person feels safe at home, school, and in the neighborhood.

Boundaries & Expectations
11. **Family boundaries**—Family has clear rules and consequences and monitors the young person's whereabouts.
12. **School boundaries**—School provides clear rules and consequences.
13. **Neighborhood boundaries**—Neighbors take responsibility for monitoring young people's behavior.
14. **Adult role models**—Parent(s) and other adults model positive, responsible behavior.
15. **Positive peer influence**—Young person's best friends model responsible behavior.
16. **High expectations**—Both parent(s) and teachers encourage the young person to do well.

Constructive Use of Time
17. **Creative activities**—Young person spends three or more hours per week in lessons or practice in music, theater, or other arts.
18. **Youth programs**—Young person spends three or more hours per week in sports, clubs, or organizations at school and/or in the community.
19. **Religious community**—Young person spends one or more hours per week in activities in a religious institution.
20. **Time at home**—Young person is out with friends "with nothing special to do" two or fewer nights per week.

Internal Assets

Commitment to Learning
21. **Achievement motivation**—Young person is motivated to do well in school.
22. **School engagement**—Young person is actively engaged in learning.
23. **Homework**—Young person reports doing at least one hour of homework every school day.
24. **Bonding to school**—Young person cares about her or his school.
25. **Reading for pleasure**—Young person reads for pleasure three or more hours per week.

Positive Values
26. **Caring**—Young person places high value on helping other people.
27. **Equality and social justice**—Young person places high value on promoting equality and reducing hunger and poverty.
28. **Integrity**—Young person acts on convictions and stands up for her or his beliefs.
29. **Honesty**—Young person "tells the truth even when it is not easy."
30. **Responsibility**—Young person accepts and takes personal responsibility.
31. **Restraint**—Young person believes it is important not to be sexually active or to use alcohol or other drugs.

Social Competencies
32. **Planning and decision making**—Young person knows how to plan ahead and make choices.
33. **Interpersonal competence**—Young person has empathy, sensitivity, and friendship skills.
34. **Cultural competence**—Young person has knowledge of and comfort with people of different cultural/racial/ethnic backgrounds.
35. **Resistance skills**—Young person can resist negative peer pressure and dangerous situations.
36. **Peaceful conflict resolution**—Young person seeks to resolve conflict nonviolently.

Positive Identity
37. **Personal power**—Young person feels he or she has control over "things that happen to me."
38. **Self-esteem**—Young person reports having a high self-esteem.
39. **Sense of purpose**—Young person reports that "my life has a purpose."
40. **Positive view of personal future**—Young person is optimistic about her or his personal future.

Novels about and for Middle and Secondary School Students

Do you want to know about the lives of middle or secondary school students? The following list contains contemporary teacher biographies, fiction, and nonfiction dealing with educational matters that affect adolescents.

The Absolutely True Diary of a Part-Time Indian, Sherman Alexie
Among School Children, Tracy Kidder
Another Planet: A Year in the Life of a Suburban High School, Elinor Burquett
Bee Season, Myla Goldberg
Bringing Up Boys: Practical Advice and Encouragement for Those Shaping the Next Generation of Men, James C. Dobson
Crank, Ellen Hopkins
The Essential 55: An Award Winning Educator's Rules for Discovering the Successful Student in Every Child, Ron Clark
Feeling Lucky?, Daniel Blanchard
Finding My Voice, Marie Lee
Fires in the Bathroom: Advice for Teachers from High School Students, Kathleen Cushman
First Time in the High School Classroom, Mary C. Clement
Freedom Writers Diary, The Freedom Writers with Erin Gruwell
Harry Potter, J. K. Rowling
Horace's Compromise: The Dilemma of the American High School, Theodore R. Sizer
Horace's Hope: What Works for the American High School, Theodore R. Sizer
Horace's School: Redesigning the American High School, Theodore R. Sizer
I Know Why the Caged Bird Sings, Maya Angelou
I Won't Learn from You: The Role of Assent in Learning, Herbert Kohl
Jaime Escalante: Sensational Teacher, Ann Byers
Lost Boys: Why Our Sons Turn Violent and How We Can Save Them, James Garbarino
Middle School, Richard Strong
A Mind at a Time, Mel Levine
Monster, Walter Dean Myers
Not Much Just Chillin': The Hidden Lives of Middle Schoolers, Linda Perlstein
Ordinary Resurrections, Jonathan Kozol
The Outsiders, S. E. Hinton

The Perks of Being a Wallflower, Stephen Chobsky
A Place Called School, John Goodlad
Queen, LouAnne Anderson
Queen Bees and Wannabes: Helping Your Daughter Survive Cliques, Gossip, Boyfriends, and Other Realities of Adolescence, Rosalind Wiseman
Rats Saw God, Rob Thomas
Reviving Ofelia: Saving the Selves, Mary Pipher
Savage Inequalities: Children in American Schools, Jonathan Kozol
The Schools Our Children Deserve, Alfie Kohn
The Secret Life of Bees, Sue Monk Kidd
A Separate Peace, John Knowles
The Shame of a Nation: The Restoration of Apartheid Schooling in America, Jonathan Kozol
Small Victories: The Real World of a Teacher, Her Students, and Their High School, Samuel G. Freedman
Speak, Laurie Halse Anderson
Teach as If Your Hair Is on Fire, Rafe Esquith
Teacher, Sylvia Ashton Warner
Teacher Man, Frank McCourt
Tears of a Tiger, Sharon Draper
There Are No Short Cuts, Rafe Esquith
The Truth about Forever, Sarah Desson
Up the Down Staircase, Bel Kaufman
Voices of a Generation: Teenage Girls on Sex, School and Self, Pamela Haag
The Water Is High, Pat Conroy
When I Was Puerto Rican, Esmeralda Santiago
When the Legends Die, Carl A. Adkins

Apply Your Knowledge

1. Select and read one of the books listed here about or for adolescents to expand your understanding of their lives.

2. Write a one-page essay summarizing what you learned about middle or secondary students by reading the book you chose.

3. Share your findings with your classmates.

---

truths while looking at five broad domains and the interplay among them. The five areas of adolescent development that he describes are the introspective domain, the somatic domain, the intellectual domain, the familial domain, and the communal domain.

The central or preeminent area where adolescents ponder their personal identity is the introspective domain that revolves around the key question, "Who am I?" This domain encompasses all the others and is affected by all perceptions, decisions, and changes in the other domains. During adolescence, students engage in constant self-talk in which they weigh, reevaluate, and critically analyze everything.

The somatic domain covers the physical changes that take place during puberty. In addition to being preoccupied

with their looks, adolescents also have concerns regarding their sexuality, fitness, drug and alcohol use, personal hygiene, and overall well-being, among other things. Often described as "walking raging hormones," adolescents are prone to mood swings and volatile behavior.

The changes that occur in the intellectual domain are central to any discussion on cognitive development. It is important for you to understand and respect your students' thought processes and require that they engage in learning that they are capable of handling. Most likely, as part of your educational psychology curriculum, you will cover Swiss psychologist Jean Piaget's developmental stage theory and focus on the types of activities, questioning, and assignments that are appropriate for students at various ages.

The familial domain looks at how adolescents interact with siblings and the evolving relationship they share with their parents and other family members. Students' relationships with relatives influence their classroom interaction. Changing roles and tensions in the family affect adolescents' self-concept and self-esteem and impact their interpersonal relationships.

We cannot underestimate the power of peer influence during this stage. The communal domain addresses the social aspect of school. Many students attend school eager to socialize. Students want to belong and explore group participation in their school, neighborhood, and local community. During adolescence, young people want to branch out and increase their sense of belonging while examining their place in the world.

Although you may think concentrating on cognitive development and its intersection with the subject you are assigned to teach is your sole responsibility, you have to teach the whole child and not limit your focus to the intellectual domain. Because adolescent students have many concerns, you must be aware of them. It is important to develop a good rapport with your students; connectedness promotes learning. Therefore, it is critical that you understand the social, emotional, and physical challenges that typify this stage in addition to the cognitive changes and limitations.

When asked to reflect on their middle school experiences, most individuals' memories are packed with tales of friendships, love interests, family ties, and other social interactions, while the subjects they studied in school are often long forgotten. Truly, adolescence is a time of complex paradoxes and contradictions. In addition to knowing about the profound changes that take place during adolescence, it is important for you to also know about the various microcultures individual students identify with and are members of.

Culture and Its Impact on Education

Cultural Identity

There are many definitions of **culture**. A simple, concise explanation defines culture as shared, learned behavior. We all have a cultural heritage that shapes who we are and helps us to make sense of our world. We are immersed in our cultural way of knowing, and it is as natural to us as the air we breathe. The specifics describing U.S. culture are debated, but most people would agree that we share identifiable cultural patterns that distinguish us from citizens of other cultures. By nature of the fact that you are living within the borders of the U.S. during the 21st century, you share certain characteristics with the dominant U.S. macroculture.

In addition, each of us belongs to many microcultural groups, also referred to as **microcultures**, *subcultures*, or *subsocieties*.[4] Microcultures are distinctive, yet their members share certain cultural patterns with all Americans. As is the case with the many microcultures we each

identify with as we move through various life stages, "we feel, think, perceive and behave, in part, because of the age group to which we belong."[5] We saw evidence of a microculture sharing common characteristics in our discussion of adolescence.

Although age is one microculture you may identify with, we often limit our definition of cultural identity to race and/or ethnicity. We confuse biological factors with cultural factors, leading us to label people on the basis of their race and/or ethnicity, but culture is much more complex than that. Lumping students together and stereotyping them on the basis of their membership in one or two microcultures is confining, faulty, and problematic. Cultural identity is composed of a number of interrelated microcultures, including—in addition to one's age, race, and ethnicity—religion, gender, class, ability, geographic location, and language.[6]

In fact, the diversity of public school students in the U.S. has increased dramatically in recent years. In 2009, estimates reported that as high as 45 % of the K–12 student population were students of color; predictions are that we will have a majority minority student population by 2020. According to the U.S. Department of Education, in 2008, 43 % of students qualified for free and reduced-price lunch programs,[7] and over 20 % of 5- to 17-year-olds spoke a language other than English at home.[8]

As we did with our discussion of adolescence, we will offer generalizations, not perpetuate stereotypes, throughout this textbook to help you to understand commonalities shared to some degree by students who belong to various microcultures. Stereotypes can be damaging, but generalizations can shed light on shared characteristics. **Stereotypes**, which are absolute and inflexible, ignore individual differences, while **generalizations** simply highlight insights that may prove to be helpful. As a teacher, it is important for you to learn about your students and their cultural backgrounds and then reflect that information in your classroom behavior.

Cultural Competency

To uphold democratic ideals and provide educational opportunities for all students, it is important that school policies are equitably enforced. Therefore, the 1,200 schools of education across this country are revamping pre-service teacher training so that you and other education students will be better prepared for the student diversity you will encounter in your future classrooms.

To meet the needs of a multicultural student body, some states are expanding licensure requirements to include a cultural competency component. *Cultural competence* focuses on the ability to effectively teach to a cross-cultural group of students. As defined by Diller and Moule, cultural competence "is the ability to successfully teach students who come from cultures other than your own. It entails mastering complex awareness and sensitivities, various bodies of knowledge, and a set of skills that, taken together, underlie effective cross-cultural teaching."[9]

Teaching Scenario — Making Community Connections: What Does Academe Have to Do with the Real World?

You have chosen one of the most challenging careers of our time given the multiple demands of the social context on teaching and learning. Today more than ever, you need to expand your awareness of the socioeconomic and political environments that influence our educational settings. In the past, the focus was limited to learners' characteristics related to cognitive development and skills. Recently, students' cultural backgrounds and prior experiences are also recognized as important factors when discussing pedagogy and curriculum design. What seems to be missing in this equation is a clear understanding that context— outside of the school—also matters as much if not more than all of these elements. Through my students' journal entries and our class discussions, it is evident that their traditional field experiences and practicum placements, which usually consist of tutoring and support activities, do not help them relate to students and schools in substantive ways. The problem that continues to plague our teacher education programs is the "distance" that exists between academic settings and the broader community. Often we find that teachers are not visible in the communities in which they teach. Few attend extracurricular events at the school, and even fewer are visible at community activities outside of the school, such as town festivals, fairs, and community meetings to address grassroots initiatives.

In an effort to overcome these challenges, as pre-service teachers you need to be more concerned, interested, and visible through community involvement outside of the schools. Mindsets and attitudes need to be transformed through experiences in the community context even before you are placed in schools and classrooms. Involvement in community organizations that serve the community at large; attendance at local poetry recitals, art exhibits, and town meetings; and perhaps even participation as volunteers in some of these venues should precede any interaction with schools. By sharing the lives of your students and their parents, you will understand the issues that affect their lives and those of their children and undoubtedly gain insights that will permeate your teaching. As future teachers, you need to be committed to meeting the needs of all students; the process needs to begin with deeper knowledge about the communities in which your students live and socialize. You need to know how their life experiences and backgrounds have influenced the choices and possibilities that students and their families have made and continue to make. Some of the issues to examine include demographics and migratory patterns; employment histories of the communities such as mills, farms, and factories that may come and go, creating joblessness and poverty in some cases; the mobility patterns affected by newcomers; the role of civic and religious organizations; and housing turnover and patterns of suburban sprawl and their impact.

Once you understand the histories and development of communities in which your schools are located, you will be better equipped to meet the needs of your students. Better dynamics with children and their parents will ensue, and your curriculum design and methods will capture and reflect more relevant content and methods. In my work, I have focused on intensifying these possibilities by involving my students in local events and exposing them to presentations and activities that the majority of students describe as their "firsts" of the kind. One such event in recent years has been accompanying my students to the Dia de los Muertos (Day of the Dead) activity at a local art gallery. The discussions of how death is viewed in different cultures were something new to the students and an important layer of information for understanding the intersections among art, death, celebration, and grieving in the Latino community. The contrasts and the richness of the experiences broadened their perspectives as teachers and as members of the community.

Think About It

1. How have your education professors modeled the importance of community involvement?

2. What community activities/events are you presently participating in?

3. How can you learn about the lives of your students and the community in which they live?

SOURCE: Contributed by Dr. Xae Alicia Reyes, associate professor of curriculum and instruction and Puerto Rican and Latino studies, University of Connecticut, Storrs (http://www.xaealiciareyes.org; http://advance .uconn.edu/2007/070439/07043009.htm).

Although there are many similarities across cultures, the differences in values, traditions, and beliefs within groups and between groups can show up in our schools. To avoid conflict, promote social harmony, and guarantee educational equity, it is important to understand these differences and to model respect for individual differences.

Cultural Sensitivity

To work on becoming culturally competent, you first need to learn about your own cultural background and become aware of your own preferences and unconscious biases. Then you need to learn about the cultural backgrounds of your students. Some of your students' cultures will be more familiar to you than others. Some students will see their home culture reflected in the school context, while other students' experiences at school might have little in common with their home environments.

In order to increase your cultural sensitivity and provide equal educational opportunity for all students, Drs. Donna Gollnick and Philip Chinn make the following suggestions. "To work effectively with the heterogeneous student populations found in schools, educators need to understand and feel comfortable with their own cultural backgrounds. They also must understand the cultural setting in which the school is located to develop effective instructional strategies. They must help their students become aware of cultural differences and inequalities in the nation and in the world. One goal is to help students affirm cultural differences while realizing that individuals across cultures have many similarities."[10]

If you pick up an article addressing the current state of education in this country, you are likely to find the terms *diversity* and *challenge* in the same headline. Instead of viewing diversity in a negative light, we need a paradigm shift that recognizes diversity as the norm. The late Dr. Mel Levine, professor of pediatric medicine, recently published an article titled "Celebrating Diverse Minds." His refreshing approach honors our country's pluralism and rejoices in uncovering each student's unique gifts and talents. Levine explains, "The real challenge for schools rests more with identifying and fortifying individuals' strengths than with caulking academic crevices."[11]

Multicultural Education

Critics and scholars alike disagree on the definition of multicultural education, yet there are core values that most associate with a multicultural education philosophy. Multicultural education is an approach based on the democratic ideals of justice and equality designed to level the playing field. It is an inclusive philosophy of schooling that values learners by validating and incorporating their cultural heritages and life experiences in the teaching-learning process. Multicultural education is infused throughout the curriculum; shapes the classroom environment; dictates procedures, practices, and policies; informs instructional strategies; and frames student-teacher interactions. Effective teaching in culturally diverse classrooms establishes high expectations for all students while promoting culturally responsive standards-based pedagogy. Therefore, one of the key roles of teacher education programs is to promote the cross-cultural understanding of prospective teachers and enhance their cultural diversity awareness and multicultural acceptance. Read the brief descriptions of some of the key researchers and practitioners in the field of multicultural education in Activity 3.2, peruse the corresponding websites, and answer the questions. Complete Activities 3.2 and 3.3 now.

Activity 3.2 | **Leaders in Multicultural Education**

Read about James A. Banks, Sonia Nieto, Geneva Gay, Carl A. Grant, and Christine Sleeter to gain a foundation in the practice and theory surrounding multicultural education. Then peruse the websites included here and answer the questions.

James A. Banks, professor of diversity studies and director of the Center for Multicultural Education at the University of Washington, Seattle, is known as the father of multicultural education. Banks is a prolific author who has written numerous books and articles about multicultural education and social studies education as well as on cultural competence and global citizenship. He edited the *Handbook of Research on Multicultural Education* with Dr. Cherry A. McGee Banks. This superb research collection includes work from several renowned scholars in the field. In addition, Banks has published numerous books, including *Teaching Strategies for Ethnic Studies, Multicultural Education: Issues and Perspectives, Cultural Diversity and Education: Foundations, Curriculum and Teaching, An Introduction to Multicultural Education*, and many others.

Sonia Nieto is professor emerita at University of Massachusetts, Amherst. Nieto's scholarly work has focused on educating culturally and linguistically diverse students in our nation's schools. She has published in several areas, including multicultural and bilingual education, curriculum reform, teacher education, and the education of Latinos and other immigrant student populations. In Nieto's best-selling book, *Affirming Diversity: The Sociopolitical Context of Multicultural Education*, she explores the meaning, necessity, and benefits of multicultural education for students of all backgrounds. Nieto describes how student success or failure in the schools of the 21st century results from a variety of personal, social, political, cultural, as well as educational factors. In the fifth edition of *Affirming Diversity*, Nieto presents 19 case studies of real students and the role that multicultural education plays in their lives.

Geneva Gay is a strong advocate for culturally responsive pedagogy. Gay has questioned why students of color can be so successful in contexts outside of school yet unsuccessful in our classrooms. She suggests several explanations for what she calls the "achievement dilemma." In her research, Gay draws from a variety of case studies against a sound theoretical background. Gay believes that culturally responsive teaching, which validates students' culture and values their life experiences, is the answer to narrowing the achievement gap. She also believes that it is important to strengthen students' relational competencies so they can coexist peacefully. Her books include *Culturally Responsive Teaching: Theory, Research, and Practice, Becoming Multicultural Educators: Personal Journey toward Professional Agency, Expressively Black: The Cultural Basis of Ethnic Identity*, and *At the Essence of Learning: Multicultural Education*.

Carl A. Grant, professor of teacher education in the departments of curriculum and instruction and Afro-American studies at the University of Wisconsin, Madison, served as the president of the National Association for Multicultural Education (NAME) from 1993 to 1999. He has published extensively in the field of multicultural education. Grant's recent publications include *An Education Guide to Diversity in the Classroom, Turning on Learning: Five Approaches for Multicultural Teaching Plans for Race, Class, Gender and Disability* (with Christine Sleeter), and *Making Choices for Multicultural Education: Five Approaches to Race, Class and Gender* (with Christine Sleeter). Grant was awarded the Philip C. Chinn Multicultural Book Award from NAME for *Global Constructions of Multicultural Education: Theories and Realities*.

Christine Sleeter is a professor at California State University, Monterey Bay; current NAME president; and coeditor of *Multicultural Education, Critical Pedagogy, and the Politics of Difference*. She published *Turning on Learning: Five Approaches for Multicultural Teaching Plans for Race, Class, Gender and Disability* and *Making Choices for Multicultural Education: Five Approaches to Race, Class and Gender* (with Carl Grant). According to Sleeter, multiculturalism is a struggle against racism and as such must reach beyond simple appreciation of diversity and address issues of institutional racism, white privilege, social injustice, and educational inequity.

Activity 3.2   *continued*

Apply Your Knowledge

To learn more about these multicultural scholars, peruse the following websites.

Diversity within Unity: Essential Principles for Teaching and Learning in a Multicultural Society, by James Banks
http://www.newhorizons.org/strategies/multicultural/
   banks.htm

About Sonia Nieto
http://www.whyweteach.com/about-sonia-nieto.php

Culturally Responsive Teaching: Theory, Research, and Practice, by Geneva Gay
http://depts.washington.edu/centerme/
   culturallyresponsiveteaching.htm

Rethinking Schools Online: Brown 50 Years Later, by Carl A. Grant
**http://www.rethinkingschools.org/archive/18_03/brow183
   .shtml**

Critical Multicultural Curriculum and the Standards Movement, by Christine Sleeter
http://education.waikato.ac.nz/journal/english_journal/uploads/
   files/2004v3n2dial1.pdf

1. What does a multicultural education approach mean to you as a future (your subject area) (_____) teacher?
2. In your discipline, describe how you would revise a lesson plan to be culturally responsive.

Activity 3.3   Classroom to Community and Back

The Northwest Regional Educational Laboratory (NWREL) produced a practitioner's guide, *Classroom to Community and Back: Using Culturally Responsive Standards-Based (CRSB) Teaching to Strengthen Family and Community Partnerships and Increase Student Achievement*, to highlight best practices in fostering family-community partnerships while implementing culturally responsive pedagogy that is standards based. By integrating family and community culture into the classroom, teachers can create a classroom climate conducive to learning, meet the needs of all students, and close the achievement gap. By valuing students' cultural heritages, validating students' life experiences, and engaging the community, teachers can make learning relevant. Teachers who incorporate the knowledge, skills, and life experiences of their students and their families can build strong family and community partnerships and support educational experiences that occur outside the classroom.

Apply Your Knowledge

You can read the *Classroom to Community and Back* guide online, download it as a free PDF file, or purchase a bound copy.

School-Family-Community Partnerships Team, Classroom to Community and Back: Using Culturally Responsive Standards-Based (CRSB) Teaching to Strengthen Family and Community Partnerships and Increase Student Achievement
http://educationnorthwest.org

Answer the following questions.

1. How could you implement culturally responsive standards-based (CRSB) teaching in your content area in your school context?
2. What strategies does NWREL suggest to integrate culturally responsive teaching, standards-based teaching, and family-community partnerships?

Multicultural Education Defined and Its Implications in Teaching

The concept of **multicultural education** has been around since the 1920s in this country, but the goals have changed through the years. We have shifted from an emphasis on multiethnic education, which includes information on various racial and ethnic groups in the curriculum, to global education that has an international focus and to a multicultural education approach that promotes pluralism and prepares all students to participate in our diverse democratic society.[12]

Because students are not identical and one's culture permeates every cell of one's being, a one-size-fits-all approach to teaching is not effective. All students have the right to learn, and multicultural education upholds that right by valuing diversity. Drs. Gollnick and Chinn define *multicultural education* as "the educational strategy in which students' cultural backgrounds are used to develop effective classroom instruction and school environments. It is designed to support and extend the concepts of culture, diversity, equality, social justice, and democracy in the formal school setting."[13]

Although often misperceived as an add-on to the standard curriculum, valuable exclusively for students of color and other "multicultural students" or for younger children or in social studies classes, the truth is that a multicultural educational approach is excellent pedagogical practice in all grades for all students and across all subject areas. The goal of multicultural education is to make sure all students "experience an equal opportunity to learn." It is your responsibility to establish a classroom climate that reflects your students' personal experiences and cultural backgrounds as well as aligning with their preferred learning styles. "The core theme of K–12 education in this century should be straightforward: high standards with an unwavering commitment to individuality."[14]

According to Futrell, Gomez, and Bedden, "Student diversity is often viewed as a major problem because of the way American schools are organized. The current organizational structure sorts students so that only about 20% receive what is defined as an excellent education.... Schools of education and school districts need to work together to reverse the proportions so that at least 80% of all students—regardless of language, culture, ethnicity, or socioeconomic status—will receive an excellent education."[15]

We also need to prepare students to make a smooth school-to-work transition since, even though the majority of students say they intend to pursue a postsecondary education, in reality, according to the National Center for Education Statistics, only about 60% of high school students go to college, and a smaller percentage, only 35%, actually earn an undergraduate degree.[16] See Activities 3.4 and 3.5.

Activity 3.4

Culturally Responsive Pedagogy: Implementing Indian Education for All (IEFA)

Montana has taken a leadership role in Indian education issues. The Office of Public Instruction is actively committed to ensuring that students learn about American and Montana Indians and their histories as well as foster respect for their unique cultures. The November 2006 edition of *Phi Delta Kappan* highlights the ongoing state initiatives of IEFA.[17]

As is the case with many minority groups in this nation, in the standard K–12 public school curriculum, Indians are often inaccurately portrayed and their contributions inadequately represented. According to the Indian Nations at Risk Task Force, many of our schools have failed to nurture the intellectual development and academic performance of American Indian students, which is evidenced by the students' negative attitudes toward school and the alarmingly high dropout rates. Omissions and misrepresentations negatively impact students and contribute to their limited success. Developing relevant culturally sensitive curriculum for students in Montana's schools inspires high achievement and promotes educational equity and excellence. In addition, efforts have been made to bridge the achievement gap between Indian students and their non-Indian counterparts. Cleary and Peacock, among others, claim, "Schools that acknowledge, accept, and teach a child's cultural heritage have significantly better success in educating students."[18] The goal of IEFA "is that Indian students will feel themselves welcomed when they see themselves reflected in their school hallways and curriculum, and that negative stereotypes will be replaced by an accurate understanding of Indian history, and the federal government's trust duty."[19]

In 2005, the Montana legislature appropriated funds for the development of IEFA to create model curriculums, assemble classroom materials, provide professional development, and fund grants for schools to develop best practices as well as appropriating monies for tribal colleges to develop tribal histories for use by K–12 schools.[20] In Montana all teachers, at all grade levels, teaching all content areas are required to address the history, culture, and contemporary issues of Montana's Indians.

Apply Your Knowledge

In addition to the references cited in the previous four footnotes, check out these websites on culturally responsive pedagogy and ponder the questions that follow.

Addressing Diversity in Schools: Culturally Responsive Pedagogy
http://www.nccrest.org/Briefs/Diversity_Brief.pdf

Culturally Responsive Teaching
http://www.intime.uni.edu/multiculture/curriculum/culture/Teaching.htm

Teaching Diverse Learners: Principles for Culturally Responsive Teaching
http://www.alliance.brown.edu/tdl/tl-strategies/crt-principles.shtml

Culturally Responsive Teaching for American Indian Students
http://www.ericdigests.org/2005-1/teaching.htm

1. Why is it important to practice culturally responsive pedagogy?
2. What can you take away from the lessons on the implementation of IEFA and apply in your school setting?

Activity 3.5

Indian Education for All and the Seven Essential Understandings

In 1999, the Montana legislature passed into law HB 528, **Indian Education for All (IEFA)**, MCA 20-1-501. Once the state of Montana recommitted to integrating IEFA across the K–12 curriculum in all disciplines, what was to be taught had to be determined. In 1999, tribal representatives from all nations in Montana were invited by the Office of Public Instruction to gather together to discuss what core knowledge holds true for each of the distinct American Indian tribes in Montana that would counteract stereotypes, generalizations, myths, and untruths. The Seven Essential Understandings Regarding Montana Indians were created. These seven guidelines articulate concepts such as the diversity among tribes, the persistence of Native ideologies, the validity of oral histories, the establishment of Indian reservations, federal policy periods, and tribal sovereignty. They guide classroom instructors and provide a framework for integrating material on American Indians' histories, cultures, and contemporary issues as well as contributions to core curricular areas.

Apply Your Knowledge

Peruse the following websites and answer the questions.

Seven Essential Understandings Summary
http://www.montanatribes.org/files/7EssUnd-Summary.pdf

The Seven Essential Understandings Regarding Montana Indians
http://opi.mt.gov/pdf/indianed/resources/essentialunderstandings.pdf

1. What did you learn about American Indians of Montana?
2. Why do you think the Seven Essential Understandings addressed the topics they did?
3. How can using the Seven Essential Understandings help you to plan lessons that infuse culturally responsive pedagogy?
4. What suggestions do you have on other material that could be included?

The Classroom in a Nation of Increasing Diversity

Our pluralistic society is becoming more and more complex. Demographic changes in the U.S. have resulted in a very racially, ethnically, religiously, and linguistically heterogeneous student body. In fact, we are one of the most diverse nations in the world. Projections based on immigration patterns and birthrates suggest that we will become even more culturally diverse in the future.

The "melting pot" metaphor, popularized in 1909 by Israel Zangwill's play of the same name,[21] has been replaced with an updated image that honors individual contributions to a diverse mix. The salad bowl, tapestry, orchestra, and mosaic metaphors of today emphasize how each ingredient or component is in itself worthy but, when combined with other ingredients or components, adds to a new, uniquely valuable creation.

As our demographics have changed, we have been re-examining, redefining, and expanding our understanding of the fundamental concepts supporting the teaching-learning process. A multicultural education approach that leverages the diversity we find in our classrooms today by recognizing and embracing student diversity is seen as the most effective model. The goal of this concept is to provide schooling so that all students—male and female students, exceptional students, linguistically diverse students, students of different religious backgrounds, students from the various socioeconomic realities, and students of all racial, ethnic, and cultural heritages—have equal opportunity to achieve academically.[22]

The variety of individual differences among students requires that teachers use strategies and tactics that accommodate those differences. To most effectively teach students who are different from you, you need skills in (a) establishing a classroom climate in which all students feel welcome and where they can learn and are supported in doing so (topic of Chapter 3); (b) techniques that emphasize cooperative and social-interactive learning and that de-emphasize competitive learning (topic of Chapter 6); (c) building on students' learning styles, capacities, and modalities; and (d) strategies and techniques that have proven successful for students of specific differences. The last two skills are the focus of this chapter.

As a licensed teacher, you are expected to know it all or at least to know where you can find all necessary information and to review it when needed. Fortunately, a wealth of information is available. Information you have stored in memory will surface and become useful at the most unexpected times. While concerned about all students' safety and physical well-being, you will want to remain sensitive to each student's attitudes, values, social adjustment, emotional well-being, and cognitive development. You must be prepared to teach one or more subjects effectively with students of different cultural backgrounds, diverse linguistic abilities, and different learning styles as well as with

students who have been identified as having special needs. It is indeed a challenge. The statistics that follow make this challenge even more obvious.

Demographic Changes

The traditional two-parent, two-child family now constitutes only about 6% of U.S. households. Approximately one-half of the children in the U.S. will spend some years being raised by a single parent. Between one-third and one-fourth of U.S. children go home after school to places devoid of any adult supervision. And, on any given day, it is estimated that as many as 300,000 children have no place at all to call home.

The U.S. population is predicted to reach 404 million by 2050 (from 2004's approximately 294 million),[23] a population boom that will be led by Hispanics and Asian Americans. A steady increase in interracial marriages and interracial babies may challenge today's conceptions of multiculturalism and race.[24]

The U.S. truly is a multilingual, multiethnic, multicultural country. According to the U.S. Census Bureau and other predictions, approximately half of the school-age population will consist of students of color by 2020.[25] In some states, nonwhite students are already in the majority. It is also estimated that more than one in six children between the ages of five and seven speak a language other than English at home. More than one-third have been labeled Limited English Proficient (i.e., conversational speaking ability only). In many large school districts, more than 100 languages are represented, with as many as 20 or more different primary languages found in some classrooms. In addition, as many as one in five children lives in poverty. This increasing ethnic, cultural, linguistic, and socioeconomic diversity is affecting schools all across the country, not only the large urban areas but also traditionally homogeneous suburbs and small rural communities.

The overall picture that emerges is a rapidly changing, diverse student population that challenges teaching skills. Teachers who traditionally have used the lecture and other techniques of direct instruction (see Chapter 9) as the dominant mode of instruction have done so with the assumption that their students were relatively homogeneous in terms of experience, background, knowledge, motivation, and facility with the English language. However, no such assumption can be made today in classrooms of such cultural, ethnic, and linguistic diversity. As a classroom teacher of today, you must be knowledgeable and skilled in using teaching strategies that recognize, celebrate, and build on that diversity. See Activity 3.6.

Styles of Learning and Implications for Teaching

The most effective classroom teachers are those who adapt their teaching styles and methods to their students, using approaches (a) that interest the students, (b) that are

Activity
3.6   **Amazing Teen Leaders**

There are adolescents who make a difference. Craig Kielburger and Mattie Stepanek were guests on *Oprah Winfrey* while Francesca Karle and Dallas Jessup shared their stories on *Montel Williams*. Their amazing accomplishments will be briefly described here.

Craig Kielburger founded Free the Children in 1995 when he was just 12 years old. After this young Canadian read about a Pakistani boy, 12-year-old Iqbal Masih, who was killed when he dared to speak out against the deplorable working conditions he and other child laborers in the carpet-making industry were forced to endure, Kielburger took action. Free the Children has grown into the world's largest network of children helping children; more than 100,000 youth from 35 different countries volunteer. Kielburger's organization focuses on education and children's rights, child-labor issues, children and poverty, and children affected by war. In 2001, Kielburger wrote and published *Take Action! A Guide to Active Citizenship* with his older brother, Marc. Kielburger has traveled the world and met with such leaders as Mother Teresa and Nelson Mandela, sharing his journey to effective advocacy.

Mattie Stepanek was a spiritual 13-year-old who was wise beyond his years. He passed away on June 22, 2004, from a rare hereditary form of muscular dystrophy. Before he died, Mattie lost two brothers and his sister to this terminal disease that his mother also suffers from. You would think this would be a heavy burden for a young child, but Mattie exuded joy, courage, and wisdom. Mattie, who wanted to be a peacemaker, started writing poetry when he was only three years old. According to Mattie, everyone has a heartsong, a song in your heart that urges you to be a better person and help others accomplish the same. That is what he shared. His books of poems, *Heartsongs, Journey through Heartsongs* and *Hope through Heartsongs*, which are his legacy, have become national best-sellers.

Francesca Karle is known as the "Hero to the Homeless." When Karle filmed her homemade documentary *On the River's Edge* to challenge the stereotypes of being homeless, she was a 17-year-old senior in high school. She filmed this compassionate depiction of the life of the homeless living along the banks of the Ohio River. Producer/director Karle got the idea for the film after volunteering in Christ Temple's monthly ministry and feeding hot meals to the homeless along the riverbank in Huntington, WV. She held a premiere in Huntington and raised over $25,000,

which she donated to organizations improving the lives of the homeless. As a result, she was honored with the Gold Award, the Girl Scouts' highest honor, and she won first place for the 2005 Best Young Film Maker at the Appalachian Film Festival.

Dallas Jessup, a 15-year-old black belt and founder/spokesperson for Just Yell Fire, created a 45-minute film to empower girls to protect themselves. After seeing an abduction of a teenage girl caught on tape by a surveillance video camera and broadcast on the television news, Jessup developed the Just Yell Fire program depicting 10 strategies to help teens be safe, get out of bad situations, and avoid rape and/or abduction. She wanted her techniques to work every time and to be simple, effective, and automatic. Students from Portland's St. Mary's Academy and La Salle High School participated in the filming of what has been described as "The Coolest High School Project Ever." Those involved in the Just Yell Fire project hope to deter predators and date rapists across the country. *Just Yell Fire* was released on September 28, 2007. It is available for free as a DVD, or it can be downloaded from the website listed here.

Apply Your Knowledge

Read more about these amazing adolescents and their accomplishments at the following websites and answer the questions that follow.

Peacemaker Hero: Craig Kielburger
http://www.myhero.com/myhero/hero.asp?hero=c_Kielburger

Mattie Stepanek's personal website
http://www.mattieonline.com

Francesca Karle: A Hero to the Homeless
http://www.cbsnews.com/stories/2005/04/12/earlyshow/series/
     heros/main687598.shtml

Just Yell Fire
http://www.justyellfire.com

1. What other teen heroes are you familiar with? What difference have they made in the world?
2. What can you do as a classroom teacher to promote teen leadership?

---

neither too easy nor too difficult, (c) that match the students' learning styles and learning capacities, and (d) that are relevant to the students' lives. This adaptation process is further complicated because each student is different. All have varying interests, abilities, backgrounds, and learning styles and capacities. As a matter of fact, not only do young people differ from one another, but each student can change to some extent from one day to the next. Therefore, you need to consider both the nature of students in general (e.g., methods appropriate for a particular seventh-grade class are unlikely to be the same as those that work best for a group of high school seniors) and each student in particular. Because you probably have already experienced a recent course in the psychology of learning, what follows is only a brief synopsis of relevant knowledge about learning.

Learning Modalities

The most basic way that individual students differ is in how they prefer to take in information. **Learning modality** refers to the *sensory portal* (or input channel) by which a learner prefers to receive sensory reception (modality preference), or the actual way a person learns best (modality adeptness). Some students prefer learning by seeing, a *visual modality*; others through instruction from others (through talk), an *auditory modality*; many others by doing and being physically involved, the *kinesthetic modality*; and others by touching objects, the *tactile modality*. A student's modality preference is not always that student's modality strength.

Although primary modality strength can be determined by observing students, it can also be mixed, and it can

<table>
<tr><td>Teaching
Scenario</td><td>A Simple Thank-You</td></tr>
</table>

Ms. Addison, a beloved middle school teacher, has received many thank-you notes from her students. This year, she was part of the sixth-grade team and taught multiple sections of cultural studies. At the end of the school year, she received this moving letter from one of her male students, a young man diagnosed with attention-deficit/hyperactivity disorder who was also diagnosed as having dyslexia, dysgraphia, and other challenges. Chad's mother assured Ms. Addison that she acted as the scribe only and that she wrote down exactly what her son dictated to her. His letter follows.

Dear Ms. Addison,

You helped me spread my knowledge of history to my fellow classmates. You inspired me to do my best in geography and in my work in school. You helped me find something that I liked to do for fun and in life as a job too. You let me talk and you listen to me. When we are talking in the hallway and in your classroom you make me feel special. When I have something to say and you don't have time for me or when kids interrupt me, you always look forward to what I say. When I am sad you always ask what is wrong and you make me feel better about myself. You give me good comments when I am down or I just want to quit in your class. You allow me quiet time when I need it and allow me to finish my work later. You laugh when I say something over when we are learning or when I say a funny comment. You make me look forward to geography. You have taught me a lot about other cultures. You make it sound interesting and that makes me want to learn more. When I am being bullied I feel I can tell you about it and who is doing the bullying and you will take care of it. I feel I can tell you anything and you won't judge me. Thank you for inspiring me to do well in school and in life. From your favorite geography student.

Chad

change as the result of experience and intellectual maturity. As one might suspect, *modality integration* (i.e., engaging more of the sensory input channels, using several modalities at once or staggered) has been found to contribute to better achievement in student learning. This concept is described in the chapters included in Part 2 of this book.

LEARNING MODALITY AND ITS IMPLICATIONS FOR TEACHING Because many middle school and high school students have neither a preference nor a strength for auditory reception, teachers should severely limit their use of the lecture method of instruction, that is, of too much reliance on formal teacher talk. Furthermore, instruction that uses a singular approach, such as auditory (e.g., talking to the students), cheats students who learn better another way. This difference can affect student achievement. A teacher, for example, who only talks to the students or uses discussions day after day is shortchanging the education of learners who learn better another way, who are, for example, kinesthetic and visual learners. One purpose of Exercise 3.1 is to get you to start integrating all of the learning modalities in your teaching. Do this exercise now.

Finally, if a teacher's verbal communication conflicts with his or her nonverbal messages, students can become confused, and this too can affect their learning. When there is a discrepancy between what the teacher says and what that teacher does, the teacher's nonverbal signal will triumph every time. A teacher, for example, who has just finished a lesson on the conservation of energy and does not turn off the room lights on leaving the classroom for lunch has, by his or her inappropriate modeling behavior, created cognitive disequilibrium and sabotaged the very purpose for the lesson.

ACTIONS DO SPEAK LOUDER THAN WORDS[26] As a general rule, most middle and secondary school students prefer and learn best by touching objects, by feeling shapes and textures, by interacting with each other, and by moving things around. In contrast, learning by sitting and listening is difficult for many of them. At one school, after discovering that nearly two-thirds of students were either tactile or kinesthetic learners, teachers and administrators grouped the students according to their modality strengths and altered reading instruction schedules every three weeks so that each group had opportunities to learn at the best time of day. As a result, student behavior, learning achievement, and attitudes improved considerably.[27]

Certain learning-style traits significantly discriminate between students who are at risk of not finishing school and students who perform well. Students who are underachieving and at risk need (a) frequent opportunities for mobility; (b) options and choices; (c) a variety of instructional resources, environments, and sociological groupings rather than routines and patterns; (d) to learn during late morning, afternoon, or evening hours rather than in the early morning; (e) informal seating rather than wooden, steel, or plastic chairs; (f) low illumination because bright light contributes to hyperactivity; and (g) tactile/visual introductory resources reinforced by kinesthetic (i.e., direct experiencing and whole-body activities)/visual resources or introductory kinesthetic/visual resources reinforced by tactile/visual resources.[28]

Regardless of the grade level and subject(s) you intend to teach, you are advised to use strategies that integrate the modalities. When well designed, thematic units and project-based learning incorporate modality integration. In conclusion, then, when teaching any group of students of mixed learning abilities, mixed modality strengths, mixed language proficiency, and mixed cultural backgrounds, the integration of learning modalities is a must for successful teaching.

Learning Styles

Related to learning modality is *learning style*, which can be defined as *independent forms of knowing and processing information*. Although some students may be comfortable beginning to learn a new idea in the abstract (e.g., visual or verbal symbolization), most need to begin with the concrete (e.g., learning by actually doing it). Some students prosper while working alone, but many others prefer working in groups. Some are quick in their studies, whereas others are slow, cautious, and meticulous. Some can sustain attention on a single topic for a long time, becoming more absorbed in their study as time passes. Others are slower starters and more casual in their pursuits but are capable of shifting with ease from subject to subject. Some can study in the midst of music, noise, or movement, whereas others need quiet, solitude, and a desk or table. The point is this: *students vary not only in their skills and preferences in the way knowledge is received but also in how they mentally process that information once it has been received.* The latter is a person's style of learning.

CLASSIFICATIONS OF LEARNING STYLES It is important to note that learning style is not an indicator of intelligence but rather an indicator of how a person learns. Although there are probably as many types of learning styles as there are individuals, David Kolb describes two major differences in how people learn: how they perceive situations and how they process information.[29] On the basis of perceiving and processing an earlier work by Carl Jung on psychological types,[30] Bernice McCarthy has described four major learning styles, presented in the following paragraphs.[31]

The *imaginative learner* perceives information concretely and processes it reflectively. Imaginative learners learn well by listening and sharing with others and integrating the ideas of others with their own experiences. Imaginative learners often have difficulty adjusting to traditional teaching, which depends less on classroom interactions and students' sharing and connecting their prior experiences. In a traditional classroom, the imaginative learner is likely to be an at-risk student.

The *analytic learner* perceives information abstractly and processes it reflectively. The analytic learner prefers sequential thinking, needs details, and values what experts have to offer. Analytic learners do well in traditional classrooms.

The *commonsense learner* perceives information abstractly and processes it actively. The commonsense learner is pragmatic and enjoys hands-on learning. Commonsense learners sometimes find school frustrating unless they can see immediate use for what is being learned. In the traditional classroom, the commonsense learner is likely to be a learner who is at risk of dropping out.

The *dynamic learner* perceives information concretely and processes it actively. The dynamic learner also prefers hands-on learning and is excited by anything new. Dynamic learners are risk takers and are frustrated by learning if they see it as being tedious and sequential. In a traditional classroom, the dynamic learner also is likely to be an at-risk student.

The Learning Cycle

To understand conceptual development and change, researchers in the 1960s developed a Piaget-based theory of learning in which students are guided from concrete, hands-on learning experiences to the abstract formulations of concepts and their formal applications. This theory became known as the three-phase learning cycle.[32] Long a popular strategy for teaching science, the learning cycle can be useful in other disciplines as well.[33] The three phases are (1) the *exploratory hands-on phase*, where students can explore ideas and experience assimilation and disequilibrium that lead to their own questions and tentative answers; (2) the *invention or concept development phase*, where, under the guidance of the teacher, students invent concepts and principles that help them answer their questions and reorganize their ideas (i.e., the students revise their thinking to allow the new information to fit); and (3) the *expansion or concept application phase*, another hands-on phase where the students try out their new ideas by applying them to situations that are relevant and meaningful to them. During application of a concept, the learner may discover new information that causes a change in his or her understanding of the concept being applied. Thus, the process of learning is cyclical.[34]

There have been more recent interpretations or modifications of the three-phase cycle, such as McCarthy's 4MAT.[35] With the 4MAT system, teachers employ a learning cycle of instructional strategies to try to reach each student's learning style. As stated by McCarthy, in the cycle learners sense and feel: they experience. Then they watch: they reflect. Then they think: they develop theories. Then they try out theories: they experiment. Finally, they evaluate and synthesize what they have learned in order to apply it to their next similar experience. They get smarter. They apply experience to experiences,[36] and in this process they are likely to be using all four learning modalities.

To evince constructivist learning theory—that is, that learning is a process involving the active engagement of learners who adapt the educative event to fit and expand their individual worldview (as opposed to the behaviorist pedagogical assumption that learning is something done to learners)[37]—and to accentuate the importance of student self-assessment, some variations of the learning cycle include a fourth phase, an *assessment phase*. However, because we, the authors of this book, believe that assessment of what students know or think they know should be a continual process, permeating all three phases of the learning cycle, we reject any treatment of assessment as a self-standing phase.

Learning Capacities: The Theory of Multiple Intelligences

In contrast to learning styles, Howard Gardner introduced what he calls *learning capacities* exhibited by individuals in differing ways.[38] Originally (and sometimes still) referred to as *multiple intelligences*, or even *ways of knowing*, capacities thus far identified are the following:

- *Bodily/kinesthetic*: Ability to use the body skillfully and to handle objects skillfully

Teaching Scenario	**Using the Theory of Learning Capacities (Multiple Intelligences) and Multitasking**

In one middle school classroom, during one week of a six-week thematic unit on weather, students were concentrating on learning about the water cycle. For this study of the water cycle, with the students' help the teacher divided the class into several groups of three to five students per group. While working on six projects simultaneously to learn about the water cycle, (1) one group of students designed, conducted, and repeated an experiment to discover the number of drops of water that can be held on one side of a new one-cent coin versus the number that can be held on the side of a worn one-cent coin; (2) working in part with the first group, a second group designed and prepared graphs to illustrate the results of the experiments of the first group; (3) a third group of students created and composed the words and music of a song about the water cycle; (4) a fourth group incorporated their combined interests in mathematics and art to design, collect the necessary materials, and create a colorful and interactive bulletin board about the water cycle; (5) a fifth group read about the water cycle in materials they researched from the Internet and various libraries; and (6) a sixth group created a puppet show about the water cycle. On Friday, after each group had finished, the groups shared their projects with the whole class.

■ *Interpersonal:* Ability to understand people and relationships

■ *Intrapersonal:* Ability to assess one's emotional life as a means to understand oneself and others

■ *Logical/mathematical:* Ability to handle chains of reasoning and to recognize patterns and orders

■ *Musical:* Sensitivity to pitch, melody, rhythm, and tone

■ *Naturalist:* Ability to draw on materials and features of the natural environment to solve problems or fashion products

■ *Verbal/linguistic:* Sensitivity to the meaning and order of words

■ *Visual/spatial:* Ability to perceive the world accurately and to manipulate the nature of space, such as through architecture, mime, or sculpture

Apply the theory of multiple intelligences by completing Exercise 3.2.

As discussed earlier and as implied in the presentation of McCarthy's four types of learners, many educators believe that many of the students who are at risk of not completing school are those who may be dominant in a cognitive learning style that is not in sync with traditional teaching methods. Traditional methods are largely of McCarthy's analytic style, where information is presented in a logical, linear, sequential fashion, and of three of the Gardner types: verbal/linguistic, logical/mathematical, and intrapersonal. Consequently, to better synchronize methods of instruction with learning styles, some teachers and schools have restructured the curriculum and instruction around Gardner's learning capacities.[39] See the sample teaching scenario shown on multiple intelligences and multitasking. Internet resources on learning styles and multiple intelligences are shown in Figure 3.2.

Learning Style and Its Implications for Teaching

The importance of the preceding information about learning styles is that you must realize at least two things:

1. *Intelligence is not a fixed or static reality but can be learned, taught, and developed.* This concept is important for students to understand, too. When students understand that intelligence is incremental, something that is developed through use over time, they tend to be more motivated to work at learning than when they believe that intelligence is a fixed entity.[40]

2. *Not all students learn and respond to learning situations in the same way.* A student may learn differently according to the situation or according to the student's ethnicity, cultural background, or socioeconomic status.[41] A teacher who, for all students, uses only one style of teaching or who teaches using only one or a few styles of learning, day after day, is shortchanging those students who learn better another way. As emphasized by Rita Dunn, when students do not learn the way we teach them, then we must teach them the way they learn.[42]

Meeting the Challenge: Recognizing and Providing for Student Differences

Assume that you are a high school history teacher and that your teaching schedule includes three sections of U.S. history. Furthermore, assume that students at your school are

Figure 3.2 Internet Resources on Learning Styles and Multiple Intelligences

- **ERIC Link to Multiple Intelligences Resources** http://www.indiana.edu/~reading/ieo/bibs/multiple.html
- **HG Project Zero** http://www.pz.harvard.edu/
- **Multiple Intelligences** http://www.education-world.com/a_curr/curr207.shtml
- **Results about Learning Styles** http://results.about.com/learning_styles/

tracked (as they are in many high schools). One of your classes is a so-called college-prep class with 30 students. Another is a regular education class with 35 students, three of whom have special needs because of disabilities. The third is a sheltered English class with 13 students: six Latino students with limited proficiency in English, three students from the former Soviet Union with very limited proficiency in English, and four Southeast Asians, two with no English skills. Again, for all three sections, the course is U.S. history. Will one lesson plan using lecture and teacher-directed discussion as the primary instructional strategies work for all three sections? The answer is an emphatic no. How do you decide what to do? Before you finish this book, we hope the answer to that question will become clear to you.

First consider the following general guidelines, most of which are discussed in further detail in later chapters as designated.

Instructional Practices That Provide for Student Differences: General Guidelines

To provide learning experiences that are consistent with what is known about ways of learning and knowing, consider the recommendations that follow and refer to them during the preactive phase of your instruction (discussed in Chapter 1):

- As frequently as is appropriate—and especially for skills development—plan the learning activities so they follow a step-by-step sequence from concrete to abstract.

- With students, collaboratively plan challenging and engaging classroom learning activities and assignments (see Chapters 8, 9, and others).

- Concentrate on using student-centered instruction by using project-centered learning, discovery and inquiry strategies, and simulations and role play (Chapter 8).

- Establish multiple learning centers within the classroom (Chapter 8).

- Maintain high (although not necessarily identical) expectations for every student; establish high standards and teach toward them without wavering (see throughout).

- Make learning meaningful by integrating learning with life—academic with vocational—helping each student successfully make the transitions from one level of learning to the next, from one level of schooling to the next, and from school to life (see throughout).

- Provide a structured learning environment with regular and understood procedures (Chapter 4).

- Provide ongoing and frequent monitoring of individual student learning (formative assessment) (Chapter 11).

- Provide variations in meaningful assignments, with optional due dates, that are based on individual student abilities and interests (Chapters 5 and 9).

- Use direct instruction to teach to the development of observation, generalization, and other thinking and learning skills (Chapter 8).

- Use reciprocal peer coaching and cross-age tutoring (Chapter 8).

- Use multilevel instruction (discussed at the end of this chapter).

- Use interactive computer programs and multimedia (Chapter 10).

- Use small-group and cooperative learning strategies (Chapter 9).

Because social awareness is such an important and integral part of a student's experience, exemplary school programs and much of their practices are geared toward some type of social interaction. Indeed, learning is a social enterprise among learners and their teachers. Although many of today's successful instructional practices rely on social learning activities and interpersonal relationships, teachers must be aware of and sensitive to individual student differences.

Recognizing and Working with Exceptional Students

If you think of placing students along a continuum, the bulk of students we refer to as *average* or *normal* would collect around the center point. Those students who deviate from the norm (either below or above) would fall somewhere between the center point and either end of the spectrum. The more they deviated from the *norm*, the farther those students would be placed away from the center. To reach their academic potential, these students would need special accommodations. Those students falling outside the norm would be classified as *exceptional learners*, also known as *students with special needs*. Included under this broad label are those with disabling conditions or impairments in any one or more of the following categories: mental retardation, hearing, speech or language, visual, emotional, orthopedic, autism, traumatic brain injury, other health impairment, or specific learning disability. Gifted and talented students fall under this umbrella term as well.

To the extent possible, students with special needs must be educated with their peers in the regular classroom. Public Law (P.L.) 94-142, the Education for All Handicapped Children Act of 1975, mandates that all children have the right to a free and appropriate education as well as to nondiscriminatory assessment. (P.L. 94-142 was amended in 1986 by P.L. 99-457. It was again amended in 1990 by P.L. 101-476, at which time its name was changed to the Individuals with Disabilities Education Act. It was again amended in 1997 by P.L. 105-17 to better ensure that all students are given access to a broad, rich general curriculum.) Emphasizing the normalization of the educational environment for students with disabilities, this legislation requires provision of the **least restrictive environment** for exceptional students. A least restrictive environment is an environment that is as normal as possible.

Students identified as having special needs may be placed in the regular classroom for the entire school day, called *full inclusion* (as is the trend).[43] Those students may also be in a regular classroom the greater part of the school day, called *partial inclusion*, or only for designated periods. Although there is no single, universally accepted definition of the term, *inclusion* is the concept that students with disabilities should be integrated into general education classrooms regardless of whether they can meet traditional academic standards.[44] (The term **inclusion** has largely replaced use of an earlier and similar term, **mainstreaming**.) As a classroom teacher, you will need information and skills specific to teaching learners with special needs who are included in your classes.

Generally, teaching students who have special needs requires more care, better diagnosis, greater skill, more attention to individual needs, and an even greater understanding of the students. The challenges of teaching students with special needs in the regular classroom are great enough that to do it well, you need specialized training beyond the general guidelines presented here.

When a student with special needs is placed in your classroom, your task is to develop an understanding of the general characteristics of different types of special needs learners, identify the student's unique needs relative to your classroom, and design lessons that teach to different needs at the same time (as discussed in the section "Multitasking" at the end of this chapter). Remember that just because a student has been identified as having one or more special needs does not preclude that person from being gifted or talented.

Congress stipulated in P.L. 94-142 that an individualized education program (IEP) be devised annually for each child with special needs. According to that law, an IEP is developed for each student each year by a team that includes special education teachers, the child's parents or guardians, and the classroom teachers. The IEP contains a statement of the student's present educational levels, the educational goals for the year, specifications for the services to be provided and the extent to which the student should be expected to take part in the regular education program, and the evaluative criteria for the services to be provided. Consultation by special and skilled support personnel is essential in all IEP models. A consultant works directly with teachers or with students and parents. As a classroom teacher, you may play an active role in preparing the specifications for the students with special needs assigned to your classroom as well as have major responsibility for implementing the program. Today, some schools report success using personalized learning plans for all students, not only those with special needs.[45]

Guidelines for Working with Students with Special Needs in the Regular Classroom

Although the guidelines represented by the paragraphs that follow are important for teaching all students, they are especially important for working with students with special needs. Familiarize yourself with exactly what the special needs of each learner are. Privately ask the student whether there is anything he or she would like you to know that may help you to facilitate his or her learning while in your class.

Adapt and modify materials and procedures to the special needs of each student. For example, a student who has extreme difficulty sitting still for more than a few minutes will need planned changes in learning activities. When establishing seating arrangements in the classroom, give preference to students according to their special needs. Try to incorporate into lessons activities that engage all learning modalities—visual, auditory, tactile, and kinesthetic. Be flexible in your classroom procedures. For example, allow the use of tape recorders or recording pens (see Chapter 10) for note taking and test taking when students have trouble with the written language.

Provide high structure and clear expectations by defining the learning objectives in behavioral terms (discussed in Chapter 5). Teach students the correct procedures for everything (Chapter 4). Break complex learning into simpler components, moving from the most concrete to the abstract rather than the other way around. Check frequently for student understanding of instructions and procedures and for comprehension of content. Use computers and other self-correcting materials for drill and practice and for provision of immediate and private feedback to the student.

Develop your **withitness**, which is your awareness of everything that is going on in the classroom, at all times, by monitoring students for signs of restlessness, frustration, anxiety, and off-task behaviors. Be ready to reassign individual learners to different activities as the situation warrants. Established classroom learning centers (discussed in Chapter 9) can be a big help.

Have all students maintain assignments for the week or some other period of time in an assignment book or in a folder that is kept in their notebooks. Post assignments in a special place in the classroom and frequently remind students of these and of assignment deadlines.

Maintain consistency in your expectations and in your responses. Learners with special needs can become frustrated when they do not understand a teacher's expectations and when they cannot depend on a teacher's reactions. Plan interesting bridging activities for learning, activities that help the students connect what is being learned with their real world. Learning that connects what is being learned with the real world helps to motivate students and to keep them on task.

Plan questions and questioning sequences and write them into your lesson plans (discussed in Chapter 11). Plan questions that you ask learners with special needs so that they are likely to answer them with confidence. Use signals to let students know that you are likely to call on them in class (e.g., prolonged eye contact or mentioning your intention to the student before class begins). After asking a question, give the student adequate time to think and respond. Then, after the student responds, build on the student's response to indicate that the student's contribution was accepted as being important.

Provide for and teach toward student success. Offer students activities and experiences that ensure each individual student's success and mastery at some level. Use of student portfolios (discussed in Chapter 11) can give evidence of progress and help in building student confidence and self-esteem.

Provide guided or coached practice. Provide time in class for students to work on assignments and projects. During this time, you can monitor the work of each student while looking for misconceptions, thus ensuring that students get started on the right track.

Provide help in the organization of students' learning. For example, give instruction in the organization of notes and notebooks. Have a three-hole punch available in the classroom so students can put papers into their notebooks immediately, thus avoiding disorganization and lost papers. During class presentations, use an overhead projector with transparencies; students who need more time can then copy material from the transparencies. Or you can use an interactive whiteboard or screencasting (see Chapter 10). Ask students to read their notes aloud to each other in small groups, thereby aiding their recall and understanding and encouraging them to take notes for meaning rather than for rote learning. Encourage and provide for peer support, peer tutoring or coaching, and cross-age teaching (Chapter 8). Ensure that the learners with special needs are included in all class activities to the fullest extent possible.[46]

Working with Culturally and Linguistically Diverse Students

Quickly determine the language and ethnic groups represented by the students in your classroom. A major problem for recent newcomers, as well as students representative of some ethnic groups, is learning a second (or third or fourth) language. Although in many schools it is not uncommon for more than half the students to come from homes where the home language is not English, standard English is a necessity in most communities of this country if a person is to become vocationally successful and enjoy a full life.

Learning basic communication skills in English can take an immigrant student at least a year and probably longer; mastering English well enough to compete with their English-speaking counterparts in cognitively challenging academic courses may take English Language Learners (ELLs) up to seven years. By default, then, an increasing number of teachers are teachers of English language learning. Helpful to the success of ELLs is the demonstration of respect for students' cultural backgrounds, long-term teacher-student cohorts (e.g., in looping), and the use of active and cooperative learning.[47]

There are numerous programs specially designed for ELLs. Students' language skills will vary greatly. Some non-English-speaking students may understand single sentences

and speak simple words or phrases in English. Sometimes students who are considered fluent in English may have an excellent command of everyday spoken English, and yet the student's overall academic achievement may still be less than desired because of language or cultural differences.[48]

Some schools use a "pullout" approach, where part of the student's school time is spent in special classes and the rest of the time the student is placed in regular classrooms. In some schools, ELLs are placed in academic classrooms that use a "sheltered" English approach. Regardless of the program, specific techniques recommended for teaching ELLs include the following:

- Allowing more time for learning activities than one normally would
- Allowing time for addressing language as well as content objectives for each lesson
- Avoiding jargon or idioms that might be misunderstood (see the accompanying scenario)
- Dividing complex or extended language discourse into smaller, more manageable units
- Giving directions in a variety of ways
- Giving special attention to key words that convey meaning and writing them on the board
- Reading written directions aloud and then writing the directions on the board
- Speaking clearly and naturally but at a slower than normal pace
- Using a variety of examples and observable models
- Using simplified vocabulary without talking down to students[49]

Additional Guidelines for Working with ELLs

While they are becoming literate in the English language, ELLs are expected to learn the same curriculum in all the various disciplines just like native English-speaking students. Although the guidelines presented in the following paragraphs are important for teaching all students, they are especially important when working with non-native English-speaking students in the regular classroom.

Present instruction that is concrete and that includes the most direct learning experiences possible. Use the most concrete (least abstract) forms of instruction.

Build on (or connect with) what the students already have experienced and know. Building on what students already know or think they know helps them to connect their knowledge and construct their understandings.

Encourage student writing. One way is by using student journals (see Chapter 11). Two kinds of journals are appropriate when working with ELLs: dialogue journals and response journals. Dialogue journals are used for students to write anything that is on their minds, usually on the right page. Teachers, parents, and classmates then respond

Teaching Scenario	**An ESL Tutor's Lessons**

Lynn is a nontraditional student working on her elementary certification in a teacher education program in Montana. Before returning to school to complete her undergraduate degree, she raised her family and worked as an English-as-a-second-language (ESL) tutor for Jefferson County Schools in Lakewood, Colorado. In the 11 years Lynn worked one-on-one with non-native English-speaking students, her experiences ranged from humorous to heartbreaking. She chuckled when she reminisced about a young Hmong student with minimal English skills named Lee Lee Lee who enrolled at one of the middle schools where she worked. Lynn said that her first task was to determine what name he went by: Lee or Lee Lee. She had a lesson in cross-cultural communication when she went to meet the family and discovered that the parents spoke no English. Lynn tried to ask her question, but the only word that was understood was Lee, which Lee Lee Lee's parents continued to repeat numerous times in the following combinations: Lee, Lee Lee and Lee Lee Lee.

One of Lynn's most disturbing memories involved Tai, a 14-year-old Vietnamese boy who was always smiling. When she encountered Tai at his junior high school, the administrators warned,

"Don't spend too much time on Tai. He's special ed. He won't be in your program long. They'll pull him out of ESL soon and place him in special education where he belongs. They are only waiting for an interpreter." So Lynn concentrated on the other 15 ELLs she was responsible for and basically ignored Tai because he was polite and cheerful and kept to himself. Much to Lynn's surprise, he didn't even interact with the other Vietnamese students for the entire six weeks he was in her class. She wondered if his peers ostracized him because he was mentally challenged. Finally, a Vietnamese speaker visited the class, but Tai remained silent when the interpreter asked him questions. The resulting diagnosis: Tai had no verbal skills. After several more weeks had passed, Lynn had built rapport and developed trust with her students. She felt comfortable enough to ask one of the more mature Vietnamese classmates why they had excluded Tai. It turned out that Tai's mother was Vietnamese but that his father was Chinese. Tai had grown up in China, not Vietnam. He had never attended school; he had never learned to read. Tai, in fact, did not speak any Vietnamese. He had remained cheerful and positive even though he was isolated. No one in the school spoke Mandarin, so he did not speak.

on the left page, thereby "talking with" the journal writers. Response journals are used for students to write (record) their responses to what they are reading or studying.[50]

Help students learn the vocabulary. Assist the ELLs in learning two vocabulary sets: the regular English vocabulary needed for learning and the new vocabulary introduced by the subject content. For example, while learning science, a student is dealing with both the regular English-language vocabulary and the special vocabulary of science.

Involve parents, guardians, or older siblings. Students whose primary language is not English may have other differences about which you will also need to become knowledgeable. These differences are related to culture, customs, family life, and expectations. To be most successful in working with linguistically different students, you should learn as much as possible about each student. To this end, it can be valuable to solicit the help of the student's parent, guardian, or even an older sibling. Parents (or guardians) of new immigrant children are usually truly concerned about the education of their children and may be very interested in cooperating with you in any way possible. In a study of schools recognized for their exemplary practices with language-minority students, the schools were recognized for being "parent friendly," that is, for welcoming parents in a variety of innovative ways.[51]

Plan for and use all learning modalities. As with teaching children in general, in working with linguistically different students in particular, you need to use multisensory approaches—learning activities that involve students in auditory, visual, tactile, and kinesthetic learning activities.

Use small-group cooperative learning. Cooperative learning strategies are particularly effective with linguistically different students because they provide opportunities

for students to produce language in a setting that is less threatening than is speaking before the entire class.

Use the benefits afforded by modern technology. For example, computer networking allows the linguistically different students to write and communicate with peers from around the world as well as to participate in "publishing" their classroom work.

Best Practices for Promoting Success for All Students

To be compatible with and be able to teach students who come from backgrounds different from yours, you need to believe that, given adequate support, *all* students *can* learn—regardless of gender, socioeconomic status, physical characteristics, language, and ethnic or cultural backgrounds. You also need to develop special skills that include those in the following guidelines, each of which is discussed in detail in other chapters. To work successfully and most effectively with students of diverse backgrounds, you should do the following:

- Build the learning around students' individual learning styles. Personalize learning for each student, much like what is done by using the IEP with learners with special needs. Involve students in understanding and in making important decisions about their own learning so that they feel ownership (i.e., a sense of empowerment and connectedness) of that learning.

- Communicate positively with every student and with the student's parents or guardians, learning as much as you can about the student and the student's culture and encouraging family members to participate in the student's learning. Involve parents, guardians, and other members of the community in the educational program so that all have a sense of ownership and responsibility and feel positive about the school program.

■ Establish and maintain high expectations—although not necessarily the same expectations—for each student. Both you and your students must understand that intelligence is not a fixed entity but a set of characteristics that—through a feeling of "I can" and with proper coaching—can be developed.

■ Teach to individuals by using a variety of strategies to achieve an objective or by using a number of different objectives at the same time (multilevel teaching).

■ Use techniques that emphasize collaborative and cooperative learning—that deemphasize competitive learning.

Recognizing and Working with Students Who Are Gifted

Historically, educators have used the term *gifted* when referring to a person with identified exceptional ability in one or more academic subjects and have used the term *talented* when referring to a person with exceptional ability in one or more of the visual or performing arts.[52] Today, however, the terms often are used interchangeably, which is how they are used here, that is, as if they are synonymous.

Sometimes, unfortunately, in the regular classroom gifted students are neglected.[53] At least part of the time, it is likely to be because there is no singularly accepted method for identification of these students. For placement in special classes or programs for the gifted and talented, school districts traditionally have used grade-point averages and standard IQ scores. However, because IQ testing measures linguistic and logical/mathematical aspects of giftedness (refer to the earlier discussion in this chapter in the section "Learning Capacities: The Theory of Multiple Intelligences"), it does not account for others, and thus gifted students sometimes are unrecognized; they also are sometimes among the students most at risk of dropping out of school.[54] It is estimated that between 10% and 20% of school dropouts are students who are in the range of being intellectually gifted.[55]

To work most effectively with gifted learners, their talents first must be identified. This can be done not only by using tests, rating scales, and auditions but also by observations in the classroom and on the campus and from knowledge about the student's personal life. With those information sources in mind, here is a list of indicators of superior intelligence:[56]

■ Ability to extrapolate knowledge to different circumstances

■ Ability to manipulate a symbol system

■ Ability to reason by analogy

■ Ability to take on adult roles at home, such as managing the household and supervising siblings, even at the expense of school attendance and achievement

■ Ability to think logically

■ Ability to use stored knowledge to solve problems

■ Creativity and artistic ability

■ Leadership ability and an independent mind

■ Resiliency: the ability to cope with school while living in poverty and/or with dysfunctional families

■ Strong sense of self, pride, and worth

■ Understanding of one's cultural heritage

To assist you in understanding gifted students who may or may not have been identified as being gifted, here are some types of students and the kinds of problems to which they may be prone, that is, personal behaviors that may identify them as being gifted but academically disabled, bored, and alienated:

■ *Antisocial* students, alienated by their differences from peers, may become bored and impatient troublemakers.

■ *Creative, high-achieving* students often feel isolated, weird, and depressed.

■ *Divergent thinking* students can develop self-esteem problems when they provide answers that are logical to them but seem unusual and off-the-wall to their peers. They may have only a few peer friends.

■ *Perfectionists* may exhibit compulsive behaviors because they feel as though their value comes from their accomplishments. When their accomplishments do not live up to expectations—their own, their parents', or their teachers'—anxiety and feelings of inadequacy arise. When other students do not live up to the gifted student's high standards, alienation from those other students is probable.

■ *Sensitive* students who also are gifted may become easily depressed because they are more aware of their surroundings and of their differences.

■ *Students with special needs* may be gifted. Attention deficit disorder, dyslexia, hyperactivity, and other learning disorders sometimes mask giftedness.

■ *Underachieving* students can also be gifted students but fail in their studies because they learn in ways that are seldom or never challenged by classroom teachers. Although often expected to excel in everything they do, most gifted students can be underachievers in some areas. Because they have high expectations of themselves, underachievers also tend to be highly critical of themselves, develop low self-esteem, and can become indifferent and even hostile.[57]

Guidelines for Working with Gifted Students

When working in the regular classroom with a student who has special gifts and talents, you are advised to do the following:

■ Collaborate with students in some planning of their own objectives and activities for learning.

■ Emphasize skills in critical thinking, problem solving, and inquiry.

- Identify and showcase the student's special gift or talent.
- Involve the student in selecting and planning activities, encouraging the development of the student's leadership skills.
- Plan assignments and activities that challenge the students to the full extent of their abilities. This does not mean overloading them with homework or giving identical assignments to all students. Rather, carefully plan so that the students' time spent on assignments and activities is quality time on meaningful learning.
- Provide in-class seminars for students to discuss topics and problems that they are pursuing individually or as members of a learning team.
- Provide independent and dyad learning opportunities. Gifted students often prefer to work alone or with another gifted student.
- Use curriculum compacting, which is allowing a student who already knows the material to pursue enriched or accelerated study. Plan and provide optional and voluntary enrichment activities. Learning centers, special projects, and computer and multimedia activities are excellent tools for provision of enriched learning activities.
- Use preassessments (diagnostic evaluation) for reading level and subject content achievement so that you are better able to prescribe objectives and activities for each student.

Recognizing and Working with Students Who Take More Time but Are Willing to Try

Students who take more time to learn typically fall into one of two categories: (1) those who try to learn but simply need more time to do it and (2) those who do not try, referred to variously as *underachievers, recalcitrant students*, or *reluctant learners*. Practices that work well with students of one category are often not those that work well with those of the second. Remember that just because a student is slow to learn doesn't mean that the student is less intelligent; some students just take longer for any number of reasons. The following guidelines may be helpful when working with a slow student who has indicated a willingness to try:

- Adjust the instruction to the student's preferred learning style, which may be different from yours and from other students in the group.
- Be less concerned with the amount of content coverage than with the student's successful understanding of content that is covered.
- Discover something the student does exceptionally well or a special interest and try to build on that.
- Emphasize basic communication skills, such as speaking, listening, reading, and writing, to ensure that the student's skills in these areas are sufficient for learning the intended content.

- Help the student learn content in small sequential steps with frequent checks for comprehension.
- If necessary, help the student to improve his or her reading skills, such as pronunciation and word meanings.
- If using a single textbook, be certain that the reading level is adequate for the student; if it is not, then for that student use other, more appropriate reading materials.
- Maximize the use of in-class, on-task work and cooperative learning, closely monitoring the student's progress. Avoid relying too much on successful completion of traditional out-of-class assignments unless the student gets coached guidance by you before leaving your classroom.
- Vary the instructional strategies, using a variety of activities to engage the visual, verbal, tactile, and kinesthetic modalities.
- When appropriate, use frequent positive reinforcement with the intention of increasing the student's self-esteem.

Recognizing and Working with Recalcitrant Students

For working with recalcitrant students, you can use many of the same guidelines from the preceding list, except that you should understand that the reasons for these students' behaviors may be quite different from those for the other category of slow learners. Slower-learning students who are willing to try are simply that—slower learning. They may be slow because of their learning style, genetic reasons, or a combination of the two. But they can and will learn. Recalcitrant learners, however, may be generally quick and bright thinkers but reluctant even to try because of a history of failure, a history of boredom with school, a poor self-concept, severe personal problems that distract from school, or any variety and combination of reasons, many of which are psychological in nature.

Whatever the case, you need to know that a student identified as being a slow or recalcitrant learner might, in fact, be quite gifted or talented in some way but may have a history of increasingly poor school attendance, poor attention to schoolwork, poor self-confidence, and an attitude problem. Consider the following guidelines when working with recalcitrant learners:

- At the beginning, learn as much about each student as you can. Be cautious in how you do it, though, because many of these students will be suspicious of any genuine interest in them shown by you. Be professional, trusting, genuinely interested, and patient. A second caution is to use the past not as ammunition, something to be held against the student, but as insight to help you work more productively with the student.
- Avoid lecturing to these students; it won't work.
- Early in the school term, preferably with the help of adult volunteers (e.g., professional community members as mentors have worked well at helping change the

Activity
3.7   **The Village Nation**

In 2003, three teachers at Cleveland High School in Los Angeles, Andre Chevalier, Bill Paden, and Fluke Fluker, were inspired to do something about the low test scores their African American students were earning on the Academic Performance Index exams. Their philosophy is exemplified by the phrase, "It takes a village," so they cofounded "The Village Nation" to promote academic and social success. The teachers tutor, hold workshops and seminars, and serve as role models for their students. During the 2007–2008 academic year, The Village Nation, in its fifth year, continued to see steady progress and growth. Test scores increased at a remarkable rate, from the pre–The Village Nation score of 578 in 2002–2003 to 697 in 2005–2006. Since school officials claim that a six-point increase in the test score is significant, this 100-plus-point change is nothing short of a miracle. Cleveland High School was even recognized as a California Distinguished School in 2005, which is a first for a school with its demographics. It is a Title 1 school; 64% of the students are Hispanic, and 25% are ELLs who claim more than 20 languages as their mother tongues. The efforts of Chevalier, Paden, and Fluker paid off. Not only have they increased test scores, but they also raised student morale and united a community.

Apply Your Knowledge

Check out The Village Nation's mission statement, philosophy, objectives, recognitions, and progress at the following websites:

http://www.thevillagenation.com
http://www2.oprah.com/tows/slide/200705/20070531/
    slide_20070531_284_107.jhtml
http://www.thevillagenation.com/site/index.php

1. What do you think is the key to The Village Nation's success?
2. What other similar programs do you know about?

student's attitude from rebellion to one of hope, challenge, and success), work out a personalized education plan with each student.

- Engage the students in learning by using interactive media, such as the Internet.

- Engage the students in active learning with real-world problem solving and perhaps community service projects.

- Forget about trying to "cover the subject," concentrating instead on the student learning some things well. A good procedure is to use thematic teaching and divide the theme into short segments. Because school attendance for these students is sometimes sporadic, try to individualize their assignments so that they can pick up where they left off and move through the course in an orderly fashion even when they have been excessively absent. Try to ensure some degree of success for each student.

- Help students develop their studying and learning skills, such as concentrating, remembering, and comprehending. Mnemonics, for example, is a device these students respond to positively and are often quick to create on their own (for examples, see Chapter 8).

- If using a single textbook, see if the reading level is appropriate; if it is not, then for that student discard the book and select other, more appropriate reading materials.

- Make sure your classroom procedures and rules are understood at the beginning of the school term and be consistent about enforcing them.

- Maximize the use of in-class, on-task work and cooperative learning, with close monitoring of the student's progress. Do not rely on successful completion of traditional out-of-class assignments unless the student gets coached guidance from you before leaving your classroom.

- Use simple language in the classroom. Be concerned less about the words the students use and the way they use them and more about the ideas they are expressing. Let the students use their own idioms without carping too much on grammar and syntax. Always take care, though, to use proper and professional English yourself.

- When appropriate, use frequent positive reinforcement with the intention of increasing the student's sense of personal worth. When using praise for reinforcement, however, try to praise the deed rather than the student. See Activity 3.7.

Teaching toward Positive Character Development

In the 1930s, again in the late 1960s, and now today, there is a resurgence in interest in the development of students' values, especially those of honesty, kindness, respect, and responsibility. Today, this interest is in what some refer to as *character education*. Whether defined as ethics, citizenship, moral values, or personal development, character education has long been part of public education in this country.[58] Stimulated by a perceived need to act to reduce students' antisocial behaviors and to produce more respectful and responsible citizens, many schools and districts today are developing curricula in character education with the ultimate goal of "developing mature adults capable of responsible citizenship and moral action."[59]

You can teach toward positive character development in two general ways: by providing a conducive classroom atmosphere where students actively and positively share in the decision making and by being a model that students can proudly emulate. Acquiring knowledge and developing understanding can enhance the learning of attitudes. Nevertheless, changing an attitude is often a long and tedious process, requiring the commitment of the teacher and the school, assistance from the community, and the

Figure 3.3 **Selected Resources on Character Education**

- **Ethics Resource Center: Character Education Links,** http://www.ethics.org/resource/character-education-helpful-links
- **Character Education Partnership,** 1025 Connecticut Avenue NW, Suite 1011, Washington, DC 20036 (800-988-8081) Web site: http://www.character.org
- **Character Education Resources,** P.O. Box 651, Contoocook, NH 03229
- **Developmental Studies Center,** 111 Deerwood Place, San Ramon, CA 94583 (415-838-7633)
- **Ethics Resource Center,** 1120 G Street NW, Washington, DC 20005 (202-434-8465)
- **Jefferson Center for Character Education,** P.O. Box 4137, Mission Viejo, CA 92690 (949-770-7602) Web site: http://www.jeffersoncenter.org
- **Josephson Institute of Ethics,** 9841 Airport Blvd. #300, Los Angeles, CA 90045 (310-846-4800)

provision of numerous experiences that will guide students to new convictions. Here are some specific practices, most of which are discussed further in later chapters:

- Build a sense of community in the school and in the classroom with shared goals, optimism, cooperative efforts, and clearly identified and practiced procedures for reaching those goals.
- Collaboratively plan with students action- and community-oriented projects that relate to curriculum themes; solicit parent and community members to assist in projects.
- Teach students to negotiate; practice and develop skills in conflict resolution, skills such as empathy, problem solving, impulse control, and anger management.[60]
- Have students research and give a presentation advocating a particular stance on a controversial issue.[61]
- Share and highlight anchor examples of class and individual cooperation in serving the classroom, school, and community.
- Make student service projects visible in the school and community.[62]
- Promote higher-order thinking about value issues through the development of skills in questioning.
- Sensitize students to issues and teach skills of conflict resolution through role play, simulations, and creative drama.

Resources on character education are shown in Figure 3.3.

When compared with traditional instruction, one characteristic of exemplary instruction today is the teacher's encouragement of dialogue among students in the classroom to discuss and to explore their own ideas. Modeling the very behaviors we expect of teachers and students in the classroom is a constant theme throughout this book.

Multitasking

To personalize the instruction to the extent possible, many teachers use *multilevel instruction* (known also as multitasking). Multitasking involves different students or groups of students working at different tasks to accomplish different objectives or working at different tasks to accomplish the same objective, all with several levels of teaching and learning going on simultaneously.

When integrating student learning, multitasking is an important and useful, perhaps even necessary, strategy. Project-centered teaching (discussed in Chapter 9) is an instructional method that easily allows for the provision of multilevel instruction. When using multilevel instruction, individual students and small groups will be doing different activities at the same time to accomplish the same or different objectives. Some students may be working independently of the teacher, others may be doing small-group work, while still others are receiving direct instruction.

To most effectively teach any group of students of mixed learning capacities and abilities, modality strengths, language proficiency, and cultural backgrounds, the use of multilevel instruction is necessary.

Summary

To teach middle and secondary students effectively, it is important for you to know what is developmentally and individually appropriate for your students. You must also be familiar with the different cultural lenses through which your students view the world. As a classroom teacher, you must acknowledge that students in your classroom have different ways of receiving information and different ways of processing that information—different ways of knowing and of constructing their knowledge. These differences are unique and important, and, as you will learn in Part 2 of this book, they are central considerations in curriculum development and instructional practice.

You must try to learn as much as you can about who your students are and how each student learns and processes information. But because you can never know everything about each student, the more you dialogue with your colleagues, vary your teaching strategies, and assist students in integrating their learning, the more likely you are to reach more of the students more of the time. In short, to be an effective classroom teacher, you should (a) learn as much about your students' cultural backgrounds and their preferred styles of learning as you can; (b) develop an eclectic style of teaching, one that is flexible and adaptable; and (c) integrate the disciplines, thereby helping students make bridges or connections between their lives and all that is being learned.

You are now ready to begin learning the specifics of how to establish and maintain a safe and effective classroom environment and plan for instruction, the topics of Part 2.

Exercise
3.1

Create an Icebreaker and a Warm-Up Activity Addressing the Learning Modalities

Now practice what you have learned about learning modalities. Middle and high school teachers often have more than 150 students each semester or each new school year. It is important for you to learn the names of your students. It is also important for your students to learn each others' names.

Describe an icebreaker activity that you would use with your class to get to know the names of your students. Be sure to include activities that address each of the learning modalities: visual, auditory, kinesthetic, and tactile.

Next, describe a warm-up activity that you would use with your class so that you could learn some personal information about your students. Be sure to include activities that address each of the learning modalities: visual, auditory, kinesthetic, and tactile.

Exercise
3.2

Modify a Lesson Plan to Integrate the Multiple Intelligences

Instructions: Get into small groups of three to five students based on the subject area you plan to teach. Suggested small groups include English/language arts, history/social studies, science, mathematics, physical education, health, music, art, and foreign language. If there are fewer than three people in a group, combine groups. In your discipline groups, decide on a course, grade level, and lesson plan. If your entire class consists of students with the same major, break into groups of three to five students each and have each group select a different grade level, course, and/or lesson plan. Review each of the eight multiple intelligences and describe an activity you would include in your lesson to address each one. Record your ideas.

Now that you have been introduced to Gardner's eight different ways of knowing, or multiple intelligences, you have the opportunity to discuss how you would modify a lesson plan in your discipline to integrate each of the different ways of knowing.

Our lesson plan titled _____ is designed for _____ graders in a _____ course. Following are the various activities we would include to address the multiple intelligences:

1. Bodily/kinesthetic
2. Interpersonal
3. Intrapersonal
4. Logical/mathematical
5. Musical
6. Naturalist
7. Verbal/linguistic
8. Visual/spatial

Now answer the following questions. After you discuss and record your answers in your small groups, be prepared to share your lesson plan activities with the rest of the class. Ask for their input on other activities you could include.

1. Which of the multiple intelligences were easiest for you to use to come up with an activity for your lesson plan? Why?
2. Which of the multiple intelligences were hardest for you to use to come up with an activity for your lesson plan? Why?

Chapter 3   POSTTEST

Short Explanation

1. Give an example of how you would use multilevel teaching in your subject field. Of what benefit is the use of multilevel teaching?

2. Explain why knowledge of teaching styles and student learning styles is important for a teacher in your subject field.

3. Explain why integration of the curriculum is important for learning in the middle and secondary school and identify some techniques used in middle and secondary schools to integrate the learning.

4. For a concept usually taught in your subject field (your choice), demonstrate specifically how you might help students bridge their learning of that concept with what is going on in their lives and with their learning in other disciplines.

5. Do you believe that middle and secondary school teachers should be concerned about student character development? Explain why or why not. If you believe in the affirmative, explain some specific ways you would address it in your own teaching.

Essay

1. Identify the topic of a lesson for middle school or secondary school students in your subject field. Describe how you would present the lesson from a behaviorist viewpoint; then describe how you would present the same lesson from a constructivist viewpoint. Is it possible to design the lesson in a way that encompasses both viewpoints? Explain your response.

2. Do you accept the view that learning is the product of creative inquiry through social interaction, with the students as active participants in that inquiry? Explain why you agree or disagree.

3. You are a high school teacher whose teaching schedule includes three sections of U.S. history. Students at your school are tracked, and one of your classes is a so-called college-prep class with 30 students; another is a regular education class with 35 students, three of whom have special needs because of disabilities; and the third is a sheltered English class with 13 students, seven of whom are Hispanics with limited proficiency in English, two of whom are from Russia with very limited proficiency in English, and four of whom are Southeast Asians, two with no ability to use English. Will one lesson plan using lecture and discussion as the primary instructional strategies work for all three sections? If so, explain why. If not, explain what you will have to do and why.

4. From your current observations and fieldwork as related to this teacher preparation program, clearly identify one specific example of educational practice that seems contradictory to exemplary practice or theory as presented in this chapter. Present your explanation for the discrepancy.

5. Describe any prior concepts you held that changed as a result of your experiences with this chapter. Describe the changes.

CHAPTER FOUR

Liz Moore/Merrill

Establishing and Maintaining a Safe and Supportive Classroom Learning Environment

I've come to the frightening conclusion that I am the decisive element in the classroom. It's my personal approach that creates the climate. It's my daily mood that makes the weather. As a teacher, I possess tremendous power to make a student's life miserable or joyous. I can be a tool of torture or an instrument of inspiration. I can humiliate or humor, hurt or heal. In all situations it is my response that decides whether a crisis will be escalated or de-escalated and a student humanized or de-humanized.[1]

—HAIM GINOTT

Chapter 4 Overview

No matter how well prepared you are, your plans will go untaught or poorly taught if presented to students in a classroom that is non-supportive and poorly managed. Thoughtfully and thoroughly planning your procedures for classroom management is as important a part of your preactive-phase decision making as is preparing units and daily lessons; and for that reason, it is a key step for instructional planning. Indeed, classroom management is perhaps the single most important factor influencing student learning. Just as you will learn to do for unit and lesson plans, you should plan and write down your management system, which you will have the opportunity to do in this chapter, long before you meet your first class of students. In this, the first chapter of Part 2, you will learn how to create a supportive classroom environment and manage the classroom effectively, for the most efficient instruction will result in the best student achievement.

Introduction

Citizens of the United States have certain inalienable rights that are protected by the Constitution. Those same rights are extended to students entering our schools; however, they do not translate into free license for students to do whatever they want. By law, all students have the right to an equal educational opportunity. With such diversity among our student body, equal educational opportunity does not always result in equitable educational opportunity, as pointed out in Chapter 1. Adjustments must be made to accommodate individual needs. This does not suggest that we should dumb down the curriculum, succumb to grade inflation, avoid distinguishing between right and wrong answers, or accept disrespectful behavior. Equal educational opportunity means that we need to create a welcoming classroom climate built on respect and design instruction in such a way that it meets the needs of *all* our students and guarantees all students the chance to learn and achieve to the greatest degree possible.[2] This cannot happen in the midst of chaos. It is our duty as educators to provide a safe and supportive environment in which all students can reach their academic potential. In this chapter, we will provide you with skills to avoid or address disruptions, a history of classroom management approaches, a review of current research and theory, and a variety of methods that you can implement in order to create a welcoming classroom environment conducive to learning.

Discipline: A Major Concern

Novice teachers, as well as seasoned professionals, are susceptible to job burnout. Discipline issues can try the patience of even the most dedicated teachers. Educators and the public alike have been concerned about student behavior for many years. Since the inception of the annual Phi Delta Kappa Gallup Poll highlighting the public's attitudes toward the public schools, school discipline has ranked as one of the public's major educational concerns, along with drug use, school funding, and violence. In fact, school discipline was named as the number one problem our schools face 16 times in the 33-year span between 1969 and 2002.[3] Lack of discipline once again was named in the top three problems in our schools in the 38th Annual Phi Delta Kappa Gallup Poll. When the results of the 2005 poll were released at a press conference in Washington, D.C., in August 2006, fighting/violence/gangs was also identified as one of the biggest problems facing schools today.[4] In the 41st and 42nd Annual Phi Delta Kappa Gallup Polls, highlighted in the September 2009 and September 2010 issues of *Phi Delta Kappan*, respectively, lack of discipline and overcrowding ranked right behind lack of school funding as the biggest problems.[5]

Common Disruptions

What are the kinds of classroom management issues that arise in the middle and secondary classrooms of today? According to research conducted by Dr. Fredric H. Jones, psychology professor and classroom management guru at the University of California, Santa Cruz, classroom disruptions can be classified into three main categories. Jones claimed that 80% of the disruptions in a typical classroom were due to students talking to their neighbors. In contrast, 15% of the disruptions were the result of students being up and out of their seats, while the final 5% were made up of a variety of disruptive behaviors, including passing notes, fiddling with pencils, rocking in chairs, and disturbing classmates. Furthermore, while students are engaged

in seat work, on average, one disruption per student every minute was observed in normal classrooms.[6]

Today, we might add that students can also be distracted by their electronic devices. Making or receiving phone calls, text messaging, tweeting to friends, picture taking, playing games, and other activities during class should be forbidden. It is important that the classroom be free of distraction and the potential for cheating. We must be attentive to the needs, sensibilities, and rights of all members of our learning community. Therefore, all portable digital devices, including cell phones, laptops, pagers, and other personal electronic devices, should be turned off and out of sight during all class meetings at all times, except under special circumstances.

The Importance of Perceptions

Unless you believe that each and every one of your students can learn, they will not. Unless you believe that you can teach each and every one of them, you will not. Unless each and every one of your students believe that they can learn and until they want to learn, they will not.

There are many influences on how teachers approach decisions about classroom management. How you go about creating a positive learning environment is greatly influenced by your personal history, including how you were disciplined at home and in your past educational experiences as a student. In addition, your personality, your previous teaching experiences with children, your teaching preparation, your personal preferences, and the school context all play a role.[7]

We all know or have heard of teachers who get the very best from all their students, even from those students that many teachers find to be the most challenging to teach. Regardless of individual circumstances, the most effective teachers are those who (a) provide adequate support to all students so they can learn, (b) expect the best from each student, (c) establish a classroom environment that motivates students to do their best, and (d) manage their classrooms so class time is efficiently used, that is, with the least amount of distraction to the learning process.

Regardless of how well you plan for instruction, certain perceptions by students must be in place to support the successful implementation of those plans. Students must perceive that (a) the classroom environment is supportive of their efforts, (b) you care about their learning and that they are welcome in your classroom, (c) the expected learning is challenging but not impossible, and (d) the anticipated learning outcomes are worthy of their time and effort to try to achieve.

Classroom Control: Its Meaning—Past and Present

Classroom control frequently is of the greatest concern to beginning teachers—and they have good cause to be concerned. As previously mentioned, even experienced teachers sometimes find control difficult, particularly at the middle and secondary school levels, where so many students come to school with so much psychological baggage that they have already become alienated as the result of negative experiences in their lives.[8] This chapter has been thoughtfully designed to help you with your concerns about control.

Historical Meaning of Classroom Control

To set the stage for your comprehension, consider what the term *classroom control* has meant historically and what it means today. In the 1800s, educators did not speak of classroom control; instead, they spoke of *classroom discipline*, and that meant *punishment*. Such an interpretation was consistent with the then-popular learning theory that assumed children were innately bad and that inappropriate behavior could be prevented by strictness or treated with punishment. Schools in the mid-1800s have been described as "wild and unruly places" and "full of idleness and disorder."[9]

By the early 1900s, educators were asking, "Why are the children still misbehaving?" The accepted answer was that the children were misbehaving as a result of the rigid punitive system. On this point, the era of progressive education began, providing students more freedom to decide what they would learn. The teacher's job, then, became one of providing a rich classroom of resources and materials to stimulate the students' natural curiosity. And because the system no longer would be contributing to misbehavior, punishment would no longer be necessary. Classes of the 1930s that were highly permissive, however, turned out to cause more anxiety than the restrictive classes of the 1800s.

Today's Meaning of Classroom Control and the Concept of Classroom Management

Today, rather than classroom discipline, educators talk of classroom *control*, the process of controlling student behavior in the classroom. The most effective teacher is one who is in control of classroom events rather than controlled by them. Classroom control is an important aspect of the broader concept of classroom management and is part of a management plan designed to (a) prevent inappropriate student behaviors, (b) help students develop self-control, and (c) suggest procedures for dealing with inappropriate student behaviors.

Effective teaching requires a well-organized, structured classroom in which motivated students work diligently at their learning tasks, free from distractions and interruptions. Establishing such a setting for learning requires careful thought and preparation and is called *effective classroom management*. Effective classroom management is the process of organizing and conducting a classroom so that it maximizes student learning.

A teacher's procedures for classroom control reflect that teacher's philosophy about how young people learn and the teacher's interpretation of and commitment to the school's stated mission. In sum, those procedures represent the teacher's concept of classroom management. Although often eclectic in their approaches, today's teachers share a concern for selecting management techniques that enhance student self-esteem and that empower students to assume control of their behavior and ownership of their learning.

Whereas some schools and school districts subscribe heavily to one approach or another, many others are more eclectic, choosing techniques that have evolved from the historical works of several leading authorities. Let's consider what some authorities have said. The guidelines and suggestions we present throughout this chapter represent an eclectic approach, borrowing from many of these authorities.

Classroom Management: Contributions of Some Leading Authorities

You are probably familiar with the term *behavior modification*, which describes several high-control techniques for changing behavior in an observable and predictable way; with B. F. Skinner's ideas about how students learn and how behavior can be modified by using reinforcers (rewards); and with how Skinner's principles of behavior shaping have been extended by others.[10] Behavior modification begins with four steps: (1) identify the behavior to be modified, (2) record how often and under what conditions that behavior occurs, (3) cause a change by reinforcing a desired behavior with a positive reinforcer (a reward), and (4) choose the type of positive reinforcers to award. At some point, almost all teachers use some type of reinforcer with their students. Following is a list of five different types of reinforcers and examples for each type. Some suggestions may seem more appropriate for middle school students; others may motivate secondary students. See Activity 4.1 to explore Alfie Kohn's views on how to instill intrinsic motivation in students.

- *Activity or privilege reinforcers*, such as choice of playing a game, running the media equipment for the teacher, caring for a classroom pet, free reading, decorating the classroom, free art time, spending time at a learning center, being free without penalty from doing an assignment or test, or running an errand for the teacher
- *Social reinforcers*, such as verbal attention or praise; nonverbal behavior, such as proximity of teacher to student; and facial (such as a wink or smile) or celebratory expressions (such as a handshake, pat on the back, or high five) of approval
- *Graphic reinforcers*, such as numerals and symbols like those made by rubber stamps
- *Tangible reinforcers*, such as candy and other edibles, badges, certificates, stickers, and books
- *Token reinforcers*, such as points, stars, or tickets that can be accumulated and cashed in later for a tangible reinforcer, such as a supervised trip to the pizzeria or ice cream store

Lee Canter and Marlene Canter developed the *assertive discipline model*. Using an approach that emphasizes both reinforcement for appropriate behaviors and consequences for inappropriate behaviors, their model emphasizes four major points. First, as a teacher, you have professional rights in your classroom and should expect appropriate student

Activity
4.1   **Alfie Kohn**

Alfie Kohn, one of the best-known critics of our educational system, attacks our preoccupation with grades and test scores in this country. This former teacher is convinced that we are being forced to "teach to the test." In fact, he refers to 21st-century schools as "test prep centers." He is concerned that tougher academic standards may result in stricter punishments. In this test-crazy society, Kohn warns that rewards may be more detrimental to student motivation than punishment. Although threats and bribes may result in temporary behavioral changes, Kohn believes they will be short lived. Consult the following websites to see Kohn's views on how to instill intrinsic motivation in students.

Carrots or Sticks? Alfie Kohn on Rewards and Punishment
http://www.educationworld.com/a_issues/chat/chat031.shtml
Alfie Kohn home page
http://www.alfiekohn.org/index.html

Apply Your Knowledge

1. How does Kohn propose to instill intrinsic motivation in students? Do you agree or disagree with his ideas? Why or why not?
2. Reflect on a time when you relied on intrinsic motivation to accomplish an academic goal. What was the result?

behavior. Second, your students have rights to choose how to behave in your classroom, and you should plan limits for inappropriate behavior. Third, an assertive discipline approach means you clearly state your expectations in a firm voice and explain the boundaries for behavior. And fourth, you should plan a system of positive consequences (e.g., positive messages home, awards and rewards, special privileges) for appropriate behavior and establish consequences (e.g., time-out, withdrawal of privileges, parent conference) for inappropriate student behavior. Consistent follow-through is necessary.[11]

With a *logical consequences* approach, Rudolf Dreikurs emphasized six points. First, be fair, firm, and friendly and involve your students in developing and implementing class rules. Second, students need to clearly understand the rules and the logical consequences for misbehavior. For example, a logical consequence for a student who has painted graffiti on a school building wall would be to either clean the wall or pay for a school custodian to do it. Third, allow the students to be responsible not only for their own actions but also for influencing others to maintain appropriate behavior in your classroom. Fourth, encourage students to show respect for themselves and for others and provide each student with a sense of belonging to the class. Fifth, recognize and encourage student goals of belonging, gaining status, and gaining recognition. And sixth, recognize but do not reinforce correlated student goals of getting attention, seeking power, and taking revenge.[12]

Continuing the work of Dreikurs, Linda Albert has developed a detailed and popular system called *cooperative discipline*. The cooperative discipline model makes use of Dreikurs's fundamental concepts, with emphasis on three Cs: capable, connect, and contribute.[13] Also building on the work of Dreikurs, Jane Nelsen provides guidelines for helping children develop positive feelings of self. Key points made by Nelsen and reflected throughout this book are (a) use natural and logical consequences as a means to inspire a positive classroom atmosphere, (b) understand that children have goals that drive them toward misbehavior (attention, power, revenge, and assumed adequacy), (c) use

kindness (student retains dignity) and firmness when administering consequences for a student's misbehavior, (d) establish a climate of mutual respect, (e) use class meetings to give students ownership in problem solving, and (f) offer encouragement as a means of inspiring self-evaluation and focusing on the students' behaviors.[14]

William Glasser developed his concept of *reality therapy* (i.e., the condition of the present rather than of the past contributes to inappropriate behavior) for the classroom. Glasser emphasizes that students have a responsibility to learn at school and to maintain appropriate behavior while there. He stresses that with the teacher's help, students can make appropriate choices about their behavior in school—they can, in fact, learn self-control.[15] Glasser suggests holding classroom meetings that are devoted to establishing class rules and to identifying standards for student behavior, matters of misbehavior, and the consequences of misbehavior. Since the publication of his first book in 1965, Glasser has expanded his message to include the student's needs of belonging and love, control, freedom, and fun, asserting that if these needs are ignored and unattended at school, children are bound to fail. Today's commitment to quality education (discussed in Chapter 2) is derived largely from the recent work of Glasser. In schools committed to quality education, students feel a sense of belonging, enjoy some degree of power, have fun learning, and experience a sense of freedom in the process.

Haim G. Ginott (1922–1973) emphasized ways for teacher and student to communicate—a *communication model*. He advised a teacher to send a clear message (or messages) about situations rather than about the child. And he stressed that teachers must model the behavior they expect from students.[16] Ginott's suggested messages are those that express feelings appropriately, acknowledge students' feelings, give appropriate direction, and invite cooperation.

Thomas Gordon emphasizes influence over control and decries use of reinforcement (i.e., rewards and punishment) as an ineffective tool for achieving a positive influence over a child's behavior.[17] Rather than using reinforcements for appropriate behavior and punishment for inappropriate behaviors, Gordon advocates encouragement and development of student self-control and self-regulated behavior. To have a positive influence and to encourage self-control, the teacher (and school) must provide a rich and positive learning environment with engaging and stimulating learning activities. Specific teacher behaviors include active listening, sending I-messages (rather than you-messages), shifting from I-messages to listening when there is student resistance to an I-message, clearly identifying ownership of problems to the student when such is the case (i.e., not assuming ownership if it is a student's problem), and encouraging collaborative problem solving.

Fredric Jones, who was mentioned following the introduction to this chapter, also promotes the idea of helping students support their own behavioral self-control. He accomplishes this by using effective nonverbal communication and implementing an incentive system. His incentive system employs a negative reinforcement method in which rewards follow good behavior.[18] Preferred Activity Time (PAT), for example, is an invention derived from Jone's model. The Jones' model makes four recommendations. First, you properly structure your classroom so that students understand the rules and procedures. Second, you maintain control by selecting appropriate instructional strategies. Third, you build patterns of cooperative work. Finally, you develop appropriate backup methods for dealing with inappropriate student behavior. See Activity 4.2 to learn more about the classroom management approaches presented here.

Jacob Kounin is well known for his identification of the *ripple effect*, or the effect of a teacher's response to one student's misbehavior on students whose behavior was appropriate. Kounin also focused on **withitness**, the teacher's ability to remain alert in the classroom and spot quickly and redirect potential student misbehavior, which is analogous to having "eyes in the back of your head."[19] In addition to being alert to everything that is going on in the classroom, another characteristic of a "withit" teacher is the ability to attend to a disruptive student without neglecting the rest of the class.

GUIDELINES FOR DEVELOPING WITHITNESS Consider the following guidelines for developing withitness:

- Avoid spending too much time with any one student or group; longer than 30 seconds may be approaching "too much time."

- Avoid turning your back to all or a portion of the students, such as when writing on the writing board.

- If two or more misbehaviors are occurring simultaneously in different locations, attend to the most serious first while giving the other(s) a nonverbal gesture showing your awareness (such as by eye contact) and displeasure (such as by a frown).

- Involve all students in your activities, not just any one student or group. Avoid concentrating on only those who appear most interested or responsive, sometimes referred to as the "chosen few."

Activity
4.2
Classroom Management Gurus

Included in this chapter are brief descriptions highlighting the key components of the various classroom management approaches promoted by Jacob Kounin, Fredric Jones, Rudolf Dreikurs and Linda Albert, Lee Canter and Marlene Canter, William Glasser, and B. F. Skinner, among others. Explore these websites for a closer look at the most popular classroom management theories and then answer the questions that follow.

Jacob Kounin
http://wik.ed.uiuc.edu/index.php/Kounin,_Jacob

http://ecommons.txstate.edu/cgi/viewcontent.cgi?article
=1081&context=honorprog&sei-redir=1#search
=%22Jacob%20Kounin%22

Fredric Jones
http://www.education-world.com/a_curr/columnists/jones/
jones001.shtml

http://www.fredjones.com

Rudolf Dreikurs and Linda Albert
http://wik.ed.uiuc.edu/index.php/Dreikurs,_Rudolf

Lee Canter and Marlene Canter
http://maxweber.hunter.cuny.edu/pub/eres/
EDSPC715_MCINTYRE/AssertiveDiscipline.html

http://wik.ed.uiuc.edu/index.php/Assertive_discipline

William Glasser
http://wik.ed.uiuc.edu/index.php/Reality_Therapy

B. F. Skinner
http://wik.ed.uiuc.edu/index.php/Skinner,_B._F.

Haim G. Ginott
http://www.eqi.org/ginott.htm

Thomas Gordon
http://www.eqi.org/tgordon.htm

http://www.gordontraining.com

Apply Your Knowledge

1. What have you learned from perusing these websites?
2. Have your ideas about one or more of the classroom management gurus talked about here changed with your more in-depth look at their classroom management philosophies?

- Keep students alert by calling on them randomly, asking questions, and calling on an answerer, circulating from group to group during team learning activities and frequently checking on the progress of individual students.

- Maintain constant visual surveillance of the entire class, even when talking to or working with an individual or small group of students and when meeting a classroom visitor at the door.

- Move around the room. Be on top of potential misbehavior and quietly redirect student attention before the misbehavior occurs or gets out of control.

- During direct instruction try to establish eye contact with each student about once every minute. It initially may sound impossible to do, but it is not; this skill can be developed with practice.

A prerequisite to being withit is the skill to attend to more than one matter at a time. This is referred to as the *overlapping ability*. The teacher with overlapping skills uses body language, body position, and hand signals to communicate with students. Consider the following examples of overlapping ability:

- Rather than having students bring their papers and problems to her desk, the teacher expects them to remain seated and to raise their hands as she circulates in the room monitoring and attending to individual students.

- The teacher takes care of attendance while visually and/or verbally monitoring the students during their warm-up activity.

- While attending to a messenger who has walked into the room, the teacher demonstrates verbally or by gestures that he expects the students to continue their work.

- While working in a small group, a student raises his hand to get the teacher's attention. The teacher, while continuing to work with another group of students, signals with her hand to tell the student that she is aware that he wants her attention and will get to him quickly, which she does.

- Without missing a beat in her talk, the teacher aborts the potentially disruptive behavior of a student by gesturing, by making eye contact, or by moving closer to the student (proximity control).

Now review Table 4.1 and complete Activity 4.3.

Developing Your Own Effective Approach to Classroom Management

As you review these classic contributions to today's approaches to effective classroom management, the expert opinions as well as the research evidence will remind you of the importance of doing the following: (a) concentrating your attention on desirable student behaviors; (b) quickly and appropriately attending to inappropriate behavior; (c) maintaining alertness to all that is happening in your classroom; (d) providing smooth transitions, keeping the entire class on task, and preventing dead time; and (e) involving students by providing challenges, class meetings,[20] ways

of establishing rules and consequences, opportunities to receive and return compliments, and chances to build self-control and self-esteem.

Using the criteria of your own philosophy, feelings, values, knowledge, and perceptions, you are encouraged to construct a classroom environment and management system that is explicit, positive, and effective for you and your students and then to consistently apply it.

Providing a Supportive Learning Environment

It is probably no surprise to hear that teachers whose classrooms are pleasant, positive, and challenging but supportive places find that their students learn and behave better than the students of teachers whose classroom atmospheres are harsh, negative, repressive, and unchallenging. What follows now are specific suggestions for making your classroom a pleasant, positive, and challenging place, that is, an environment that supports students in their development of meaningful understandings.

Create a Positive Classroom Atmosphere

All students should feel welcome in your classroom and accepted by you as individuals of dignity. Although these feelings and behaviors should be reciprocal—that is, expected of the students as well—they may need your frequent modeling of the behaviors expected of them. You must help students know that any disapproval by you of a specific student's behavior is not a denial of that individual as a worthwhile person. Make it clear that the offending student is still welcomed to come to your class to learn as long as he or she agrees to follow expected procedures. Specific things you can do to create a positive classroom environment, some of which are repeated from preceding chapters and others addressed in later chapters, are the following:

- Admonish behavior, not persons.

- Ensure that no prejudice is ever displayed against any individual student.

- Attend to the classroom's physical appearance and comfort. It is your place of work; show pride in that fact.

- Be an interesting person and an optimistic and enthusiastic teacher.

- Encourage students to set high yet realistic goals for themselves and then show them how to take the necessary steps toward meeting their goal—letting each know that you are confident in his or her ability to achieve.

- Help students develop their skills in interactive and cooperative learning.

- Involve students in every aspect of their learning, including the planning of learning activities, thereby giving them part ownership and responsibility in their learning.

- Use interesting and motivating learning activities. Make the learning enjoyable, at least to the extent possible and reasonable.

Table
4.1   Comparing Approaches to Classroom Management

Authority	To Know What Is Going On	To Provide Smooth Transitions	To Maintain Group Alertness	To Involve Students	To Attend to Misbehavior
Canter/Jones	Realize that the student has the right to choose how to behave in your class with the understanding of the consequences that will follow his or her choice.	Insist on decent, responsible behavior.	Set clear limits and consequences; follow through consistently; state what you expect; state the consequences and why the limits are needed.	Use firm tone of voice; keep eye contact; use nonverbal gestures and verbal statements; use hints, questions, and direct messages in requesting student behavior; give and receive compliments.	Follow through with your promises and the reasonable, previously stated consequences that have been established in your class.
Dreikurs/ Nelsen/ Albert	Realize that the student wants status, recognition, and a feeling of belonging. Misbehavior is associated with mistaken goals of getting attention, seeking power, getting revenge, and wanting to be left alone.	Identify a mistaken student goal; act in ways that do not reinforce these goals.	Provide firm guidance and leadership.	Allow students to have a say in establishing rules and consequences in your class.	Make it clear that unpleasant consequences will follow inappropriate behavior.
Ginott/Kohn	Communicate with the student to find out his/her feelings about a situation and about himself/ herself.	Invite student cooperation.	Model the behavior you expect to see in your students.	Build students' self-esteem.	Give a message that addresses the situation and does not attack the student's character.
Glasser/ Gordon/ Rogers/ Gathercoal/ Freiberg	Realize that the student is a rational being; he/she can control his or her own behavior.	Help the student make good choices; good choices produce good behavior, and bad choices produce bad behavior.	Understand that class rules are essential.	Realize that classroom meetings are effective means for attending to rules, behavior, and discipline.	Accept no excuses for inappropriate behavior; see that reasonable consequences always follow.
Kounin	Develop withitness, a skill enabling you to see what is happening in all parts of the classroom at all times.	Avoid jerkiness, which consists of thrusts (giving directions before your group is ready), dangles (leaving one activity dangling in the verbal air, starting another one, and then returning to the first activity), and flip-flops (terminating one activity, beginning another one, and then returning to the first activity you terminated).	Avoid slowdowns (delays and time wasting) that can be caused by overdwelling (too much time spent on explanations) and by fragmentation (breaking down an activity into several unnecessary steps). Develop a group focus (active participation by all students in the group) through accountability (holding all students accountable for the concept of the lesson) and by attention (seeing all the students and using unison and individual responses).	Avoid boredom by providing a feeling of progress for the students, offering challenges, varying class activities, changing the level of intellectual challenge, varying lesson presentations, and using many different learning materials and aids.	Understand that teacher correction influences behavior of other nearby students (the ripple effect).
Skinner	Realize the value of nonverbal interaction (i.e., smiles, pats, and handshakes) to communicate to students that you know what is going on.	Realize that smooth transitions may be part of your procedures for awarding reinforcers (i.e., points and tokens) to reward appropriate behavior.	Set rules, rewards, and consequences; emphasize that responsibility for good behavior rests with each student.	Involve students in "token economies," in contracts, and in charting behavior performance.	Provide tangibles to students who follow the class rules; represent tangibles as "points" for the whole class to use to "purchase" a special activity.

SOURCE: Kellough, Richard D., *A Resource Guide for Teaching: K–12*, 4th edition, ©2003. Reprinted by permission of Pearson Education, Inc., Upper Saddle River, NJ.

Activity 4.3   **Jacob Kounin's Model**

Classroom management theorist Jacob Kounin focused on preventive discipline. Kounin was the first to research the interaction between a teacher's actions and students' behaviors. He believed that being aware of what is going on in the classroom, intervening when students misbehave, and attending to several events simultaneously lead to the successful integration of teaching and discipline. Kounin suggested the following techniques to promote desired behaviors and prevent misbehaviors from happening.

Positive Behaviors to Implement

Withitness—A teacher who is aware of everything that is happening in the classroom is demonstrating withitness (also referred to as "eyes in the back of your head")

Overlapping—The ability to attend to several events/activities/tasks at the same time

Smoothness—The ability to make smooth transitions from one activity to the next

The ripple effect—The ability to correct the misbehavior of one student in order to stop other students from misbehaving

Group alerting—The ability to keep all students engaged and in suspense

Behaviors to Avoid

Dangling—Jumping from one topic to another and inserting unrelated material

Flip-flops—Switching from one topic being discussed and inserting material from a previous lesson

Thrust—Giving unclear directions for a task at hand, which leads to reexplaining the directions to students individually

Apply Your Knowledge

Answer the following questions and then share your responses with your classmates.

1. Which of the preventive techniques listed above do you think aid in successful classroom management?
2. Describe a teacher you had in middle or secondary school who had "eyes in the back of his or her head."
3. Kounin has been criticized for placing the "blame" for student misbehavior on teachers. What do you think about this?

- Send positive messages home to parents or guardians, even if you have to get help, and write the message in the language of the student's home.
- Recognize and reward truly positive behaviors and individual successes, no matter how meager they might seem to you.
- Have fun. Remember, you set the tone for your classroom. Enthusiasm is infectious, so be a carrier.

Behaviors to Avoid

Two items in the preceding list are statements about giving encouragement. When using encouragement to motivate student learning, you should avoid a few important behaviors because they inhibit learning:

- Avoid comparing one student with another or one class of students with another.
- Avoid encouraging competition among students.
- Avoid giving up or appearing to give up on any student.
- Avoid telling a student how much better he or she could be.
- Avoid using qualifying statements, such as "I like what you did, but …" or "It's about time."

Get to Know Your Students as People

For classes to move forward smoothly and efficiently, they should fit the learners' cultural backgrounds, learning styles, learning capacities, developmental needs, and interests. To make the learning meaningful and long lasting, build curriculum around students' interests, capacities, perceptions, and perspectives. Therefore, you need to know your students well enough to be able to provide learning experiences that they will find interesting, relevant, valuable, intrinsically motivating, challenging, and rewarding. Knowing your students is as important as knowing your subject—and maybe more important. Eminent Swiss psychologist Carl Jung summed it up this way: "An understanding heart is everything in a teacher, and cannot be esteemed highly enough. One looks back with appreciation to the brilliant teachers, but with gratitude to those who touched our human feelings. The curriculum is so much necessary raw material, but warmth is the vital element for the growing plant and for the soul of the child."[21] The following paragraphs describe a number of things you can do to get to know your students as people.

QUICKLY LEARN AND USE STUDENT NAMES Like everyone else, students appreciate being recognized and addressed by name. Not only do you need to learn your students' names, but it is important that classmates know each others' names as well. Quickly learning and using your students' names is an important motivating strategy and will help you with your classroom management. You may need to work hard at quickly learning the names of the students in your classes, but it is worth the extra effort. Be sure to take extra care to learn the proper spelling and pronunciation of non-English first and surnames. Avoid renaming students of Asian descent, other minority groups, or non-native English speakers with common Anglo names unless that is their preference.

One technique for learning names quickly is to use a seating chart. Laminate the seating chart onto a neon-colored (it gives students a visual focus) clipboard that you can carry in class with you. Many teachers prefer to assign

Teaching Scenario	A Name Is Just a Name

Takashi's family moved from Kodiak, Alaska, to a suburb of Des Moines, Iowa, when he was a junior in high school. Yes, it was a culture shock. Being of Japanese American heritage, Takashi had Asian physical traits. At his new school, Takashi was constantly asked where he was from, a question that he had never heard back home. Fellow students who made that inquiry were not wondering what state he came from. The inference was that he could not be American and must be from Asia or somewhere else outside the United States. Although offended by the narrow picture that the students at his school had of what an American looks like, Takashi was most bothered by the fact that his homeroom teacher often ignored him completely, skipped over him when calling roll, or mispronounced his name and called him Takaki, Kastati, or Kikitai. His teacher's insensitivity would always prompt a roar of laughter and relentless teasing from his peers. It hurt and angered him that his teacher did not make the effort to learn the correct pronunciation of his name. After all, she knew the names of all the other students and used them appropriately.

permanent seats and then make seating charts from which they can unobtrusively check the roll while students are doing seat work.

It is usually best to get your students into the lesson before taking roll and before doing other housekeeping chores. Ways of assigning student seating are discussed later in this chapter (see the section "The First Day").

Digital photography makes it easy for you to create visual likenesses of each of your students that can be labeled with their names and frequently viewed. Addressing students by name every time you speak to them can also help you to learn and remember their names. Another helpful way to learn students' names is to return papers yourself by calling their names and then handing the papers to them, paying careful attention as you look at each student and make mental notes that may help you to associate the name with the face.

CLASSROOM SHARING DURING THE FIRST WEEK OF SCHOOL

During the first week of school, many teachers take some time each day to have students present information about themselves and/or about the day's assignment. This is time well spent. It helps students feel valued and comfortable and builds a sense of community. Perhaps you can select five or six students each day to answer questions such as "What name would you like to be called by?," "Where did you attend school last year?," "Tell us about your hobbies and other interests," or "What interested you about last night's reading, or yesterday's lesson?" Some students are reluctant to talk off the cuff or in front of a large group. In order for introverted students, non-native English speakers, or others who might appreciate a "heads-up" to have time to prepare their answers, you might provide a list of questions for students to take home the night before and reflect on. You might also consider having your students share information of this sort with each other in groups of three or four while you visit each group in turn.

Still another approach is the "me-in-a-bag" activity. Each student is to bring to school a paper bag (limit the size) that contains items brought from home that represent that person. Then students are given time in class to share the items brought, explaining how each item represents them.

How the student answers such questions or participates in such activities can be as revealing as is the information (or the lack thereof) that the student shares. From the sharing, you sometimes get clues about additional information you would like to obtain about the student.

OBSERVE STUDENTS IN THE CLASSROOM—DEVELOP AND PRACTICE YOUR WITHITNESS

During learning activities, the effective teacher is constantly moving around the classroom and is alert to the individual behavior (nonverbal and verbal) of each student in the class, whether the student is on task or daydreaming and perhaps thinking about other things. Be cautious, however; just because a person is gazing out the window does not mean that he or she is not thinking about the learning task. Group work is a particularly good time to observe students and get to know more about each one's skills and interests.

OBSERVATIONS OF AND CONVERSATIONS WITH STUDENTS OUTSIDE THE CLASSROOM

Another way to learn more about students is by observing them outside class: at school athletic events, at dances, at performing arts events, at lunchtime (finding it an excellent time to get to know their students as well as to provide informal guidance, some teachers open their classrooms at noon for a brown-bag lunch with any student who wishes to come), during advisory or homeroom, in the hallways, and at club meetings. Observations outside the classroom can give information about student personalities, friendships, interests, and potentials. For instance, you may find that a student who seems lackadaisical or uninterested in your classroom is a real fireball on the playing field or at some other student gathering.

CONFERENCES AND INTERVIEWS WITH STUDENTS

Conferences with students (and sometimes with family members as well) afford yet another opportunity to show that you are genuinely interested in each student as a person and as a student. Some teachers make brief telephone calls to each student's parents and/or guardians during the first couple of weeks of school to introduce themselves, review their expectations, and share their concern for the child's success in their classroom. Other secondary teachers send home disclosure statements, a sort of contract that lays out the expectations for success in a particular course, that parents and students are expected to read and sign. Examples of disclosure statements are included in Chapter 6. This initial communication lays the groundwork for positive problem solving should the need arise in the future. By being proactive, you can establish allies early on.

Some teachers and teaching teams plan a series of conferences during the first few weeks in which, individually or in small groups of three or four students, students are interviewed by the teacher or by the teaching team. Block scheduling is especially conducive to teacher-parent-student conferences. Such conferences and interviews are managed by using open-ended questions. The teacher indicates by the questions, by listening, and by nonjudgmental and empathic responses (i.e., being able to put him- or herself in the shoes of the student, thereby understanding where the student is coming from) a genuine interest in the students. Keep in mind, however, that students who feel they have been betrayed by prior adult associations may at first be distrustful of your sincerity. In such instances, don't force it. Be patient but do not hesitate to take advantage of the opportunity afforded by talking with individual students outside of class time. Investing a few minutes of time in a positive conversation with a student during which you indicate a genuine interest in that student can pay real dividends when it comes to that student's interest and learning in your classroom.

STUDENT WRITING AND QUESTIONNAIRES Much can be learned about students by what they write (or draw). It is important to encourage writing in your classroom and to read everything that students write (except for personal journals) and ask for clarification when needed. The journals and portfolios discussed in Chapter 11 are useful for this purpose.

Some teachers use open-ended interest-discovering and autobiographical questionnaires. Student responses to questionnaires can provide ideas about how to tailor assignments to individual students. However, you must assure students that their answers are optional and that you are not invading their right to privacy.

In an interest-discovering questionnaire, students are asked to answer questions such as "When you read for fun or pleasure, what do you usually read?," "What are your favorite movies, videos, or television shows?," "Who are your favorite music video performers?," "Who are your favorite athletes?," "Describe your favorite hobby or other non-school-related activity," and "What are your favorite sport activities to participate in and to watch?"

In an autobiographical questionnaire, students are asked to answer questions such as "Where were you born?," "What do you plan to do following high school?," "Do you have a job?," "If so, what is it?," "Do you like it?,"

"How do you like to spend your leisure time?," "Do you like to read?," "What do you like to read?," and "Do you have a favorite hobby? What is it?" Many teachers model the process by beginning with reading to the students their own autobiographical answers to the questions.

CUMULATIVE RECORD, DISCUSSIONS WITH COLLEAGUES, AND EXPERIENTIAL BACKGROUNDS The cumulative record for each student is held in the school office. It contains information recorded from year to year by teachers and other school professionals. The information covers the student's academic background, standardized test scores, and extracurricular activities. However, the Family Educational Rights and Privacy Act (FERPA) of 1974 and its subsequent amendments and local policies may forbid your reviewing the record, except perhaps in collaboration with an administrator or counselor when you have a legitimate educational purpose for doing so. Although you must use discretion before arriving at any conclusion about information contained in the cumulative record, the record may afford information for getting to know a particular student better. Remember, though, a student's past is history and should not be held against that student but rather should be used as a means for understanding a student's experiences and current perceptions. Start fresh with your students; everyone deserves a second chance.

To better understand a student, it is sometimes helpful to talk with the student's other teachers, adviser, or counselor to learn of their perceptions and experiences with the student. As discussed in Chapter 1, one of the advantages of schools that use looping or that are divided into "houses" or both is that teachers and students get to know one another better.

Another way of getting to know your students is to spend time in the neighborhoods in which they live. One principal at a middle school in Portland, Oregon, asks all of her new hires to ride their students' school buses the first week of school to get to know their communities. Observe and listen, finding and noting things that you can use as examples or as learning activities.

Preparation Provides Confidence and Success

For successful classroom management, beginning the school term well may make all the difference in the world. Remember that you have only one opportunity to make a first and lasting impression. Therefore, you should appear at the first class meeting (and every class meeting thereafter) as well prepared and confident as possible.

Perhaps in the beginning, you will feel nervous and apprehensive, but being ready and well prepared will help you at least to appear to be confident. Being well prepared provides the confidence necessary to cloud feelings of nervousness. A slow under-the-breath counting to 10 at the start can be helpful, too. Then, if you proceed in a businesslike, matter-of-fact way, the impetus of your well-prepared beginning will, most likely, cause the day, week, and year to proceed as desired.

Effective Organization and Administration of Activities and Materials

Taking time for preemptive classroom management is time well spent. In a well-managed classroom, student movement about the classroom is routinized, controlled, and purposeful to the learning activities. Reflecting on a room arrangement that will help support your instructional activities, organize supplies and materials, and provide flexibility will limit distractions, off-task behavior, and chaotic transitions. In a well-managed classroom, students know what to do, have the materials needed to do it well, and stay on task while doing it. The classroom atmosphere is supportive; the assignments and procedures for doing them are clear; the materials of instruction are current, interesting, and readily available; and the classroom proceedings are businesslike. At all times, the teacher is in control of events rather than controlled by them, seeing that students are spending their time on appropriate tasks. Some teachers are so masterful that they appear to be laid-back naturals when it comes to classroom management, but make no mistake, they have these systems in place. For your teaching to be effective, you must perfect skills in managing the classroom.

Natural Interruptions and Disruptions to Routine

As you plan and prepare to implement your management system, you must also be aware of your own moods and high-stress days and anticipate that your own tolerance levels may vary. Middle school and high school students, too, are susceptible to personal problems that can be the sources of high stress. As you come to know your students well, you will be able to ascertain when certain students are under an inordinate amount of stress and anxiety.

You must understand that classroom routines may be interrupted occasionally for perfectly natural reasons, especially on certain days and at certain times during the school year. Other, more serious incidents may disrupt your plans as well. Carrying out business as usual after the 9/11 tragedy, a student suicide, a school shooting, or other devastating circumstances is not realistic. Sometimes you need to put your lesson plan aside and let students go through a grieving process.

Even under normal circumstances, students will not have the same motivation and energy level on each and every day, nor will you. Energy levels also vary throughout the school day. Your anticipation of and thoughtful and careful planning for the preactive phase of instruction—periods of high or low energy levels—will preserve your own mental health. Depending on a number of factors, periods of high energy levels might include (a) the beginning of each school day; (b) before a field trip, a holiday, or a school event, such as a dance, homecoming, picture day, or a school assembly; (c) the day of a holiday; (d) the day following a holiday;

(e) grade report day; (f) immediately before or/and after lunch; (g) on a shortened day or the day a substitute teacher is present; and (h) toward the end of each school day, toward the end of school each Friday afternoon, and toward the end of the school term or year.

Although there may be no hard evidence, many experienced teachers will tell you that particularly troublesome days for classroom control are those days when there is a strong north wind or a full moon. One teacher jokingly (we suspect) said that on days when there are both a strong north wind and a full moon, she calls in sick.

How should you prepare for these so-called high-energy days? There are probably no specific guidelines that will work for all teachers in all situations in each instance from the list. However, these are days to which you need to pay extra attention during your planning, days that students could possibly be restless and more difficult to control, days when you might need to be especially forceful and consistent in your enforcement of procedures or even compassionate and more tolerant than usual. Plan instructional activities that might be more readily accepted by the students. PATs that serve as skill drills or reviews for tests make learning fun.[22] In no instance is it our intent to imply that learning ceases and playtime takes over. What little instructional time is available to a teacher during a school year is too precious for that ever to happen.

Classroom Procedures and Guidelines for Acceptable Behavior

It is impossible to overemphasize the importance of getting the school term off to a good beginning, so let's start this section by discussing how that is done.

Designing Your Room Arrangement

Before classes begin, it is important for you to set up your classroom in such a way as to support learning. How you choose to arrange your classroom will be a reflection of your teaching style. Do not leave your classroom arrangement up to the discretion of the custodial staff. It may be convenient to have desks placed in rows for cleaning purposes, but this layout is not conducive to interactive, hands-on collaborative group activities.[23] Eliminate barriers and be sure to leave yourself ample room in the aisles for easy student access. Think about the various small-group and whole-class activities you would like to have your students engage in. Also, verify that all students can see the board, overhead projector screen, or other necessary equipment from their seats.

In addition to placing the furniture strategically and using the space you have in an efficient manner, you also want to remove barriers and eliminate congestion in high-traffic areas so that you and the students can move freely and easily throughout the classroom when appropriate. You need to arrange your room so that you and your students are comfortable, all of them can see you, and you can monitor their work.

Teaching materials and classroom supplies should be stored so that they are easily accessed. When deciding where to put things, you have to keep in mind what your preferred teaching style is and the kinds of activities you will ask your students to engage in.[24] You will spend a lot of time in your classroom, so make it a cheerful place.

Starting the School Term Well

Students size you up in the first three minutes of your first encounter. In addition to exuding confidence, there are three important keys to getting the school term off to a good beginning. First, be prepared and be fair. Preparation for the first day of school should include establishing and reviewing your classroom procedures and basic expectations for the students' behavior while they are under your supervision. The procedures and expectations must be consistent with school policy and seem reasonable to your students, and in enforcing them, you must be a fair and consistent professional. However, being coldly consistent is not the same as being fair and professional. Students need structure, but, just like good parenting, good classroom facilitation requires flexibility.

As a teacher, you are a professional who deals in matters of human relations and who must exercise professional judgment. You are not a robot, nor are your students. Human beings differ from one another, and seemingly similar situations can vary substantially because the people involved are different. Consequently, your response (or lack of response) to each of two separate but quite similar situations may differ. To be most effective, learning must be enjoyable for students; it cannot be enjoyable when a teacher consistently acts like a marine drill sergeant. If a student breaks a rule, rather than assuming why, seeming not to care why, or overreacting to the infraction, find out why before deciding your response. See, for example, the Teaching Scenario "Late Homework Paper from a Student At Risk" in Chapter 9.

Second, in preparing your classroom management system, remember that too many rules and detailed procedures at the beginning can be overwhelming. To avoid confusion, it is best at first to present only the minimum number of procedural expectations necessary for an orderly start to the school term. By the time students are in middle school grades, unless they are recent newcomers to this country, they have likely been exposed to the general rules of expected behavior, although great variation in the expectations and enforcement of said expectations may have existed. Some of your students' prior teachers may not always have been consistent or even fair about applying these expectations. For middle school teachers who are members of a teaching team, a unified approach to classroom expectations may be presented to the students.

Although there are similarities in expectations, expectations change from teacher to teacher, from school to school, and from year to year. For some high school students, it may prove difficult to change classes every 45 or 50 minutes and be confronted with different expectations. To make it even more challenging, some secondary teachers do not believe in writing out classroom rules or guidelines and posting them in their classroom, whereas some use one simple word, *respect*, or the phrase "the Golden Rule" because they expect high school students to be well acquainted with the norms for acceptable behavior.[25] Above all, teach your students to be responsible for their behavior. However, by establishing and sticking to a few explained general expectations (see discussion that follows in the section "The First Day") and to those that may be specific to your subject area, you can leave yourself some room for judgments and maneuvering.

Third, consequences for not following established procedures must be reasonable, clearly understood, and fairly applied. The procedures should be quite specific so that students know exactly what is expected and what is not and what the consequences are when procedures are not followed. Check out Exercise 4.1 now.

Procedures Rather Than Rules; Consequences Rather Than Punishment

To encourage a constructive and supportive classroom environment, we encourage you and your students to practice thinking in terms of procedures (or standards and guidelines)[26] rather than rules and of consequences rather than punishment. The rationale is this: to many people, the term *rules* has a more negative connotation than does the term *procedures*. When working with a cohort of students, some rules are necessary, but some people feel that using the term *guidelines* has a more positive ring to it. For example, a classroom rule might be that when one person is talking, we do not interrupt that person until he or she is finished. When that rule is broken, rather than reminding students of the rule, the emphasis can be changed to a procedure simply by reminding the students, "What is our guideline (or standard expectation) when someone is talking?"

Although some people will disagree, we concur with the contention that thinking in terms of and talking about procedures and consequences are more likely to contribute to a positive classroom atmosphere than using the terms *rules* and *punishment*. Of course, some argue that by the time students are in middle school and high school, you might as well tell it like it is. Especially if your group of students is linguistically and culturally mixed, you will need to be as direct and clear as possible to avoid sending confusing or mixed signals. After considering what experienced teachers have to say, the final decision is only one of many that you must make and that will be influenced by your own thinking and situation. It might be a decision made in collaboration with members of your teaching team. It is, however, important that expectations are communicated clearly to the students and followed consistently by you and other members of your teaching team.

It is important to get student cooperation, so you want them to have buy-in. From time to time, it may be effective to remind middle school students to apply the rules. For instance, you might ask them to reflect on and describe what a good listener acts like, looks like, participates like, and so forth before a whole-class group discussion where you expect students to raise their hands and wait to be called on before speaking and/or to respond to their classmates' statements. You might decide to have your secondary students involved in the determination of appropriate classroom rules. If you have in mind what you would like as classroom guidelines ahead of time, you could guide students to include your ideas, and/or you can reserve final veto power if you dislike any of their suggestions.

Once you have decided your initial expectations or created your expectations to include your students' input, you are ready to explain them to your students and to begin rehearsing a few of the procedures on the very first day of class. You will want to do this in a positive way. Students work best in a positive atmosphere; when teacher expectations are clear to them; when procedures are stated in positive terms, are clearly understood and agreed on, and have become routine; and when consequences for behavior that is inappropriate are reasonable, clearly understood, and fairly applied. Check out Activity 4.4 now.

The First Day

On the first day, you will want to cover certain major points of common interest to you and your students. The following paragraphs offer guidelines and suggestions for meeting your students the first time.

GREETING THE STUDENTS AND FACILITATING THE FIRST ACTIVITY Welcome your students with a smile as they arrive and then conduct the entire class with a friendly but businesslike demeanor. This means that you are not frowning or off in a corner of the room doing something else as students arrive. As you greet the students at the classroom door, tell them to take a seat and start on the first activity at their desk. This ensures that students have

---

Activity 4.4 **Classroom Rules/Guidelines Found Posted in Middle and Secondary Classrooms in Billings, Montana**

Read through these sample middle and secondary classroom rules/guidelines.

Ms. B's Seventh-Grade Math Rules

1. Follow directions the first time they are given.
2. Eyes on the teacher when she is teaching.
3. Stay in your seat when the teacher is teaching.
4. Treat others the way you want them to treat you.

Guidelines for Successful Sixth Graders

1. Respect yourself, your classmates, your teacher, and your school.
2. Treat others the way you would like to be treated.
3. Speak kind words.
4. Take accountability for your actions.
5. Stretch your mind.

Rules for Middle School Language Arts

Take turns. Follow rules. Share with others. Say please and thank you. Raise your hand. Be polite.

Mr. M's Middle School Physical Education Rules

No gum. No roughhousing. Keep your hands, feet, and objects to yourself. Obey the Golden Rule. Take care of personal hygiene in the restroom/locker room. One person at a time is allowed to leave the gym with the hall pass.

Classroom Rules for Ninth-Grade Health Enhancement

1. Be respectful
   - Raise your hand before talking.
   - Treat others the way you wish to be treated.
2. Be responsible
   - Complete assignments on time.
   - Own your behavior and accept consequences.
3. Cooperate
   - Work with your peers and teacher.

High School Language Arts Classroom

I have the right to teach.

Classroom Expectations for High School Chorus Members

No gum, drinks, or food.
No talking to neighbors.
No pushing or shoving.
No doing homework for other classes.
No late arrivals.
No unexcused absences.

Mr. G's High School Biology Classroom Expectation

Respect is required by everyone in this classroom in all circumstances.

Mrs. O's High School Social Studies Rules

1. Lateness will not be tolerated.
2. Come to class ready to work.
3. Do your assignments neatly and hand them in on time.
4. Cooperate with your teacher and classmates.
5. Listen to all directions.
6. Do not use the pencil sharpener during instructional time.
7. Do not vandalize school property.
8. Do not interrupt your classmates' learning.
9. Speak only if you are called on.
10. Stay on task in class.
11. Do not cheat.
12. Do not touch your classmates' belongings.

Apply Your Knowledge

Record your responses to the following questions:

1. What similarities and/or differences do you observe in the different classroom rules/guidelines listed here?
2. What do the rules/guidelines tell you about the respective teacher's classroom management style?
3. What is the tone set by the classroom rules/guidelines? Explain.

something to do immediately on arriving at your classroom. And starting the learning immediately on arrival should be the routine every day thereafter.

That first activity might be a questionnaire each student completes. This is a good time to instruct students on the expected standard for heading their papers. After giving instructions on how papers are to be handed in, rehearse the procedure by collecting this first paper. Or you may ask students to provide answers to a few discipline and personal questions on the back of a 3 × 5 card that you use to take attendance throughout the semester/year.

STUDENT SEATING One option for student seating is to have student names on the first activity paper and placed at student seats when students arrive at that first class meeting. That allows you to have a seating chart ready on the first day from which you can quickly take attendance and learn student names. Another option, not exclusive of the first, is to tell students that by the end of the week, each should be in a permanent seat (either assigned by you or self-selected) from which you will make a seating chart that will help you to learn their names quickly and take attendance efficiently each day. It is important that students know that you will move them if they have chosen seat assignments that do not support their learning. Let them know, too, that from time to time you will redo the seating arrangement (if that is true). For small classes, a seating chart is probably unnecessary.

INFORMATION ABOUT THE CLASS After the first assignment has been completed, discussed, and collected, explain to students what the course is about, in other words, what they will be learning and how they will learn it (covering study habits and your expectations regarding the quantity and quality of their work). This is a time you may choose to get student input into the course content in order to give students an opportunity for some empowerment. Although it is not common practice, some secondary teachers put this information in a course syllabus (see the samples in Chapter 5), give each student a copy, and review it with them, specifically discussing the teacher's expectations about how books will be used; about student notebooks, journals, portfolios, and assignments; about what students need to furnish; and about the location of resources in the classroom, school media center, and elsewhere.

CLASSROOM PROCEDURES AND ENDORSED BEHAVIOR Now discuss in a positive way your expectations regarding classroom behavior, procedures, and routines (discussed next). Students work best when teacher expectations are easily understood, with established routines. In the beginning, it is important that there be no more procedures than necessary to get the class moving effectively for daily operation. Five or fewer expectations should be enough, such as the following:

- Arrive promptly with needed materials and stay on task until excused by the teacher (the teacher, not a bell, excuses students).

- Demonstrate respect for the rights, the person, and the property of others.
- Remain seated and listen attentively when someone else is talking.
- Use appropriate and nonoffensive language.
- Work on anchor assignments whenever you have time in class. (We will discuss anchor assignments, any ongoing assignment such as portfolio organization, journal writing, or project work, in Chapter 7.)

Too many procedural expectations at first can be restricting and even confusing to students. As said earlier, most students already know these things, so you shouldn't have to spend much time on the topic except for those items specific to your course, such as the nature of the anchor assignment and apparel and safety expectations for laboratory courses, technology education, art classes, and physical education. Be patient with yourself on this, for finding and applying the proper level of control for a given group of students is one of the skills that you will develop and refine with experience.

Although many schools traditionally have posted in the halls and in the classrooms a list of prohibited behaviors, exemplary schools tend to focus on the positive: on endorsed attitudes and behaviors. Displaying a list of "do nots" does not encourage a positive school or classroom atmosphere; a list of "dos" does. For example, at Constellation Community Middle School (Long Beach, CA), all students receive regular daily reminders when, after reciting the Pledge of Allegiance, they recite the school's five core principles: (1) anything that hurts another person is wrong, (2) we are each other's keepers, (3) I am responsible for my own actions, (4) I take pride in myself, and (5) leave it better than when you found it.[27]

Establishing Classroom Expectations, Procedures, and Consequences

When establishing classroom behavior expectations and procedures, remember this point: the learning time needs to run efficiently (i.e., with no "dead spots," or times when students have nothing to do), smoothly (i.e., routine procedures are established, and transitions between activities are smooth), and with minimum distraction. As discussed in the preceding section, when stating your expectations for student classroom behavior, do so in a positive manner, emphasizing procedures, desired attitudes, and behaviors and stressing what students should do rather than what they should not do. Respect for the teacher, for themselves, for fellow classmates, for school property, for the process, and so forth should be emphasized.

What Students Need to Understand from the Start

As you prepare the guidelines, standards, and expectations for classroom behavior, you (and, if relevant, your teaching team) need to consider some of the specifics about what students need to understand from the start. These specific points, then, should be reviewed and rehearsed with the students, sometimes several times, during the first week of school and then followed consistently throughout the school term.

Important and specific things that students need to know from the start will vary considerably, depending on whether you are working with sixth graders in a middle school or high school seniors and whether you are teaching an English class or a shop class. Generally, though, each of the following paragraphs describes things that all students need to understand from the beginning.

SIGNALING THE TEACHER FOR ATTENTION AND HELP At the start of the school term, most teachers who are effective classroom managers expect students to raise their hands until the teacher acknowledges (usually by a nonverbal gesture, such as eye contact and a nod) that the student's hand has been seen. With that acknowledgment, the recommended procedure is that the student should lower his or her hand and return to work.

There are a number of important reasons for expecting students to raise their hands before speaking. Two are that it allows you to (1) control the noise and confusion level and (2) be proactive in deciding who speaks. The latter is important if you are to be in control of classroom events rather than controlled by them and if you are to manage a classroom with equality, with equal attention to individuals regardless of their gender, ethnicity, proximity to the teacher, or any other personal characteristic. We are not talking about students having to raise their hands before talking with their peers during group work; we are talking about not allowing students to shout across the room to get your attention and boisterously talk out freely during instruction.

Another important reason for expecting students to raise their hands and be recognized before speaking is to discourage impulsive outbursts and encourage them to grow intellectually. An instructional responsibility shared by all teachers is to help students develop intelligent behaviors (discussed in Chapter 8). Learning to control impulsivity is one of the intelligent behaviors. Teaching youth to control their impulsivity is a highly important responsibility that, in our opinion, is too often neglected by too many teachers (and by too many parents).

ENTERING AND LEAVING THE CLASSROOM From the time that the class is scheduled to begin until it officially ends, teachers who are effective classroom managers expect students to be in their seats or at their learning stations and attentive to the teacher or the learning activity until excused by the teacher. For example, students should not be allowed to begin meandering toward the classroom exit in anticipation of the passing bell or the designated passing time. Otherwise, their meandering toward the door will begin earlier and earlier each day, and the teacher will increasingly lose control. Besides, it is a waste of a very valuable and very limited resource—instructional time. As mentioned earlier, PATs can be used as a productive alternative when students become restless or when students complete an activity earlier than anticipated.

MAINTAINING, OBTAINING, AND USING MATERIALS FOR LEARNING AND ITEMS OF PERSONAL USE Students need to know where, when, and how to store, retrieve, and care for items, such as their coats, backpacks, books, pencils, and medicines; how to get papers and materials; and when to use the classroom pencil sharpener and wastebasket. Classroom control is easiest to maintain when (a) items that students need for class activities and for their personal use are neatly and safely arranged (e.g., backpacks stored under tables or chairs rather than in aisles) and located in places that require minimum foot traffic, (b) there are established procedures that students clearly expect and understand, (c) there is the least amount of student off-task time, and (d) students do not have to line up for anything. Therefore, you will want to plan the room arrangement, equipment and materials storage, preparation of equipment and materials, and transitions between activities to avoid needless delays, confusion, and safety hazards. Remember this well: problems in classroom control will most certainly occur whenever some or all students have nothing to do, even if only briefly.

LEAVING CLASS FOR A PERSONAL MATTER Normally, most students of middle school and high school age should be able to get a drink of water or go to the bathroom between classes if necessary; however, sometimes they do not or, for medical reasons or during long block classes, cannot. Reinforce the notion that they should do those things before coming into your classroom or during the scheduled times but be flexible enough for the occasional student who has an immediate need. Whenever permitting a student to leave class for a personal reason, follow established school procedures, which may for reasons of security mean that students can leave the room only in pairs and with a hall pass or when accompanied by an adult, such as a campus security person.

REACTING TO A VISITOR OR AN INTERCOM ANNOUNCEMENT Unfortunately, class interruptions do occur, and in some schools they occur far too often and for reasons that are not as important as interrupting a teacher and students' learning would imply. For an important reason the principal, a vice principal, or some other person from the school's office may interrupt the class to see the teacher or a student or to make an announcement to the entire class. Students need to understand what behavior is expected of them during those interruptions. When there is a visitor to the class, the expected procedure should be for students to continue their learning task unless directed otherwise by you. To learn more about class interruptions, do Exercise 4.2 now.

WHEN LATE TO CLASS OR LEAVING EARLY You must abide by school policies on early dismissals and late arrivals. Make your own procedures routine so that students clearly understand what they are to do if they must leave your class early (e.g., for a medical appointment) or when they arrive late. Procedures in your classroom—and indeed throughout the school—should be such that late arriving and early dismissal students do not have to disturb you or other teachers or the learning in progress.

When students are allowed to interrupt the learning in progress because the teacher has not established such procedures and these interruptions happen repeatedly and regularly, the covert message conveyed by the hidden curriculum, at least in that classroom if not in the entire school, is that instruction is relatively low on the list of priorities. Do not let this happen.

CONSEQUENCES FOR INAPPROPRIATE BEHAVIOR Most teachers who are effective classroom managers routinize their procedures for handling inappropriate behavior and ensure that the students understand the consequences for inappropriate behavior. The consequences are posted in the classroom and, depending on the school, may be similar to the five-step model shown in Figure 4.1.

Whether offenses subsequent to the first one are those that occur on the same day or within a designated period of time, such as one week, is one of the many decisions that must be made by a teacher or by members of a teaching team, department, or the entire faculty, with administrative approval.

EMERGENCY DRILLS (PRACTICE) OR REAL EMERGENCIES Students need to clearly understand what to do, where to go, and how to behave in emergency conditions, such as those that might occur because of a fire, storm, earthquake, or disruptive campus intruder. Students must be expected to behave during practice drills as well as in real emergencies.

To further your understanding of classroom management and to begin the development of your own management system, do Exercises 4.3 and 4.4.

Using Positive Rewards

As you probably learned in an educational psychology course, reinforcement theory contends that a person's gratification derived from receiving a reward strengthens the tendency for that person to continue to act in a certain way, while the lack of a reward (or the promise of a reward) weakens the tendency to act that way. For example, according to the theory, if students are promised a reward of PAT on Friday if they work well all week long, then the students are likely to work toward that reward, thus improving their standards of learning. PAT is your bargaining chip. You should be happy to award students PAT because while they are having fun, they will be learning content. Some educators argue that (a) once the extrinsic reinforcement (i.e., the reward from outside the learner) has been removed, the desired behavior tends to diminish and that (b) rather than *extrinsic* sources of reinforcement, focus should be on increasing the student's internal sense of accomplishment, an *intrinsic* reward. Perhaps, for the daily work of a teacher in a classroom of many diverse individuals, the practical reality is somewhere in between. After all, the reality of classroom teaching is less than ideal, and all activities cannot be intrinsically rewarding. Further, for many young people, intrinsic rewards are often too remote to be effective.

The promise of extrinsic rewards is not always necessary or beneficial. Students generally will work harder to learn something because they want to learn it (i.e., it is intrinsically motivating) than they will merely to earn PAT, points, grades, candy, or some other form of reward (called an *extrinsic motivator*). In addition, regarding the promise of PAT on Friday, many young people are so preoccupied with "now" that, for them, the promise on Monday of PAT on Friday probably will have little desired effect on their behavior on Monday. To them, Friday seems to be a long way off from Monday.

Activities that are interesting and intrinsically rewarding are not further served by the addition of extrinsic rewards. This is especially true when working with students who are already highly motivated to learn. Adding extrinsic incentives to learning activities that are already highly motivating tends to reduce student motivation. For most students, the use of extrinsic motivators should be minimal and is probably most useful in skills learning, where there

F i g u r e 4 . 1 **Sample Consequences for Inappropriate Behavior**

First offense results in a direct but reasonably unobtrusive (often nonverbal) reminder from the teacher to the student.

Second offense results in a private but direct verbal warning.

Third offense results in a time-out in an isolation area (but one with adult supervision) followed by a private teacher-student (or teacher-student-parent) conference.

Fourth offense results in a suspension from class until there is a student-parent-teacher (and perhaps counselor) conference.

Fifth offense results in a referral to the vice principal or principal or counselor, sometimes followed by a limited or permanent suspension from that class or a total expulsion from school.

is likely to be a lot of repetition and the potential for boredom. If students are working diligently on a highly motivating student-initiated project of study, extrinsic rewards are not necessary and could even have negative effects.

Managing Class Meetings

The guidelines for the first meeting with your students hold true for every meeting thereafter. When it is time for the class period to begin, you should start the learning activities at once, with no delay. By beginning your class meeting without delay, you discourage the kind of fooling around and time wasting that might otherwise occur. To minimize problems with classroom control, you must practice this from the very first day of your teaching career.

Note: At the beginning of your student teaching, you may need to follow the opening procedures already established by your cooperating teacher. If your cooperating teacher's procedures for classroom management are largely ineffective, it is important for you to remember that you are a guest in that classroom. If you have a good working relationship established with your cooperating teacher, you may try talking directly to him or her and making suggestions. If the lines of communication are strained, chalk this up as a learning experience. Remember, sometimes we learn more about teaching by observing what we do not want to do in our classrooms than by having someone model stellar behavior. In a worst-case scenario, you should talk with your university supervisor about a different placement.

Once class has begun, the pace of activities should be lively enough to keep students alert and busy, without dead time, but not so fast as to discourage or lose some students. The effective teacher runs a businesslike classroom; at no time does any student sit or stand around with nothing to do. To maintain a smooth and brisk pace and to lessen distractions and prevent dead time, consider the guidelines that follow.

Opening Activities

Although many schools no longer use a bell system for the beginning and ending of every class period, many teachers still refer to the initial class activity as the bell activity. More frequently, perhaps, it is referred to as the warm-up activity or opener.

At the beginning of each class, in order to take attendance and to attend to other routine administrative matters, most teachers expect the students to be in their assigned seats. You should greet the students warmly and start their learning quickly. Unless you really want responses, it perhaps is best to avoid greeting students with a rhetorical question such as "How was your weekend?" If you are teaching in a school where you must monitor attendance at the beginning of each class meeting and are not yet comfortable with your overlapping skill, an effective management procedure is to have the overhead projector on each day when students arrive in class, with the day's agenda and immediate assignment or warm-up activity clearly

written on a transparency and displayed on the screen or written on the board or on your Smart Board, which then is referred to after your greeting. Once administrative matters are completed (usually in a matter of a minute or two), the day's regular lesson should begin, which could mean that students will move to other stations within the classroom.

When there are no announcements or other administrative matters to cover, you should try to begin the day's first lesson immediately. Then, within a few minutes after the students have begun their lesson activities, take attendance. Some teachers recommend beginning the day's lesson immediately while giving a reliable classroom aide or student assistant the responsibility of taking attendance and dealing with other routine administrative tasks. However, when another person performs the daily attendance routines, it remains your responsibility to check and sign the relevant attendance forms. Perhaps the best routine, one that requires your practice and overlapping skill, is to do both simultaneously—take attendance while starting a learning activity. Whichever the case, once the class period has begun, routines and lesson activities should move forward briskly and steadily until the official end of the class period or, in the case of extended class periods or blocks, until a scheduled break.

Warm-up activities include any variety of things, such as a specific topic or question that each student responds to by writing in his or her journal or the same topic or question that pairs (dyads) of students discuss and write about in their journals. Other activities include a problem to be solved by each student or student pair, the exchange and discussion of a homework assignment, the completion of the write-up of a laboratory activity, and the writing of individual or student dyad responses to textbook questions. Now do Exercise 4.5 to learn further how experienced teachers open their class meetings.

Smooth Implementation of the Lesson

Lessons should move forward briskly and purposefully, with natural transitions from one lesson activity to the next and with each activity starting and ending conclusively, especially when using direct (teacher-centered) instruction. As a beginning teacher, it will take time to develop finesse in your application of this guideline; during your student-teaching experience, your cooperating teacher and college or university supervisor will understand that it takes time and will help you develop and hone your skill in the application of this principle. Transitions (discussed in the section that follows), in particular, are a most troublesome time for many beginning teachers. Transitions are less troublesome when planned carefully during the preactive phase of instruction and written into the lesson plan.

When giving verbal instructions to students, do so succinctly, without talking too long and giving so much detail that students begin to get restless and bored. Adolescents are quickly bored with long-winded verbal instructions from a teacher. To address the linguistic needs of the

English Language Learners as well as the preferences of the visual learners in your class, you may consider displaying directions on the board or on an overhead.

With whole-class instruction, before starting a new activity, be sure that the present activity is satisfactorily completed by most students. Students who finish early can work on an anchor or transitional activity. End each activity conclusively before beginning a new activity, and with a relevant and carefully prepared transition, bridge the new activity with the previous one so that students understand the connection. Helping students understand connections is a continuing focus and theme for the classroom teacher.

With your skill in withitness, you will carefully and continuously monitor all students during the entire class period. If one or two students become inattentive and begin to behave inappropriately, quietly (i.e., using indirect or nonobtrusive intervention) redirect their attention without interrupting the rest of the class.

To help in the prevention of dead time and management problems, especially when using multiple learning tasks and indirect (student-centered) instruction, you will want to establish and rehearse the students in the use of anchor or transitional activities, which are ongoing, relevant tasks that students automatically move to whenever they have completed their individual or small-group classroom learning activities. Examples of an anchor activity include working on their portfolios or writing in their journals.

Transitions: A Difficult Skill for Beginning Teachers

Transitions are the moments in lessons between activities or topics, that is, times of change. It will probably take you a while to sharpen the skill of smooth transitions. Planning and consistency are necessary in mastering this important skill. With a dependable schedule and consistent routines, transitions usually occur efficiently and automatically, without disruption. Still, it is probable that for classroom teachers, the greatest number of discipline problems occur during times of transitions, especially when students must wait for the next activity. To avoid problems during transitions, eliminate wait time by thinking and planning ahead. During the preactive phase of instruction, plan your transitions and write them into your lesson plan.

Transitions in lessons are of two types, and at times both are used. The first is achieved by the teacher's connecting one activity to the next so that students understand the relationship between the two activities. That is a lesson transition. The second type of transition occurs when some students have finished a learning activity but must wait for others to catch up before starting the next. This we call a *transitional* or, as we will discuss in Chapter 7, an *anchor activity*. The transitional (or anchor) activity is one intended to keep all students academically occupied, allowing no time when students have nothing to do but wait. A common example occurs during testing when some students have finished the test while others have not. The effective

teacher plans a transitional activity and gives instructions or reminders for that activity or for an ongoing anchor activity before students begin the test.

Teachers who are most effective are those who, during the preactive phase of instruction, plan and rehearse nearly every move they and the students will make, thinking ahead to anticipate and avoid problems in classroom control. Transitions are planned and students are prepared for them by using clearly established transition routines. While in transition and waiting for the start of the next activity, students engage in these transitional activities. You can plan a variety of transitional activities relevant and appropriate to the topics being studied although not necessarily related to the next activity of that particular day's lesson. Transitional activities may include any number of meaningful activities, such as journal writing, worksheet activity, lab reports, portfolio work, homework, project work, and even work on an assignment for another class.

As a beginning teacher, it will take time to develop finesse in your application of these guidelines for effective lesson management. Well aware of that fact, your cooperating teacher and college or university supervisor will be patient and help you develop and sharpen your skills during your student-teaching experience.

Student Misbehavior

Student behavior that is inappropriate in the classroom can range from minor acts to very serious ones. Sometimes the causes of student misbehavior are the result of problems that originate outside the classroom and spill over into it. Others are simply misbehaviors that result from the fact that whenever 30 or so young people are grouped together for a period of time, mischief is likely to result. Still others are the result of something the teacher did or did not do. Read attentively the guidelines and suggestions that follow in the remaining pages of this chapter.

Categories of Student Misbehavior

Described next, in order of increasing seriousness, are categories of student misbehavior that classroom teachers sometimes have to contend with.

TRANSIENT NONDISRUPTIVE BEHAVIOR This least serious category includes these common and usually nondisruptive behaviors: fooling around, chatting with a neighbor, and momentarily being off task. Fortunately, in most instances, this type of behavior is transient, and sometimes it might even be best if you pretend for a moment or so not to be aware of it.[28] If it persists, all it may take to get the student back on task is an unobtrusive (silent and private) redirection. Examples of silent and private redirection techniques include a stare or a stare accompanied by a frown (when eye contact with the student is made) or moving to stand next to the student. If this doesn't work, then go to the second-level intervention by quickly name-dropping (calling the student by name but without making an issue of it). If this doesn't work, go to a third-level intervention by calling on the student by name and reminding the student of the correct procedure or of what the student is supposed to be doing.

Avoid asking an off-task student any question, such as a content question, "Bob, what are the end products of photosynthesis?," when you know full well the student is not paying attention or an inquiry, "Bob, why are you doing that?" Avoid also making a threat, such as "Bob, if you don't turn around and get to work I will send you outside." It is important not to make "mountains out of molehills," or you could cause more problems than you would resolve. Maintain students' focus on the lesson rather than the off-task behavior.

Examples of trivial nondisruptive behaviors that you need not worry about unless they become disruptive are emotionally excited student behavior because the student is really "into the lesson," brief whispering during a lesson, or short periods of inattentiveness, perhaps accompanied by visual wandering or daydreaming. Teacher responses to student behavior and enforcement of procedures such as raising hands and being recognized before speaking will naturally vary, depending on the particular subject, size of the class, lesson activity, and maturity of the students.

In addition, there is sometimes a tendency among beginning teachers, especially when they have a problem with students being disruptive, to assume that the entire class of students is being unruly; in fact, more often it is only one, two, or maybe three students. When this is so, you want to avoid saying to the entire class of students anything that implies that you perceive all of them as being unruly. That false accusation will only serve to alienate the majority of the students who are being attentive to the learning task.

CLASS DISRUPTIONS This category includes talking out of turn, walking about the room without permission, and persistent clowning, all of which students know are behaviors that are unacceptable in the classroom. In handling such misbehaviors, it is important that you explain their consequences to students and then, following your stated procedures, promptly and consistently deal with the violations. Too many beginning teachers (and veteran teachers, too) tend to ignore these class disruptions (seemingly in the hope that, if not recognized, they will discontinue). You must not ignore minor infractions of this type, for if you do, they most likely will escalate beyond your worst expectations. It is important to take care of discipline before instruction. Without displaying any anger (otherwise, students are winning the battle for control), simply and quickly enforce your consequences and keep the focus on the lesson, not on the inappropriate behavior. In other words, maintain your control of classroom events rather than become controlled by them. Or, putting it another way, with respect to classroom management, be proactive rather than reactive.

DEFIANCE, BACK TALK, CHEATING, LYING, AND STEALING When a student refuses to do what you say, the student's defiance may be worthy of temporary or permanent removal from the class. Depending on your judgment of the seriousness of the act of defiance, you may simply give the student a time-out, or you may suspend the student from class until there has been a conference about the situation, perhaps involving the teacher, members of your teaching team, the student, the student's parent or guardian, and a school official.

Back talk may come in the form of insults and/or profanity. Students may insult you by commenting on your personal hygiene, your grooming, your dress, or any number of other topics. Profanity, consisting of vulgar or inappropriate language or swearing, is about who is in control (i.e., who has the power). Teachers need to remember that when these power struggles are taking place, silence is the key to success. Do not escalate the situation by responding in kind. Fredric Jones sums it up this way: "It takes one fool to start Back Talk, but it takes two fools to make a conversation out of it."[29]

Any cheating, lying, and stealing may be an isolated act, and the student may only need a one-on-one talk to find out what precipitated the incident and what might be done to prevent it from ever happening again. A student who habitually exhibits any of these behaviors may need to be referred to a specialist. Whenever you have reason to suspect immoral behavior, you should discuss your concerns with members of your teaching team and a school counselor or psychologist.

VIOLENCE Today's teachers are sometimes confronted with major problems of misbehavior that have ramifications beyond the classroom or that begin elsewhere and spill over into the classroom. If this happens, you may need assistance and should not hesitate to ask for it. As a teacher, you must stay alert. In the words of Johnson and Johnson,

> Teaching is different from what it used to be. Fifty years ago, the main disciplinary problems were running in halls, talking out of turn, and chewing gum. Today's transgressions include physical and verbal violence, incivility, and in some schools, drug abuse, robbery, assault, and murder. The result is that many teachers spend an inordinate amount of time and energy managing classroom conflicts. When students poorly manage their conflicts with each other and with faculty, aggression results. Such behavior is usually punished with detentions, suspensions, and expulsions. As violence increases, pressure for safe and orderly schools increases. Schools are struggling with what to do.[30]

Today's schools are adopting a variety of types of schoolwide and classroom instructional programs designed to reduce or eliminate violent, aggressive student behaviors. Educators are being encouraged to enhance their ability to spot signs of trouble by increasing their efforts at establishing caring, responsive, and supportive relationships with students.[31] Check out Activity 4.5 to learn about **relational aggression** and how schools are addressing it, and read

Activity 4.5   Relational Aggression and the Empower Program

You've heard of bullying and **cyberbullying,** right? But have you heard of covert bullying? Another name for this psychological, social/emotional aggression is relational aggression. Did you see *Mean Girls* when it was released in 2004? In this blockbuster hit, Lindsay Lohan plays a naïve new student trying to join the "in" crowd, "The Plastics," in a Chicago high school. Although fictional, *Mean Girls* is based on Rosalind Wiseman's research on how female high school social cliques operate and their negative effects. To reveal the problem of relational aggression, a form of bullying often employed by teenage girls, Wiseman published *Queen Bees and Wannabes: Helping Your Daughter Survive Cliques, Gossip, Boyfriends, and Other Realities of Adolescence* in 2002. This best-seller focused the spotlight on the cruel behavior that characterizes relational aggression, namely, lying, sharing secrets, gossiping, betraying, and using other dishonest tactics to destroy, damage, or manipulate relationships or attack victims' social standing and/or shun and exclude them.

Dismayed by the behaviors she observed, Wiseman, a Washington, D.C., native and high school teacher, cofounded the not-for-profit Empower Program to help adolescents deal with conflict, avoid bullying, and eliminate violence in their schools.

The Empower Program's mission is to create a world in which young people are empowered to stop violence. Through "Owning Up," a comprehensive award-winning curriculum, the Empower Program teaches adolescents to transform silence into action. The curriculum emphasizes "hands-on activities, role-playing, writing, question and answer sessions and discussions to get to the root of problems," according to the Empower Program website. Other curricula include classes designed for both boys and girls that explore social hierarchies, violence, safety, and other topics.

Apply Your Knowledge

Check out the following website to learn more about relational aggression, the "Owning Up" curriculum, and Wiseman's work:

The Empower Program
http://www.empowered.org

1. How is male and female bullying similar and or different?
2. What cliques or groups existed when you attended middle and high school?

Teaching Scenario   Cyberbullying

Abbie was new to Elgin School District. Her family had moved from Atlanta to Portland during the summer between her freshman and sophomore years. Abbie was an attractive, athletic, fun-loving 15-year-old. She was very sad to be leaving her old friends but was excited about getting to know her new tenth-grade classmates. Her sassy southern accent, sincere smile, and confident demeanor earned her instant popularity. Sarah and Lindsey, members of the cool clique, welcomed Abbie into their social circle. Life was good at Elgin High. Abbie enrolled in college-prep courses, joined the yearbook committee, and sang in the concert choir. She also had aspirations to try out for the cheerleading squad along with Sarah and Lindsey. Everything changed in early October when Abbie and Lindsey were selected, but Sarah did not make the cheerleading squad. To make matters worse, starting quarterback Craig Wilson, the object of Sarah's lust, was rumored to have a crush on Abbie. The trio's friendship deteriorated quickly. Sarah, seeking revenge, set up a defamatory MySpace personal website where she "dissed" Abbie. She spread cruel, malicious gossip; called her a "ho" and slut; and shared intimate secrets. She even videotaped Abbie undressing and showering in the locker room and uploaded the videos. The website was live for several days, so the entire student body had access before the authorities got involved.

Unfortunately, this incident is not an isolated event. Cyberbullying—bullying and harassing others using electronic devices—is a prevalent occurrence among young children and adolescents. Using an assortment of email, instant messaging, cell phones, pagers, social networking websites, blogs, lists, and so on, students commit character assassination, which can have devastating effects on the victims. During the 2003–2004

academic year, I-SAFE America surveyed 1,500 fourth to eighth graders across the U.S. on cyberbullying. Their feedback, summarized here, is available at **http://www.isafe.org/channels/sub.php?ch=op&sub_id=media_cyber_bullying:**

- 42% of kids have been bullied while online. One in four has had it happen more than once.
- 35% of kids have been threatened online. Nearly one in five has had it happen more than once.
- 21% of kids have received mean or threatening email or other messages.
- 58% of kids admit someone has said mean or hurtful things to them online. More than 4 out of 10 say it has happened more than once.
- 53% of kids admit having said something mean or hurtful to another person online. More than one in three have done it more than once.
- 58% have not told their parents or an adult about something mean or hurtful that happened to them online.

Think About It

For more information on how to deter, detect, and take action, check out these websites on preventing cyberbullying:

http://www.nyssca.org/Linked%20Documents/
    Cyberbullying%20pp-New%20NYSSCA.pdf
http://www.cyberbullying.us
http://www.stopcyberbullying.com
http://www.cyberbully.org
http://www.challengeday.org

Teaching Scenario	Name-Calling Is Unacceptable

Dear Principal Kirk and Vice Principal Thompson,

I am the concerned parent of an eighth-grade student named Greg McAlister who attends Centennial Middle School. For some time now Greg has felt bullied at school as kids call him "Ginger" referring to his red hair (he says it is even worse for another student named Jack in eighth grade who also has red hair). To address this issue, my husband and I suggested that Greg talk to his eighth-grade counselor about these bullying episodes—he says that he did but that the counselor shrugged it off. When Greg gets on the bus each morning, he tells us that many kids stand up and shout "Ginger" at him. We have tried to address bullying issues on the bus with the bus company and have had no success (the bus driver blatantly allows bullying on her bus). Greg says that on a daily basis kids in the cafeteria shout out at Jack and him—calling them Gingers.

I was unaware, until today, that Ginger is a very derogatory term used internationally to describe red-haired people. A little Internet searching, and I found appalling evidence that this is true. South Park recently aired an episode called "Kick the Ginger," and there became an international "Kick the Ginger" day.

Here are some of the related YouTube sites I uncovered:

South Park's Kick a Ginger Day Leads to Hate Crimes Charges
http://www.youtube.com/watch?v=EBOjl8lG9GI

Kick a Ginger Day Nov. 20—South Park Cause of Bullying?
http://www.youtube.com/watch?v=SXBHWe-7_G4

Ginger Kids (Commentary)
http://www.youtube.com/watch?v=ddsK_Qzt86s&feature=related

My Google search on "ginger" and "bullying" produced a long string of articles about school bullying, as well. Some articles even discuss children committing suicide over the relentless teasing about their red hair and actual murders have taken place in the United Kingdom—as hate crimes against "gingers."

"Kick a Ginger" Middle School Beating Inspired by South Park?
http://www.cbsnews.com/8301-504083_162-5682034-504083 .html

Red Hair Bullying Cases Could End Up in Court: "Gingerism" the Grounds for Constructive Dismissal
http://www.theregister.co.uk/2007/06/14/red_hair_bullying

I am alarmed that "gingering" is being tolerated at Centennial! In bullying there are multiple victims—the target of the bullying, those witnessing it, and the bullies themselves. If I do not take action, I will be part of the problem—part of the enabling—part of propagation of the ugliness of bullying—and part of the problem of school violence.

I am assuming that neither of you were previously aware of the problem of children being called "Gingers." I am also assuming that Highland School District already has a policy in place that forbids bullying. I want to hear back from you on what actions you plan to take to put an end to the tolerance of letting children call other children "Gingers."

Being professionals, I am sure that you will take my concerns seriously and will discuss with professional school counselors appropriate ways to address this issue (saying that a mom of a ginger complained to the administration would obviously only escalate the problem for my child and other red-haired children). Perhaps referring to today's article in the Highland Gazette or some of the above listed references could be part of an overall strategy.

I realize that all school administrators are worried about a multitude of issues—not the least of which is the alarming decrease in funding. However, central to your mission is the safety and well-being of children, and for this reason bullying is an issue worth addressing. I am looking forward to hearing about your action plans.

Sincerely, Megan McAlister, concerned parent

---

about how schools are getting students to step outside their comfort zones and befriend students in other cliques with "Mix It Up" in Activity 4.6.

There Are Success Stories

There are success stories; examples are described in the following paragraphs.

After instituting nontraditional flexible scheduling (discussed in Chapter 1), it is not uncommon for schools to report an improved school climate with significant improvement in student attitudes, behavior, attendance, and academic success.[32]

After instituting looping (keeping students with the same teacher for multiple years) and creating a focus on character development, Kennedy Middle School (Eugene, OR) reports higher student achievement and improved student behavior.[33]

A diet high in saturated fat and refined sugar has been proven to negatively impact the health and behavior of our

students. In his film *Super Size Me*, Morgan Spurlock documents what happens to him as a result of eating McDonald's food three times a day for 30 days. Some people think that Spurlock's experiment is an unfair attack on the fast-food industry in this country, but the connection between fast-food menus and obesity in our youth is undeniable.

Does diet negatively affect student behavior as well? Spurlock investigated school lunch programs and questioned if eliminating junk food could reduce discipline problems. His documentary highlighted an alternative high school in the Midwest that instituted a healthy lunch program. The at-risk students attending Appleton Central Alternative High School in Appleton, Wisconsin, were offered wholesome breakfasts and lunches with a lot of healthy choices, including fresh fruit and salads, cooked meats, and whole-grain breads. After instituting these dietary changes, the school reported a remarkable decline in behavioral problems. Since the program's inception in 1997, Principal LuAnn Coenen has reported a decline in

A c t i v i t y
4.6   **"Mix It Up"**

Youth subcultures populate our middle and high schools. Students often self-segregate on the basis of gender, sexual orientation, ethnicity, race, linguistic identity, religious beliefs, socioeconomic status, fashion/style/appearance, athleticism, academic ability, or artistic interests. The most common groupings include jocks, cool kids, preppies, nerds/geeks, druggies/stoners, Goths, gangbangers, skaters, the Masonites, Thespians, bandies, Metal Heads, Hip-Hoppers, and Emos. These friendship groupings often result in exclusive cliques, with impenetrable social boundaries. Fitting in can be challenging; often, teens in certain groups are unfriendly and unwelcoming to "outsiders." Being ostracized can be devastating. When surveyed, 70% of adolescents in a Teaching Tolerance poll said that the separation of cliques in their schools was most obvious in the cafeteria. At lunchtime, students don't usually interact with nonmembers of their cliques.

In an effort to encourage students to step outside their comfort zones, learn how to get along better with people who are different from them, and resist bullying, Teaching Tolerance started "Mix It Up at Lunch Day" in 2001. Mix It Up encourages students to cross social boundaries and meet new people at their schools. In 2005, more than 4 million participants at 9,000 schools were involved.

Apply Your Knowledge

Check out the Mix It Up success stories at **http://www.tolerance.org/mix-it-up**.

1. What activities can students and teachers engage in before and after the Mix It Up experience to talk about the cliques in their school?
2. What other ideas do you have to encourage adolescents to expand their friendship circle?

---

the number of dropouts, an elimination of truant behavior, a decrease in drug use and suicide, an improvement in grades, and overall better behavior among the students. "Suddenly, the revolving discipline plans, metal detectors, security officers, and all the other tactics schools currently use to deal with rowdy students were no longer needed. . . . The improvement in student behavior is obvious to all. Teachers report fewer daily discipline issues and classroom disruptions."[34]

When teachers, counselors, students, parents, and community representatives work together, it is not uncommon for a school to report improved student attendance and a decline in the dropout rate. A successful effort at helping students make a connection with the value and goals of school has been through school and business partnerships. A special form of partnership called mentoring has had success with at-risk students as they become more receptive to schooling. The mentoring component of the partnership movement is a one-on-one commitment by community volunteers to improve the self-esteem, attitudes, and attendance of youngsters. Around the country, there are a number of successful mentoring programs.[35]

Successful strategies include incorporating modern technology, making classes more student centered, altogether eliminating the lower curriculum track and raising expectation standards for all students, and linking the school with parents and community representatives. By providing newsletters and other correspondence in Spanish and/or other languages spoken in the homes of the students and hiring administrative staff and teachers who are bilingual, more parents will feel comfortable about becoming involved. Time and again, schools report that using these combined strategies results in a decline in suspensions and an increase in student attendance and academic success, with a decrease in the student dropout and failure rates.

The school becomes a positive force in enhancing students' lives and in improving their academic achievement and their desire to come to and remain in school.[36]

Teacher Response to Student Misbehavior: Direct and Indirect Intervention

The goal in responding to student misbehavior is to intervene and redirect the student's focus and to do so successfully with the least amount of classroom disturbance. Typically, teachers respond to student classroom misbehaviors in one of three ways: hostile, assertive, or nonassertive. Hostile and nonassertive responses should be avoided. Unlike a hostile response, an assertive response is not abusive or derogatory to the student. Unlike a nonassertive response, an assertive response is a timely and clear communication to the student about what the teacher wants and an indication that the teacher is prepared to back that want with action.[37]

Too often, teachers intervene with verbal commands—direct intervention—when nonverbal actions such as eye contact, proximity, gesturing (e.g., finger to the lips or raised hand), and body language—indirect and unobtrusive intervention strategies—are less disruptive and often more effective in redirecting a misbehaving student. Although the offenses might be identical, the teacher's intervention for one student might have to be direct, while for another student indirect intervention is enough to stop the misbehavior.

ORDER OF BEHAVIOR INTERVENTION STRATEGIES To redirect a student's attention, your usual first effort should be indirect (nonverbal) intervention (e.g., proximity, eye contact, gesturing, body posture, or silence). Your second effort could be the simplest (i.e., the most private) direct (verbal) intervention (e.g., "David, please follow

Teaching Scenario	**Bears and Cats Mentoring Program**

The Bears and Cats Mentoring Program was a win-win partnership designed to establish supportive mentoring relationships between undergraduate secondary education majors in a teacher education program at a liberal arts college in the Pacific Northwest and at-risk freshmen at the local high school. The ultimate goal of the program was to maximize the high school students' academic and social potential and provide these students with additional resources and support. Participants completed brief surveys and were matched with partners according to their preferences, interests, and schedules. The college students served as influential role models by sharing their educational experiences, professional goals, and other interests with their ninth-grade mentees. Among the most critical attributes of the mentors were support, expertise, knowledge, experience, and encouragement. Mentors and their protégés met weekly on the high school campus during lunch, before and after school, and occasionally during morning breaks. Sometimes the pairs simply chatted, sometimes they worked on homework, and other times the mentors accompanied their high school counterparts to school club meetings, assemblies, and other activities. According to the principal, these relationships were very positive. The high school teachers witnessed significant improvement in writing ability, self-directed learning, teamwork, critical thinking skills, and career and workplace knowledge and an increased desire to attend college. The mentors showed genuine interest in their mentees' lives, which translated into self-confidence and success in high school. In a thank-you letter sent to the mentors at the end of the academic year the principal wrote, "Research on resiliency (the ability to keep going when hurdles in life present themselves) shows that the single most important factor in high-risk students who are resilient is a meaningful connection with an adult. You have been that connection for our kids."

Think About It

1. What mentoring opportunities are available in your teacher education program? In your community?

procedures"). Your third effort, one that closely follows the second in time interval (i.e., within the same class period), should follow your rules and procedures as outlined in your management system, which might mean a time-out or detention and a phone call to the student's parent or guardian (in private, of course). Normally, such a third effort is not necessary. A fourth effort, still rarer, is to suspend the student from class (and/or school) for some period of time until decisions about the future of that student in school are made by school officials in consultation with the student, the parents or guardians, and other professionals such as the school psychologist.

Direct intervention should be reserved for repetitive and serious misbehavior. When using direct intervention, you should give a direct statement, either reminding the student of what he or she is supposed to be doing or telling the student what to do. You should avoid asking a rhetorical question such as, "David, why are you doing that?" When giving students directions about what they are supposed to be doing, you may be asked by a student, "Why do we have to do this?" To that question, you may give a brief academic answer but do not become defensive or make threats. And rather than spending an inordinate amount of time on the misbehavior, try to focus the student's attention on a desired behavior. See Activity 4.7.

One reason that direct intervention should be held in reserve is because by interrupting the lesson to verbally intervene, you are doing exactly what the student who is being reprimanded was doing—interrupting the lesson. Not only is that improper modeling, but it can create a host of management problems beyond your wildest nightmares. Another reason for saving direct intervention is that, when used too often, direct intervention loses its effectiveness.

Teacher-Caused Student Misbehavior: Scenarios for Review

As a classroom teacher, one of your major responsibilities is to model appropriate behavior and not to contribute to or cause problems in the classroom. Some student misbehaviors and problems in classroom control are caused or escalated by the teacher. (Yes, you may unwittingly contribute to your students' misbehavior.) In some cases, problems can be prevented or easily rectified if the teacher behaves or acts differently.

In addition to sometimes ignoring minor inappropriate behaviors, you should also avoid using negative methods of procedures enforcement and ineffective forms of punishment, such as exemplified by the following scenarios. You and your classmates might decide to treat these scenarios as case studies for small groups to consider and then discuss before the whole class.

- *Capricious.* Because of her arbitrary and inconsistent enforcement of classroom rules, Fran Fickle, a ninth-grade English teacher, has lost the respect and trust of her students as well as control of her language arts classes. Students are constantly testing Fran to see what they can get away with.

- *Extra assignments.* When students in Margaret Malopropros's seventh-grade reading class misbehave, she habitually assigns extra reading and written work as punishment, even for the most minor offenses. This behavior has simply reinforced the view of many of her students that school is drudgery, so they no longer look forward to her classes, and behavior problems in her class have steadily increased since the beginning of the school year.

Activity 4.7   **CARE Courtesy and Respect Empower**

"Nerd!" "Geek!" "Wuss!" "Bitch!" "Ho!" "I'll beat your a——!" "You're so gay!" These taunts, jeers, threats, and insults are all too common in our hallways, playgrounds, locker rooms, and lunchrooms as well as in our classrooms. They may seem harmless, but absenteeism, truancy, drug abuse, suspensions/expulsions, homicides, and suicides among adolescents are on the rise. In fact, crime plagues our schools, and all too often criminal incidents involve targeted violence. In order to address this problem, schools across the U.S. have implemented a variety of antiviolence schoolwide campaigns to stop violence where it starts. One such program, CARE (Courtesy and Respect Empower), was developed by Jim Bryngelson of Billings, MT.

Bryngelson believes that many of the antiviolence efforts are too expensive, too complex, and, all too often, ineffective. Bryngelson created the School Violence Continuum, an awareness tool that highlights the importance of addressing all problems proactively, even milder behaviors that seem less serious such as put downs, insults, threats, trash talk, and bullying, to prevent escalated violent behaviors. Relying heavily on the Violence Continuum, CARE focuses on "*any* behavior that violates a school's educational mission or climate of respect." According to Bryngelson, victims, bystanders, and even bullies themselves must be focused on in prevention efforts.

The original CARE program was called "Respect and Manners" and was first adopted by Principal David Munson. CARE was designed to be a community campaign to reduce violence by introducing positive weekly expected behaviors and creating safe, orderly environments. The simple concept focuses on a weekly bombardment of a simple manner message. Input from the staff and parents is used to select the manner to be focused on

and the various methods to be used to emphasize it throughout the week, including daily announcements, poster competitions, role plays, essay contests, and media coverage.

Apply Your Knowledge

Check out the following website to read more about CARE and violence prevention:

Just What Is School Violence?
http://www.ncdjjdp.org/cpsv/pdf_files/newsbrief5_02.pdf

1. Why is it important to involve the entire school community in violence prevention?
2. Why must teachers prevent put downs, insults, and bullying?
3. What other violence prevention efforts are you familiar with?

The School Violence Continuum

SOURCE: Reprinted with permission. Copyright 1998. Jim Bryngelson, CARE Initiative of Montana.

■ *Embarrassment.* When eighth-grade social studies teacher Denise Degradini was having difficulty controlling the behavior of one of her students, she got on the classroom phone, called the student's parent, and, while the entire class of 33 students could hear the conversation, told the parent about her child's behavior in class and how she was going to have to give the student a referral if the student's behavior did not improve. From that one act, Denise lost all respect from her students. Class academic achievement grades plummeted for the rest of the year.

■ *Group punishment.* Because Fred Flock has not developed his withitness and overlapping skills, he has developed the unfortunate habit of punishing the entire group for every instance of misbehavior. Yesterday, for example, because some students were noisy during a video presentation, he

gave the entire class an unannounced quiz on the content of the film. Not only has he lost the respect of the students, but students are hostile toward him, and his problems with classroom control are steadily growing worse.

■ *Harsh and humiliating punishment.* Vince Van Pelt, a high school physical education teacher, has lost control of his classes and the respect of his students. His thrashing, whipping, tongue-lashing, and use of humiliation are ineffective and indicative of his loss of control. Parents have complained and one is suing him. The district has given Mr. Van Pelt official notice of the nonrenewal of his contract.

■ *Loud talk.* The noisiest person in Steve Shrill's high school English class is Mr. Shrill. His constant and mistaken efforts to talk over the classes have led to his own yelling and screaming, to complaints from neighboring teachers about the noise in his classes, and to a reprimand from the principal.

- *Lowered marks.* Eunice Erudite, an eighth-grade language arts/social studies core teacher, has a policy of writing a student's name on the board each time the person is reprimanded for misbehavior. Then, when a student has accumulated five marks on the board, she lowers his or her academic grade by one letter. As a result of her not separating their academic and social behaviors, her students are not doing as well as they were at the start of the year. Parents and students have complained about this policy to the administration, arguing that the grades Ms. Erudite is giving do not reflect the students' academic progress or abilities.

- *Nagging.* Paul Peck's continual and unnecessary scolding and criticizing of students upsets the recipient students and arouses resentment from their peers. His nagging resolves nothing and, like a snowball building in size as it rolls down the hill, causes Mr. Peck, a ninth-grade social studies teacher, more and more problems in the classroom.

- *Negative direct intervention.* In the seventh-grade humanities block class, Joshua swears more and more frequently and with graphic and startling language. Other students are beginning to behave similarly. Rather than giving Joshua alternative ways of expressing his feelings, Polly Premio, one team teacher, verbally reprimands Joshua each time this happens and threatens to call his parents about it. Ms. Premio doesn't realize that by giving her attention to Joshua's swearing, she is rewarding, reinforcing, and causing the increase in Joshua's unacceptable behavior.

- *Negative touch control.* When Ezzard, an eighth-grade bully, pushes and shoves other students out of his way for no apparent reason other than to physically manipulate them, his teacher, Tony Trenchant, grabs Ezzard and yanks him into his seat. What "roughneck" Tony the teacher doesn't realize is that he is using the very behavior (physical force) that he is trying to stop Ezzard from using. This simply confuses students and teaches them (especially Ezzard) that the use of physical force is okay if you are bigger or older than the recipient of that force. In this situation, unfortunately, hostility begets hostility.

- *Overreact.* Randall, a 10th-grade student, was reading a magazine when his English teacher, Harriet Harshmore, grabbed it from Randall's hands, called it pornographic, ripped out the offending pages, and tossed them into a wastebasket. The magazine was *National Geographic*, and the "pornographic" article was on evolution and included drawings of unclothed humans. Harriet was later reprimanded by the school superintendent, who said that although he supported her right to put a stop to what she considered a class disruption, Ms. Harshmore had crossed the line when she damaged the magazine.

The magazine, apparently a rare collector's issue, had been brought from Randall's home at his teacher's encouragement to bring reading material from home.

- *Physical punishment.* Mr. Fit, a ninth-grade geography teacher, punishes students by making them go outside and run around the school track when they misbehave in his class. Last week, Sebastian, a student whom he told to go out and run four laps for "mouthing off in class," collapsed and died while running. Mr. Fit has been placed on paid leave and is being sued for negligence by Sebastian's parents.

- *Premature judgments and actions.* Because of Kathy Kwik's impulsiveness, she does not think clearly before acting, and more than once she has reprimanded the wrong student. Because of her hasty and faulty judgments, students have lost respect for her. For them, her French I class has become pure drudgery.

- *Taped mouths.* Miss Ductless taped the mouths of 20 of her sixth-grade students in order to keep them quiet. Later in the school day, several of the students went to the school nurse complaining of allergic reactions caused by the duct tape. Until a full investigation is made, Miss Ductless has been relieved of her teaching duties.

- *Threats and ultimatums.* Threats and ultimatums from ninth-grade math teacher Bonnie Badger are known to be empty; because she does not follow through, her credibility with the students has been lost. Like wildfire, the word has spread around—"We can do whatever we want in old Badger's class."

- *Too hesitant.* Because Tim Timideo is too hesitant and slow to intervene when students get off task, his classes have increasingly gotten further and further out of his control, and it is still early in the school year. As a result, neighbor teachers are complaining about the noise from his classroom and Tim has been writing more and more referrals.

- *Writing as punishment.* Because they were "too noisy," high school biology teacher Steve Scribe punished his class of 28 students by making each one hand copy 10 pages from encyclopedias. When they submitted this assignment, he tore up the pages in front of the class and said, "Now, I hope you have learned your lesson and from now on will be quiet." On hearing about this, all six teachers of the school's English department signed and filed a complaint with the principal about Mr. Scribe's use of writing as punishment.

Preventing a Ship from Sinking Is Much Easier Than Saving a Sinking One: Mistakes to Avoid

During your beginning years of teaching, no one, including you, should expect you to be perfect. You should, however, be aware of common mistakes teachers make that often are the causes of student inattention and misbehavior. Many classroom control problems are teacher caused and preventable. In this section, you will find descriptions of mistakes commonly made by beginning (and even experienced) teachers. To have a most successful beginning to your career, you will want to sharpen your skills to avoid these mistakes; this requires both knowledge of the potential errors and reflection on your own behaviors in relation to the errors.

1. Inadequately attending to long-range and daily planning. A teacher who inadequately plans ahead is heading for trouble. Inadequate long-term and sketchy daily planning is a precursor to ineffective teaching and, eventually, to teaching failure. Students are motivated best by teachers who clearly are working hard and intelligently for them. Plan, plan, plan; there is no such thing as overplanning.

2. Emphasizing the negative. Too many warnings to students for their inappropriate behavior—and too little recognition for their positive behaviors—do not help to establish the positive climate needed for the most effective learning to occur. Reminding students of procedures is more positive and will bring you quicker success than reprimanding them when they do not follow procedures. Remember, there is no reality, only perception. Some describe the glass as half empty where others see the same glass as half full. Keep a positive attitude.

   Too often, teachers try to control students with negative language, such as "There should be no talking," "No gum or candy in class or else you will receive detention," and "No getting out of your seats without my permission." Teachers sometimes allow students, too, to use negative language to each other, such as "Shut up!" Negative language does not help instill a positive classroom climate. To encourage a positive atmosphere, use concise, positive language. Tell students precisely what they are supposed to do rather than what they are not supposed to do. Disallow the use of disrespectful and negative language in your classroom.

3. Not requiring students to raise hands and be acknowledged before responding. Whereas ineffective teachers often are ones who are controlled by class events, competent teachers are those who are in control of class events. You cannot be in control of events and your interactions with students if you allow students to shout out their comments, responses, and questions whenever they feel like it. The most successful beginning teacher is one who quickly establishes his or her control of classroom events.

   In addition, indulging their natural impulsivity does not help students to grow intellectually. When students develop impulse control, they think before acting. Students can be taught to think before acting

or shouting out an answer. One of several reasons that teachers should insist on a show of student hands before a student is acknowledged to speak is to discourage students from the impulsive, disruptive, and irritating behavior of shouting out in class.[38]

4. Allowing students' hands to be raised too long. When students have their hands raised for long periods before you recognize them and attend to their questions or responses, you are providing them with time to fool around. Although you don't have to call on every student as soon as he or she raises a hand, you should acknowledge him or her quickly, such as with a nod or a wave of your hand, so that the student can lower his or her hand and return to work. Then you should get to the student as quickly as possible. The students should clearly understand these procedures, and you should practice them consistently.

5. Spending too much time with one student or one group and not monitoring the entire class. Spending too much time with any one student or a small group of students is, in effect, ignoring the rest of the students. As a novice teacher you cannot afford to ignore the rest of the class, even for a moment.

6. Beginning a new activity before gaining the students' attention. A teacher who consistently fails to insist that students follow procedures and who does not wait until all students are in compliance before starting a new activity is destined for major problems in classroom control. You must establish and maintain classroom procedures. Starting an activity before all students are in compliance is, in effect, telling the students that they don't have to follow expected procedures. You cannot afford to tell students one thing and then do another. In the classroom, your actions will always speak louder than your words.

7. Pacing teacher talk and learning activities too quickly. Pacing instructional activities is one of the more difficult skills for beginning teachers to master. Students need time to disengage mentally and physically from one activity before engaging in the next. You must remember that this takes more time for a room of 25 or so students than it does for just one person, you. This is a reason that transitions, as discussed in Chapter 5, need to be scheduled and written into your lesson plan.

8. Using a voice level that is always either too loud or too soft. A teacher's voice that is too loud day after day can become irritating to some students, just as one that cannot be heard or understood can become frustrating.

9. Assigning a journal entry without giving the topic careful thought. If the question or topic about which students are supposed to write is ambiguous or obviously hurriedly prepared—without your having given thought to how students will interpret and respond to it—students will judge that the task is busywork (e.g., something to keep them busy while you take

Teaching Scenario   "Don't Smile before Christmas"

Lily had always dreamed about being a teacher. She was so excited when she completed her certification program and began her secondary English student teaching assignment. She was only 20, but she was a mature, confident individual. Everyone predicted she would be as successful in her classroom practice as she had been in her coursework. During the fall 2006 semester, she had a placement with Mr. Jones at Bogart, a high school with 1,200 students in grades 9 through 12. She had three preps and was responsible for two sections of freshman English, one section of English IV, and an elective course, Science Fiction. Lily was a very competent, conscientious student teacher who was always well prepared. She learned the names of her students quickly. She established routines and set high expectations for everyone. She always had copies of her detailed lesson plans available for her cooperating teacher and university supervisor to review well ahead of time. She was a taskmaster who made efficient use of class time. There was just one problem: Lily never smiled. She had heard the catchphrase several times in her teacher preparation program, "Don't Smile before Christmas," and she was strictly adhering to that policy.

After her university supervisor had observed a few classes, she asked Lily if she enjoyed teaching and if she liked her students. Her stern demeanor made it difficult to discern. Lily seemed confused and offended by the questions. She responded defensively, "I love to teach. I learned that as a young teacher, I shouldn't befriend the students. I was told that the students are there to learn and I am here to teach. I'm afraid that if I'm friendly with them, they will never respect me. In my classroom management course, the professor told us to be strict, to stop bad behavior as soon as it starts, and to be sure to show the students who is boss. He warned that if we come across as easygoing, tolerant, or approachable, our students would take advantage of us."

A few more weeks passed, and Lily made little effort to loosen up. Lily's university supervisor visited again and felt the same negativity and fear in her classroom. Although the students

were obedient and compliant, they were very disengaged. Lily remained unconvinced by her supervisor's comments; nonetheless, she prepared a midterm survey to ask her students how well she was doing. She was shocked by their feedback. Jake's comments were typical: "She's not a very happy person. . . . I think she hates us. . . . I don't know why she wants to teach. We have so much more fun with Mr. Jones." Once again the university supervisor suggested that Lily drop her guard a little and let the students get to know her, appreciate her sense of humor, and have fun while learning. The transformation was immediate and impressive.

Students should have limits and structure is important. Still, teachers need to nurture the interpersonal relationships in the teaching–learning process. The best advice for new teachers comes from Lily: "Create a safe, welcoming environment, model appropriate behavior, embrace diversity, empower students to reach their academic potential, and for gosh sakes, smile."

Think About It

Students may not like your content area; in a few years, they may not even remember what subject you taught, but they will never forget how you made them feel. Reflect on your favorite middle and secondary school teachers and answer the following questions.

1. Who were your favorite middle and secondary school teachers? What did you like about them?
2. What characteristics did they have in common?
3. Brainstorm a list of qualities you think effective teachers should possess.
4. Visit **http://www.fastcompany.com/magazine/53/teaching.html**. Read Chuck Salter's article, "Attention Class! 16 Ways to Be a Smarter Teacher." What commonalities did you find between your list and Salter's?

---

attendance). If they do it at all, it will be with a great deal of commotion and much less enthusiasm than were they writing on a topic that had meaning to them.

10. Standing too long in one place. Most of the time in the classroom, you should be mobile, "working the crowd."

11. Sitting while teaching. As a middle or secondary school teacher, unless you are physically unable to stand, in most situations there is no time to sit while teaching. It is difficult to monitor the class while seated. You cannot afford to appear that casual.

12. Being too serious and no fun. No doubt, good teaching is serious business. But students are motivated by and respond best to teachers who obviously enjoy working with students and helping them learn.

13. Falling into a rut by using the same teaching strategy or combination of strategies day after day. A teacher in such a rut is likely to become boring to students. Because of their multitude of differences, students are

motivated by and respond best to a variety of well-planned and meaningful learning activities.

14. Inadequately using silence (wait time) after asking a content question. When expected to think deeply about a question, students need time to do it. A teacher who consistently gives insufficient time to students to think is teaching only superficially, at the lowest cognitive level, and is destined to have problems in student motivation and classroom control.

15. Poorly or inefficiently using instructional tools. The ineffective use of teaching tools such as books, the overhead projector, writing board, and computer says to students that you are not a competent teacher. Would you want an auto mechanic who did not know how to use the tools of her trade to service your car? Would you want a brain surgeon who did not know how to use the tools of her trade to remove your tumor? Working with adolescents in a classroom is no less important. Like a competent mechanic or surgeon, a competent teacher

selects and effectively uses the best tools available for the job. If you plan on integrating technology into a lesson, always be sure to have a backup plan in case things do not go as planned.

16. Ineffectively using facial expressions and body language. As said earlier, your gestures and body language communicate more to students than your words do. For example, one teacher didn't understand why his class of seventh graders would not respond to his repeated expression of "I need your attention." In one 15-minute segment, he used that expression eight times. Studying videotape of that class period helped him understand the problem. His dress was very casual, and he stood most of the time with his right hand in his pocket. At five feet eight inches, with a slight build, a rather deadpan facial expression, and an unexpressive voice, he was not a commanding presence in the classroom. After seeing himself on tape, he returned to the class wearing a tie, and he began using his hands, face, and body more expressively. Rather than saying, "I need your attention," he waited in silence for the students to become attentive. It worked.

17. Relying too much on teacher talk for classroom control. Beginning teachers have a tendency to rely too much on teacher talk. Too much teacher talk can be deadly. Unable to discern between the important and the unimportant verbiage, students will quickly tune a teacher out.

     Some teachers rely too much on verbal interaction and too little on nonverbal intervention techniques. Verbally reprimanding a student for his or her interruptions of class activities is reinforcing the very behavior you are trying to stop. In addition, verbally reprimanding a student in front of his or her peers can backfire on you. Instead, develop your indirect, silent intervention techniques, such as eye contact, mobility, frown, silence, body stance, and proximity.

18. Inefficiently using teacher time. During the preactive phase of your instruction (the planning phase), think carefully about what you are going to be doing every minute and then plan for the most efficient and therefore the most productive use of your time in the classroom. Consider the following example. During a brainstorming session, a teacher is recording student contributions on a large sheet of butcher paper that has been taped to the wall. She solicits student responses, acknowledges those responses, holds and manipulates the marker, walks to the wall, and writes on the paper. Each of those actions requires decisions and movements that consume precious instructional time and that can distract her from her students. An effective alternative would be to have a reliable student helper do the writing while the teacher handles the solicitation and acknowledgment of student contributions. That way, she has fewer decisions and fewer actions

to distract her. And she does not lose eye contact and proximity with the classroom of students. If you choose to ask a student to serve as your scribe, be sure that he or she captures what you want or need him or her to.

19. Talking to and interacting with only half the class. While leading a class discussion, there is a tendency among some beginning teachers to favor (by their eye contact and verbal interaction) only 40% to 65% of the students, sometimes completely ignoring the others for an entire class period. Knowing that they are being ignored, those students will, in time, become uninterested and perhaps unruly. Remember to spread your interactions and eye contact throughout the entire class. Students who are eager to participate make the teacher's job easy. It is important to remember, though, that some students' learning styles are different and that they may need more encouragement, a "heads-up," longer wait time, and so forth in order to participate.

20. Collecting and returning student papers before assigning students something to do. If while turning in papers or waiting for their return students have nothing else to do, they get restless and inattentive. Students should have something to do while papers are being collected or returned.

21. Interrupting while students are on task. It is not easy to get an entire class of students on task. Once they are on task, you do not want to be the distracter. Try to give all instructions before students begin their work. The detailed instructions should be written in your lesson plan; that way you are sure not to forget anything. Once they are on task, if there is an important point you wish to make, write it on the board. If you want to return papers while students are working, do it in a way and at a time that is least likely to interrupt them from their learning task.

22. Using "Shhh" as a means of quieting students. When you do that, you simply sound like a balloon with a slow leak. The sound should be deleted from your professional vocabulary.

23. Using poor body positioning. Develop your skill of withitness by always positioning your body so you can continue to visually monitor the entire class even while talking to and working with one student or a small group. Avoid turning your back to even a portion of the class.

24. Settling for less when you should be trying for more—not getting the most from student responses. The most successful schools are those with teachers who expect and get the most from all students. Don't hurry a class discussion; "milk" student responses for all you can, especially when discussing a topic that students are obviously interested in. Ask a student for clarification or reasons for his or her response. Ask for verification. Have another student paraphrase what a student said. Pump students for deeper thought and meaning. Too

often, the teacher will ask a question, get an abbreviated (often a one-word and low-cognitive-level) response from a student, and then move on to another subject. Instead, follow up a student's response to your question with a sequence of questions, prompting and cueing to elevate the student's thinking to higher levels.

25. Using threats. Avoid making threats of any kind. One teacher, for example, told her class that if they continued with their inappropriate talking (as if the entire classroom of students were talking inappropriately), they would lose their break time. She should have had that consequence as part of the understood procedures and consequences and then taken away the break time for some students if warranted.

26. Punishing the entire class for the misbehavior of a few. Although the rationale behind such action is clear (i.e., to get group pressure working for you), often the result is the opposite. Students who have been behaving well are alienated from the teacher because they feel they have been punished unfairly for the misbehavior of others. Those students expect the teacher to be able to handle the misbehaving students without punishing those who are not misbehaving, and they are right.

27. Using global praise. Global praise is pretty useless. An example is, "Class, your rough drafts were really wonderful." This is hollow and says nothing—simply another instance of useless verbiage from the teacher. Instead, be specific—tell what it was about their drafts that made them so wonderful. As another example, after a student's oral response to the class, rather than simply saying "Very good," tell the student what was so good about the response.

28. Using color meaninglessly. The use of color on transparencies and the writing board is nice but will shortly lose its effectiveness unless the colors have meaning. If, for example, everything in the classroom is color coded and students understand the meaning of the code, then use of color can serve as an important mnemonic to student learning.

29. Verbally reprimanding a student from across the room. This is yet another example of a needless interruption of all students. In addition, because of peer pressure (students tend to support one another), it increases the "you versus them" syndrome. Reprimand when necessary but do it quietly and as privately as possible.

30. Interacting with only a chosen few students rather than spreading interactions around to all. As a beginning teacher, especially, it is easy to fall into a habit of interacting with only a few students, especially those who are vocal and who make significant contributions. Your job, however, is to teach all the students. To do that, you must be proactive, not reactive, in your interactions.

31. Not intervening quickly enough during inappropriate student behavior. When allowed to continue, inappropriate student behavior only gets worse, not better. It will not go away by itself. It's best to nip it in the bud quickly and resolutely. A teacher who ignores inappropriate behavior, even briefly, is in effect approving it. In turn, that approval reinforces the continuation and escalation of inappropriate behaviors.

32. Not learning and using student names. To expedite your success, you should quickly learn and use students' names. A teacher who does not know or use names when addressing students is, in effect, viewed by the students as impersonal and uncaring.

33. Reading student papers only for correct (or incorrect) answers and not for process and student thinking. Reading student papers only for correct responses reinforces the false notion that the process of arriving at answers or solutions is unimportant and that alternative solutions or answers are impossible or unimportant. In effect, it negates the importance of the individual and the very nature and purpose of learning.

34. Not putting time plans on the board for students. Yelling out how much time is left for an activity interrupts student thinking and implies that their thinking is unimportant. Avoid interrupting students once they are on task. Show respect for their on-task behavior. In this instance, write on the board before the activity begins how much time is allowed for it. Write the time it is to end. If during the activity a decision is made to change the end time, then write the changed time on the board.

35. Asking global questions that nobody likely will answer. Examples are "Does everyone understand?" and "Are there any questions?" and "How do you all feel about . . . ?" It is a brave young soul who in the presence of peers is willing to admit ignorance. It is a waste of precious instructional time to ask such questions. If you truly want to check for student understanding or opinions, then do a spot check: ask specific questions, allow think time, and then call on individuals.

36. Failing to do frequent comprehension checks (every few minutes during most direct instruction situations) to see if students are understanding. Too often teachers simply plow through a big chunk of the lesson or the entire lesson, assuming that students are understanding it. Or, in the worst-case scenario, teachers rush through a lesson without even caring if students are getting it. Students are quick to recognize teachers who really don't care.

37. Using poorly worded, ambiguous questions. Key questions you will ask during a lesson should be planned and written into your lesson plan. Refine and make the questions precise by asking them to yourself or a friend and try to predict how students will respond to particular questions.

38. Trying to talk over student noise. This simply tells students that their making noise while you are talking is acceptable behavior. When this happens, everyone, teacher included, usually gets increasingly louder during the class period. All that you will accomplish when

trying to talk over a high student noise level is a sore throat by the end of the school day and, over a longer period of time, the potential for nodules on your vocal cords.

39. Wanting to be liked by students. Forget it. If you are a teacher, then teach. Respect is earned as a result of your effective teaching. Being liked may come later.

40. Permitting students to be inattentive to an educationally useful media presentation. This usually happens because the teacher has failed to give the students a written handout of questions or guidelines for what they should acquire from the program. Sometimes students need an additional focus. Furthermore, a media presentation is usually audio and visual. To reinforce student learning, add the kinesthetic, such as the writing required when a handout of questions is used. This provides minds-on and hands-on activities that enhance learning.

41. Starting in stutters. A stutter start is when the teacher begins an activity, is distracted, begins again, is distracted again, tries again to start, and so on. During stutter starts, students become increasingly restless and inattentive and sometimes even amused by the teacher's futility, making the final start almost impossible for the teacher to achieve. Avoid stutter starts. Begin an activity clearly and decisively. This is best done when lesson plans are prepared thoughtfully and in detail.

42. Introducing too many topics simultaneously. It is important that you not overload students' capacity to engage mentally by introducing different topics simultaneously. For example, during the first 10 minutes of class, a teacher started by introducing a warm-up activity, which was a journal entry with instructions clearly presented on the overhead; the teacher also verbally explained the activity, although she could have simply pointed to the screen, thereby nonverbally instructing students to begin work on the activity (without disrupting the thinking of those who had already begun). One minute later, the teacher was telling students about their quarter grades and how later in the period they would learn more about those grades. Then she returned to the warm-up activity, explaining it a second time (a third time if one counts the detailed explanation already on the screen). Next, she reminded students of the new tardy rules (thereby introducing a third topic). At this time, however, most of the students were still thinking and talking about what she had said about quarter grades, few were working on the warm-up activity, and hardly any were listening to the teacher talking about the new tardy rules. There was a lot of commotion among the students. The teacher had tried to focus student attention on too many topics at once, thus accomplishing little and losing control of the class in the process.

43. Failing to give students a pleasant greeting on a Monday or following a holiday or to remind them to have a pleasant weekend or holiday. Students are likely to perceive such a teacher as uncaring or impersonal.

44. Sounding egocentric. Whether you are or are not egocentric, you want to avoid appearing so. Sometimes the distinction is subtle but apparent, such as when a teacher says, "What I am going to do now is . . . " rather than "What we are going to do now is . . . ." If you want to strive for group cohesiveness—a sense of "we-ness"—then teach not as if you are the leader and your students are the followers but rather in a manner that empowers your students in their learning.

45. Taking too much time to give verbal instructions for an activity. Students become impatient and restless during long verbal instructions from the teacher. It is better to give brief instructions (two or three minutes should do it) and get the students started on the task. For more complicated activities, teach three or four students the instructions and then have those students do workshops with five or six students in each workshop group. This frees you to monitor the progress of each group.

46. Taking too much time for an activity. No matter what the activity, during your planning think carefully about how much time students can effectively spend to it. A general rule for most classes (age level and other factors will dictate variation) is that when only one or two learning modalities are involved (e.g., auditory and visual), the activity should not extend beyond about 15 minutes; when more than two modalities are engaged (e.g., add tactile or kinesthetic), then the activity might extend longer, say for 20 or 30 minutes.

47. Being uptight and anxious. Consciously or subconsciously, students are quick to detect a teacher who is afraid that events will not go well. And it's like a contagious disease—if you are uptight and anxious, your students will likely become the same. To prevent such emotions, at least to the extent they damage your teaching and your students' learning, you must prepare lessons carefully, thoughtfully, and thoroughly. Unless there is something personal going on in your life that is making you anxious, you are more likely to be in control and confident in the classroom when you have well-prepared lessons. How do you know if your lesson is well prepared? You will know. It's when you develop a written lesson plan that you are truly excited about and looking forward to implementing, and then before doing so, you review it one more time.

If you have a personal problem going on in your life that is distracting and making you anxious (and occasionally most of us do), you need to concentrate on ensuring that your anger, hostility, fear, or other negative emotions do not adversely affect your teaching and your interactions with students. Regardless of your personal problems, your classes of students will face you each day expecting to be taught reading, mathematics, history, science, physical education, or whatever it is you are supposed to be helping them to learn.

48. Using a one-size-fits-all technique; failing to apply the best of what is known about how young people learn. Too many teachers unrealistically seem to expect success having all 33 students doing the same thing at the same time rather than having several alternative activities simultaneously occurring in the classroom, called multilevel teaching or multitasking. For example, a student who is not responding well (i.e., being inattentive and disruptive) to a class discussion might behave better if given the choice of moving to a quiet reading center in the classroom or to a learning center to work alone. If after trying an alternative activity the student continues to be disruptive, then you may have to try still another alternative activity. You may have to send the student to another supervised location out of the classroom, one previously arranged by you, until you have time after class or after school to talk with the student about the problem.

49. Overusing punishment for classroom misbehavior—jumping to the final step without trying alternatives. Teachers sometimes mistakenly either ignore inappropriate student behavior (see number 31) or skip steps for intervention, resorting too quickly to punishment. They immediately send the misbehaving student outside to stand in the hall (not a wise choice because the student is not supervised) or too quickly assign detention (usually an ineffective form of punishment). In-between steps to consider include the use of alternative activities in the classroom (as in number 48).

50. Being imprecise and inconsistent. Perhaps one of the most frequent causes of problems in classroom control for beginning teachers is when they fail to say what they mean or mean what they say. A teacher who gives only vague instructions or who is inconsistent in his or her behavior confuses students (e.g., does not enforce his or her own classroom procedural expectations). A teacher's job is not to confuse students.

You have heard and will repeatedly hear how important it is to be consistent. Students who believe that rules are unfairly and inconsistently enforced are usually the ones who are most likely to misbehave.[39]

Now direct your attention to other specific instances of teacher behaviors, some of which reinforce or cause student misbehavior, by completing Exercises 4.6 and 4.7. Then review the categories that make up a classroom management plan by completing Activity 4.8 on your own and then with your integrated team members.

Activity 4.8 **Things to Consider When Developing a Classroom Management Plan for Your Integrated Unit**

I. Physical Arrangement of the Classroom
Describe the physical layout of the classroom and the placement of the furniture. Describe where you would place the following: the teacher's desk, student desks, worktables, computer(s), overhead projector, screen, storage areas, file cabinets, bulletin boards, whiteboards, decorations, supplies, and so on and the rationale for your choices.

II. Classroom Guidelines/Rules
List your classroom guidelines/rules. Include three to five rules, stated in positive language. Then break down each rule or guideline with more specific directions.

III. Classroom Procedures
Describe the method or process students are to follow; in other words, explain how you want things to be done in your classroom by detailing normal classroom procedures here. For example, "Students are expected to . . . ."

IV. Disciplinary Situations
Of course, there are times when students choose to ignore the rules. When that happens, there should be consequences in place. Describe various potential conflicts (address varying levels of severity) that may arise and the respective consequences your teaching team has agreed on.

A. Minor Conflicts and Consequences
Getting up out of their seat without permission. Talking to classmates. Doing unrelated work during class. Passing notes. Throwing trash.

B. Moderate Conflicts and Consequences
Cheating on tests/quizzes. Plagiarizing papers. Stealing. Displaying blatant disrespect and/or hostility.

C. Major Conflicts and Consequences
Acting violently. Threatening violent behavior. Possessing weapons.

D. Interpersonal Conflicts
Name-calling and put-downs. Bullying. Threatening to enact physical harm.

V. Description of Our Classroom Management Model
This narrative description is based on key ideas from the following seven models of discipline: Kounin model, neo-Skinnerian model, Ginott model, Glasser model, Dreikurs model, Canter model, and Jones model. Consult the summary comparing approaches to classroom management in Table 4.1 and explore some of the websites listed in Activity 4.2, "Classroom Management Gurus."

Apply Your Knowledge

With the members of your integrated unit team, discuss your individual responses, come to a consensus, and write your classroom management plan. Start your discussion by sharing, reviewing, and comparing the responses you recorded individually in Exercises 4.3, 4.4, 4.5, and 4.6. Then talk about your vision for how you will integrate instruction and discipline in your integrated unit.

Include the following categories in your written description of your classroom management plan: (I) physical arrangement of the classroom, (II) classroom guidelines/rules, (III) classroom procedures, (IV) disciplinary situations, and (V) description of your classroom management model.

Summary

Students are more likely to learn when they feel that the learning is important or worth the time. In this chapter, we described factors important for learning to occur. As a classroom teacher, you should not be expected to solve all the societal woes that can spill over into the classroom. Yet as a professional, you have certain responsibilities, including the following: to prepare thoughtfully and thoroughly for your classes, to manage and control your classes, and to be able to diagnose, prescribe, and remedy those learning difficulties, disturbances, and minor misbehaviors that are the norm for classrooms and for the age-group with which you are working. If you follow the guidelines provided in this book, you will be well on your way to developing a teaching style and management system that, for the most part, should provide teaching that runs smoothly and effectively, without serious problems.

It is important to select strategies most appropriate to your teaching plans and that complement your management system. Chapters that follow in Part 3 present guidelines for doing that.

Exercise 4.1

Student Handbooks

Instructions: Search the Web to locate a variety of middle school and/or high school student handbooks. You might start by reviewing some at the suggested websites that follow. You might also check the student handbook for the schools in your local district, the school(s) you attended when you were in middle/high school, or schools in a city/state you may be interested in relocating to for your first teaching position. Compare and contrast the various schools' discipline codes and answer the questions that appear at the end of this exercise. Once you have written the answers to the questions, share them with your classmates in small groups.

Suggested middle and high school student handbooks to peruse follow.

Aitkin High School, Aitkin, MN	http://www.aitkin.k12.mn.us/highs1.html
Arlington Independent School District Junior High, Arlington, TX	http://www.aisd.net/pdf/HSCDHandbook/JHHandbook.pdf
Arlington Middle School, Poughkeepsie, NY	http://teacherweb.com/NY/Arlington/ArlingtonMiddleSchool/photo2.stm
East Chapel Hill High School, Chapel Hill, NC	http://www2.chccs.k12.nc.us/education/components/scrapbook/default.php?sectiondetailid=18380
Goldenview Middle School, Anchorage, AL	http://www.asdk12.org/schools/goldenview/pages/FormBank/780handbook.pdf
Kapolei Middle School, HI	http://www2.kapoleims.k12.hi.us/campuslife/depts/technology/AUP.pdf
Estes Park Middle School, Estes Park, CO	http://psdr3.k12.co.us/education/components/docmgr/default.php?sectiondetailid=246&catfilter=ALL&record_filter_file_ext=pdf
Olentangy Local School District, Lewis Center, OH	http://www.olentangy.k12.oh.us/district/board/policy/handbooks/middle/index.html
Charles M. Russell High School, Great Falls, MT	http://cmrweb.gfps.k12.mt.us/2010-2011Student%20Handbook.pdf%20-%20Adobe%20Acrobat%20Pro.pdf
Sebring Middle School, Sebring, FL	http://www.highlands.k12.fl.us/~sms/
Warner Middle/High School, Warner Springs, CA	http://www.sdcoe.k12.ca.us/districts/warner/pdf/HSHandbook0607.pdf

Answer the following questions:

1. What different elements did you find included in the various student handbooks you examined?

2. Which of the elements do you think should be addressed in a student handbook? Why or why not?

3. Discuss what you think is an appropriate policy on the following issues: cheating, tardiness, truancy, dress, alcohol/substance abuse, vandalism, sexual harassment, intimidation/bullying, open campus, use of cell phones and other electronic devices, inappropriate language/profanity/vulgar gestures, and gang-related activity.

Exercise
4.2

Observing a Classroom for Frequency of External Interruptions

Instructions: It is disconcerting to know how often teachers and students in some school classrooms are interrupted by announcements from the intercom, a phone call, or a visitor at the door. After all, no one would even consider interrupting a surgeon during the most climactic moments of an open-heart operation or a defense attorney at the climax of her summation. But it seems far too often that teachers are interrupted just at the moment they have their students at a critical point in a lesson. Once lost because of an interruption, student attention and that teachable moment are difficult to recapture.

Arrange to visit a school classroom and observe for classroom interruptions created from outside the classroom. School administrators and office personnel must sometimes be reminded that the most important thing going on in the school is that which teachers have been hired to do—teach. The act of teaching must not be frivolously interrupted. In our opinion, except for absolutely critical reasons, teachers should never be interrupted after the first five minutes of a class period and before the last five minutes. That policy should be established and rigidly adhered to. Otherwise, after many years of being a student, the lesson learned is that the least important thing going on at the school is that which is going on in the classroom. No wonder, then, that it is so difficult for teachers in some schools to gain student attention and respect. That respect must be shown starting from the school's central office. Because the turnaround and refocus must somehow begin now, for our effort toward that end we have added this exercise to this book.

1. School and class visited: _____

2. Time (start and end of class period): _____

3. Interruptions (tally for each interruption) _____
   Intercom: _____
   Phone: _____
   Visitor at door: _____
   Emergency drill: _____
   Other (specify): _____

4. Total number of interruptions: _____

5. My conclusion: _____

6. Share and compare your results and conclusion with your classmates.

Exercise
4.3

Teachers' Behavior Management Systems

Instructions: The purpose of this exercise is to interview two teachers, one from a middle or junior high and the other from a high school, to discover how they manage their classrooms. Use the outline format that follows, conduct your interviews, and then share the results with your classmates, perhaps in small groups.

1. Teacher interviewed: _____

2. Date: _____   3. Grade level: _____

4. School: _____

5. Subject(s): _____

6. Please describe your classroom management system. Specifically, I would like to know your procedures for the following:
   a. How are students to signal that they want your attention and help?
   b. How do you call on students during question and discussion sessions?
   c. How and when are students to enter and exit the classroom?
   d. How are students to obtain the materials for instruction?
   e. How are students to store their personal items?
   f. What are the procedures for students going to the drinking fountain or bathroom?
   g. What are the procedures during class interruptions?
   h. What are the procedures for tardies or early dismissals?
   i. What are the procedures for turning in homework?

7. Describe your expectations for classroom behavior and the consequences for misbehavior.

In discussion with classmates following the interviews, consider the following:
Many modern teachers advocate the use of a highly structured classroom, and then, as appropriate over time during the school year, they share more of the responsibility with the students. Did you find this to be the case with the majority of teachers interviewed? Was it more or less the case in middle schools, junior highs, or high schools? Was it more or less the case with any particular subject areas?

Beginning the Development of My Classroom Management System

Instructions: The purpose of this exercise is to begin preparation of the management system that you will explain to your students during the first day or week of school. Answer the questions that follow and share those answers with your peers for their feedback. Then make changes as appropriate. (On completion of this chapter, you may want to revisit this exercise to make adjustments to your management plan as you will from time to time throughout your professional career.)

1. My teaching subject area and anticipated grade level:

2. Attention to procedures. Use a statement to explain your procedural expectation for each of the following:
   a. How are students to signal that they want your attention and help?
   b. How do you call on students during question and discussion sessions?
   c. How and when are students to enter and exit the classroom?
   d. How are students to obtain the materials for instruction?
   e. How are students to store their personal items?
   f. What are the procedures for students going to the drinking fountain or bathroom?
   g. What are the procedures during class interruptions?
   h. What are the procedures for tardies or early dismissal?
   i. What are the procedures for turning in homework?

3. List of student behavior expectations that I will present to my class (no more than five):
   Rule 1:
   Rule 2:
   Rule 3:
   Rule 4:
   Rule 5:

4. Explanation of consequences for broken rules:

5. How procedures, rules, or consequences may vary (if at all) according to the grade level taught or according to any other criteria, such as in team teaching:

Observation and Analysis of How Teachers Start Class Meetings

Instructions: Select three teachers, all of the same subject and grade level, to observe how they begin their class meetings. Observe only the first five minutes of each class. After collecting this data, share, compile, and discuss the results as follows.

Grade level and subject discipline I observed:

1. Make a check next to each of the following observations that you made, and for each teacher place a number (1, 2, 3, and so on) next to the things that teacher did first, second, third, and so on during that initial five minutes from the time students begin entering the classroom until after the official clock start of class (i.e., when class was supposed to begin).

	Teacher 1	Teacher 2	Teacher 3
Greeting the students			
Giving an assignment (i.e., a warm-up activity)			
Taking attendance			
Talking with another adult			
Talking with a classroom aide			
Talking with one or a few students			
Readying teaching materials or equipment			
Working at desk			
Handing out student papers or materials			
Other (specify)			

2. For these three teachers, did you observe a common beginning?

3. Compile your results with those of your classmates. Write the results here.

4. Compare the results of observations for all subjects and middle and secondary school grade levels. What are the similarities and differences?

5. Are there any conclusions you can reach as a class about teachers of particular grade levels and disciplines and how they spent the first five minutes with their students?

Applying Measures of Control

Instructions: The purpose of this exercise is for you to determine when you might use each of the various options available when there is a student behavior problem in your classroom. For each of the following, as specifically as possible identify both a situation in which you would and one in which you would not use that measure. Then share your responses with others in your class.

1. Eye contact and hand signal to the student.
   Would:
   Would not:

2. Send student immediately to the office of the vice principal.
   Would:
   Would not:

3. Ignore the student.
   Would:
   Would not:

4. Assign the student to detention.
   Would:
   Would not:

5. Send a note home to parent or guardian about the student's misbehavior.
   Would:
   Would not:

6. Touch a student on the shoulder.
   Would:
   Would not:

7. Provide candy as rewards.
   Would:
   Would not:

8. Provide a time-out from academic time.
   Would:
   Would not:

9. Verbally redirect the student's attention.
   Would:
   Would not:

10. Use a verbal reprimand.
    Would:
    Would not:

Selecting Measures of Control

Instructions: The purpose of this exercise is to provide situations to help you in determining which measures of control you would apply in similar situations. For each of the following, write what you would do in that situation. Then share your responses with your classmates.

1. A student reveals a long knife and threatens to cut you.

2. During a test, a student appears to be copying answers from a neighboring student's answer sheet.

3. Although you have asked a student to take his seat, he refuses.

4. While talking with a small group of students, you observe two students on the opposite side of the room tossing paper airplanes at each other.

5. During small-group work, one student seems to be aimlessly wandering around the room.

6. Although chewing gum is against your classroom rules, at the start of the class period you observe a student chewing what appears to be gum.

7. During band rehearsal, you (as band director) observe a student about to stuff a scarf down the saxophone of another student.

8. During the viewing of a film, two students on the side of the room opposite you are quietly whispering.

9. At the start of the period, while a student is about to take his seat, a boy pulls the chair from beneath him. He falls to the floor.

10. Suddenly, for no apparent reason, a student gets up and leaves the room.

Chapter 4   POSTTEST

Short Explanation

1. Identify at least four guidelines for using positive reinforcement for a student's appropriate behavior.

2. Explain why it is important to prevent behavior problems before they occur. Describe at least five preventive steps you will take to minimize your classroom management problems.

3. Explain how and why your classroom management procedures and expectations might differ depending on the students involved and the learning activities planned.

4. Is it better to be very strict with students at first and then relax once your control has been established or to be relaxed at first and then tighten the reins later if students misbehave? Explain your answer.

5. Explain what you would do if two unacceptable student behaviors occurred simultaneously in different locations in your classroom.

Essay

1. Some experts say that 90% of control problems in the classroom are teacher caused. Do you agree or disagree? Explain why or why not.

2. Some supervisors of student teachers prefer that the student teacher never conduct a class while seated. Is it ever appropriate for a (nondisabled) teacher to be seated while teaching? Explain why it is or is not.

3. It has been said that students are more likely to learn when they feel that the learning is important or worth their time. Explain how a teacher in your subject field can make that happen, that is, students feeling that the learning is important and worth their time.

4. It is not uncommon to find that a particular student achieves well and behaves well in one teacher's class but not in another's. What explanations can there be for such a difference in a student's behavior and achievement?

5. From your current observations and fieldwork related to your teacher preparation program, clearly identify one specific example of educational practice that seems contradictory to exemplary practice or theory presented in this chapter. Present your explanation for the discrepancy.

CHAPTER FIVE

Valerie Schultz/Merrill

Selecting Content and Preparing Instructional Objectives

If your plan is for one year, plant rice; if your plan is for ten years, plant trees; if your plan is for a hundred years, educate children.

—CONFUCIUS

Specific Objectives

At the completion of this chapter, you will be able to:

▶ Explain the relationship of planning to the preactive and reflective thought-processing phases of instruction.

▶ Describe the primary focus of national curriculum standards for your subject field.

▶ Explain the value and limitations of student textbooks for your subject field.

▶ Demonstrate an ability to plan the long-range sequence of content for teaching in your subject field and identify the value of collaborative planning.

▶ Write concise and measurable cognitive, affective, and psychomotor instructional objectives.

Chapter 5 Overview

Now that you know how to set up a classroom management system, your classroom is organized, and your guidelines and procedures have been established, it is time to focus on what you are going to teach. We begin this chapter by emphasizing the importance of planning. Then we will take you through the process of selecting content for a course and preparing the specific learning outcomes expected as students learn that content. From that content outline and the related and specific learning outcomes, a teacher prepares units and daily lessons (discussed in Chapters 6 and 7). Although planning is a critical skill for a teacher, a well-developed plan will not guarantee the success of a lesson or unit or even the overall effectiveness of a course. But the lack of a well-developed plan will almost certainly result in poor teaching. Like a good map, a good plan helps you reach your destination with more confidence and with fewer wrong turns.

Introduction

Planning the instruction constitutes a large part of a teacher's job. As a teacher, you will be responsible for planning at three levels: (1) courses for a semester or academic year, (2) units of instruction, and (3) lessons. Throughout your career, you will be engaged almost continually in planning at each of these three levels. Planning for instruction is a steady and cyclical process that involves the preactive and reflective thought-processing phases discussed in Chapter 1. The importance of mastering the process at the very beginning of your career cannot be overemphasized, as it is the basis of this chapter.

Clarification of Terms

Let us begin the discussion by clarifying a few relevant terms. A **course** can be defined as a complete sequence of instruction that presents a major division of a subject matter or discipline. Courses are laid out for a year, a semester, a quarter, or, in the case of mini-courses or intensive courses, a few weeks. Each course is composed of units. A **unit** is a major subdivision of a course, comprising planned instruction about some central theme, topic, issue, or problem for a period of several days to several weeks. Units that take much longer than three weeks (with the exception of interdisciplinary units) tend to lose their effectiveness as recognizable units of instruction. Each unit is composed of lessons. A **lesson** is a subdivision of a unit, usually taught in a single class period or, on occasion, for two or three successive periods.

The heart of good planning is decision making. For every plan, you must decide what your goals and objectives are, what specific subject matter should be taught, what materials are available and appropriate for instruction, and what methods and techniques should be employed to accomplish the objectives. Making these decisions can be complicated because there are so many choices. Therefore, you must be knowledgeable about the principles that are the foundation for effective course, unit, and lesson planning. Since the principles of all levels of educational planning are much the same, it makes mastering the necessary skills easier than you might think.

Reasons for Planning Thoughtfully and Thoroughly

Thoughtful and thorough planning is vital for effective teaching to occur. Such planning helps produce well-organized classes and a purposeful classroom atmosphere and also reduces the likelihood of problems in classroom control. A teacher who has not planned or who has underprepared will have more problems than imaginable. While planning, you should keep in mind these two goals: (1) select strategies that keep students physically and mentally on task and that ensure student learning and (2) do not waste anyone's time.

Careful planning has several other benefits as well. Planning well helps guarantee that you know the subject, for in planning you will more likely become a master of the material and the methods to teach it. No one can know everything about a discipline, but careful planning can save you from fumbling through half-digested, poorly understood content and making errors along the way. Thoughtful planning is likely to make your classes livelier, more interesting, more accurate, and more relevant and thus make your teaching more successful.

Another important reason for careful planning is to ensure program coherence. Periodic lesson plans constitute an integral part of a larger plan, represented by course goals and objectives. The students' learning experiences should be thoughtfully planned in sequence and then orchestrated by a teacher who understands the rationale for their respective positions in the curriculum—not precluding, of course, an occasional diversion from planned activities.

Unless your course stands alone, following nothing and leading to nothing (which is unlikely), there are prerequisites to what you want your students to learn, and there are learning objectives to follow that build on this learning. Good planning addresses both the *scope* (breadth and depth of the content coverage) and the *sequence* (what comes before and what follows) of the content.

Another important reason for careful planning is that the diversity of students in today's schools demands that the teacher address those individual differences—such as diverse cultural backgrounds and life experiences, different learning styles and capacities, and various levels of proficiency in the use of English. Still another reason for planning is to ensure program continuation. In case a substitute teacher is needed or other members of the teaching team must fill in, the program continues without you.

Careful and thoughtful planning is important, too, for teacher self-assessment. After an activity, a lesson, or a unit, as well as at the end of a semester and the school year, you will assess what was done and the effect it had on student achievement (the reflective phase of instruction, discussed in Chapter 1). Finally, supervisors and administrators expect you to plan well. Your plans represent a criterion recognized and evaluated by administrators—the experienced know that inadequate attention to planning usually results in incompetent teaching.

Components of Instructional Planning

Eight components should be evident in a complete instructional plan:

1. *Statement of philosophy.* This is a general statement about why the plan is important and how students will learn its content.

2. *Needs assessment.* The wording of the statement of philosophy should demonstrate an appreciation for the cultural diversity of the school context, with a corresponding perception of the needs of society, the community, and the learners and of the functions served by the school. The statement of philosophy and needs assessment should be consistent with the school's mission or philosophy statement.

3. *Aims, goals, and objectives.* The plan's stated aims, goals, and objectives should be consistent with the school's mission or philosophy statement. The distinctions among aims, goals, and objectives are discussed in this chapter.

4. *Sequence.* The sequence of a plan refers to its relationship to the preceding and subsequent curricula. A presentation of the sequence, or the *vertical articulation*, shows the plan's relationship to the learning that preceded and the learning that follows, from kindergarten through grade 12 (in some instances, to the learning that follows high school graduation, such as in tech prep high schools where the curriculum is articulated with that of a neighboring postsecondary vocational school).

5. *Integration.* The integration component concerns the plan's connection with other curricula and cocurricular activities across the grade level. For example, the language arts curriculum at a middle school may be closely integrated with that school's social studies curriculum, or at a high school, several of the humanities courses may be

integrated. The integration component is also referred to as the *horizontal articulation* of a plan. "Writing across the curriculum," as used in many schools, is an example of both vertical and horizontal integration.

6. *Sequentially planned learning activities.* This is the presentation of the organized and sequential units and lessons, which must be appropriate for the subject and grade level and for the age and diversity of the students. Preparing an instructional plan is the topic of Chapter 6.

7. *Resources needed.* This is a listing of resources, such as books, speakers, field trips, and media. Resources are integrated throughout Chapters 6, 9, and 10.

8. *Assessment strategies.* These strategies, which must be consistent with the objectives, include procedures for diagnosing what students know or think they know prior to the instruction (preassessment) as well as the evaluation of student achievement during (formative assessment) and at completion of the instruction (summative assessment). Assessment is the topic of Chapter 11.

Planning a Course

When planning a course, you must decide exactly what is to be accomplished in that time period for which students take the course, whether for an academic year, a semester, or some shorter time period. Planning ahead what it is that you want students to learn and then designing instructional activities that will facilitate their learning those things constitutes *outcome-based education*. Planning ahead, designing activities to accomplish those goals and objectives, and then assessing student achievement against those goals and objectives is called *criterion-referenced education*. An education that is outcome based should also be one that

is criterion referenced and vice versa. To plan what is to be accomplished, you should (a) review school and other public documents for mandates and guidelines; (b) probe, analyze, and translate your own convictions, knowledge, and skills into behaviors that foster the intellectual development of your students; and (c) talk with colleagues and learn about their expectations.

Documents That Provide Guidance for Content Selection

Curriculum publications of your state department of education, district subject matter standards and courses of study, school-adopted printed and nonprinted materials, and resource units are all valuable sources you will use in planning the school year. Your college or university library may have some of these documents. Others may be obtained from cooperating teachers or administrative personnel at local schools and sites on the Internet. For sample Internet sites, see Figure 5.1. Many of these documents are generated through the process of state accreditation.

To receive *accreditation* (which is usually renewed every three to six years), a high school is reviewed by an accreditation team. Prior to the team's visit, the school prepares self-study reports for which each department reviews and updates the curriculum guides that provide information about the objectives and content of each course and program offered. In some states, middle schools and junior high schools also are accredited by state or regional agencies. In other states, those schools can volunteer to be reviewed for improvement. The accreditation process, which can be expensive, is paid for with school or district funds. Now do Activity 5.1.

Figure 5.1 **Sample Internet Resources on National and State Curriculum Standards and Frameworks**

General and multiple disciplines
- http://www.mcrel.org
- http://www.goenc.com

Discipline-specific national standards
- **Economics** http://www.ncee.org
- **English/reading** http://www.ncte.org
- **ISTE: International Society for Technology in Education** http://www.iste.org
- **Mathematics** http://www.nctm.org
- **Psychology** http://www.apa.org/ed/
- **Science** http://www.nsta.org
- **Social studies: National Council for the Social Studies** http://www.ncss.org/
- **Sport and Physical Education** http://www.aahperd.org/naspe/standards/national standards/

Standards state by state, discipline by discipline
- http://www.statestandards.com

Academic Benchmarks
- http://www.academicbenchmarks.com/search/
- http://www.academicbenchmarks.org/search/

Activity
5.1   **Oprah's National High School Essay Contest**

In 1996, Oprah launched the world's most popular book club. By selecting many new books for 15 years, Oprah has done more to promote literacy than anyone. She has turned obscure titles into best-sellers. She has converted reluctant readers into bookworms.

In February 2006, Oprah conducted a national essay contest focusing on the Oprah's Book Club selection titled *Night* by Elie Wiesel. She encouraged high school students to write a 1,000-word essay answering the question, "Why is Elie Wiesel's Holocaust memoir *Night* relevant today?"

In order to participate, students had to be legal residents of the United States enrolled full-time in grades 9 through 12 in a public or private school. Nearly 50,000 high school students across the country shared what *Night*, the moving account of Wiesel's experience in Nazi concentration camps during World War II, meant to them.

Apply Your Knowledge

To meet the 50 winners and read excerpts from their essays, check out the following website.
Oprah's National High School Essay Contest
http://myown.oprah.com/search/index.html?q
 =Oprah%E2%80%99s%20National%20High%20School
 %20Essay%20Contest

To peruse the books Oprah has selected for her Book Club selections, visit the following website.
Oprah's Book Club Selections
http://en.wikipedia.org/wiki/Oprah's_Book_Club

National Curriculum Standards

Curriculum standards are a definition of what students should know (content) and be able to do (process and performance). At the national level, curriculum standards did not exist in the U.S. until they were developed and released for mathematics education in 1989. Shortly after the release of the mathematics standards, support for national goals in education was endorsed by the National Governors Association, and the National Council on Education Standards and Testing recommended that in addition to those for mathematics, national standards for subject matter content in K–12 education be developed for the arts, civics/social studies, English/language arts/reading, geography, history, and science. Initial funding for the development of national standards was provided by the U.S. Department of Education. In 1994, the U.S. Congress passed the Goals 2000: Educate America Act, amended in 1996 with an Appropriations Act, encouraging states to set standards (see Table 1.3 in Chapter 1). Long before, however, as was done for mathematics by the National Council of Teachers of Mathematics, national organizations devoted to various disciplines were already articulating standards.

The national standards represent the best thinking by expert panels, including teachers from the field, about what are the essential elements of a basic core of subject knowledge that all students should acquire. They serve not as national mandates but rather as voluntary guidelines to encourage curriculum development to promote higher student achievement. State and local curriculum developers decide the extent to which the standards are used. Strongly influenced by the national standards, nearly all 50 states have completed or are presently developing state standards for the various disciplines.

By 1992, for example, most states, usually through state curriculum frameworks, were following the 1989

standards for mathematics education to guide what and how mathematics is taught and how student progress is assessed. The essence of many of those recommendations—a hands-on, inquiry-oriented, performance-based approach to learning less but learning it better—can also be found in the standards that were subsequently developed for other disciplines.

STANDARDS BY CONTENT AREA The following alphabetical listing describes standards development for content areas of the K–12 curriculum. Although the date when the standards were first published is listed, standards are revised on a regular basis. Consult the various disciplines for specific updates. Many of the standards are available on the Internet (see Figure 5.1).

Arts (Visual and Performing). Developed jointly by the American Alliance for Theater and Education, the National Art Education Association, the National Dance Association, and the Music Educators National Conference, the National Standards for Arts Education were published in 1994.

Economics. Developed by the National Council on Economic Education, standards for the study of economics were published in 1997.

English/Language Arts/Reading. Developed jointly by the International Reading Association, the National Council of Teachers of English, and the University of Illinois Center for the Study of Reading, standards for English education were published in 1996.

Foreign Languages. *Standards for Foreign Language Learning: Preparing for the 21st Century* was published by the American Council on the Teaching of Foreign Languages (ACTFL) in 1996.[1]

Geography. Developed jointly by the Association of American Geographers, the National Council for Geographic Education, and the National Geographic Society, standards for geography education were published in 1994.[2]

Health. Developed by the Joint Committee for National School Health Education Standards, *National Health Education Standards: Achieving Health Literacy* was published in 1995.[3]

History/Civics/Social Studies. The Center for Civic Education and the National Council for the Social Studies developed standards for civics and government, and the National Center for History in the Schools developed the standards for history, all of which were published in 1994.

Mathematics. In 1989, the National Council of Teachers of Mathematics (NCTM) published *Curriculum and Evaluation Standards for School Mathematics*. Revised standards were developed and released in 2000. See the mathematics site of the National Council of Teachers of Mathematics in Figure 5.1.

Physical Education. In 1995, the National Association of Sport and Physical Education (NASPE) published *Moving into the Future: National Standards for Physical Education.*

Psychology. In 1999, the American Psychological Association released voluntary national standards for what students should be taught in high school psychology courses.

Science. In 1995, with input from the American Association for the Advancement of Science and the National Science Teachers Association, the National Research Council's National Committee on Science Education Standards and Assessment published the standards for science education.

Technology. With initial funding from the National Science Foundation and the National Aeronautics and Space Administration and in collaboration with the International Technology Education Association, National Educational Technology Standards (NETS) are being developed. For an update, see the technology site designation in Figure 5.1.

Supplements to the national standards are available from the Bureau of Indian Affairs for the arts (dance, music, theater, and visual), civics and government, geography, health, language arts, mathematics, science, and social studies.[4] The *American Indian Supplements* may be used by Indian nations as guides in their preparation of tribally specific local standards. They are also useful to school districts serving American Indian children in adapting state standards to be more culturally relevant to their communities.

As discussed in Chapter 2, the Common Core Standards in English-language arts and mathematics have been adopted by most states. Still, the national standards presented here are commonly used in middle and secondary schools across the U.S. in a variety of subject areas in lieu of state and local standards. Proceed now to Exercises 5.1, 5.2, and 5.3, through which you will explore national standards and state and local curriculum documents. Then, to learn more about the Common Core Standards Initiative, peruse **http://www.corestandards.org/about-the-standards**. Also, read about civic education and **cultural literacy** by reviewing and completing Activities 5.2 and 5.3, respectively.

Activity 5.2 **Civic Education**

Our schools strive to produce educated Americans ready to actively participate in our democratic system of government. Since 1971, Close Up has led our nation in civic education. Close Up is a Washington, D.C.–based experiential program that educates, inspires, and empowers middle and high school students and new Americans to become active citizens. Each year, through their learning programs and their multimedia publications, they promote active citizenship to more than 1 million students and teachers in 15,000 schools across the country. Close Up also publishes *Current Issues*, the nation's leading supplemental social studies text, and produces a television show, *Close Up at the Newseum*, which airs weekly.

Another website resource, The American Promise, was created to help teachers, professors, and educators bring democracy into their classrooms. This site is a supplement to the videos and teaching guide produced for the original public television series. The American Promise website offers many downloadable curricular materials and free classroom sets of materials.

The Center for Civic Education outlines the K–12 standards for civic education and government, which specify what students should know and be able to do in the field of civics and government. A work in progress, it is comprised of prompts and strategies in literature, reading, writing, and math that use *We the People* and *Foundations in Democracy* curricular materials as a base.

Apply Your Knowledge

Check out the following websites to learn more about efforts to promote civic competence.

Center for Civic Education
http://www.civiced.org/index.php?page=stds

Close Up Foundation
http://www.closeup.org

The American Promise
http://www.farmers.com/FarmComm/AmericanPromise/about_main.html

Activity
5.3   **Cultural Literacy**

Professor E. D. Hirsch, Jr. is now retired from the University of Virginia, but his research on literacy and the achievement gap have profoundly influenced educators, parents, and students for over three decades. In 1986, Hirsch founded the Core Knowledge Foundation and then wrote *Cultural Literacy: What Every American Needs to Know* the following year. In 1988, he cowrote *The Dictionary of Cultural Literacy*. Then, in 1997, Hirsch started publishing the popular eight-volume Core Knowledge series. You have probably seen *What Your Kindergartner Needs to Know: Preparing Your Child for a Lifetime of Learning*, *What Your First Grader Needs to Know: Fundamentals of a Good First-Grade Education*, and so on, which highlight what students should be taught at each respective grade level throughout their elementary schooling.

In the late 1970s, Hirsch noticed that students at the University of Virginia and students at a traditionally black community college in the same state scored differently on reading tests. Hirsch concluded that expertise in decoding was not enough; he claimed that the determining factor in reading comprehension was wide-ranging background knowledge. Hirsch then formulated his cultural literacy theory to ensure that a standardized curriculum exposed all students to the same cultural canon.

Although Hirsch is a liberal, his theories have been criticized for failing to address differences in learning styles and for being culturally insensitive. His critics have argued that Hirsch promotes a "lily-white" curriculum based on "drill and kill" trivia mastery. For a critical view of Hirsch's work, read what Alfie Kohn has to say about cultural literacy in *The Schools Our Children Deserve*.

In 1996, Hirsch published *The Schools We Need and Why We Don't Have Them*. In this book, Hirsch claims that the American education system continues to produce students who are not knowledgeable because we focus on teaching higher-order skills like critical thinking instead of the necessary fact-based curriculum he supports. In his most recent book, *The Knowledge Deficit* (2006), Hirsch continues to claim that the cause of disappointing reading performance is a lack of background knowledge.

Apply Your Knowledge

Find out more about E. D. Hirsch, Jr. cultural literacy, and Core Knowledge schools by perusing the following websites and their links and answering the questions below.

Core Knowledge

http://www.coreknowledge.org

Narrowing the Two Achievement Gaps, a presentation at the 18th Education Trust National Conference, November 9, 2007, Washington, D.C., by E. D. Hirsch Jr.

http://www.coreknowledge.org/blog/?p=28

"The Influential E. D. Hirsch," article by Walter Feinberg in *Rethinking Schools Online*

http://www.rethinkingschools.org/archive/13_03/ hirsch.shtml

"The Educational Theory of E. D. Hirsch," by analyst Jen Coppola

http://www.newfoundations.com/GALLERY/Hirsch.html

1. What does it mean to be culturally literate?
2. Test your knowledge of American geography, history, and other trivia by completing a few quizzes online. You can access Geography Quizzes at **http://www.triv.net/html/geography.htm** and History Quizzes at **http://www.triv.net/html/history.htm**. Depending on your interest and knowledge, select those quizzes that sound interesting to you. How did you do? What information was covered in your American geography and history quizzes that would make E. D. Hirsch's "right stuff" lists that is information/material all teachers should know, regardless of the grade and/or subject they teach?
3. Should all teachers be expected to know basic U.S. history and geography regardless of the grade or subject they teach or intend to teach? Why or why not?

Student Textbooks

For several reasons—the recognition of the diversity of learning styles, capacities, and modalities of students; the increasing cost of textbooks; and the availability of non-printed materials—textbook appearance, content, and use have changed considerably in recent years and will likely continue to change in the years to come.

School districts periodically adopt new textbooks (usually every five to eight years). If you are a student teacher or a first-year teacher, this will most likely mean that someone will say to you, "Here are the textbooks you will be using."

Even if you are handed a textbook that your school or district has adopted, you should make additions and modifications to your curriculum choices. The suggestions listed here will help you select supporting textbooks and materials for your classes that provide realistic and balanced portrayals of females, various racial and ethnic groups, people with disabilities, English Language Learners, and other traditionally misrepresented or underrepresented groups.

After you have some teaching experience under your belt, you may be asked to serve on a textbook selection committee. Textbook selection plays a key role in promoting an unbiased curriculum. Therefore, it is important that you view textbooks critically. There are some specific types of bias you want to avoid and some basic guidelines you can follow when contemplating textbook adoption. Sadker and Sadker highlight seven forms of textbook bias that you should be on the lookout for and avoid: *invisibility* (excluding certain groups altogether), *stereotyping* (portraying all members of certain groups in a limited role or negative light), *imbalance and selectivity* (presenting only one perspective), *unreality* (omitting unpleasant truths), *fragmentation and isolation* (not integrating information about certain groups or including that information as an "add-on"), *linguistic bias* (selecting language with negative connotations to describe certain groups), and *cosmetic bias* (making minimal surface changes to appear to address diversity).[5]

Broad guidelines for selecting a student textbook and support materials that are free of bias include the following: the textbook preface should make reference to diversity and/or multiculturalism; the concepts, historical events, and issues should be presented from a variety of perspectives; and there should be diversity among the contributing authors.[6] In addition, verify that the teacher's edition provides lesson adaptations and accommodations for students with special needs, English Language Learners, gifted and talented students, and so forth. Make sure the commitment to diversity is replicated in all supporting materials as well.

Benefit of Student Textbooks to Student Learning

It is unlikely that anyone could rationally argue that textbooks are of no benefit to student learning. Textbooks can provide (a) an organization of basic or important content for the students, (b) a basis for deciding content emphasis, (c) previously tested activities and suggestions for learning, (d) information about other readings and resources to enhance student learning, and (e) a foundation for building higher-order thinking activities (e.g., inquiry discussions and student research) that help develop critical thinking skills. The textbook, however, should not be the "be all and end all" of the instructional experiences. Now complete Activity 5.4.

Problems with Reliance on a Single Textbook

The student textbook is only one of many teaching tools and not the ultimate word. Of the many ways in which you may use textbooks for student learning, the least acceptable is to show a complete dependence on a single book and require students simply to memorize material from it. This is the lowest level of learning; furthermore, it implies that you are unaware of other significant printed and nonprinted resources and have nothing more to contribute to student learning.

Another potential problem brought about by reliance on a single textbook is that because textbook publishers prepare books for use in a larger market—that is, for national or statewide use—a state- and district-adopted book may not adequately address issues of special interest and importance to the community in which you teach.[7] That is one reason why some teachers and schools provide supplementary printed and nonprinted resources.

Still another problem brought about by reliance on a single source is that the adopted textbook may not be at the appropriate reading level for many students. For example, in a recent study of the readability of high school chemistry textbooks, 80 % of the books were found to have reading levels beyond high school. In other words, most high school students would not be able to read and comprehend the majority of books adopted for use in teaching high school chemistry.[8] In today's heterogeneous classrooms, the level of student reading can vary by as much as two-thirds of the chronological age of the students. This means that if the chronological age is 12 years (typical for seventh graders), then the reading-level range would be eight years—that is, the class may have some students reading at only the third-grade level while others are reading at the 11th-grade level. This is the case in Ms. Sunday's sixth-grade geography classes in Estes Park, CO, where some students read at the second- and third-grade levels. Examine student textbooks and teacher's editions of those books by doing Exercise 5.4.

Guidelines for Textbook Use

Generally, students benefit by having their own copies of a textbook in the current edition. However, because of budget constraints, this may not always be possible. The book may be outdated, or quantities may be limited. When the latter is the case, students may not be allowed to take the books home or perhaps may only occasionally do so. In other classrooms, there may be no textbook at all. Some classrooms have two sets of the textbook, one set that remains for use in the classroom and another set that is assigned to students to use at home for home studying. With that

---

Activity 5.4 | **MiddleWeb**

MiddleWeb was established in 1996. With more than 1.4 million visitors each year, MiddleWeb is one of the most frequently visited websites for middle school educators. It provides a wealth of resources to all of those dedicated to raising the achievement of middle schoolers. MiddleWeb provides resources for schools, districts, parents, and public school advocates in addition to teachers. Sponsored by Stenhouse Publishers, MiddleWeb is considered to be one of the best middle-grades resources on the Web. They even feature humorous and touching weblog diaries in which middle school teachers share their challenges and triumphs.

Apply Your Knowledge

Check out the news stories, chats, online conferences, freebies, weblog diaries, and great links for teachers on MiddleWeb at **http://www.middleweb.com.** Next, answer the questions below.

1. What did you learn from the articles on curriculum design, teaching strategies, and assessment procedures you read?
2. Sign up for the MiddleWeb free biweekly newsletter. What information did you find most helpful?

arrangement, students do not have to carry around heavy books in their backpacks. The following general guidelines apply to using the textbook as a learning tool.

Progressing through a textbook from the front cover to the back in one school term is not necessarily an indicator of good teaching. The textbook is one resource; to enhance their learning, students should be encouraged to use a variety of resources. Encourage students to search for additional sources to update the content of the textbook. This is especially important in certain disciplines such as science and social sciences where the amount of new information is growing rapidly and students may have textbooks that are several years old. The library and the Internet should be researched by students for the latest information on certain subjects. Keep supplementary reading materials for student use in the classroom. School and community librarians and resource specialists usually are delighted to cooperate with teachers in the selection and provision of such resources.

Individualize learning for students of various reading abilities. Consider differentiated reading and workbook assignments in the textbook and several supplementary sources (see the section "Multitext and Multireadings Approaches"). Except to make life simpler for the teacher, there is no advantage in all students working out of the same book and exercises. Some students benefit from the drill, practice, and reinforcement afforded by workbooks that accompany textbooks, but this is not true for all students, nor do all benefit from the same activity. In fact, the traditional workbook may eventually become extinct as it is replaced by the modern technology afforded by computer software and online resources. As the cost of hardware and software programs becomes more affordable for schools, the use of computers by individual students is also becoming more common. Computers and other interactive media provide students with a psychologically safer learning environment in which they have greater control over the pace of the instruction, can repeat instruction if necessary, and can ask for clarification without the fear of having to do so publicly.

Whether the students are reading their textbooks or supplemental library materials or scanning informational websites, they need guidance in order to increase their reading comprehension and maximize their critical thinking. Several methods have been invented by teachers to help students develop their higher-level thinking skills and their comprehension of expository material. Some of these methods are the following:

- *K-W-L method.* Students recall what they already know (K) about a topic, determine what they want to learn (W), and later assess what they have learned (L).
- *POSSE method. Predict* ideas, *organize* ideas, *search* for structure, *summarize* main ideas, and *evaluate* understanding.
- *PQRST method. Preview, question, read, state* the main idea, and *test* yourself by answering the questions you posed earlier.

- *RAP method. Read* paragraphs, *ask* questions about what was read, and *put* it in your own words.
- *SQ3R method. Survey* the chapter, ask *questions* about what was read, and *read, recite,* and *review.*
- *SQ4R method. Survey* the chapter, ask *questions* about what was read, *read* to answer the questions, *recite* the answers, *record* important items from the chapter into notebooks, and then *review* it all.
- *SRQ2R method (survey, read, question, recite, review).* Use **reciprocal teaching** in which students are taught and practice the reading skills of summarizing, questioning, clarifying, and predicting.[9]

Just because something is in print or on the Internet does not guarantee its accuracy or truth. Textbooks and Web pages are often riddled with typographical errors, half-truths, omissions, and inaccuracies. Encourage students to be alert for errors in the textbook both in content and in printing—perhaps by giving them some sort of credit reward, such as points, when they bring an error to your attention. This helps students develop the skills of critical reading, critical thinking, and healthy skepticism. For example, a history book is reported to have stated that the first person to lead a group through the length of the Grand Canyon was John Wesley Powell. Critically thinking students quickly made the point that perhaps Powell was the first white person to do this, but Native Americans had traveled the length of the Grand Canyon for centuries.[10]

Introducing the Textbook

Students seldom know how to use their textbooks efficiently and effectively. Therefore, on the first day before they begin to read, you might introduce students to the textbook in a lesson in which you and they discuss these elements of the text:

1. *Title page.* What information does it give? When was the book written? Has it been revised? Who is the publisher? Where was it published? Do these factors indicate any likelihood of bias?

2. *Preface.* What does the author claim he or she intended to do? What was his or her purpose?

3. *Table of contents.* How much weight is given to various topics? How can we use the information contained in the table of contents to help study the text?

4. *List of maps, charts, and illustrations.* What is the importance of these devices? How can one use them to aid study? Choose examples of each—maps, charts, tables, graphs, and illustrations—and have students find essential information in them.

5. *Appendix.* What does appendix mean? What is it for?

6. *Index.* Use drill exercises to give students practice in using the index. These can be made into games or contests.

7. *Glossary.* What is a glossary? Why is it included? Use exercises that call for looking up words and then using them in sentences.

8. *Study aids at the ends of chapters.* How can study questions be used? Which are thought questions? Which are fact questions?

9. *Chapter headings, section headings, paragraph leads, introductory overviews, preliminary questions, and summaries.* What are the purposes of each of these? Use exercises that call for getting meaning from aids such as these without reading the entire text.

Multitext and Multireadings Approaches

Expressing dissatisfaction with the single-textbook approach to teaching, some teachers have substituted a multitext strategy in which they use one set of books for one topic and another set for another topic. This strategy provides some flexibility, although it really is only a series of single texts.

Other teachers—usually the more knowledgeable and proficient—use a strategy that incorporates many readings for a topic during the same unit. This multireading strategy gives the students a certain amount of choice in what they read. The various readings allow for differences in reading ability and interest level. By using a study guide, all the students can be directed toward specific concepts and information, but they do not have to all read the same selections. To implement this type of multireading approach, (a) select your instructional objectives; (b) solicit the help of your school librarian—generally, school librarians are quite willing to help you put a list of readings together; (c) select a number of readings that shine light on your objectives, being sure there are several readings for each objective to provide variation in students' reading levels and interests as you make your selections; (d) build a study guide that

directs the students toward the objectives and suggests readings appropriate to each objective; and (e) let the students select what they will read to meet the provisions of the guide. Now learn more about all the resources that are available at the Library of Congress by doing Activity 5.5.

Other Printed Materials

Besides the student textbook and maybe an accompanying workbook, a vast array of other printed materials is available for use in teaching—and many materials are available without cost. Printed materials include books, workbooks, pamphlets, magazines, brochures, newspapers, professional journals, periodicals, and duplicated materials. When thinking about what materials to use, be alert for (a) appropriateness of the material in both content and reading level; (b) articles in newspapers, magazines, and periodicals related to the content that your students will be studying or to the skills they will be learning; (c) assorted workbooks that emphasize thinking and problem solving rather than rote memorization (with an assortment of workbooks, you can have students working on similar but different assignments, depending on their interests and abilities—an example of multilevel teaching); (d) pamphlets, brochures, and other duplicated materials that students can read for specific information and viewpoints about particular topics; and (e) relatively inexpensive paperback books that both provide multiple book readings for your class and make it possible for students to read **primary sources**.

For free and inexpensive printed materials, look for sources in your college, university, or public library or in the resource center at a local school district; such sources are listed in Figure 5.2. Additionally, teachers can obtain free and inexpensive teaching materials through

Activity 5.5

The Library of Congress: More Than 10 Million Primary Sources Online

The largest library in the world, the Library of Congress, was established in 1800. The library strives to maintain its collection of cultural resources and make them available to members of Congress as well as the American people. In fact, it has a multitude of resources available to teachers. The extensive collection includes over 130 million books, recordings, photographs, maps, and manuscripts.

Some of the resources you may be interested in are found in the following categories: America's Library, Center for the Book, Citing Electronic Resources, Classroom Features and Activities, Everyday Mysteries, Guide to Law Online, Images on Popular Topics, International Resources, Lesson Plans, Places in the News, Poetry and Literature Center, Prints and Photographs Reading Room, Portals to the World, Reference Sites Compiled by the Library, Research Centers, Teacher's Guide to Folklife Resources, Teaching with Primary Sources Program, Thematic Resources, Veterans History Project, Webcasts for Teachers, and Wise Guide to local government.

Apply Your Knowledge

Check out the many resources available on the Library of Congress website at **http://www.loc.gov/teachers**.

1. Visit the Today in History link. What did you learn about what happened in history on a certain date that you did not know before visiting this website? How can this information support your teaching?

2. Visit the Lesson Plans link and select the lesson titled Using Primary Sources in the Classroom. Complete "I. Source Type: Objects." How could you use this link in your content area? Share your ideas with your classmates.

3. Visit the Lesson Plans link and under Lessons by Title select the H–P category. Review the unit plan titled "Indian Boarding Schools: Civilizing the Native Spirit." Check out the various resources listed on the Resource Page. Which ones did you find the most informative? How do you think this unit can be used in a sixth- to ninth-grade U.S. history course?

<u>**Figure 5.2**</u> **Resources for Free and Inexpensive Printed Materials**

- Civil Aeronautics Administration, *Sources of Free and Low-Cost Materials*. Washington, DC: U.S. Department of Commerce.
- Educators Progress Service, Inc., *Educator's Guide to Free Materials; Educator's Guide to Free Teaching Aids*. 214 Center Street, Randolph, WI 53956 (414) 326-3126.
- *Educator's Guide to Free Audio and Video Materials; Educator's Guide to Free Films; Educator's Guide to Free Filmstrips; Guide to Free Computer Materials; Educator's Guide to Free Science Materials*, Educator's Progress Service, Inc., 214 Center Street, Randolph, WI 53956 (414) 326-3126.
- *Freebies: The Magazine with Something for Nothing*. PO Box 5025, Carpinteria, CA 93014-5025.
- Freebies editors, *Freebies for Teachers*. Los Angeles: Lowell House, 1994.
- *A Guide to Print and Nonprint Materials Available from Organizations, Industry, Governmental Agencies and Specialized Publishers*. New York: Neal Schuman.
- *Video Placement Worldwide (VPW)*. Source of free sponsored educational videos and print materials on the Internet at **http://www.vpw.com**
- Professional periodicals and journals.
- *Catalog of Audiovisual Materials: A Guide to Government Sources* (ED 198 822). Arlington, VA: ERIC Documents Reproduction Service.

connections on the Internet. When considering using materials that you have obtained free or inexpensively, you will want to ensure that the materials are appropriate for use with the age-group with whom you work and that they are free of bias or an unwanted message.[11]

The Future for School Textbooks

Within the span of your professional career, you likely will take part in a revolution in the design of school textbooks. Already some school districts and states allow teachers in certain disciplines (where the technology is available) to choose among traditional student textbooks, ebooks, and interactive media programs.

With the revolution in microcomputer-chip technology, student textbooks have taken on a whole new appearance. There have been and will continue to be dramatic changes in the importance and use of student texts as well as new problems for the teacher, some of which are predictable. Student texts may become credit-card size, increasing the chance of students' losing their books. On the positive side, the classroom teacher will probably have available a variety of textbooks to better address the variety of reading levels, interests, learning styles, and abilities of individual students. Distribution and maintenance of reading materials could create an even greater demand on the teacher's time. Regardless, dramatic and exciting changes have begun to occur in a teaching tool that previously had not changed much throughout the history of education in this country. As an electronic multimedia tool, the textbook of the 21st century may be an interactive device that offers text, sound, and video and allows for worldwide communication.

Collaborative Planning

As noted, the textbook is only one resource for determining content to be studied. Your students and teaching colleagues are resources, too. Although you will do much of your instructional planning alone, many teachers also do a considerable amount of shared planning in instructional teams, both at the department level and between departments, and involve their students in phases of the planning as well.

By integrating teachers, we can integrate the curriculum. In middle schools and high schools across the U.S., teachers are working collaboratively in teams to produce interdisciplinary theme-based units. In an effort to make learning more relevant to students' lives, educators at the middle and secondary levels are taking advantage of natural connections between the disciplines. In Chapter 6, we will discuss planning for integrated teaching in detail.

Team Planning

In some schools, teachers plan together in teams (as discussed in Chapter 1). Planning procedures are much the same as recommended previously in this chapter, the difference being that the team members might split the planning responsibilities. Coming back together to share their individual planning, the team members work cooperatively to develop a final plan. Team planning works best when members of the team share a common planning time that is a minimum of four hours a week and that is separate from their individual preparation periods.

Teacher-Student Collaboration in Planning

Many teachers today encourage students to participate in the planning of some phase of the learning activities, units, and courses. Such participation tends to give students a proprietary interest in the activities, thereby increasing their motivation. In addition, sharing instructional accountability with them is more likely to ensure student achievement in learning. What students have contributed to the plan often seems more relevant to them than what others have planned for them, and students like to see their own plans succeed. Thus, teacher-student collaboration in planning can be a very effective motivational tool.

Preparing for the Year

You have reviewed the rationale and the components for instructional planning and examined state and local curriculum documents and student reading materials. While doing so, you undoubtedly have reflected on your own biases regarding content you believe should be included in a subject at a particular grade level. Now it is time to obtain practical experience in long-range planning.

Some educators believe that writing objectives (learning targets) should be the first step in preparing to teach. It is our contention that a more logical first step is to prepare a sequential general major topic outline. The second step is to detail the outline, that is, to add second- and third-level headings. Then, the third step is to write the instructional objectives from your detailed outline—the final focus of this chapter. Once you have decided the content and objectives, you are ready to create the subdivisions known as units of instruction and then prepare those units with their daily lessons (the topics of Chapter 7).

For most beginning teachers, topic outlines and instructional objectives are presented in the course of study or the teacher's edition of the student textbook, with the expectation that these will be used in teaching. Yet someone had to have written those outlines and objectives, and that someone was one or several teachers. As a teacher candidate, you should know how it is done, for someday you will be concentrating on it in earnest.

For now, then, the next step is for you to experience preparing a yearlong (or, in some instances, a semester-long) content outline for a subject and grade level that you intend to teach. Be cautioned that beginning teachers often have unrealistic expectations about the amount of content that

teenagers can study, comprehend, and learn over a given period of time. Reviewing school and other public documents and talking with experienced teachers in your local schools can be very helpful in developing a realistic selection and sequencing of content as well as the time frame for teaching that content. Keeping that caution in mind and recognizing that during implementation you may make adjustments to the original content outline, work on preparing a content outline by doing Exercise 5.5.

Preparing for and Dealing with Controversy

Controversial content and issues abound in teaching, especially in certain disciplines: for example, in English/language arts, over the use of certain books; in social studies, over values and moral issues; in science, over biological evolution; and in health, over lifestyle choices. As a general rule, if you have concern that a particular topic or activity might create controversy, it probably will. During your teaching career, you undoubtedly will have to make decisions about how you will handle such matters. When selecting content that might be controversial, consider the paragraphs that follow as guidelines.

Maintain a perspective with respect to your own goal, which is at the moment to obtain your teaching credential, then a teaching job, and then tenure. Student teaching is not a good time to become involved in controversy. If you communicate closely with your cooperating teacher and your college or university supervisor, you should be able to prevent any major problems dealing with controversial issues.

Teaching Scenario — **The Oprah Winfrey Leadership Academy for Girls**

Former President Nelson Mandela, Sidney Poitier, Tina Turner, Mariah Carey, Spike Lee, and Quincy Jones were among the dignitaries and celebrities who helped Oprah celebrate the grand opening of her Leadership Academy for Girls in a village outside Johannesburg, South Africa. The boarding school for girls in grades 7 through 12 opened its doors in January 2007, welcoming the 152 lucky scholarship winners the media mogul herself handpicked from among 1,500 potential students. Oprah was very involved in all aspects of the planning of the school and took care to create a welcoming, aesthetically pleasing environment for her girls. The art decorating the buildings on the campus includes beadwork, paintings, sculpture, and murals celebrating South African culture. In addition, every detail of the dorm and classroom facilities was chosen with the utmost care.

At the Leadership Academy, the students will receive instruction in leadership skills, decision making, critical thinking, and social responsibility to prepare them to lead South Africa. Oprah even plans on teaching via satellite from Chicago. The creation of this innovative school is the realization of Oprah's dream to help build a peaceful, prosperous South Africa. Because of her personal early struggles, Oprah feels very connected to these young girls who have faced incredible adversity and yet still possess a "can-do spirit." Oprah has done a lot to promote literacy, and she is a strong advocate of educational opportunity for all students. By creating this Leadership Academy, Oprah hopes to share her love of learning with these exceptional young adolescents.

Think About It

To find out more about the Oprah Winfrey Leadership Academy, see the following websites or read the article titled "Building a Dream" in the January 2007 issue of *O The Oprah Magazine*, pp. 154–161, 217.

Building a Dream: The Oprah Winfrey Leadership Academy
http://www.oprah.com/index.html

Oprah Winfrey's $40 Million Girls' School Opens
http://www.people.com/people/article/0,,20005603,00.html

Sometimes, during normal discussion in the classroom, a controversial subject will emerge spontaneously, catching the teacher off guard. If this happens, think before saying anything. You may wish to postpone further discussion until you have had an opportunity to talk over the issue with members of your teaching team or your supervisors. Controversial topics can seem to arise from nowhere for any teacher, and this is perfectly normal. Young people are in the process of developing their moral and value systems, and they need and want to know how adults feel about issues that are important to them, particularly those adults they hold in esteem—their teachers. Students need to discuss issues that are important to society, and there is absolutely nothing wrong with dealing with those issues as long as certain guidelines are followed.

First, students should learn about all sides of an issue. Controversial issues are open ended and should be treated as such. They do not have right answers or correct solutions. If they did, there would be no controversy. (As used in this book, an *issue* differs from a *problem* in that a problem generally has a solution, whereas an issue has many opinions and several alternative solutions.) Therefore, the focus should be on process as well as on content. A major goal is to show students how to deal with controversy and to make wise decisions on the basis of carefully considered information. Another goal is to help students learn how to disagree without being disagreeable—how to resolve conflict. To that end, students need to learn the difference between conflicts that are destructive and those that can be constructive, in other words, to see that conflict (disagreement) can be healthy and have positive value. A third goal, of course, is to help students learn about the content of an issue so that, when necessary, they can make decisions based on knowledge, not on ignorance.

Second, as with all lesson plans, one that deals with a topic that could lead to controversy should be well thought out ahead of time. Potential problem areas and resources must be carefully considered and prepared for in advance. Problems for the teacher are most likely to occur when the plan has been poorly thought out.

Third, at some point all persons directly involved in an issue have a right to input: students, parents and guardians, community representatives, and other faculty. This does not mean, for example, that people outside the public school have the right to censor a teacher's lesson plan, but it does mean that parents or guardians and students should have the right *without penalty* not to participate and to select an alternate activity. Most school districts have written policies that deal with challenges to instructional materials. As a beginning teacher, you should become aware of the policies of your school district. In addition, professional associations such as the National Council of Teachers of English (NCTE), the National Council for the Social Studies (NCSS), and the National Science Teachers Association (NSTA) have published guidelines for dealing with controversial topics, materials, and issues.

Fourth, we see nothing wrong with students knowing a teacher's opinion about an issue as long as it is clear that the students may disagree without reprisal or academic penalty. However, it is probably best for a teacher to wait and give his or her opinion only after the students have had full opportunity to study and report on facts and opinions from other sources. Sometimes it is helpful to assist students in separating facts from opinions on a particular issue being studied by setting up on the overhead or writing board a fact-opinion table, with the issue stated at the top and then two parallel columns, one for facts and the other for related opinions.

A characteristic that has made this country so great is the freedom granted by the First Amendment for all its people to speak out on issues. This freedom should not be excluded from public school classrooms. Teachers and students should be encouraged to express their opinions about the great issues of today, to study the issues, to suspend judgment while collecting data, and then to form and accept each other's reasoned opinions. We must understand the difference between teaching truth, values, and morals and teaching about truth, values, and morals. (Aspects of character education are presented in both Chapter 3 and later in this chapter.)

As a public school teacher, there are limits to your academic freedom, much greater than are the limits on a university professor. You must understand this fact. The primary difference is that the students with whom you will be working are not yet adults (unlike postsecondary students); they must be protected from dogma and allowed the freedom to learn and to develop their values and opinions, free from coercion from those who have power and control over their learning. You should also keep in mind that cultural differences may arise in classroom discussions or activities. It is important to be respectful of all opinions, expect all students to act with integrity, and not let differences be divisive.

Now that you have read our opinion and suggested guidelines, what do you think about this topic, which should be important to you as a teacher? For the development and expression of your opinion, proceed to Exercise 5.6.

Aims, Goals, and Objectives: A Clarification

Now that you have examined content typically taught in the grades 7 through 12 curriculum and have experienced preparing a tentative content outline for a subject that you intend to teach for that content learning, it is time for you to learn to write specific learning targets for that content learning. Such learning targets are called *instructional objectives*. They are statements describing what the student will be able to do on completion of the instructional experience. Whereas some authors distinguish between instructional objectives (hence referring to objectives that are not behavior specific) and behavioral or performance objectives (objectives that are behavior specific), the terms are used here as if they are synonymous to emphasize the importance of writing instructional objectives in terms that are measurable.

As a teacher, you frequently will encounter the compound structure that reads "goals and objectives," as you likely found in the curriculum documents that you reviewed earlier in this chapter. A distinction needs to be understood. The easiest way to understand the difference between the words *goals* and *objectives* is to look at your intent.

Goals are targets that you intend to reach, that is, ideals that you would like to accomplish. Goals may be stated as teacher goals or collaboratively as team goals. Ideally, in both, the goal is the same. If, for example, the goal is to improve students' knowledge of how a democratic legislative body works, it could be stated as follows: "To help students improve their knowledge of how a democratic legislative body works" (teacher or course goal).

Educational goals are general statements of intent and are prepared early in course planning. (*Note:* Some writers use the phrase "general goals and objectives," but that is incorrect usage. Goals are general; objectives are specific.) Goals are useful when planned collaboratively with students and/or when shared with students as advance mental organizers—for instance, to establish a mind-set. The students then know what to expect and will begin to prepare mentally to learn it. From the goals, objectives are prepared. **Objectives** are not intentions. They are the actual behaviors that teachers intend to cause students to display. Objectives are what students do.

The most general educational objectives are often called aims; the objectives of schools, curricula, and courses are called goals; the objectives of units and lessons are called instructional objectives. **Aims** are more general than goals, and goals are more general than objectives. Instructional objectives are quite specific. Aims, goals, and objectives represent the targets, from general to specific statements of learning expectations, toward which curriculum and instruction are designed and aimed.

Instructional Objectives and Their Relationship to Curriculum and Assessment

As implied in the preceding paragraphs, goals guide the instructional methods; objectives drive student performance. Assessment of student achievement in learning should be an assessment of that performance. An assessment procedure that matches the instructional objectives is sometimes referred to as assessment that is aligned or authentic (discussed in Chapter 11). When objectives, instruction, and assessment match the stated goals, we have what is referred to as an aligned curriculum.

Goals are general statements, usually not even complete sentences and often beginning with the infinitive *to*, that identify what the teacher intends for the students to learn. Objectives, stated in performance terms, are specific actions and should be written as complete sentences that include the verb *will* to indicate what each student is expected to be able to do as a result of the instructional experience. When writing instructional objectives for their unit and lesson plans, some beginning teachers err by stating what they intend to do rather than what the anticipated student performance is. The value of stating learning objectives in terms of student performance is well documented by research.[12]

Although instructional goals may not always be quantifiable (i.e., readily measurable), instructional objectives should be measurable. Furthermore, those objectives then become the essence of what is measured in instruments designed to assess student learning; they are the learning targets. Consider the examples shown in Figure 5.3.

Learning Targets and Goal Indicators

The main purpose for writing objectives in performance terms is to be able to assess with precision whether the instruction has resulted in the desired behavior. In many school districts, the educational goals are established as learning targets, competencies that the students are expected to achieve. These goals are then divided into performance objectives, sometimes referred to as *goal indicators*. Instruction is designed to teach toward those objectives. When students perform the competencies called for by these objectives, their education is considered successful. This is known variously as *results-driven*, *criterion-referenced*, *competency-based*, *performance-based*, or *outcome-based* education. Expecting students to achieve one set of competencies before moving on to the next set is called **mastery learning**. The success of the student achievement, teacher performance, and the school may each be assessed according to these criteria.

Figure 5.3 **Examples of Goals and Objectives**

> **Goals**
> 1. To acquire knowledge about the physical geography of South America.
> 2. To develop an appreciation for music.
> 3. To develop an enjoyment for reading.
>
> **Objectives**
> 1. On a map the student will identify specific mountain ranges of South America.
> 2. The student will identify ten different musical instruments by listening to a tape recording of the Boston Pops Symphony Orchestra and identifying which instrument is being played at specified times as determined by the teacher.
> 3. The student will read two books, three short stories, and five newspaper articles at home within a two-month period. The student will maintain a daily written log of these activities.

Overt and Covert Performance Outcomes

Assessment is not difficult to accomplish when the desired performance is **overt behavior**, that is, behavior that can be observed directly. Each of the sample objectives of the preceding section is an example of an overt objective. Assessment is more difficult to accomplish when the desired behavior is a **covert behavior**, that is, when it is not directly observable. Although certainly no less important, behaviors that call for *appreciation, discovery,* or *understanding,* for example, are not directly observable because they occur within a person. Because covert behavior cannot be observed directly, the only way to tell whether the objective has been achieved is to observe behavior that may indicate that achievement. The objective, then, is written in overt language, and evaluators can only assume or trust that the observed behavior is, in fact, reasonably close to being indicative of the expected learning outcome.

Furthermore, when assessing whether an objective has been achieved—that learning has occurred—the assessment device must be consistent with the desired learning outcome. Otherwise, the assessment is not aligned; it is invalid. When the measuring device and the learning objective are compatible, we say that the assessment is authentic. For example, a person's competency to teach specific skills in mathematics to high school sophomores is best (i.e., with highest reliability) measured by directly observing that person *doing* that very thing—teaching specific skills in mathematics to high school sophomores. Using a standardized paper-and-pencil test of multiple-choice items to determine a person's ability to teach specific mathematical skills to high school sophomores is not authentic assessment.

Balance of Behaviorism and Constructivism

Whereas behaviorists assume a definition of learning that deals only with changes in overt behavior, constructivists hold that learning entails the construction or reshaping of mental schemata and that mental processes mediate learning. Thus, people who adhere to constructivism or cognitivism are concerned with both overt and covert behaviors.[13] Does this mean that you must be one or the other, a behaviorist or a constructivist? Probably not. For now, the point is that when writing instructional objectives, you should write most or all of your basic expectations (minimal competency expectations) in overt terms (the topic of the next section). However, you cannot be expected to foresee all learning that occurs or to translate all that is learned into performance terms—most certainly not before it occurs.

Teaching toward Multiple Objectives, Understandings, and Appreciations

Any effort to write all learning objectives in behavioral terms neglects, in effect, the individual learner for whom it claims to be concerned. Such an approach does not allow for diversity among learners. *Learning that is most meaningful to students is not so neatly or easily predicted or isolated.* Rather than teaching one objective at a time, much of the time you should direct your teaching toward the simultaneous learning of multiple objectives, understandings, and appreciations. However, when you assess for learning, assessment is more accurate when objectives are assessed one at a time. More on this matter of objectives and their use in teaching and learning follows later in this chapter. Let's now review how objectives are prepared.

Preparing Instructional Objectives

When preparing instructional objectives, you must ask yourself, "How is the student to demonstrate that the objective has been reached?" The objective must include an action that demonstrates that the objective has been achieved. Inherited from behaviorism, this portion of the objective is sometimes called the *anticipated measurable performance.*

The ABCDs of Writing Objectives

When completely written, an instructional objective has four key components. To aid your understanding and remembering, you can refer to these as the ABCDs of writing behavioral objectives.

One component is the *audience.* The A of the ABCDs refers to the students for whom the objective is intended. To address this, sometimes teachers begin their objectives with the phrase "The student will be able to . . ." or, to personalize the objective, "You will be able to . . . ." (*Note:* To conserve space and to eliminate useless language, in examples that follow we eliminate use of "be able to" and write simply "The student will . . . ." For brevity, writers of objectives sometimes use the abbreviation "TSWBAT . . ." for "The student will be able to . . . .")

The second key component is the expected *behavior,* the B of the ABCDs. This second component represents the important learning target. The expected behavior (or performance) should be written with verbs that are measurable—that is, with action verbs—so that it is directly observable that the objective, or target, has been reached. As discussed in the preceding section, some verbs are too vague, ambiguous, and not clearly measurable. When writing objectives, you should avoid verbs that are not clearly measurable, covert verbs, such as *appreciate, comprehend,* and *understand* (see Figure 5.4). For the three examples given earlier, for Objectives 1 and 2 the behaviors (action or overt verbs) are *will identify,* and for Objective 3, the behaviors are *will read* and *will maintain.* Now, to test and to further your understanding, do Exercise 5.7.

F i g u r e 5 . 4 **Verbs to Avoid When Writing Overt Objectives**

appreciate	familiarize	learn
believe	grasp	like
comprehend	indicate	realize
enjoy	know	understand

Most of the time, when writing objectives for your unit and lesson plans, you will not bother yourself with including the next two components. However, as you will learn, they are important for the assessment of learning.

The third ingredient is the *conditions*, the C of the ABCDs, the setting in which the behavior will be demonstrated by the student and observed by the teacher. Conditions are forever changing; although the learning target should be clearly recognizable long before the actual instruction occurs, the conditions may not. Thus, conditions are not often included in the objectives teachers write. For the first sample objective, the conditions are "on a map." For the second sample objective, the conditions are "by listening to a tape recording of the Boston Pops Symphony Orchestra" and "specified times as determined by the teacher." For the third sample, the conditions are "at home within a two-month period."

The fourth ingredient, which again is not always included in objectives written by teachers, is the *degree* (or level) of expected performance—the D of the ABCDs. This is the ingredient that allows for the assessment of student learning. When mastery learning is expected, the level of expected performance is usually omitted (because it is understood). In teaching for mastery learning, the performance-level expectation is 100 %. In reality, however, the performance level will most likely be between 85 % and 95 %, particularly when working with a group of students rather than with an individual student. The 5 % to 15 % difference allows for human error, as can occur when using written and oral communication. Like conditions, standards will vary, depending on the situation and purpose, and thus are not normally included in the unit and lessons that teachers prepare. Now, to reinforce your comprehension, do Exercise 5.8.

Performance level is used to assess student achievement, and sometimes it is used to evaluate the effectiveness of the teaching. Student grades might be based on performance levels; evaluation of teacher effectiveness might be based on the level of student performance. Now, with Exercise 5.9, try your skill at recognizing measurable objectives.

Classifying Instructional Objectives

When planning instructional objectives, it is useful to consider the three domains of learning objectives: The **cognitive domain** involves mental operations from the lowest level of the simple recall of information to complex, high-level evaluative processes. The **affective domain** involves feelings, attitudes, and values and ranges from the lower levels of acquisition to the highest level of internalization and action. The **psychomotor domain** ranges from the simple manipulation of materials to the communication of ideas and finally to the highest level of creative performance.

The Domains of Learning and the Developmental Needs of Youth

Educators attempt to design learning experiences to meet the following areas of developmental needs of youth: intellectual, physical, emotional/psychological, and moral/ethical. As a teacher, you must include objectives that address learning within each of these categories of needs. While the intellectual needs are primarily within the cognitive domain and the physical needs are within the psychomotor domain, the other needs are mostly within the affective domain.

Too frequently, teachers focus on the cognitive domain while assuming that the psychomotor and affective domains will take care of themselves. Many experts argue that teachers should do just the opposite: that when the affective domain is directly attended to, the psychomotor and cognitive domains naturally develop. In any case, you should plan your teaching so your students are guided from the lowest to highest levels of operation within each of the three domains, separately or simultaneously. The three developmental hierarchies are discussed next to guide your understanding of each of the five areas of needs. Notice the illustrative verbs within each hierarchy. These verbs help you fashion your objectives when you are developing unit plans and lesson plans. Caution must be urged, however, for there can be considerable overlap among the levels at which some action verbs may appropriately be used. For example, the verb *identify* is appropriate in each of the following objectives at different levels (identified in parentheses) within the cognitive domain:

- The student will identify the correct definition of the term *osmosis*. (knowledge)
- The student will identify examples of the principle of osmosis. (comprehension)
- The student will identify the osmotic effect when a cell is immersed into a hypotonic solution. (application)
- The student will identify the osmotic effect on turgor pressure when the cell is placed in a hypotonic solution. (analysis)

COGNITIVE DOMAIN HIERARCHY In a widely accepted taxonomy of objectives, Bloom and his associates arranged cognitive objectives into classifications according to the complexity of the skills and abilities they embodied.[14] The result was a ladder ranging from the simplest to the most complex intellectual processes. Within each domain, prerequisite to a student's ability to function at one particular level of the hierarchy is the ability to function at the preceding level or levels. In other words, when a student is functioning at the third level of the cognitive domain, that student is automatically also functioning at the first and second levels. Rather than an orderly progression from simple to complex mental operations as illustrated by Bloom's Taxonomy, other researchers prefer an organization of cognitive abilities that ranges from simple information storage and retrieval, through a higher level of discrimination and concept attainment, to the highest cognitive ability to recognize and solve problems.[15]

The six major categories (or levels) in Bloom's Taxonomy of cognitive objectives are (1) *knowledge*—recognizing and recalling information; (2) *comprehension*—understanding the meaning of information; (3) *application*—using information; (4) *analysis*—dissecting information into its component parts to comprehend the relationships; (5) *synthesis*—putting components together to generate new ideas; and (6) *evaluation*—judging the worth of an idea, notion, theory, thesis, proposition, information, or opinion. In this taxonomy, the top four categories or levels—application, analysis, synthesis, and evaluation—represent what are called *higher-order cognitive thinking skills*.[16]

Although space does not allow elaboration here, Bloom's Taxonomy includes various subcategories within each of these six major categories. It is probably less important that an objective be absolutely classified than it is for a teacher to be cognizant of hierarchies of thinking and doing and to understand the importance of attending to student intellectual behavior from lower to higher levels of operation in all three domains. Discussion of each of Bloom's six categories follows.

Knowledge. The basic element in Bloom's Taxonomy concerns the acquisition of knowledge, that is, the ability to recognize and recall information. (As discussed in Chapter 9, this is similar to the *input level* of thinking and questioning.) Although this is the lowest of the six categories, the information to be learned may not itself be of a low level. In fact, it may be of an extremely high level. Bloom includes here knowledge of principles, generalizations, theories, structures, and methodology as well as knowledge of facts and ways of dealing with facts.

Action verbs appropriate for this category include *choose, cite, complete, define, describe, identify, indicate, list, locate, match, name, outline, recall, recognize, select,* and *state*.

The following are examples of objectives at the knowledge level. Note especially the verb (in italics) used in each example:

- From memory, the student *will recall* the letters in the English alphabet that are vowels.
- The student *will list* the organelles found in animal cell cytoplasm.
- The student *will identify* the major parts of speech in the sentence.
- The student *will name* the positions of players on a soccer team.

The remaining five categories of Bloom's Taxonomy of the cognitive domain deal with the use of knowledge. They encompass the educational objectives aimed at developing cognitive skills and abilities, including comprehension, application, analysis, synthesis, and evaluation of knowledge.

Comprehension. Comprehension includes the ability to translate, explain, or interpret knowledge and to extrapolate from it to address new situations. Action verbs appropriate for this category include *change, classify, convert, defend, describe, discuss, estimate, expand, explain, generalize, infer, interpret, paraphrase, predict, recognize, retell, summarize,* and *translate*.

Examples of objectives in this category are the following:

- From a sentence, the student *will recognize* the letters that are vowels in the English alphabet.
- The student *will describe* each of the organelles found in animal cell cytoplasm.
- The student *will recognize* the major parts of speech in the sentence.
- The student *will recognize* the positions of players on a soccer team.

Application. Once learners understand information, they should be able to apply it. Action verbs in this category of operation include *apply, calculate, demonstrate, develop, discover, exhibit, modify, operate, participate, perform, plan, predict, relate, show, simulate, solve,* and *use*. Examples of objectives in this category are the following:

- The student *will use* a word in a sentence that contains at least two vowels.
- The student *will predict* the organelles found in plant cell cytoplasm.
- The student *will demonstrate* in a complete sentence each of the major parts of speech.
- The student *will relate* how the positions of players on a soccer team depend on each other.

Analysis. This category includes objectives that require learners to use the skills of analysis. Action verbs appropriate for this category include *analyze, arrange, break down, categorize, classify, compare, contrast, debate, deduce, diagram, differentiate, discover, discriminate, group, identify, illustrate, infer, inquire, organize, outline, relate, separate,* and *subdivide*. Examples of objectives in this category include the following:

- From a list of words, the student *will differentiate* those that contain vowels from those that do not.
- Under the microscope, the student *will identify* the organelles found in animal cell cytoplasm.
- The student *will analyze* a paragraph for misuse of major parts of speech.
- The student *will illustrate* on the writing board the different positions of players on a soccer team.

Synthesis. This category includes objectives that involve such skills as designing a plan, proposing a set of operations, and deriving a series of abstract relations. Action verbs appropriate for this category include *arrange, assemble, categorize, classify, combine, compile, compose, constitute, create,* *design, develop, devise, document, explain, formulate, generate, hypothesize, imagine, invent, modify, organize, originate, plan, predict, produce, rearrange, reconstruct, revise, rewrite, summarize, synthesize, tell, transmit,* and *write.* Examples of objectives in this category are the following:

- From a list of words, the student *will rearrange* them into several lists according to the vowels contained in each.
- The student *will devise* a classification scheme of the organelles found in animal cell and plant cell cytoplasm according to their functions.
- The student *will write* a paragraph that correctly uses each of the major parts of speech.
- The student *will illustrate* on the chalkboard an offensive plan that uses the different positions of players on a soccer team.

Evaluation. This, the highest category of Bloom's Taxonomy of the cognitive domain, includes offering opinions and making value judgments. Action verbs appropriate for this category include *appraise, argue, assess, choose, compare, conclude, consider, contrast, criticize, decide, discriminate, estimate, evaluate, explain, interpret, judge, justify, predict, rank, rate, recommend, relate, revise, standardize, support,* and *validate.* Examples of objectives in this category are the following:

- The student *will listen* to and *evaluate* other students' identifications of vowels from sentences written on the board.
- While observing living cytoplasm under the microscope, the student *will justify* his or her interpretation that certain structures are specific organelles of a plant or animal cell.
- The student *will evaluate* a paragraph written by another student for the proper use of major parts of speech.
- The student *will interpret* the reasons for an opposing team's offensive use of the different positions of players on a soccer team.

AFFECTIVE DOMAIN HIERARCHY Krathwohl, Bloom, and Masia developed a useful taxonomy of the affective domain.[17] The following are their major levels (or categories), from least internalized to most internalized: (1) *receiving*—being aware of the affective stimulus and beginning to have favorable feelings toward it; (2) *responding*—taking an interest in the stimulus and viewing it favorably; (3) *valuing*—showing a tentative belief in the value of the affective stimulus and becoming committed to it; (4) *organizing*—placing values into a system of dominant and supporting values; and (5) *internalizing*—demonstrating consistent beliefs and behavior that have become a way of life. Although there is considerable overlap from one category to another within the affective domain, these categories do give a basis by which to judge the quality

of objectives and the nature of learning within this area. A discussion of each of the five categories follows.

Receiving. At this level, which is the least internalized, the learner exhibits willingness to give attention to particular phenomena or stimuli, and the teacher is able to arouse, sustain, and direct that attention. Action verbs appropriate for this category include *ask, choose, describe, differentiate, distinguish, hold, identify, locate, name, point to, recall, recognize, reply, select,* and *use.* Examples of objectives in this category are the following:

- The student *demonstrates sensitivity* to the property, beliefs, and concerns of others.
- The student *listens attentively* to the ideas of others.
- The student *pays attention* to the directions for enrichment activities.

Responding. At this level, learners respond to the stimulus they have received. They may do so because of some external pressure, because they find the stimulus interesting, or because responding gives them satisfaction. Action verbs appropriate for this category include *answer, applaud, approve, assist, command, comply, discuss, greet, help, label, perform, play, practice, present, read, recite, report, select, spend (leisure time in), tell,* and *write.* Examples of objectives at this level are the following:

- The student *reads* for enrichment.
- The student *discusses* what others have said.
- The student *cooperates* with others during group activities.

Valuing. Objectives at the valuing level deal with learner's beliefs, attitudes, and appreciations. The simplest objectives concern the acceptance of beliefs and values; the higher ones involve learning to prefer certain values and to finally become committed to them. Action verbs appropriate for this level include *argue, assist, complete, describe, differentiate, explain, follow, form, initiate, invite, join, justify, propose, protest, read, report, select, share, study, support,* and *work.* Examples of objectives in this category include the following:

- The student *protests* against racial or ethnic discrimination.
- The student *synthesizes* a position on biological evolution.
- The student *argues* a position against abortion or pro-choice for women.

Organizing. This fourth level in the affective domain concerns the building of a personal value system. Here the learner is conceptualizing and arranging values into a system that recognizes their relative importance. Action verbs appropriate for this level include *adhere, alter, arrange, balance, combine, compare, defend, define, discuss, explain, form, generalize, identify, integrate, modify, order, organize,* *prepare, relate,* and *synthesize.* Examples of objectives in this category are the following:

- The student *forms judgments* concerning proper behavior in the workplace.
- The student *integrates* certain behaviors into a personal work ethic.
- The student *defends* the important values of a particular subculture.

Internalizing. This is the last and highest category within the affective domain, at which the learner's behaviors have become consistent with his or her beliefs. Action verbs appropriate for this level include *act, complete, display, influence, listen, modify, perform, practice, propose, qualify, question, revise, serve, solve,* and *verify.* Examples of objectives in this category are the following:

- The student's behavior *displays* a well-defined and ethical code of conduct.
- The student *practices* accurate verbal and nonverbal communication.
- The student *performs* independently.

PSYCHOMOTOR DOMAIN HIERARCHY Whereas identification and classification within the cognitive and affective domains are generally agreed on, there is less agreement on the classification within the psychomotor domain. Originally, the goal of this domain was simply to develop and categorize proficiency in skills, particularly those dealing with gross and fine muscle control. The classification of the domain presented here follows this lead but includes at its highest level the most creative and inventive behaviors, thus coordinating skills and knowledge from all three domains. Consequently, the objectives are in a hierarchy ranging from simple gross locomotor control to the most creative and complex, requiring originality and fine locomotor control—for example, from simply turning on a computer to designing a software program. From Harrow, we offer the following taxonomy of the psychomotor domain: (a) *moving,* (b) *manipulating,* (c) *communicating,* and (d) *creating.*[18]

Moving. This level involves gross motor coordination. Action verbs appropriate for this level include *adjust, carry, clean, grasp, jump, locate, obtain,* and *walk.* Sample objectives for this category are the following:

- The student *will jump* a rope 10 times without missing.
- The student *will correctly grasp* the putter.
- The student *will carry* the microscope to the desk correctly.

Manipulating. This level involves fine motor coordination. Action verbs appropriate for this level include *assemble, build, calibrate, connect, play, thread,* and *turn.* Sample objectives for this category are the following:

- The student *will assemble* a kite.

- The student *will play* the C scale on the clarinet.
- The student *will turn* the fine adjustment until the microscope is in focus.

Communicating. This level involves the communication of ideas and feelings. Action verbs appropriate for this level include *analyze, ask, describe, draw, explain,* and *write.* Sample objectives for this category are the following:

- By *asking* appropriate questions, the student will demonstrate active listening skills.
- The student *will draw* what he or she observes on a slide through the microscope.
- The student *will describe* his or her feelings about the cloning of humans.

Creating. Creating is the highest level of this domain and of all domains and represents the student's coordination of thinking, learning, and behaving in all three domains. Action verbs appropriate for this level include *create, design,* and *invent.* Sample objectives for this category are the following:

- The student *will design* a mural.
- The student *will create, choreograph,* and *perform* a dance pattern.
- The student *will invent* and build a kite pattern.

Now, with Exercise 5.10, assess your recognition of performance objectives according to the domain to which they belong. Then, with Exercise 5.11, begin writing your own objectives for use in your teaching.

Using the Taxonomies

Theoretically, the taxonomies are constructed so that students achieve each lower level before being ready to move to the higher levels. But, because categories and behaviors overlap, as they should, this theory does not always hold in practice. Furthermore, as explained by others, feelings and thoughts are inextricably interconnected; they cannot be neatly separated, as the taxonomies would imply.[19]

The taxonomies are important in that they emphasize the various levels to which instruction must aspire. For learning to be worthwhile, you must formulate and teach to objectives from the higher levels of the taxonomies as well as from the lower ones. Student thinking and behaving must be moved from the lowest to the highest levels of thinking and behavior. When it is all said and done, it is, perhaps, the highest level of the psychomotor domain (creating) to which we aspire.

In using the taxonomies, remember that the point is to formulate the best objectives for the job to be done. In schools that use outcome-based education (known also as *results-driven education*) models, those models describe levels of mastery standards (rubrics) for each outcome. The taxonomies provide the mechanism for ensuring that you do not spend a disproportionate amount of time on facts and other low-level

Figure 5.5 **Sample Learning Outcome Standards**

Results-based education helps produce people who are lifelong learners, who are effective communicators, who have high self-esteem, and who are:

Problem solvers	• are able to solve problems in their academic and personal lives.
	• demonstrate higher-level analytical thinking skills when they evaluate or make decisions.
	• are able to set personal and career goals.
	• can use knowledge, not just display it.
	• are innovative thinkers.
Self-directed learners	• are independent workers.
	• can read, comprehend, and interact with text.
	• have self-respect with an accurate view of themselves and their abilities.
Quality producers	• can communicate effectively in a variety of situations (oral, aesthetic/artistic, nonverbal).
	• are able to use their knowledge to create intelligent, artistic products that reflect originality.
	• have high standards.
Collaborative workers	• are able to work interdependently.
	• show respect for others and their points of view.
	• have their own values and moral conduct.
	• have an appreciation of cultural diversity.
Community contributors	• have an awareness of civic, individual, national, and international responsibilities.
	• have an understanding of basic health issues.
	• have an appreciation of diversity.

learning and can be of tremendous help where teachers are expected to correlate learning activities to one of the school's or district's outcome standards (see Figure 5.5).

Preparing objectives is essential to the preparation of good items for the assessment of student learning. Clearly communicating your performance expectations to students and then specifically assessing student learning against those expectations makes the teaching most efficient and effective, and it makes the assessment of the learning closer to being authentic. This does not mean to imply that you will always write performance objectives for everything taught, nor will you always be able to accurately measure what students have learned. As said earlier, learning that is meaningful to students is not as easily compartmentalized as the taxonomies of educational objectives suggest.

Observing for Connected (Meaningful) Learning: Logs, Portfolios, and Journals

In learning that is most important and that has the most meaning to students, the domains are inextricably interconnected. Consequently, when assessing for student learning, both during the instruction (**formative assessment**) and at the conclusion of the instruction (**summative assessment**), you must look for those connections.

Ways of looking for connected learning include (a) maintaining a teacher's (or team's) log with daily or nearly daily entries about the progress of each student, (b) having students maintain personal learning journals in which they reflect on and respond to their learning, and (c) having students assemble individual learning portfolios that document their thinking, work, and learning experiences.

Dated and chronologically organized items that students place in their portfolios can include notes and communications; awards; brainstorming records; photos of bulletin board contributions and of charts, posters, displays, and models made by the student; records of peer coaching; visual maps; learning contract; record of debate contributions; demonstrations or presentations; mnemonics created by the student; peer evaluations; reading record; other contributions made to the class or to the team; record of service work; and test and grade records. Student journals and portfolios are discussed further in Chapter 11.

Character Education

Related especially to the affective domain, although not exclusive of the cognitive and psychomotor domains, is an interest in the development of students' values, especially those of honesty, kindness, respect, and responsibility, an interest in what is sometimes called **character education** (see also Chapter 3). For example, Wynne and Ryan state that "transmitting character, academics, and discipline—essentially, 'traditional' moral values—to pupils is a vital educational responsibility."[20] Thus, if one agrees with that interpretation, then the teaching of moral values is the transmission of character, academics, and discipline and clearly implies learning that transcends the three domains of learning presented here. Stimulated by a perceived need to reduce student antisocial behaviors (such as drug abuse and violence) and to produce more respectful and responsible citizens, with a primary focus on the affective domain, many schools are developing curricula in character education and instruction in conflict resolution. The ultimate goal of those efforts is to develop in students values that lead to responsible citizenship and moral action. Specific techniques and resources on character education are presented in Chapter 3.

Learning That Is Not Immediately Observable

Unlike behaviorists, constructivists do not limit the definition of learning to that which is observable behavior. You shouldn't either. Bits and pieces of new information are stored in short-term memory, where the new information is "rehearsed" until ready to be stored in long-term memory. If the information is not rehearsed, it eventually fades from short-term memory. If it is rehearsed and made meaningful through connections with other stored knowledge, then this new knowledge is transferred to and stored in long-term memory either by building existing schemata or by forming new schemata. As a teacher, your responsibility is to provide learning experiences that will result in the creation of new schemata as well as the modification of existing schemata.

To be an effective teacher, the challenge is to use performance-based criteria but simultaneously use a teaching style that encourages the development of intrinsic sources of student motivation, allowing, providing, and encouraging learning that goes beyond what might be considered predictable, immediately measurable, and representative of minimal expectations.

Summary

As you reviewed curriculum documents and student textbooks, you probably found most of them well organized and useful. In your comparison and analyses of courses of study and the teacher's editions of student textbooks, you probably discovered that some are accompanied by sequentially designed resource units from which the teacher can select and build specific teaching units. A resource unit usually consists of an extensive list of objectives, a large number and variety of activities, suggested materials, and extensive bibliographies for teacher and students from which the teacher will select those that best suit his or her needs to build an actual teaching unit.

As you also may have discovered, some courses of study contain actual teaching units that have been prepared by teachers of that particular school district. An important question often asked by beginning teachers, as well as by student teachers, is this: How closely must I follow the school's curriculum guide or course of study? You need the answer before you begin teaching. To obtain that answer, you need to talk with teachers and administrators of that particular school.

In conclusion, your final decisions about what content to teach are guided by all of the following: (a) articles in professional journals; (b) discussions with other teachers; (c) local courses of study and state curriculum documents; (d) the differences, interests, and abilities of your students; and (e) your own personal convictions, knowledge, and skills.

After discovering what you will teach comes the process of preparing the plans. The next two chapters guide you through the planning process. Although teachers' editions of textbooks and other curriculum documents make the process easier, they should never substitute for your own specific planning.

In attempting to blend the best of behaviorism and constructivism, many teachers do not bother to try to write specific objectives for all the learning activities in their teaching plans. Clearly, though, when teachers do prepare specific objectives (by writing them or borrowing from other sources) and teach toward those objectives, student learning is better.

Most school districts require teachers to use objectives that are specifically stated. There is no question that clearly written instructional objectives are worth the time, especially when the teacher teaches toward those objectives and evaluates students' progress and learning against them—that is called *performance-based teaching* or *outcome-based* or *criterion-referenced assessment*. It is not imperative that you write all the instructional objectives that you will need. In fact, many of them are usually already available in textbooks and other curriculum documents.

As a teacher, you should plan specifically what you intend your students to learn, convey your expectations to your students, and then assess their learning against that specificity. There is a danger inherent in such performance-based or criterion-referenced teaching, however. Because it tends toward high objectivity, it could become too objective and thus have negative consequences. The danger is that, if students are treated as objects, the relationship between teacher and student is impersonal and counterproductive to real learning. Highly specific and impersonal teaching can be discouraging to serendipity, creativity, and the excitement for real discovery and meaningful learning. It can also have a negative impact on the development of students' self-esteem.

Performance-based instruction works well when teaching toward mastery of basic skills, but mastery learning often assumes that there is some foreseeable end point to learning—an assumption that is obviously amiss. With performance-based instruction, the source of student motivation tends to be mostly extrinsic. Teacher expectations, grades, society, and peer pressure are examples of extrinsic sources that drive student performance. To be an effective teacher, you must use performance-based criteria but simultaneously use a teaching style that encourages the development of intrinsic sources of student motivation. Your teaching style must allow for, provide for, and encourage coincidental learning—learning that goes beyond the predictable and immediately measurable and that represents minimal expectations. Part 3 is designed to assist you in meeting that challenge.

Now, with your content outline (Exercise 5.5) and instructional objectives (Exercise 5.11) in hand, you are ready to prepare detailed instructional plans, which are discussed in Chapters 6 and 7.

Examining National Curriculum Standards

Instructions: The purpose of this exercise is for you to become familiar with the national curriculum standards for various subjects of the K–12 curriculum. Using the addresses of sources provided in Figure 5.1 on national curriculum standards and other sources, such as professional journals, review the standards for your subject or subjects. Use the following questions as a guideline for small- or large-group class discussions. Following small-group subject-area discussion, share the developments in each field with the rest of the class.

Subject Area

1. Name of the standards document reviewed:

2. Year of document publication:

3. Developed by:

4. Precise K–12 goals specified by the new standards:

5. Are the standards specific as to subject matter content for each grade level? Explain.

6. Do the standards offer specific strategies for instruction? Describe.

7. Do the standards offer suggestions for teaching children who are culturally and linguistically diverse and/or who are students with special needs? Describe.

8. Do the standards offer suggestions or guidelines for dealing with controversial topics?

9. Do the standards offer suggestions for specific resources? Describe.

10. Do the standards refer to assessment? Describe.

11. In summary, compared with what has been taught and how it has been taught in this field, what is new with the standards?

12. Is there anything else about the standards you would like to discuss in your group?

Examining State Curriculum Documents

Instructions: The purpose of this exercise is for you to become familiar with curriculum documents published by your state department of education. You must determine if that department publishes a curriculum framework for various subjects taught in schools. State frameworks provide valuable information about both content and process, and teachers need to be aware of these documents. You may want to duplicate this form so that you can use it to evaluate several documents. After examining documents that interest you, use the following questions as a guideline for small- or large-group class discussions.

1. Are there state curriculum documents available to teachers in your state? If so, describe them and explain how they can be obtained.
   Title of document:
   Source:
   Most recent year of publication:
   Other pertinent information:

2. Examine how closely the document follows the eight components presented in this chapter. Are any components omitted? Are there additional components? Specifically, check for these components:

		Yes	No
2.1	Statement of philosophy?	_____	_____
2.2	Evidence of a needs assessment?	_____	_____
2.3	Aims, goals, and objectives?	_____	_____
2.4	Schemes for vertical articulation (sequence)?	_____	_____
2.5	Schemes for horizontal articulation (scope)?	_____	_____
2.6	Recommended instructional procedures?	_____	_____
2.7	Recommended resources?	_____	_____
2.8	Assessment strategies?	_____	_____
2.9	Other:	_____	_____

3. Are the documents specific as to subject matter content for each grade level? Describe evidence of both vertical and horizontal articulation schemes.

4. Do the documents offer specific strategies for instruction? If yes, describe.

(continued)

Exercise 5.2 **Examining State Curriculum Documents** *continued*

5. Do the documents offer suggestions and resources for working with culturally and linguistically diverse students, for students with special needs, and for students who are intellectually gifted and talented? Describe.

6. Do the documents offer suggestions or guidelines for dealing with controversial topics? If so, describe.

7. Do the documents distinguish between what shall be taught (mandated) and what can be taught (permissible)?

8. Do the documents offer suggestions for specific resources?

9. Do the documents refer to assessment strategies? Describe.

10. Is there anything else about the documents you would like to discuss in your group?

Exercise
5.3 **Examining Local Curriculum Documents**

Instructions: The purpose of this exercise is for you to become familiar with curriculum documents prepared by local school districts. A primary resource for what to teach is referred to as a *curriculum guide*, or *course of study*, which normally is developed by teachers of a school or district. Samples may be available in your university library or in a local school district resource center. Or perhaps you could borrow them from teachers you visit. Obtain samples from a variety of sources and then examine them using the format of this exercise. (You may duplicate this form for each document examined.) An analysis of several documents will give you a good picture of expectations. If possible, compare documents from several schools, districts, and states.

Title of document:
District or school:
Date of document:

1. Examine how closely the documents follow the eight components. Does the document contain the following components?

	Yes	No
1.1 Statement of philosophy?	_____	_____
1.2 Evidence of a needs assessment?	_____	_____
1.3 Aims, goals, and objectives?	_____	_____
1.4 Schemes for vertical articulation (sequence)?	_____	_____
1.5 Schemes for horizontal articulation (scope)?	_____	_____
1.6 Recommended instructional procedures?	_____	_____
1.7 Recommended resources?	_____	_____
1.8 Assessment strategies?	_____	_____

2. Does the document list expected learning outcomes? If so, describe what they are.

3. Does the document contain detailed unit plans? If so, describe them by answering the following questions:
   3.1 Do they contain initiating activities (how to begin a unit)?
   3.2 Do they contain specific learning activities?
   3.3 Do they contain suggested enrichment activities (as for gifted and talented students)?
   3.4 Do they contain culminating activities (activities that bring a unit to a climax)?
   3.5 Do they contain assessment (for determining student achievement)?
   3.6 Do they contain activities for learners with special needs? For learners who are different in other respects?

4. Does the document provide bibliographic entries for
   ■ The teacher?
   ■ The students?

5. Does the document list audiovisual and other materials needed?

6. Does the document help you clearly understand what the teacher is expected to teach?

7. Are there questions not answered by your examination of this document? If so, list them for class discussion.

Exercise
5.4

Examining Student Textbooks and Teacher's Editions

Instructions: The purpose of this exercise is for you to become familiar with textbooks that you may be using in your teaching. Student textbooks are usually accompanied by a teacher's edition that contains specific objectives, teaching techniques, learning activities, assessment instruments, test items, and suggested resources. Your university library, local schools, and cooperating teachers are sources for locating and borrowing these enhanced textbooks. For your subject field of interest, select a textbook that is accompanied by a teacher's edition and examine the contents of both using the following format. If there are no standard textbooks available for your teaching field (such as might be the case for art, home economics, industrial arts, music, and physical education), then select a field in which there is a possibility you might teach. Beginning teachers are often assigned to teach in more than one field—sometimes, unfortunately, in fields for which they are untrained or have only minimal training. After completion of this exercise, share the book and your analysis of it with your classmates.

Title of book:
Author(s):
Publisher:
Date of most recent publication:

1. Analyze the teacher's edition for the following elements.

	Yes	No
a. Are its goals consistent with the goals of local and state curriculum documents?	_____	_____
b. Are there specific objectives for each lesson?	_____	_____
c. Does the book have scope and sequence charts for teacher reference?	_____	_____
d. Are the units and lessons sequentially developed, with suggested time allotments?	_____	_____
e. Are there any suggested provisions for individual differences?		
For reading levels?	_____	_____
For students with special needs?	_____	_____
For students who are gifted and talented?	_____	_____
For students who have limited proficiency in English?	_____	_____
f. Does it recommend specific techniques and strategies?	_____	_____
g. Does it have listings of suggested aids, materials, and resources?	_____	_____
h. Are there suggestions for extension activities (to extend the lessons beyond the usual topic or time)?	_____	_____
i. Does the book have specific guidelines for assessment of student learning?	_____	_____

2. Analyze the student textbook for the following elements.

	Yes	No
a. Does the textbook treat the content with adequate depth?	_____	_____
b. Does the textbook treat ethnic minorities and women fairly?*	_____	_____
c. Is the format attractive?	_____	_____
d. Does the textbook have good-quality binding with suitable type size?	_____	_____
e. Are illustrations and visuals attractive and useful?	_____	_____
f. Is the reading clear and understandable for the students?	_____	_____

3. Would you like to use this textbook? Give reasons why or why not.

*For a detailed procedure that is more specific to subject areas, see Carl A. Grant and Christine E. Sleeter, *Turning on Learning: Five Approaches for Multicultural Teaching Plans for Race, Class, Gender, and Disability* (Upper Saddle River, NJ: Prentice Hall, 1989), 104–9.

Preparing a Content Outline

Instructions: The purpose of this exercise is for you to organize your ideas about subject content and the sequencing of content. Unless instructed otherwise by your instructor, you should select the subject (e.g., algebra I, biology, English, U.S. history) and the grade level (7–12).

With *three levels of headings* (see the example that follows), prepare a sequential topic outline (on a separate piece of paper as space is not provided here) for a subject and grade level you intend to teach. Identify the subject by title and clearly state the grade level. This outline is of topic content only and does not need to include student activities associated with the learning of that content (i.e., do not include experiments, assignments, or assessment strategies). For example, for the study of earth science, three levels of headings might include the following:

I. Earth's surface
 A. Violent changes in Earth's surface
  1. Earthquakes
  2. Volcanoes
 B. Earth's land surface
  1. Rocks
and so forth.

If the study of earth science was just one unit for a grade level's study of the broader area of science, then three levels of headings for that study might include the following:

I. Earth science
 A. Earth's surface
  1. Violent changes in Earth's surface
and so forth.

Share your completed outline to obtain feedback from your classmates and university instructor. Because content outlines are never to be carved in stone, make adjustments to your outline when and as appropriate.

Here are some content outline evaluation guidelines:

- Does the outline follow a logical sequence, with each topic logically leading to the next?
- Does the content assume prerequisite knowledge or skills that the students are likely to have?
- Is the content inclusive and to an appropriate depth?
- Does the content consider individual student differences?
- Does the content allow for interdisciplinary studies?
- Are there serious content omissions?
- Is there content that is of questionable value for this level of instruction?

Save this completed exercise for later when you are working on Exercise 5.7.

Dealing with Controversial Content and Issues

Instructions: The purpose of this exercise is for you to discover controversial content and issues that you may face as a teacher in your specific content area and to consider what you can and will do about them. After completing this exercise, share it with members of your class who intend to teach the same subject as you.

1. After studying current periodicals and talking with colleagues in the schools you visit, list two potentially controversial topics that you are likely to encounter as a teacher of your subject. (Two examples are given for you.)

Issue	Source
Intelligent Design	*National Center for Science Education,* September 2002
Why Human Cloning Is Wrong	*Singularity High School Science Journal,* June 2006

2. Take one of these issues and identify opposing arguments and current resources.

3. Identify your own position on this issue.

4. How well can you accept students (and parents or guardians) who assume the opposite position?

5. Share the preceding with other teacher candidates. Note comments that you find helpful or enlightening.

Exercise
5.7

Recognizing Verbs That Are Acceptable for Overt Objectives—A Self-Check Exercise

Instructions: The purpose of this exercise is for you to check your recognition of verbs that are suitable for use in overt behavioral objectives. From the following list of verbs, circle those that *should not* be used in overt objectives—that is, those verbs that describe covert behaviors that are not directly observable and measurable. Check your answers against the answer key found on page 360. Discuss any problems with the exercise with your classmates and instructor.

1. apply	2. appreciate	3. believe
4. combine	5. comprehend	6. compute
7. create	8. define	9. demonstrate
10. describe	11. design	12. diagram
13. enjoy	14. explain	15. familiarize
16. grasp*	17. identify	18. illustrate
19. indicate	20. infer	21. know
22. learn	23. name	24. outline
25. predict	26. realize	27. select
28. solve	29. state	30. understand

*Words in English often have multiple meanings. For example, *grasp* as listed here could mean "to take hold," or it could mean "to comprehend." For the former, it would be an acceptable verb for use in overt objectives; for the latter, it would not.

Exercise
5.8

Recognizing the Parts of Criterion-Referenced Behavioral Objectives—A Self-Check Exercise

Instructions: The purpose of this exercise is to practice your skill in recognizing the four components of a behavioral objective. In the following two objectives, identify the parts of the objectives by underlining once the *audience*, twice the *behavior*, three times the *conditions*, and four times the *performance level* (degree or standard of performance). Check against the answer key found on page 360; discuss any problems with your classmates and instructor.

1. You will write a 500-word account of the battle between the forces of Gondor and its allies against those of Mordor and its allies, as related in *The Lord of the Rings*, completely from memory. This account will be accurate in all basic details and include all the important incidents of the battle.

2. Given an interurban bus schedule, at the end of the lesson the student will be able to read the schedule well enough to determine at what time buses are scheduled to leave randomly selected points, with at least 90% accuracy.

Exercise
5.9

Recognizing Objectives That Are Measurable—A Self-Check Exercise

Instructions: The purpose of this exercise is to assess your skill in recognizing measurable objectives—those stated in behavioral terms. Place a check before each of the following that is a student-centered behavioral objective or a learning objective that is clearly measurable. Although the audience, conditions, and degree of the ABCD structure may be absent, ask yourself, "As stated, is it a student-centered and measurable objective?" If it is, then place a check in the blank. An answer key found on page 360. After checking your answers, discuss any problems with your classmates and instructor.

____√____ 1. The students will understand that the basic issue that resulted in secession was the extension of slavery.

_____ 2. Digestion is the chemical change of foods into particles that can be absorbed.

_____ 3. To explain what an acid is and what an acid's properties are.

_____ 4. Introduction to vector qualities and their use.

____√____ 5. The students will be able to convert Celsius temperatures to Fahrenheit temperatures.

(continued)

Exercise 5.9   **Recognizing Objectives That Are Measurable—A Self-Check Exercise** *continued*

_____ ✓ **6.** The students will understand that vibrating bodies provide the source of all sounds and sound waves.

_____ ✓ **7.** At the end of the lesson, with at least 90% accuracy, the students will be able to read a bus schedule well enough to determine at what time buses are scheduled to arrive at and leave from designated stations.

_____ ✓ **8.** Given a number of quadratic equations with one unknown, the students will be able to solve the equations correctly in 80% of the cases.

_____ ✓ **9.** The students will appreciate the problems faced by those who have emigrated from Southeast Asia to the United States.

_____ **10.** A study of the external features and internal organs of the frog through video films of dissections.

_____ **11.** To discuss the reasons why the field of philosophy was well developed by the ancient Greeks.

_____ **12.** Animals' physical adaptation to their environments.

Exercise
5.10

Assessing Recognition of Objectives According to Domain—A Self-Check Exercise

Instructions: The purpose of this exercise is for you to assess your ability to recognize objectives according to their domains. Classify each of the following instructional objectives by writing in the blank space the appropriate letter according to its domain: *C* = cognitive, *A* = affective, *P* = psychomotor. Check your answers with the key found on page 360, and then discuss the results with your classmates and instructor.

_____ **1.** The student will continue shooting free throws until the student can successfully complete 80% of the attempts.

_____ **2.** The student will identify on a map the mountain ranges of the eastern United States.

_____ **3.** The student will summarize the historical development of the Democratic Party of the United States.

_____ **4.** The student will demonstrate a continuing desire to learn more about using the classroom computer for word processing by volunteering to work at it during free time.

_____ **5.** The student will volunteer to tidy up the storage room.

_____ **6.** After listening to several recordings, the student will identify the respective composers.

_____ **7.** The student will translate a favorite Cambodian poem into English.

_____ **8.** The student will accurately calculate the length of the hypotenuse.

_____ **9.** The student will indicate an interest in the subject by voluntarily reading additional library books about earthquakes.

_____ **10.** The student will write and perform a piano concerto.

Exercise
5.11

Preparing My Own Instructional Objectives

Instructions: The purpose of this exercise is for you to begin the construction of objectives for your own teaching. For a subject content and grade level of your choice (perhaps from your content outline in Exercise 5.5), prepare 10 specific objectives. (Audience, conditions, and performance level are not necessary unless requested by your course instructor.) Exchange completed exercises with your classmates, and then discuss and make changes where necessary.

Subject field: Grade level:

1. Cognitive knowledge:

2. Cognitive comprehension:

3. Cognitive application:

4. Cognitive analysis:

5. Cognitive synthesis:

6. Cognitive evaluation:

7. Affective (low level):

8. Affective (highest level):

9. Psychomotor (low level):

10. Psychomotor (highest level):

Chapter 5 POSTTEST

Short Explanation

1. When you have prepared a course topic outline, how will you know if the content of that outline is appropriate content for the subject and grade level for which the outline is intended?

2. Explain the intent of having national and Common Core Standards for each core subject taught in public schools. Who prepared these standards in your field? For your subject field, what are some of the major features that distinguish the standards from traditional teaching of that subject?

3. Explain how a textbook can be helpful to a student's learning in your discipline. How might reliance on a single textbook be a hindrance to student learning?

4. Give an example of a covert learning objective from your teaching field and describe how you would decide whether a student had reached the objective.

5. Identify the three levels of planning for which a classroom teacher is responsible.

Essay

1. It is sometimes said that teaching less can be better. Think back to your own schooling. What do you really remember? Do you remember lectures and worksheets, or do you remember projects, your presentations, the lengthy research you did, and your extra effort for artwork to accompany your presentation? Maybe you remember a compliment by a teacher or a pat on the back by peers. Most likely, you do not remember the massive amount of content that was covered. Write a one-page essay expressing and defending your agreement or disagreement with the original statement of this paragraph.

2. Do you believe that your students should have input in the planning of a course? Explain why or why not.

3. Describe the meaning of the term *quality education* as it relates to your teaching field.

4. From your current observations and fieldwork as related to this teacher preparation program, clearly identify one specific example of educational practice that seems contradictory to exemplary practice or theory as presented in this chapter. Present your explanation for the discrepancy.

5. Describe any prior concepts you held that changed as a result of your experiences with this chapter. Describe the changes.

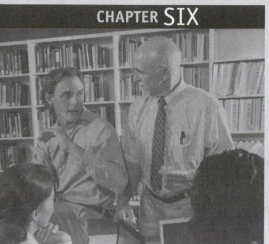
Shutterstock

CHAPTER SIX

Course Syllabi, Instructional Units, and Curriculum Integration

This important work of several decades ago, as well as much of what has since been in the forefront of educational thought, stresses the importance of teachers finding ways to make subject matter relevant to students, to involve students in setting their own goals, to vary the ways of learning to use approaches that employ all of the senses, and to be sure that there are opportunities for relating the knowledge to experiences or actually using it.[1]

—JOHN I. GOODLAD

Specific Objectives

At the completion of this chapter, you will be able to:

▸ Explain the levels and steps involved in planning for instruction.

▸ Design a course syllabus and/or a disclosure document.

▸ Describe why curriculum mapping is effective and prepare a curriculum map for your discipline.

▸ Develop different types of instructional units.

▸ Explain the characteristics, usefulness, and general procedures for developing an interdisciplinary thematic unit of instruction.

Chapter 6 Overview

Having prepared a topic content outline (Exercise 5.5) and related instructional objectives (Exercise 5.11), you have begun development of an instructional plan. This chapter and Chapter 7 are designed to acquaint you with the basic components and procedures necessary for developing effective units and lessons. Although the teacher's edition of the student textbook and other resource materials will expedite your planning, this should not substitute for it. You must know how to create a good instructional plan. In this chapter, you will learn about different types of instructional plans and the basics of how to plan and develop several types of units of instruction. With that knowledge, you will start to develop an instructional plan with daily lessons. In Chapter 7, you will explore in more detail how to prepare individual lesson plans and learn specifically how to create a unit plan.

Introduction

Seldom, if ever, can a teacher enter a classroom of students unprepared or underprepared and yet teach effectively. Spur-of-the-moment teaching rarely results in dynamic, meaningful, logically presented lessons from which students develop a clear understanding of knowledge, skills, or concepts. Such lessons require careful thought and preparation. The teacher must decide which aspects of the subject should be the focus of each lesson, how a topic should be adapted to a particular group of students, how a lesson should build on preceding lessons, and how a lesson should prepare students for lessons to come. Without careful attention to these matters, lessons tend to be dull, drifting aimlessly toward no good purpose. Here we will discuss the lesson-writing process and various types of units.

Planning for Instruction: A Three-Level and Seven-Step Process

As introduced at the beginning of Chapter 5, complete planning for instruction occurs at three levels—the semester or year, the units, and the daily lessons. There are seven steps in the planning process. This section identifies and describes each of those steps. Some of the planning guidelines that follow were addressed previously and are included here to show you where they fit in the seven-step planning procedure.

The seven steps of instructional planning involve the following:

1. *Course, grade level, and school goals.* Consider and understand your curriculum goals and their relationship to the mission and goals of the school. Your course does not exist in isolation but is an integral part of the total school curriculum.

2. *Expectations.* Consider topics and skills that you are expected to teach, such as those found in the course of study (Chapter 5).

3. *Academic year, semester, or trimester plan.* Think about the goals that you want the students to reach months from now. Working from your tentative topic outline and with the school calendar in hand, you will begin by deciding how much time should be devoted to each topic (or unit), penciling those times onto the outline. (Unless you are doing your planning at a computer, we suggest pencil because you will probably modify these many times.)

4. *Course schedule.* This schedule becomes a part of the course syllabus that you can present to students at the start of the school year. However, the schedule must remain flexible to allow for the unexpected, such as the cancellation or interruption of a class meeting or the extended study of a particular topic.

5. *Plans for each class meeting.* Working from the calendar plan or the course schedule, you are now ready to prepare plans for each class meeting, keeping in mind the abilities and interests of your students while making decisions about appropriate strategies and learning experiences. (Strategies are the focus of Part 3.) The preparation of daily plans takes considerable time and continues throughout the year as you arrange and prepare instructional notes, demonstrations, discussion topics and questions, and classroom exercises as well as arrange for guest speakers, audiovisual materials and media equipment, field trips, and tools for the assessment of student learning. Because the content of each class meeting is often determined by the accomplishments of and your reflections on the preceding one, your lessons are never "set in concrete" but need continual revisiting and assessment by you.

6. *Instructional objectives.* Once you have the finalized schedule and as you prepare the daily plans, you will complete your preparation of the instructional objectives (begun in Exercise 5.11). These instructional objectives are critical for proper development of the next and final step.

7. *Assessment.* The final step is to decide how to assess student achievement. Included in this component are your decisions about how you will accomplish diagnostic assessment or **preassessment** (assessment of what students know or think they know at the start of a new unit of study or a new topic), *formative assessment* (ongoing assessment during a unit of study on what the students are learning), and *summative assessment* (assessment of learning at the conclusion of a unit of study on what the students learned). Also included in the assessment component are your decisions about assignments and the grading procedures (discussed in Chapter 11).

You will proceed through these steps as you develop your first instructional plan. Before we get into that, consider the nature of the course syllabus.

The Syllabus

A syllabus is a written statement of information about the workings of a particular class or course. As a student in postsecondary education, you have seen a variety of syllabi written by professors, each with their individual ideas about what general and specific logistic information is most important for students to know about a course. The syllabi from your college courses serve as contracts of sorts laying out expectations. Not all public school teachers use a course syllabus, but many do, at least as described and illustrated here. Therefore, we will explore the use of syllabi in this discussion. In addition to using a syllabus with their students, middle- and secondary-level teachers may also use the syllabus to highlight what is covered in their course when they meet with parents. Still other teachers use a modified version of their syllabus as a disclosure document, a contract of sorts, with their students and their students' parents.

We believe that teachers should at least cover this information with their students even if they do not distribute a syllabus to their classes. Related to that belief are several questions that are answered next: Why should teachers prepare a syllabus? What purpose does it fulfill? How do I develop one? Can students have input into its contents and participate in its development? Where do I start? What information should be included? How rigidly should it be followed?

Use and Development of a Syllabus and/or Disclosure Document

The syllabus and/or disclosure document contains information about the class or course and is usually presented to students on the first day or during the first week of school. It may also be reviewed in class and in parent-teacher meetings and require signatures from students and parents or guardians. Often the disclosure document is just an abridged version of the syllabus. (See the samples shown in Figures 6.1 through 6.6) The syllabus and/or disclosure document may be developed completely by you or in collaboration with colleagues. The sample advanced placement biology syllabus and disclosure document (see Figures 6.1 and 6.2, respectively) were developed by a team of biology teachers at Bozeman High School in Bozeman, Montana. Both are stellar educators. Paul Anderson was recently named the 2011 Montana Teacher of the Year by the Montana Professional Teaching Foundation and was selected as a national finalist by a panel of educators from 14 large U.S. education organizations. His colleague, Scott Taylor, won the 2007 Distinguished Educator Award, Bozeman Public Schools. You can read about their teaching at **http://www.ccsso.**

org/Documents/NTOY/Applications/2011NTOYfinMTapp.pdf. The advanced placement psychology syllabus and disclosure document were designed by an individual instructor, Joyce Jarosz Hannula (see Figures 6.3 and 6.4, respectively), as were the sixth-grade geography syllabus, designed by Anastasia Sunday, and the geometry syllabus, designed by Paula Maguire, both of which serve as the course syllabus and disclosure document for their respective courses (see Figures 6.5 and 6.6). Be sure to note the varying levels of specificity included in the different samples. Compare and contrast the documents created for use with middle school and high school students. Also, check out the lesson plans that both Joyce Jarosz Hannula (Lesson Plan 7.11) and Anastasia Sunday (Lesson Plan 7.2) contributed.

Figure 6.1 Advanced Placement (AP®) Biology Course Syllabus

Philosophy

Our AP® Biology course aims to develop a student's understanding of basic biological concepts and to develop a scientific vocabulary that allows them to communicate these concepts. We also enable students to apply the scientific process in solving problems and encourage students to become critical thinkers that can challenge assumption, process, and conclusion. The course also aids in the preparation for college-level study and the AP® Biology exam to be held in May.

Course Overview

Our AP® Biology course conforms to the standards instituted by the College Board for all AP courses and covers all of the topics in the AP Biology Course Description. The course emphasizes the biological concepts as specified in the three overarching topics listed in the Topic Outline in the Course Description:

- Molecules and Cells (25%; Units 1–3)—biochemistry, cells, energy transformations.
- Heredity and Evolution (25%; Units 4–6)—heredity, molecular genetics, evolution.
- Organisms and Populations (50%; Units 7–11)—taxonomy, plant structure and function, animal structure and function, embryology and development, behavior, ecology.

Texts

The textbook for the course is the fifth edition of Neil A. Campbell and Jane B. Reece's Biology. Students also use the AP Biology Lab Manual for Students. Additional labs are teacher-generated or come from other sources.

Course Planner

The two major goals of our AP® Biology class are to help students develop a conceptual framework for biology and an appreciation for science as a process. We organize our class into the following eleven units. **Evolution** is the foundation of modern biological thought and it therefore is found through each of the following units of study.

Unit 1: Intro and Biochemistry

Unit 2: Cell Biology

Unit 3: Cellular Energetics

Unit 4: Mendelian Genetics

Unit 5: Molecular Genetics

Unit 6: Evolutionary Biology

Unit 7: Diversity of Life

Unit 8: Animal Structure/Function I

Unit 9: Animal Structure/Function II

Unit 10: Plants

Unit 11: Ecology

Each unit integrates the eight major themes described in the AP Course Description.

We especially emphasize the importance of evolution as a unifying theme within the life sciences. Unit 6 (Evolutionary Biology) integrates the following themes within the curriculum.

Theme 1—Science as Process—The students will study the work of Charles Darwin to better understand that the theory of natural selection was developed through experimentation and observation.

Theme 2—Evolution—The students will study natural selection to better understand that the widespread use of antibiotics has selected for antibiotic resistance in disease-causing bacteria.

Theme 3—Energy Transfer—The students will understand that complex organisms evolved from simpler ancestors as islands of low entropy in an increasingly random universe without violating the second law of thermodynamics.

Theme 4—Continuity and Change—The students will understand that evidence of evolution as genetic change pervades biology.

Theme 5—Relationship of Structure to Function—The students will understand that functional structure occurs at all biological levels. For example the folded inner membrane of a mitochondria and the folded gills of a fish increase the surface area.

Theme 6—Regulation—The students will understand that many regulatory mechanisms, such as thermoregulation, have evolved in humans to help maintain homeostasis.

Theme 7—Interdependence in Nature—The students will understand that symbiosis is one of the driving evolutionary mechanisms in the living world.

Theme 8—Science, Technology and Society—The students will understand that as we continue to alter the global environment, through deforestation, the resulting extinctions will rival that at the end of the Cretaceous period.

(continued)

Figure 6.1 **Advanced Placement (AP®) Biology Course Syllabus**   *continued*

Schedule

Unit	Unit Description	Topics Covered	Reading	Activities
1	Intro and Biochemistry (13 class periods)	Intro to AP Biology Scientific method Intro to biochemistry Water Carbon chemistry Biochemistry Metabolism Enzymes	1–9 9–19 22–33 37–45 48–55 58–79 83–88 88–97	AP Lab 11—Animal behavior Molecular Modeling AP Lab 1—Enzyme Catalysis
2	Cell Biology (13 class periods)	Cell anatomy Membrane structure Cell cycle and mitosis	100–127 130–143 206–213	Organelle presentations Cell microscopy lab AP Lab 2—Osmosis AP Lab 3a—Mitosis
3	Cellular Energetics (10 class periods)	Respiration Photosynthesis	147–165 168–184	AP Lab 4—Respiration AP Lab 5—Photosynthesis
4	Mendelian Genetics (12 class periods)	Meiosis Mendelian theory Chromosomes DNA	224–237 239–258 261–275 278–290	AP Lab 3b—Meiosis AP Lab 7—Genetics of organisms
5	Molecular Genetics (15 class periods)	Transcription Translation Viral structure Bacterial genetics Eukaryotic genetics DNA Technology	294–304 304–314 319–329 330–337 344–358 364–385	 Protein folding of *Trp* cage AP Lab 6a—Transformation AP Lab 6b—Electrophoresis DNA Technology presentations
6	Evolutionary Biology (13 class periods)	Intro to evolution Population genetics Speciation Phylogeny Life Origins	412–425 428–442 445–460 464–485 488–498	 AP Lab 8—Population Genetics Camouflage lab Shoe cladistics
7	Diversity of Life (12 class periods)	Prokaryotes Eukaryotic diversity Fungi Animal evolution Invertebrates Vertebrates	502–517 520–540 574–587 589–596 599–626 630–658	Microscopy (prepared slides) Fungi observation lab Diversity presentations
8	Animal Structure/Function I (16 class periods)	Structure/function Nutrition Circulation Immune system Excretory system	776–789 792–808 811–836 840–859 865–889	Tissue microscopy AP Lab 10—Physiology of circulatory system Lung volume activity Immunity comic strip
9	Animal Structure/Function II (16 class periods)	Chemical signals Animal reproduction Animal development Nervous systems Sensory and motor systems	893–910 912–933 936–954 960–984 992–1018	Nerve speed calculation Sense of smell lab
10	Plants (10 class periods)	Plant diversity Plant structure Transport in plants Plant control systems	546–571 670–689 695–710 751–773	AP Lab 9—Transpiration Flower dissection
11	Ecology (12 class periods)	Intro to ecology Behavioral biology Population ecology Community ecology Ecosystems Conservation biology	1026–1049 1053–1078 1082–1101 1107–1126 1131–1150 1154–1170	AP Lab 12—Dissolved oxygen and aquatic primary productivity

Figure 6.1 **Advanced Placement (AP®) Biology Course Syllabus** *continued*

Teaching Strategies

Detailed outlines of the material covered in each unit are provided to the students at the beginning of the school year through access to our AP Biology website. Students are encouraged to add additional information to the outlines during the lecture component of the classroom. **A sample lecture outline is included below.** PowerPoint presentations of each unit contain outlines of the material as well as diagrams, animations, and videos that help to further explain the material. Classroom discussion is also a very important portion of the lecture component.

Students are not required to take the AP Biology examination in the spring but most of them end up taking the test. A number of teacher strategies are used throughout the year to adequately prepare for the test.

–Unit tests contain a mix of multiple-choice and free response questions that are very similar to those found on the AP Biology Exam.

–Free response questions are graded on a 10-point scale identical to the scale used on the AP Biology Exam.

–Students are encouraged to use AP review websites and test preparation books to prepare for the AP Biology Exam in the spring.

–Extra review sessions are added in the spring to adequately prepare for the exam.

Each topic of every unit has an assigned reading section. Homework questions are used to detail the important concepts within each of these reading sections. Additional videos and DVDs are used to supplement the material within the textbook. Students work in groups to give presentations on recent advances in DNA technology. Students give group presentations on topics such as gel electrophoresis and the Sanger method of DNA sequencing that serve as the primary lecture device during the unit on molecular genetics.

Lab Component

The important theme of science as a process is re-emphasized during the laboratory section of the class. The scientific method is used in most of the laboratories as a guide to planning and executing a proper laboratory. Laboratories account for roughly 25% of the time in AP Biology.

We use inquiry laboratories whenever possible to force the students to properly apply sound scientific methodology. We have modified virtually all of the AP Labs as found in the AP Lab Manual so that they are much more student-designed, rather than procedural. Once students are given a basic protocol, they design their own procedures and independent variables to test. We hope that students gain an appreciation for the scientific process through a continuous emphasis on *supporting* hypotheses, rather than *proving* them. Critical discussion of causation versus correlation is also a major theme in our lab activities.

The lab write-ups include the following components:

I. **Problem** (defined as a question)
II. **Hypothesis** (if ... then format, taking into account changes in variables)
III. **Identification of independent variable** (what is being manipulated, including relevant units)
IV. **Identification of dependent variable** (what is being measured, including relevant units)
V. **Controlled variables** (several required—what, if not held constant, could affect the dependent variable)
VI. **Procedure** (detailed and repeatable; addresses all variables: independent, dependent, controlled)
VII. **Results** (data effectively compiled in table format, relevant calculations if applicable)

VIII. **Graph(s)** (proper format, trends noted, slope calculated if applicable)
IX. **Conclusion/analysis** (addresses original stated problem, explains findings—addressing concepts of the activity, statistical analysis if applicable, sampling error addressed)

An example of our modified version of the Osmosis and Diffusion lab has been included at the bottom of this document.

Lab Schedule

Unit 1

• AP Lab 11—Animal Behavior—Students use choice chambers and pill bugs to study animal behavior. Students also use the scientific method to study the effect of their own independent variable on pill bug choice.

• Molecular modeling—Students use molecular modeling kits to build simple organic molecules.

• AP Lab 1—Enzyme Catalysis—Students use catalase, hydrogen peroxide and discs of filter paper to study the effects of catalase concentration on reaction rate. Students are given basic instructions on protocol and measurement techniques, but are required to choose their own independent variables and to consider such procedural components as sample size.

Unit 2

• Cell microscopy lab—Students use microscopes to observe and sketch human cheek cells.

• AP Lab 2—Osmosis—Students complete AP Lab 2 "Osmosis and Diffusion" (see attached).

• AP Lab 3a—Mitosis—Students complete AP Lab 3a "Mitosis" using onion mitosis slides.

Unit 3

• AP Lab 4—Respiration—Students complete AP Lab 4. Earthworms are also added to one of the respirometers.

• AP Lab 5—Photosynthesis—Students use discs cut from leaves to study the effects of many variables on the rate of photosynthesis.

Unit 4

• AP Lab 3b—Meiosis—Students complete AP Lab 3b "Meiosis." Due to continual problems with the *Sordaria* culture involved, we use several photographs of parentheca.

• AP Lab 7—Genetics of Organisms—Students complete AP Lab 7 "Genetics of Organisms." Data is given to the students for this section as the actual breeding consumes too much time.

Unit 5

• Protein folding of Trp cage—Students transcribe and transform an actual protein that is found in the saliva of a Gila monster. Flexible noodles are used to model the protein.

• AP Lab 6a—Transformation—Students use pGlo to transform E.Coli bacteria.

• AP Lab 6b—Electrophoresis—Students complete AP Lab 6b.

Unit 6

• AP Lab 8—Population Genetics—Students use different colored beads to complete AP Lab 8.

• Camouflage Lab—Students model natural selection using colored disks of paper on the floor of the science lab. **Evolution** occurs as the number of disks which blend in with the floor increase over time.

(continued)

Figure 6.1 **Advanced Placement (AP®) Biology Course Syllabus** *continued*

- Shoe classification—Students classify shoes from their class-mates using a dichotomous key.

Unit 7

- Microscopy—Students view prepared slides of diversity of prokaryotic and eukaryotic life.
- Fungi—Students observe and then sketch mushrooms and fungal spores.
- Diversity presentations—Students prepare visual models and give classroom presentations on individual phylum or class within the diversity of life.

Unit 8

- Tissue lab—Students observe and sketch representative slides of major human tissues.
- AP Lab 10—Students complete AP Lab 10 "Physiology of Circulatory System" and study the effect of temperature on respiration rate in goldfish.
- Lung volume—Students calculate individual vital lung capacities and compare with various student characteristics to determine possible correlations.

Unit 10

- AP Lab 9—Transpiration—Students complete AP Lab 9 "Leaf Transpiration."

Unit 11

- AP Lab 12—Dissolved Oxygen—Students complete AP Lab 12 using a nearby creek.

Student Evaluation

Students are evaluated on their performance on unit tests, homework, projects and laboratory write-ups. Unit tests account for roughly 50% of their grade in AP Biology and consist of multiple-choice and free response questions. The remainder of a student's grade in AP Biology is based on his or her performance on homework assignments, projects, and laboratories, which vary for each unit of study.

Sample Lecture Outline

Evolution Unit Outline
Descent with Modification: A Darwinian View of Life
Types of Evolution

- Microevolution—population changes
  –Generation to generation
- Macroevolution—population changes
  –Over geologic time

Pre-Darwin History

- Aristotle
- Natural Theology
- Taxonomy—Linnaeus
- Catastrophism—Cuvier
- Gradualism—Hutton
- Jean-Baptiste Lamarck

  –Blacksmith arm
  –Stretching giraffe necks

The Darwinian Revolution

- The Voyage of the Beagle
- Charles Lyell's *Principles of Geology*
- Alfred Wallace
- *The Origin of Species*

Natural Selection—Darwin's Observations

1. Species could overpopulate
2. Population sizes remain stable.
3. Resources are limited.
4. No two individuals are alike.
5. Much of the variation is heritable.

Microevolution
Evidence for Evolution

- Biogeography
- The Fossil Record
- Comparative Anatomy
  –Homologous structures
- Comparative Embryology
- Molecular Biology

Descent with Modification
"Evolution is just a theory."
The Evolution of Populations
Individuals are selected, but populations evolve.
Darwin's Natural Selection + Mendel's Genetics = Modern Synthesis
Population Genetics

- Population—localized group of individuals
  –Same species.
- Species—individuals can interbreed and produce fertile offspring.
- Gene Pool—all of the genes in a population.

Hardy-Weinberg Theorem

- The frequency of alleles in a population will remain constant in normal mating.
- If p and q are the frequencies of alleles.
- Then $p^2 + 2pq + q^2 = 1$

  –p^2 and q^2 are homozygous
  –pq are heterozygous

Hardy-Weinberg Equilibrium

- The frequency of alleles in a population will remain constant in normal mating UNLESS ... The Population is Evolving.
- Microevolution—generation to generation change in a population's alleles.

The Five Causes of Microevolution

1. Genetic Drift—changes in a small population due to chance.
   –Bottleneck effect
   –Founder effect
2. Gene Flow—migration of individuals/genes
3. Mutations—change in organism's DNA
4. Nonrandom Mating—inbreeding or assortative mating.
5. Natural Selection—differential success in reproduction.

Genetic Variation in Populations

- Within populations
  –Polymorphism
    - Garter Snakes
    - Blood Types
- Between Populations

  –Geographical variation
    - Cline—graded changes

Polymorphism
Genetic Variation
Creating Variation

1. Mutation
   –New alleles

Figure 6.1 **Advanced Placement (AP®) Biology Course Syllabus** *continued*

2. Sexual Recombination
–Crossing over
–Independent assortment
–Random fertilization
Preserving Variation
1. Diploidy
–2 Chromosomes
2. Balanced polymorphism
• Heterozygote advantage
• Sickle-cell anemia
• Hybrid vigor
• Hybrid corn
• Frequency-dependent selection
• Right mouthed cichlids
Effects of Natural Selection
1. Stabilizing Selection
• 7 lb. babies
2. Directional Selection
• Moth color
3. Diversifying Selection
• Speckled background
Osmosis and Diffusion Lab

Osmosis and Diffusion

I. Demonstration of osmosis
Procedure:
1. Obtain a 30-cm piece of 2.5-cm dialysis tubing that has been soaking in water. Tie off one end of the tubing to form a bag. To open the other end of the bag, rub the end between your fingers until the edges separate.
2. Place 15 mL of the 15% glucose/1% starch solution in the bag. Tie off the other end of the bag, leaving sufficient space for the expansion of the bag's contents. Record the color of the solution in **Table 1.1**.
3. Test the 15% glucose/1% starch solution in the bag for the presence of glucose with Testape@. Record the results.
4. Fill a 250 mL beaker or cup 2/3 full with distilled water. Add approximately 4 mL of Lugol's solution to the distilled water and record the color in **Table 1.1**. Test the solution for glucose and record the results in **Table 1.1**.
5. Immerse the bag in the beaker of solution.
6. Allow your set-up to stand for approximately 30 minutes or until you see a distinct color change in the bag or the beaker. Record the final color of the solution in the bag, and of the solution in the beaker, in **Table 1.1**.
7. Test the liquid in the beaker and in the bag for the presence of glucose. Record the results.

Table 1.1

	Initial contents	Initial sol'n color	Final solution color	Initial presence of glucose	Final presence of glucose
Bag	15%gluc/ 1%starch				
Beaker	H_2O + IKI				

Part I Questions
1. Which substance(s) are entering the bag and which are leaving the bag? What experimental evidence supports your answer?
2. *Explain* the results you obtained. Include the concentration differences and membrane pore size in your discussion.
3. Quantitative data uses numbers to measure observed changes. How could this experiment be modified so that quantitative data could be collected to show that water diffused into the dialysis bag?
4. Based on your observations, rank the following by relative size, beginning with the smallest: glucose molecules, water molecules, IKI molecules, membrane pores, starch molecules.

II. Demonstration of osmosis
A. Problem:
B. Hypothesis:
C. Independent variable:
D. Dependent variable:
E. Controlled variables:
F. Procedure:
1. Obtain six 20-cm strips of presoaked dialysis tubing.
2. Use a rubber band to seal off one end of each piece of dialysis tubing to form six bags. Pour approximately 15 ml of each of the following solutions into 6 separate bags:
• distilled water
• 0.2M sucrose
• 0.4M sucrose
• 0.6M sucrose
• 0.8M sucrose
• 1.0M sucrose.
3. Remove most of the air from the bags by drawing the dialysis bag between two fingers. Tie off the other end of the bag with a rubber band. Leave sufficient space for the expansion of the contents in the bag.
4. Rinse each bag gently with distilled water to remove any sucrose spilled during filling.
5. Carefully blot the outside of each bag and record its initial mass.
6. Fill six 250 ml beakers 2/3 full with distilled water.
7. Immerse each bag in one of the beakers of distilled water and label the beaker to indicate the molarity of the solution in the dialysis bag. Be sure to completely submerge each bag.
8. Let them stand for 30 minutes.
9. At the end of 30 minutes remove the bags from the water. Carefully blot and determine the mass of each bag.

Analysis:
• Data table
• Graph
• Conclusion/explanation of results addressing the following concepts: concentration gradient, osmosis, selective permeability, and error analysis

Part II Questions
1. Predict what would happen to the mass of each bag in this experiment if all the bags were placed in a 0.4M sucrose solution instead of distilled water. Explain your response.
2. Predict what would happen if the bags were left in the water for an extended period of time. Assume the bags will not disintegrate. Explain your answer.

(continued)

F i g u r e 6.1 **Advanced Placement (AP®) Biology Course Syllabus** *continued*

3. Predict what would happen to an experimental dialysis bag containing 3.0M sucrose. Explain.
4. Why did you calculate the *percent* change in mass rather than using the change in mass?

III. Determination of molar concentration of potato cells

Get together with your group and discuss how you would determine the molar concentration of potato cells. (Hint: The cell membrane of the potato acts like a dialysis membrane.)

Be sure to:

• include a hypothesis
• develop a thorough and understandable procedure
• clearly define variables
• carry out your experiment using the materials available to you
• identify any controls (at least ten!)
• include pertinent data tables and graphs
• present and *explain* your findings in the conclusion, including any explanation of error

Available materials: potatoes, corers, knives, parafilm, rulers, sucrose solutions of varying molarity, distilled water, beakers, large test tubes, test tube racks, mass balance

Ecology Unit Reading Questions

1. List several abiotic and biotic components that contribute to an organism's environment.
2. Put the following in order from smallest to largest in scope: community, ecosystem, organism, population.
3. Why would we expect to find plants with different pigments at or near the surface of water than at a depth of, say, ten meters?
4. Identify what causes the temperature of a temperate lake to be uniform in spring and autumn, yet stratified during winter and summer. Be sure to include relevant properties of water in your answer.
5. Describe the vertical stratification of deep aquatic biomes. Make a sketch of a lake and label AND describe the various regions.
6. Contrast an oligotrophic and eutrophic lake.
7. Contrast wetlands and estuaries.
8. Define pelagic zone.
9. Describe the defining characteristics of the following biomes: tropical forest, temperate forest, savanna, chaparral, temperate grassland, temperate deciduous forest, taiga (coniferous forest), tundra. Be sure to include the abiotic and biotic factors associated with each (especially vegetation).
10. What is a strict conformer? Give an example of one (with explanation) not found in this section.
11. Define: maturation, habituation, imprinting, trial-and-error.
12. (3 pts) A rodent-like animal called the ruby-headed meadow scamper exhibits an unusual behavior. When a male scamper finds a food source, it makes a chirping sound. This signals female scampers to run to the food site and perform an elaborate dance. If the dance "appeals" to the first scamper, it will share its food booty with the dancing scamper; otherwise, it will display aggressive behavior and chase her away.

    Construct a brief, *testable*, hypothesis that would infer an experiment to determine if the dance is a product of a) maturation, b) imprinting, or c) trial-and-error learning (a sentence or two each should suffice).

13. What is the *benefit* in being a low-social-status animal? (Think opportunity cost!)
14. In an environment with relatively poor resource availability, would natural selection tend to favor monogamous or polygamous mating systems in birds/mammals? Explain.
15. Define, in your own words, inclusive fitness.
16. What is the coefficient of relatedness with an uncle? A grandparent? A half-sister (same father, different mother)?
17. Describe the following dispersion patterns: clumped, uniform, and random. What environmental conditions might favor each type?
18. Define fecundity, generation time, and cohort.
19. If a population's annual birthrate is 0.25, and the death rate is 0.20, and started with a population of 1,000 individuals, how big would the population be at the end of five years? Graph this population. Is this growth rate zero, linear, or exponential?
20. What factors affect r_{max}? How does carrying capacity affect a population?
21. Contrast r-selecting and K-selecting populations. Give an example of a species that follows each strategy.
22. Give an example of a density-dependent factor and a density-independent factor. (Not found in the book!!!!)
23. Describe the growth of the human population. Is it exponential?
24. Which do you think is more important—species richness (diversity) or relative abundance? Explain your view.
25. Explain how interspecific competition might affect community structure.
26. Describe the competitive exclusion principle, and explain how competitive exclusion may affect community structure.
27. Compare a species' fundamental niche and its realized niche.
28. Explain how resource partitioning can affect species diversity.
29. Two snakes have very similar markings: the coral snake and the false coral snake. Each has a distinct yellow, red, and black striping pattern; however, the coral snake is extremely poisonous, while the false coral snake is not. What type of mimicry is this? What would you predict about the relative abundance of each? CHECK FALSE CORAL SNAKE NAME!!!
30. Distinguish among parasitism, mutualism, commensalism.
31. Distinguish between primary and secondary succession.
32. Describe the factors involved in limiting a species to a particular range.
33. List the factors that can limit productivity of an ecosystem.
34. Explain why productivity declines at each trophic level.
35. Distinguish between the energy pyramids and biomass pyramids.
36. Use diagrams to describe the following cycles: hydrologic (water) cycle, carbon cycle, nitrogen cycle, and phosphorous cycle.
37. Describe how the carbon cycle differs in terrestrial and aquatic biomes.
38. Explain how toxic compounds usually have the greatest effect on top-level carnivores.
39. Describe how increased atmospheric concentrations of carbon dioxide could effect the Earth.

SOURCE: Contributed by Scott E. Taylor and Paul Andersen, AP Biology Teachers, Bozeman High School, Bozeman, MT. Used with permission.

<u>F i g u r e   6 . 2</u>   **Advanced Placement (AP®) Biology Disclosure Document**

Instructors: Scott E. Taylor and Paul Andersen

Text: <u>Biology: Concepts and Connections</u>, 6th edition, Campbell
       AP Biology Study Guide *highly* recommended (several available)

AP Biology Moodle Website: http://bit.ly/apbiology

Materials needed:
Composition-type, quadrilined (graph paper) lab notebook (9¾" × 7½")
Three-ring-binder with pocket that fits lab book
A calculator and colored pencils will frequently be useful

Special needs: Any students with special needs should feel free to consult with the instructors. We will be made aware of any IEPs that exist.

AP Biology aims to:
- develop a student's understanding of basic biological concepts and to develop a scientific vocabulary that allows them to communicate these concepts.
- enable the students to apply the scientific process in solving problems.
- aid in the preparation for college-level study and the AP exam.
- encourage students to become critical thinkers that can challenge assumption, process, and conclusion.

Course overview:
This course is designed to prepare the student for the AP Biology test given

8:00am Monday, May 9, 2011.

     AP Biology is extremely rigorous and demanding of time; several pages of reading in a college biology text will be expected most nights. The most successful students are naturally gifted and highly motivated with good study skills. Since much of the course builds upon previous concepts, it is imperative that students keep up with the material.

     The curriculum is based on the recommendations of the College Board, the governing body of AP. It is a comprehensive course commensurate with an introductory college biology course.

Course outline:
  I. <u>Molecules and cells</u> (25%)—biochemistry, cells, energy transformation
  II. <u>Heredity and Evolution</u> (25%)—heredity, molecular genetics, evolution
 III. <u>Organisms and Populations</u> (50%)—taxonomy, plant structure & function, animal structure & function, embryology and development, behavior, ecology

The focus of this class is on understanding biological concepts. If you know and understand the material, you will do well in this class and on the AP exam. This class is structured for those taking the AP exam, but it is not required.

Remember: The students who have studied all year long and who have prepared **will most likely pass the AP Biology exam**! It is impossible to cram for the exam; there is simply too much content to be mastered.

Grading:
Grades will be based on a percentage derived from the following:
- **Unit Tests** will be worth 100 points. Tests will include both objective and free response components. The raw score will be the score earned on the test.
- **Unit Formative Assignments** will be worth between 20 and 50 points. In order to get the minimum of 20/20 points, students **must** to do three things:
  1. **Read** relevant text sections before class
  2. **View** chapter podcasts before class
  3. **Complete** unit lab activities

     Students may earn up to 50/50 points per unit by completing a variety of supplemental tasks which will be discussed in class and on the class Moodle website.

     Examples include comprehensive class notes, peer mentoring, student-created content, chapter outlining, and contributing to the course Moodle website. Students will be able to continue receiving credit for such tasks, **as long as they can be correlated to progress on tests**. Otherwise, students must attempt new supplemental methods to gain additional points. <u>Points will be awarded at the rate of 10 points per 3 hours of work (no rounding).</u> You must fill out a time sheet.

- **Semester tests** are worth **20%** of the semester grade. Bonus points *may* be added.

Grade Scale:		
	90%	A
	80%	B
	70%	C
	60%	D
	<60%	F

(continued)

Figure 6.2 **Advanced Placement (AP®) Biology Disclosure Document** *continued*

   Bozeman High School (BHS) uses <u>weighted grades</u>. In an AP class, an A is worth 5.0, B   is worth 4.0, etc. It should be noted that an F still results in a 0.0 for GPA purposes.

Plagiarism/academic dishonesty is a serious issue at BHS. In addition to more obvious examples, the following acts also constitute academic dishonesty:

• Discussing exams with students who have not yet taken them

• Copying homework or labs (this is NOT considered "working together")

The penalty for breaching acceptable conduct is a zero on a test or unit formative assignments, the score on that particular assignment or test becomes a zero grade.

I have read and understand the AP Biology 2010-2011 Disclosure Document.

_____   _____

Student Printed Name   Parent/Guardian Signature

_____

Student Signature

SOURCE: Contributed by Scott E. Taylor and Paul Andersen, AP Biology Teachers, Bozeman High School, Bozeman, Montana. Used with permission.

Figure 6.3 **Advanced Placement (AP®) Psychology Syllabus**

Instructor: Joyce Jarosz Hannula

Text: Myers, David. **Psychology: Myers In Modules**, Ninth Edition, New York: Worth Publishers, 2010

Study Guide, in paperback and/or on DVD

Note-taking Guides (created by instructor)

Course Objectives:

AP Psychology is a year-long course and is offered as elective credit for juniors and seniors with seniors having first priority. Our general objectives are listed in the **APA High School Program: Statement for the High School Psychology Course:**

• Students should study the major core concepts and theories of psychology. They should be able to define key terms and to use these terms in their everyday vocabulary. Students should be able to compare and contrast major theories in psychology.

• Students should learn the basic skills of psychological research. They should be able to devise simple research projects, interpret and generalize from results, and evaluate the general validity of research reports.

• Students should be able to apply psychological concepts to their own lives. They should be able to recognize psychological principles when they are encountered in everyday situations.

• Students should develop critical thinking skills. They should become aware of the danger of blindly accepting or rejecting any psychological theory without careful, objective evaluation.

• Students should actively develop reading, writing, and discussion skills.

• Students should learn about the ethical standards governing the work of psychologists. They should maintain high ethical standards and sensitivity in applying the principles of psychology to themselves, other peoples, and other organisms.

Syllabus and Specific Objectives:

We will study the following units during the first 18-week semester. Each unit is approximately two weeks in duration and includes formative assessment and summative assessments including reading quizzes as well as an objective unit exam. Exams reflect the multiple choice AP exam structure and range from comprehension to application and synthesis of information.

Unit I: Psychology—A New Science with a Long Past

Themes: Contributions of Philosophy and Biology; Schools of Thought—Theoretical Approaches and Their Founders, Current APA Divisions; Enduring Issues

Objectives:

• Define the study of psychology
  (All specific objectives are student-based—"The student will be able to ....")

• Identify the basic perspectives including psychoanalytic, behavioral, humanistic, cognitive, biological, social-cultural, evolutionary, and positive psychology

• Identify current professional specialties including clinical, counseling, educational, industrial and organizational psychology

Figure 6.3 **Advanced Placement (AP®) Psychology Syllabus** *continued*

- Define research areas including developmental, social, experimental physiological, cognitive, personality and psychometrics
- Define and contrast enduring issues in psychology including nature versus nurture, stability versus change, rationality versus irrationality
- Describe the purpose and function of the APA and discuss its divisions

Unit II: Good Research vs. Bad Research
Themes: Understanding the Need for Psychological Research; Basic Research Methodology; Descriptive and Experimental Design; Data Analysis Using Elementary Descriptive Statistics; Ethical Guidelines for Human and Nonhuman Research
Objectives:
- Specify goals of research: measurement, description, understanding, prediction, application and control
- Describe the scientific method
- Identify the mental set that leads to good research
- Describe, compare, and contrast basic research methods including descriptive and experimental designs
- Evaluate appropriate research methodology including sampling, control, independent and dependent variable and significance
- Indicate common flaws in research including experimenter bias, sampling bias, placebo effects, and self-report distortion
- Analyze data using elementary descriptive statistics including central tendency, variability and correlation
- Evaluate appropriate conclusions based on correlational data
- Describe conditions determined by APA under which animal and/or human research is essential and ethical
- Activity—Design and conduct and evaluate a limited descriptive or experimental study
- Present research to classmates; answer questions; offer strategies for replication
- Practice essay on methods of research, evaluating strengths and weaknesses of designs

Unit III: Personality, Part I: A Historical Perspective
Themes: Freud, Neo-Freudians, Implications of the Psychonalytical Perspective
Objectives:
- Explain the historical conditions and impact of the Psychoanalytic Perspective
- Identify key contributors including Charcot, Freud and the Neo-Freudians
- Define key concepts including the unconscious, id, ego, superego and defense mechanisms and stages of psychosexual development
- Relate key components of therapeutic approach including role of hypnosis, free association, transference, fixations, resistance and projective tests
- Evaluate contemporary use of Psychoanalysis and Freudian terminology

Unit IV: Learning and Behaviorism: Founders and Theories
Themes: Pavlov, Watson, Thorndike, Skinner, Bandura, Seligman; Classical Conditioning; Operant Conditioning, Cognitive Approaches
Objectives:
- Define the nature of learning
- Explain the work of Pavlov as well as principles and process of classical conditioning
- Identify UCS, UCR, CS, CR and apply to various examples
- Demonstrate use of appropriate terminology: acquisition, extinction, spontaneous recovery, generalization, and discrimination
- Identify cognitive contributions and biological influences on Classical Conditioning theory
- Discuss applications of Classical Conditioning to immune responses, drug abuse, and behavior across various species
- Identify key theorists including Thorndike, Skinner and Watson
- Explain the work of Thorndike, Skinner and Watson as well as principles and processes of operant conditioning
- Demonstrate use of appropriate terminology including acquisition, extinction, shaping
- Identify applications of types of reinforcers and major schedules of reinforcement
- Discuss the impact of punishment on human behavior
- Identify and evaluate applications of operant conditioning in contemporary culture
- Define Bandura's contributions to our understandings of observational learning
- Define modeling and the impact of pro and anti-social models
- Activity: Conduct a Naturalistic Observation of Parent and Child Interactions
- Activity: Behavior Modification Contract
- Essay practice: Physical punishment: reasons for use and detrimental effects

(continued)

Figure 6.3 **Advanced Placement (AP®) Psychology Syllabus** *continued*

Unit V: Memory: Process and Systems

Themes: Encoding, Storage and Retrieval; Biology of Memory; Forgetting; Current Research in Memory Construction, Eyewitness Testimony, and Cultural Influence

Objectives:

- Explain memory in terms of encoding, storage and retrieval model
- Identify the sensory systems and impact of Iconic and Echoic memory and Selective attention
- Distinguish between types and effects of encoding, including automatic, effortful, acoustic, visual, and semantic
- Define encoding failure and forgetting
- Explain the role of the hippocampus and cerebellum and the divisions of explicit and implicit memory
- Describe long-term memory and define long-term potentiation
- Explain and demonstrate accurate use of the terms: recall, recognition relearning, retrieval cues, state and content dependent memory
- Discuss the definition and impact of interference, repression and memory construction and schema
- Describe the research of Loftus and associates and its impact on perceptions of the accuracy of eyewitness testimony

Unit VI: Biological Basis of Behavior

Themes: Historic and Contemporary Tools for Studying the Brain and Nervous Systems, Endocrine system; Current Research in Brain Injury and Plasticity

Objectives:

- Identify the methods of studying the brain, historical and current
- Label the basic structures of a neuron
- Describe the discovery neurotransmitters, the role of neurotransmitters, and the general effects of neurotransmitter imbalances
- Identify the major divisions and functions of the central, somatic, and autonomic nervous system, the endocrine system and the sensory organs
- Describe the overall organization of the brain as well as the functions of the various structures within the brain including the brainstem, limbic system and cerebral cortex
- Identify the impact of damage to each of these structures including reorganization and plasticity
- Describe current brain research
- Activity—create a human replication of the neuron's structure and movement of an action potential
- Activity—create a brain model or video documenting the brain's key structures and their functions
- Activity—view AWAKENINGS, Columbia Pictures, 1990, as an introduction to brain disorders and the impact of neurotransmitter imbalance; Complete a note-taking guide

Unit VII: Language and Thought

Themes: Shared Structures and Theories of Language Development and Influence; Other Species: Research on Language and Cognitive Abilities; Cognitive Studies; Decision Making; Patterns, Logic, Obstacles and Error

Objectives:

- Demonstrate understanding of phonemes, morphemes, words, grammar, syntax and semantics
- Explain the stages of human language acquisition
- Identify key theories of language acquisition including the Behaviorists and Chomsky
- Describe the linguistic relativity hypothesis and the controversies regarding its application
- Discuss the seminal and current research on animal communication and language
- Activity—Video clips: The First Signs of Washoe; Genie
- Essay—Memory, interference and schema's impact on perception

Unit VIII: Motivation and Emotion—Why Do We Do the Things We Do???

Themes: Key Theories of Motivation, Hunger and Thirst, Sexual Motivation, Achievement, Affiliation, Maslow and the Hierarchy of Needs; Theories of Emotion, Nonverbal Communication, Gender and Culture Studies

Objectives:

- Identify the basic theories and understanding in human motivation including instinct, drives, Maslow's Hierarchy, hunger, sexual motivation, achievement motivation, and affiliation
- Distinguish between behaviors in terms of intrinsic and extrinsic motivation

Figure 6.3 **Advanced Placement (AP®) Psychology Syllabus** *continued*

- Describe hunger and eating in terms of externals and internals
- Identify the role of the hypothalamus, insulin and glucose in feelings of hunger and satiation
- Define anorexia and bulimia nervosa and discuss options for therapy
- Review current research on the nature and dynamics of sexual orientation
- Compare and contrast management styles and evaluate the impact of theory X and Y managers, including cultural influences
- Describe universal physiological responses and expressions involved in human emotion
- Explain the major theories of emotion including James-Lange, Cannon-Bard, Schacter-two factor and Opponent Process
- Define the facial feedback hypothesis and catharsis and explain their implications in behavioral responses
- Explain the principles of operation and effectiveness of the polygraph

Unit IX: Stress and Health or How to Survive Christmas and/or College
Themes: Sources, Coping and the Biology of Stress; Reducing Stress; Stress and Personality; Stress and Illness; Post-traumatic Stress Disorder
Objectives:

- Identify major causes and types of stress including conflict types approach-approach, approach-avoidance, avoidance-avoidance, and multiple approach-avoidance
- Describe emotional, physiological and behavioral responses including the inverted U hypothesis of arousal, the general adaptation syndrome, the role of the hypothalamus, the pathways of response, and the reduction of immune system functions
- Explain and discuss the impact of stress on psychological functioning including tasks, burnout, physical and psychological disorders, such as PTSD, as well as self-improvement
- Describe the findings on the impacts of smoking, lack of exercise, poor nutrition, and risky sexual behavior as response to stress
- Compare healthy methods of coping to unhealthy responses
- Relate reactions to illness including decisions to seek treatment, communication with health professionals, and adherence to medical instructions/advice
- Activity • Integrative Essay Practice with topics in previous units
- Activity—Student Stress Response Scale, http://eric.ed.gov/ERICWebPortal/Home.portal?_nfpb=true&_pageLabel=RecordDetails&ERICExtSearch_SearchValue_0=ED350345&ERICExtSearch_SearchType_0=eric_accno&objectId=0900000b80126532

  Semester Exam—Our exam time is a hundred minutes; you will have an objective test with approximately 150 questions. This test will help you prepare for the AP exam, as it is written in a similar style and includes questions from released exams.

Unit X: Sensation and Perception: What Kind of Perceivers Are We?
Themes: Study of Psychophysics; Systems of Sensation; Human Systems of Perception; Comparison of Our Systems to Other Species
Objectives:

- Explain the basic principles of psychophysics including absolute threshold, Weber's law, signal detection theory, point of transduction sensory adaptation, and subliminal perception
- Identify how wavelength, amplitude and purity affect perception of visual and auditory stimulus
- Label and explain the functions of the key eye structures and visual receptors including lens, pupil, retina, optic disk, fovea, rods, cones, ganglion and bipolar cells
- Describe how depth perception is created by binocular cues, retinal disparity, monocular cues and pictorial cues
- Discuss how theories of color vision, trichromatic and opponent process are complementary in explaining color vision
- Describe and apply concepts in perception including inattentional blindness, feature analysis, and the Gestalt principles of figure and ground, proximity, closure, similarity, simplicity and continuity
- Identify, label and explain key structures involved in audition including the pinna, eardrum, ossicles, cochlea and basilar membrane
- Define auditory localization
- Trace the pathways to sensation in the chemical senses including the roles of the taste buds, the thalamus (taste) and the olfactory cilia
- Recognize the qualities of super tasters and the difficulties caused by the loss of a sense of smell
- Describe the role of sensory receptors in the skin: pressure, temperature and pain
- Discuss the gate control theory and cultural influences in the perception of pain
- Explain the role of the kinesthetic system and the vestibular system
- Activity: color vision after effects, optical illusions, smell and taste labs
- Activity: sound localization
- Activity: skin sensory receptors for temperature

(continued)

Figure 6.3 **Advanced Placement (AP®) Psychology Syllabus** *continued*

Unit XI: Human Development Across the Life Span

Themes: Prenatal Development, Development in Childhood, Adolescence and Adulthood

Objectives:

- Chart the stages of prenatal development from zygote, to embryo to fetus
- Describe the effects of maternal consumption of alcohol, tobacco and other drugs on the developing fetus
- Discuss the impact of maternal malnutrition, illness, and AIDS
- Chart the motor development of the infant, including considerations of the impact of maturation and environment
- Describe the theories of cognitive, moral and Personality development, including the work of Piaget, Vygotsky, Kohlberg, and Erikson
- Address Piaget's specific stages of development, including the process of schema assimilation and accommodation
- Defend a position on continuous development versus stage theory approaches
- Describe the position of nativists and evolutionary theorists in regard to the genetic aptitudes of the child
- Explain key theories of attachment including the work of Harry Harlow and John Bowlby
- Define the four infant-mother attachment categories and discuss the impact of a relatively secure attachment
- Compare cultural patterns of attachment
- Define and evaluate the period of adolescence including the concepts of pubescence, puberty, primary sex characteristics, early maturers, later maturers, the delay of prefrontal cortex maturity, Erikson's' and Marcia's theories of development of Identity and family/parent relationships
- Describe adult development in terms of transitions to marriage and family, social clock, Erikson's stages, cognitive changes, fluid and accumulated intelligence, and physical and sensory changes
- Define and describe the impact of dementia and Alzheimer's disease; explain theories regarding cause
- Compare and contrast longitudinal and cross-sectional studies in terms of advantages and disadvantages
- Summarize the results and implications of twin and adoption studies on the nature-nurture question
- Activity—Child Development Project: interview with a child, ages 3 to 6
- Activity—Essay Practice—AP Released Question—Child visits a fire station

Unit XII: Personality, Part II

Themes: Short Review of Psychoanalytic and Neo-Freudians; Behavioral Perspective, Social-Cognitive Perspective, Trait and Biological Perspective, Genetic Approach

Objectives:

- Review basic components of psychoanalytic theory
- Review tenets of Neo-Freudians including Adler, Jung and Horney
- Describe how Skinner's theory of operant conditioning would apply to personality development
- Discuss Bandura's social cognitive theory and its application to personality including the key concepts of observational learning, modeling, reciprocal determinism, and self-efficacy
- Describe the central tenets of the Humanistic perspective including the contributions of Maslow and Rogers
- Define key Humanistic terminology including hierarchy of needs, self-actualization person-centered theory, incongruence, unconditional positive regard, empathic listening, and congruent self-concept
- Explain the basic assumptions and procedures of Rogers's client-centered therapy
- Trace the development of Trait theory from Allport to the Big Five
- Detail the contributions of Hans Eysenk, identifying the five continuums of Trait theory, including the emphasis on genetic patterns
- Review the evolutionary approach with its emphasis on reproductive fitness and analyze the adaptive elements suggested in the Big Five traits.
- Relate the current research on twins and discuss heritability estimates for personality
- Analyze the impact of culture on personality by evaluating various cultures and the dimensions of the Big Five; include historical applications such as war, governmental influence, natural disaster, economic success and religion
- Activity—elect to take a Big Five and Myers-Briggs Personality test online
  http://www.personalityresearch.org/bigfive.html
  http://www.humanmetrics.com/cgi-win/JTypes1.htm
- Activity—develop a personal theory of personality
- Activity— practice two timed essays during a single class period

F i g u r e 6 . 3 **Advanced Placement (AP®) Psychology Syllabus** *continued*

Unit XIII: Psychological Disorders and Therapeutic Approaches

Themes: Introduction to Psychological Disorders; Anxiety Disorders, Somatoform Disorders, Dissociative Disorders, Mood Disorders, Schizophrenic Disorders, Personality Disorders; Treatments: Approaches for the Classes of Disorders; Current Issues in Treatment, Institutional Treatment and Cultural Implications

Objectives:

- Explain and discuss the criteria and continuum for judgments about normal versus abnormal behaviors

- Discuss the development of the DSM-IV understanding the classification system based and recorded on five axes

- Describe the similarities and differences between generalized anxiety disorder, phobic disorders, panic disorder, obsessive-compulsive disorder, Tourette's syndrome, and posttraumatic stress disorder

- Explain the possible role of genetic predisposition, disturbances in neural circuits, classical conditioning, operation conditioning and stress

- Discuss each perspective's application of therapeutic approaches including medication, (anti-depressant and anti-anxiety) systematic desensitization, counter-conditioning, relaxation therapy, free association, client-centered therapy and cognitive therapy

- Identify the types of Somatoform disorders including somatization disorders, conversion disorders, and hypochondria and include discussion of the etiology of this group of disorders including histrionic personality traits, distorted thinking, and the benefits of the "sick" role

- Describe treatment approaches including free association, cognitive therapy, client-centered therapy, and group therapies

- Define dissociative disorders differentiating between dissociative amnesia, dissociative fugue, dissociative identity disorder or MPD

- Explain possible causes including extreme stress, role-playing, and severe emotional trauma during childhood

- Discuss options for treatment including free association, client-centered therapy, rational emotive therapy, and the passage of time

- Define the types of mood disorders: major depressive and bipolar; differentiate between the normal ranges of depression and mania and medical ranges

- Explain suggested etiology including twin studies, serotonin and norepinephrine imbalances, hippocampus abnormalities, negative explanatory styles, inadequate social skills, and stress

- Review the major perspectives/approaches to treatment including medications (SSRIs and mood stabilizers such as Lithium), cognitive therapy, client-centered therapy, social skills training, group therapy, and in major depression only, ECT

- Define symptoms of schizophrenia and differentiate between types including paranoid, catatonic, disorganized, and undifferentiated and positive and negative symptoms

- Indicate factors in the etiology including genetic vulnerability, disturbances in dopamine synapses, disruption of normal brain maturation, stress, and specific family and cultural profiles

- Discuss therapies, specifically drug treatments, and institutionalization

- Assess cultural variations in disorders

- Define meta-analysis and apply to outcomes of psychotherapy

- Describe outcomes from the research on the effectiveness of alternative therapies

- Activity: various clips from documentaries, and Annenburg's Mind and Brain Series: http://www.learner.org/resources/series150.html

- Activity: Timed Essay Schizophrenia, released AP exam questions

Unit XIV: Social Psychology

Themes: Attribution Theory; Attitudes Resulting in Behaviors, Actions Effect on Behavior; Conformity Obedience, Group Influence, Group Interaction, Prejudice, In-group and Outgroup, Scapegoating, Aggression, Attraction, Altruism

Objectives:

- Define attribution, differentiating between external and internal attributions

- Define the following terms indicating bias: fundamental attribution error, actor-observer bias, defensive attribution, self-serving bias

- List and discuss the three components of an attitude and describe the findings from studies on attitudes as predictors of behavior

- Define the tendency for action to affect attitude through the following: foot-in-the-door phenomenon, role-playing, Festinger's cognitive dissonance theory

- Explain how source credibility and likeability, two-sided arguments, fear appeals and the central route to persuasion produces attitude change

- Explain Asch's experiments on conformity and Milgram's studies of obedience

(continued)

F i g u r e   6 . 3   **Advanced Placement (AP®) Psychology Syllabus**   *continued*

- Discuss Asch's conclusions on the impact of group size, presence of a dissenter and conformity in collectivist cultures
- Differentiate between normative social influence and informative social influence
- Discuss the generalizibility of Milgram's research and the impact of his work on ethical standards
- Describe Zimbardo's Prison simulation and debate its accuracy in predicting the impact of social roles and situational factors
- Explain how the presence of others influences individual behavior, including the following concepts: social facilitation, social loafing, deindividuation, group polarization, and group think
- Discuss the social, emotional and cognitive roots of prejudice, including the definition of prejudice, the impact of social inequality, scapegoating, and in-group bias
- Describe the biological and psychological factors in aggressive behavior, including genetic influences, biochemical influences, the frustration-aggression principle, operant conditioning, and observational learning
- Explain the role of social traps and enemy perceptions in promoting conflict
- Discuss research concerned with the question: "Why do fools fall in love?" Include mere exposure effect, physical attractiveness, similarity, passionate love, companionate love, the role of equity and self-disclosure (Generally we cover this material on Valentine's day, while we consume chocolate)
- Define altruism and explain the impact that the murder of Kitty Genovese produced in researching social behavior, including discussion of the bystander effect, and the social exchange theory
- Activity—film clips from the Asch's Conformity, Stanford Prison Studies and Milgram's Obedience Studies
- Activity—each concept above offers engaging activities for the class. See website for examples: http://jfmueller.faculty.noctrl .edu/crow/
- Activity—essay practice—Released, integrative AP essays, two timed essays

Unit XV: States of Consciousness:

Themes: Nature of Consciousness, Circadian Rhythms, Sleep, Sleep Disorders, Dreams and Theories of Dreaming, Hypnosis (covered with Psychoanalytic Theory), Meditation, Drugs and Altered Consciousness

- Define consciousness and explain what is meant by variations in consciousness
- Explain circadian rhythms, effects of disruptions, and current understandings of biological adjustment through light and melatonin
- Describe the stages of sleep, and the major events in each stage
- Discuss the impact of sleep deprivation and list sleep disorders and potential treatments: insomnia, narcolepsy, sleep apnea, nightmares, night terrors and sleepwalking
- Discuss the nature of dreaming and detail theories including activation synthesis, wish fulfillment, problem solving, and research associated with memory organization and retention
- Review the controversy regarding hypnosis as an altered state of consciousness versus social role-playing
- Relate the studies regarding the definition and benefits of meditation
- Describe factors influencing impact of drugs such as age, expectations, method of administration and tolerance
- Activity: Cooperative Learning in groups of two to three, students will present classes of abused drugs, including narcotics, sedatives, stimulants, hallucinogens, cannabis, alcohol, date rape drugs, nicotine, inhalants and MDMA. Group members will present history of drug use, mechanisms of drug action, short and long-term risks

Unit XVI: Post AP Test:

Students design, prepare and present Psychology Fair to parents, community high school students and teachers.

Additional materials:

Students are provided with access to current research via computer labs, which allow entry to various data bases.

Students view various clips from the following series:

Discovering Psychology, The Annenberg, CPB Collection, 1989

The Brain and The Mind Teaching Modules, WNET New York, 1990

We often evaluate current materials in the media, such as the focus on the Brain in January, 2007, **Time**

Released Exams and Essays, New Jersey: The College Board and Educational Testing Service

Additional Teacher Resources:

Gazzaniga, Michael and Heatherton, Todd, **Psychological Science, 2nd edition**, New York: W.W. Norton and Company, 2006

Kowalski, R. and Westen, D, **Psychology: 4th edition**, New Jersey, John Wiley & Sons, Inc., 2005

Weiten, Wayne, **Psychology, Themes and Variations, 7th edition**, California, Thomson Wadsworth, 2007

Figure 6.3 **Advanced Placement (AP®) Psychology Syllabus**   *continued*

Zimbardo, Johnson, Weber and Gruber, **Psychology, AP Edition**, Boston: Pearson, 2007

Research indicates student performance increases when note-taking guides that outline key content are used. Included below are two teacher-created guides

Emotions: Mods 37 and 38
Components of emotion:

     1
     2
     3

Theories: James—Lange
              Cannon—Bard
              Two-Factor

Physiological

Sympathetic Nervous System

Parasympathetic

  Mnemonics to remember the difference

Physiological states accompanying specific emotions

Nonverbal Communication

Facial Muscles

Polygraph

Culture and Emotional Expression

Gestures

Facial Expression

Effects of Facial Expression

Experiencing Emotion

Fear—amygdala

Anger—catharsis

Feel Good—Do good

Adaptation Level

Relative Deprivation

Notes for Adolescence and Adulthood

In addition to Kohlberg and Erikson—take notes, answering these questions
  1. What is the difference between authoritarian, authoritative and permissive parenting?
  2. What is the difference between primary and secondary sex characteristics?
  3. What does Carol Gulligan suggest Erikson has overlooked?
  4. Describe general changes in middle and late adulthood. Include <u>sensory, health, hormonal and emotional</u> changes
  5. Define cross-sectional study—when are these studies most useful?
  6. Define longitudinal study—when are these studies most useful?
  7. What is the difference between crystallized and fluid intelligence?
  8. What is a social clock? How is the American social clock different from other country's? (Choose your country or culture to contrast)

SOURCE: Contributed by Joyce Jarosz Hannula, AP Psychology Teacher and Instructional Coach, Bozeman High School, Bozeman, Montana. Used with permission.

Figure 6.4 Advanced Placement (AP®) Psychology Disclosure Document

Instructor: Joyce Jarosz Hannula

Course Objectives:

This course offers a yearlong survey of the basic principles and perspectives in psychology. You will examine the progression of psychology from a philosophical curiosity about the nature of humankind to the current biological approach. General objectives for each student include the following:

- To gain a thorough knowledge of research methodology, major theories, and concepts and to use specific terminology comfortably and knowledgeably.
- To develop reading comprehension, composition, and discussion skills.
- To hone critical thinking skills, becoming aware of the danger of blindly accepting or rejecting theory without careful and repeated evaluation.
- To understand the ethical standards governing the work of psychologists and maintain personal standards and sensitivity in applying the principles of psychology to themselves as well as others.
- To prepare for the successful completion of the AP Psychology Exam.

Required:

- Readings from David Myers, <u>Psychology</u>
- Occasional outside readings/research
- Participation in experiential learning assignments/activities
- A binder or folder for note-taking guides

Attendance:

You are responsible for all material presented in class. Missed work for activities must be completed in a timely manner. Please initiate requests for make-up. **Do not wait for me to ask you about missing scores.**

Assessments:

All assignments are listed on the white board at the front of the room. Please check the board daily and refer to the course syllabus. Exams will be announced at least one week before the date the exam is to be taken. Roughly two-thirds of the course grade is based upon objective tests. One-third is based upon participation, projects, and essay exams. Late papers will be penalized 1/2 grade per day late. No make-up will be accepted beyond a reasonable make-up time. Activity make-up=one day or each day missed. Illness—please visit with me to determine a reasonable and specific plan. Also, become familiar with the student handbook; carefully read the sections on academic standards and dishonesty.

Psychology offers us an engaging study of human behavior. I appreciate your curiosity, unique talents, and perspectives on a daily basis. In the same manner, please value the diversity of your classmates as we explore our far-reaching and engaging course of study.

Please don't hesitate to ask questions—regarding content, procedures, or personal interests; as James Thurber wrote, "It is better to know some of the questions than all of the answers."

Please sign below indicating that you have read and understand the course disclosure document.

Student: _____ Parent(s)_____

SOURCE: Contributed by Joyce Jarosz Hannula, Psychology Teacher and Instructional Coach, Bozeman High School, Bozeman, MT. Used with permission.

Figure 6.5 Sixth-Grade Geography Syllabus

Dear Parents and Students,

This year we will strive to develop a global perspective and an understanding of the fundamental themes and skills important to the study of North American, Central and South American, and European Geography. The course focuses on the following questions: Where is it? What is it like? What is the relationship between people and their environment? How and why do people, ideas and goods move from place to place? In what ways do areas of the world share similar characteristics?

We will also focus on basic mapping skills and understandings about what culture and history are in relation to geography and spend some quality time talking about Colorado History.

Class Expectations—Bobcat ROARS!

I expect all of my students to follow the Park School District ROARS policy in and out of the classroom while at Estes Park Middle School (EPMS). All students are expected to be:

R = Respectful

O = On Time

A= Attentive

R = Responsible

S = Safe

When students follow ROARS there will be positive consequences. They include praise in class, "good news" calls or postcards home, positive notes in the agenda book and/or postings on the wall of excellence.

What if a student chooses not to follow the Bobcat ROARS?

Every student has the opportunity to be successful at EPMS. To be successful, I expect my students to follow ROARS. If they choose not to, consequences will result.

One Chance—Students have the opportunity to do what is expected in class. The first time a student chooses not to follow ROARS, I will issue a verbal or non-verbal reminder alerting the student that the ROARS expectations are not being followed.

One Choice—Students have the responsibility of making their own choices. Students will need to decide to do what is expected of them after a reminder is given.

One Consequence—The consequence can be a reward for choosing to do what is expected in class. Or the consequence can be a penalty for choosing to do what is not expected in class. The consequence depends on the student's choice. Once a negative consequence is carried out, students always have a "clean slate" in class.

(continued)

Figure 6.5 **Sixth-Grade Geography Syllabus**   *continued*

Class Materials:

Students are required to bring their agenda, a notebook, a pen or pencil, colored pencils, loose leaf paper and the textbook (when required) to class everyday.

Grades:

Geography course grade consists of four parts:

20% Assessment—Quizzes, Test

30% Assignments—Group Projects

25% Learning Activities—Class work, homework, activities, foldable study guide, interactive notebook

25% Participation

Assessments: Students can retake a test before the last week of the quarter and the grade will be averaged. Projects will be done with partners or in group work. Each member is responsible for contributing to project work and supporting fellow group members and classmates. Students will be required to make up all missed assignments.

Learning Activities: Ample time will be given for class work to be completed in class. If a student is unable to finish his/her class work during the allotted time in class, he/she will be able to complete the work as homework, which will be due the next day.

Late work:

Late work will be accepted for full credit if completed that day in the ZAP program. After that, 10% will be deducted from your score as long as your work is completed in a reasonable amount of time.

Absences:

When students are absent, it is their responsibility to check the missing homework file. Assignments and notes will be available each day. The student should also see a classmate or agenda items for the day(s) absent. Students have two days for every day absent to make up missed work. After that time, it will be considered late work (see above).

What if a student needs help?

PLEASE ASK QUESTIONS IN CLASS! Mrs. Sunday is available every day after school until 4:00 (when possible) for extra help. Lunchtime help can be arranged when scheduling permits.

Contact Information:

Mrs. Sunday can be reached by school phone at 970-586-4439 ext. 3220 and the school email is **Anastasia_Sunday@psdr3.k12.co.us**. I am looking forward to a great year with your student.

_____ Parent and/or Guardian Signature

_____ Student Signature

SOURCE: Contributed by Anastasia Sunday, 6th Grade Geography Teacher, Estes Park Middle School, Estes Park, CO. Used with permission.

Figure 6.6 **Geometry Syllabus—Mrs. Maguire's Classroom Expectations and Procedures**

Course Grading:

A = 90–100%

B = 80–89%

C = 70–79%

D = 60–69%

F = 59% or below

- Grades will be calculated with assessments counting 70% of the grade and homework counting 30% of the grade.
- It is essential that students keep track of their own progress. Once Infinite Campus is accessible to parents you will be able to check grades at any time.
- Grades will be updated at the end of the day every Thursday.

Grades Will Be Based on:

- Homework = 10 points
- Bellwork Quizzes (weekly) = 20 points
- Quizzes = 50 points
- Tests = 100 points
- Projects 30–100 points

Homework:

1. Homework will be due at the beginning of class. Students will be allowed one late homework assignment per quarter; oth-

erwise late homework is worth ½ credit. This late assignment may only be one day late to receive credit.
2. Homework in mathematics will be graded according to the following Homework Rubric:
   - 3 points—All assigned problems genuinely attempted in pencil.
   - 3 points—Notes taken on all inaccurate answers during class, in pen.
   - 3 points—All work shown.
   - 1 point—Neatness and use of complete sentences.
   - Extra point: 1 point—All answers were correct when assignment is reviewed in class.
3. Problem sets for each chapter will be handed out ahead of time and students are encouraged to work ahead, especially when extended absences are anticipated.

_____

Geometry Expectations & Procedures

Please retain the syllabus as a reference. Return this portion only indicating that you have read and understand the information.

Student Name (printed): _____

Student Signature: _____ Date: _____

Parent/Guardian Signature: _____

(continued)

Figure 6.6 Geometry Syllabus—Mrs. Maguire's Classroom Expectations and Procedures *continued*

Materials:

1. Necessary:
   - Pencils
   - Pens
   - Notebook for notes, homework, etc.
   - Graph Paper
   - Compass
   - Protractor
   - Scientific or Graphing Calculator

2. Appreciated Donations:
   - Dry Erase Markers
   - Kleenex
   - Film Canisters

Online Textbook and Resources:

Key Curriculum offers a variety of resources for students and parents along with an online textbook. To access these resources go to the URL: **http://www.keymath.com/DG4**. Once at the site enter your class pass. The class pass is lhsgeometry and the period number of your geometry class. Example, you are in period 1 geometry. Your class pass is lhsgeometry1.

Daily Classroom Expectations:

- Expectations are set high to allow for an environment that encourages respectful and responsible students.

- One of your rights as a student is the right to learn without distraction from other students. You, in turn, have the responsibility to the other students in the class and to the teacher to not disturb their efforts.

Standards:

- Detailed standards and benchmarks can be found at **www .stvrain.k12.co.us**
- Notice that 9th and 10th grade standards include more than just geometry. The class will be supplemented with algebra and other math skills throughout the year.

This is my fifteenth year as an educator and my twelfth year here at Lyons. I am so excited to be a part of our high achieving high school and am looking forward to working with both the students and parents. Please never hesitate to call me or email me, as we are all working together to achieve the same goal (the success of each student).

School Number: **Email:**

SOURCE: Paula Maguire, Math Teacher, Lyons Middle/Senior High School, Lyons, CO. Used with permission.

As you shall learn, the syllabus can also be developed collaboratively with students. However it is developed, the syllabus should be designed so that it helps establish a rapport among students, parents or guardians, and the teacher; helps students feel at ease by providing an understanding of what is expected of them; and helps them to organize, conceptualize, and synthesize their learning experiences.

The syllabus should provide a reference, helping eliminate misunderstandings and misconceptions about the nature of the class—its rules, expectations, procedures, requirements, and other policies. The syllabus should also serve as a plan to be followed by you and the students, and it should serve as a resource for substitute teachers and (when relevant) members of a teaching team. When teaming, each team member should have a copy of every other member's syllabus. In essence, the syllabus stands as documentation for what is taking place in the classroom for those outside the classroom (i.e., parents or guardians, administrators, other teachers, and students). For access by parents and other interested persons, some teachers include at least portions of their course syllabus, such as homework assignment specifications and due dates, with the school's website on the Internet.

Usually, the syllabus (at least portions of it) is prepared by the teacher long before the first class meeting. If you maintain a syllabus template on your computer, then it is a simple task to customize it for each group of students you teach. You may find that it is more useful if students participate in the development of the syllabus, thereby empowering the students with a sense of ownership of the syllabus and a commitment to its contents. By having

input into the workings of a course and knowing that their opinions count, students will take more interest in what they are doing and learning. This has been demonstrated, for example, at East Paulding High School (Dallas, GA), where students in applied communications participate in developing the course syllabus by choosing literature selections, preparing study guides, creating project assignments, and devising assessment criteria.[2] Figure 6.7 shows the steps you can use as a collaborative learning experience in which students spend time during the first (or an early) class meeting brainstorming the content of their syllabus.

Content of a Syllabus

The syllabus should be concise, matter-of-fact, uncomplicated, and brief—perhaps no more than two pages, although several of the samples included here are much longer than that—and should include the following information:

- *Descriptive information about the course.* This includes the teacher's name, course title, class period and days of class meetings, beginning and ending times, and room number.

- *Importance of the course.* This information should describe the course, cite how students will profit from it, and tell whether the course is a required course and (if relevant) from which program in the curriculum: a core curriculum course, a cocurriculum course, an exploratory or elective course, a vocational course, an Advanced Placement course, or some other arrangement.

- *Goals and objectives.* Include the major goals and a few of the major objectives.

Figure 6.7　**Steps for Involving Students in the Development of Their Course Syllabus**

Step 1

Sometime during the first few days of the course, arrange students in heterogeneous groups (mixed abilities) of three or four members to brainstorm the development of their syllabus.

Step 2

Instruct each group to spend five minutes listing everything they can think of that they would like to know about the course. Tell the class that group *recorders* must be chosen to write their lists of ideas on paper and then, when directed to do so, to transfer the lists to the writing board or to sheets of butcher paper to be hung in the classroom for all to see (or on overhead transparencies—a transparency sheet and pen are made available to each group). Tell them that each group should select a group *spokesperson* who will address the class, explaining the group's list. Each group could also appoint a *materials manager* whose job is to see that the group has the necessary materials (e.g., pen, paper, transparency, chalk) and a *task master* whose job is to keep the group on task and to report to the teacher when each task is completed.

Step 3

After five minutes, have the recorders prepare their lists. When using transparencies or butcher paper, the lists can be prepared simultaneously while recorders remain with their groups. If using the writing board, then recorders, one at a time, write their lists on areas of the board that you have designated for each group's list.

Step 4

Have the spokesperson of each group explain the group's list. As this is being done, you should make a master list. If transparencies or butcher paper are being used, rather than the writing board, you can ask for them as backup to the master list you have made.

Step 5

After all spokespersons have explained their lists, you ask the class collectively for additional input. "Can anyone think of anything else that should be added?"

Step 6

You now take the master list and design a course syllabus, being careful to address each question and to include items of importance that students may have omitted. However, your guidance during the preceding five steps should ensure that all bases have been covered.

Step 7

At the next class meeting, give each student a copy of the final syllabus. Discuss its content. (Duplicate copies to distribute to colleagues, especially those on your teaching team, interested administrators, and parents and guardians at back-to-school night.)

■ *Materials required.* Explain what materials are needed—such as a textbook, notebook, binder, portfolio, supplementary readings, or safety goggles—and specify which are supplied by the school, which must be supplied by each student, and which materials must be available each day.

■ *Types of assignments.* These should be clearly explained in as much detail as possible this early in the school term. There should be a statement of your estimate of time required (if any) for homework each night. There should also be a statement about where daily assignments will be posted in the classroom (the same place each day), the procedures for completing and turning in assignments, and (if relevant) procedures for making corrections to assignments already turned in (see information on second opportunities in the next paragraph). Include your policy regarding late work. Parents will want to know your expectations of them regarding helping their children with assignments. (Homework is discussed in Chapter 11.)

■ *Attendance expectations.* Explain how attendance is related to grades and to promotion (if relevant) as well as the procedure for making up missed work. Typical school policy allows that for an excused absence, missed work can be completed without penalty if done within a reasonable period of time after the student returns to school. To strongly encourage regular attendance, the policy of Talent Development secondary schools is that a student automatically fails a course when the student accumulates five or more absences per quarter. However, to encourage students, the policy also includes recovery strategies. For example, each absence can be nullified if the student accumulates five consecutive days of perfect attendance. Policy also provides students with second opportunities for success on assignments although at some cost so as to encourage a strong first effort.[3]

■ *Assessment and marking/grading procedures.* Explain the assessment procedures and the procedures for determining marks or grades. Will there be quizzes, tests, homework, projects, and group work? What will be their formats, coverage, and weights in the procedure for determining grades? For group work, how will the contributions and learning of individual students be evaluated?

■ *Other information specific to the course.* Field trips, special privileges, computer work, parental expectations, homework hotline, classroom procedures and expectations (discussed in Chapter 4), academic honesty, and procedures regarding cell phones, personal digital assistants, laptops, and other electronic devices should be included here. To affirm that your policies as indicated in the first draft of your syllabus are not counter to any existing school policies, if you are a beginning teacher or are new to the school, you probably should share your first draft of the syllabus with members of your team or the department chairperson for their feedback. Now do Exercises 6.1 and 6.2.

The Instructional Unit

The *instructional unit* is a major subdivision of a course (for one course, there are several to many units of instruction), and is comprised of instruction planned around a central theme, topic, issue, or problem. Organizing the entire year's content into units makes the teaching process more manageable than when no plan or only random choices are made by a teacher.

The instructional unit, whether an interdisciplinary thematic unit (known also as an *integrated unit*) or a stand-alone standard subject unit, is not unlike a chapter in a book, an act or scene in a play, or a phase of work when undertaking a project such as building a house. Breaking down information or actions into component parts and then grouping the related parts makes sense out of learning and doing. The unit brings a sense of cohesiveness and structure to student learning and avoids the piecemeal approach that might otherwise unfold. You can learn to articulate lessons within, between, and among unit plans and focus on important elements while not ignoring tangential information of importance. Students remember chunks of information, especially when those chunks are related to specific units.

Types of Instructional Units

Although the steps for developing any type of instructional unit are essentially the same, units can be organized in a number of ways, basically differentiated and described as follows.

CONVENTIONAL UNIT A conventional unit (known also as a standard unit) consists of a series of lessons centered on a topic, theme, major concept, or block of subject matter. In a standard unit each lesson builds on the previous lesson by contributing additional subject matter, providing further illustrations, and supplying more practice or other added instruction, all of which are aimed at bringing about mastery of the knowledge and skills on which the unit is centered.

INTEGRATED UNIT When a conventional unit is centered on a theme, such as "transportation," then the unit may be referred to as a **thematic unit**. When, by design, the thematic unit integrates disciplines, such as one that combines the learning of science and mathematics or history/social studies and English/language arts (or all four of the core disciplines), then it is called an **integrated (interdisciplinary) thematic unit**.

SELF-INSTRUCTIONAL UNIT A self-instructional unit (known also as a *modular unit*) is a unit of instruction that is designed for individualized or modularized self-instruction. Such a unit is designed for independent, individual study; because it covers much less content than the units previously described, it can generally be completed in a much shorter time, usually an hour or less. The unit consists of instruction, references, self-check exercises, problems, and all other information and materials that a student needs to independently carry out the unit of work. Consequently, students can work on the units individually at their own speed, and different students can be working on different units at the same time. Students who successfully finish a modular unit can move on to another unit of work without waiting for the other students to catch up. Such units are essential ingredients of continuous-progress (multiage or nongraded) programs. Self-instructional units are useful in courses taught via distance education (see Chapter 10). And, finally, whether for purposes of remediation, enrichment, or makeup, self-instructional units work especially well when done at and in conjunction with a learning center. (Learning centers are discussed further in Chapter 8.)

CONTRACT UNIT A contract unit is an individualized unit of instruction for which a student agrees (contracts) to carry out certain activities. Some contract units have a variable-letter-grade agreement built into them. For example, the contract may contain specified information such as the following:

- For an A grade, you must complete activities 1 through 5 plus satisfactorily complete six of the optional related activities and receive no less than a B on the posttest.
- For a grade of B, you must complete activities 1 through 5 plus satisfactorily complete four of the optional related activities and receive no less than a B on the posttest.
- For a grade of C, you must complete activities 1 through 5 plus satisfactorily complete two of the optional related activities and receive no less than a C on the posttest.
- To pass with a D grade, you must complete activities 1 through 5 and pass the posttest.

Planning and Developing Any Unit of Instruction

For the several types of unit plans—a conventional unit, a contract unit, a self-instructional unit, and an interdisciplinary thematic unit—steps in planning and developing the unit are the same and are described in the following paragraphs.

1. *Select a suitable theme, topic, issue, or problem.* These may be already laid out in your course of study or textbook or already agreed to by members of the teaching team. However, many schools change their themes or add new ones from year to year.
2. *Select the goals of the unit and prepare the overview.* The goals are written as an overview or rationale, covering

what the unit is about and what the students are to learn. In planning the goals, you should (a) become as familiar as possible with the topic and materials used; (b) consult curriculum documents, such as courses of study, state frameworks, and resource units, for ideas; (c) decide the content and procedures (i.e., what the students should learn about the topic and how); (d) write the rationale or overview, where you summarize what you expect the students will learn about the topic; and (e) be sure your goals are congruent with those of the course or grade-level program.

3. *Select suitable instructional objectives.* In doing this, you should (a) include understandings, skills, attitudes, appreciations, and ideals; (b) be specific, avoiding vagueness and generalizations; (c) write the objectives in performance terms; and (d) be as certain as possible that the objectives will contribute to the major learning described in the overview.

4. *Detail the instructional procedures.* These procedures include the subject content and the learning activities, established as a series of lessons. Proceed with the following steps in your initial planning of the instructional procedures:

   a. By referring to curriculum documents, resource units, and colleagues as resources, gather ideas for learning activities that might be suitable for the unit.

   b. Check the learning activities to make sure that they will actually contribute to the learning designated in your objectives, discarding ideas that do not.

   c. Make sure that the learning activities are feasible. Can you afford the time, effort, or expense? Do you have the necessary materials and equipment? If not, can they be obtained? Are the activities suited to the intellectual and maturity levels of your students?

   d. Check available resources to be certain that they support the content and learning activities.

   e. Decide how to introduce the unit. Provide *introductory activities* that will arouse student interest; inform students of what the unit is about; help you learn about your students—their interests, their abilities, and their experiences and present knowledge of the topic; provide transitions that bridge this topic with that which students have already learned; and involve the students in the planning.

   f. Plan *developmental activities* that will sustain student interest, provide for individual student differences, promote the learning as cited in the specific objectives, and promote a project.

   g. Plan *culminating activities* that will summarize what has been learned, bring together loose ends, apply what has been learned to new situations, provide students with an opportunity to demonstrate their learning, and provide transfer to the unit that follows.

5. *Make lesson plan modifications to meet the needs of all of your students.* When planning your unit and its components, the daily lessons and specific activities, be sure to consider the accommodations you will make for the learners with special needs. Vary instructional strategies and consider students' learning modalities, learning styles, and learning capacities as well as the suggested guidelines discussed in Chapter 3.

6. *Plan for preassessment and assessment of student learning.* Preassess what students already know or think they know. Assessment of student progress in achievement of the learning objectives (formative evaluation) should permeate the entire unit (i.e., as often as possible, assessment should be a daily component of lessons). Plan to gather information in several ways, including informal observations, checklist observations of student performance and their portfolios, and paper-and-pencil tests. As discussed in Chapter 11, assessment must be congruent with the instructional objectives.

7. *Provide for the materials and tools of instruction.* The unit cannot function without materials. Therefore, you must plan long before the unit begins for media equipment and materials, references, reading materials, reproduced materials, and community resources. Librarians and media center personnel are usually more than willing to assist in finding appropriate materials to support a unit of instruction.

Unit Format, Inclusive Elements, and Time Duration

Follow the seven steps previously noted to develop any type of unit. In addition, two general points should be made. First, although there is no single best format for a teaching unit, there are minimum inclusions. Particular formats may be best for specific disciplines or grade levels, topics, and types of activities. During your student teaching, your college or university program for teacher preparation and/or your cooperating teacher(s) may have a format that you will be expected to follow. Regardless of the format, the following elements should be evident in any unit plan: (a) identification of grade level, subject, topic, and time duration of the unit; (b) statement of rationale and general goals for the unit; (c) major objectives of the unit; (d) materials and resources needed; (e) lesson plans; (f) assessment strategies; and (g) a statement of how the unit will attend to variations in students' reading levels, experiential and cultural backgrounds, and special needs.

Second, there is no set time duration for a unit plan, although for specific units curriculum guides will recommend certain time spans. Units may extend for a minimum of several days or, as in the case of some interdisciplinary thematic units, for several weeks to an entire school year. However, be aware that when conventional units last more than two or three weeks, they tend to lose the character of clearly identifiable units. For any unit of instruction, the exact time duration will be dictated by several factors, including the topic, problem, or theme; the age, interests, and maturity of the students; and the scope of the learning activities.

Curriculum Integration

In recent years, it has become apparent to many teachers that to be most effective in teaching important understandings to the diversity of students in today's classrooms, much of the learning in each discipline can be made more effective and longer lasting when that learning is integrated with the whole curriculum and made meaningful to the lives of the students rather than when simply taught as an unrelated and separate discipline at the same time each day.

In an exercise Dr. Heidi Hayes Jacobs refers to as **curriculum mapping**, middle and high school teachers start the process of designing integrated curriculum by listing what they each teach in their disciplines in a calendar year. Hayes Jacobs refers to this plan as the road map of their year, with each month corresponding to a signpost on the road map. Instead of having teachers list what they are required, expected, and hope to teach, she has teachers focus on what they actually cover in order to brainstorm opportunities for integrating the curriculum. According to Hayes Jacobs, integrating curriculum is really about integrating teachers. Discipline isolation can be avoided if we teach teachers to look for obvious connections among their content areas. It requires space and time for teachers to

plan together. As a result, students become engaged, empowered learners who take responsibility for their learning.[4] Complete Activity 6.1 now.

Procedural and Conceptual Knowledge

It is also quite clear that if learning is defined as being only the accumulation of bits and pieces of information, then we already know how that is learned and how to teach it. However, the accumulation of pieces of information (which is called *declarative knowledge*) is at the lowest end of a spectrum of types of learning and leads to what is sometimes referred to as *procedural knowledge* (which is knowing how to do something). For higher levels of thinking and for learning that is most meaningful and longest lasting, that is, knowing when to use declarative and procedural knowledge, referred to as conceptual knowledge, the results of research support the use of (a) a curriculum where disciplines are integrated and (b) instructional techniques that involve the learners in social interactive learning, such as cooperative learning, peer tutoring, and cross-age teaching.[5]

The Spectrum of Integrated Curriculum

When learning about **integrated curriculum**, it is easy to be confused by the plethora of terms that are used, such as

---

Activity
6.1

Curriculum Mapping

Schools and districts nationwide are mapping their curricula. In an effort to align the scope and sequence of K–12, be accountable, and establish open communication with parents, teachers are reporting what they actually teach. Curriculum Mapper, an online tool designed to simplify the curriculum mapping process, was developed by Dr. Heidi Hayes Jacobs. Curriculum Mapper helps teachers examine the curriculum both vertically and horizontally, organize their content, focus on skill development, and create appropriate assessments. Estes Park Middle School, located in Estes Park, CO, has successfully implemented this dynamic reporting process. With the use of Curriculum Mapper, the faculty at Estes Park Middle School keep track of how the standards are being addressed and what is being taught when, during a specific school year and across a student's 13-year K–12 academic career.

Check out Park School District R3's mission statement, the district's newsletters available in both Spanish and English, other school news, and general school information available on the website listed below. Next, check out the information on Estes Park Middle School English teacher Susan Ryder, 2007 Colorado Teacher of the Year recipient. Then access the link for Estes Park Middle School by scrolling down to the bottom of the right-hand corner to "Curriculum Mapping" and click on the "Middle" school link. The necessary User ID (6180) and password (bobcats) to grant you access to the Curriculum Mapper are available on the website along with specific easy-to-follow instructions.

The teachers and staff in Park School District R3 all have their curriculum maps posted on their website. Check out the 2006–2007 academic year curriculum maps for sixth-grade geography and eighth-grade mathematics designed by Anastasia Sunday

and Kathy Klipstein, respectively. Review what they have entered in the following categories for each month of the school year: content and essential questions, skills, assessment, resources, and potential enhancements. Then review their sample lesson plans in Chapter 7 of this textbook. You can also check out the curriculum maps designed by the high school faculty as well as the other sixth- through eighth-grade curriculum maps created by the middle school teachers.

Apply Your Knowledge

Peruse the Park School District R3 website and the curriculum maps developed by faculty at Estes Park Middle School at the following address:

Park School District R3
http://psdr3.k12.co.us

Then follow the Curriculum Mapper links to find out more about this online tool designed to simplify the curriculum mapping process for middle and high school teachers. See how integrating standards and tracking curriculum is made easy.

Curriculum Mapper—Dr. Heidi Hayes Jacobs
http://www.youtube.com/watch?v58etEUVzo2GE

Curriculum Mapping—Kassblog Heidi Hayes Jacobs
http://www.kassblog.com/2011/02/
    curriculum-mapping-heidi-hayes-jacobs

Welcome to Curriculum Mapping 101
http://www.curriculummapping101.com/index.html

thematic instruction, *multidisciplinary teaching*, *integrated studies*, *interdisciplinary curriculum*, *interdisciplinary thematic instruction*, and *integrated curriculum*. In essence, regardless of which of these terms is being used, the reference is to the same thing.

Before going further, because it is not always easy to tell where curriculum leaves off and instruction begins, let's assume for now that, for the sake of better understanding the meaning of *integrated curriculum*, there is no difference between what is **curriculum** and what is **instruction**. In other words, for the intent of this discussion, there is no relevant difference between the two terms. Whether we use the term *integrated curriculum* or the term *integrated instruction*, we are referring to the same thing.

Definition of Integrated Curriculum

Integrated curriculum (or any of its synonyms mentioned in the preceding discussion) refers to both a way of teaching and a way of planning and organizing the instructional program so that the discrete disciplines of subject matter are related to one another in a design that (a) matches the developmental needs of the learners and (b) helps to connect their learning in ways that are meaningful to their current and past experiences. In that respect, integrated curriculum is the antithesis of traditional, isolated subject matter–oriented teaching and curriculum designations.

Integrated Curricula Past and Present

The reason for the variety of terminology is, in part, because the concept of integrated curriculum is not new. It has had a roller-coaster ride throughout most of the history of education in the U.S. Therefore, over time, efforts to integrate student learning have had varying labels.

Without reviewing that history, suffice to say that prior to now, in some form or another, the most recent popularity stems from the late 1950s, with some of the discovery-oriented, student-centered projects supported by the National Science Foundation. Some of these are *Elementary School Science* (ESS), a hands-on and integrated science program for grades K–6; *Man: A Course of Study* (MACOS), a hands-on, anthropology-based program for fifth graders; and *Environmental Studies* (name later changed to *ESSENCE*), an interdisciplinary program for use in all grades, K–12, regardless of subject matter orientation. The popularity of integrated curriculum also stems from the "middle school movement," which began in the 1960s (discussed in Chapter 1), and from the "whole-language movement" in language arts, which began in the 1980s.

Current interest in the development and implementation of integrated curriculum and instruction has risen from at least three sources: (1) the success at curriculum integration that has been enjoyed by many schools, (2) the literature-based movement in reading and language arts, and (3) recent research in cognitive science and neuroscience about how children learn.

An integrated curriculum approach may not necessarily be the best approach for every school or the best tactic for every student's learning, nor is it necessarily the manner by which every teacher should or must always plan and teach. As evidenced by practice, the truth of this statement becomes obvious.

Levels of Curriculum Integration

In attempts to connect students' learning with their experiences, efforts fall at various places on a spectrum or continuum, from the least integrated instruction (level 1) to the most integrated (level 5), as illustrated in Figure 6.8.[6]

It is not our intent that this illustration be interpreted as going from worst-case scenario (top) to best-case scenario (bottom), although some experts may interpret it in exactly

Figure 6.8 **Levels of Curriculum Integration**

Level	Subject	Collaboration	Solo or Team		
Level 1	Subject-specific topic outline	No student collaboration in planning	Teacher solo	Least Integrated	Student input into decision making is low.
Level 2	Subject-specific	Minimal student input	Solo or teams		
Level 3	Multidisciplinary	Some student input	Solo or teams		Student input into decision making is high.
Level 4	Interdisciplinary thematic	Considerable student input in selecting themes and in planning	Solo or teams		
Level 5	Integrated thematic	Maximum student and teacher collaboration	Solo or teams	Most Integrated	Student input into decision making is very high.

that way. It is meant solely to illustrate how efforts to integrate fall on a continuum of sophistication and complexity. The paragraphs that follow describe each level of the continuum.

LEVEL 1   This is the traditional organization of curriculum and classroom instruction, where teachers plan and arrange the subject-specific scope and sequence in the format of topic outlines, much as you did for Exercise 5.5. If there is an attempt to help students connect their learning and their experiences, then it is up to individual classroom teachers to do it. A student who moves during the school day from classroom to classroom, from teacher to teacher, from subject to subject, and from one topic to another is likely learning in a level 1 instructional environment. A topic in science, for example, might be earthquakes. A related topic in social studies might be the social consequences of natural disasters. These two topics may or may not be studied by a student at the same time.

LEVEL 2   When the same students are learning English/language arts, social studies/history, mathematics, or science through a thematic approach rather than a topic outline, they are learning at level 2. At this level, themes for one discipline are not necessarily planned and coordinated to correspond to or integrate with themes of another or to be taught simultaneously. The difference between what is a topic and what is a theme is not always clear. For example, earthquakes and social consequences of natural disasters are topics, whereas natural disasters could be the theme or umbrella under which these two topics could fall. At this level, the students may have some input into the decision making involved in planning themes and content.

LEVEL 3   When the same students are learning two or more of their core subjects (English/language arts, social studies/history, mathematics, and science) around a common theme, such as the theme *natural disasters*, from one or more teachers, they are then learning at level 3 integration. At this level, teachers agree on a common theme, and then they *separately* deal with that theme in their individual subject areas, usually at the same time during the school year. Therefore, what the student is learning from a teacher in one class is related to and coordinated with what the student is concurrently learning in another or several other classes. Some authors may refer to level 2 or 3 as *coordinated curriculum*. At level 3, students may have some input into the decision making involved in selecting and planning themes and content.

LEVEL 4   When teachers and students do collaborate on a common theme and its content and when discipline boundaries begin to disappear as teachers teach about this common theme, either solo or as an interdisciplinary teaching team (as discussed in Chapter 1), level 4 integration is achieved.

LEVEL 5   When teachers and their students have collaborated on a common theme and its content, when discipline boundaries are truly blurred during instruction, and when teachers of several grade levels and/or of various subjects teach toward student understanding of aspects of the common theme, then this is level 5, an integrated thematic approach.

Procedure for Planning and Developing an Interdisciplinary Thematic Unit

The seven steps outlined earlier in this chapter are essential for planning any type of teaching unit, including the interdisciplinary unit, which is made of smaller subject-specific units. The primary responsibility for the development of interdisciplinary thematic units can depend on a single teacher or on the cooperation of several teachers representing several disciplines. Remember, as discussed in Chapter 1, that this interdisciplinary team may meet daily during a common planning time. Flexible scheduling allows for instructional blocks so that team members can have such common time, and unit lessons likewise can be less constrained by time.

A teaching team may develop from one to four interdisciplinary thematic units a year. Over time, then, a team will have several units that are available for implementation. However, the most effective units are often those that are the most current or the most meaningful to students. This means that ever-changing global, national, and local topics provide a veritable smorgasbord from which to choose, and teaching teams must constantly update old units and develop new and exciting ones.

One teaching team's unit should not conflict with another's at the same or another grade level. If a school has two or more teams at the same grade level that involve the same disciplines, for example, the teams may want to develop units on different themes and share their products. As another example, a ninth-grade team must guard against developing a unit quite similar to one that the students had earlier or will have later at another grade level. Open lines of communication within, between, and among teams and schools are critical to the success of thematic teaching.

Because developing interdisciplinary thematic units is an essential task for many of today's teachers, teacher candidates should learn this process now. One other point needs to be made: an interdisciplinary thematic unit can be prepared and taught by one teacher, but more often it is prepared and taught by a team of teachers. When the latter is the case, the instructional strategy is referred to as *interdisciplinary thematic team teaching*. A thematic unit may be designed by the core curriculum teachers, or a teaching team might consist of fewer than four disciplines, for example, just math and science or English and history or an academic discipline and a vocational class or some other combination of subjects. Here are a few recent examples:

- *Manatee High School (Bradenton, FL)*. Students from mathematics and vocational business studies worked together on a backyard swimming pool project; students from a computer-assisted drafting class and an honors geometry class actually designed and built a nine-hole miniature golf course; and students from marketing classes and foreign language classes worked together to examine international laws and customs.

- *North Penn High School (Lansdale, PA).* Students in child development, mathematics, and manufacturing classes combined their efforts to design and produce equipment for the school's child development program playground, including a 40-foot-long simulated train consisting of a locomotive and four cars. All students submitted papers for their English classes about the project.

- *Tolsia High School (Fort Gay, WV).* Students from English and vocational classes worked together at designing and building a scale-model medieval town complete with castles.

- *Waialua High School (Waialua, HI).* Students from applied technology, mathematics, art, and English classes combine knowledge and skills to build and race electric cars and make presentations on the construction and design of their cars.

The following steps are used to develop an interdisciplinary thematic unit:

1. *Agree on the nature or source of the unit.* Team members should view the interdisciplinary approach as a collective effort in which all members (and other faculty) can participate if appropriate. Write what you want the students to receive from interdisciplinary instruction. Troubleshoot possible stumbling blocks.

2. *Discuss subject-specific frameworks, goals, and objectives; curriculum guidelines; textbooks and supplemental materials; and units already in place for the school year.* Focus on what you must teach and explain the scope and sequence of the teaching so that all team members understand the constraints and limitations.

3. *Choose a topic.* From the information provided by each subject-specialist teacher in step 2, start listing possible topics that can be drawn from within the existing course outlines. Give-and-take is essential here, as some topics will fit certain subjects better than others. The chief goal is to find a topic that can be adapted to each subject without detracting from the educational plan already in place. This may require choosing and merging content from two or more other units previously planned. The theme is then drawn from the topic. When considering a theme, you should ask these questions:
   a. Is the theme within the realm of understanding and experience of the teacher involved?
   b. Will the theme interest all members of the team?
   c. Do we have sufficient materials and resources to supply information we might need?
   d. Does the theme lend itself to active learning experiences?
   e. Can this theme lead to a unit that is of the proper duration, not too short and not too long?
   f. Is the theme helpful, worthwhile, and pertinent to the course objectives?
   g. Will the theme be of interest to students, and will it motivate them to do their best?
   h. Is the theme novel enough so that teachers can share in the excitement of the learning?

4. *Establish two timelines.* The first is for the team only and is to ensure that the deadlines for specific work required in developing the unit will be met by each member. The second timeline is for both students and teachers and shows how long the unit will be, when it will start, and in which classes it will be taught.

5. *Develop the scope and sequence for content and instruction.* To develop the unit, follow the six steps for planning and developing a unit of instruction outlined earlier in this chapter. This should be done by each team member as well as by the group during common planning time so that members can coordinate dates and activities in logical sequence and depth. This is an organic process and will generate both ideas and anxiety. Under the guidance of the team leader, members should strive to keep this anxiety at a level conducive to learning, experimenting, and arriving at group consensus.

6. *Share goals and objectives.* Each team member should have a copy of the goals and objectives of every other team member. This helps to refine the unit and lesson plans and to prevent unnecessary overlap and confusion.

7. *Give the unit a name.* The unit has been fashioned and is held together by the theme you have chosen. Giving the theme a name and using that name tells the students that this unit of study is integrated, important, and meaningful to both school and life.

8. *Share subject-specific units, lesson plans, and printed and nonprinted materials.* Exchange the finalized unit to obtain one another's comments and suggestions. Keep a copy of each teacher's unit(s) as a resource and see if you could present a lesson using it as your basis (some modification may be necessary).

9. *Field-test the unit.* Beginning at the scheduled time and date, present the lessons. Team members may trade classes from time to time. Team teaching may take place when two or more classes can be combined for instruction (if a classroom space large enough is available), such as is possible with block scheduling.

10. *Evaluate and perhaps adjust and revise the unit.* Team members should discuss their successes and failures during their common planning time and determine what needs to be changed and how and when that should be done to make the unit successful. Adjustments can be made along the way (formative assessments), and revisions for future use can be made after the unit (summative assessment).

The preceding steps are not absolutes and should be viewed only as guides. Differing teaching teams and levels of teacher experience and knowledge make the strict adherence to any plan less productive than the use of group-generated plans. For instance, some teachers have found that the last point under step 3 could state exactly the opposite; they recommend that the topic for an interdisciplinary unit should be one that a teacher or a teaching team already knows well. In practice, the process that works well—one that results in meaningful learning for the students and in their positive feelings about themselves, about learning, and about school—is the appropriate process. Now collaborate on interdisciplinary units by completing Exercises 6.3 and 6.4.

Summary

Developing units of instruction that integrate student learning and that provide a sense of meaning for the students requires coordination throughout the curriculum—which is defined here as consisting of all the planned experiences students encounter while at school. Hence, for students, learning is a process of discovering how information, knowledge, and ideas are interrelated—learning to make sense out of self, school, and life. Molding chunks of information into units and units into daily lessons helps students process and make sense out of knowledge. Having developed your first unit of instruction, you are on your way to becoming a competent planner of instruction. There is no single best way to organize a daily plan, no "one-size-fits-all" lesson plan format, and no foolproof formula that will guarantee a teacher an effective lesson. With experience and the increased competence that comes from reflecting on that experience, you will develop your own style, your own methods of implementing that style, and your own formula for preparing a lesson plan. Like a map, your lesson plan charts the course, places markers along the trails, pinpoints danger areas, highlights areas of interest and importance along the way, and ultimately brings the traveler to the successful completion of the objective.

The best-prepared units and lessons, though, will go untaught or only poorly implemented if presented in a poorly managed classroom. Refer to Chapter 4 to review how to provide a supportive classroom environment—to effectively manage the classroom for the most efficient instruction and student achievement.

Exercise 6.1

Content of a Course Syllabus

Instructions: The purpose of this exercise is for you to begin your thinking about preparing a syllabus for use in your teaching. From the following list of items that might appear on a course syllabus, identify (by circling) all those you would include in your own course syllabus. And, for each, explain why you would or would not include that item. Then share the syllabus with your classmates. After sharing, you might want to make revisions in your own list.

1. Name of teacher (my name):

2. Course title (and/or grade level):

3. Room number:

4. Beginning and ending times:

5. Time when students could schedule a conference with teacher:

6. Course description:

7. Course philosophy or rationale (underline which):

8. Instructional format (such as lecture-discussion, student-centered learning groups, or laboratory centered):

9. Absence policy:

10. Tardy policy:

11. Classroom procedures and rules for behavior:

12. Goals of course:

13. Objectives of course:

14. Policy about plagiarism:

15. Name of textbook and other supplementary materials:

(continued)

Exercise 6.1   **Content of a Course Syllabus**   *continued*

16. Policy about use and care of textbook and other reading materials:

17. Materials to be supplied by student:

18. Assignments:

19. Policy about homework assignments (due dates, format, late assignments, weights for grades):

20. Course relationship to adviser-advisee program, core, cocurricular, exploratories, or some other aspect of the school curriculum:

21. Grading procedure:

22. Study skills:

23. Themes to be studied:

24. Field trips and other special activities:

25. Group work policies and types:

26. Other members of the teaching team and their roles:

27. Tentative daily schedule:

28. Other (specify):

29. Other (specify):

30. Other (specify):

Exercise 6.2   **Preparing a Course Syllabus—An Exercise in Collaborative Thinking**

Instructions: The purpose of this exercise is to prepare (in a group) a syllabus for a course that you intend to teach. Using your results from Exercise 6.1, work in groups of three or four members who will teach the same content area to develop one syllabus for a course you and other group members may someday teach. Each group should produce one course syllabus that represents that group's collaborative thinking; the finished product should be duplicated and shared with the entire class. Discuss within your group the pros and cons of having student input into the course syllabus (see Figure 6.7). Share the results of that discussion with the entire class.

Exercise 6.3   **Generating Ideas for Interdisciplinary Units**

Instructions: The purpose of this exercise is for you to use brainstorming to generate a list of potential topics suitable as interdisciplinary units. Divide your class into groups of three to five. Each group is to decide the grade or age level for which their ideas will be generated. If the group chooses, cooperative learning can be used; group members are then assigned roles such as facilitator, recorder, reporter, monitor of thinking processes, on-task monitor, and so on. Each group is to generate as many topics as possible. One member of each group should record all ideas. Reserve discussion of ideas until no further topics are generated. Lists can be shared with the entire class.

Grade-level interest of the group:

1. Existing subject-area content units (as the group knows them to be or as they are predicted to exist):

2. Current topics of
   a. Global interest:
   b. National interest:
   c. Statewide interest:
   d. Local interest:
   e. Interest to the school:
   f. Interest to students of this age:

Exercise
6.4

Integrating the Topic

Instructions: The purpose of this exercise is for you to practice weaving interdisciplinary themes into our curricula. In groups of three or four, choose one idea that was generated during Exercise 6.3 and derive a list of suggestions about how that theme could be woven into the curricula of various classes, programs, and activities, as indicated below. It is possible that not all areas listed are relevant to the grade level to which your group is addressing its work. Cooperative learning can be used, with appropriate roles assigned to group members. One person in the group should be the recorder. On completion, share your group's work (the process and product of which will be much like that of an actual interdisciplinary teaching team) with the class. Copies should be made available to those who want them.

Unit theme:

1. In core classes
   a. English:
   b. Social studies:
   c. Mathematics:
   d. Science:
   e. Reading:
   f. Physical education:
   g. Art:
   h. Music:

2. In cocurricular programs and activities
   a. Electives:
   b. Clubs:
   c. School functions:
   d. Assemblies:
   e. Intramurals:
   f. Study skills:

3. In exploratories:

4. In homerooms:

5. Explain how multicultural components could be incorporated into the unit.

6. As individuals and as a group, how productive was this exercise?

Chapter 6   Posttest

Short Explanation

1. Explain the concept of unit and lesson planning and where and how it fits in a curriculum built around a block schedule with classes that are sometimes integrated disciplines and that are each perhaps up to 150 minutes long.

2. Explain three reasons why a beginning teacher needs to prepare detailed lesson and unit plans, even when the textbook program you are using provides them.

3. Describe a situation during instruction when, if ever, you can or should divert from the written plan.

4. Describe the elements you would include in your syllabus? Would you share the same syllabus with your students and their parents? Why or why not?

5. Define and describe each of the various levels of curriculum integration.

Essay

1. Describe three different types of activities that could be used to introduce a unit of instruction for a particular grade level in your subject field.

2. Explain the importance of organizing instruction into units. Is there ever a time when you might not do so? Explain.

3. Describe the advantages and disadvantages of interdisciplinary thematic instruction for a teacher of your subject area and grade-level interest.

4. From your current observations and fieldwork related to this teacher preparation program, clearly identify one specific example of educational practice that seems contradictory to exemplary practice or theory presented in this chapter. Present your explanation for the discrepancy.

5. Describe any prior concepts you held that changed as a result of your experiences with this chapter. Describe the changes.

Designing Lesson and Unit Plans to Engage All Students

Alamy Images

Making a living and having a life are not the same thing. Making a living and making a life that's worthwhile are not the same thing. Living the good life and living a good life are not the same thing. A job title doesn't even come close to answering the question, "What do you do?"[1]

—ROBERT FULGHUM

Specific Objectives

At the completion of this chapter, you will be able to:

▸ Describe the format and basic elements of a lesson plan.

▸ Prepare a teaching unit complete with daily lesson plans, demonstrating an understanding of the basic components of a lesson plan.

▸ Differentiate among preassessment, formative assessment, and summative assessment and describe how each is used.

▸ Explain the concept of planning as a continual process and the best way to integrate technology into lesson plans to engage all students.

▸ Explain the place and role of each of the four decision-making and thought-processing phases in unit planning and unit implementation.

Chapter 7 Overview

In Chapter 6, we reviewed the basics of preparing an instructional plan. We described the components of course syllabi, examined several types of instructional units, and reviewed the various levels of curriculum integration. This chapter focuses on lesson and unit planning and is designed to acquaint you with the basic elements and procedures necessary for developing effective units and lessons to engage your students and to provide insight into how to critically evaluate the process and products. It includes numerous examples of lesson and unit plans for a variety of subject areas and grade levels and descriptions of the individuals who contributed the plans along with suggestions on how the lesson and unit plans could be modified to include even more technology and/or how the lesson and unit plans could be modified to best meet the needs of diverse learners.

Introduction

The lesson plans included in this chapter were contributed by pre-service teachers, teacher candidates, in-service teachers, and master teachers, as well as teacher educators. Many of these exemplary lesson plans have integrated technology and provided suggestions on how the plans can be extended to other disciplines effectively. We have also provided a variety of additional suggestions on how best to differentiate the lessons to reach all students as well as alternative ways to make these lesson and unit plans even more technology rich. If you plan to use the lesson and unit plans presented here or if you will have these lesson and unit plans serve as models for future lessons you create, ultimately, you as the teacher will have to adapt, alter, and adjust these lesson plans and our suggestions to meet the needs of your own particular groups of students. You will have to develop a lesson plan style that is comfortable for you, usable in your teaching, and effective in facilitating student learning. This chapter will help you to accomplish that.

Lesson Planning: Rationale and Assumptions

As described at the beginning of Chapter 6, step 5 of the seven steps of instructional planning is the preparation for class meetings. The process of designing a lesson is important in learning to provide the most efficient use of valuable and limited instructional time and the most effective learning for the students to meet the unit goals.

Notice the title of this section refers not to the *"daily lesson plan"* but rather to the "lesson plan." The focus is on how to prepare a lesson plan, which may or may not be a daily plan. In some instances, a lesson plan may extend for more than one class period or for days, perhaps two or three. In other instances, the lesson plan is, in fact, a daily plan and may run for an entire class period. In block scheduling, one lesson plan may run for part of or for an entire two-hour block of time. See the section "The Problem of Time" later in this chapter.

Effective teachers are always planning for their classes. For the long range, they plan the scope and sequence and develop content. Within this long-range planning, they develop units, and within units they design the activities to be used and the assessments of learning to be done. They familiarize themselves with books, materials, media, and innovations in their fields of interest. Yet, despite all this planning activity, the lesson plan remains pivotal to the planning process. Consider now the rationale, description, and guidelines for writing detailed lesson plans.

Rationale for Preparing Written Lesson Plans

Carefully prepared and written lesson plans show everyone— first and foremost your students, then your colleagues, your administrator, and, if you are a student teacher, your cooperating teacher and your college or university supervisor—that you are a committed professional. Sometimes, beginning teachers are concerned with being seen by their students using a written plan in class, thinking it may suggest that the teacher has not mastered the material. On the contrary, a lesson plan is tangible evidence that you are working at your job and demonstrates respect for the students, yourself, and the profession. A written lesson plan shows that preactive thinking and planning have taken place. There is absolutely no excuse for appearing before a class without evidence of being prepared.

Written and detailed lesson plans provide an important sense of security, which is especially useful to a beginning teacher. Like a rudder of a ship, a lesson plan helps keep you on course. Without it, you are likely to drift aimlessly. Sometimes a disturbance in the classroom can distract from the lesson, causing the teacher to forget an important part of the lesson. A written and detailed lesson plan provides a road map to guide you and help keep you on track.

Written lesson plans help you to be or become a reflective decision maker. Without a written plan, it is difficult or impossible to analyze how something might have been planned or implemented differently after the lesson has been taught. Written lesson plans serve as resources for the next time you teach the same or a similar lesson and are useful for teacher self-evaluation as well as the evaluation of student learning and of the curriculum.

Written lesson plans help you organize material and search for loopholes, loose ends, or incomplete content. Careful and thorough planning during the preactive phase of instruction includes anticipation of how the lesson activities will develop as the lesson is being taught. During this anticipation, you will actually visualize yourself in the classroom teaching your students, using that visualization to anticipate possible problems.

Written plans provide evidence for administrators that specific content was taught. This is especially important since teachers are often judged on how well their students perform on standardized tests.

Written plans help other members of the teaching team understand what you are doing and how you are doing it. This is especially important when implementing an interdisciplinary thematic unit. *Written lesson plans also provide substitute teachers with a guide to follow if you are absent.*

The preceding reasons clearly express the need to write detailed lesson plans. The list is not exhaustive, however, and you may discover additional reasons why written lesson plans are crucial to effective teaching. In summary, two points must be made: (1) lesson planning is an important and ongoing process, and (2) teachers must take time to plan, reflect, write, test, evaluate, and rewrite their plans to reach optimal performance.

Assumptions about Lesson Planning

Not all teachers need elaborate written plans for every lesson. Sometimes, effective and skilled veteran teachers need only a sketchy outline. Sometimes, they may not need written plans at all. Veteran teachers who have taught the topic many times in the past may need only the presence of a class of students to stimulate a pattern of presentation that has often been successful (though frequent use of old patterns may lead one into the rut of unimaginative and uninspiring teaching).

Considering the diversity among middle school and secondary school teachers, their instructional styles, their students, and what research studies indicate, certain assumptions about lesson planning can be made:

1. Although not all teachers need elaborate written plans for all lessons, all effective teachers do have clearly defined goals and objectives in mind and a planned pattern of instruction for every lesson, whether that plan is written out or not.

2. Beginning teachers need to prepare detailed written lesson plans. Failing to prepare is preparing to fail.

3. Some subject matter fields, topics, or learning activities require more detailed planning than others.

4. The depth of knowledge a teacher has about a subject or topic influences the amount of planning necessary for the lessons.

5. The skill a teacher has in remaining calm and in following a train of thought in the presence of distraction will influence the amount of detail necessary when planning activities and writing the lesson plan.

6. A plan is more likely to be carefully and thoughtfully plotted when it is written out.

7. The diversity of students within today's public school classroom necessitates careful and thoughtful consideration about individualizing the instruction; these considerations are best implemented when they have been thoughtfully written into lesson plans.

8. There is no particular pattern or format that all teachers need to follow when writing out plans. Some teacher preparation programs have agreed on certain lesson plan formats for their teacher candidates; you need to know if this is the case for your program.

In summary, well-written lesson plans provide many advantages. They give a teacher an agenda or outline to follow in teaching a lesson, they give a substitute teacher a basis for presenting appropriate lessons to a class—thereby retaining lesson continuity in the regular teacher's absence—and they are certainly very useful when a teacher is planning to use the same lesson again in the future. Lesson plans provide the teacher with something to fall back on in case of a memory lapse, an interruption, or some distraction, such as a call from the office or a fire drill. In addition, using a written plan demonstrates to students that you care and are working for them. Above all, lesson plans provide beginning teachers security because, with a carefully prepared plan, a beginner can walk into a classroom with confidence and professional pride gained from having developed a sensible framework for that day's instruction.

Thus, as a beginning teacher, you should make considerably detailed lesson plans. Naturally, this will require a great deal of work for at least the first year or two, but the reward of knowing that you have prepared and presented effective lessons will compensate for that effort.

A Continual Process

Lesson planning is a continual process even for experienced teachers, for there is always a need to keep materials and plans current and relevant. Because no two classes of students are ever identical, today's lesson plan will need to be tailored to the peculiar needs of each classroom of students. Moreover, because the content of instruction and learning will change as each distinct group of students with their own needs and interests give input, new thematic units are developed, new developments occur, or new theories are introduced, your objectives and the objectives of the students, school, and teaching faculty will change.

For these reasons, lesson plans should be in a constant state of revision. Once the basic framework is developed,

however, the task of updating and modifying becomes minimal. If your plans are maintained on a computer, making changes from time to time is even easier.

Well Planned but Open to Last-Minute Change

The lesson plan should provide a tentative outline of the time period given for the lesson but should always remain flexible. A carefully worked out plan may have to be set aside because of the unpredictable, serendipitous effect of a "teachable moment" (see the Teaching Scenario "A Lost Opportunity") or because of unforeseen circumstances, such as a delayed school bus, an impromptu school assembly program, an emergency drill, or the cancellation of school due to inclement weather conditions. Student teachers often are appalled at the frequency of interruptions during a school day and of disruptions to their lesson planning that occur. A daily lesson planned to cover six aspects of a given topic may end with only three of the points having been considered. Although far more frequent than necessary in too many schools, these occurrences are natural in a school setting, and the teacher and the plans must be flexible enough to accommodate this reality.

Although you may have your lesson plans completed for several consecutive lessons, as can be inferred by the vignette involving Casey and her students, what actually transpires during the implementation of today's lesson may necessitate late adjustments to the lesson you have planned for tomorrow.

The Problem of Time

A lesson plan should provide enough materials and activities to consume the entire class period or time allotted. As mentioned earlier, it should be well understood that, in your planning for teaching, you need to plan for every minute of every class period. The lesson plan, then, is more than a plan for a lesson to be taught; it is a plan that accounts for the entire class period or time that you and your students are together in the classroom. Because planning is a skill that takes years of experience to master, especially when teaching a block of time that may extend for 90 or more minutes and that involves more than one discipline and perhaps more than one teacher, as a beginning teacher you should overplan rather than run the risk of having too few activities to occupy the time the students are in your classroom. One way of ensuring that you overplan is to include "if time remains" activities in your lesson plan. For an example of overplanning, see Lesson Plan 7.8A and Lesson Plan 7.8C, which have a variety of proposed activities in the lessons included in the unit plan designed by Dr. Nivea Lisandra Torres titled "The Immigrant Experience in Literature: Literature for and about Hispanic Students" and the "Sheltered Instruction Observation Protocol Lesson Plan: Identifying the Main Idea in a Reading Selection."

When a lesson plan does not provide sufficient activity to occupy the entire class period or time that the students are available for the lesson, a beginning teacher often loses

Teaching Scenario: A Lost Opportunity

Casey was teaching an eighth-grade humanities block, a two-hour block course that integrates student learning in social studies, reading, and language arts. On this particular day, while Casey and her students were discussing the topic of Manifest Destiny, a student raised his hand and, when acknowledged by Casey, asked, "Why aren't we [the United States] still adding states [i.e., taking more territory into the United States]?" Casey immediately replied, "There aren't any more states to add." By responding too quickly, Casey missed one of those "teachable moments," moments when the teacher has the students thinking and asking questions.

What could Casey have done? She could have asked a series of questions to get the students thinking critically about when the most recent additions to the U.S. were and why today there still are U.S. territories, that is, places that are overseen by the federal government and share some rights and responsibilities but are not states. For instance, Casey could have asked the following questions: When did Alaska gain statehood (January 3, 1959)? Before this time, Alaska was given territorial status; what changed for Alaskans when President Eisenhower signed the official declaration making Alaska the 49th state? When was Hawaii added as the 50th state to the United States (August 21, 1959)? Did all Hawaiians support statehood 50 or more years ago? If not, why did some people object to having Hawaii become a state? What happened in the recent 50th-anniversary celebration that highlighted the fact that many Native Hawaiians remain antistatehood? Why hasn't Puerto Rico become a state? Guam? The Philippines? And so forth. Aren't those possibilities for new states? Why *aren't* more states or territories being added today? What are the political and social ramifications of being a territory of the U.S. today, and how do they differ from those of the 1800s? It might also be interesting to discuss perspective. For instance, do you think Indigenous people would have the same definition/meaning of Manifest Destiny? Why or why not? How might that perspective differ among Indigenous people living in the 48 contiguous states versus Alaska and Hawaii?

control of the class as behavior problems mount. Thus, it is best to prepare more than you likely can accomplish in a given period of time. This is not to imply that you should involve the students in meaningless busy work. Students can be very perceptive when it comes to a teacher who has finished the plan and is attempting to bluff through the minutes that remain before dismissal.

If you ever do get caught short—as most teachers do at one time or another—one way to avoid embarrassment is to have students work on what is referred to as an *anchor assignment* (or transitional activity). This is an ongoing assignment, and students understand that whenever they have spare time in class, they should be working on it. Example anchor activities include a review of material that has been covered that day or in the past several days, allowing students to work on homework, journal writing, portfolio organization, and long-term project work. Regardless of how you handle time remaining, it works best when you plan for it and write that aspect into

your lesson plan and when the procedures for doing it are well understood by the students.

A Caution about "The Daily Planning Book"

A distinction needs to be made between actual lesson plans and the book for daily planning that many schools require teachers to maintain and even submit to their supervisors a week in advance. Items that a teacher writes in the boxes in a daily planning book (see Figure 7.1) most assuredly are not lesson plans; rather, the pages are a layout by which the teacher writes into the boxes to show what lessons will be taught during the day, week, month, or term. Usually, the book provides only a small lined box for time periods for each day of the week. These books are useful for outlining the topics, activities, and assignments projected for the week or term, and supervisors sometimes use them to check the adequacy of teachers' course plans. However, they are too sketchy to be called lesson plans.

Figure 7.1 Daily Lesson Plan Book

DAILY LESSON PLAN BOOK				
Grade _____ Subject _____ Lesson _____ Teacher _____				
Date	*Content*	*Materials*	*Procedure*	*Evaluation*
Monday				
Tuesday				
Wednesday				
Thursday				
Friday				

Constructing a Lesson Plan: Format, Components, and Samples

Although it is true that each teacher develops a personal system of lesson planning—the system that works best for that teacher in his or her unique situation—a beginning teacher needs a more substantial framework from which to work. The best format to use is constantly evolving. This section provides a *preferred* lesson plan format (Figure 7.2). Review the preferred lesson plan format; the lesson plan template was provided by the Department of Education at Linfield College in McMinnville, OR. Unless or until your program of teacher preparation insists otherwise, use it with your own modifications until you find or develop a better model.

For Guidance, Reflection, and Reference

While student teaching and during your first few years as a beginning teacher, your lesson plans should be printed from a computer or, if that isn't possible, written out in an intelligible style. If you keep electronic copies of your lesson plans, adaptations and modifications can be easily recorded. If you have a spelling problem, then we suggest that you use a spell-check program and print your plans from the computer. There is good reason to question teachers who say they have no need for a written plan because they have their lessons planned in their heads. The hours and periods in a school day range from several to many, as does the number of students in each class. When multiplied by the number of school days in a week, a semester, or a year, the task of keeping so many things in one's head becomes mind-boggling. Few persons could effectively do that. Until you have considerable experience behind you, you will need to prepare and maintain detailed lesson plans for guidance, reflection, and reference.

Basic Elements of a Lesson Plan

A written lesson plan should contain the following basic elements: (a) descriptive data, (b) goals and objectives, (c) rationale, (d) procedure, (e) assignments and assignment reminders, (f) materials and equipment, (g) accommodations for students with special needs, (h) a section for assessment of student learning, and (i) reflection on the lesson and ideas for lesson revision. These nine components need not be present in every written lesson plan, nor must they be presented in any particular order. They are neither inclusive nor exclusive; therefore, you might choose to include additional components or subsections.

Several sample lesson plans are included in this chapter so that you can examine a variety of styles and look for examples of each of the components described in the various lesson plans included here to see how they compare. As mentioned earlier, contributions are from seasoned professionals, teacher educators, pre-service teachers, and teacher candidates during their student-teaching assignment. Figure 7.2 illustrates a format that includes several

of the previously mentioned components and sample subsections of those components. Some contributors followed this format closely, and others used a variety of other lesson plan formats. Following are detailed descriptions of the major components of the preferred format.

Descriptive Data

A lesson plan's descriptive data include demographic and logistical information that identifies details about the class. Anyone reading this information should be able to identify when and where the class meets, who is teaching it, and what is being taught. Although as the teacher you know this information, someone else may not. Members of the teaching team, administrators, and substitute teachers (and, if you are the student teacher, your university supervisor and cooperating teacher) appreciate this information. Most teachers discover which items of descriptive data are most beneficial in their situation and develop their own identifiers. Remember this: the mark of a well-prepared, clearly written lesson plan is the ease with which someone else (such as another member of your teaching team or a substitute teacher) could implement it. The descriptive data include the following:

1. Name of course or class and grade level. These serve as headings for the plan and facilitate orderly filing of plans.
2. Instructional strategies used for creating and teaching the lesson.
3. Name of the unit. Inclusion of this facilitates the orderly control of the hundreds of lesson plans a teacher constructs.
4. Topic to be considered within the unit. This is also useful for control and identification.
5. Time allotted for the lesson plan. Specify how long a class period is.

Goals and Objectives

The goals are general statements of intended accomplishments from that lesson. Teachers and students need to know what the lesson is designed to accomplish. In clear, understandable language, the general goal statement provides that information. Because the goals are also included in the unit plan, sometimes a teacher may include only the objectives in the daily lesson plan. The instructional objectives state what you want your students to be able to do as a result of the experiences that you provide.

SETTING THE LEARNING OBJECTIVES A crucial step in the development of any lesson plan is setting the objectives. It is at this point that many lessons go wrong and where many beginning teachers have problems.

A common error and how to avoid it. Teachers sometimes confuse *learning activity* (*how* the students will learn it) with the *learning objective* (*what* the student will learn as a result of the learning activity). For example, teachers sometimes mistakenly list what they intend to do—such as "lecture on photosynthesis" or "lead a discussion on the

Figure 7.2 **Preferred Lesson Plan Format with Nine Components**

LESSON PLAN

1. Descriptive Data

Teacher _____ Class _____ Date _____ Grade level _____

Room number _____ Period _____ Unit _____

Lesson number _____ and Topic _____

2. Goals and Objectives

Instructional Goals:

Specific Objectives:

   Cognitive:

   Affective:

   Psychomotor:

3. Rationale

4. Procedure (Procedure with time plan, modeling examples, transitions, guided practice experiences, etc.)

Content:

_____ minutes. Activity 1 (set introduction):

_____ minutes. Activity 2:

_____ minutes. Activity 3 (the exact number of activities in the procedure will vary):

_____ minutes. Final Activity (lesson conclusion or closure):

If time remains:

5. Assignments and Reminders of Assignments

Special notes and reminders to myself:

6. Materials and Equipment Needed

Audiovisual:

Other:

7. Accommodations for Students with Special Needs. (Specifically describe what you plan to do to ensure the success of each and every one of your students who is identified as having special needs.)

8. Assessment of Student Learning

Assessment of student learning tied directly to instructional objectives.

9. Reflection/Evaluation (Discuss the relative success or failure of your lesson)

Reflective thoughts about lesson:

Suggestions for revision:

SOURCE: Adapted from Linfield College Education Department Lesson Plan Template from 2004. Used with permission.

causes of the Civil War"—and fail to focus on just what the learning objectives in these activities truly are—that is, what the students will be able to do (performance) as a result of the instructional activity. Or, rather than specifying what the student will be able to do as a result of the learning activities, the teacher mistakenly writes what the students will do in class (the learning activity)—such as, "In pairs the students will do the 10 problems on page 72"—as if that were the learning objective.

When you approach this step in your lesson planning, to avoid error ask yourself, "What should students learn *as a result* of the activities of this lesson?" Your answer to that question is your objective. Objectives of the lesson are included as specific statements of performance expectations, detailing precisely what students will be able to do as a result of the instructional activities.

NO NEED TO INCLUDE ALL DOMAINS AND HIERARCHIES IN EVERY LESSON Not all three domains (cognitive, affective, and psychomotor) are necessarily represented in every lesson plan. As a matter of fact, any given lesson plan may be directed to only one or two (or a few) specific objectives. Over the course of a unit of instruction, however, all domains and most, if not all, levels within each should be addressed.

Rationale

The rationale is an explanation of why the lesson is important and why the instructional methods chosen will achieve the objectives. Parents, students, teachers, administrators, and others have the right to know why specific content is being taught and why the methods employed are being used. Prepare yourself well by setting a goal for yourself of always being prepared with intelligent answers to those two questions. Teachers become reflective decision makers when they challenge themselves to think about *what* (the content) they are teaching, *how* (the learning activities) they are teaching it, and *why* (the rationale) it must be taught.

Procedure

The **procedure** consists of the instructional activities for a scheduled period of time. The substance of the lesson—the information to be presented, obtained, and learned—is the content. Appropriate information is selected to meet the learning objectives, the level of competence of the students, and the grade level or course requirements. To be sure your lesson actually covers what it should, you should write down exactly what minimum content you intend to cover. This material may be placed in a separate section or combined with the procedure section. Be sure that your information is written down because it is important to be able to refer to it quickly and easily when you need to.

If, for instance, you intend to conduct the lesson using discussion, you should write out the key discussion questions. Or, if you are going to introduce new material using

a 10-minute lecture, then you need to outline the content of that lecture. The word *outline* is not used casually—you need not have pages of notes to sift through, nor should you ever read declarative statements to your students. You should be familiar enough with the content so that an outline (in as much detail as you believe necessary) will be sufficient to carry on the lesson, as in the following example of a content outline:

Causes of Civil War

a. Primary causes
  1. Economics
  2. Abolitionist pressure
  3. Slavery
  4. etc.

b. Secondary causes
  1. North-South friction
  2. Southern economic dependence
  3. etc.

The procedure or procedures to be used, sometimes referred to as the *instructional components*, make up the *procedure* component of the lesson plan. It is the section that outlines what you and your students will do during the lesson. Appropriate instructional activities are chosen to meet the objectives, to match the students' learning styles and special needs, and to ensure that all students have an equal opportunity to learn. Ordinarily, you should plan this section of your lesson as an organized entity having a beginning (an introduction or set), a middle, and an end (called the **closure**) to be completed during the lesson. This structure is not always needed because some lessons are simply parts of units or long-term plans and merely carry on activities spelled out in those long-term plans. Still, most lessons need to include in the procedure (a) an *introduction*, the process used to prepare the students mentally for the lesson, sometimes referred to as the set, or initiating activity; (b) *lesson development*, the detailing of activities that occur between the beginning and the end of the lesson, including the transitions that connect activities; (c) *plans for practice*, sometimes referred to as the follow-up—that is, ways that you intend on having students interact in the classroom (such as individual practice, in dyads, or in small groups) while receiving guidance or coaching from each other and from you; (d) the *lesson conclusion* (or closure), the planned process of bringing the lesson to an end, thereby providing students with a sense of completeness and, with effective teaching, accomplishment and comprehension by helping students to synthesize the information learned from the lesson; (e) a *timetable* that serves simply as a planning and implementation guide; (f) a *plan* for what to do if you finish the lesson and time remains; and (g) *assignments*, that is, what students are instructed to do as follow-up to the lesson, either as homework or as in-class work, thus providing students an opportunity to practice and enhance what is being learned. Let's now consider some of those elements in detail.

INTRODUCTION TO THE LESSON Like any good performance, a lesson needs an effective beginning. In many
respects, the introduction sets the tone for the rest of the
lesson by alerting the students that the business of learning
is to begin. The introduction should be an attention-getter.
If it is exciting, interesting, or innovative, it can create a
favorable mood for the lesson. In any case, a thoughtful
introduction serves as a solid indicator that you are well
prepared. Although it is difficult to develop an exciting
introduction to every lesson taught each day, many
options are available by which to spice up the launching
of a lesson. You might, for instance, begin the lesson by
briefly reviewing the previous lesson, thereby helping
students connect the learning. Another possibility is to
review vocabulary words from previous lessons and to
introduce new ones. Still another possibility is to use the
key point of the day's lesson as an introduction and then
again as the conclusion. Sometimes teachers begin a lesson
by demonstrating a discrepant event (i.e., an event that is
contrary to what one might expect), sometimes referred to
as a "hook." Yet another possibility is to begin the lesson
with a writing activity on some controversial aspect of the
ensuing lesson. Sample introductions might include the
following:

- *For English, study of interpretations.* As students enter
  the classroom, the state song, for example, "I Love You,
  California," is playing softly in the background. After a
  warm greeting, the teacher begins by showing the state
  seal on the overhead and asks, "Does anyone know what
  this is?"
- *For U.S. history, study of Westward Expansion.* The
  teacher asks, "Who has lived somewhere else other than
  (*name of your state*)?" After students show hands and
  answer, the teacher asks individuals why they moved to
  (*name of your state*). The teacher then asks students to
  recall why the first European settlers came to the U.S.
  and then moves into the next activity.
- *For science, study of the science process skill of predicting.*
  The teacher fills a glass to the brim with colored water
  (colored so it is more visible) and asks students, in dyads
  (pairs), to predict how many pennies can be added to the
  glass before any water spills over its rim.
- *For Western civilizations, the study of history of religion.*
  You have five minutes to write an argument in support
  of or against the following statement: "The recent hate
  crimes in our nation can be related to what we are learning about the history of religion."

In short, you can use the introduction of the lesson to
review past learning, tie the new lesson to the previous
lesson, introduce new material, point out the objectives of
the new lesson, help students connect their learning with
other disciplines or with real life, or—by showing what
will be learned and why the learning is important—induce
in students some motivation and a mind-set favorable to
the new lesson.

LESSON DEVELOPMENT The developmental activities
make up the bulk of the plan and are the specifics by which
you intend to achieve your lesson objectives. They include
activities that present information, demonstrate skills,
provide reinforcement of previously learned material, and
provide other opportunities to develop understanding and
skill. Furthermore, by actions and words, during lesson
development the teacher models the behaviors expected
of the students. Students need such modeling. By effective
modeling, the teacher can exemplify the anticipated
learning outcomes. Activities of this section of the lesson
plan should be described in some detail so that (a) you will
know exactly what it is you plan to do and (b) during the
intensity of the class meeting you do not forget important
details and content. For this reason, you should consider,
for example, noting answers (if known) to questions you
intend to ask and solutions (if known) to problems you
intend to have students solve.

LESSON CONCLUSION Having a concise closure to the
lesson is as important as having a strong introduction.
The concluding activity should summarize and bind
together what has ensued in the developmental stage and
should reinforce the principal points of the lesson. Ways
to accomplish these ends include (a) restating or outlining
the key points of the lesson, (b) having students devise
one-sentence summaries, and (c) providing answers that
represent a review but having the students create the
questions. Sometimes the closure is not only a review of
what was learned but also the summarizing of a question
left unanswered that signals a change in your plan of
activities for the next day. In other words, it becomes a
transitional closure.

TIMETABLE Estimating the time factors in any lesson
can be very difficult, especially for a new teacher. A good
procedure is to gauge the amount of time needed for each
learning activity and note that alongside the activity and
strategy in your plan, as shown in the preferred sample
lesson plan format. However, placing too much faith in your
time estimate may be foolish; an estimate is more for your
guidance during the preactive phase of instruction than for
anything else. Beginning teachers frequently find that their
planned discussions and presentations do not last as long
as was expected. To avoid being embarrassed by running
out of material, try to make sure you have planned enough
meaningful work to consume the entire class period. (See
the section "The Problem of Time" earlier in this chapter.)
Another important reason for including a time plan in
your lesson is to give information to students about how
much time they have for a particular activity, such as a
quiz or a group activity. Students appreciate that sort of
thoughtfulness on the part of the teacher.

Assignments

When an assignment is to be given, it should be noted in
your lesson plan. The time to present an assignment to the

students is optional, but it should never be yelled as an afterthought as the students are exiting the classroom at the end of the period. Whether they are to be begun and completed during class time or done out of school, assignments should be written on the writing board, in a special place on the bulletin board, in each student's assignment log maintained in a binder, on a handout, or in some combination of these. Be sure that assignment specifications are perfectly clear to all students. Many teachers give assignments to their students on a weekly or other periodic basis. When given on a periodic basis rather than daily, assignments should still be included in your daily lesson plans in order to remind yourself to remind students of them.

Once assignment specifications and due dates are given, it is a good idea not to make major modifications to them, and it is especially important not to change assignment specifications several days after an assignment has been given. Last-minute changes in assignment specifications can be very frustrating to students who have already begun or completed the assignment; it shows little respect to those students. (See also "Learning from Assignments and Homework" in Chapter 11.)

ASSIGNMENT VERSUS PROCEDURE Understand the difference between assignments and procedures. An assignment tells students *what* is to be done, while procedures explain *how* to do it. Although an assignment may include procedures, spelling out procedures alone is not the same thing as giving an academic assignment. When students are given an assignment, they need to understand the reasons for doing it and have some notion of ways the assignment might be done.

BENEFITS OF COACHED PRACTICE Allowing time in class for students to begin work on homework assignments and long-term projects is highly recommended; it provides an opportunity for the teacher to offer personalized attention to students. Being able to coach students is the reason for using in-class time to begin assignments. The benefits of *coached practice* include being able to (a) monitor student work so a student doesn't go too far in a wrong direction, (b) help students develop their metacognitive skills (i.e., to reflect on their thinking), (c) assess the progress of individual students, (d) provide for peer tutoring, and (e) discover or create a "teachable moment." For the latter, for example, while observing and monitoring student practice, the teacher might discover a commonly shared student misconception. The teacher then stops and discusses that issue in an attempt to clarify the misconception, or the teacher may collaboratively, with students, plan a subsequent lesson focusing on the common misconception.

SPECIAL NOTES AND REMINDERS In their lesson plan format, many teachers have a regular place for special notes and reminders concerning such things as announcements to be made, school programs, long-term assignment due dates, and individual work for certain students. You should be able to reference this section quickly.

Materials and Equipment to Be Used

Materials of instruction include books, media, handouts, and other supplies necessary to accomplish the lesson objectives. You must be *certain* that the proper and necessary materials and equipment are available for the lesson; to be certain requires planning. Teachers who, for one reason or another, have to busy themselves during class looking for materials or equipment that should have been readied before class began are likely to experience classroom control problems.

Accommodations for Students with Special Needs

For every student in your class who has an Individualized Education Program (IEP), you need to specifically describe what you plan to do to ensure his or her success. By consulting the guidelines provided in Chapter 3, you can describe the steps you will take to accommodate that student.

Assessment

Details of how you will assess how well students are learning (formative assessment) and how well they have learned (summative assessment) should be included in your lesson plan. This does not mean to imply that both types of assessment will be in every daily plan. Comprehension checks for formative assessment can be in the form of questions that you ask and that the students ask during the lesson (in the procedural section) as well as various kinds of checklists.

For summative assessment, teachers typically use review questions at the end of a lesson (as a closure) or the beginning of the next lesson (as a review or transfer introduction), in independent practice or summary activities at the completion of a lesson, and in tests.

Reflection and Revision

In most modern lesson plan formats, there is a section reserved for the teacher to make notes or reflective comments about the lesson. Reflections about the lesson are useful for you and for those who are supervising you if you are a student teacher or a teacher being mentored or considered for tenure. Sample reflective questions you might ask yourself are shown in Figure 7.3.

As you will see in the variety of middle- and secondary-level lesson plans featured here, common elements are often included, but the level of detail varies greatly. Compare the following 10 key elements in the sample lesson plans in this chapter: (1) descriptive data (subject, grade level, lesson, unit, time frame, and so on), (2) standard(s) (which specific subject/grade standard is being addressed), (3) goals (from the teacher's point of view) and instructional objectives (cognitive, affective, and psychomotor), (4) rationale (why teach this lesson and how it fits into the curriculum), (5) procedure (procedure with time plan, modeling examples, transitions, guided practice experiences, and so on; warm-up/introduction, content, activities, closure), (6) assignments and reminders of assignments, (7) materials and equipment needed, (8) accommodations for students with

Figure 7.3 **Questions for Lesson Self-Relection**

- What is my overall feeling about today's lesson—good, fair, or bad? What made me feel this way?
- Did students seem to enjoy the lesson? What makes me think so?
- Did the objectives seem to be met? What evidence do I have?
- What aspects of the lesson went well? What makes me believe so?
- Were I to repeat the lesson, what changes might I make? Why?
- Which students seemed to do well? Which ones should I give more attention to? Why and how?
- To what extent was this lesson personalized according to student learning styles, abilities, interests, talents, and needs? Could I do more in this regard? Why or why not?
- Did the students seem to have sufficient time to think and apply? Why or why not?
- Would I have been proud had the school superintendent been present to observe this lesson? Why or why not?

special needs (specifically describe what you plan to do to ensure the success of each and every one of your students who is identified as having special needs), (9) assessment of student learning (assessment of student learning tied directly to instructional objectives), and (10) reflection/evaluation (discuss the relative success or failure of your lesson; suggestions for revision). Then examine the additional lesson plans created by pre-service teachers, in-service teachers, curriculum designers, and teacher educators that appear in this chapter.

Writing and, later, reading your reflections can not only provide ideas that may be useful if you plan to use the lesson again at some later date but can also offer catharsis, easing the tension caused from teaching. To continue working effectively at a challenging task (i.e., to prevent intellectual **downshifting**, or reverting to earlier learned, lower-cognitive-level behaviors) requires significant amounts of reflection. After you have reviewed the sample lesson plan formats, proceed to Exercise 7.1, where you will analyze a lesson that failed; then, as instructed by your course instructor, do Exercises 7.2A, 7.2B, and 7.3.

Reviewing and Analyzing the Lesson Plans

As mentioned before, the lesson and unit plans included here were contributed by a diverse group of educators with varying degrees of experience. Most were written by individuals, and some were collaborative efforts among dyads or groups. These sample lesson and unit plans were contributed by both middle- and secondary-level educators willing to share their journeys. Some have extensive experience in lesson planning and teaching, and others have provided their first attempt at writing a lesson plan. The sample lesson plans in this chapter represent many subject areas, including language arts/English, mathematics, science, social studies, geography, history, psychology, English as-a-second-language, English as-a-foreign-language, French, art, and music.

We will introduce you to each educator who contributed a lesson or unit plan here, highlight the strengths of each contribution, make suggestions on how the lesson plan can

be further enhanced by adding more technology, and discuss how best to differentiate instruction where appropriate. First, we will review the contributions of lesson and unit plans designed to be used with middle school students. Then we will review the lesson and unit plans created for use with secondary-level students.

Middle School–Level Lesson and Unit Plans

In this section, middle school lessons in science, geography, mathematics, music, Indian Education for All/science, and English as-a-foreign-language and their contributors are described.

LESSON PLAN 7.1 The lesson plan, titled "The James Webb Space Telescope: Why Space Telescopes Are Important," was contributed by Ryan Hannahoe and Peter Detterline. Ryan Hannahoe is an education and public outreach intern on the James Webb Space Telescope mission at the NASA Goddard Space Flight Center and an elementary education student, with an emphasis on science education, at Montana State University, Bozeman. Peter Detterline is an instructor of astronomy at Kutztown University, and he serves as the director of the Boyertown Area School District Planetarium. This is an exemplary, inquiry-based, multidisciplinary lesson plan integrating science, art, and technology; it addresses national standards in each of these disciplines. In this lesson, designed for sixth to eighth-graders, students are asked to reflect on why telescopes are important and why a space telescope is needed as opposed to a ground-based telescope and to record their ideas in their journals. Next, the instructors engage the students in a mini-lead-in that has them focusing on various objects as they look through a misted window representing the Earth's atmosphere with their naked eyes and later with binoculars and/or a telescope, among other variations. The instructors then have teams of students create scale models of the Hubble Space Telescope's and of the James Webb Space Telescope's primary mirrors. Once they complete their models, students compare the Hubble and its successor, the Webb Space Telescope, and share their findings. This hands-on interactive lesson is designed to have students appreciate why space-based telescopes are important.

As an addition to this lesson plan, after students have completed their models, compared the Hubble and Webb telescopes, and recorded their findings in their journals, or perhaps between steps 8 and 9 under "Instructional Procedures" outlined in the lesson plan, it might work well to have students peruse the references included in this lesson plan and other websites, such as Ryan Hannahoe's site Astronomical Imaging at **http://ryanhannahoe.nmskies.com**, the NASA James Webb Space Telescope site at **http://www.wst.nasa.gov/teachers/html**, and the Hubble Telescope site at **http://hubblesite.org**, to explore what makes the telescopes tick and how they are serviced by astronauts and ground crews and to look at images, animations, and videos and then share what they find in a PowerPoint or Prezi presentation for their classmates.

Lesson Plan 7.1   The James Webb Space Telescope

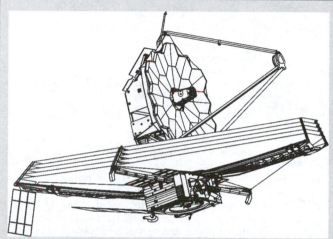

Credit: Illustration courtesy of NASA

Grade Level: 6 to 8

Lesson Duration: 2 × 50 minute periods

Rationale: Later this decade, the James Webb Space Telescope (Webb) will launch from Earth to unlock some of the most thought provoking questions of our time. Webb is the successor of the Hubble Space Telescope (Hubble), and stands 3 stories high and spans the size of a tennis court. This gargantuan telescope will reside 1-million miles from our planet; this is nearly 4 times the distance from the Earth to the Moon. Webb will study the formation of galaxies, planets outside of our Solar System, and newborn stars by using the infrared part of the Electromagnetic Spectrum. The 6.5 meter segmented mirror of Webb has a light-gathering power of 7 times that of Hubble. To give students a perspective on the need of large space-based telescopes, students will explore why these types of telescopes are necessary, and students will work together to construct a scale model of the Hubble and Webb mirrors. This multi-disciplinary lesson will cover topics in art, science, and technology.

Key Concepts: The importance of large space telescopes and perspective

Content Standards:

National Science Education Standards (1996: Grades 5–8)
- A: Abilities of Technological Design
  - Implement a proposed design
- F: Science in Personal and Social Perspectives
  - Science and technology in society

International Society for Technology in Education Standards (2007: Grades K–12)
- 1: Creativity and Innovation
  - B: Create original works as a means of personal or group expression

- C: Use models and simulations to explore complex systems and issues

National Standards for Visual Art (1994: Grades 5–8)
- 5: Reflecting upon and assessing the characteristics and merits of their work and the work of others
  - Students compare multiple purposes for creating works of art
- 6: Making connections between visual arts and other disciplines
  - Students describe ways in which the principles and subject matter of other disciplines taught in school are interrelated with the visual arts

Learning Outcomes:
- Students will *describe* why space-based telescopes are important.
- Students will, as a class, *create* a scale model of the Webb primary mirror and an artistic representation of a galaxy on the reverse side of that model.
- Students will *compare* each mirror model and each galaxy representation. Students will additionally *reflect* on what differences exist between each model and how subjects like art and science can be interrelated.

Instructional Procedure:

1. Begin the lesson by having students take out their science journals. Ask students *"Why are telescopes important?"* and *"Why do we need a space telescope as opposed to a ground-based telescope?"* Allow them time to write their responses in their journals. Have students pair up and ask them to share their responses with a classmate and then share with the class.

2. Have students gather around a window in the classroom or in the school. Spray the window with water by using a water mister. Guide students' understanding using an analogy that this window represents the Earth's atmosphere. Have students focus their sight on a distant object on the other side of the glass. Ask them to describe the appearance of the object in as much detail as possible, and to discuss some of the challenges they face in viewing the object. Have them record these responses in their journal.

3. Repeat step 2, but this time have the students look at the same object through the window with a set of binoculars or a small telescope mounted on a tripod. Ask them to again describe the appearance of the object in as much detail as possible. Can they see more detail using the optical aid or less? Why? What is the problem of observing objects in space from Earth? Have them record their responses in their journals.

4. Lift up the window and have the students look at that same object with only their eyes. Ask them to describe the appearance of the object in as much detail as possible. How is this image different from the first time they viewed the object with the window closed? Have them record their responses in their journals.

(continued)

Lesson Plan 7.1 **The James Webb Space Telescope** *continued*

5. Repeat step 4, but this time have the students look through the window with binoculars or a small telescope mounted on a tripod.Ask them to again describe the appearance of the object in as much detail as possible and again to record their answers in their journals.

6. Have students break into small groups and share their journal observations. Have each group share their answers with the class. Guide students' understanding that telescopes need to be in space so that we do not see a blurry image. Ask them *"Which view did they like the best?"*and then *"How could you see more detail to view the image even better?"* Student responses should discuss the need for a bigger pair of binoculars or telescope to see an object in more detail.

7. Relate the view seen with their eyes through the open window to that of the Hubble Space Telescope. Explain to students that we need larger telescopes in space to see celestial objects in more detail. The view of the object through binoculars or a small telescope compared to the unaided view is the kind of difference that you would see with a larger telescope in space compared to a smaller one in space, such as the James Webb Space Telescope compared to the Hubble Space Telescope.

8. Break the class into two groups.One group will be the Hubble Space Telescope Team (3 or more students) and the other the James Webb Telescope Team (the rest of the class will need to be 18 students). Explain to the students that they will be making a scale model of the Hubble and the Webb mirrors.

Space Telescope Mirror Comparison

HEIGHT IN METERS

Hubble
Primary Mirror

Webb
Primary Mirror

Credit: Illustration courtesy of A. Feild (STScI/AURA)

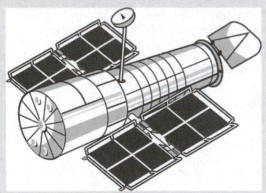

Credit: Illustration courtesy of NASA

The Hubble Space Telescope Team
From the Resources Section at the end of this lesson, share Hubble facts with students. Students should have the understanding that they will be sharing what they believe is important from this information with the rest of the class.

9. Give the students an 8" × 8" sheet of cardstock and a similar size of tinfoil. Have the students use a guide to trace and then cut out a circle with a diameter of 7.3"of cardstock and tinfoil. The students should then glue the tinfoil, shiny-side-up, to one of the sides of the cardstock circle.

10. Reference the illustration at the end of this lesson that depicts the primary mirror of Hubble. The illustration shows a galaxy. Assign the students to draw the galaxy on the non-tinfoil side of their model. Have students clean up their area when finished.

James Webb Space Telescope Team
As the Hubble Team begins working on their telescope model have the Webb team work on theirs. From the Resources Section at the end of this lesson, share Webb facts with students. The students should have the understanding that they'll be sharing

what they believe is important from this information with the rest of the class.

11. Explain to students that they are going to be making a scale model of Webb's primary mirror. Distribute one 5" × 5" sheet of cardstock and a similar size of tinfoil to the students. They will need 18 pieces to complete the mirror model.

12. Have each student use a guide to trace and then cut out a hexagon with a diameter of 4". The students should have one hexagon made of cardstock and one of tinfoil. The student should then glue the tinfoil, shiny-side-up, to one of the sides of the cardstock hexagon.

13. Reference the illustration at the end of this lesson that depicts the 18 mirror segments of Webb. Each mirror segment shows a portion of a galaxy. Assign a mirror segment to the students so that they can draw the corresponding portion of that galaxy on the non-tinfoil side of their model.

14. Once students have completed their drawings, have them assemble the model by taping the edges of the segments together by using clear tape (this is best if done on the tinfoil side of the model).

15. Using a meter stick and some masking tape, have students create a full scale mirror segment of the James Webb Space Telescope on the floor. It needs to be a hexagon with a diameter of 1.32 meters. Make certain that students understand that this is a real-scale model of just one of the 18 mirror segments. Have students look at their Webb mirror segment model for reference. Have students clean up their area.

16. Have the Hubble Space Telescope Team show their mirror and share with the class some of the interesting things they learned about their telescope. Likewise, have the James Webb Telescope Team show their mirror and share with the class some of the interesting things that they learned about their telescope.

17. Have students look at the size of the mirror segment of the James Webb Space Telescope and compare it to the Hubble mirror. Have a group of students stand in a circle with a 2.4 m diameter (the diameter of the Hubble mirror). Ask them *"Why do you think the Webb is better if the Hubble mirror is larger?"* The students should understand that the Webb consists of 18 segments all working together to form a large array of mirrors with a greater light collecting area than that of Hubble. Have students look at their Webb mirror segment model for reference. Ask them *"How many Webb mirror segments could fit in the classroom?"* and *"How many classrooms would it take to create a full scale model using all 18 segments?"*

(continued)

Lesson Plan 7.1 **The James Webb Space Telescope** *continued*

18. Have students return to their desks and take out their science journals. Ask them to think about everything they learned today and to summarize it in three to five sentences. The summary should be conversational (as if talking to a friend who is not in the class), factual (using words that they can understand), and without personal opinions (we already know it is cool—just the facts please). Students should also write a few sentences on how they think the discoveries made by Webb will affect the world and them personally. Collect science journals from students when they are finished.

Plan for Assessment:

Formative Assessment: As an informal, formative assessment, students should complete both before/after observations of the "looking through the window" portion of this lesson. Completion credit can be awarded depending on both observations made and that each student offers discussion in their journals.

Summative Assessment: Students will complete either a Hubble mirror or a Webb mirror segment portion. Students will also turn in their science journals at the end of the lesson. Students will be evaluated based off of the checklist below:

✓ Students, in their journal, discussed why space-based telescopes are important.

✓ Students, in their journal, offered a meaningful summary reflection that included 3 or more points discussed in this lesson.

✓ Students turned in their mirror segment with a portion of a galaxy drawn on the reverse side

Materials:

✓ Computer and LCD projector with lesson graphics loaded on it

✓ Colored crayons or pencils

✓ Enough cardstock and tinfoil for 5" × 5" and 8" × 8" segments for the number of students outlined above (Be sure to have extra!)

✓ Glue

✓ Rulers

✓ Meter stick

✓ Science journals or other writing material for students' reflection

✓ Scissors

✓ Set of binoculars or small telescope mounted on a tripod

✓ Clear tape

✓ Masking tape

✓ Water spray mister

References:

Webb: How does Webb compare with Hubble?
   http://www.jwst.nasa.gov/comparison_about.html

Webb: Quick Facts
   http://www.jwst.nasa.gov/facts.html
   http://jwstsite.stsci.edu/webb_telescope/technology_at_the
   _extremes/quick_facts.php

Webb: Challenge: Make it big
   http://jwstsite.stsci.edu/webb_telescope/technology_at_the
   _extremes/make_it_big.php

About the Authors:

Ryan Hannahoe is an education and public outreach intern on the James Webb Space Telescope mission at the NASA Goddard Space Flight Center. Ryan is also an elementary education student at Montana State University – Bozeman.

Peter Detterline is an instructor of astronomy at Kutztown University, and he serves as the director of the Boyertown Area School District Planetarium.

Additional resources:

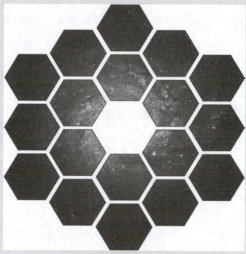

Credit: Galaxy image courtesy of NASA, ESA, and the Hubble Heritage Team (STScI/AURA)

The above represents an image of a face-on spiral galaxy that appears on our Webb mirror model; this has been slightly altered for the purpose of this lesson and is not to scale.

For additional resources discussed in this lesson plan, please visit:

http://www.jwst.nasa.gov/education/JWST-Lesson_Plan
-RHannahoe-PDetterline.pdf

SOURCE: Contributed by Ryan Hannahoe and Peter Detterline. Used with permission.

LESSON PLAN 7.2 Anastasia Sunday is certified to teach social studies and highly qualified to teach science and technology. Currently, she is a sixth-grade geography teacher at Estes Park Middle School in Estes Park, CO. She is a seasoned professional with 15 years of middle- and secondary-level teaching experience. Two of her lesson plans focusing on photographs as primary sources are included here so you can see the progression of her planning. In her lesson plans, she blends her passion for social studies and technology to teach her students how to analyze, read, and interpret photographs with a critical eye while addressing the question, "What characterizes a primary source?" The lesson plan titled "Geography Sixth-Grade Lesson Plan: Analyzing Photographs" (see Lesson Plan 7.2A) is the first draft, and Lesson Plan 7.2B is the revised lesson plan with technology integrated throughout. Sunday believes it is important that

Lesson Plan 7.2A **Geography Sixth-Grade Lesson Plan: Analyzing Photographs**

One-day lesson. 60 minutes.

Essential Questions:

How do historians use photographs as historical data?

How much can a picture tell you about the environment around you?

How do pictures inform you about culture?

Intelligences used: Kinesthetic, interpersonal, intrapersonal, spatial

Standards: Standard H.1 Students understand the chronological organization of history and know how to organize events and people into major eras to identify and explain historical relationships.

Expectation H.1.3 Students use chronology to examine and explain historical relationships.

Expectation H.2.3 Students apply knowledge of the past to analyze present-day issues and events from multiple, historically objective perspectives.

Materials:

Pictures depicting life in the 1800s in Canada (15 pictures—2 to a pair)

Paper/Pencil

Overhead

Overheads of pictures

Large paper to hang around the room

Large markers for students to write on paper

Procedures:

Tape large pieces of paper around the room. Label each piece of paper with the following labels: First Reaction, Collect Data, Make Generalizations, Draw Inference, and Draw Conclusion. Explain vocabulary to students.

Have students work in groups of two. Pair/share. Then split them into two groups. Each group is analyzing a different photograph depicting activities of daily life in Canada. Students will be working from individual to pairs to large group format. Students will gather all the information and then they will be given markers to go and write their paired information on the large pieces of paper.

1. First reaction. Jot down whatever first impressions you have about the photograph individually. Wait one minute and have them share with a partner. (Do this with all labels.)
2. Collect data. Make list of such things as the number of people in the picture, their appearance, the types of clothing, and the weather.
3. Make generalizations. Use the list and other observations to make statements about the photo. For example, "The people in the photo represent members of the same social group (they are all wearing similar kinds of clothing)."
4. Draw inferences. Go beyond the photo to try to determine why the photo was taken, whether it was posed, when it was taken, what one might see outside the frame of the photo . . . .
5. Draw conclusions. What facts about life in Canada can you learn from the photo? How does the photo help you understand the culture/daily life of the people who lived there?

Have the students put their information on the pieces of paper and then have them compare photographs with each other. They should find the same information.

Vocabulary: Generalization, inference, conclusion, primary source

Modifications and Assessment: It happens during the lesson. Working individual, groups. Tag appropriate, higher level thinking.

SOURCE: Contributed by Anastasia Sunday, Cultural Studies Teacher, Estes Park Middle School, Estes Park, CO. Used with permission.

Lesson Plan 7.2B **Geography Sixth-Grade Lesson Plan: Analyzing Photographs**

Lesson Plan: Analyzing Photographs of Canada: A Gallery Walk of Canadian Photographs—Are Photographs Primary Sources?

Submitted by: Anastasia Sunday (Estes Park Middle School, Estes Park, Colorado)

Grade Levels: Grades 5-7
Subjects: Geography and History
Duration: 1-2 days (50 minute class periods)

Standards:

• This lesson meets the National Council for the Social Studies (NCSS) national standards for social studies teachers which state that student experiences will encourage increasingly abstract thought as they use data and apply skills in analyzing human behavior in relation to their physical and cultural environment. Historical analysis enables us to identify continuities over time in core institutions, values, ideals, and traditions, as well as processes that lead to change within societies and institutions, and that result in innovation and the development of new ideas, values and ways of life. (Themes 1,2,3)

• This lesson meets Colorado State requirements to develop an understanding of how people view, construct, and interpret history.

Description:
Students will analyze a gallery of Canadian photographs that depict the culture, the geography and the history of Canada. These photographs will be chosen from Google Images and other Canadian Web

sites that best represent Canada. A variety of photographs that have been manipulated as well as others that are accurate will be included.

The students will have to determine whether each photograph is representative of Canadian culture, if it belongs in the Canadian gallery and if it should be considered a primary source, or not. Students will have the opportunity to manipulate a Canadian primary source photograph, to see how easy it is to doctor a photograph with technology.

Goal:
The goal is to introduce students to a variety of images to see if they can select ones that are representative of Canadian culture (a task that also assesses prior knowledge the students already have about Canada) and to demonstrate that not all photographs can be considered primary sources. The goal is for students to analyze and interpret historical sources and to be able to formulate historical questions.

Objectives:
Students will be able to:

• identify ways different cultures record history.
• interpret documents and data from multiple primary and secondary sources while formulating historical questions.
• make generalizations about the photographs.
• draw inferences and make conclusions about life in Canada based on the photographs.
• identify why all photographs are not considered primary sources.

(continued)

Lesson Plan 7.2B **Geography Sixth-Grade Lesson Plan: Analyzing Photographs** *continued*

Internet Resources for Background Information:

- http://www.collectionscanada.gc.ca/education/008-3010-e.html — primary sources
- http://editor.pho.to — edit pictures free software works (no download required)
- http://freedownloaders.net/downloads/gimp/?t202id=246&c1=GCN&t202kw=Photo%20editor%20software — edit photos free software (download required)
- http://www.canadaphotos.info — great photos to use for landscapes for gallery walk
- http://commfaculty.fullerton.edu/lester/writings/day.html — fake cover National Geographic 1991
- http://www.media-awareness.ca/english/resources/educational/teachable_moments/photo_truth.cfm — media literacy ... great photograph combining all the things that make Ottawa beautiful in one shot

Materials:

- pictures from Google images depicting life in Canada from 1800 to the present
- papers/pencils
- handouts
- computers
- http://www.collectionscanada.gc.ca/education/008-3010-e.html
- Smartboard or projector/overhead projector
- pictures from Google Images depicting similar aspects of life in countries other than those included in the gallery on Canada. They include other places in the world such as photos of Big Ben in London, landscapes, Maroon bells in Colorado, and famous people who are not from Canada.

Procedures:

1. Hand out a piece of paper that has the following information: First Reaction, Collect Data, Make Generalizations, Draw Inferences, and Draw Conclusions. Explain vocabulary to students.
2. Have students work in groups of two. Pair/Share. Each group will analyze a different photograph depicting activities of daily life in Canada and perform the following tasks on a handout created by the teacher for the students:

   - First Reaction: Jot down all first impressions you have about the photograph.
   - Collect Data: Make a list of details such as the number of people in the picture, their appearance, the type of clothing they are wearing, what you can assume about the weather, etc.
   - Make Generalizations: Use the list you generated and other observations to make statements about the photo. For example, "The people in the photo represent members of the same social group (they are all wearing similar clothing)."

- Drawing Inferences: Go beyond the photo to try to determine why the photo was taken, whether it was posed, when it was taken, what one might see outside the frame of the photo, etc.
- Drawing Conclusions: What facts about life in Canada can you learn from the photo? How does the photo help you understand the culture/daily life of the people who live there?

3. After students have analyzed one photo have them continue to gallery walk and visit many images and jot down information about the photographs, such as any similarities or differences they see in the photographs. What are some of the cultural aspects of Canada they can assume from viewing the photographs? Students should spread out and walk around the room to see the images clearly.
4. Ask students if any images seem out of place. On the gallery walk add in 2-3 images that have been manipulated or are from some other location that the students might recognize. Ask students to explain photographs as a primary source. See the link in Materials for background information.
5. Not all photographs can be considered primary sources because they can be changed and/or manipulated. Show students some examples of Canadian photos that have been changed. For example, put Big Ben where the Peace Tower is on the Parliament building using a photo editing program or change the Parliament building into an oil painting and then make it a black and white photograph. Use the photo of Ottawa, and ask the students what is wrong with this picture?

Evaluation/Assessment:

A. Collect student handouts with all their written responses about the Canadian photographs.
B. Have students turn in a reflective essay answering the following questions.
   1. How much can a picture tell you about the environment around you?
   2. How do pictures tell you about culture?
   3. How do historians use photographs as historical data?
   4. Are photographs primary sources?
C. Ask students to attempt to manipulate a picture from Canadian culture and change something using an editing program online. The teacher or a different student can evaluate the level of success anonymously.

Possible Extension:

Have students create their own gallery walk with pictures they collect from Google depicting the culture of Canada. Have students add a variety of photographs from several aspects of Canadian culture in their gallery walk to represent all aspects of Canada. Have students comment on the photograph of their teacher seated in the Canadian Parliament. Students should answer the question, "What's wrong with this picture of Ottawa?"

SOURCE: Contributed by Anastasia Sunday, 6th Grade Geography Teacher, Estes Park Middle School, Estes Park, CO. Used with permission.

students know that so-called primary sources can easily be manipulated with Photoshop and paint programs. In fact, in her revised lesson plan, she has integrated altered photographs into the Gallery Walk she prepared for her students and has provided students with instruction on how to manipulate photographs themselves (see Lesson Plan 7.2B).

After attending the STUDY CANADA Summer Institute for K–12 Educators professional development workshop in Ontario and Quebec (read about her experience in Chapter 12), Sunday revised her 60-minute lesson plan. In her revised lesson plan, she guides students to use photographs to organize history chronologically and to become acquainted with all aspects of Canadian culture: history, geography, politics, pop culture, sports, the arts, and so on. For additional contributions by Sunday in this textbook, check out Figure 6.5, Sixth-Grade Geography Syllabus," in Chapter 6; Figure 11.10,

"Grading Rubric for Sixth-Grade Geography, South America Unit PowerPoint Project," in Chapter 11; and the following Teaching Scenarios: "Communicating with Parents Using Infinite Campus" in Chapter 11 and "STUDY CANADA Summer Institute for K–12 Educators" in Chapter 12.

LESSON PLAN 7.3 Kathy Klipstein is a middle school mathematics teacher who has been teaching seventh- and eighth-grade math for 15 years at Estes Park Middle School in Estes Park, CO. She has a master's degree in educational technology. She blends her love of math and her knowledge and skills in integrating technology across her curriculum to create technology-rich lesson plans like the "Technology-Integrated Mathematics Lesson Plan" she contributed here (see Lesson Plan 7.3). This lesson plan enables students to use a free online graphing calculator (GCalc) in algebra 1 to work at their own pace and get help with homework. Graphing calculators are expensive and easily lost. The websites that Klipstein has included in her lesson plan are excellent resources for students who are exploring how to use a graphing calculator. In fact, teachers and students worldwide use GCalc every day for their graphing needs. GCalc is designed to provide a basic, easy-to-use, well-balanced set of graphing functionality that is very helpful

to middle school students studying algebra. It has great graphics, is interactive, and is easily accessible. Since all students may not be able to afford a personal graphing calculator and some schools cannot afford purchasing a classroom set of graphing calculators (while others may have a class set of graphing calculators to be used in school but do not supply graphing calculators for students to use outside of class), using free resources online is a great alternative.

LESSON PLAN 7.4 Dr. Stephanie L. Standerfer is an associate professor of music education at Shenandoah Conservatory at Shenandoah University in Winchester, Virginia. She taught public school vocal and general music in grades K–12 for nine years in Colorado and Virginia before completing her graduate studies and serving as a teacher educator. Standerfer's research has focused on differentiating K–12 curriculum, experiential education, teaching music literacy, and National Board Certification for music teachers. According to Standerfer, if K–12 classroom music teachers plan ahead and tap into their creativity, differentiating music instruction to meet the needs of all students in a variety of choral, instrumental, and general music courses can be accomplished. In her lesson plan "Music Lesson" (see Lesson Plan 7.4), she introduces her students

Lesson Plan 7.3 **Technology-Integrated Mathematics Lesson Plan**

Title: Online Graphing Calculator Activity
Equipment/Supplies needed: Computer lab with Internet access
Subject: Algebra 1
Instructor: Kathy Klipstein
Grade Level: 8th
Colorado Math Standard 2
Lesson Length: 35–45 minutes, optional second day for Activity 3
Task Objectives: Enable students to find outside sources for help in algebra; Explore the common functions of a typical graphing calculator using technology

Process Strategy Activity:
1. The following is a very informative Web site for those of you exploring with graphing calculators. You can choose the model you have and find exact steps for entering info for the calculator to solve. For example, if you wondered how to find absolute value correctly using your calculator, the specific steps for your model calculator with pictures of the buttons are provided.
   http://www.prenhall.com/divisions/esm/app/calc_v2/
2. For those of you who do not have a graphing calculator and those who just like to explore, this next Web site provides free access for graphing equations.
   http://www.gcalc.net

Please experiment with changing the data on the column at the right of the page to see the effects on your screen. (For example, change one thing at a time like the X MIN to -5. What happened?)

List your changes and results for class discussion on Friday.

Move your mouse around inside the graph. What does the gray box on the top left corner with x = and y = do?

Click the gray boxes below the graph one at a time and see what happens. Please try to put settings back to the original after each change. Otherwise close and reopen the page.

Graph the following equations:

a) $y = 3x$ Directions: type 3x only, ***leave out the y =*** in the function bar located above the gray **x = y** box on the top left corner.

Then notice the change for the color from the menu on the right and graph $y = 3x + 4$; again, don't type the y = part. ☺ You will see your new line in a different color.

Now graph $y = -3x$

Then $y = -3x + 4$

Lastly, $y = -3x - 4$. Please summarize for me what you notice about the different equations and their graphs. For example, what effect does changing the y-intercept have and what effect does changing the slope have?

Now create at least 5–10 examples of your own to further explore your ideas. List your equations and tell one or two things you noticed.

3. Go to:

http://www.algebrahelp.com/

Click on the link for "Lessons" on the top right.

Choose at least two topics from the Lessons Index that you have had difficulty with in this class and read through the explanations provided.

Depending on time you might like to use the resources provided at the end of the explanations to practice and check your understanding.

Please do your best to thoroughly explore the above information and be prepared to report back to your classmates regarding your discoveries.

Resources: http://www.prenhall.com/divisions/esm/app/calc_v2/, www.gcaLc.net, www.algebrahelp.com

SOURCE: Contributed by Kathy Klipstein, Mathematics Teacher, Estes Park Middle School, Estes Park, CO. Used with permission.

Lesson Plan 7.4 Music Lesson: Sixth- Through Eighth-Grade General Music, "Erie Canal"

Lesson Title: Erie Canal
Grade Level: 6–8 General Music
Materials: Assignment sheet, access to computers and library resources for research, recording of "Erie Canal"

Standards:

National Standards for Arts Education—Music Content Standards for Grades K–12
  1. Singing, alone and with others, a variety of repertoire.
  4. Composing and arranging music within specified guidelines.
  6. Listening, analyzing, and describing music.
  9. Understanding music in relation to history and culture.

Objectives:
As a result of this lesson students will know/identify: (facts, terms)
  1. basic facts about the history of the Erie Canal (dates of construction, politicians and workers involved, location and major cities).
  2. the historical information presented in the song.
  3. the basic functioning of a canal system including locks, towpath, aqueducts, and barges.
  4. the function of work songs.
As a result of this lesson students will be able to: (observable skills)
  5. write descriptively about the history of the Erie Canal.
  6. create a new verse describing how "Erie Canal" was a work song.
  7. sing one of the student-created parodies with a small group.

Post-Assessment:
The teacher will assess student understanding of the historical information about the song and the canal based upon the rubric below. The parody will be assessed on how well the new lyrics fit the melody and if it explains the function of the song as a work song. The students' performances of a selected parody will be assessed on pitch and rhythmic accuracy or improvement of singing skill.

RAFT Rubric:
  4 The student has a complete and detailed understanding of the information regarding the Erie Canal including important people involved, history of its construction, current usage, and location.
  3 The student has an understanding of the Erie Canal but not in great detail.
  2 The student has an incomplete understanding of the Erie Canal and/or misconceptions about some of the information. However, the student maintains a basic understanding of the topic.
  1 The student's understanding of the Erie Canal is incomplete and has misconceptions.
  0 No judgment can be made.
*Rubric adapted from Marzano, R. J. (2000) *Transforming Classroom Grading*, ASCD.

Steps in Lesson:
  1. Have students listen to a recording of "Erie Canal." As they listen have them take notes of what the song is about. Ask students to volunteer answers after listening.
  2. Distribute the music to the song. Have students listen to the song a second time and circle words or phrases they do not know. Have students create a cumulative list after listening.
  3. Explain how a lock system works. Either draw or show diagrams.
  4. Listen to the song for a third time and have students hum the melody as they listen. Have students then sing the song as a group.
  5. Distribute the RAFT assignment sheet in class along with the grading rubric by which they will be assessed.
  6. Students must choose a role from the first column and complete the corresponding task. In order to complete tasks, students will need to research the history of the Erie Canal.
  7. Randomly group students into group of 8–9. Each group should review the parodies written by each group member and choose one to perform for the class. Give students time to practice together.
  8. Review the list of unknown words and phrases from step 2. Have students explain each based on their research.
  9. Allow students to display their work and perform their group parodies for the class.

Name: _____
Date Assigned: _____
Date Due: _____

RAFT

Directions: Choose one role from the following list. Complete the task in the indicated format for the indicated audience about the indicated topic. Make sure to have someone peer-edit your work before submitting it!

Role	Audience	Format	Topic
De Witt Clinton	Business owners in Albany	Speech	A canal will benefit you because . . .
Irish Canal Worker	His mother in Ireland	Letter	Let me tell you about my day...
General store owner in Schenectady	Possible customers	Website information	Let me tell you how we can make prices low, low, LOW!
Environment	Industry	Complaint	What you do to me...
Rochester Townspeople	Canal Workers	Debate	The state of our town
Thomas Jefferson	Canal Workers	Speech	Aiding westward expansion

Create a parody verse explaining the function of "Erie Canal" as a work song. Be able to sing your parody!

SOURCE: Contributed by Dr. Stephanie Standerfer, Music Education, Montana State University–Bozeman. Used with permission.

to "work songs." Standerfer shares basic information about how a lock system works and specifics about the Erie Canal, including its location, history, construction, and current use. Students are instructed to listen to the song a few times and then, in groups, write and perform a parody verse.

Technology can easily be integrated into this music lesson. First, students could research the Erie Canal by perusing the Internet. One site that might be of particular interest to middle school students lets them join Ayla, a fellow middle school student, on an informative boat ride on the Three@Sea down the Erie Canal. Students can access her voyage at **http://www.youtube.com/ watch?v=LePSecHFkIQ**. There are also multiple recordings of the song "Erie Canal" by popular artists. Students could listen to Suzanne Vega's version and follow the lyrics at **http://www.youtube.com/watch?v=CT78NL34kOc**; listen to Pete Seeger at **http://www.youtube.com/ watch?v=JxKy1_c6DeM&feature=fvwrel**; listen to Bruce Springsteen's live concert performance singing "Erie Canal" in 2006 at **http://www.youtube.com/watch?v= VhHWAyFFv9s&feature=fvwrel**; or listen to the Corndodgers' 2009 recording and enjoy the accompanying images of the Erie Canal at **http://www.youtube.com/ watch?v=GQZUQtlT828&feature=related**. Another fun way to integrate technology would be to have students create their own SchoolTube videos of their parody verses and upload them to the Internet. That way, they could receive comments on their performance from students and music lovers around the globe.

LESSON PLAN 7.5 The next lesson plan was created by a group of students enrolled in Multicultural Education, a core course in the Teacher Education Program at Montana State University. This course is a broad interdisciplinary examination of the complex school-society relationship in the U.S. designed to help pre-service teachers become culturally competent, reflective practitioners by focusing on specific knowledge, skills, and dispositions related to teaching in a pluralistic context. In Multicultural Education, students complete an Embedded Signature Assignment that addresses Interstate Teacher Assessment and Support Consortium (INTASC) Standard 3: "The teacher understands how students differ in their approaches to learning and creates instructional opportunities that are adapted to diverse learners." For this assignment, pre-service middle- and secondary-level teachers work collaboratively. They design and present lesson plans that integrate Indian Education for All in their respective disciplines (see Chapter 3 for a description of Indian Education for All and the Seven Essential Understandings). Each group is asked to critically evaluate several websites and a resource and design and present an integrated culturally responsive lesson plan to their classmates.

The lesson plan titled "Plains Indians' Dependence on the Bison and Other Natural Resources" included here was created by Colby Carruthers, Leslie Jackson, Dan Burfeind, Hillary Stacey, and Megan Hamilton (see Lesson Plan 7.5A). This science lesson is a WebQuest that the students created in QuestGarden. It is designed to help eighth graders understand the important role the bison played for Plains Indians, how the different body parts were used, and how the bison populations changed over time. The group created handouts for the in-class activity and also included a grading rubric in addition to listing numerous Internet resources in their WebQuest. This assignment was the first time most of these group members designed and delivered a lesson plan. Check out their WebQuest at **http://questgarden .com/122/85/4/110329150026** to see how the group integrated technology as well as how the group designed

Lesson Plan 7.5A **Plains Indians' Dependence on the Bison and Other Natural Resources, Handouts, and Evaluation Rubric**

Indian Education for All Lesson Plan for Multicultural Education

Plains Indians' Dependence on the Bison and Other Natural Resources

By Colby Carruthers, Leslie Jackson, Dan Burfeind, Hillary Stacey, and Megan Hamilton

Science Grade 8

Montana State Standards

Science Standards:

3.4- Investigate and explain the interdependent nature of populations and communities in the environment and describe how species in these populations adapt by evolving.

5.5- Describe how the knowledge of science and technology influences the development of the Montana American Indian cultures.

Library Media Standards:

2.3- Locate information within multiple resources.

Montana's Essential Understandings:

1 There is great diversity among the 12 tribal Nations of Montana in their languages, cultures, histories and governments. Each Nation has a distinct and unique cultural heritage that contributes to modern Montana.

3 The ideologies of Native traditional beliefs and spirituality persist into modern day life as tribal cultures, traditions, and languages are still practiced by many American Indian people and are incorporated into how tribes govern and manage their affairs. Additionally, each tribe has its own oral histories, which are as valid as written histories. These histories pre-date the "discovery" of North America.

5 Federal policies, put into place throughout American history, have affected Indian people and still shape who they are today. Much of Indian history can be related through several major federal policy periods.

Goals

• Students will understand that the bison were crucial to the lives of the Plains Indians in many ways.

(continued)

Lesson Plan 7.5A   **Plains Indians' Dependence on the Bison and Other Natural Resources, Handouts, and Evaluation Rubric**   *continued*

- Students will understand how and why the bison population changed over time.
- Students will understand how Native Americans during this time period utilized their natural resources.

Instructional Objectives

- Students will be able to describe the Plains Indians' usage of each body part of the bison.
- Students will compare and contrast resources of certain Native Americans before the decimation of the bison population (~1800's) to Native Americans today.
- Students will determine factors in the decline of the wild bison population.
- Students will construct a resource web of a Native American tribe before the decimation of the bison population (circa 1800's) of their choice using research tactics taught during the WebQuest lesson.

Rationale

From this lesson, students will have a better understandings of a way of life other than their own. They will become sensitive to the traditions and natural resources of certain Native American tribes. Students will begin to examine the interdependence of a population of people (Plains Indians) with a natural resource (bison). They will also practice library media skills through the WebQuest by gathering information from a collection of websites.

Procedure

Warm up/introduction: After a lesson on population, we will transition into a unit on natural resources. Students will be shown an attention-grabbing video illustrating a buffalo jump (30 seconds).

Content: Then they will begin to construct a KWL chart (know, want to know, learned) as an entire class, up on the whiteboard, about how Plains Indians depended on the bison and other natural resources.

After constructing the chart we will discuss misconceptions that may be present such as bison versus buffalo terminology. We will also identify specific tribes that are Plains Indians. This section of the lesson will take about 30 minutes total or half of a class period.

The next day students will head down to the library to do the WebQuest and worksheet project that aligns with it. They will perform their own research (guided by the WebQuest) to satisfy the four learning objectives. They will be assessed by completion of the project worksheet. The WebQuest will take an entire class period and the students may finish it at home or after school if they are not done.

WebQuest URL
http://questgarden.com/122/85/4/110329150026/

Closure: The next class period we will summarize what they learned in their research by completing the class KWL chart.

In-class activity for example of lesson: Slideshow of parts of the bison. Peers in the class will work with partners at their tables to guess what the specific parts of the bison was used for. They will write their predictions on a worksheet between the two of them. Afterwards we will go over each specific part of the bison and what exactly it was used for and discuss incorrect guesses or additional information together.

Plan for Differentiated Instruction

- Readiness: The sources the students will be using for their research vary by readiness level. The students can avoid Web sites that use high-level vocabulary or they can seek out Web sites that are of a higher level should they need compacting.
- Interests: The students get to choose which specific tribe they are interested in for a part of the project. They also get to choose which Web sites they visit and which learning styles fit them best. Some Web sites contain more visuals, audio, or text than others.

- Scaffolding: Certain Web sites require more research while others explicitly lay out information.

Materials and Equipment Needed
Audiovisual: Introduction video
Multimedia: PowerPoint, whiteboards for KWL activity, Questgarden.com (Used to create Web site)
Other: Bison artifacts from Plains Indians, a computer for each student, a WebQuest activity sheet for each student

Detailed list of materials/resources used to construct the lesson plan
Books: Calloway, C.G. (2008). *First People: A Documentary Survey of American Indian History.* Boston: Bedford/St. Martins.
Websites: Montana Office of Public instruction;
http://opi.mt.gov/programs/indianed/
http://www.nebraskastudies.org/0300/frameset_reset.html?
http://www.nebraskastudies.org/0300/stories/0301_0109.html
http://www.youtube.com/watch?v=KgOweOUCeps
http://fwp.mt.gov/hunting/bison.html
http://fieldguide.mt.gov/detail_AMALEO1010.aspx
http://www.saskschools.ca/~gregory/firstnations/
http://www.buffalofieldcampaign.org/index.html
www.spartacus.schoolnet.co.uk/WWplains.htm
www.tribaldirectory.net/articles/american-buffalo.html
www.questgarden.com

Assessment of Student Learning
Pre-assessment- First section of KWL chart
Formative assessment- Completion of KWL chart
Summative assessment- Completion of WebQuest activity and worksheet

Reflection/Evaluation
Group evaluation: We divided the work by working through all parts of the project together. It was nice having a small group because we always could find large blocks of time to meet. Some of us had specific areas of expertise that especially helped: Colby knew lots of information on Native American topics, Hillary knew how to construct a WebQuest, Dan was very good at finding helpful resources, Megan had lots of knowledge on how to write a lesson plan, and Leslie had good ideas for activities. The presentation mostly went as planned. We could have planned out the final activity better. There were a few awkward moments in the slide show of pictures of bison parts at the end. We have learned a wealth of information about the Plains Indians tribes of Montana and North Dakota. In finding information it was often hard to distinguish between certain tribes and the information tended to be a little Pan-Indian. We learned how to incorporate themes and concepts from the perspectives of diverse cultural groups. This was good practice for all of us on writing and planning lessons. We learned how much time it takes to prepare one single lesson.

Peer evaluations: In the future we could improve the presentation by the following ideas and many others. For the end activity, we would have them work as groups on just the bison parts listed on the worksheet and then go through all of the pictures only once. Most of the suggestions we received were to not read off the slides or our note cards and this could have been avoided with extensive preparation. Some of the suggestions were contradictory such as some suggested more excitement and some said we had good energy. A few of the more helpful suggestions were to focus on more science and current day issues than on history. This could help us improve the lesson for the students as well.

For the lesson, we could delve into topics such as current day uses of the bison by certain Native American tribes. We could try harder to avoid Pan-Indianism by focusing more on the specific tribes of the Plains Indians.

SOURCE: Contributed by Colby Carruthers, Leslie Jackson, Dan Burfeind, Hillary Stacey, and Megan Hamilton, students enrolled in Multicultural Education at Montana State University–Bozeman during the Spring 2011 semester. Used with Permission.

L e s s o n   P l a n   7.5B **Plains Indians' Dependence on the Bison and Other Natural Resources, Handouts, and Evaluation Rubric**

Part I: Write the usage of each body part underneath the word.
Learning Objective: Students will be able to describe the Plains Indians' usage of each body part of the bison.

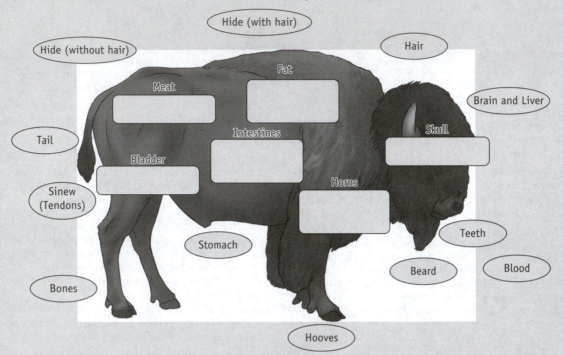

Part II: Fill in the table below to compare and contrast how Native Americans before the decimation of the bison population (circa 1800's) and people in Montana today satisfy these needs. Learning Objective Students will compare and contrast resources of certain Native Americans before the decimation of the wild bison population(~1800's) to those of Native Americans today.

Aspect of Life	Part of the bison used by Native Americans of the 1800's	Native Americans today
Clothing		
Housing		
Eating		
Cleaning		
Farming		
Entertainment		
Hunting		

Part III: Short Essay
Learning Objective: Students will determine factors in the decline of the wild bison population.
What were some of the factors that led to the decline of the population of the wild bison? Explain your answer in a paragraph with 5 to 7 sentences. Cite your sources at the bottom of the paragraph.

Part IV: Resource Web
Learning Objective: Students will construct a resource web of a Native American tribe before the decimation of the wild bison population (circa 1800's) of their choice using research tactics taught during the WebQuest lesson.
Construct a web of resources the tribe of your choice used from their geographical location during the 1800's and before. Identify the resource and what it was used for. You must describe at least 5 resources in your web following the pattern below. Cite the sources of your information below the web.

<u>L e s s o n   P l a n   7 . 5 C</u> **Plains Indians' Dependence on the Bison and Other Natural Resources, Handouts, and Evaluation Rubric**

This is how your work will be evaluated.

	Beginning 1	Developing 2	Qualified 3	Exemplary 4	Score
Describe the Usages of Bison Parts	Several but not all of the usages of parts are described in one to two words	All of the usages of bison parts are described in one to two words	All of the usages of bison parts are described in at least two words and some are described in detail	All of the usages of bison parts are described in detail with more than one usage described for most parts.	
Compare and Contrast Resources	Several items in the chart are filled out with one word	All of the items in the chart are filled out with one-word examples	All items in the chart are filled out with several containing two or more examples	All items in the chart are filled out with two or more examples	
Decline of Bison Population	Essay is poorly written with numerous mistakes in grammar or is not written in complete sentences. OR the factors described do not make sense.	Essay contains several grammatical errors or does not satisfy the length and content requirements.	Essay contains few grammatical errors and two factors are described, meeting the length requirements.	Essay contains no grammatical errors and two or more factors are thoroughly explained. The length requirement is met or exceeded.	
Construction of Resource Web	There are not 5 resources described or they do not make sense. Web is pan-Indian instead of specific.	5 resources are present but the focus may be on more than one tribe instead of just one.	5 resources or more are present and described. Focus is explicitly on one tribe.	More than 5 resources are described in detail. Focus is explicitly on one tribe.	

a rubric for evaluating what students learn about the usages of bison parts (see Lesson Plan 7.5A, 7.5B, and 7.5C).

LESSON PLAN 7.6 Roger Aguirre Lopez is a middle school teacher of English as-a-foreign-language in Chimbote, Peru. He has been teaching English at the middle school level for 10 years. He is an active member of his school, where he has played a key role in promoting English-language acquisition among his students as well as helping his colleagues improve their English skills. He also leads an English club that allows students to practice their language skills outside of class. Aguirre recently was the recipient of a Teaching Excellence and Achievement scholarship, a program of the Bureau of Educational and Cultural Affairs of the U.S. State Department, administered by the International Research and Exchanges Board. As a result, Aguirre joined other scholarship recipients (middle and high school teachers from around the world) and attended classes at Montana State University and completed an internship in the Bozeman Public Schools. He developed lesson plans while studying in the United States; the lesson plan included here, "Animal Life," focuses on teaching middle school students how to properly use the comparative and superlative in English. Aguirre has used technology in a

creative way to help his students learn the grammatical structures by encouraging them to describe the most common features of several animals (see his lesson plan, PowerPoint slides, and handout in Lesson Plan 7.6A, 7.6B, and 7.6C, respectively).

Secondary School–Level Lesson Plans

In this section, secondary school lesson and unit plans focused on Indian Education for All/social studies, language arts, English as-a-second-language, history, advanced placement (AP) psychology, mathematics, French, and art and their contributors are described.

LESSON PLAN 7.7 Discovering that there is not one universally accepted "truth" but rather multiple perspectives when it comes to recounting historical events is challenging for many secondary students as well as for their teachers to accept. In "Model Social Studies High School Lesson Plan," Mike Jetty, Indian education specialist at the Montana Office of Public Instruction, shares insights from his conversation with James Loewen, author of *Lies My Teacher Told Me*. Jetty's lesson plan is framed around Essential Understanding 6, "History is a story most often related through the subjective experience of the teller. With the inclusion of more and varied voices, histories are being rediscovered and revised. History told from an

Lesson Plan 7.6A **Animal Life: The Comparative and the Superlative, Handout, PowerPoint**

Micro - Lesson Plan Template

Date March 7th 2011	**Instructor Name**	ROGER AGUIRRE LOPEZ	**Instructor Country**	PERU
Micro - Lesson Title	ANIMAL LIFE - The comparative & the superlative		**Teaching Discipline(s)**	ENGLISH 1

Learning Objectives
- Students will be able to describe the most common features of several animals by using the comparative and the superlative in questions and answers.
- Students will be able to evaluate the differences between the comparative and superlative in their grammatical structure as well as their use.

Accessories/Teaching Aids Required PowerPoint presentation, laptop, and multimedia projector

Reference Material (if any public materials are used, please list the sources of these materials here)
Handout prepared by the teacher.

Micro - Lesson Outline (please describe the activity, strategy, topic you will demonstrate to the "student" group)

The teacher introduces the lesson by asking questions about the animals shown in a PowerPoint presentation: Which animal do you like the most? And why? After some answers have been given, the teacher encourages students to guess the lesson topic. The students look at the pictures of animals on the screen and guess the answers to the questions about the most common features of the animals. The teacher emphasizes the answers to point out the use of the comparative and the superlative in the sentences given. Next, the students reflect on the use of the comparative and the superlative by looking at a chart that summarizes the rules on how to form the comparative and the superlative of short and long adjectives. After that, all the students are invited to form two teams where they should establish roles. The teacher gives the students a handout containing a quiz about animals; they discuss the questions and the answers in groups while the teacher encourages the members of the teams to work cooperatively. After some minutes of discussion, the teams participate in the game "Jeopardy" where there are two topics (comparative & superlative) and three questions for each one. Each team chooses the question in turns: the task consists of completing the questions using the correct form of the comparative or superlative of the adjectives given in the parenthesis and choosing the correct choice; if the answer is correct, the group will get the established score. The teacher checks the students' participation in the teamwork, and provides feedback to their answers.

As a follow-up activity, the students are asked to work in pairs to make questions based on the lists of words provided in the handout and exchange answers. This will be considered as a speaking activity to be performed in the next lesson.

Assessment (how you will assess learning during this lesson)

The students in groups will discuss the topic using questions and answers about several features of animals while the teacher will walk around the classroom to check how well the students are doing the activity and providing extra help when needed. Participation and cooperation in their group will be taken into account to assess the students' progress.

Best teaching practices this lesson demonstrates

In this lesson the students will become involved in active learning tasks, working in cooperative groups, and playing an active role within the teamwork.

This Lesson Plan Template has been adapted from a template available for free at: **www.TeachersPrintables.net**

SOURCE: Contributed by Roger Aguirre Lopez, English as-a-foreign-language Teacher and Teaching Excellence and Achievement (TEA) Program Fellow at Montana State University, Spring 2011. Used with permission.

Indian perspective frequently conflicts with the stories mainstream historians tell" (see the descriptions of Indian Education for All and the Seven Essential Understandings in Chapter 3).

In this lesson, Jetty, a leader in Indian education with more than 20 years of experience promoting the accurate teaching of American Indian cultures, histories, and contemporary issues, and Loewen, well-known historian, professor, and author, address the following: why it is important to examine historical events from multiple perspectives, why Dr. Loewen's book is titled *Lies My Teacher Told Me*, and to what extent certain myths and/or lies about American Indians are perpetuated in history textbooks today.

All educators can learn from the comments and insights that Jetty and Loewen shared during this interview. In addition to accessing the article that Jetty wrote called "History Through Red Eyes: A Conversation with James Loewen" and the other suggested readings in the lesson plan, students could be encouraged to explore other Internet resources to uncover bias in textbooks. They could also be directed to the Montana Office of Public Instruction's Indian Education website at **http://opi.mt.gov/Programs/IndianEd/curricsearch.html** to peruse the extensive collection of Indian Education for All curricular materials designed to promote culturally responsive pedagogy and to review the document "Evaluating American Indian Materials and Resources for the Classroom: Textbooks, Literature, DVDs, Videos, and Websites" at **http://opi.mt.gov/pdf/IndianEd/Resources/09Eval_Textbooks.pdf**.

ANIMAL LIFE

ENGLISH 1

I. **Answer the following questions.**

1. How many animals can you name?

2. Which animal do you like the most? Why?

II. **Complete the questions and check the answer you think is correct.**

ANIMAL LOVERS QUIZ

(comp. SLOW)	1. Which animal is _slower than_ a turtle?	☐ a snake	☑ a snail	☐ a crocodile
(super. LONG)	2. Which animal lives _the longest_ ?	☐ a tortoise	☐ an elephant	☐ a whale
(comp. HEAVY)	3. Which animal is _____ a pig?	☐ a monkey	☐ a hippopotamus	☐ a cheetah
(super. DANGEROUS)	4. Which animal is _____?	☐ a wolf	☐ a vulture	☐ a lion
(comp. INTELLIGENT)	5. Which is _____ a monkey?	☐ the dolphin	☐ the whale	☐ the cat
(super. GOOD)	6. Which animal is _____ pet?	☐ a rooster	☐ a cow	☐ a puppy
(comp. HIGH)	7. Which animal can jump _____ a dog?	☐ a kangaroo	☐ a bear	☐ a camel
(super. FAST)	8. Which is _____ animal?	☐ a zebra	☐ a cheetah	☐ an ostrich
(super. TALL)	9. Which animal is _____?	☐ a rhinoceros	☐ a giraffe	☐ an elephant
(super. DIRTY)	10. Which one is _____ animal?	☐ a cat	☐ a horse	☐ a pig
(super. SMALL)	11. Which is _____ bird?	☐ seagull	☐ hummingbird	☐ vulture
(comp. BIG)	12. Which one is _____ an elephant?	☐ blue whale	☐ bear	☐ rhinoceros

III. **Make questions with these words and find out the answers. Use the superlative.**

What ...
Who ...

long
popular ✓
dry
tall
expensive
large

country
person in ...
city in ...
sport ✓
river
metal

?

1. _What is the most popular sport?_   _Soccer is the most popular sport._

2. ....

1

Roger Aguirre López – PERU 2011

Lesson Plan 7.6C Animal Life: The Comparative and the Superlative, PowerPoint

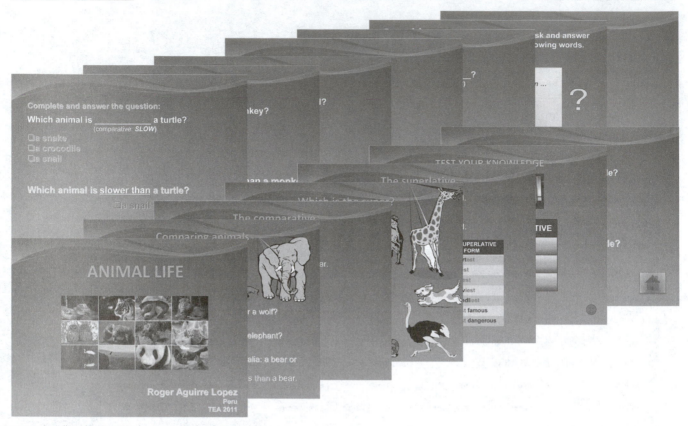

SOURCE: Contributed by Roger Aguirre Lopez. Used with Permission

LESSON PLAN 7.8 Dr. Nivea Lisandra Torres has worked in the Windham School District and throughout Connecticut and the Northeast as a classroom teacher, principal, and assistant superintendent. She also serves as an adjunct professor of second language acquisition at the Neag School of Education at the University of Connecticut, Storrs. Torres is an exceptional bilingual who has excellent command of both English and Spanish. She has been engaged in professional development activities for faculty and curriculum design for English Language Learners and diverse students for several years. In her unit plan included here, Lesson Plan 7.8, titled "The Immigrant Experience in Literature," she focuses on a Latina author to help students explore key concepts: an immigrant's journey to belong and the adolescent's search for identity. During this three-week unit plan, Torres has students read *When I Was Puerto Rican* by Esmeralda Santiago, discuss key themes, write essays, record journal entries, and watch the film *Almost a Woman*, based on Santiago's memoir. In her unit, Torres also includes a Sheltered Instruction Observation Protocol (SIOP) lesson (see Lesson Plan 7.8C) to address both content and language objectives for English Language Learners, a Cultural Relevance Rubric (see Lesson Plan 7.8B), and the Windham Public Schools Rubric for Narrative Writing (see Lesson Plan 7.8A). She also suggests that English and social studies teachers could complement the unit by connecting historical and literary aspects.

In addition to the many activities suggested in this unit plan, students could also be asked to conduct research on Puerto Rico—in the past and present. They could peruse the Internet to find information about famous and well-known Puerto Ricans, including other authors. They could also search for basic facts about the culture, history, geography, demographics, religion, language, politics, education system, celebrations, and relationship to the U.S. as well as look at several images.

To further integrate technology into this unit plan and address the language development of English Language Learners, you could have students go to Quizlet at **http://quizlet.com/2467206/when-i-was-a-puerto-rican-flash-cards**, where the students could create flash cards and play a variety of games to learn and use vocabulary from Santiago's novel. The reflective journal that students are asked to write could be done as an interactive blog site (see Chapter 10). The instructor could create a classroom blog site where students could contribute to an online journal. Students could share their entries, obtain feedback, edit their posts, share music and photos, and embed YouTube clips as well as add commentary. Students could also create a TeacherTube video and include audio. They might also create story maps or posters at WritingGuide Poster Sessions at **http://writing.colostate.edu/guides/speaking/poster**.

Lesson Plan 7.7 Model Social Studies High School Lesson Plan, Topic 11, The Colonization Era—An Interview with Dr. James Loewen

Montana
Office of Public Instruction
Denise Juneau, State Superintendent

opi.mt.gov

Model Lesson Plan
Social Studies
High School

Topic 11—The Colonization Era—An Interview with Dr. James Loewen

Stage 1 Desired Results

Established Goals:

Students will investigate, interpret, and analyze the impact of multiple historical and contemporary viewpoints concerning events within and across cultures (SS4:B12.6).

Suggested time frame: Two 50- minute class periods.

Understandings:	Essential Questions:
History is a story most often related through the subjective experience of the teller. With the inclusion of more and varied voices, histories are being rediscovered and revised.	Why is it important to examine historical events from multiple perspectives?
History told from an Indian perspective frequently conflicts with the stories mainstream historians tell. (Essential Understanding 6)	Why would author James Loewen title his book "Lies My Teacher Told Me"?
	To what extent do myths or lies about American Indians get perpetuated in history textbooks?
Students will be able to ...	*Students will know ...*
Briefly describe some American Indian perspectives regarding early colonization.	Students will be introduced to the multiple American Indian viewpoints regarding issues associated with colonization.

Stage 2 Assessment Evidence

Performance Tasks:

Participate in class discussion, read and react to an article about how American Indians are usually portrayed in history textbooks.

Stage 3 Learning Plan

Learning Activities:

Briefly introduce students to the topic of colonization. Lead a class discussion/brainstorming session to see what they already know. List out topics/issues on the board and discuss. Emphasize the point that colonization has had (and still does) a huge impact on how American Indians have been written about and portrayed in history textbooks. In almost all cases, tribal histories were filtered through a European American (usually male) cultural lens.

Tell students they will be reading an article from the Phi Delta Kappan, the second largest educational journal in the U.S. The interview is with author Dr. James Loewen, who is well known for his national bestseller "Lies My Teacher Told Me."

Ask students, Why would author James Loewen title his book "Lies My Teacher Told Me"?

Has anyone ever read it or heard about the book? Can anyone think of specific examples in our country's history where American Indians have been lied about? Was it intentional or were people just working with limited knowledge?

Brainstorm a list of potential American Indian topics/events that may be interpreted from multiple viewpoints. Examples include: Columbus and "discovery," the roles of American Indians in the early colonial times, Pocahontas, influence Indians had on early colonial thinking, westward movement, Lewis and Clark, etc... . Discuss the list with the class and then share the following guidelines with them before handing out the article.

Things to keep in mind as you study about a particular event in history:

- With regard to events such as Lewis and Clark and the Corps of Discovery, Montana tribal histories offer differing points of view from those expressed in your American history textbook.
- Your history textbook and a tribal history each represent "points of view"; the point of view changes, depending on whose story is being told.
- Identifying and respecting another culture's viewpoints of historical events is basic to your understanding of how histories can influence our ideas and points of view.
- Events from the past, and how they are viewed by tribes and by the U.S. government, still cause issues of concern today.
- The "discovery" of an area is not necessarily a discovery. Indigenous people had been in the area explored by the expedition for hundreds, probably thousands of years.

(continued)

Distribute copies of the article to all students and have them read in class. Allow at least 10-15 minutes for reading the article.

Ask students to write up a one-page reaction paper to the article. Did they learn anything new? Did this conflict with what they have been previously taught? Do these perspectives differ from what is in your history textbook?

After students have had a chance to read and discuss the article have them write up a one page reaction paper to article.

Lead a class discussion on the major issues covered in the article.

List on the board new information gained as a result of reading this article.

After the whole class discusses the article, allow students time to add to or revise their one-page reaction papers.

Tell them their one-page reaction papers will be due at the beginning of the next class.

Extension activity:

Have students work in small groups to look at all the references regarding American Indians. Ask them to pay particular attention to issues of bias. Have them examine the terminology in the textbook. Groups could report their research results to the rest of the class. If examples of bias or misinformation are found have them write the textbook publisher asking them to consider rewriting the section.

Resources:

Jetty, Mike. "**History Through Red Eyes: A Conversation with James Loewen.**" *Phi Delta Kappan,* Vol. 88, No. 03 (November 2006): 218-222. **http://www.pdkintl.org/**

Additional Recommended Resources:

Loewen, James W. *Lies My Teachers Told Me*: *Everything Your American History Textbook Got Wrong.* New York: The New Press, 1995. 372 pp. ISBN:1-56584-100X

Supahan, Sarah. *Points of View vs. Historical Bias*: *Recognizing Bias in Texts about Native Americans—An Integrated Thematic Unit.* Klamath-Trinity Joint Unified School District's Indian Education Program, Indians of Northwest California. Available through **www .oyate.org**

Article appeared in the November 2006 issue of the Phi Delta Kappan—Reprinted with permission.

History Through Red Eyes: A Conversation with James Loewen

James Loewen's Lies My Teacher Told Me *was a challenge to our preconceived notions of who we are as a people and of our national history. Mike Jetty recently sat with Loewen to get his thoughts on the potential for Montana's Indian Education for All Act to bring about significant change.*

By Mike Jetty

JAMES Loewen is an author, historian, and professor. Through *Lies My Teacher Told Me*, he has helped to reconstruct the way history is viewed and taught in public schools all across America. During a recent conversation, he shared his views on how American Indian topics and events are traditionally taught and offered his insights into what we can do to accommodate multiple perspectives in our examination of history. Below, I present his comments and insights as he told them to me.

* * *

My first teaching assignment was at Tougaloo College, a historically black institution in Tougaloo, Mississippi. In my first year, I taught a course developed by the history department that was titled "The Freshman Social Science Seminar." In it we introduced students to sociology, anthropology, political science, economics, and psychology in the context of African American history. This made sense because 99% of our students were African American.

The second semester of the course began with events immediately following the Civil War. I had a new group of students in the second semester, and I didn't want to do all the talking on the first day of class, so I asked them, "We're starting with Reconstruction. What is that period?"

What followed was an "Aha!" experience for me. Or it might be better called an "Oh no!" experience. Sixteen out of 17 students said, "Reconstruction was that period right after the Civil War when blacks took over the government of the Southern states. But they were too soon out of slavery, so they screwed up, and white folks had to take control again."

Now, there are at least three complete misstatements—lies I would call them—in that sentence, and I was just floored by it. Blacks never took over the government of the Southern states; the Reconstruction governments did not, on the whole, screw up; and whites didn't resume control at the end of Reconstruction. However, a certain group of "whites" did take control, using terrorist tactics. It was, in fact, the original Ku Klux Klan.

So I thought, "What must your teachers have done to you to make you believe that the one time your group was center stage in American history, they screwed up, and whites had to take control back again?"

If it were true, that would be fine. But it is *not* true. What these students had learned we might call BS—that would be Bad Sociology—in the black public schools. What they had learned was being taught by black teachers in all-black schools. But it was white supremacist history because their teachers were just blindly teaching what was in the textbooks. Seeing the outcome made me aware that history can be a weapon and that it can be used against you, just as it had been against my black students.

When I put together a team of students and faculty members at Tougaloo and Millsaps College (a nearby all-white college), we confronted the lies and myths in Mississippi history by writing a new history textbook for the Mississippi history course that was required in public schools. But our book just wasn't racist enough, so the state refused to adopt it. Because Mississippi is a textbook-adoption state, we actually had to sue to get it adopted. The case was *Loewen et al.* v. *Turnipseed et al.*

After eight years in Mississippi, I moved to the University of Vermont, where I continued to teach first-year students in huge introductory sociology classes. There I learned that distorted history was not a phenomenon peculiar to Mississippi. Although in the early 1970s Mississippi exhibited it in a more exaggerated form—as Mississippi exhibited many national maladies in a more exaggerated form back then—this was a national problem.

As I had done in Mississippi, I went to nearby high schools to learn where my students were getting the bizarre ideas they brought to college. Many of these ideas had to do with "savage" Indians. *Lies My Teacher Told Me* is based on my intensive reading of 12 high school American history textbooks. I claim to be the only American ever to attempt such a feat. It was a desperate career move that no one should try at home.

I have to say that the task of puncturing myths was much harder for me in Vermont than in Mississippi. It's fairly easy for someone coming into Mississippi from outside to see what the white supremacists have gotten wrong about the state's past. But myths about Indians are national myths—or lies. They are harder to detect, because almost all of us "know" things about Native Americans that are wrong. So it's harder for us, especially for non-Indians, to step outside our education and culture and realize when we are making the same kinds of mistakes.

This is particularly true because we have a national myth that we might even call an archetype—the archetype of progress. It tells us that the U.S. started out great and that we've been getting better in every way ever since. I really do believe that is the underlying myth that provides the basic story line of American history as it is taught in most K-12 schools—and certainly as taught in the textbooks that are presented K-12.

As to myths about American Indians, we started out quite harshly some decades ago. We once taught about the "savage" Indians. We—that is, everybody non-Indian, but particularly whites—learned that we settled a mostly virgin continent. There were very few Indians, we learned, so we didn't really displace that many people. And the "savage" Indians were just backward and in the way, so they had no choice but to acquiesce to the progressive new civilization that was being formed here on American soil. So we didn't really do anything wrong. That is, of course, a myth.

In the last 30 years, that myth has become much softer, much nicer, if you will. The word "savage" is rarely applied to Indian people. And sometimes they're not even called primitive, although I think it's sometimes implied. The most common notion today is that Indians had their own culture and it was just fine, but they had a tragic unwillingness or inability to adopt or adapt to European culture. As a result, they fell by the wayside.

This is a much nicer story, but it, too, is a myth. In *Lies My Teacher Told Me* this point is illustrated by the story of Joseph Vann, a Cherokee Indian from Georgia. He and many other Cherokee had taken on the cotton culture and managed to adapt quite successfully. Vann lived in a plantation house straight out of *Gone with the Wind* and owned many slaves. Yet he was not allowed to acculturate, and his beautiful house made him a target. So Chief Vann was forced to leave Georgia for Oklahoma because the white sheriff wanted his house. Later, the entire Cherokee nation, which was literate and agricultural and generally prosperous, was driven out of Georgia. They were forced on the Trail of Tears to Oklahoma. This did not happen because they couldn't or refused to acculturate. It happened simply because they were different, and part of that difference was racial.

Clearly, Native Americans were never really allowed to acculturate. And that's one of the specific things we get wrong. Right from the start, you can see it's tied to the myth of progress: we—the non-Indians—are the progressive ones. Most American Indians were in fact agriculturalist when the white folks and black folks first arrived. The myth tells us that they were nomadic, that they were hunters and gatherers. But most were not. Most grew crops. And if we think about the myth, we realize that the Pilgrims' pumpkin pie and squash and corn were all Indian foods. So obviously the Pilgrims had to have learned something about farming from the Native Americans. Yet we have the myth that Native peoples were not agriculturalist and did not live in settled villages. We have the myth that we civilized them.

One of the things we do with these stereotypes and myths is put them on the landscape. For example, one of my favorite hated places on the landscape—if you can have a favorite hated place—is near Ground Zero in Manhattan. There stands a statue meant to celebrate the Dutch purchase of Manhattan from Native Americans. The Dutchman is wearing a coat. The Native American is almost naked, wearing just a breechcloth and a wonderful feather headdress. The Dutchman is handing $24 worth of beads to the Native American. This statue is located at the exact spot where this purchase *never took place*!

The statue is particularly embarrassing because the purchase that never took place is *supposed* to have happened in about 1630. And the Indian represented in the statue is, of course, the stereotypical Plains Indian. However, the Plains Indian culture did not even emerge until about a hundred years later, when Native peoples were being forced westward onto the plains by the French and British and when horses escaped from the Spanish and made their way northward from Mexico. These two events combined to create the wonderful Plains Indian horse culture, a culture that lasted only about a century, from about 1790 to about 1890, when Plains Indians were forced onto reservations.

Not only had the culture not yet emerged, but any Indian who wore the headdress depicted in the statue in the eastern woodlands would be crazy. Such a headdress works great if you are riding around on the prairies of South Dakota or Montana, but it wouldn't work at all in what were then the woodlands of Manhattan Island. Within five minutes, a branch would knock the headdress off. And, of course, no two people at the same time and place would be dressed as differently as the people depicted by this statue. I've been in New York City in February, and if this purchase (that never took place) had taken place in February, that would be one cold Indian. I've also been there in August, and if this purchase (that never took place) had occurred in August, that would be a very hot Dutchman.

(continued)

Lesson Plan 7.7   **Model Social Studies High School Lesson Plan, Topic 11, The Colonization Era—An Interview with Dr. James Loewen**
continued

What the statue really depicts is a primitive person and a civilized person. When we look at it, that registers at some level. Yet we don't notice it because it already fits with our stereotype that Indians were primitive and white folks were civilized. Looking further into the legend, it turns out, of course, that the Dutch purchased the island from the wrong Indians. They bought it from the Canarsee Indians, who lived in Brooklyn. And beads were not involved at all.

We should also examine our terminology. As we often use them, our words become counterfactual. For example, we use the word "discover" to mean the first white person to see something. And we don't just say this about Columbus discovering America, but about the settlers discovering the Mississippi River and so on. We use the term "settler" for whites moving westward and the terms "savage" or "renegade" for Native people who were already living there and had lived there for centuries.

Although part of our problem is terminology, it isn't enough for teachers just to clean up their language. That would be a good start, but it would be even better if they get students to think about these terms and if they find misuse of terms in a textbook or some other source, that they then write the textbook author or publisher and see if they can get the language changed. Even if the publishers don't do anything, it will engage the students and make everybody smarter. And it could even get the textbooks improved.

And fall, with Columbus Day and Thanksgiving, is a terrible time for learning about Native Americans — to learn *non-true* facts, that is. Historically, many well-intentioned teachers have perpetuated lies and myths regarding these two events as they have been traditionally taught in schools throughout the U.S.

Today, kids as young as second- and third-graders are still told these stories. They are the distortions of the conquerors, and they make the Indians look stupid. And that means that our crimes against Indians are continuing as long as we teach such nonsense. This kind of education has a terrible effect on Native children. I have spoken at American Indian reservations from Maine to Washington State, and I've learned that many Native Americans hated history as it was taught to them in school. How history was taught affected them deeply. It affected their self-confidence; it affected their ability to function in our world. It also has a terrible impact on non-Indian people: it makes us ethnocentric and stupid about other cultures.

The easy mythologies we lulled ourselves with over the decades don't make us more patriotic or better citizens. They serve only to make us stupider. But what's happening in Montana with Indian Education for All really can change how we view history and how we project ourselves into the future. The law is similar to one just passed in Mississippi requiring K-12 education to include teaching about the struggle for civil rights in that state. These laws will help Indian children in Montana and black children in Mississippi, but I believe they will have even more transforming impact on non-Natives and non-blacks. If educators and textbook producers and other folks make use of these laws, we really can make some significant changes in what we teach our children. That will be an important change.

MIKE JETTY (Spirit Lake Dakota Nation) is an Indian education specialist with the Montana Office of Public Instruction, Helena.

PDK PHI DELTA KAPPA *International*
PDK Home | Site Map | Search

Last modified November 2, 2006 **http://www.pdkintl.org/ kappan/k_v88/k0611jet.htm** PDK International respects your privacy © 2006 Phi Delta Kappa International

SOURCE: Contributed by Mike Jetty, Indian Education Implementation Specialist, Office of Public Instruction, Helena, Montana. Used with permission.

Lesson Plan 7.8A   **Unit Plan: The Immigrant Experience in Literature: Literature for and about Hispanic Students, Cultural Relevance Rubric, and Sheltered Instruction Observation Protocol (SIOP) Lesson Plan**

Background:

This unit is intended for a heterogeneous group of high school students. While the target audience is ninth–twelfth graders in a small urban community of Connecticut, high school students, in general, would benefit from exposure to a multi-cultural text and film by a Hispanic writer. Presently, 50.2% of the student body in this district is composed of Hispanic students.

Unit Goals:

The following goals are part of a unit titled *The Immigrant Experience in Literature: Literature for and about Hispanic Students*. This unit focuses on Hispanic authors and the challenges of a daunting new life in the United States. Interdisciplinary activities between English and social studies teachers would complement the unit by connecting the historical and literary aspects of this topic. The general unit should examine at least three to five Hispanic writers, but the focus of this design is on one: Esmeralda Santiago.

• To include Latino authors that are not traditionally a part of the English curriculum.

• To enable all English students to develop a wider knowledge of contemporary Latino authors and their literary contributions.

• To improve student to text connections by including multicultural texts that are representative of the ethnic groups within the student body.

• To improve student interest and motivation in reading by including multicultural texts that are age-appropriate and of high interest.

(continued)

Lesson Plan 7.8A **Unit Plan: The Immigrant Experience in Literature: Literature for and about Hispanic Students, Cultural Relevance Rubric, and Sheltered Instruction Observation Protocol (SIOP) Lesson Plan** *continued*

- To improve student appreciation, participation, and interest in the English class by including multicultural texts that honor their culture, heritage, and language.

A. Unit Objectives:

Content Objectives:

ELL Standards:

> Goal 2: Use English to achieve in all academic settings.
>
> Content Standard 2-2: Use English to read and write in academic settings.

After completing this unit:

- Students will have a wider knowledge of a contemporary Latino author (Esmeralda Santiago) and her literary contributions.
- Students will improve their text connections by identifying themselves with the chosen text (*When I Was Puerto Rican*).
- Students will develop an appreciation and interest for the English class by seeing their culture, heritage, and language valued by the classroom teacher.
- Students will be able to interpret a given text.
- Students will analyze the causes and effect in the novel.
- Students will read the novel and represent the sequence of events through words, pictures, or drama.

Language Objectives:

ELL Standards:

Goal 2: Use English to achieve in all academic settings.

Content Standard 2-1: Use English to participate orally in academic settings.

- Students will participate in full-class, group and paired activities.

- Students will express their opinions.
- Students will take turns when speaking.
- Students will develop working definitions for the following terms: "immigrant," "isolation," "identity," "Americanized."

B. Concepts to Which Unit Is Related:

- The immigrant's search for belonging
- The adolescent's search for identity
- An adolescent's fight for independence
- The concept of becoming "Americanized"

C. Grade Level:

- Ninth–Twelfth Grade Intermediate and Advanced ESL (English as a Second Language) students

D. Unit Length:

- Three Weeks

E. Evaluative Criteria/Assessment:

- A Personal Narrative/Memoir
- Comparison/Contrast Essay: Comparing Text to a Movie Adaptation
- Journal Entries

*Note: See Appendix for Rubric

Week	Lesson Objectives	Activities
1	• With the use of the prompt *"Once I was… Now I am,"* students will write a five-paragraph personal experience essay with no more than five grammatical errors. • Prior to reading *When I Was Puerto Rican*, students will read book and chapter titles to make 5 predictions about what the book will be about. • After reading the first five chapters of the book, students will work in groups to map at least five events along with their causes and effects that have happened so far.	• During the first week, students will work on personal experience writing as a "building background" activity to the reading selection. They will use the prompt *"Once I was… Now I am."* Students will be encouraged to reflect on their own experiences in moving to another country, state, or school. For students who have not experienced this, they will be encouraged to interview a classmate and/or family member and ask them about their experiences. Upon completing the essay, a "stand and share" activity will take place. • Students will work on making predictions about the reading selection based on the title of the book and the chapter headings. These will be recorded on a poster board and verified by the class as the reading progresses. • Throughout the course of this unit, students will be required to keep a "reflective journal." They will be asked to record their feelings, emotions, reactions to the reading selection and how it relates to their personal experiences and/or situations others might have experienced. • As students read along, they will work in cooperative learning groups to record key events in the story and their possible causes and effects.

(continued)

Lesson Plan 7.8A **Unit Plan: The Immigrant Experience in Literature: Literature for and about Hispanic Students, Cultural Relevance Rubric, and Sheltered Instruction Observation Protocol (SIOP) Lesson Plan** *continued*

Week	Lesson Objectives	Activities
2	• With the use of the novel *When I Was Puerto Rican,* students will create two to three story maps to clarify sequence of events in the story. • After reading halfway through the book, students will work in groups to create character charts that list at least 5 characters. • Working in guided reading groups, students will read at least five chapters of *When I Was Puerto Rican* during a one-week period.	• Once students have read half of the novel they will design story maps that list the sequence of events in the story. Using these story maps they will then work on making predictions for the last chapters and checking these with the predictions that were made at the beginning of the unit. • Students will continue writing in their journals. Those who feel like sharing their entries with the class will be encouraged to do so. • At this point in the novel most of the characters have been presented. Therefore, students will work in cooperative learning groups to create character traits. In doing so, they can talk about which characters they most identify with and why. • Students will be divided in guided reading groups according to their reading levels. The teacher will serve as a facilitator and model during this process.
3	• Working in guided reading groups, students will read the last five chapters of *When I Was Puerto Rican* during a one-week period. • After reading the novel, *When I Was Puerto Rican,* students will write a three-paragraph reflective journal entry about the differences and/or similarities between the novel and their lives. • After viewing the film version *Almost a Woman* (based on *When I Was Puerto Rican*), students will write a five-paragraph comparison/contrast essay between the text and the film version. A sample Venn diagram will be distributed. This will be used as a pre-writing activity. • With the use of a "Cultural Relevance Rubric," students will determine the relevance of *When I Was Puerto Rican* to their own personal lives.	• During the last week of this unit, students will spend time completing the novel and reflecting on the impact that it had on them. Discussions will take place as to the contribution that Esmeralda Santiago (author) makes to literature. Topics such as search for identity, assimilation, acquiring a second language, and others will be part of class discussions and students' writing. • Students will view the film version of the novel (at least two class periods) and then talk about the differences and similarities between the two in preparation for their final reaction papers. Students will also be encouraged to discuss how the film might mirror their lives. • Finally, students will rate the book using a "Cultural Relevance Rubric" and determine how the book connects to their lives. They will then write a final journal entry based on these responses.

APPENDIX

Windham Public Schools

Rubric for Narrative Writing

Score Point: 6
Well-developed narratives; writers expand on all key events and characters
• Fully elaborated with specific details
• Strong organizational strategy/sequencing
• Fluent

Score Point: 5
Developed narratives; writers expand on most key events and characters
• Moderately well-elaborated with mostly specific details
• Generally strong organizational strategy/sequencing
• Moderately fluent

Score Point: 4
Somewhat-developed narratives; some expansion of key events and characters
• Adequately elaborated with mix of general and specific details
• Satisfactory organizational strategy/sequencing
• Somewhat fluent

Score Point: 3
Minimally developed narratives; little expansion of key events and characters; some details just listed
• More general than specific details
• Some evidence of organization/sequencing
• Some awkwardness may be present

Score Point: 2
Undeveloped narratives; usually brief responses, details just listed
• Mostly general details
• May be disorganized/weak sequencing
• May be awkward and confused

Score Point: 1
Very sparse narratives
• May have few/vague details
• Too brief to indicate sequencing
• Awkward and confused

SOURCE: Contributed by Dr. Nivea Lisandra Torres, Windham Public Schools, ELL and Curriculum Specialist, Mansfield Center, CT. Used with permission.

Lesson Plan 7.8B Unit Plan: The Immigrant Experience in Literature: Literature for and about Hispanic Students

Cultural Relevance Rubric

adapted from Ann Freeman, 2000

	Just like us .... Not at all			
Are the characters in the story like you and your family?	4	3	2	1
Have you ever had an experience like one described in this story?	4	3	2	1
Have you lived in or visited places like those in the story?	4	3	2	1
Could this story take place this year?	4	3	2	1
How close do you think the main characters are to you in age?	4	3	2	1
Are there main characters in the story who are: boys (for boys) or girls (for girls)?	4	3	2	1
Do the characters talk like you and your family do?	4	3	2	1
How often do you read stories like these?	4	3	2	1

SOURCE: Contributed by Dr. Nivea Lisandra Torres, Windham Public Schools, ELL and Curriculum Specialist, Mansfield Center, CT. Used with permission.

Lesson Plan 7.8C Sheltered Instruction Observation Protocol (SIOP) Lesson Plan

Topic: Identifying the Main Idea in a Reading Selection

Background:

The class has been studying a unit on *"The Immigrant Experience in Literature: Literature for and about Hispanic Students."* This unit focuses on Hispanic authors and the challenges of a daunting new life in the United States. This particular lesson focuses on the concept of self-worth and identity and how a life-changing experience marks the character's life.

English Proficiency Level: Intermediate/Advanced
Grades: 9–12

Preparation:

Connecticut State English Language Arts Standard:
1: Reading and Responding;
1.1. Students use appropriate strategies before, during and after reading in order to construct meaning.

ELL State Standard:
2-2 Use English to read and write in academic settings.

Content Objective:
Students will identify the main idea of the reading selection: *An Awakening...Summer 1956* by Nicholasa Mohr.

Language Objective:
Students will discuss and explain the terms "awakening," "self-worth," and "exclusion" as they relate to the story and their personal lives.

Allotted Time:
Multi-day class (depending on students' English proficiency this lesson could require 2 45-minute class periods) with review and continued practice on the following day.

Resources/Materials:
Board/Chart Paper
Markers
Index Cards
Overhead Projector
Transparency with Main Idea Graphic Organizer
Textbook: *Latino Caribbean Literature,* Globe Fearon: Reading Selection: *An Awakening ...Summer 1956* by Nicholasa Mohr

Presentation/Building Background:
The teacher will initiate the lesson and build background with a pre-reading activity. Students will be asked to respond in their journals to the following question: *What are some qualities and characteristics that you possess that make you feel proud of who you are?*
  Students will have the opportunity to share their responses with their peers and the class.

Next, students will be asked to think of a time when they might have been unfairly judged or treated because of their gender, nationality, or ethnicity. Some students might feel comfortable sharing their experiences with the class, while others will prefer to simply record their experiences in their journal.

Practice/Application:
• Students will read the selection in their reading groups. The teacher will provide assistance as necessary during the reading of the selection. Each group will receive an index card with one of the three target terms written on it (**awakening, self-worth, exclusion**). This word will serve as a focus point during the reading and as a prompt for discussion post-reading.
• Once all groups have finished reading the selection, they will have 5 minutes to discuss among themselves how the word they were given relates to the story and possibly to their own experiences. Students will have the opportunity to select a recorder, presenter, and time keeper for this activity.
• The presenter for each group will share with the class their definition of the assigned term as it relates to the story. Each group's definition will be posted on the class Word Wall.
• Finally, each group will be given a main idea graphic organizer. Each group will have 10 minutes to discuss among themselves what the main idea of the selection is. Each group will be asked to change the assigned roles of recorder, presenter, and time keeper for this new task.
• The presenter will record the group's main idea on a chart paper outline of the main idea graphic organizer.
• The class will discuss the main ideas posted and reach a consensus on a main idea for the selection.

Review/Assessment:
• Each student will be asked to write in their journal a sentence describing the story's main idea with the use of any of the target words (**awakening, self-worth, exclusion**).
• Students will be asked to share orally a response for one of the following review prompts:
  "After today's lesson, I learned..."
  "After today's lesson, I wonder..."
  "After today's lesson, I am surprised..."

Homework: Respond to the following question in paragraph format: Which part of the selection had the greatest impact on you? Why?

SOURCE: Contributed by Dr. Nivea Lisandra Torres, Windham Public Schools, ELL and Curriculum Specialist, Mansfield Center, CT. Used with permission.

LESSON PLAN 7.9 Dr. Melanie Reap has a background in both science and agricultural education. Reap is the Department of Education chairperson at Winona State University in Winona, MN, where she teaches courses in the elementary education and the science education programs. She taught middle and high school science and agriculture for five years in a remote western Texas district before becoming a teacher educator. Reap has been using historical narrative to teach science, as evidenced in Lesson Plan 7.9A and 7.9B included here. Her lesson "Surviving the Donner Party: A Learning Cycle" and the accompanying "Example Donner Lesson Extensions for Secondary Language Arts and Social Studies" make up an exemplary interdisciplinary lesson integrating the use of a variety of technologies, primary source documents, and activities. According to Reap, the massive westward movement in U.S. history presents a compelling interaction of social, cultural, religious, and economic forces. Specifically, Reap claims, analysis of the story of the Donner Party allows the discovery of patterns of influence of gender, age, and family structure on survival in an extreme situation. In this lesson, she has students examine the westward movement through a new lens by reviewing personal narratives of those who experienced the journey. The lesson plan is guided by four questions and includes several websites and a selected bibliography. In addition to reviewing the vast data that Reap provides, she suggests that students watch the 1992 PBS documentary *Donner Party* by Ric Burns, study topographic maps of the route, and analyze artifacts such as bones, diaries, Google images, and forensics of the Donner party to learn what happened to its members.

This lesson presents possibilities for extensions in social studies, geography, physical education, health, physics, psychology, math, and other disciplines as well. The numerous suggestions on how to integrate technology in this lesson plan could be complemented by having students create various tables, pie charts, bar graphs, line graphs, and so on to display the data they compile from their searches in addition to creating an Excel spreadsheet. Also, in addition to or instead of showing the PBS documentary in class, students could participate in a collaborative learning jigsaw activity where different groups could watch different segments of "The Donner Party, Parts 1 through 9," available on the Internet at **http://www.youtube.com/watch?v=s1ceO0gtlJ4**, and share their findings with their classmates. Students could also peruse the website Digital History: Using New Technologies to Enhance Teaching and Research at **http://www.digitalhistory.uh.edu/database/article_display .cfm?HHID=303M** and other sites to find materials on westward expansion and the Donner Party.

You could also ask students to research current survivors like Aron Ralston, a mountain climber from Colorado whose extraordinary survival story of how he cheated death in Blue John Canyon has been captured in his book *Between a Rock and a Hard Place* and told in the movie *127 Hours*. Students could also read one of Will Hobbs's novels. Hobbs is a former reading and language arts teacher who taught secondary students for 17 years in Durango, CO. Adolescents really enjoy his more than 20 wilderness adventures. You can peruse his publications at **http://www.willhobbsauthor .com/books/books.html**, and students can communicate with him via his blog. Students can also read a novel by Canadian-born author Gordon Korman, who wrote his first book, *This Can't Be Happening at Macdonald Hall*, when he was 12 years old for a coach who suddenly found himself teaching seventh-grade English. Or students could read his Island Trilogy: *Shipwreck*, *Survival*, and *Escape*, which are action/adventure novels that highlight the challenges of six shipwrecked kids who were in real danger of dying every minute. Reviews of Korman's books can be found at **http:// gordonkorman.com**.

Students might also be encouraged to search the Internet to uncover other harrowing survival stories involving cannibalism like the Uruguayan Andes flight disaster in South America, where a chartered flight carrying 45 people, including a rugby team and their friends and family, crashed in the Andes in 1972. More than a quarter of the passengers died in the crash, several others died soon after, and an avalanche killed nine more individuals. The last of the 16 survivors were rescued more than two months after the crash. Faced with starvation and radio news reports that the search for them had been abandoned, the survivors fed on the dead passengers who had been preserved in the snow. Students could watch the documentary *Stranded* and compare it to the film *Alive*. They could also read the account of the tragedy in *Miracle in the Andes* by rugby team member and crash survivor Nando Parrado. A comparison between the circumstances the members of the Donner Party faced and the passengers on the Andes flight encountered could be made.

LESSON PLAN 7.10 Jennifer Norton has been teaching at Argonaut High School in the Amador County Unified School District in Jackson, CA, since 1992. She has taught courses in world history, AP European history, English, and AP art history. She has also served as a museum teacher fellow with the U.S. Holocaust Memorial Museum (USHMM) since 2005 and conducts workshops across the western region. She also developed a Holocaust and genocide studies elective for her students at Argonaut High School. In the summer of 2009, Norton was one of 16 educators in the U.S. to be awarded a Fulbright-Hayes grant to Poland. She is currently finishing her master's degree in history with an emphasis on the Holocaust.

The exemplary lesson plan and supporting materials that Norton contributed here are titled "Working with Documents: Pre-War Nazi Antisemitism," the "Key to Select Sources," and "Internet and Text Resources for Creating Document-Based Lessons" (see Lesson Plan 7.10A and 7.10B). In this lesson, students acquire skills in decoding, analyzing, and finding meaning and relevance in a wide range of primary source documents. In fact, Norton has students

Lesson Plan 7.9A Model Lesson Plan Integrating Technology

Surviving the Donner Party: A Learning Cycle

Exploration

Materials per group:

Donner Party lists on Excel spreadsheet (see Resources below)

Calculators

Scratch paper

Procedure:

Distribute the calculators and scratch paper and have the groups analyze the data. They will be looking for patterns in the data such as:

1. Who lived?
2. Who died?
3. When in the year did they die?
4. Did the age or gender of a person play a role in survival?

Allow enough time for the students to explore the data, discover the patterns, and create charts and graphs in Excel. Some patterns are not as obvious as others; allow a minimum of 30 minutes for an average class.

Explanation

Materials per group of two or three:

Ideally, a computer projector should be used to project the Excel charts and graphs. If that is not possible, have the students transfer the graphs to chart paper or overhead transparencies.

Blank overhead acetate or large piece of chart paper

Overhead pens or markers

Procedure:

Have students compile their data and present their findings to the class.

The question to be answered through the analysis of the data is:

What factors led to survival?

Sample statistics derived from the raw data:

• Of the 81 people who made it to the mountain camps, 47 were male and 34 were female.

• In the mountain camps, 27 males (57%) and 9 females (26%) died.

• Mean age of the survivors was 17 yrs; of those who died, 25 yrs.

• Median age of survivors was 14 yrs; of those who died, 25 yrs.

• Of those 5 years old and under—7 lived, 12 died.

• Of those between ages 6 and 15—20 lived and 3 died.

• Of those between ages 16 and 30—13 lived and 15 died.

• Of those older than 30—6 lived and 10 died.

• Of 19 adult males without families, 3 died on the trail, and 13 died in the mountains (or 84% perished).

• Of those with a family affiliation, 62% survived.

Many factors led to the survival of people in this pioneer group. Two-thirds of the males died while only one-third of the females died. Those with family affiliation survived; only three traveling alone did. The very young and the elderly did not survive regardless of gender or family affiliation.

Expansion

Example from Geography:

Analysis of the demographic data can be developed in many ways; for example, you may wish to explore the biology behind the demise/survival of individuals or the role of family affiliation in survival. One question that certainly arises is: Where were these people trapped and how did they become trapped?

Materials per group:

A blank map of the United States west of the Mississippi River

A map of the western United States showing geographic features

A topographic map of the Sierra Nevada Mountains near Truckee, CA and Donner Pass (available at **http://www.topozone.com**)

Photographs/video showing east and west sides of the Sierra Nevada OR The Donner Party, a documentary made by Ric Burns for The American Experience, PBS (very useful but may be too intense for sensitive viewers).

(**Note:** Most maps of the westward expansion show the Donner Party route. Hard copies of topographic maps are available from most state land-grant university libraries, the United States Geological Survey, or specialty map stores.)

Provide the students a list of points to plot on their blank map so that they trace the pioneer party's route. Pay close attention to the location of Hastings Cut-off, the Wasatch Mountains, the Great Salt Lake, the Great Basin Desert, the Humboldt and Truckee rivers, the Ruby Mountains, and the pass through the Sierra Nevada Mountains near present-day Truckee Lake and Donner Lake.

After plotting the route, have the students analyze the topographic maps of the Sierra Nevada Mountains. Compare photos (or watch video) of the east and west sides of the mountains and the mountains in the four seasons (emphasize snow amounts). Alternatively, if it is fall or winter, students could download current snow conditions at Truckee, California, by going to **http://www.weather.com**.

Snowfall in the Sierra Nevada Mountains is very high due to the uplift of moisture-laden air from the Pacific, which condenses and falls as rain or snow. Most moisture falls on the mountains and very little falls east of the Sierras. The area beyond the mountains (Great Basin Desert) is called a rain shadow.

The Donner Party got to the pass late in the season (October) because they took Hastings Cut-off. As they tried to go over the pass, it began to snow. They had no road and became bogged down in the heavy snow. They had to remain in the mountains until help arrived in March.

Resources

• A list of Donner Party members that gives the names, family association, age, sex, rescue status, and final condition (lived/died) can be found at the Web sites listed. One of the best lists is from the article "Living through the Donner Party" by Jared Diamond in the March 1992 issue of Discover magazine. You may also contact Dr. Melanie A. Reap at mreap@winona.edu.

• Useful Web sites:
  http://www.utahcrossroads.org/DonnerParty/
  http://members.aol.com/danmrosen/donner/index.htm
  http://raiboy.tripod.com/Donner/index.html
  http://www.spartacus.schoolnet.co.uk/WWdonnerP.htm
  http://www.topozone.com
  http://www.weather.com

• Selected Bibliography:
  Diamond, Jared. (March 1992). "Living through the Donner Party." Discover, 100–107.

(continued)

Lesson Plan 7.9A **Model Lesson Plan Integrating Technology** *continued*

Hastings, L. W. (originally published in 1845, reprint by Applewood Books). *The emigrants' guide to Oregon and California*. Bedford, MA: Applewood Books.

King, Joseph A. (1992). *Winter of entrapment: A new look at the Donner Party*. Lafayette, CA: K&K Publications.

Mullen, Jr., F. (1977). *The Donner Party chronicles*. Carson City, NV: Nevada Humanities Commission.

Murphy, Virginia Reed. (1980 edition). *Across the plains in the Donner Party: A personal narrative of the overland trip to California, 1846–47*. Golden, CO: Outbooks.

SOURCE: Contributed by Dr. Melanie A. Reap, Department Chair, Winona University. Used with permission.

Lesson Plan 7.9B **Example Donner Lesson Extensions for Secondary Language Arts and Social Studies (Technology Rich)**

Language Arts/Literature

Many of the Donner Party survivors and rescuers left accounts of their ordeal. The following are key primary sources:

Virginia Reed Murphy—*Across the Plains in the Donner Party: A Personal Narrative of the Overland Trip to California 1846–47*. Outbooks Press, Golden, CO: ISBN 0-89646-063-0.

Eliza P. Donner Houghton—*The Expedition of the Donner Party and Its Tragic Fate*. University of Nebraska Press, Lincoln, NE: ISBN 0-8032-7304-5.

Patrick Breen—*The Diary of Patrick Breen, One of the Donner Party*. Online at the University of California, Berkeley, CA.

URL—**http://sunsite.berkeley.edu/cgi-bin/ebind2html/2/breen?cap**

Lansford W. Hastings—*The Emigrants' Guide to Oregon and California*. Applewood Books, Bedford, MA: ISBN 1-55709-245-1.

Kristin Johnson (Ed.)—*Unfortunate Emigrants: Narratives of the Donner Party*. Utah State University Press, Logan, UT: ISBN 0-87421-208-1.

(Note: Kristin Johnson's book is a compilation of the statements and memoirs of Donner Party members, rescuers, and those who encountered the group during their journey. Many of these accounts have not been in print for decades. It is a very rich resource.)

Activities based on these resources:

1. Compare Hastings' "travel guide" with modern travel guides, especially for California and Nevada. What made Hastings' guide so compelling to the emigrants? Do modern guides use similar techniques?
2. Compare two or three accounts of an incident from Johnson's book. Why do they differ? How are they the same? What is the picture painted by their words? Are there hidden agendas at work in the retelling of the story?
3. How do Virginia Reed Murphy and Eliza Donner Houghton's memoirs align with what we know from our scientific investigation of survival?
4. Patrick Breen's diary was written by him during the ordeal. It is a first-hand, real-time account of what happened.

Compare it to the accounts written after rescue—many of which were written years later.

Social Studies (Geography)

The Donner Party got into trouble because they followed the advice in Hastings' book. However, Hastings himself was a victim of two things—his ego and his lack of information about the route. His "cutoff" looked good on the maps of the day; but we know that it killed people. The following two activities highlight the use of maps. If it is available, a GIS program would allow students even more interaction with the topography of the route and could extend the activities.

Activity 1—Modern versus old

Hand out the route of the Donner Party from St. Joseph, Missouri to San Francisco—use only place names, rivers, and mountain ranges. Have students plot the route using maps of that era. Two online resources for historical maps are:

http://www.lib.utexas.edu/maps/map_sites/hist_sites.html#US

http://alabamamaps.ua.edu/historicalmaps/unitedstates/1826-1850b.html

Repeat using modern road maps.

Discuss: Was Hastings that off base in his estimation of the "cutoff"? What is your supporting evidence?

Activity 2—How would you get there?

You are going to walk, yes walk, from St. Joseph, Missouri to San Francisco, CA. However, you are not required to "keep to the roads" during your journey. Using modern topographic maps of the route, plot your best path to travel. Estimate the length of the route and time it will take you to finish the journey (average 20 miles per day on flat areas, 10 miles per day in very mountainous areas). Justify your decisions and present your path to the class.

SOURCE: Contributed by Dr. Melanie A. Reap, Department Chair, Winona University. Used with permission.

critically analyze various primary source documents, images, and artifacts to explore Hitler's antisemitism in its context of Nazi racial ideology as well as its role in Europe. Norton believes that the contextualization of history, that is, making careful distinctions about sources of information and striving for balance in establishing whose perspectives inform one's study, is crucial when teaching about the Holocaust. Educators can use Norton's lesson plan as it appears here, or the lesson plan can serve as a model for unique lessons.

In addition to perusing the numerous websites highlighted in Norton's lesson, students can also be encouraged to search the archives of the Library of Congress, which has cataloged over 1,200 resources in its digital collection pertaining to the Holocaust, including Web pages, legislation, photographs, prints, drawings, books, manuscripts, films, videos, and software. Its resources can be accessed at **http://www.loc.gov/search/?q=Holocaust&fa=digitized:true**.

Lesson Plan 7.10A Working with Documents: Pre-War Nazi Antisemitism

Overview and Rationale
Using Primary Source Materials to Teach about the Holocaust

Primary sources are the basis for all historical research and scholarship. In addition to their textbooks, students in social studies classes need to be exposed to a rich variety of primary sources, and learn how to understand and interpret them.

The Holocaust is a subject that affords a wealth of primary source materials. Much of the Permanent Exhibit of the USHMM is made from primary source materials: newspaper articles and pictures; newsreel and other film sources; clothing and other artifacts; posters and advertisements; journals, letters, and other documents left by the victims, perpetrators, bystanders, and rescuers.

Many of these primary source documents and photos can be accessed on the museum's Web site, in addition to the wealth of material available on other Holocaust-related Web sites that are linked to the museum's Web site, so creating a lesson using primary sources is not difficult to do. Students will have a higher degree of engagement with materials that come from the actual participants, and they can, at the same time, gain valuable strategies for and practice in decoding and interpreting primary source documents for meaning, context and point of view.

The following lesson has been developed to support the USHMM guidelines for teaching about the Holocaust, and can be used as is, or serve as a model for unique lessons individually created by teachers in their own classrooms.

Before students can work effectively with primary sources, they must become used to analyzing and interpreting them effectively and in a discriminating manner. Without developing this skill, students will often simply report on or restate the content of a document, apparently accepting it as a factual statement and not as an expression of an individual's point of view, replete with the speaker's biases and opinions. Students must be trained to consider the source of the document and its speaker's attributes, such as occupation, nationality, social class, and religion, as well as the intended audience and purpose of the source.

Given practice in considering all these factors, students will become discerning analysts and gain a much deeper understanding of, and confidence in, working with primary sources.

When I begin the Holocaust unit each year in my AP European and world history classes, I can always anticipate these questions: "What did Hitler have against the Jews, anyway?" and "Why did he hate the Jews so much?" These questions indicate that my students, like many others across the country, have neither any experience with antisemitism nor any understanding of its historical contexts or modern incarnations.

While not all Holocaust historians agree about the degree to which antisemitism is implicated in the origins or the implementation of the "Final Solution," they nearly universally accept that it played a part. Not only is it important for students to explore Hitler's antisemitism in its context of Nazi racial ideology, but also to understand the historical "background noise" of antisemitism in Europe that may have paved the way for the participation of thousands of Holocaust perpetrators and collaborators and the complicity of thousands more bystanders. Students should have the opportunity to make connections between the antisemitic myths and stereotypes common in Europe since medieval times and still evident in churches and literature today and the tidal wave of antisemitic Nazi propaganda to which the German people were subjected in the years 1933–1945.

I spend about four weeks on the Holocaust unit, in which I see my students on alternate days for 87 minutes. In this type of class schedule, I can complete this lesson in one or two class periods.

Purpose of Lesson
This lesson supports the museum's guidelines concerning contextualization of the history, making careful distinctions about sources of information and striving for balance in establishing whose perspective informs your study when teaching about the Holocaust. Students assess the relative importance of racial antisemitism as a factor in the conception and implementation of the Holocaust by studying and analyzing primary source images and documents. Through this lesson, students will begin to comprehend the increasingly tragic consequences of European antisemitism, culminating in the genocidal actions of the Nazi state and its collaborators.

Goals for Student Understanding
Desired Learning Outcomes

- Students acquire skill in decoding, analyzing, and finding meaning and relevance in a wide range of primary source materials.
- Students see the connections among and understand the purposes of a variety of Nazi publications and Nazi policies in pre-war Germany.
- Students will develop a broader context for understanding the events of the Holocaust.
- Students will develop an understanding of the appalling costs within a culture or society of the unchecked stereotyping and persecution of a specific group.

The Lesson
This lesson uses, in an adapted form, the Document Analysis Worksheets created by the National Archives and available in their original form at **http://www.archives.gov/education/lessons/ worksheets/index.html**

Accompanying each worksheet is a sample document intended to help students learn how to ask questions of a varying range of primary sources and make informed conclusions based on specific analytical devices.

Finally, students are asked to respond to specific questions relating to their analysis of the documents.

Culminating Activity
Once students have had a chance individually, in pairs or in groups to fill out the Document Analysis Worksheets, they should answer a range of questions which will measure their understanding and interpretation of the documents. These questions will help students synthesize the information they have gleaned from the documents and think about the topic as a coherent whole.

Questions for this part of the lesson should test the following skills:

1. Comprehension of a source
2. Corroboration by cross-referencing of sources
3. Evaluation of sources for purpose and utility
4. Making judgments about an interpretation
5. Relation of sources to contextual knowledge

A. Study the sources.
   Is there a particular audience that many of the sources address? If so, who is targeted? List the specific sources and explain how the audience is addressed in each. What explanations can you give for targeting this audience?
B. Study Sources 2 and 6.
   Think about the kinds of future Nazi actions and activities for which these sources might be preparing the German people. Use the sources and your own knowledge to list as many of these as you can.
C. Study Sources 4 and 5.
   What emotions are these documents trying to create in the German people? Why might this be necessary? List all the

(continued)

Lesson Plan 7.10A **Working with Documents: Pre-War Nazi Antisemitism** *continued*

words the images in these two documents suggest that might help the Nazis to get their message across.

D. Study Source 3.

Based on your knowledge of events in Germany in 1933–1939, what might be the intended purpose of the activity/event pictured? Can you find other sources that support this same purpose? If so, which ones? How?

E. Study Sources 1 and 3.

What difficulties and contradictions are inherent in Nazi attempts to define and classify Jews as a "non-Aryan race"

in Source 1? While the Nazi ideology was based on supposed racial differences between Jews and non-Jews, why do you think both of these sources use religion to make this distinction? How do the Nazis show their concerns for public opinion in these sources? In what way do sources 2 and 5 relate to these two sources?

F. Evaluate the usefulness of these documents in helping you to understand the purposes, methods, and intended audience of Nazi propaganda in the pre-war years. Suggest other sources that might have helped your understanding.

Written Document Analysis Worksheet

1. TYPE OF DOCUMENT (Check one):

___ Newspaper   ___ Diary   ___ Press release   ___ Report

___ Letter   ___ Telegram   ___ Advertisement   ___ Others_____

___ Memorandum

2. DATE(S) OF DOCUMENT: _____

3. AUTHOR (OR CREATOR) OF THE DOCUMENT: _____

POSITION (TITLE): _____

4. FOR WHAT AUDIENCE WAS THE DOCUMENT WRITTEN? _____

5. DOCUMENT INFORMATION (There are many possible ways to answer A–E.)

A. List three things the author said that you think are important:

_____

_____

_____

B. Why do you think this document was written?

_____

_____

C. What evidence in the document helps you know why it was written? Quote from the document.

_____

_____

D. List at least two things the document tells you about events and/or life at the time it was written:

_____

_____

_____

_____

_____

E. Write a question to the author that is left unanswered by the document:

_____

_____

(continued)

Source 1

Nuremberg Law for the Protection of German Blood and German Honor (*September 15, 1935***)**

Moved by the understanding that purity of the German Blood is the essential condition for the continued existence of the German people, and inspired by the inflexible determination to ensure the existence of the German Nation for all time, the Reichstag has unanimously adopted the following law . . .

Article 1

1. Marriages between Jews and subjects of the state of German or related blood are forbidden. Marriages nevertheless concluded are invalid, even if concluded abroad to circumvent this law.

Article 2

Extramarital intercourse between Jews and subjects of the state of German or related blood is forbidden.

Article 3

Jews may not employ in their households female subjects of the state of German or related blood who are under 45 years old.

The Reich Citizenship Law: First Regulation
    (***November 14, 1935***)

Article 2

2. An individual of mixed Jewish blood is one who is descended from one or two grandparents who were racially full Jews, in so far as he or she does not count as a Jew according to Article 5, paragraph 2. One grandparent shall be considered as full-blooded if he or she belonged to the Jewish religious community.

Article 3

Only the Reich citizen, as bearer of full political rights, exercises the right to vote in political affairs or can hold public office....

Article 4

1. A Jew cannot be a citizen of the Reich. He has no right to vote in political affairs and he cannot occupy public office.

2. Jewish officials will retire as of December 31, 1935. If these officials served at the front in the world war, either for Germany or her allies, they will receive in full, until they reach the age limit, the pension to which they were entitled according to the salary they last received; they will, however, not advance in seniority.

Article 5

1. A Jew is anyone who is descended from at least three grandparents who are racially full Jews.

2. A Jew is also one who is descended from two full Jewish parents, if (a) he belonged to the Jewish religious community at the time this law was issued, or joined the community later, (b) he was married to a Jewish person, at the time the law was issued, or married one subsequently, (c) he is the offspring of a marriage with a Jew, in the sense of Section I, which was contracted after the Law for the Protection of German Blood and German Honor became effective, (d) he is the offspring of an extramarital relationship with a Jew, according to Section I, and will be born out of wedlock after July 31, 1936. **http://www.ess.uwe.ac.uk/documents/gerblood.htm**

Poster Analysis Worksheet

1. What are the main colors used in the poster? _____

2. What symbols (if any) are used in the poster? _____

3. If a symbol is used, is it
   clear (easy to interpret)? _____

   memorable? _____

   dramatic? _____

4. Are the messages in the poster primarily visual, verbal, or both? _____

5. Who do you think is the intended audience for the poster? _____

6. What does the Government hope the audience will do? _____

7. What Government purpose(s) is served by the poster? _____

8. The most effective posters use symbols that are unusual, simple, and direct. Is this an effective poster? Why? _____

Source 2

Poster titled "The Nuremberg Law for the Protection of German Blood and German Honor," circa 1935.

This poster is no. 70 in a series titled *Theory of Inheritance and Racial Hygiene,* published by Publisher for National Literature, Stuttgart.

The German text at the bottom reads, "Maintaining the purity of blood ensures the survival of the German people."

The illustration includes:

• A stylized map of the borders of central Germany

• A schematic of the forbidden degrees of marriage between Aryans and non-Aryans

• Point 8 of the Nazi party platform (against the immigration of non-Ayrans into Germany): "Any further immigration of non-citizens is to be prevented. We demand that all non-Germans, who have immigrated to Germany since 2 August 1914, be forced immediately to leave the Reich."

• The text of the "Law for the Protection of German Blood." "1. Marriages between Jews and nationals of German or kindred blood are forbidden. Marriages concluded in defiance of this law are void, even if, for the purpose of evading this law, they are concluded abroad." "3. Relations outside marriage between Jews and nationals of German or kindred blood are forbidden."

(continued)

Lesson Plan 7.10A **Working with Documents: Pre-War Nazi Antisemitism** *continued*

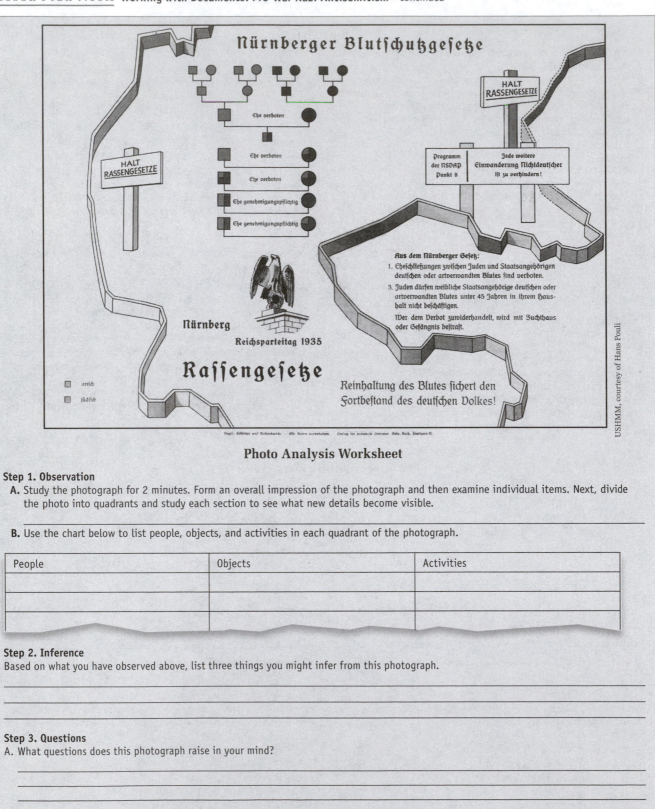

USHMM, courtesy of Hans Pouli

Photo Analysis Worksheet

Step 1. Observation

A. Study the photograph for 2 minutes. Form an overall impression of the photograph and then examine individual items. Next, divide the photo into quadrants and study each section to see what new details become visible.

B. Use the chart below to list people, objects, and activities in each quadrant of the photograph.

People	Objects	Activities

Step 2. Inference

Based on what you have observed above, list three things you might infer from this photograph.

Step 3. Questions

A. What questions does this photograph raise in your mind?

B. Where could you find answers to them?

(continued)

Lesson Plan 7.10A **Working with Documents: Pre-War Nazi Antisemitism**   *continued*

Source 3

A Jewish student wearing a suit and bow tie is marched across the Weidenhaüser Bridge in Marburg, Germany, carrying a sign that reads, "I have defiled a Christian maiden."

USHMM, courtesy of Marburg, Amt fuer Presse-und Oeffentlichkeitsarbeit.

Cartoon/Illustration Analysis Worksheet

Level 1

Visuals
List the objects or people you see in the cartoon.

_____
_____
_____
_____

Words (not all cartoons include words)
Identify the cartoon caption and/or title.

_____

Locate three words or phrases used by the cartoonist to identify objects or people within the cartoon.

_____

Record any important dates or numbers that appear in the cartoon.

_____

Level 2

Visuals
Which of the objects on your list are symbols?

_____

What do you think each symbol means?

_____
_____
_____

Words
Which words or phrases in the cartoon appear to be the most significant? Why do you think so?

_____
_____

List adjectives that describe the emotions portrayed in the cartoon.

_____
_____

(continued)

Lesson Plan 7.10 A **Working with Documents: Pre-War Nazi Antisemitism** *continued*

Level 3

Describe the action taking place in the cartoon. _____

Explain how the words in the cartoon clarify the symbols. _____

Explain the message of the cartoon. _____

What special interest groups would agree/disagree with the cartoon's message? Why? _____

Sources 4 and 5

Circa 1938 Germany

The cover of a children's book titled, "The Poisonous Mushroom," published in Germany in 1938.

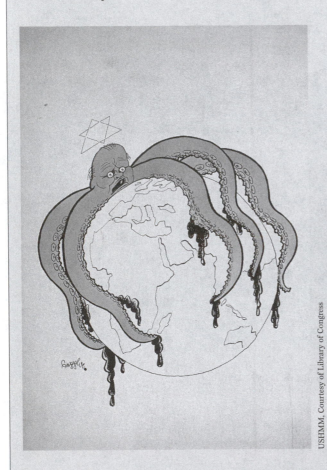

USHMM, Courtesy of Library of Congress

USHMM, Courtesy of Hiemer, Ernst. Der Giftpilz: [The Poisonous Mushroom]. Der Sturmer, C. 1938.

Artifact Analysis Worksheet

1. Type of Artifact

   Describe the material from which it was made: bone, pottery, metal, wood, stone, leather, glass, paper, cardboard, cotton, wood, plastic, other material.

   _____

2. Special Qualities of the Artifact

   Describe how it looks and feels: shape, color, texture, size, weight, movable parts, anything printed, stamped, or written on it.

   _____

(continued)

Lesson Plan 7.10A **Working with Documents: Pre-War Nazi Antisemitism** *continued*

3. Uses of the Artifact
   A. What might it have been used for? _____
   B. Who might have used it? _____
   C. Where might it have been used? _____
   D. When might it have been used? _____

4. What Does the Artifact Tell Us
   A. What does it tell us about technology of the time in which it was made and used?
       _____
   B. What does it tell us about the life and times of the people who made it and used it?
       _____
       _____
       _____

   C. Can you name a similar item today? If so, give as many examples as you can:
       _____
       _____
       _____

Source 6: German board game introduced in the 1930s

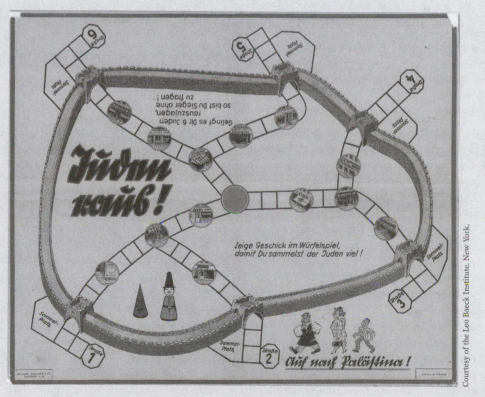

Courtesy of the Leo Baeck Institute. New York.

The illustration includes:

- The name of the game, "Juden Raus," on the left side of the game board in bold type, means, "Jews Out!"
- The three members of a Jewish family (lower right) are shown as crude antisemitic stereotypes and are being expelled from a medieval gated, walled city over the words "Off to Palestine."
- The game pieces all wear medieval "Jew's Hats" and have exaggerated cartoonish, antisemitic faces.
- Other illustrations on the game board are antisemitic characterizations of Jewish facial features and Jewish occupations.
- The instructions written in the middle of the game board read, "Skill with the dice will gather you many Jews."

Credit: Stephanie Bruchfeld and Paul A. Levine, *Tell ye your children…*, The Swedish Government Offices Living History Project, Stockholm, 1998

SOURCE: Contributed by Jennifer Norton, Teacher, Argonaut High School, Jackson, California; Museum Teacher Educator, Regional Education Corps, United States Holocaust Memorial Museum. Used wih permission.

(continued)

Lesson Plan 7.10B   Internet and Text Resources for Creating Document-Based Lessons (Technology Rich)

USHMM Web site: **www.ushmm.org**

USHMM links page—all reputable sites dealing with the Holocaust **http://www.ushmm.org/research/library/weblinks/**

National Archives Web site—Document Analysis Worksheets **http://www.archives.gov/education/lessons/worksheets/index.html**

The Einsatzgruppen Archives (Note: This site contains a warning from Google, but I have not found it unsafe) **http://www.einsatzgruppenarchives.com/**

German Propaganda Archive—Randall Bytwerk at Calvin College **http://www.calvin.edu/academic/cas/gpa/**

PBS Web site—America and the Holocaust: Deceit and Indifference **http://www.pbs.org/wgbh/amex/holocaust/**

PBS Web site—Auschwitz **http://www.pbs.org/auschwitz/**

PBS Web site—Shtetl **http://www.pbs.org/wgbh/pages/frontline/shtetl/**

Russian Jewish History—particularly good for anti-Semitism pre-20th century **http://www.friends-partners.org/partners/beyond-the-pale/**

Paul Halsall, Jewish History Sourcebook **http://www.fordham.edu/halsall/jewish/jewishsbook.html**

Simon Wiesenthal Center Web site—good resources **http://www.museumoftolerance.com/site/pp.asp?c=arLPK7PILqF&b=249685**

Fortunoff Video Archive for Holocaust Testimonies **http://www.library.yale.edu/testimonies/excerpts/index.html**

Fred R. Crawford Witness to the Holocaust Project files **http://sage.library.emory.edu/collection-0608.html**

Imperial War Museum Holocaust *Resource* Reflections **http://london.iwm.org.uk/server/show/ConWebDoc.1454**

Into the Arms of Strangers Web site—Kindertransport testimony from England **http://www2.warnerbros.com/intothearmsofstrangers/**

Nuremberg Trial Project Web site—full text of all trial transcripts **http://nuremberg.law.harvard.edu/php/docs_swi.php?DI=1&text=overview**

Avalon Project at Yale University—excellent source for Primary Sources/Nuremberg Trials **http://www.yale.edu/lawweb/avalon/imt/imt.htm**

Yad Vashem Holocaust Resource Center—Documents, Artifacts, etc. **http://www1.yadvashem.org/Odot/prog/index_before_change_table.asp**

Yad Vashem Web site—*The Auschwitz Album* **http://www1.yadvashem.org/exhibitions/album_auschwitz/home_auschwitz_album.html**

Excellent Holocaust Web site—Eichmann Trial Transcripts **http://www.nizkor.org/hweb/people/e/eichmann-adolf/transcripts/Sessions/index-01.html** (Eichmann trial transcripts)

UK Web site for Secondary Schools—Excellent resource for all types of short primary sources **http://www.spartacus.schoolnet.co.uk**

SOURCE: Contributed by Jennifer Norton, Teacher, Argonaut High School, Jackson, CA; Museum Teacher Educator, Regional Education Corps, United States Holocaust Memorial Museum. Used with permission.

Students could be asked to peruse the vast number of films depicting the atrocities of the Holocaust. Numerous sites list books and films about the Holocaust, including Wikipedia. You can locate films by date, title, or country of origin. Students could review scenes or films in their entirety for bias. One website that has a detailed list of films produced from the 1940s to 2006 is **http://en.wikipedia.org/wiki/List_of_Holocaust_films**. Students could also research other resources to uncover songs of the prison camps, collections of photographs, propaganda, Holocaust photo essays, and many other resources. They could critically analyze their resources by completing the corresponding analysis worksheets included in this lesson plan. Students could also participate in a virtual tour of the Holocaust History Museum at **http://www1.yadvashem.org/yv/en/museum/virtual_tour.asp** or peruse the online exhibitions of the U.S. Holocaust Memorial Museum at **http://www.ushmm.org/museum/exhibit/online**.

Students could also use the Internet to conduct research on other genocides. Students could explore the meaning of genocide and the historical contexts surrounding genocide as well as investigate genocide today. They could listen in on a Voices on Genocide Prevention podcast at **http://blogs.ushmm.org/COC2/C9**. Students could search the Internet to find primary documentation covering instances of genocide against Indigenous populations of the Western Hemisphere and explore accounts of genocide in countries worldwide,

including Cambodia, Congo, Sudan, Ivory Coast, Rwanda, Guatemala, Bosnia and Herzegovina, and Darfur.

LESSON PLAN 7.11 The AP psychology unit plan on social diversity, included here as Lesson Plan 7.11, was contributed by Joyce Jarosz Hannula, who is a master teacher with over 30 years of teaching experience at the secondary and postsecondary levels. Initially certified in secondary English, Hannula has taught courses in remedial English, composition, and technical writing. Most recently, she designed and taught numerous courses in general and AP psychology. She also served as the chair of the social studies department at Bozeman High School in Bozeman, MT. In addition, she serves as an adjunct professor at Montana State University, where she has taught courses in the Teacher Preparation Program and the English Department and for the Office of International Programs. In fact, she has served as the academic coordinator for several U.S. State Department International Research and Exchanges Board programs arranging and overseeing internships for international middle and secondary teaching fellows from around the world. Hannula places the international teachers with middle and secondary teachers in Bozeman Public Schools. Through this connection, she has been invited to offer professional development workshops for teachers in Russia, Armenia, Ukraine, and other overseas destinations. She relies on her vast multicultural experience in her teaching.

<u>**Lesson Plan 7.11**</u>   **AP Psychology Unit Plan/Course Project**

Grade Level: 11 and 12

Topic of Lesson: Social Diversity and Individual Response

General Course Objectives:

1. Students shall take part in community-building and self-awareness activities during both semesters. These activities are designed to increase personal awareness of stereotyping and promote acceptance of differences.
2. The impact of a lesson or the teaching of a concept is more lasting when it is frequently revisited. Thus, these activities will be presented in several units and ultimately reinforced in a larger unit on Social Diversity.

Learning Objectives:

At the completion of this unit, students should be able to:

1. Describe and evaluate the impact of community-building and self-awareness exercises
2. Demonstrate an understanding of schema and how it impacts stereotypes as applied to memory formation
3. Define the terms, in-group bias, scapegoating, prejudice, and discrimination
4. Explain the role stress plays in human interaction, specifically in terms of prejudice and discrimination
5. Discuss how cultural differences in norms and roles influence individual behavior and stereotyping
6. Discuss the impact of ethnic and racial diversity on a culture
7. Identify biological gender similarities and differences in terms of, and the results of, stereotyping based on these characteristics
8. Explain how gender identity is influenced by cultural, historical, and life-span differences in behavior.
9. Describe factors that contribute to prejudice and discrimination
10. Analyze prejudice and discrimination as applied to populations with mental disorders
11. Discuss and demonstrate effective methods of reducing prejudice and of affirming the value of social and cultural diversity

Necessary Resources:

1. Course text: Meyers, David G. (2001) *Psychology*, New York: Worth Publishers
2. Community Building Activities including first day opener, "Breaking Down Barriers," Peer Interview Questions, Self-Awareness Exercise, and Multicultural Quiz.
3. Internet Lab for student group research
4. PowerPoint program, Lightware Projector
5. Printed assignment sheets for group research and middle school presentations

Specific Activities:

1. This unit is developed a bit differently than the typical linear, move-on-we're-going-on scope and sequence. In order to "teach" tolerance, the unit must become a thread woven through the classroom content and experience. In order to increase self-awareness and build community within the classroom, several activities will be used throughout both semesters.

    These activities include "Breaking Down Barriers—Studying the Effects of Stereotypes" on the first day of class, to peer interviews three times during the course of the year, to an eye-witness testimony exercise, demonstrating how schema interferes with recall, to "Who am I," in the personality unit, and finally, before the specific content of the Social Diversity unit is introduced, to an attribution exercise in order to assess stereotyping.

2. Following the attribution exercise, students will take a quiz on Multicultural Awareness to measure awareness and link what is known to what is not known or not understood. (**www.mhhe .com/socscience/education/multi/activities/awarenessquiz _key.htlm**)
3. Students will complete reading of Chapter 19, defining the terms "in-group bias," "scapegoating," "prejudice" and "discrimination."
4. Students will watch and discuss selected portions of "Eye of the Storm."
5. Students will be placed into groups of four to five, depending on the size of the class. To increase community within the classroom, the instructor will create heterogeneous groupings. Each group will research and develop a ten-minute PowerPoint presentation on one of the following topics as it relates to **stereotyping and discrimination:**
    a.   Recent reports of violence and crime
    b.   Gender
    c.   Historical economic, religious, and social factors within a culture
    d.   Recent immigrants to the United States
    e.   Media's influence
    f.   Schools as a unique culture
    g.   Strategies for affirming and accepting diversity
6. After each presentation, students within the group will lead a classroom discussion based upon their topic.
7. All students will submit a list of five appropriate quiz questions on the day following each group presentation. Four of these are to be written as fill-in-the-blank or true-false formats. One is to be written as a short-answer question.
8. Students will complete a group assessment and self-assessment of their cooperative projects.
9. Students will complete a unit exam.
10. Review and reinforcement will be provided by application of these concepts in the chapter on Mental Disorders.
11. At the conclusion of the year, students will be asked to prepare a presentation for several middle school classrooms. This presentation should address the issues of diversity and intolerance within a school culture and should incorporate the research findings on learning, intolerance and self-awareness presented throughout the year. A sample lesson will be presented and experienced by the students (Once upon a time: **www.media-awareness.ca/english/resources/educational/ lessons**). Time and direction will be provided for Internet search and lesson practice.

Evaluation Criteria:

Objective 1: This objective will be evaluated in terms of active participation during the various exercises. Final evaluation will be based upon total participation (80%) and a final one-page, written self-assessment totaling 20%.

Objectives 2, 3, 7, 9, and **10** will be assessed initially by multiple-choice questions. Students should be able to identify basic definitions and demonstrate comprehension.

Objectives 2, 4, 5, 6, 7, 8, and **9** will be measured by teacher and peer evaluation and self-evaluation of PowerPoint presentations (60% of unit score) and short-answer question essays (40% of unit score) based on key concepts in each objective. Please see attached rubrics.

(continued)

Lesson Plan 7.11   **AP Psychology Unit Plan/Course Project**   *continued*

Objective 11 will be evaluated by self, group, and instructor assessment based upon effective planning, accuracy of content, engagement of group members and audience response/participation—appropriate, of course, to the middle school audience.

Bibliography:

Resources for Student Cooperative Learning Unit

www.socialpsychology.com (mega site)

www.alleydog.com (mega site)

www.cops.uni-sb.de/ronald/home/html (stereotyping)

www.auaa.org (discrimination)

www.social_Psychology.net (stereotypes)

www.colorado.edu/conflict/peace/treatment/fixstereo.htm (solutions)

www.courseworkbank.co.uk/coursework/value_sterotypes_21/ (stereotypes)

www.ccsf.edu/resources/tolerance/lesson/div01.html (stereotypes, history, religion)

http://www.yaaams.org/ (recent news stories—Young African American site)

http://www.worldcatlibraries.org/ (general reference)

http://www.media-awareness.ca/english/resources/educational/lessons/elementary/gender_portrayal/once_upon_a_time.cfm (gender and media)

http://www.educatingjane.com/educators.htm (gender and media)

www.hrw.org/reports/ (Human Rights Watch, Acts of Discrimination and Violence in the schools)

http://www.media-awareness.com/english/issues/stereotyping/ethnics_and_minorities/ (Economics of Racial Stereotyping)

www.quoteland.com/

www.bartleby.com/

www.quotationreference.com/ (sites for accessing quotations on tolerance and diversity)

This list will develop as students conduct Internet research.

Teacher Use:

http://Oregonstate.edu/fye/resources/notebook/section4c11htm (opening day exercise)

www.usu.edu/psy3510/prejudice.htlm (measuring attributions exercise)

www.mhhe.com/socscience/education/multi/activities/awarenessquiz_handout.html (multicultural awareness quiz)

http://www.mediaawareness.ca/english/issues/stereotyping/whiteness_and_privilege (gender issues and media)

http://www.adl.org/what_to_tell/print.asp (community building)

www.tolerance.org/teach/activities/activity.jap?ar

www.media-awareness.ca/english/resources/educational/lessons (sample student activities for middle school assignment)

www2./wwgbh.org/MBCWEIS/LTC/ALRI/teachtoltwo.html (Shadow of Hate)

Note— Sites for Listservs or Chats/discussion groups are not available here since the browser at Bozeman High School blocks these sites and students must access and use information in cooperative groups in the computer labs.

SOURCE: Contributed by Joyce Jarosz Hannula, Psychology Teacher and Instructional Coach, Bozeman High School, Bozeman, MT. Used with permission.

In her unit plan, Hannula weaves the importance of promoting tolerance and acceptance with an appreciation of the richness that diversity brings to the teaching-learning process. This comprehensive unit plan is designed to span the semester and provides students with ample opportunities to revisit key concepts like in-group bias, stereotyping, scapegoating, and discrimination. Hannula has integrated technology throughout this unit plan. Highlights include having students watch Jane Elliott's *Eye of the Storm*, access and complete a multicultural awareness quiz online, complete Web searches of current events touching on various aspects of diversity, peruse a variety of online resources, and create a PowerPoint presentation.

To incorporate even more technology, students could also visit the Implicit Association Test (IAT) on the Southern Poverty Law Center's website at **http://www.tolerance.org/activity/test-yourself-hidden-bias** to uncover their hidden biases. Drs. Anthony Greenwald and Mahazarin R. Banaji have created quizzes that students can take online and then receive feedback regarding their attitudes and preferences. The IATs were originally developed to explore the unconscious roots of thinking and feeling, but this website was constructed to help people gain greater awareness about their own unconscious preferences and beliefs. Having students take the IATs is a great way to introduce the concept of bias.

Students could also complete a variety of quizzes on equity and diversity, classism and poverty, and digital sexism, among other things, at **http://www.edchange.org/multicultural/quizzes.html**. Students could also listen to social justice speeches, songs, and quotations at the Critical Multicultural Pavilion and on other websites.

Since Hannula has her AP psychology juniors and seniors create a presentation for middle school students, technology could easily be incorporated. Students could explore Prezi in addition to PowerPoint to create their presentations. They could also create posters at Writing Guide Poster Sessions at **http://writing.colostate.edu/edu/guides/speaking/poster**. For additional contributions by Hannula in this textbook, see Figures 6.3 and 6.4 in Chapter 6 and Figures 11.13 and 11.14 in Chapter 11.

LESSON PLAN 7.12 To see how students can use Algebra Tiles to build models to represent the factorization of polynomials, review the "Sample Mathematics Lesson Plan," which was prepared by Jordanne Nevin during the semester she student-taught. Nevin was a math education major at Linfield College in McMinnville, OR, when she completed her student-teaching assignment at the local high school. After a few years of teaching high school mathematics, Nevin completed her first year as an administrator in the Kent School District in Washington. After she finished her master's degree and earned her Professional and Administration Certificates, she thought she was done with her education; however, she has decided to apply to doctoral programs to explore best practices in teaching math to traditionally underserved student populations.

Lesson Plan 7.12 **Sample Mathematics Lesson Plan**

LINFIELD COLLEGE
Education Department

Student ID Number:	Time/Period: 11:06–12:16/3rd	Date: March 18, 2004
Lesson/Unit Title: Algebra Tiles Activity	Subject: Algebra 1C	Grade Level: 10–12

Instructional Objectives:
(State what you want your students to be able to do as a result of the experiences that you provide. These objectives should represent a variety of cognitive levels, and each one should be tied to one or more specific instructional strategies and assessments in your plan.)

1. Select appropriate Algebra Tiles to use for activities (Knowledge).
2. Build models to represent factorization of polynomials (Application/Psychomotor).
3. Construct and test Algebra Tiles representation of factored polynomials for accuracy (Synthesis/Psychomotor).

Terms or Vocabulary:

Algebra Tiles

Learning Materials or Aids:
Overhead, overhead manipulatives (Algebra Tiles), student-made Algebra Tiles, two algebra activity recording sheets

Adaptations:
(Specifically describe what you plan to do to ensure the success of each and every one of your students who is identified as having special needs.)

In order to ensure success for each of my students, I will continue practicing the techniques that I currently employ in the classroom. One of these strategies is to always give a verbal and visual representation of the information being presented. I also frequently check for understanding and encourage students to ask questions or share comments. I have asked all of my students to choose a seat in the class where they feel that they can be the most successful, and I trust that they have done so. If any seating arrangements are disruptive to students' success, I will move that student to a location in which I feel he or she can be more productive in class.

I have two students with Individualized Education Programs (IEPs) in this class, only one of which has a specification for mathematics. This particular student has an annual goal of solving equations with one unknown as well as maintaining his current skills and performance level. He shows excellent progress and maintenance in these areas every day. On top of my frequent checks for understanding, I will ask him personally after each lesson if he has any questions on what was covered and how he would evaluate his progress and success/failure on his previous night's homework. For my other student with an IEP, I implement all of the above mentioned strategies and do a daily one-on-one check for understanding and comprehension.

I also have one student who is an English language learner (ELL). My cooperating teacher and I have set up a situation for him where he may leave class during work time and go get help from one of the English as a second language (ESL) teachers.

Instructional Strategies:
(Describe the instructional experiences that you will provide for your students.)

- Class will begin with a brief greeting and some disciplinary tasks that need to be addressed such as appropriate behavior in class, using time well, and the job of both the students and myself.
- After our greeting, students will be asked to work on their warm-up activity that covers last night's homework.
- I will go over all of the problems on the warm-up activity on the board and/or overhead in order to clarify anything that the students may still be stuck on.
- After the warm-up activity is complete, I will ask students to pair up by sliding their desks next to the person in the row across from them. They will be instructed to compare their homework answers and come to an agreement on any problems that either student missed (about how to solve the problem correctly).
- I will answer any questions that the students still have on their homework before moving on to the Algebra Tiles activity.
- Students are expected to have their Algebra Tiles ready for use in class. If they do not they will be provided with problems from the textbook to work on while the rest of the class works on their Algebra Tiles activity.
- I will do an introduction to Algebra Tiles and explain to the students that they will understand better once they begin working with them, which is why I have two activity sheets for them to complete. By the end of these activities, my hope is that the majority of my students feel comfortable factoring with Algebra Tiles.
- As a class we will work through Activity 1 and Activity 3 in the textbook. I will then ask students to work silently on the first Algebra Tiles activity sheet.
- Students will be given time to work on their own. Once students start to finish their first nine problems, I will do some teaching with my overhead manipulatives geared toward the introduction to our next lesson.

Assessment:
(Specifically describe how you will know if each of your objectives has been met during this lesson.)

Assessment of objectives 1–3 will take place during the Algebra Tiles activity, as well as when I collect the activity sheets at the beginning of the next lesson, to monitor students' understanding.

Closure:
(Describe how you will effectively conclude your lesson.)

Students will be dismissed with a quick rundown of their behavior and a reminder about their homework assignment. They are expected to finish the two Algebra Tiles activity sheets and read Section 9.3 in their textbook.

Reflection/Evaluation:
(Discuss the relative success or failure of your lesson.)

Excellent day! After putting so much effort into yesterday's lesson and having it be mediocre, I was feeling down and knew that today needed to begin with a new strategy and a sterner attitude on my part. In order to ensure success in today's lesson, I started with a

(continued)

Lesson Plan 7.12   **Sample Mathematics Lesson Plan**   *continued*

check of how my students felt about their homework. At least half of the class got halfway through the assignment, but thought it was very difficult, while many others told me that they didn't even try because it was too hard. Hearing those comments reassured me that a talk about expectations was needed. I spent about 5 minutes explaining to my students that I expect them to take responsibility for their learning. I am available to help them at many times during the day and I am more than willing to make time for any student. But they need to take the initiative to ask for help. During this discussion I also made it clear that I want all of my students to be communicating with each other during class, but at the appropriate times and about appropriate material. I also made sure to note how wonderful their questions are and urged them to continue asking them, but prompted them to use their textbook, notes, and classmates as resources before me. My students understood my concerns for them and seemed satisfied with my expectations.

I asked the students to attempt all of the problems on their warm-up activity to the best of their ability. After giving ample time to finish the six warm-up problems, I explained that I would not collect last night's homework because I wanted everyone to feel confident enough to move ahead. I asked my students to take notes as I went over the warm-up problems on the overhead. By the time I finished the first two, at least five students had had an "ah ha" moment, and everything began to click. I was especially excited when one of my students who had failed last trimester came in with every problem on his homework attempted. He told me that he really understood it after the warm-up problems, which made me very happy. The student who made this comment was the same student I spoke with after the pretest. I am very proud of his accomplishments so far. He has had his homework complete every day this first week. Since he earned only 40% of his homework points last trimester this is a major feat. I made sure to catch him before he left class today and let him know that I appreciated his effort and am very glad that he has chosen to take the Internet course on top of this class because I enjoy having him in class.

Although many students seemed to understand the material better as we worked through it, I did have to continue to remind them to take notes and participate so they could remember what we were learning for future lessons and tests.

The next portion of class was our introduction to Algebra Tiles. I did not get to spend enough time on this for the students to really understand the concept of Algebra Tiles. If they are resourceful tonight and use their textbook to assist in their understanding, I'm

sure they will be successful. If they aren't, however (which is more likely), we may spend a bit more time than planned tomorrow learning about how Algebra Tiles work and how to use them for particular sections of the book.

Another huge success today was during lunch, which is right after I teach this class. One of my female students came in for help about 5 minutes after lunch started. She is a new student to the school and is still adapting to the environment. I asked if she was adjusting, and she said no, trying to hide that she was crying. I don't know exactly why she was so upset, but I think that part of it was her frustration with the material in class. She was struggling quite a bit and seemed to be feeling left behind. She did not understand the Algebra Tiles activity sheets, so I got my overhead manipulatives and sat down in the desk next to hers to start working through the activity sheets I had given for homework. She seemed to feel more comfortable as I explained to her that I had never used Algebra Tiles before this week and we were learning how to use them together. We did a few problems and then talked about how the examples in the book can really help with comprehension as long as we are willing to read all the way through them and not just look at the pictures. She stayed in my room for the rest of lunch working with the overhead manipulatives to finish her activity sheets. She was back to her cheerful demeanor by the end of lunch and thanked me for my help.

I believe that my students are beginning to understand why I am asking them to learn how to factor using Algebra Tiles and appreciate how willing and excited I am to help them. What makes me so happy about today is that I got through these lessons and reached many of my students after being stern with them at the beginning of class and requiring more attention and participation from them. My next big task is to somehow plan a lesson allowing students time to work with each other so that I can meet individually with a few of my students with issues. I have one boy who sleeps every day, or just doesn't work. I would like to talk with him about what we can do as a team to meet his needs some time in the next few days. I have been feeling overwhelmed with a full class load, new students, a work sample, and curriculum, not to mention my life outside of the classroom. I am certain, however, that I will become more comfortable with my workload in the next few weeks.

SOURCE: Contributed by Jordanne Nevin during her student teaching. Used with permission.

Nevin's lesson plan included here is from the work sample comprehensive unit plan that she was required to complete during her student teaching. She decided to create a work sample for her remedial algebra course, which was open to sophomores, juniors, and seniors. This is one of the first lesson plans that Nevin created for her unit plan. She prepared it to share with her university supervisor on one of her observation visits. Lesson Plan 7.12 incorporates many of the lesson plan components and developmentally appropriate learning activities discussed in this book. In the sections labeled "Instructional Strategies" and "Reflection/ Evaluation," Nevin uses the first-person narrative to candidly describe the challenges and successes she experienced while trying to teach her students to factor using Algebra Tiles. She even admits that this technique for factoring polynomials was new to her. Clarifying the differences

among procedures, instructional strategies, and activities would make this lesson stronger, as would tying assessment to instructional objectives. Nonetheless, it is evident that Nevin spent a lot of time thinking about the best way to differentiate instruction to meet the needs of all her students.

The integration of technology into this lesson plan could help Nevin accomplish her objectives. In addition to having students create manipulatives, they could build their own models of Algebra Tiles at **http://faculty.prairiestate .edu/skifowit/htdocs/manip/alg_tile.htm**, a great interactive website that is designed to help middle and secondary school algebra students graphically depict addition and subtraction, multiplication, factoring, and completing the square. Students could also use **http://illuminations.nctm .org/ActivityDetail.aspx?ID=216** to learn how to represent and solve algebraic equations. At this website, sponsored by the National Council of Teachers of Mathematics, students can use Algebra Tiles to represent variables and constants as well as solve algebra problems. The warm-up problems included in this lesson could be demonstrated by students or the teacher on an interactive whiteboard. The teacher could also use screencasting software or create a podcast to capture her explanation of how to use Algebra Tiles so that students who were absent from class or who needed to have the explanation repeated could easily do so. Students could also use recording pens and create a pencast with an audio and/or visual explanation of their problem-solving process so that the teacher could listen to and respond to their work (see Chapter 10).

LESSON PLAN 7.13 Erin Pleinman studied French at Montana State University and wrote this thematic unit plan titled "Le week-end et les vacances" during her student-teaching assignment. Pleinman spent part of her childhood in France, where she attended middle school, mastered the French language, and came to love French culture. She completed her student-teaching assignment at Bozeman High School in Bozeman, MT, where she had the opportunity to work with students studying all levels of French. When she graduated, she was hired as a long-term substitute teacher and taught French at Bozeman High School and Sacajawea Middle School in Bozeman. For the past three years, Pleinman has taught French I through IV at Belgrade High School in Belgrade, MT.

The 11-day unit plan included here was designed as a review of vocabulary, verb conjugations, grammar, and sentence structure for French I and II students. In addition to reviewing material, Pleinman also added new elements to this unit, including an introduction to the passé composé verb tense, leisure-activity vocabulary, and grammar specific to travel, weekend, and vacation activities.

In this unit, Pleinman has students create a postcard and a poster highlighting their fictitious travels in order to practice using expressions of time and the proper past tense. There are many ways that technology can be integrated into this unit plan to enhance those projects. Students could use a publishing program to create their postcards or visit one of the many websites that provide free postcard templates. The instructor could create a classroom blog site where students could share their postcards.

There are also numerous instructional videos, software packages, and websites to support language development and practice. Students could practice vocabulary by accessing Make French Flash Cards at **http://french.about.com/cs/teachingresources/a/flashcards.htm**. Students could access free online French-English dictionaries at **http://www.french-linguistics.co.uk/dictionary** to help them write their postcards and develop their posters. The Writing Guide Poster Sessions website at **http://writing.colostate.edu/guides/spekaing/poster** would give students the opportunity to create multimedia posters. Students could also benefit from conversing with francophone pen pals. There are numerous websites that help set up student relationships, including International Pen Pals at **http://www.europa-pages.co.uk/penpal_form.html**.

Lesson Plan 7.13A Sample French Unit Plan Overview

Thematic Unit: Le week-end et les vacances

Teacher: Mademoiselle Pleiman
Grade: Level II French (freshmen, sophomores, juniors, seniors)
Period 2 and 7
Duration: 11 days, 50 minute class periods
Class size: 28 students/26 students

Rationale: This unit will review French vocabulary, verbs, grammar and sentence structure taught in French I and French II up to this time. This unit will also add new vocabulary, verbs, grammar (specifically the **passé composé** of verbs) and sentence structure specific to travel, weekend, and vacation activities. By making the content meaningful to the students through the use of culture, travel, and their own love for vacation time, this unit will help students to review previous knowledge from French I and French II and gain knowledge needed to continue successfully in French II.

General Instructional Goals:
Students will be able to:

- Describe what they did yesterday, last weekend, last summer, or during their last vacation using the past tense of verbs.
- Describe more generally about what happened in the past using the past tense of verbs and expressions of time.
- Apply the past tense as well as leisure activity vocabulary to describe their own weekend activities.

- Create a postcard using vocabulary described in Unit 2 of textbook, specifically weekend and vacation activities as well as the past tense of verbs.
- Create an end of unit project, a poster about their favorite vacation or about an imaginary vacation. This project will include use of everything they have learned throughout this unit as well as tap into their artistic abilities.
- List new vocabulary presented each day throughout the unit in a variety of ways (writing, listening, reading, and speaking). New vocabulary includes many new regular and irregular verbs as well as vocabulary about weekends, vacations, and expressions of time and for conversation.

Unit Topic Sequence:

- **Day 1:** Introduction to unit topic and pre-quiz to measure what they may or may not know about the unit content. Introduction to the verb **voir**. Introduction to the past participles of some irregular verbs conjugated with **avoir** (**être, avoir, faire, mettre, prendre** and **voir**).
- **Day 2:** Introduction of the verb **aller** in the past tense (hand out). Creating a postcard from a favorite "vacation." Review of certain expressions of time.
- **Day 3:** Finishing the postcards, final draft on card stock.
- **Day 4:** Short reading assignment about weekend activities, followed by comprehension and application questions.

(continued)

Lesson Plan 7.13A Sample French Unit Plan Overview *continued*

Quelqu'un, quelque chose et leurs contrairs. Expression of time and gestures.

- **Day 5:** Introduction to lesson 8 in textbook. Verbs **sortir, partir** and **dormir** in the present tense and in the passé composé.
- **Day 6:** Introduction to all sixteen **VANDERTRAMP** verbs ("**être** verbs"); the past tense with **être.**
- **Day 7:** Continue to review and practice all sixteen **VANDERTRAMP** verbs ("**être** verbs"). **"La maison d' être."** Students will be presented with ideal vacation poster project rubric.
- **Day 8:** In class create a poster of their favorite or ideal vacation. The poster will contain a paragraph about their vacation as well as pictures. Review of passé composé.
- **Day 9:** Turning in and presenting posters. Post-assessment quiz. Reading assignment.
- **Day 10:**   Review for unit test.
- **Day 11:** Unit test.

Lesson plans:
SEE DAILY LESSON PLANS

Evaluations:
Teacher will reflect and evaluate the entire unit upon its completion.

Assessment of Students:

- Students will be informally assessed throughout entire unit during activities and classroom discussions for their pronunciation, recollection of proper usage of verbs, vocabulary, and grammar and sentence structure used in unit.

- Students will be assessed on their writing and proper use of verbs, vocabulary, and grammar and sentence structure used in unit by turning in postcards, partner activity worksheets (like the phone dialogues), warm-up activities and sentences describing their weekend and vacation activities.
- Students will be given an identical pre-assessment and a post-assessment quiz to measure how much they have learned throughout the unit.
- Students will take a unit test at the end of the unit to assess their overall understanding of the entire unit.
- Students will be creating a poster about their favorite vacation; this poster will be a summative assessment that will use the vocabulary, verbs, and verb tenses from the entire unit.

Materials:

- Handouts: Le passé composé d'aller, Vandertramp handouts, La carte postale, Le passé composé, *Qui a de la chance?* (short story)
- Pre-assessment quiz.
- Post-assessment quiz.
- Transparencies.
- DVD—Vidéo scène 7.
- Teacher's edition of textbook.
- Rubric for vacation poster project.
- Unit test.

SOURCE: Contributed by Erin Pleiman during her student teaching, Montana State University–Bozeman, Student. Used with permission.

Lesson Plan 7.13B Sample French Lesson Plan

Unit: Le week-end et les vacances (leçon 7 et 8, Unité 3 dans le texte).
Leçon: Le passé composé du verbe aller
Date: le vendredi 9 novembre
Class : Français II
Duration: 50 minutes

General Objectives:

- Students will recall the regular use of the **passé composé** with **–er, -ir** and **–re** verbs. Students will apply that knowledge to understand irregular verbs in the **passé composé** including the verb **aller.** Students will create sentences with new verb(s) in the **passé composé.** Students will create a postcard illustrating their knowledge of how to write sentences describing past events from a vacation or weekend.

Learning Outcomes:
Students will be able to:

- Recall **les participes passes irréguliers** by writing sentences in the **passé composé** during the warm-up activity and during the review of the homework from yesterday.
- Recall and restate the use of the **passé composé** by asking a partner the question, **qu'est-ce que tu as fait hier soir?** Students will respond using **passé composé.**
- Practice the **passé composé** of **aller** by reading a handout, listening to the teacher's explanation.
- Practice the **passé composé** of **aller** by creating sentences while looking at pictures on the overhead projector.
- Restate and practice the **passé composé** of **aller** by writing the answers to **Activité 6, p. 125.**

- Apply their new knowledge by creating a postcard. This postcard will review old vocabulary and verbs in the past tense. This postcard will also allow students to practice the **passé composé** of **aller** by describing where they went on vacation.

Rationale for Lesson:

- Through various activities that include reading, writing, listening, and speaking, students will recall old information (specifically the passé composé) as well learn new information (le verbe *aller* au passé composé). The theme of "favorite vacations" will make this lesson meaningful to the students, in turn helping the students internalize the presented information.

Instructional Procedures:

- **Focusing Event: 3 minutes**
Introduce the verb **aller** on the board. What does it describe in the past?

—Warm up and review: 5 minutes
Directions on the board will direct students to open their notes and their books (p. 123). There will be four sentences in the present tense on the board. Students will be asked to write the sentences in their notes in the **passé composé.** Four students will come up to the board and write the sentences in the **passé composé.**

- **Teaching Methods and Student Activities:**

—Opener: Qu'est-ce que tu as fait hier soir? 3–5 minutes
Students will ask a student next to them to answer this question to begin thinking and speaking in French. Once they ask the question and receive an answer their partner will ask them the same question.

(continued)

Lesson Plan 7.13B **Sample French Unit Plan**   *continued*

—**Review homework: 5–7 minutes**
As a class, students and teacher will go over homework. Students will volunteer the answers to the homework. Students will be asked to correct each others' mistakes. Teacher will ask students to pass homework forward and one student will go around and collect homework. Homework will be graded and returned on Monday.
→ Teacher will transition into **le passé composé d'aller** by asking students to help teacher conjugate the verb **être** on the board.

—**The passé composé of aller handout: 10 minutes**
As the class is helping recall the verb **être,** teacher will pass out a handout on the verb **aller** in the **passé composé.** This handout is meant to facilitate their understanding of the **passé composé** of **aller** and the **agreement** of the past participle with the subject in gender and number.

Students will volunteer to read handout out loud. Teacher will explain as the class follows along on handout, writing explanations on the board as needed.

Students will translate the sentences at the bottom of handout as practice; students will come to the board and write out the sentences.

→ As students translate the sentences teacher will walk around and help students that are having difficulties. Teacher will also post a transparency on the overhead for practice.

—**Practice: 5 minutes**
The transparency will ask students to conjugate the verb **aller** in the **passé composé.** The transparency will have pictures of people coming to and from places. Students will be asked to create sentences about the people using the passé composé of **aller** out loud. Teacher will write sentences on the board.

—**Practice: 5–7 minutes**
Students will be asked to write the answers to **Activité 3** p. 125. The three days of the activity will be divided by the three sections of the classroom. Each section of the class will do their work quietly, and when they have finished they will share answers with the class.
→ Teacher will transition by asking students if they like vacation. Where have they been?

—**Postcard project: 15 minutes**
Before teacher passes out the postcard handout students will be asked if they have ever received a postcard from anyone.
Teacher will hand out stacks of postcards for students to look at. Students will then be asked to brainstorm favorite destination spots. Teacher will be writing them on the board.
Students will then be asked about things to do on vacation. Class will brainstorm ideas of activities and teacher will write them on the board in French.

What would you write on a postcard? Weather, activities, what you saw, etc.
Teacher will pass out postcard handout and explain directions.
Students will turn to p. 127 for an example of a postcard.
Students will be told to write a postcard to a friend or family member "from their favorite destination."
Students will be told: please make the postcard an actual letter format with heading, body and closing and at least six sentences using the past tense.
Once students are finished they will be instructed to have their postcard proofread by a classmate.
Teacher will be circulating throughout activity observing students' activity, keeping them on task and providing help when needed.

• **Closure:**
Teacher will instruct students to put away their books and notes. Teacher will remind students to bring in a picture, photograph, or drawing on Monday in order to finish postcard.

• **Assessment Procedures:**
—Warm-up will evaluate student recollection of regular verbs in the passé composé.
—Homework from previous lesson: Exercise 3 p. 123 will assess how well students apply knowledge of new irregular past participles to create sentences about the past weekend.
—Overhead projector practice of using the verb **"aller"** in a sentence will allow teacher to assess understanding of use of new verb as well as assess student recollection of vocabulary to describe places.
—In-class practice of the verb **aller** by completing **Activité 3** p. 125 will assess students' understanding of subject agreement of the past participle with gender and number of the verb **aller** in the passé composé.
—Postcard project will assess the students' ability to use the passé composé of regular verbs, irregular verbs, and **aller** by describing where they went on vacation.

• **Evaluation Procedure:**
Teacher will reflect and evaluate the entire unit and each lesson upon its completion.

• **Materials:**
Le verbe aller handout
Overhead projector
Transparency—où vont-ils?
Postcard project handout
Sample postcards

SOURCE: Contributed by Erin Pleiman during her student teaching, Montana State University–Bozeman, Student. Used with permission.

LESSON PLAN 7.14 Dr. Kimberly Boehler created this lesson plan when she was a graduate student at Montana State University, where she was working on her doctorate in adult and higher education. While she was completing her graduate studies, she also served as an adjunct instructor in curriculum and instruction and taught art methods courses. Her lesson plan titled "Islamic Art" was created for that course. Boehler currently serves as an adjunct instructor in curriculum and instruction at Montana State University and as an art education professor at Southern Oregon University in Ashland. She is also coauthor of *Art Connections: Integrating Art Throughout the Curriculum* (Culver City, CA: Good Year Books, 1995).

In this lesson, Boehler emphasizes that Islamic art is the mirror of a culture and its worldview. Students learn that the Prophet Muhammad discouraged figurative imagery and that Islamic design centers on geometric designs and the symbolic meaning of certain numbers, such as 7, 4, and 8, which are common, as are certain shapes: the circle, the hexagon, and the triangle.

Since students are asked to create a page for a book focusing on shape, color, symmetry, repetition, rhythm, movement, and so on in Islamic art, the students' contributions could be scanned into the computer, and a class bound book could be created for each member of the class. Students are also encouraged to talk or write about their personal artwork

Lesson Plan 7.14 Islamic Art

A Summary of National Art Standards:

National Standards in art as well as most state standards evolved from curriculum guidelines defined by Discipline Based Art Education. Most art educators agree that best practice in art teaching will consistently include content from four component areas. These are: Art Process (practice with medium and technique, develop skills), Make Connections (become familiar with exemplary art works, understand that culture and historical context directly connected to the meaning of art works), Art Criticism (learning the language and conceptual ideas for looking deeply and talking about works of art), and finally Aesthetics (The big questions such as, What is art? What does it mean to be an artist? Is there a right and wrong way to make art?).

All of the four components included in standards-based art curriculum must be considered carefully so that students can demonstrate skills and knowledge in each. Also in art integration it is extremely important that lessons are well developed so that all students have opportunity for success and not just those students who are identified as "creative or artistic." With this in mind, each art classroom should have a structure for helping students feel comfortable with the third component which is Art Criticism or talking about art: Below is the See Scale, a tool which provides a formal vocabulary for students to use as they talk and think about art.

The "See" Scale
The Qualities of a Work of Art

What I see:

The Design Elements
    Line
    Shape/Form
    Color/Value
    Space
    Texture

The way things are arranged:

The Design Principles
    Balance: Symmetry, Asymmetry
    Unity: Repetition, Rhythm
    Interest: Contrast, Emphasis, Movement,
             Variety

The way I think it was made:

Characteristics and vocabulary for materials and process

What I think is being expressed:

Theories are a way of reflecting on the "big idea" of the artwork:
    Is it Imitational?
    Is it Formal?
    Is it Expressive?
    Is it Functional?

Based on *Aesthetic Scanning*, E.B. Feldman

Islamic Art: Working With Geometric Pattern

Big Idea: Joining Heaven and Earth with Geometry

Keep in mind:

    Integration opportunity: Math, Social Studies.

    Islam means to achieve peace.

Islamic design considers certain numbers to be symbolically meaningful; common are 7, 4, and 8. Various shapes also have symbolic meaning: the circle, hexagon, and triangle.

What will students learn about the Islamic Art tradition?

    Muhammad discouraged figurative imagery.

Geometric design can be for the service of Islam or it can be found in secular design. The style is favored because its geometry is considered to be intermediary between material and spiritual world.

    Islamic Art traditionally is not considered expressive.

Islamic Art: Holistic Rubric

Design/Plan:

    Created on one page for bound book

    Design fills page

    Drawn in pencil

    Uses both geometric and organic shapes

    All shapes drawn with tools or stencil

Elements and Principles:

    Shape (geometric, organic)

    Color (primary, secondary, intermediate)

    Symmetrical or radial symmetry

    Repetition, rhythm, (movement?)

    (What Theory? I, E, F, F?)

Painting:

    Erase all pencil lines except design

Decide on one hue group to use (or be able to identify all hue choices)

Making the historical, cultural, and aesthetic connection:

    Students talk or write about personal work

Students talk/write about how personal work is similar or different from traditional work of this culture.

Geometric and Organic Shapes as Symbols of Heaven and Earth

Drawing the Design

Begin: (The purpose of steps 1 and 2 is to divide the space into a geometric design of choice while contemplating the numerical potential for meaning.)

Use compass or ruler to draw one geometric shape that touches four sides of the paper (such as a square, circle, star, or octagon). This shape should be symmetrical and/or radially symmetrical.

Use compass or ruler and repeat another geometric shape to divide the space again into 4 or 8 or more sections.

Next: Draw an organic shape onto cardboard to use as a template.

    This template will be traced/repeated onto the geometric design in a symmetrical or radially symmetrical pattern.

Painting the Design
Finally: Paint the shapes to complete the design. (If my objective is to teach color vocabulary, I might suggest using one primary hue, one secondary hue, and one intermediate hue along with black or white. These choices can be open ended or guided based on teacher objectives.)

        Lesson Overview:

Connection:
Islamic Art; Geometric and Organic Shapes as Symbols of Heaven and Earth

Process and Skill:
Mechanical drawing (using tools) of geometric shapes and organic shapes

Talk about Art:
Elements: Shape (Geometric & Organic) and Color

Principles: Balance (Symmetrical and Radial Symmetry)
                Unity (Repetition, Rhythm)
                Interest (Contrast, Variety)

Theory: What theory can be used to describe the art work?

SOURCE: Contributed by Dr. Kimberly Boehler, Doctoral Candidate, Montana State University–Bozeman, Department of Education. Used with permission.

in this lesson. This could be done in an interactive blog site where students could upload their designs and talk about them. In addition, students could be encouraged to research the history and cultures where Islam is practiced. They could search the Internet for images of Islamic art, Arabic calligraphy, Islamic art and architecture, and mosques around the world, as well as other art-related topics.

LESSON PLAN 7.15 "The Blackfeet Confederacy Timeline" lesson plan was created by a group of secondary social studies teacher candidates enrolled in Multicultural Education, a core course in the Teacher Education Program at Montana State University that is described in detail in the section on Lesson Plan 7.5 in this chapter. The five group members—Chantal Gee, Heather Tyler, Tony Coppola, Rob Baither, and Adam Rudolph—had varying degrees of experience creating lesson plans and had different expertise. For some group members, this was the first lesson they ever created. For all group members, creating a presentation using Prezi was a new endeavor. This two-week unit plan integrating Indian Education for All and addressing Essential Understandings 1, 2, 5, and 6 (see Chapter 3), as well as covering Montana Social Studies Standards, was designed to be used with high school juniors in a course in American history. The group members included cognitive, affective, and psychomotor instructional objectives and learned Prezi to create an engaging interactive presentation. They used the Four Directions of Native American Studies website and its many links. They included a well-thought-out explanation of differentiated instruction to engage all students and included varied scaffolding, compacting, flexible use of time, varying text by reading level, group work, and varying supplementary materials. They also included a sample rubric.

Students are even encouraged to create a podcast or a digital story and share that with their classmates as an option to presenting "live" in front of their classmates. Since this was the first time the teacher candidates created a Prezi presentation, they included a description of Prezi.com, their process in creating their interactive time line, a comparison between Prezi and PowerPoint listing the pros and cons of each presentation software program, practical advice for instructors and students to use Prezi, an explanation of copyright laws and fair use guidelines, and valuable links to be able to create a Prezi.com.

Lesson Plan 7.15A The Blackfeet Confederacy Timeline, Lesson/Unit Plan with a Dynamic Timeline (What Is Prezi.com)

The Blackfeet Confederacy Timeline
Indian Education for All Group Lesson Plan and Presentation
By: Chantal Gee, Heather Tyler, Tony Coppola, Rob Baither and Adam Rudolph
1. Descriptive Data:
   a. Subject: Timelines based on Native American nations and relationships with the U.S. government
   b. Grade Level: Juniors in high school, United States History
   c. Time Frame: Two weeks for research plus three days for in-class presentations
2. Montana Social Studies Standards:
   a. Standard 3: Students apply geographic knowledge and skills (e.g., location, place, human/environment interactions, movement, and regions).
   b. Standard 4: Students demonstrate an understanding of the effects of time, continuity, and change on historical and future perspectives and relationships
   c. Standard 6: Students demonstrate an understanding of the impact of human interaction and cultural diversity on societies.
3. Indian Education for All (IEFA) Essential Understandings:
   a. Essential Understanding 1: There is great diversity among the 12 tribal Nations of Montana in the languages, culture, histories, and governments. Each Nation has distinct and unique cultural heritage that contributes to modern Montana.
   b. Essential Understanding 2: There is great diversity among individual American Indians as identity is developed, defined and redefined by entities, organizations, and people. A continuum of Indian identity, unique to each individual, ranges from assimilated to traditional. There is no generic American Indian.
   c. Essential Understanding 5: Federal Policies, put into place throughout American History, have affected Indian people and still shape who they are today. Much of the Indian

history can be related through several major federal policy periods.
   d. Essential Understanding 6: History is a story often related through the subjective experience of the teller. With the inclusion of more and varied voices, histories are being rediscovered and revised. History told from an Indian perspective frequently conflicts with the stories mainstream historians tell.
4. Goals:
   a. Instructional Objectives:
      i. Cognitive: Students will be able to …
         1. produce a presentation by synthesizing the timeline and research paper
         2. evaluate their paper and group presentation according to the rubric
         3. collect events about their chosen tribe
         4. organize the information into an interactive timeline
         5. analyze the research into a concise Word document
      ii. Affective: Students will be able to …
         1. demonstrate knowledge of the tribe they are researching and address any misconceptions or preconceived notions that the group may have had before beginning their research.
      iii. Psychomotor: Students will be able to …
         1. create a well-crafted presentation, using technologically advanced presentational material, such as Prezi.com.
5. Rationale:
   a. This lesson plan will fit nicely into Montana-based classrooms where Indian Education for All is a mandated government program for all public school students. This lesson plan could also be used across the United States to either promote culturally responsive programs like Indian Education for All or to spread general awareness about Native Americans that may not be presented without this lesson plan.

(continued)

<u>Lesson Plan 7.15A</u> **The Blackfeet Confederacy Timeline, Lesson/Unit Plan with a Dynamic Timeline (What Is Prezi.com)** *continued*

6. Procedure:
   a. According to the information provided on the website for the Four Directions Institute of Native American Studies (**www.fourdir.com**) compose a timeline for any Indian Tribe based in the United States. Use the website to choose the tribe that your group would like to study. On the website there is a simple timeline for hundreds of different tribes. We suggest looking at several different tribes before you make your decision. Each group member will select two specific events mentioned on the timeline and they will research them on their own. Every event does not need to be researched, just make sure that every group member researches two events. The website mentioned above also lists several other websites for each tribe to help you find the information needed for the research section. In addition to Internet sources each group member must find a hard-copy resource; these may include magazine or newspaper articles, books, and encyclopedias. Each member will also hand in a one-page summary of the information that he/she acquired about his/her subjects. Once each member has acquired the information on his/her event the group will create an interactive timeline, using **www.prezi.com**, to share with the class. Every event listed from the website timeline must be included, and the individually researched events will be shared in great detail with the class. The group member who researched the specific events will be the one presenting them to the class. The presentation must include pictures, images, and very few words; this will help keep the presenter from reading directly from the presentation. The presentation must be at least twenty minutes long for the group members to receive full credit for the presentation portion of the project. Each group will be given two weeks to study their specific tribes and create their Prezi. We will be spending each class period in the library to help aid with their research. On Monday, Tuesday, and Wednesday of the third week each group will present their timeline to the rest of the class. Every project must be turned in on Monday including a hard or digital copy of the Prezi and the groups' individual research papers, regardless of presentation date.

7. Plan for Differential Instruction:
   a. The following plans for differentiation will foster student interest and achieve readiness for this particular lesson plan. All these options are **engaging to the student, are student-centered and represent sound pedagogy.**
   i. Varied Scaffolding:
      1. The instructor will give the students step-by-step instruction on how to conduct proper research practices and etiquette, how to use MLA style documentation, and the dos and don'ts of writing a research document and presenting that research. If needed, the instructor will scaffold the student by providing help and suggestion where needed to help the student achieve his or her zone of proximal development in this content area.
   ii. Compacting:
      1. For those students who need a greater challenge, the instructor will offer a more challenging scope to the assignment. Some suggestions for this will be:

limiting the number of web-based resources, this will force the student to use hardcopies for their research portion which will require more work, create an additional body of work other than the assignment based on the rubric, such as a research portfolio, which the students may present to the class at the end of the assignment. Another option would be to take their research and compete in the annual History Competition. This competition challenges students in the 7th through 12th grades at a state and eventually at the national level where the students compete in a media-based format, a debate format or tri-fold board presentation. This event summons higher cognitive abilities and further challenges the student in this content area of social studies.

iii. Flexible Use of Time:
   1. This form of differentiation allows students to use their time on the project differently than the prescribed time of the instructor. Students will be allowed to use more or less of the library and research time based on the individual student's needs. Students who use this option will be able to work at their own pace to reach the goal of finishing the presentation on time and in accordance with the standards of the rubric.

iv Varied Texts by Reading Level:
   1. Students with higher or lower reading abilities will benefit from this differentiation tool. If the students need to use less scholarly sources to arrive at the same conclusion outlined in the rubric, this will be a great option for them. The goal of the lesson plan is for the student to research a Native American tribe, write a well-documented research paper using MLA format and present it to their classmates. The quality of the source is important, but if the student doesn't understand what he/she is presenting, then the lesson will be in vain. Using varied texts by reading level will allow the student to better comprehend what he/she is researching and hence understand it on a cognitive level.

v. Group Work:
   1. Working in a small group will foster cognitive development. Whether the students guide one another in proper research practices or help one another discover a quality source on their topic, the students will definitely gain insight from working in groups on this particular lesson.

vi. Varied Supplementary Materials:
   1. For students who do not do well on presentations or have difficulty speaking in front of classmates, this plan for differentiation will play in their favor. Other options for creating a presentation include, but are not limited to: creating a Podcast, creating a Digital Story or using pictures, graphs, etc. to present their research to the class. The above mentioned options for presenting student research are engaging and student centered. Both these will foster collaboration and resonate quality pedagogy.

(continued)

8. Materials and Equipment Needed During the Lesson:

a. Computer with Internet access so the following addresses can be accessed

  i. Prezi.com—used to set up their interactive timeline

  ii. Internet—research, **www.fourdir.com**

  iii. Along with any additional websites that the students choose to use for their research

b. Library so that the students can have easy access to the following hard-copy sources

  i. Books, magazines, journals, articles, and/or any primary sources

9. Assessment: Here is a sample rubric that could be handed to the students to help guide them through their research, writing their papers, and creating their Prezi.

a. Points will be distributed as follows:

  i. Research Section:

    1. 20 points for being on task during library time

    2. 50 points for the written summary of the research information

      a. 30 points for the information provided

      b. 15 points for minimal spelling and grammatical errors

      c. 5 points for a Works Cited or Reference Page in MLA format

      d. The paper should be as follows:

        i. One page, double spaced, Times New Roman font, name, group name, and date in the top right-hand corner (not double spaced), title at the top of the page will be the name of your event

  ii. Presentation Section:

    1. 60 points

      a. 20 points for the inclusion of all of the events given in the website timeline, along with the well-researched events

      b. 25 points for being well prepared, all of the group members know the material, all of them take a turn speaking during the presentation, and the presentation looks completed and is visually pleasing

      c. 5 points for the presentation being at least twenty minutes

      d. 5 points for questions answered during the question and answer section with the rest of the class

      e. 5 points for a Works Cited or Reference Slide in MLA format

  iii. Group Cooperation:

    1. 20 points: Each member of the group will grade the other members of the group based on the work that they contributed to the project.

  iv. For a total of 150 points

10. Reflection/Evaluation:

a. Out of the 26 feedback slips we received 14 of them had some sort of critique. This is a good sign for the group. The critiques ranged from individual comments to group comments. Here is a list of critiques that need/should be addressed.

  i. Strayed a bit from the Blackfeet: With this comment I can say with a degree of certainty that it was done on purpose. This was meant to demonstrate that information is important for all tribes.

  ii. More concise slides: I believe that this addresses the really wordy ones. That is something that was not bullet-pointed. We had to include these slides because they are important. We provided handouts with that in mind, but they are correct that you should not do this if you are presenting this to a class. The problem is the presentation is not a multiday event; hence the long slides.

  iii. Let everyone speak: We did notice that some of us talked more than others. This was not intentional but we tried to make it equal for all.

  iv. Reading off the board or talking to the wall: This seems to be an individual critique. Since there was no elaboration on whom needs to address this issue, I cannot comment. We printed off the slides and what was on them to allow the individual presenter to speak to the audience.

  v. Add to the timeline: In regards to Native American events. We thought about doing this but this is not a tutorial on Prezi.com, so we did not include that.

  vi. Focus more on the Standards: because this is a college course we thought that the audience should be able to draw the parallels between the standards and the activity. In many ways we thought: "Would you ask your students to explain the standards?" In the case of this presentation we should have clearly addressed them for the benefit of the class.

b. We commented that we could have included more information or slides. The original thinking was time; we thought we would go over the limit. So we did cut back on many of the things we had prepared (such as the whole timeline we created, edit the Prezi with Native American events over the decades, and highlighting more events in the timeline.) But overall from the comments we received from the class the group feels that we did a really good job.

SOURCE: Contributed by Chantal Gee, Heather Tyler, Tony Coppola, Rob Baither and Adam Rudolph, Secondary Education Majors enrolled in Multicultural Education at Montana State University, Bozeman, Montana during the Spring 2011 semester. Used with permission.

Lesson Plan 7.15B The Blackfeet Confederacy Timeline, Lesson/Unit Plan with a Dynamic Timeline (What Is Prezi.com)

Lesson/Unit Plan with a Dynamic Timeline:
This lesson was set up for an upper division high school class in the subject area of history. The timeline provided directly relates to Indian Education for All (IEFA).

What is Prezi.com?:
Prezi.com is a website that allows educators to create a presentation like PowerPoint. The major difference is in the presentation. PowerPoint creates slides that transition from slide A to slide B, slide B to slide C and so on. With a Prezi presentation, the user will actually witness the actual motion of moving from slide to slide. The user/observer can also see information from a large perspective and then create an action that will highlight smaller parts of the text. Another advantage of Prezi is the fact that videos can be embedded in the project (PowerPoint creates a link and will use an Internet browser to open the video). Prezi acts like a giant map full of information in which the creator can control how much information is seen at a time and in which direction the creator wants the viewer to see the information.

Step One: Setting up the Prezi account.
Prezi.com is open to everyone; however, there are different levels of access. Montana State University has an agreement with Prezi that allowed us to use the Educational version of Prezi. This option is found by using the "Student/Teacher Licenses" link. It has the same benefits of the "Enjoy" version minus the support category. The largest hurdle in the K–12 school environment is the need to overcome accessibility to Prezi.com. One major consideration when using the "Public/Free" version is that anything the author creates or utilizes will be a public resource. This must be kept in mind when including pictures, video, information, and the like in your Prezi due to copyright laws. A resource pertaining to a question about fair use and/or copyright laws is **http://fairuse.stanford.edu/**; there is good information about these topics at this address. The use for educational purposes falls under fair use, and if you are using an image, video, and/or other work created or authored by another person then **A CITATION SHOULD BE USED**. If copyright, fair use, and regulations are followed, the presentation serving as a Public Resource will work just fine.

Step Two: Presenting the information.
When incorporating technology into the classroom one must think of its relative advantage. Could an educator teach the lesson as effectively or the same without incorporating the technology aspect? The advantage in this case has a lot to do with the ARCS model. The ARCS model falls under Motivational Design (Keller). Each letter stands for a key element in this model, A = Attention R = Relevance C = Confidence and S = Satisfaction. In the case of history we looked at "Relevance." Regardless of how an instructor justifies using the Prezi dynamic timeline, there is an essential need for content. A Prezi project should not turn into an art/media project; the students need to learn from this lesson.

The lesson should begin by building student knowledge towards the subject. The classic lecture would be a fine way to present the material and it should be incorporated into the final timeline. As a group, we found some great websites that presented timelines for Native American Tribes that can be used as the backbone for the comprehensive timeline. These resources can be found at the end of the Prezi we created. Groups can then open pre-selected websites and choose a tribe. This will start the technology section of the lesson. In addition, we chose to take one topic from the timeline and research it in further detail. This way, each group member was responsible for a part of the project. Once these two basic steps are accomplished, students can move into the Prezi.com.

Step Three: The Prezi timeline.
This in many ways will be the most difficult part of the project. The best advice is to experiment. I created two Prezis before this project. Here are some pointers that will assist with this task:

* *Watch the tutorial.* This will give basic information to create a Prezi presentation.
* *Explore, create, and fine tune.* Information can be thrown anywhere in the Prezi and dragged into place, resized, and/or aligned with other information.
* *We are educators, not graphic designers.* A teacher's first Prezi may not look that great; as long as the information is there and has a clear direction, the goal is accomplished.
* *Keep the movements to a minimum.* The first time I set up this Prezi there were close to 115 movements! That is way too much; we honestly thought that our classmates would become sick by watching all of those movements. We decided to hit main points with the movements. Broad looks at the centuries, key events that group members researched, and general goals of our lesson became the key movements.
* *Include different forms of media.* This could come in the form of video, pictures, sounds, music, etc. ..., which will engage the students. Students will also have the advantage of learning how to take these forms of media from the Internet (using correct citations and credit to the creator) and place them in other media platforms.

Basics to the timeline:
* The arrow drawing: As evidenced in our project, we used it a lot. The teacher could create a blank template in any image creator that would have the basic "left, right" arrow that the students could build off. This would save the students some time.
* The arrows coming off the timeline: These are not necessary, just an artistic touch. The students could simply place the description of the event over the date.
* Media: We chose to include pictures with the events that we individually researched. One can choose to include as many pictures as they desire, as long as they relate to the timeline and are cited properly.
* Adding events: To add the text of the timeline simply click anywhere on the screen (I chose to do this away from the timeline, that is, in an open space), type the desired text, resize, and drag into place.

Presentation:
Once students have their timelines assembled, it is time to present them. A television, overhead projector, or any other large media player (i.e. interactive whiteboard) that is connected to a computer needs to be available. The students will need to pull up their Prezi account and presentation. Use the "full screen" option in the lower right-hand corner of the display screen. Students can either use the arrows at the bottom of the screen to "move" through their presentation or utilize/use the arrow keys on the keyboard.
Link to the Prezi we created:
https://prezi.com/secure/570f6ce129e030bc6d74b7d1176ad2f925d9e673/

Link to the Tribal timeline website:
http://www.fourdir.com/tribes_index.htm

Questions about the Prezi:
http://prezi.com/learn/

SOURCE: Contributed by Rob Baither, Secondary Education Major enrolled in Multicultural Education at Montana State University, Bozeman, Montana during the Spring 2011 semester. Used with permission.

LESSON PLAN 7.16 Abderrahman Ouarab is a high school teacher of English as-a-foreign language in Kenitra, Morocco. He has been teaching English at a public secondary school, Abdelmalek Essaadi, for the past 23 years. He became a teacher after graduating from the university and spending one year at a teacher training school. Ouarab is multilingual and speaks several languages, including Moroccan Arabic, French, and English. Like Roger Aguirre Lopez, who contributed Lesson Plan 7.6 featured here, Ouarab was the recipient of a Teaching Excellence and Achievement scholarship along with other middle and high school teachers from around the world and attended classes at Montana State University and completed an internship in the Bozeman Public Schools. Like Aguirre, Ouarab developed lesson plans while studying in the U.S. his lesson plan included here is titled "Follow-Up Activity on the First Conditional VS the Second Conditional."

In his lesson plan, Ouarab covers factual or true conditional sentences as well as examples of hypothetical conditional sentences. He explains that the first conditional is formed with clauses in the present and future tenses and that the second conditional form is used to talk about "impossible"

situations; Ouarab stresses that it is important to use the subjunctive form *were* instead of *was* in these examples. After a review of the two conditional structures, he has students participate in a matching activity. Each student receives a clause and searches for the student holding the best match.

There are many ways to complement this lesson plan by integrating technology. Students can access a variety of websites to review the conditional grammar rules and see numerous examples of the two different uses of the conditional sentences in English. Students can access tutorials on the conditional at **http://www.englishpage.com/conditional/conditionalintro.htm**l, **http://www.englishpage.com/grammar/Conditional**, and **http://www.english-grammar-lessons.com/secondconditional/menu.php**. By perusing the Internet, students can find other resources to help them learn and practice using the conditional tense. Using music lyrics to study the conditional is another fun way to engage students. The YouTube video found at **http://www.youtube.com/watch?v = Udmj4AV1XdU** features the lyrics and melody to "Time in a Bottle" by Jim Croce. Students can practice the conditional clauses by listening to "Time in a Bottle" and practicing the expressions.

Lesson Plan 7.16 **Follow-Up Activity on the First Conditional VS the Second Conditional**

Micro - Lesson Plan Template		
Date	Micro - Lesson Title: Follow-Up Activity on the First Conditional VS the Second Conditional	Instructor Name: Abderrahman Ouarab
Teaching Discipline(s): English as a Fore ign Language, High school students in English II		Instructor Country: Morocco
Learning Objectives (Please identify 1-2 objectives of this micro-lesson) - The students will be able to identify the difference between the first conditional and the second conditional. - The students will be able to use their knowledge of the rules of both conditionals by matching jumbled up clauses.		
Accessories/Teaching Aids Required Paper with prepared clauses which demonstrate first conditional structure.		
Reference Material (if any public materials are used, please list the sources of these materials here) None		

Micro - Lesson Outline (please describe the activity, strategy, topic you will demonstrate to the "student" group)
  1. The teacher reviews the rules of the first conditional as well as the second conditional. (2 minutes)
  2. Then he/she writes the rules on the board. (1 minute)
  3. Each student will get <u>one piece of paper</u>. (1 minute)
  4. On each piece of paper there is a clause of a conditional sentence.
  5. The students will have <u>to move around</u> the class in order to find out who has the clause that matches the one they have. (5 minutes)
  6. Each pair of students comes to the board with their papers and they read them to the class. The teacher and the other students check the correctness. (4 minutes)
 	
The sentences are:
1- If I had enough money, I'd travel to Japan.
2- If Layla wakes up early tomorrow, she'll catch the 6 o'clock train.
3- If you work hard, you'll succeed.
4- If you don't listen to me, you'll regret it.
5- If people were more tolerant, there would be no war.
6- If I were you, I wouldn't take that job.
7- If my friend asks me for help, I won't hesitate to give him a hand.
8- If our team had good players, we'd compete for the championship.
9- If you talk too much, people won't listen to you.
10- If there were more police officers on the streets, there would be less crime.		

(continued)

Lesson Plan 7.16 **Follow-Up Activity on the First Conditional VS the Second Conditional** *continued*

Assessment (please describe how you will assess learning during this micro-lesson)
Teacher reads or presents on the board five unfinished conditional sentences and students volunteer to finish them. The unfinished sentences are:

1- If I ruled the world, I

_____

_____

2- If I could change one thing in my country, I

_____

_____

3- If I win the lottery, I

_____

_____

4- I'll marry her/him if she/he

_____

_____

5- If it rains, I

_____

_____

Please describe what best teaching practices this lesson will demonstrate:
Cooperative learning is a beneficial method for practicing grammar in a meaningful way.

SOURCE: Contributed by Abderrahman Ouarab, High School English as-a-foreign language Instructor in Morocco and Teaching Excellence and Achievement (TEA) Program Fellow at Montana State University, Spring 2011. Used with permission.
This Lesson Plan Template has been adapted from a template available for free at: **www.TeachersPrintables.net**

Summary

Developing units of instruction that integrate student learning and that provide a sense of meaning for the students requires coordination throughout the curriculum—which is defined here as consisting of all the planned experiences students encounter while at school. Hence, for students, learning is a process of discovering how information, knowledge, and ideas are interrelated—learning to make sense out of self, school, and life. Molding chunks of information into units and units into daily lessons helps students process and make sense of knowledge. Having developed your first unit of instruction, you are on your way to becoming a competent planner of instruction. There is no single best way to organize a daily plan, no "one-size-fits-all" lesson plan format, and no foolproof formula that will guarantee a teacher an effective lesson. With experience and the increased competence that comes from reflecting on that experience, you will develop your own style, your own methods of implementing that style, and your own formula for preparing a lesson plan. Like a map, your lesson plan charts the course, places markers along the trails, pinpoints danger areas, highlights areas of interest and importance along the way, and ultimately brings the traveler to the successful completion of the objective.

The best-prepared units and lessons, though, will go untaught or will be only poorly implemented if presented in a poorly managed classroom. Refer to Chapter 3 to review how to provide a supportive classroom environment—to effectively manage the classroom for the most efficient instruction and student achievement.

Exercise
7.1
Analysis of a Lesson That Failed

Instructions: The planning and structure of a lesson are often predictors of the success of its implementation. The purpose of this exercise is to read the following synopsis of the implementation of a lesson, answer the discussion questions individually, and use your responses as a basis for class discussion in small groups about the lesson.
The Setting: ninth-grade life science class; 1:12–2:07 P.M., spring semester

(continued)

Exercise 7.1   **Analysis of a Lesson That Failed**   *continued*

Synopsis of Events

1:12	Bell rings.
1:12–1:21	Teacher directs students to read from their texts while he or she takes attendance.
1:21–1:31	Teacher distributes a handout to each student; students are to label the parts of a flower shown on the handout.
1:31–1:37	Silent reading and labeling of the handout.
1:37–1:39	Teacher verbally gives instructions for working on a real flower (e.g., by comparing it with the drawing on the handout). Students may use microscope if they want.
1:39–1:45	Teacher walks around room, giving each student a real flower.
1:45–2:05	Chaos erupts. There is much confusion, with students wandering around, throwing flower parts at each other. Teacher begins writing referrals and sends two students to the office for misbehavior. Teacher is flustered, directs students to spend remainder of period quietly reading from their texts. Two more referrals are written.
2:05–2:07	A few students begin meandering toward the exit.
2:07	End of period (much to the delight of the teacher).

Questions for Class Discussion

1. Do you think the teacher had a lesson plan? If so, what (if any) were its good points? Its problems?

2. If you believed that the teacher had a lesson plan, do you believe that it was written and detailed? Explain your response. What is your evidence?

3. How might the lesson have been prepared and implemented to avoid the chaos?

4. Was the format of the lesson traditional? Explain.

5. Have you experienced a class such as this? Explain.

6. Which teacher behaviors were probable causes of much of the chaos? (*Hint:* See the section "The Learning Experiences Ladder" in Chapter 8.)

7. What teacher behaviors could have prevented the chaos and made the lesson more effective?

8. Within the 55-minute class period, students were expected to operate rather high on the Learning Experiences Ladder (see Chapter 8). Consider this analysis: 9 minutes of silent reading, 10 minutes of listening, 6 minutes of silent reading and labeling, 2 minutes of listening, 6 minutes of action (the only direct experience), and an additional 22 minutes of silent reading. In all, there were approximately 49 minutes (89% of the class time) of abstract verbal and visual symbolization. Is this a problem?

9. What have you learned from this exercise?

Exercise
7.2A   **Preparing a Lesson Plan**

Instructions: Use the model lesson format (Figure 7.2) or an alternative format that is approved by your instructor to prepare a _____minute lesson plan (length to be decided in your class) for a grade and course of your choice. After completing your lesson plan, evaluate it yourself, modify it, and then have your modified version evaluated by at least three peers, using Exercise 7.2B for the evaluation, before turning it in for your instructor's evaluation. This exercise may be connected with Exercise 7.3.

Exercise
7.2B   **Self- and Peer Assessment of My Lesson Plan**

Instructions: You may duplicate blank copies of this form for evaluation of the lesson you developed for Exercise 7.2A. Have your lesson plan evaluated by three of your peers and yourself. For each of the following items, evaluators should check either "yes" or "no" and write instructive comments. Compare the results of your self-evaluation with the other evaluations.

	No	Yes	Comments
1. Are descriptive data adequately provided?			
2. Are the goals clearly stated?			
3. Are the objectives specific and measurable?			
4. Are objectives correctly classified?			
5. Are objectives only low order, or is higher-order thinking expected?			
6. Is the rationale clear and justifiable?			
7. Is the plan's content appropriate?			

(continued)

Exercise 7.2B **Self- and Peer Assessment of My Lesson Plan** *continued*

	No	Yes	Comments
8. Is the content likely to contribute to achievement of the objectives?			
9. Given the time frame and other logistical considerations, is the plan workable?			
10. Will the opening (set) likely engage the students?			
11. Is there a preassessment strategy?			
12. Is there a proper mix of learning activities for the time frame of the lesson?			
13. Are the activities developmentally appropriate for the intended students?			
14. Are transitions planned?			
15. If relevant, are key questions written out and key ideas noted in the plan?			
16. Does the plan indicate how coached practice will be provided for each student?			
17. Is adequate closure provided in the plan?			
18. Are the materials and equipment that are needed identified, and are they appropriate?			
19. Is there a planned formative assessment: formal or informal?			
20. Is there a planned summative assessment?			
21. Is the lesson coordinated in any way with other aspects of the curriculum?			
22. Is the lesson likely to provide a sense of meaning for the students by helping bridge their learning?			
23. Is an adequate amount of time allotted to address the information presented?			
24. Is a thoughtfully prepared and relevant student assignment planned?			
25. Could a substitute who is knowledgeable follow the plan?			

Additional comments:

Exercise
7.3

Preparing an Instructional Unit

Instructions: The purpose of this exercise is threefold: (1) to give you experience in preparing an instructional unit, (2) to assist you in preparing an instructional unit that you can use in your teaching, and (3) to start your collection of instructional units that you may be able to use in your teaching. This is an assignment that will take several hours to complete, and you will need to read ahead in the book. Our advice, therefore, is that the assignment be started early, with a due date much later in the course. Your course instructor may have specific guidelines for your completion of this exercise; what follows is the essence of what you are to do.

First, divide your class into two teams, each with a different assignment pertaining to this exercise. The units completed by these teams are to be shared with all members of the class for feedback and later use.

Team 1

Members of this team, individually, will develop standard teaching units, perhaps with different grade levels in mind. (You will need to be knowledgeable about material in Chapters 8 through 11.) Using a format that is practical, individuals on this team will each develop a minimum two-week unit for a particular grade level. Regardless of format chosen, each unit plan should include the following elements:
1. Identification of (a) grade level, (b) subject, (c) topic, and (d) time duration.
2. Statement of rationale and general goals.
3. Separate list of instructional objectives for each daily lesson. Wherever possible, the unit should include objectives from all three domains—cognitive, affective, and psychomotor.
4. List of the materials and resources needed and where they can be obtained (if you have that information). These should also be listed for each daily lesson.
5. Each of the daily lessons.
6. List of all items that will be used to assess student learning *during* and at *completion* of the unit of study.
7. Statement of how the unit will attend to variations in students' reading levels, socioethnic backgrounds, and special needs.

Team 2

In collaboration, members of this team will develop interdisciplinary thematic units. Depending on the number of students in your class, team 2 may be comprised of several teams, with each one developing an ITU. Each team should be composed of no fewer than two members (e.g., a math specialist and a science specialist) and no more than four (e.g., social studies, language arts/reading, mathematics, and science).

Chapter 7 POSTTEST

Short Explanation

1. Explain why supervisors of student teachers expect student teachers to plan and prepare their classroom management systems in writing and to do very detailed and written unit and lesson planning.

2. Explain why lesson planning is or should be a continual process.

3. Explain the importance of preassessment of student learning. When do you do a preassessment? How can it be done? What is done with the information obtained?

4. Explain the concept of a student-negotiated curriculum. Is it used today in middle school and secondary school teaching? Why or why not? Would you use it? Why or why not?

5. Explain the importance of the idea that all teachers are teachers of reading, writing, studying, and thinking. Do you agree or disagree with the statement? Why?

Essay

1. Describe the lesson and unit planning process.

2. Explain the importance of writing clear instructional objectives in all three domains: cognitive, psychomotor, and affective. Provide examples from your subject area.

3. Select a lesson plan from the many samples included in this chapter and describe recommendations you could make to accommodate the following students: a student with attention-deficit/hyperactivity disorder, an English Language Learner, a gifted and talented student, and a recalcitrant student. Support your claims.

4. From your current observations and fieldwork related to this teacher preparation program, clearly identify one specific example of educational practice that seems contradictory to exemplary practice or theory presented in this chapter. Present your explanation for the discrepancy.

5. Describe any prior concepts you held that changed as a result of your experiences with this chapter. Describe the changes.

CHAPTER EIGHT

Student-Centered Instructional Strategies

Alamy Images

An understanding heart is everything in a teacher, and cannot be esteemed highly enough. One looks back with appreciation to the brilliant teachers, but with gratitude to those who touched our human feelings. The curriculum is so much necessary raw material, but warmth is the vital element for the growing plant and for the soul of the child.[1]

—CARL JUNG

Specific Objectives

At the completion of this chapter, you will be able to:

▶ Demonstrate an understanding of the advantages and disadvantages of direct and indirect instructional strategies and of when each type is likely to be most appropriate and demonstrate how and why in one class period you would combine direct and indirect instructional strategies.

▶ Give examples in your subject area of learning experiences from each of these categories and when, why, and how you would use each category: verbal, visual, vicarious, simulated, and direct.

▶ Describe situations in your subject area when you would use each of the following: dyad teaching, learning centers, small-group learning, and cooperative learning groups.

▶ Differentiate as well as discuss the relationships among problem solving, inquiry, and discovery.

▶ Demonstrate an understanding of ways that teaching your subject area can help students develop their thinking and writing skills.

Chapter 8 Overview

Rather than focusing your attention on the selection of a particular model of teaching, our preference is to emphasize the importance of an eclectic approach in which you will select the best instructional strategy from various models. For example, there will be times when you want to use a direct, teacher-centered instructional strategy, perhaps by using a mini-lecture or a demonstration. There will also be times when you will want to use an indirect, student-centered or social-interactive instructional strategy, such as the use of cooperative learning and other small-group activities. And perhaps there will be even more times when you will be doing both simultaneously. In this chapter, we present and discuss a number of teaching strategies that all have two common elements: (1) social interaction and (2) problem solving. These strategies require that students interact with one another and draw conclusions, learn concepts, and form generalizations through induction, deduction, and observation or through application of principles. The premises underlying these strategies are that a person learns to think by thinking and sharing his or her thoughts with others and that knowledge gained through active learning and self-discovery is more meaningful, permanent, and transferable than knowledge gained through rote memorization and expository techniques.

Introduction

Teachers are urged to accept the principle that learning is an active process. They are told that the goals of education encompass not only the acquisition of knowledge but also the guidance of every person to his or her fullest potential. Such guidance involves development of a multitude of skills, including those needed for critical thinking, independent inquiry and problem solving, and active participation in group endeavors.

Group activity is a part of life—in the circles of family and friends as well as in the work, civic, religious, economic, governmental, social, and recreational realms. At one time or another, everyone is involved in activities with others as either a participant or an observer. These activities include those at the workplace, legislative committees, collective negotiations in business and labor, radio and television talk shows, roundtable discussions, religious and club activities, various symposia and panels, and town hall meetings. Group participatory skills are learned skills, not innate ones. The school has a role to play in the development of those skills both by encouraging awareness and analysis and by using experiential approaches. Therefore, teachers need to add to their repertoire of strategies a variety of techniques that provide students with opportunities to interact with one another. Here we will select a mode of instruction and highlight the strengths and weaknesses of student-centered instructional strategies.

Principles of Classroom Instruction and Learning: A Synopsis

A student does not learn to write by learning to recognize grammatical constructions of sentences. Neither does a person learn to play soccer solely by listening to a lecture on soccer. Learning is superficial unless the instructional methods and learning activities are (a) developmentally appropriate for the learners and (b) intellectually appropriate for the understanding, skills, and attitudes desired. Memorizing, for instance, is not the same as understanding. Yet far too often, memorization seems all that is expected of students in many classrooms. The result is low-level learning, a mere verbalism or regurgitation of information. That is not intellectually appropriate, and it is not teaching but just the orchestration of short-term memory exercises. A mental model of learning that assumes that a brain is capable of doing only one thing at a time is invidiously incorrect.[2]

When selecting the mode of instruction, you should bear in mind the following six basic principles of classroom instruction and learning:

1. To a great degree, it is the mode of instruction that determines what is learned.
2. Students must be actively involved in their own learning and in the assessment of their learning.
3. You must hold high expectations for the learning of each student (although not necessarily identical expectations for every student) and not waver from those expectations.
4. Students need constant, steady, understandable, positive, and reliable feedback about their learning.
5. Students should be engaged in both independent study and cooperative learning and give and receive individualized instruction.
6. No matter what content area you are prepared to teach, you are also a teacher of reading, writing, thinking, and study skills.

Conceptual knowledge refers to the understanding of relationships, whereas *procedural knowledge* entails the recording in memory of the meanings of symbols, rules, and procedures needed in order to accomplish tasks. Unless it is connected in meaningful ways to the formation of conceptual knowledge, the accumulation of memorized procedural knowledge is fragmented and ill fated and will be remembered for only a brief time.

To help students establish conceptual knowledge, learning, for them, must be meaningful. To help make learning meaningful for your students, you should use direct and real experiences as often as practical and possible. Vicarious experiences are sometimes necessary to provide students with otherwise unattainable knowledge; however, direct experiences that engage all the students' senses and all their learning modalities are more powerful. Students learn to write by writing and by receiving coaching and feedback about their progress in writing. They learn to play soccer by playing soccer and by receiving coaching and feedback about their developing skills and knowledge in playing the game. They learn these things best when they are actively (hands on) and mentally (minds on) engaged in doing them. This is real learning, learning that is meaningful; it is *authentic learning*.

Culturally Responsive Pedagogy

In **culturally responsive pedagogy**, the cultural beliefs, traditions, values, and mores of the students and their families are reflected in all aspects of the teaching/learning process. To promote culturally responsive pedagogy, teachers learn special strategies to align the school and home environments, use culturally relevant materials, support all learning modalities, employ classroom management techniques that are culturally acceptable, and have students engage in higher-order thinking and problem-solving skills that directly apply to their real-life experiences. This student-centered curricular approach helps *all* students meet the content standards in academically challenging content courses.[3] Complete Activities 8.1, 8.2, and 8.3 now.

Direct versus Indirect Instructional Modes: Strengths and Weaknesses of Each

When selecting an instructional strategy, there are two distinct choices (modes): should you deliver information to students directly, or should you provide students with access to information?

The *delivery mode* (known also as the *didactic*, *expository*, or *traditional style*) is designed to deliver information. Knowledge is passed on from those who know (the teachers, with the aid of textbooks) to those who do not (the students). Within the delivery mode, traditional and time-honored strategies are textbook reading, the lecture (formal teacher talk), questioning, and teacher-centered or teacher-planned discussions.

In the *access mode*, instead of direct delivery of information and direct control over what is learned, you provide

Activity
8.1
Cradleboard Teaching Project: Science through Native American Eyes

Do you want to teach your students about the principles of friction? Let them participate in a friendly interactive animated computer game version of Snow Snake. Do you want to help your students discover how sound travels? Let them play a virtual flute to discover how different finger positions create a range of tones. Do you want to show your students what Pueblo adobe houses, Plains Indians' tepees, Great Lakes wigwams, and Iroquois longhouses look like? Let them click on an interactive map of North America to examine the architectural styles of these and other lodging that Native Americans designed.

Take the time to examine a unique interactive multimedia program by the Cradleboard Teaching Project and learn how to integrate *Science through Native American Eyes*. The first program of its kind, this instructional software addresses scientific concepts from a Native American perspective while meeting national content standards for middle school science. The founder of the Cradleboard Teaching Project, Dr. Buffy Sainte-Marie, the singer-songwriter, Academy Award winner, and *Sesame Street* regular turned educator, has designed this program to make Indigenous ways of knowing come alive. According to the members of the Nihewan Foundation, "The Cradleboard Teaching Project turns on the lights in public education about Native American culture—past, present, and most important for the children—the future."

Frustrated by the inaccurate portrayal of Native Americans and the inadequate representation of Native Americans' contributions in the standard K–12 public school curriculum, Sainte-Marie has undertaken the creation of a series of 15 core curriculum units in geography, history, music, and social studies in addition to science for elementary, middle, and secondary students. The Cradleboard Teaching Project is designed to empower Native American students by boosting their self-identity while providing schools with a fun, interactive way to teach about Native American culture.

Science through Native American Eyes is designed to meet the needs of diverse learners. Instructional tools include videos, animation, music, experiments, and tests. The curriculum highlights Principles of Sound, Principles of Friction, and Native American Lodges. Preassessment, formative assessment, and summative assessment are all incorporated. Students can take an entry quiz to determine what they already know, quizzes over each section they explore, and exit exams in each key area to see what they have learned. This attractive multimedia presentation includes a dream catcher main menu containing a flute (principles of sound), sled (principles of friction), house (science in traditional Native American lodges), and other user-friendly graphics that invite students to explore core concepts.

Special features include teacher tips, lesson plans, vocabulary with spoken pronunciation, help pages throughout, an interactive grade book for recording and tracking student progress, an image library of rare photos and illustrations, and a collection of contemporary flute, drum, and string instrument musical selections.

Apply Your Knowledge

To learn more about the Cradleboard Teaching Project's multimedia CD-ROM *Science through Native American Eyes*, other Native American resources, student exchanges, or the social studies, science, and geography interactive online curricula, check out the following websites:

Cradleboard Teaching Project
http://www.cradleboard.org/main.html

Cradleboard Curricula
http://sparkaction.org/node/501

The Nihewan Foundation for Native American Education
http://www.nihewan.org

Activity
8.2
English as-a-Second-Language

There are numerous professional organizations, multiple clearinghouses, and a variety of websites addressing the needs of English Language Learners (ELLs). Some of the more popular resources include Teachers of English to Speakers of Other Languages (TESOL); the National Association of Bilingual Education (NABE); the National Clearinghouse for English Language Acquisition; the U.S. Department of Education; the Center for Research on Education, Diversity, and Excellence (CREDE); the Center for Advanced Research on Language Acquisition (CARLA); the Center for Applied Linguistics (CAL); and the ERIC Clearinghouse on Language and Linguistics. Their corresponding websites cover second-language acquisition, language teaching strategies, current legislation, and best practices.

Apply Your Knowledge

Visit the English-as-a-second-language page on the University of Alabama at Birmingham School of Education's website at **http://www.ed.uab.edu/esl**.

1. Visit the website's links for TESOL, NABE, CREDE, CARLA, or one of the other organizations listed above. Peruse these links to uncover a wealth of resources, including lesson plans, games/activities, professional development opportunities, and journal articles. Prepare a tour of the website to share the resources you uncovered with your classmates.

2. Visit the language technology links at **http://www.sussex.ac.uk/languages/resources/tech** to peruse the diverse collection of computer-aided language learning software, teaching videos, and other resources available on the Internet. Select a resource to share with your classmates.

3. Visit Dave Sperling's ESL Café at **http://eslcafe.com**. What student resources are available? How might you use them with the ELLs in your classroom?

Activity 8.3   Sheltered Instruction Observation Protocol (SIOP)

The number of non-native English language speakers in our public schools continues to increase. As a regular classroom teacher, you will have English Language Learners (ELLs) in your classes. In order to help ELLs learn grade-specific content as well as master the English language, the implementation of sheltered instruction was researched. Drs. Jana Echevarria, Mary Ellen Vogt, and Deborah J. Short (2004) developed the Sheltered Instruction Observation Protocol (SIOP) model. The SIOP model is currently used in most states and in hundreds of schools across the U.S. as well as in several other countries. This research-based methodology is not an add-on but a comprehensive strategy to meet the academic and linguistic needs of ELLs. There are eight components in the SIOP model: lesson preparation, building background, comprehensible input, strategies, interaction, practice/application, lesson delivery, and review/assessment. See also Dr. Torres's SIOP Lesson Plan 7.8C in Chapter 7.

Apply Your Knowledge

Peruse the following SIOP websites:

SIOP: Making Content Comprehensible for ELLs
http://www.everythingesl.net/inservices/using_siop_model_08621.php.php

Classroom Connections: Teaching English Learners the SIOP Way
http://www.prel.org/products/paced/fall06/siop.pdf

Effective Instructional Strategies for English Language Learners in Mainstream Classrooms
http://education.jhu.edu/newhorizons

The SIOP Institute: Sample SIOP Lesson Plans/Research
http://www.siopinstitute.net/index.html

The SIOP Model of Sheltered Instruction
http://www.cal.org/siop

1. What challenges do ELLs face in content courses?
2. How do the SIOP sample lesson plans compare to standard lesson plans you are used to creating?

SOURCE: J. Echevarria, M. E. Vogt, and D. J. Short, *Making Content Comprehensible for English Learners: The SIOP Model*, 2nd ed. (Boston: Pearson/Allyn and Bacon, 2004).

---

students with access to information by working *with* the students. In collaboration with the students, experiences are designed that help students build their existing schemata and obtain new knowledge and skills. Important instructional strategies include cooperative learning, inquiry, and investigative student-centered project learning, each of which most certainly will use questioning, although the questions more frequently will come from the students than from you, the textbook, or some other source extrinsic to the student. Discussions and lectures on particular topics also may be involved. But when used in the access mode, discussions and lectures occur during or after (rather than preceding) direct, hands-on learning by the students. In other words, rather than preceding student inquiry, discussions and lectures *result from* student inquiry and then may be followed by further student investigation.

You are probably more experienced with the delivery mode. To be most effective as a classroom teacher, however, you must become knowledgeable about and skillful in using access strategies. For young learners, strategies within the access mode clearly facilitate their positive learning and acquisition of conceptual knowledge and help build their self-esteem.

You should appropriately select and effectively use strategies from both modes but with a strong favoring of access strategies. Thus, from your study of this and the next chapter, you will become knowledgeable about specific techniques so you can make intelligent decisions about

choosing the best strategy for particular goals and objectives for your subject and the interests, needs, and maturity level of your own unique group of students.

Figure 8.1 provides an overview of the specific strengths and weaknesses of each mode. By comparing those, you can see that the strengths and weaknesses of one mode are nearly mirror opposites of the other. As noted earlier, although as a teacher you should be skillful in the use of strategies from both modes, for the most developmentally appropriate teaching for most groups of learners, you should concentrate more on using strategies from the access mode. Strategies within that mode are more student centered, hands-on, and concrete; students interact with one another and are actually (or are closer to) doing what they are learning to do—that is, the learning is likely more authentic. Learning that occurs from the use of that mode is longer lasting; that is, it fixes into long-term memory. And, as the students interact with one another and with their learning, they develop a sense of "can do," enhancing their self-esteem.

Selecting Learning Activities

Returning to our soccer example, can you imagine a soccer coach teaching students the skills and knowledge needed to play soccer but without ever letting them play the game? Can you imagine a science teacher instructing students on how to read a thermometer without ever letting them actually read a real thermometer? Can you imagine

<u>F i g u r e 8 . 1</u> **Delivery and Access Modes: Their Strengths and Potential Weaknesses**

Mode	Strengths	Potential Weaknesses
Delivery Mode	• Much content can be covered within a short span of time, usually by formal teacher talk, which then may be followed by an experiential activity. • The teacher is in control of what content is covered. • The teacher is in control of time allotted to specific content coverage. • Strategies within the delivery mode are consistent with competency-based instruction. • Student achievement of specific content is predictable and manageable.	• The sources of student motivation are mostly extrinsic. • Students have little control over the pacing of their learning. • Students make few important decisions about their learning. • There may be little opportunity for divergent or creative thinking. • Student self-esteem may be inadequately served.
Access Mode	• Students learn content, and in more depth. • The sources of student motivation are more likely intrinsic. • Students make important decisions about their own learning. • Students have more control over the pacing of their learning. • Students develop a sense of personal self-worth.	• Content coverage may be more limited. • Strategies are time-consuming. • The teacher has less control over content and time. • The specific results of student learning are less predictable. • The teacher may have less control over class procedures.

a geography teacher teaching students how to read a map without ever letting them put their eyes and hands on a real map? Can you imagine a piano teacher teaching a student to play piano without ever allowing the student to touch a real keyboard? Unfortunately, still today, too many teachers do almost those exact things—they try to teach students to do something without letting the students practice doing it.

In planning and selecting appropriate learning activities, an important rule is to select activities that are as close to the real thing as possible, that is, have them learn through direct experiencing. When students are involved in direct experiences, they are using more of their sensory input channels: their learning modalities (i.e., auditory, visual, tactile, and kinesthetic). And when all the senses are engaged, learning is more integrated and is most effective, most meaningful, and longest lasting. This "learning by doing" is *authentic learning*—or, as often referred to, **hands-on/minds-on learning**.

The Learning Experiences Ladder

Figure 8.2 depicts what is called the *Learning Experiences Ladder*, a visual depiction of a range of the kinds of learning experiences from which a teacher may select. Hands-on/minds-on learning is at the bottom of the ladder. At the top are abstract experiences, where the learner is exposed only to symbolization (i.e., letters and numbers) and uses only one or two senses (auditory or visual). The teacher lectures while the students sit, watch, and hear. Visual and verbal symbolic experiences, although impossible to avoid when teaching, are less effective in ensuring that planned and meaningful

learning occurs. This is especially so with learners who have special needs, learners who are culturally different, and ELLs. Thus, when planning learning experiences and selecting instructional materials, you are advised to select activities that engage the students in the most direct experiences possible.

As can be inferred from the Learning Experiences Ladder, when teaching about tide pools (the first example for each step), the most effective mode is to take the students to a tide pool (direct experience), where students can use all their senses (see, hear, touch, smell, and perhaps even taste if the water is not polluted with toxins) to experience the tide pool. If a field trip to a tide pool is not possible, students could experience a tide pool through a multimedia presentation or virtual reality adventure via the Internet. The least effective mode is for the teacher to merely talk about the tide pool (verbal experience, the most abstract and symbolic experience), engaging only one sense: auditory.

Of course, for various reasons—such as time, matters of safety, lack of resources, or geographic location of your school—you may not be able to take your students to a tide pool. You cannot always use the most direct experience, so sometimes you must select an experience higher on the ladder. Self-discovery teaching is not always appropriate. Sometimes it is more appropriate to build on what others have discovered and learned. Although learners do not need to reinvent the wheel, the most effective and longest-lasting learning is that which engages most or all of their senses. On the Learning Experiences Ladder, those are the experiences that fall within the bottom three categories—direct, simulated, and vicarious. This is true for

Figure 8.2 **The Learning Experiences Ladder**

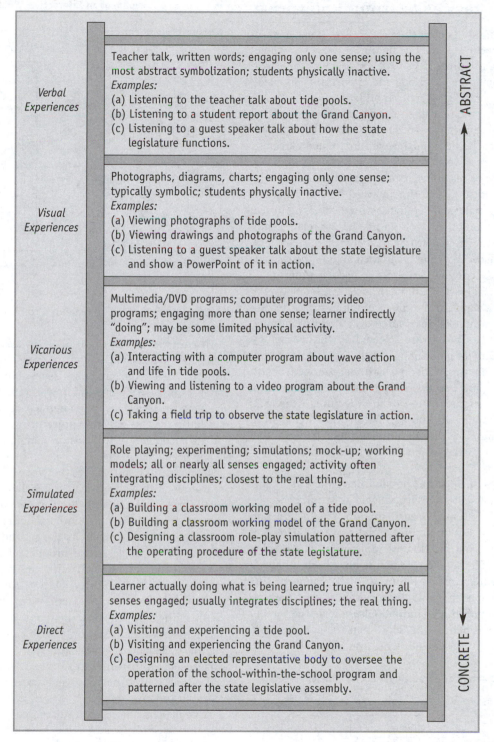

Verbal Experiences

Teacher talk, written words; engaging only one sense; using the most abstract symbolization; students physically inactive.
Examples:
(a) Listening to the teacher talk about tide pools.
(b) Listening to a student report about the Grand Canyon.
(c) Listening to a guest speaker talk about how the state legislature functions.

Visual Experiences

Photographs, diagrams, charts; engaging only one sense; typically symbolic; students physically inactive.
Examples:
(a) Viewing photographs of tide pools.
(b) Viewing drawings and photographs of the Grand Canyon.
(c) Listening to a guest speaker talk about the state legislature and show a PowerPoint of it in action.

Vicarious Experiences

Multimedia/DVD programs; computer programs; video programs; engaging more than one sense; learner indirectly "doing"; may be some limited physical activity.
Examples:
(a) Interacting with a computer program about wave action and life in tide pools.
(b) Viewing and listening to a video program about the Grand Canyon.
(c) Taking a field trip to observe the state legislature in action.

Simulated Experiences

Role playing; experimenting; simulations; mock-up; working models; all or nearly all senses engaged; activity often integrating disciplines; closest to the real thing.
Examples:
(a) Building a classroom working model of a tide pool.
(b) Building a classroom working model of the Grand Canyon.
(c) Designing a classroom role-play simulation patterned after the operating procedure of the state legislature.

Direct Experiences

Learner actually doing what is being learned; true inquiry; all senses engaged; usually integrates disciplines; the real thing.
Examples:
(a) Visiting and experiencing a tide pool.
(b) Visiting and experiencing the Grand Canyon.
(c) Designing an elected representative body to oversee the operation of the school-within-the-school program and patterned after the state legislative assembly.

ABSTRACT

CONCRETE

adult learners, primary-grade children, or students of any age-group.

Direct, Simulated, and Vicarious Experiences Help Connect Student Learning

Another value of direct, simulated, and vicarious experiences is that they tend to be interdisciplinary; that is, they blur or bridge subject-content boundaries. That makes those experiences especially useful for teachers who want to help students connect the learning of one discipline with that of others and to bridge what is being learned with their own life experiences. Direct, simulated, and vicarious experiences are more like real life. That means that the learning resulting from those experiences is authentic. Now reflect on your school experiences and complete Exercises 8.1, 8.2, and 8.3.

The Total Class as a Group Enterprise

To start your thinking about the processes of participation and group interaction, it may be helpful to view the whole class as a group. In efforts to provide experiences for learners, teachers sometimes overlook the opportunity to make sessions with the total class more interactive.

Consider for a moment the major characteristics of the traditional—and prevalent—teacher-centered, recitation-type strategy: teacher-led and teacher-dominated sessions; questions of a relatively superficial, information-seeking nature; repeating or restating (reciting) what has previously been learned, studied, read, or memorized; the "hearing" of lessons to detect right and wrong answers; checking to see if students have done their work; a one-to-one relationship between the questioner and hearer and between the teller and answerer; and all decision making in the hands of the teacher regarding purpose, content, process, and participation.

A flowchart of participation in such a session would probably reveal a significant number of tallies for the teacher, with a smaller number distributed over a relatively small number of students who were selected by the teacher to participate. The major mode of operation would tend to be a question and an answer, with an occasional comment about the accuracy or character of student responses. There also might be the occasional lecture or mini-lecture. Figure 8.3 is a diagram showing the flow of interaction found in a typical recitation. Note that the interaction is between the teacher and individual students only. There is no cross flow between students.

In contrast, consider the possibilities inherent in the concept of a whole-class activity, viewed as genuine discussion with student interactive participation. The focus is not on hearing lessons but on inquiry and discovery. Figure 8.4 is a diagram showing the flow of interaction in a whole-class discussion. In that class, students have been arranged in an open square. Arrows pointing to the center of the square indicate that the person is speaking to the group as a whole. Arrows pointing to individuals indicate the person that the speaker is addressing. Note that the conversation includes cross talk between students and talk addressed to

Figure 8.3 **Diagram of a Traditional Recitation-Type Strategy**

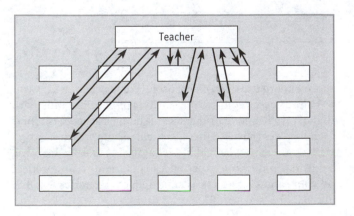

Figure 8.4 **Diagram of an Interactive, Whole-Class Discussion**

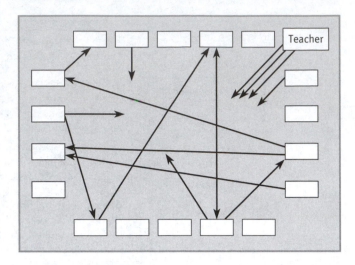

the group as a whole. The teacher's role in the discussion is that of facilitator.

In contrast to the traditional strategy, an interactive, whole-class discussion is characterized by probing exploration of ideas, concepts, and issues; building on student responses in a developmental flow; interaction among class members; shifting leadership among participants; questioning, sharing, differing, and conjecturing on the part of all; student participation in decision making; and hypothesizing and problem solving.

The essential difference between the two types of classrooms is that the first (the teacher-centered discussion) is based on the view that knowledge consists of a series of correct answers, with students as more or less passive participants, whereas the second is based on the view that knowledge is the product of creative inquiry through social interaction, with the students as active participants in that inquiry. Only through genuine student involvement and interaction can the contributions and thinking of each participant be seen as being welcomed and accepted. And only with such interaction can hypotheses be tested, views expressed and analyzed, questions raised, controversies examined, and insights developed, along with other desirable cognitive and affective processes and outcomes.

A whole-class discussion (discussed further in Chapter 9) is not the only strategy you have at your disposal to promote interactive learning. Many other strategies will provide the opportunity for students to participate interactively in the learning process. For our purposes here, the tactics and strategies are broadly classified into four categories: (1) dyad groups; (2) cooperative learning groups; (3) the relatively formal, planned, short-term, presentation-type technique; and (4) those group strategies that involve more student interaction and work of a long-term nature (e.g., projects) with varied purposes, including the analysis of the group process itself.

Learning in Pairs

It is sometimes advantageous to pair students (dyads) for learning. Various dyads are described as follows.

Peer Tutoring, Mentoring, and Cross-Age Coaching

Peer tutoring, **mentoring**, or peer-assisted learning is a strategy whereby one classmate tutors another. It is useful, for example, when one student helps another who is an ELL or when a student skilled in math helps another who is less skilled. It has been demonstrated repeatedly that peer tutoring is a significant strategy for promoting active learning.[4] Furthermore, peer tutoring increases academic achievement not only for those receiving tutoring but also for those students doing the tutoring.[5]

Cross-age **coaching** is a strategy where one student is coached by another from a different and usually higher grade level. This is similar to peer tutoring, except that the coach is from a different age level than the student being coached.[6] Many middle schools and high schools have service learning projects that involve students mentoring younger elementary school children. Sometimes students from nearby colleges and universities mentor local middle school and high school students. (See the Teaching Scenario "Bears and Cats Mentoring Program" in Chapter 4.)

Paired Team Learning

Paired team learning is a strategy whereby students study and learn in teams of two. Students identified as gifted work and learn especially well when paired. Specific uses for paired team learning include drill partners, book report pairs, homework partners,[7] and project assignment pairs.

Think-Pair-Share

Think-pair-share is a strategy where students, in pairs, examine a new concept or topic about to be studied. After the students of each dyad discuss what they already know or think they know about the concept, they present their perceptions to the whole group. This technique is useful for discovering students' **misconceptions**, also called **naive theories**, about a topic. Introducing a writing step, the modification called *think-write-pair-share*, the members of the dyad think and write their ideas or conclusions before sharing with the larger group.

The Learning Center

Another significantly beneficial way of pairing students for instruction is by using the **Learning Center (LC)**. An LC is a special station located in the classroom where one student (or two if student interaction is necessary or preferred at the center) can quietly work and learn more about a special topic or improve specific skills at his or her own pace. All materials needed are provided at that station, including clear instructions for operation of the center. Whereas the LC used to be thought of as being effective in elementary or self-contained classrooms, now, with block scheduling and longer class periods, the LC has special relevance for all teachers regardless of grade level. Familiar examples are the personal computer station and the reading center.

The value of LCs as instructional devices undoubtedly lies in the following facts. LCs can provide instructional diversity. While working at a center, the student is giving time and quality attention to the learning task (learning toward mastery) and is likely to be engaging his or her most effective learning modality or integrating several modalities or all of them. To adapt instruction to students' personal needs and preferences, it is possible to design a learning environment that includes several LCs, each of which uses a different medium and modality or focuses on a special aspect of the curriculum. Students then rotate through the various LCs according to their needs and preferences.

There are three types of LCs. In the *direct-learning center*, performance expectations for cognitive learning are quite specific, and the focus is on mastery of content. In the *open-learning center*, the goal is to provide opportunity for exploration, enrichment, motivation, and creative discovery. In the *skill center*, as in a direct-learning center, performance expectations are quite specific, but the focus is on the development of a particular skill or process.

Although in all instances the primary reason for using an LC is to differentiate instruction—that is, to provide collections of materials and activities adjusted to the various readiness levels, interests, and learning profiles of students—there are additional reasons. These are to provide (a) a mechanism for learning that crosses discipline boundaries; (b) a special place for a student with special needs; (c) opportunities for creative work, enrichment experiences, and multisensory experiences; and (d) opportunities to learn from learning packages that use special equipment or media of which only one or a limited supply may be available for use in your classroom (e.g., science materials, a microscope, a computer, a DVD player, or some combination of these).

To construct an LC, you should follow these guidelines. The center should be designed with a theme in mind, preferably one that integrates the students' learning by providing activities that cross discipline boundaries. Decide the purpose of the center and give the center a name, such as "the center for the study of wetlands," "walking tour of Florence," "traveling to Québec City," "structure and function," "patterns in nature," "the United Nations," "patterns of discrimination," "editing a video," "the center for worldwide communication," and so on. The purpose of the center should be clearly understood by the students. Centers should always be used for educational purposes, *never* for punishment.

The center should be designed to be attractive, purposeful, and uncluttered and should be identified with an attractive sign. LCs should be activity oriented (i.e., dependent on the students' manipulation of materials, not just paper-and-pencil tasks).

Topics for the center should be related to the instructional program—for review and reinforcement, remediation, or enrichment. The center should be self-directing (i.e., specific instructional objectives and procedures for using the center should be clearly posted and understandable to the student users). An audio- or videocassette or a computer program is sometimes used for this purpose. The center should also be self-correcting (i.e., student users should be able to tell by the way they have completed the task whether they have done it correctly and have learned). The center should contain a variety of activities geared to the varying abilities and interest levels of the students. A choice of two or more activities at a center is one way to provide for this.

Materials to be used at the center should be maintained at the center, with descriptions for use provided to the students. Materials should be safe for student use, and the center should be easily supervised by you or another adult. Some centers may become more or less permanent centers, that is, remain for the school term or longer, whereas other centers may change according to what is being studied at the time.

Learning in Small Groups

Small groups are those involving three to eight students in either a teacher- or a student-directed setting. Using small groups for instruction, including the cooperative learning group, enhances the opportunities for students to assume greater control over their own learning, sometimes referred to as *empowerment*.

Purposes for Using Small Groups

Small groups can be formed to serve a number of purposes. They might be useful for a specific learning activity (e.g., reciprocal reading groups, where students take turns asking questions, summarizing, making predictions about, and clarifying a story), or they might be formed to complete an activity that requires materials that are in short supply (to complete a science experiment or a project), lasting only as long as the project does. Teachers have various rationales for assigning students to groups. Groups can be formed by grouping students according to (a) personality type (e.g., sometimes a teacher may want to team less assertive students together to give them the opportunity for greater management of their own learning), (b) social pattern (e.g., sometimes it may be necessary to break up a group of rowdy friends, or it may be desirable to broaden the association among students), (c) common interest, (d) learning styles (e.g., forming groups either of mixed styles or of styles in common), or (e) their abilities in a particular skill or their knowledge in a particular area. One specific type of small-group instruction is the cooperative learning group.

Cooperative Learning

Lev Vygotsky (1896–1934) studied the importance of a learner's social interactions in learning situations. Vygotsky argued that learning is most effective when learners cooperate with one another in a supportive learning environment

under the careful guidance of a teacher. Cooperative learning, group problem solving, problem-based learning, and cross-age tutoring are instructional strategies used by teachers that have grown in popularity as a result of research evolving from the work of Vygotsky.

The Cooperative Learning Group

The *cooperative learning group (CLG)* is a **heterogeneous group** (i.e., mixed according to one or more criteria, such as ability or skill level, learning style, learning capacity, gender, and language proficiency) consisting of three to six students who work together in a teacher- or student-directed setting, emphasizing support for one another (see Exercise 8.4). Often a CLG consists of five students of mixed ability, learning styles, gender, and ethnicity, with each member of the group assuming a particular role.

THE THEORY AND USE OF COOPERATIVE LEARNING The theory of **cooperative learning** is that when small groups of students of mixed backgrounds and capabilities work together toward a common goal, members of the group increase their friendship and respect for one another. As a consequence, each individual's self-esteem is enhanced, students are more motivated to participate in higher-order thinking, and academic achievement is accomplished.[8]

There are several techniques for using cooperative learning. Of special interest to teachers are general methods of cooperative learning, such as "student team-achievement division," where the teacher presents a lesson, students work together in teams to help each other learn the material, individuals take quizzes, and team rewards are earned based on the individual scores on the quizzes; "teams-games-tournaments," where tournaments (rather than quizzes) are held in which students compete against students with similar achievements and then winners contribute toward their team's score; and group investigations.[9] Yet the primary purpose of each is for the groups to learn—which means, of course, that individuals within a group must learn. Group achievement in learning, then, is dependent on the learning of individuals within the group. Rather than competing for rewards for achievement, members of the group cooperate with one another by helping one another learn so that the group reward will be a good one.

ROLES WITHIN THE CLG It is advisable to assign roles (specific functions) to each member of the CLG. These roles should be rotated either during the activity or from one time to the next. Although titles may vary, five typical roles are the following:

- *Group facilitator.* To lead the group by soliciting everyone's input and facilitating the group discussion.
- *Recorder.* To record all group activities and processes and perhaps to periodically assess how the group is doing. Either the recorder or the group facilitator may report the group process and accomplishments to the teacher and/or to the entire class.

■ *Taskmaster.* To see that all members carry out their respective roles, to keep the group on task, and to make sure the group completes the task at hand within the time frame allotted.

■ *Materials manager.* To obtain, maintain, and return materials needed for the group to function.

■ *Thinking monitor.* To identify and record the sequence and processes of the group's thinking. This role encourages metacognition and the development of thinking skills.

It is important that students understand and perform their individual roles and that each member of the CLG performs his or her tasks as expected. No student should be allowed to ride on the coattails of the group. To emphasize and reinforce how important each role is and to be able to readily recognize the role any student is serving during a CLG activity, one teacher made a trip to an office supply store and had permanent badges made for the various CLG roles. During CLGs, then, each student attaches the appropriate badge to his or her clothing. Another instructor distributed props, such as an oversized pencil to the recorder, an hourglass to the taskmaster, a basket to the materials manager, and so on so that he could easily identify each student's role as he walked through the classroom.

WHAT STUDENTS AND THE TEACHER DO WHEN USING CLGs For learning to take place, each member of the CLG must understand and assume two roles or responsibilities—the role he or she is assigned as a member of the group and that of seeing that all others in the group are performing their roles. Sometimes this requires interpersonal skills that students have yet to learn or to learn well. This is where the teacher must assume some responsibility, too. Simply placing students in CLGs and expecting each member and each group to function and to learn the expected outcomes may not work. In other words, skills of cooperation must be taught, and if all your students have not yet learned the skills of cooperation, then you will have to teach them. This doesn't mean that if a group is not functioning you immediately break up the group and reassign members to new groups. Part of group learning is learning the process of how to work out conflict. A group may require your assistance to work out a conflict. With your guidance, the group should be able to discover what the problem is that is causing the conflict, identify some options, and then mediate at least a temporary solution. If a particular skill is needed, then, with your guidance, students can identify and learn that skill.

WHEN TO USE CLGs CLGs can be used for problem solving, investigations, opinion surveys, experiments, review, project work, test making, or almost any other instructional purpose. Just as you would for small-group work in general, you can use CLGs for most any purpose at any time, but, as with any other type of instructional strategy, it should not be overused.

OUTCOMES OF USING CLGs When the process is well planned and managed, the outcomes of cooperative learning include (a) improved communication and increased acceptance among diverse students; (b) quality learning with fewer off-task behaviors; (c) improved ability to perform four key thinking strategies—problem solving, decision making, critical thinking, and creative thinking; and (d) increased academic achievement. In the words of Good and Brophy, "Cooperative learning arrangements promote friendships and prosocial interaction among students who differ in achievement, sex, race, or ethnicity, and they promote the acceptance of mainstreamed handicapped students by their nonhandicapped classmates. Cooperative methods also frequently have positive effects, and rarely have negative effects, on affective outcomes such as self-esteem, academic self-confidence, liking for the class, liking and feeling liked by classmates, and various measures of empathy and social cooperation."[10]

COOPERATIVE GROUP LEARNING, ASSESSMENT, AND GRADING Normally, the CLG is rewarded on the basis of group achievement, though individual members within the group can later be rewarded for individual contributions. Because of peer pressure, when using CLGs you must be cautious about using group grading.[11] Some teachers give bonus points to all members of a group to add to their individual scores when everyone in the group has reached preset criteria. In establishing preset standards, the standards can be different for individuals within a group, depending on each member's ability and past performance. It is important that each member of a group feel rewarded and successful. Often, students' complaints of CLG experiences center on unfair grading. Hold students individually responsible while promoting group accountability. For determination of students' report card grades, measure individual student achievement later through individual results on tests and other sources of data. Exercise 8.4 provides you with the opportunity to reflect back on a positive experience working in a CLG.

Why Some Teachers Have Difficulty Using CLGs

Sometimes, teachers have difficulty when they think they are using CLGs, and they either give up trying to use the strategy or simply tell students to divide into groups for an activity and call it cooperative learning.[12] As emphasized earlier, for the strategy to work, each student must have been given training in and have acquired basic skills in interaction and group processing and must realize that individual achievement rests with that of their group. And, as mentioned earlier, CLGs must not be overused—teachers must vary their strategies.

For CLGs to work well, advanced planning and effective management are a must. Students must be instructed in the necessary skills for group learning. Each student must be assigned a responsible role within the group and be held accountable for fulfilling that responsibility. And, when a CLG activity is in process, groups must be continually monitored by the teacher for possible breakdown of this process within a group. In other words, while students are working in groups, the teacher must exercise his or her skills of withitness (see Chapter 4). When a potential breakdown is noticed, the teacher quickly intervenes to help the group get back on track.

Teaching Thinking for Intelligent Behavior

Thinking can be thought of as the mental process by which a person makes sense out of experience.[13] Teachers should help students develop their thinking skills. In teaching for thinking, we are interested not only in what students know but also in how students behave when they don't know. Gathering evidence of the performance and growth of intelligent behavior requires observing students as they try to solve the day-to-day academic and real-life problems they encounter. By collecting anecdotes and examples of written, oral, and visual expressions, we can see students' increasingly voluntary and spontaneous performance of intelligent behaviors.

Characteristics of Intelligent Behavior

Characteristics of intelligent behavior that you should model, teach, and observe developing in your students, as identified by Costa,[14] are described in the following paragraphs.

PERSEVERANCE Perseverance is making a continual steady effort and sticking to a task until it is accomplished. Consider the following examples:

- Nearly single-handedly and against formidable odds, Clara Barton persevered to form the American Red Cross in 1882.
- Refusing to be intimidated by the chemical industry, powerful politicians, and the media, Rachel Carson was persistent in her pursuit to educate society about the ill effects of pesticides on humans and the natural world and refused to accept the premise that damage to nature was the inevitable cost of technological and scientific progress. Her book *Silent Spring*, published in 1963, was the seed for the beginning of the development of today's more responsible ecological attitude.
- Because of childhood diseases, Wilma Rudolph, at the age of 10, could not walk without the aid of leg braces. Just 10 years later at the age of 20, she was declared to be the fastest-running woman in the world, having won three gold medals in the 1960 Olympics.

DECREASING IMPULSIVITY When students develop impulse control, they think before acting. Impulsive behavior can worsen conflict and inhibit effective problem solving.[15] Students can be taught to think before shouting out an answer, before beginning a project or task, and before arriving at conclusions with insufficient data. One of

several reasons that teachers should usually insist on a show of hands before a student is acknowledged to respond or ask a question is to help students develop control over the impulsive behavior of shouting out in class.[16]

LISTENING TO OTHERS WITH UNDERSTANDING AND EMPATHY Some psychologists believe that the ability to listen to others, to empathize with and to understand their point of view, is one of the highest forms of intelligent behavior. Empathic behavior is considered an important skill for conflict resolution. Piaget refers to this behavior as *overcoming egocentrism*. In class meetings, brainstorming sessions, think tanks, town meetings, advisory councils, board meetings, and legislative bodies, people from various walks of life convene to share their thinking, to explore their ideas, and to broaden their perspectives by listening to the ideas and reactions of others.

COOPERATIVE THINKING: SOCIAL INTELLIGENCE Humans are social beings. Real-world problem solving has become so complex that seldom can any person go it alone. Not all students come to school knowing how to work effectively in groups. They may exhibit competitiveness, narrow-mindedness, egocentrism, ethnocentrism, or criticism of others' values, emotions, and beliefs. Listening, consensus seeking, giving up an idea to work on someone else's, empathy, compassion, group leadership, cooperative learning, knowing how to support group efforts, and altruism are behaviors indicative of intelligent human beings, and they can be learned by students at school and in the classroom.

FLEXIBILITY IN THINKING Sometimes referred to as *lateral thinking*, flexibility in thinking is the ability to approach a problem from a new angle using a novel approach. With modeling by the teacher, students can develop this behavior as they learn to consider alternative points of view and to deal with several sources of information simultaneously.

METACOGNITION Learning to plan, monitor, assess, and reflect on one's own thinking, known as **metacognition**, is another characteristic of intelligent behavior. CLGs, journals, portfolio conferences, self-assessment, and thinking aloud in dyads are strategies that can be used to help students develop this intelligent behavior. Thinking aloud is good modeling for your students, helping them to develop their own cognitive skills of thinking, learning, and reasoning.[17]

STRIVING FOR ACCURACY AND PRECISION Teachers can observe students growing in this behavior when students take time to check over their work, review the procedures, refuse to draw conclusions with only limited data, and use concise and descriptive language.

SENSE OF HUMOR The positive effects of humor on the body's physiological functions are well established: a drop in the pulse rate, an increase of oxygen in the blood, the activation of antibodies that fight against harmful microorganisms, and the release of gamma interferon, a hormone that fights viruses and regulates cell growth. Humor liberates creativity and provides high-level thinking skills, such as anticipation, finding novel relationships, and visual imagery. The acquisition of a sense of humor follows a developmental sequence similar to that described by Piaget[18] and Kohlberg.[19] Initially, young children may find humor in all the wrong things—human frailty, ethnic jokes, sacrilegious riddles, or obscene profanities. Later, creative adolescents thrive on finding incongruity and will demonstrate a whimsical frame of mind during problem solving.

QUESTIONING AND PROBLEM POSING Young people are usually full of questions, and, unless discouraged, they do ask them. We want students to be alert to and recognize discrepancies and phenomena in their environment and to freely inquire about their causes. In exemplary educational programs, students are encouraged to ask questions (see Chapter 9) and then from those questions develop a problem-solving strategy to investigate their questions.

DRAWING ON KNOWLEDGE AND APPLYING IT TO NEW SITUATIONS A major goal of formal education is for students to apply school-learned knowledge to real-life situations. To develop skills in drawing on past knowledge and applying that knowledge to new situations, students must be given an opportunity to practice doing that very thing. Problem recognition, problem solving, and project-based learning are ways of providing that opportunity.

TAKING RISKS Students should be encouraged to venture forth and explore their ideas. Teachers should model this behavior and can provide opportunities for students to develop this intelligent behavior by using techniques such as **brainstorming**, exploratory investigations, projects, and cooperative learning.

USING ALL THE SENSES As discussed earlier in this chapter, as often as is appropriate and feasible, students should be encouraged to use and develop all their sensory input channels for learning (i.e., verbal, visual, tactile, and kinesthetic).

INGENUITY + ORIGINALITY + INSIGHTFULNESS = CREATIVITY All students must be encouraged to do and be discouraged from saying "I can't." Students must be taught in such a way as to encourage intrinsic motivation rather than reliance on extrinsic sources. Teachers need to offer criticism in such a way that the student understands that the criticism is constructive and not a criticism of self. In exemplary programs, students learn the value of feedback.

WONDERMENT + INQUISITIVENESS + CURIOSITY + THE ENJOYMENT OF PROBLEM SOLVING = A SENSE OF EFFICACY AS A THINKER Young children express wonderment, an expression that should never be stifled. Through effective teaching, adolescents can recapture that sense of wonderment as they are guided by an effective teacher into a feeling of "I can" and an expression of "I enjoy."

We should strive to help our own students develop these characteristics of intelligent behavior. Now, let's review additional research findings that offer important considerations in the facilitation of student learning and intelligent behavior.

Direct Teaching for Thinking and Intelligent Behavior

The curriculum of any school includes the development of skills that are used in thinking. Because the academic achievement of students increases when they are taught thinking skills directly, many researchers and educators concur that direct instruction should be given to all students on how to think and behave intelligently.[20]

Research Imperatives for the Teaching of Thinking

Four research perspectives have influenced the direct teaching of thinking. The *cognitive view of intelligence* asserts that intellectual ability is not fixed but can be developed. The *constructivist approach to learning* maintains that learners actively and independently construct knowledge by creating and coordinating relationships in their mental repertoire. The *social psychology view of classroom experience* focuses on the learner as an individual who is a member of various peer groups and a society. The *perspective of information processing* deals with the acquisition, elaboration, and management of information.[21]

Direct Teaching of Skills Used in Thinking

Rather than assuming that students have developed thinking skills (such as *classifying, comparing, concluding, generalizing, inferring,* and others; see Figure 8.6), teachers should devote classroom time to teaching them directly. When teaching a thinking skill directly, the subject content becomes the vehicle for thinking. For example, a social studies lesson can teach students how to distinguish fact and opinion, a language arts lesson instructs students how to compare and analyze, and a science lesson can teach students how to set up a problem for their inquiry.

Inquiry Teaching and Discovery Learning

Both **inquiry teaching** and **discovery learning** are useful tools for learning and for teaching thinking skills. Intrinsic to the effectiveness of both inquiry and discovery is the assumption that students would rather actively seek knowledge than receive it through traditional expository (i.e., information delivery) methods such as lectures, demonstrations, and textbook reading. Although inquiry and discovery are important teaching tools, there is sometimes confusion about exactly what inquiry teaching is and how it differs from discovery learning. The distinction should become clear as you study the following descriptions of these two important tools for teaching and learning.

Problem Solving

Perhaps a major reason why inquiry and discovery are sometimes confused is that, in both, students are actively engaged in problem solving. Problem solving is *the ability to define or describe a problem, determine the desired outcome, select possible solutions, choose strategies, test trial solutions, evaluate outcomes, and revise these steps where necessary.*[22]

Inquiry versus Discovery

Problem solving is *not* a teaching strategy but a higher-order intellectual behavior that facilitates learning. What a teacher can and should do is provide opportunities for students to identify and tentatively solve problems. Experiences in inquiry and discovery can provide those opportunities. With the processes involved in inquiry and discovery, teachers can help students develop the skills necessary for effective problem solving. Two major differences between discovery and inquiry are (a) who identifies the problem and (b) the percentage of decisions that are made by the students.

What is called *Level I inquiry* is actually traditional, didactic, "cookbook" teaching, where both the problem and the process for resolving it are defined for the student. The student then works through the process to its inevitable resolution. If the process is well designed, the result is inevitable because the student discovers what was intended by the program's designers. This level is also called *guided inquiry* or *discovery* because the students are carefully guided through the investigation to (the predictable) discovery.

Level I is in reality a strategy within the *delivery mode*, the advantages of which were described earlier in this chapter. Because Level I inquiry is highly manageable and the learning outcome is predictable, it is probably best for teaching basic concepts and principles. Students who never experience learning beyond Level I are missing an opportunity to engage their highest mental operations, and they seldom (or never) get to experience more motivating, real-life problem solving. Furthermore, those students may come away with the false notion that problem solving is a linear process, which it is not. As illustrated in Figure 8.5, true inquiry is cyclical rather than linear. For that reason, Level I is *not* true inquiry because it is a linear process. Real-world problem solving is a cyclical rather than a linear process. One enters the cycle whenever a discrepancy or problem is observed and recognized, and that can occur at any point in the cycle.

True Inquiry

By the time students are in middle and secondary school, they should be provided experiences for true inquiry that begins with *Level II*, where students actually decide and design processes for their inquiry. In true inquiry, there is an emphasis on the tentative nature of conclusions, which makes the activity more like real-life problem solving where decisions are always subject to revision if and when new data so prescribe.

Figure 8.5 The Inquiry Cycle

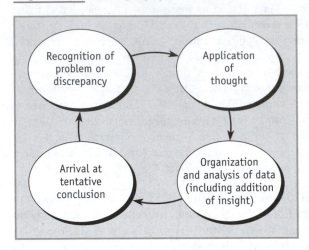

At *Level III* inquiry, students recognize and identify the problem as well as decide the processes for resolving it and reach conclusions. In *project-centered teaching*, students are usually engaged at this level of inquiry. By the time students are in middle grades and certainly by the time they are in secondary school, Level III inquiry should be a major strategy for instruction. However, it is not easy; like most good teaching practices, it is a lot of work, but the intrinsic rewards make the effort worthwhile. As exclaimed by one teacher using interdisciplinary thematic instruction with student-centered inquiry, "I've never worked harder in my life, but I've never had this much fun, either."

The Critical Thinking Skills of Discovery and Inquiry

In true inquiry, students generate ideas and then design ways to test those ideas. The various processes used represent the many critical thinking skills. Some of those skills are concerned with generating and organizing data; others are concerned with building and using ideas. Figure 8.6

Figure 8.6 Inquiry Cycle Processes

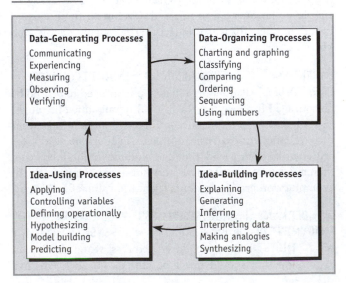

| Teaching Scenario | **Problem Solving and Decision Making in the Real World Is an Integrated and Interdisciplinary Inquiry Activity[23]** |

On any given day or specified time period, teachers and students can look at a problem or subject of study from the point of view of many separate disciplines. Such an interdisciplinary approach has been adopted to some degree not only by educators but by other professionals as well. It is *the* mode of meaningful learning and real-life problem solving.

For example, consider the fact-finding and decision-making approach of public officials in the state of Colorado when confronted with the task of making decisions about projects proposed for watersheds in their state. While gathering information, the officials brought in Dave Rosgen, a state hydrologist. Rosgen led the officials into the field to demonstrate specific ways by which he helped control erosion and rehabilitate damaged streams. He took the officials to Wolf Creek, where they wore high waders. Rosgen led the group down the creek to examine various features of that complex natural stream. He pointed out evidence of the creek's past meanders, patterns that he had incorporated into his rehabilitation projects. In addition to listening to this scientist's point of view, the public officials listened to other experts to consider related economic and political issues before making final decisions about projects that had been proposed for watersheds in that state.

During interdisciplinary thematic units, students study a topic and its underlying ideas as well as related knowledge from various disciplines on an ongoing basis. The teacher, sometimes with the help of students and other teachers and adults, introduces experiences designed to elicit specific ideas and skills from various disciplines, just as Rosgen introduced information from hydrology to develop literacy skills through the unit. For instance, the teacher might stimulate communication skills through creative writing and other projects. Throughout the unit, the students are guided in exploring ideas related to different disciplines to integrate their knowledge.

Some processes in the cycle are discovery processes, and others are inquiry processes. Inquiry processes include the more complex mental operations (including all of those in the idea-using category). Project-centered teaching provides an avenue for inquiry processes, as does problem-centered teaching.

Inquiry learning is a higher-level mental operation that introduces the concept of the discrepant event, something that establishes cognitive disequilibrium (using the element of surprise to challenge students' prior notions) to help students develop skills in observing and being alert for discrepancies. Such a strategy provides opportunities for students to investigate their own ideas about explanations.[24] Inquiry, like discovery, depends on skill in problem solving; the difference between the two is in the amount of decision-making responsibility given to students. Experiences afforded by inquiry help students understand the importance of suspending judgment and also the tentativeness of answers and solutions. With those understandings, students eventually are better able to deal with life's ambiguities. When students are not provided these important educational experiences, their education is incomplete.

One of the most effective ways of stimulating inquiry is to use materials that provoke students' interest. These materials should be presented in a nonthreatening, noncompetitive context so that students think and hypothesize freely. The teacher's role is to encourage students to form as many hypotheses as possible and then support their hypotheses with reasons. After the students suggest several ideas, the teacher should begin to move on to higher-order, more abstract questions that involve the development of generalizations and evaluations. True inquiry problems have a special advantage in that they can be used with almost any group of students. Members of a group approach the problem as an adventure in thinking and apply it to whatever background they can muster. Background experience may enrich a student's approach to the problem but is not crucial to the use or understanding of the evidence presented to him or her. Figure 8.7 is a Level II inquiry about locating a colony. As a class, do the inquiry now.

provides four main categories of these thinking processes and illustrates the place of each within the inquiry cycle.

Project-Centered Learning: Guiding Learning from Independent and Group Investigations, Papers, and Oral Reports

For the most meaningful student learning to occur, **independent study**, individual writing, student-centered projects, and oral reports should be major features of your instruction. There will be times when the students are interested in an in-depth inquiry of a topic and will want to pursue a particular topic for study. This undertaking of a learning project can be flexible: an individual student, a team of two, a small group, or the entire class can do the investigation. The *project* is a relatively long-term investigative study from which students produce something called the *culminating presentation*. It is a way for students to apply what they are learning. The culminating presentation is a final presentation that usually includes an oral and written report accompanied by a hands-on item of some kind (e.g., a display, play or skit, book, song or poem, multimedia presentation, diorama, poster, map, chart, and so on). Some high schools have adopted what they call the Senior Project, which is required for graduation,[25] as a culminating experience and exhibition of student learning.

Values and Purposes of Project-Centered Learning

The values and purposes of encouraging project-centered learning are to do the following:

■ Develop individual skills in cooperation and social interaction.

F i g u r e 8 . 7   **Locating a Colony: A Level II Inquiry**

Presentation of the Problem. In groups of three or four, students receive the following information.

Background. You (your group is considered as one person) are one of 120 passengers on the ship, the *Prince Charles*. You left England 12 weeks ago. You have experienced many hardships, including a stormy passage, limited rations, sickness, cold and damp weather, and hot, foul air below deck. Ten of your fellow immigrants to the New World, including three children, have died and been buried at sea. You are now anchored at an uncertain place, off the coast of the New World, which your captain believes to be somewhere north of the Virginia Grants. Seas are so rough and food so scarce that you and your fellow passengers have decided to settle here. A landing party has returned with a map they made of the area. You, as one of the elders, must decide at once where the settlement is to be located. The tradesmen want to settle along the river, which is deep, even though this seems to be the season of low water levels. Within ten months they expect deep-water ships from England with more colonists and merchants. Those within your group who are farmers say they must have fertile, workable land. The officer in charge of the landing party reported seeing a group of armed natives who fled when approached. He feels the settlement must be located so that it can be defended from the natives and from the sea.

Directions, step one: You (your group) are to select a site on the attached map which you feel is best suited for a colony. Your site must satisfy the different factions aboard the ship. A number of possible sites are already marked on the map (letters *A–G*). You may select one of these locations or use them as reference points to show the location of your colony. When your group has selected its site, list and explain the reasons for your choice. When each group has arrived at its tentative decision, these will be shared with the whole class.

Directions, step two: After each group has made its presentation and argument, a class debate is held about where the colony should be located.

Notes to teacher: For the debate, have a large map drawn on the writing board or on an overhead transparency, where each group's mark can be made for all to see and discuss. After each group has presented its argument for its location and against the others, we suggest that you then mark on the large map the two, three, or more hypothetical locations (assuming that, as a class,

there yet is no single favorite location). Then take a straw vote of the students, allowing each to vote on his or her own, independently rather than as members of groups. At this time you can terminate the activity by saying that if the majority of students favor one location, then that, in fact, is the solution to the problem—that is, the colony is located wherever the majority of class members believe it should be. No sooner will that statement be made by you than someone will ask, "Are we correct?" or "What is the right answer?" They will ask such questions because, as students in school, they are used to solving problems that have right answers (Level I inquiry teaching). In real-world problems, however, there are no "right" answers, though some answers may seem better than others. It is the process of problem solving that is important. You want your students to develop confidence in their ability to solve problems and understand the tentativeness of "answers" to real-life problems.

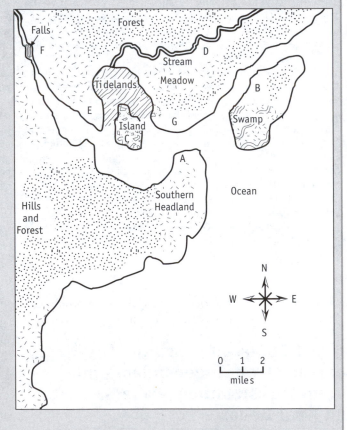

SOURCE: Adapted by permission from unpublished material provided by Jennifer Devine Pfeifer and Dennis Devine.

■ Develop student skills in writing, communication, and higher-level thinking and doing.

■ Foster student engagement and independent learning and thinking skills.

■ Optimize personal meaning of the learning to each student by considering, valuing, and accommodating individual interests, learning styles, learning capacities, and life experiences.

■ Provide opportunity for each student to become especially knowledgeable and experienced in one area of subject content or in one process skill, thus adding to the student's knowledge and experience base and sense of importance and self-worth.

- Provide opportunity for students to become intrinsically motivated to learn because they are working on topics of personal meaning, with outcomes and even timelines that are relatively open ended.

- Provide opportunity for students to make decisions about their own learning and to develop their skills in managing time and materials.

- Provide opportunity for students to make some sort of a real contribution.

As has been demonstrated time and again, when students choose their own projects, integrating knowledge as the need arises, motivation and learning follow naturally.[26]

GUIDELINES FOR GUIDING STUDENTS IN PROJECT-CENTERED LEARNING In collaboration with the teacher, students select a topic for the project. What you can do is to stimulate ideas and provide sample model studies. You can stimulate ideas by providing lists of things students might do; by mentioning each time an idea comes up in class that this would be a good idea for an independent, small-group, or class project; by having former students tell about their projects; by showing the results of other students' projects; by suggesting Internet resources and readings that are likely to give students ideas; and by using class discussions to brainstorm ideas.

Sometimes a teacher will write the general problem or topic in the center of a graphic web and ask the students to brainstorm some questions that will lead to ways for students to investigate, draw sketches, construct models, record findings, predict items, compare and contrast, and discuss understandings. In essence, brainstorming such as this is the technique often used by teachers in collaboration with students for the selection of an interdisciplinary thematic unit of study.

Allow students to individually choose whether they will work alone, in pairs, or in small groups. If they choose to work in groups, then help them delineate job descriptions for each member of the group. For project work, groups of four or fewer students usually work better than groups of more than four. Even if the project is one the whole class is pursuing, the project should be broken down into parts with individuals or small groups of students undertaking independent study of these parts.

You can keep track of the students' progress by reviewing weekly updates of their work. Set deadlines with the groups. Meet with groups daily to discuss any questions or problems they have. Based on their investigations, the students will prepare and present their findings in culminating presentations.

Provide coaching and guidance. Work with each student or student team in topic selection as well as in the processes of written and oral reporting. Allow students to develop their own procedures but guide their preparation of work outlines and preliminary drafts, giving them constructive feedback and encouragement along the way. Aid students

in their identification of potential resources and in the techniques of research. Your coordination with the library and other resource centers is central to the success of project-centered teaching. Frequent drafts and progress reports from the students are a must. During each of these stages, provide students with constructive feedback and encouragement. Provide written guidelines and negotiate timelines for the outlines, drafts, and the completed project.

Promote sharing. Insist that students share both the progress and the results of their study with the rest of the class. The value of this type of instructional strategy comes not only from individual contributions but also from the learning that results from the experience and the communication of that experience with others.

Without careful planning and unless students are given steady guidance, project-based teaching can be a frustrating experience for both the teacher and the students, not to mention a beginning teacher who is inexperienced in such an undertaking. Students should choose and do projects because they want to and because the project seems meaningful. Therefore, students with guidance from you should decide *what* project to do and *how* to do it. Your role is to advise and guide students so they experience success. There must be a balance between structure and opportunities for student choices and decision making. Without frequent reports on progress by the student and guidance and reinforcement from the teacher, a student can get frustrated and quickly lose interest in the project.

WRITING SHOULD BE A REQUIRED COMPONENT OF PROJECT-CENTERED LEARNING Provide options but insist that writing be a part of each student's work. Research examining the links among writing, thinking, and learning has helped emphasize the importance of writing. Writing is a complex intellectual behavior and process that helps the learner create and record his or her understanding—that is, construct meaning. So, insist that writing be a part of the student's work (see the section that follows).

When teachers use project-centered teaching, a paper and an oral presentation are usually automatically required of all students. It is recommended that you use the *I-Search paper* instead of the traditional research paper. Using the I-Search paper method, under your careful guidance, the student (a) lists things that he or she would like to know and from the list selects one that becomes the research topic; (b) conducts the study while maintaining a log of activities and findings that, in fact, becomes a process journal; (c) prepares a booklet that presents the student's findings and that consists of paragraphs and visual representations; (d) prepares a summary of the findings, including the significance of the study and the student's personal feelings; and (e) shares the project as a final oral report with the teacher and classmates.

ASSESS THE FINAL PRODUCT The final product of the project, including papers, oral reports, and presentations, should be graded. The method of determining the grade should be clear to students from the beginning as well as the weight of the project grade toward the term grade. Provide students with clear descriptions (**rubrics**) of how evaluation and grading will be done. (See Chapter 11 for sample rubrics.) **Evaluation** should include meeting deadlines for drafts and progress reports. The final grade for the study should be based on four criteria: (1) how well it was organized, including meeting draft deadlines; (2) the quality and quantity of both content and procedural knowledge gained from the experience; (3) the quality of the students' sharing of that learning experience with the rest of the class; and (4) the quality of the students' final written or oral report.

Writing across the Curriculum

Because writing is a discrete representation of thinking, every teacher should consider himself or herself to be a teacher of writing. In exemplary schools, student writing is encouraged in all subjects across the curriculum.

Kinds of Writing

A student should experience a variety of kinds of writing rather than the same form, class after class, year after year. Perhaps most important is that writing should be emphasized as a process that illustrates one's thinking rather than solely as a product completed as an assignment. Writing and thinking develop best when a student experiences during any school day various forms of writing to express his or her ideas, such as the following:

Analysis. The writer speculates about the causes and effects of a specific event.

Autobiographical incident. The writer narrates a specific event in his or her life and states or implies the significance of the event.

Evaluation. The writer presents a judgment on the worth of an item—book, movie, art work, or consumer product—and supports this with reasons and evidence.

Eyewitness account. The writer tells about a person, group, or event that was objectively observed from the outside.

Firsthand biographical sketch. Through incident and description, the writer characterizes a person he or she knows well.

Problem solving. The writer describes and analyzes a specific problem and then proposes and argues for a solution.

Report of information. The writer collects data from observation and research and chooses material that best represents a phenomenon or concept.

Story. Using dialogue and description, the writer shows conflict between characters or between a character and the environment.

Student Journals

Many teachers across the curriculum have their students maintain journals in which the students keep a log of their activities, findings, and thoughts (i.e., *process journals*, as previously discussed) and write their thoughts about what it is they are studying (*response journals*). Actually, two types of response journals are commonly used: *dialogue journals* and reading-response journals. Dialogue journals are used for students to write anything that is on their minds, usually on the right side of a page, while peers, teachers, and parents or guardians respond on the left side of a page, thereby "talking with" the journal writer. Response journals are used for students to write (and perhaps draw—a "visual learning log") their reactions to what is being studied.

Purpose and Assessment of Student Journal Writing

Normally, academic journals are not personal diaries with the writer's recollection of daily events and thoughts about the events. Rather, the purpose of journal writing is to encourage students to write, to think about their writing, to record their creative thoughts about *what they are learning*, and to share their written thoughts with an audience—all of which help in the development of their thinking skills, in their learning, and in their development as writers. Students are encouraged to write about experiences, both in school and out, that are related to the topics being studied. They should be encouraged to record their feelings about what and how they are learning.

Journal writing provides practice in expression and should not be graded by the teacher. Negative comments and evaluations from the teacher will discourage creative and spontaneous expression by students. Teachers should read the journal writing and then offer constructive and positive feedback, but teachers should avoid making negative comments or grading the journals. For grading purposes, most teachers simply record whether a student does, in fact, maintain the required journal. The National Council of Teachers of English (NCTE) has developed guidelines for journal writing. Your school English/language arts department may have a copy of these guidelines, or you can contact NCTE directly or via the Internet.

Learning by Educational Games

Educational games include a wide variety of learning activities, such as simulations, role-play and sociodrama activities, mind games, board games, computer games, and sporting games, all of which provide valuable learning experiences for participants. That is, they are experiences that tend to involve several senses and several learning modalities, tend to engage higher-order thinking skills, and tend to be quite effective as learning tools.

Of all the arts, drama involves the learner-participant most fully—intellectually, emotionally, physically, verbally, and socially. Interactive drama, which is role playing, a simplified form of drama, is a method by which students can become involved with literature. Studies show that comprehension increases and students are highly motivated to read if they are involved in analyzing and actively responding to the characters, plot, and setting of the story being read.

Cindy was a French major who completed her student-teaching assignment at Newberg High School in Oregon during the spring 2005 semester. Thanks to Madame Hammond, the school had a thriving French department. Cindy had responsibility for three different preps: French I, French II, and French IV. She decided to complete the required unit for her student teaching in French I. She developed a two-week clothing unit. To help students learn the vocabulary, Cindy created flash cards with pictures of the different articles of clothing being introduced. She also designed posters and other visual aids that showed her students how the vocabulary words were spelled in the target language. Students played Vocabulary Bingo and wrote and performed short dialogues. Cindy had students complete the exercises in the textbook to practice their written and spoken skills. She also had them listen to *dictées* and read short excerpts. Students were expected to identify clothing when the article was seen or the word for it was spoken. Cindy prepared quizzes to review the vocabulary associated with the various articles of clothing, including the colors, the seasons, activities, and the simple present tense.

For the culminating activity of the unit, the students prepared a fashion show. Students were paired in dyads. One partner was the model, the other the announcer. Together the partners selected a theme, music, and wardrobe and prepared a detailed description of the model's apparel. Student models were to dress for a certain occasion, and the announcer was expected to describe the style and colors of the clothing and the accessories while his or her partner showed off what he or she was wearing. The categories included A Day at the Beach, Back-to-School Duds, Hit the Slopes, The Après Ski Party, Comfort First, Just Chillin', Rockin' Out, and All Dolled Up.

The day of the fashion show, Cindy rolled out a runner of red craft paper to pave the runway that crossed the classroom floor. The students donned oversized glasses, striped toe socks, painted ties, fake furs, and funny hats. The class assistant served as the disc jockey. As the music played, the models sashayed down the runway. When the models reached the end of the runway, they turned around and then showed off their fashions as their partners read the corresponding descriptions. The students enjoyed acting like divas as they competed for prizes. They practiced their vocabulary and expressed their creativity with this innovative, fun lesson. Cindy and her cooperating teacher were very happy with the results.

Simulations, a more complex form of drama, serve many of the developmental needs of young people. They provide for interaction with peers and allow students to work together on a common project. They engage students in physical activity and give them an opportunity to try out different roles, helping them to better understand themselves. Role-play simulations can provide concrete experiences that help students to understand complex concepts and issues, and they provide opportunities for exploring values and developing skill in decision making.

Educational games can play an integral role in interdisciplinary teaching and serve as valuable resources for enriching the effectiveness of students' learning. As with any other instructional strategy, the use of games should follow a clear educational purpose, have a careful plan, and be congruent with the instructional objectives.

Purposes of Educational Games

Games can be powerful tools for teaching and learning. A game can have one to several of the following purposes: (a) add variety and change of pace, (b) assess student learning, (c) enhance student self-esteem, (d) motivate students, (e) offer a break from the usual rigors of learning, (f) provide learning about real-life issues through simulation and role playing, (g) provide learning through tactile and kinesthetic modalities, (h) provide problem-solving situations and experiences, (i) provide skill development and motivation through computer usage, (j) provide skill development in inductive thinking, (k) provide skill development in verbal communication and debate, (l) reinforce convergent thinking, (m) review and reinforce subject matter learning, (n) encourage learning through peer interaction, (o) stimulate critical thinking, (p) stimulate deductive thinking, (q) stimulate divergent and creative thinking, and (r) teach both content and process. Sources for useful educational games include professional journals (see Figure 8.8) and the Internet. Now complete Activity 8.4 to learn about Grammar Punk, a fun, innovative way to teach middle and secondary students grammar and punctuation.

Integrating Strategies for Integrated Learning

In today's exemplary classrooms, instructional strategies are combined to establish the most effective teaching-learning experience. For example, in an integrated middle school language-arts program, teachers are interested in their students' speaking, reading, listening, thinking, study, and writing skills. These skills (and not textbooks) form a holistic process that is the primary aspect of integrated language arts.

In the area of speaking skills, oral discourse (discussion) in the classroom has a growing research base that promotes methods of teaching and learning through oral language. These methods include cooperative learning, instructional scaffolding, and inquiry teaching.

In cooperative learning groups, students discuss and use language for learning that benefits both their content learning and their skills in social interaction. Working in heterogeneous groups, students participate in their own learning and can extend their knowledge base and cultural awareness with students of different backgrounds. When students share information and ideas, they are completing

Figure 8.8 Sample Professional Journal Articles and Web Sites on Educational Games and Simulations

- N. Balasubramanian and B. G. Wilson, Games and Simulations, http://site.aace.org/pubs/foresite/GamesAndSimulations/.pdf
- J. Bassett, The Pullman Strike of 1894, *OAH Magazine of History 11*(2), 34–41 (Winter 1997).
- D. Bogan and D. Wood, Simulating Sun, Moon, and Earth Patterns, *Science Scope 21*(2), 46, 48 (October 1997).
- J. Collom, Illot-Mollo and Other Games, *Teachers & Writers 30*(5), 12–13 (May/June 1999). Instructions for two word games useful in secondary writing classrooms.
- C. Collyer, Winter Secrets: An Instant Lesson Plan, *Pathways: The Ontario Journal of Outdoor Education 9*(2), 18–20 (April 1997). Instructions for two games about predator-prey relationships.
- S. A. Farin, Acting Atoms, *Science Scope 21*(3), 46 (November/December 1997).
- J. Gorman, Strategy Games: Treasures From Ancient Times, *Mathematics Teaching in the Middle School 3*(2), 110–116 (October 1997). Presents several games for integrating history and mathematics.
- S. Hightshoe, Sifting through the Sands of Time: A Simulated Archaeological Special Feature, *Social Studies and the Young Learner 9*(3), 28–30 (January/February 1997).
- M. J. Howle, Play-Party Games in the Modern Classroom, *Music Educators Journal 83*(5), 24–28 (March 1997). Introduces games that were popular on the 19th-century American frontier.
- T. Levy, The Amistad Incident: A Classroom Reenactment, *Social Education 59*(5), 303–308 (September 1995).
- T. M. McCann, A Pioneer Simulation for Writing and for the Study of Literature, *English Journal 85*(3), 62–67 (March 1996).
- H. Morris, Universal Games from A to Z, *Mathematics in School 26*(4), 35–40 (September 1997). See also F. Tapson, Mathematical Games, pp. 2–6 of same issue.
- K. D. Owens et al., Playing to Learn: Science Games in the Classroom, *Science Scope 20*(5), 31–33 (February 1997).
- R. J. Quinn and L. R. Wiest, Exploring Probability through an Evens-Odds Dice Game, *Mathematics Teaching in the Middle School 4*(6), 358–362 (March 1999).
- J. V. Vort, Our Town's Planning Commission Meeting, *Journal of Geography 96*(4), 183–190 (July/August 1997).

Activity 8.4

Teaching Grammar

Most teachers hate teaching it; most students hate learning it. At the MEA/MFT (Montana Education Association/Montana Federation of Teachers) annual 2007 conference in Belgrade, MT, participating teachers were entertained by Sam Beeson's lively presentation on Grammar Punk. Beeson is a high school English teacher at American Fork High School in American Fork, UT, author of *Kissing Kringle* and *Santa's First Flight*, and the creator of the popular Grammar Punk Curriculum and Dice System. This grammar program was designed for students in grades 7 through 12, and the Grammar Punk Curriculum and Dice System also is frequently used in freshman and sophomore college writing courses as well as in high school classrooms. In fact, Beeson has field-tested Grammar Punk with students ranging from second graders to college students as well as with both native and non-native English speakers.

When Beeson first started teaching, he was surprised and horrified to find out that as an English teacher he was responsible for teaching grammar. He was prepared with lessons on American and British literature, but he wasn't sure how to make grammar accessible to all his students in order to help them improve their written communication skills. After consulting the research on how grammar has been traditionally taught and the lack of

transfer to students' writing, Beeson became very frustrated. He found that students not only despised learning grammar but also often retained and applied very little of what they were taught. So he developed the Grammar Punk Curriculum, which explains all the rules and the basics of grammar and punctuation in a creative, hands-on manner to which students respond very positively. Beeson believes better command of grammar rules helps students become better writers. Beeson's goal, to make grammar and punctuation understandable and fun, resulted in this unique curriculum; with Grammar Punk, students master grammar rules and improve their writing skills.

Apply Your Knowledge

Check out the Grammar Punk curriculum and resources and what teachers think of the program at the following websites:

Grammar Punk
http://www.grammarpunk.com

UEA Convention Brings Teachers Together
http://www.heraldextra.com/content/view/196514/4

difficult learning tasks, using divergent thinking and decision making, and developing their understanding of concepts. As issues are presented and responses are challenged, student thinking is clarified. Students assume the responsibility for planning within the group and for carrying out their assignments. When needed, the teacher models an

activity with one group in front of the class, and when integrated with student questions, the modeling can become inquiry teaching. Activities can include the following:

- *Brainstorming.* Members generate ideas related to a key word and record them. Clustering or chunking, mapping, and the Venn diagram (all discussed in the following text) are variations of brainstorming.

■ *Chunking or clustering.* Groups of students apply mental organizers by clustering information into chunks for easier manipulation and remembering.

■ *Memory strategies.* The teacher and students model the use of acronyms, mnemonics, rhymes, or clustering of information into categories to promote learning. Sometimes, such as in memorizing one's Social Security number, one must learn information by rote, that is, without any connection to any prior knowledge. To do that, it is helpful to break the information to be learned into smaller chunks, such as dividing the nine-digit Social Security number into smaller chunks of information (with, in this instance, each chunk separated by a hyphen). Learning by rote is also easier if one can connect that which is to be memorized to some prior knowledge. Strategies such as these are used to bridge the gap between rote learning and meaningful learning and are known as *mnemonics.* Mnemonic devices include acronyms, rap, music, and peg systems. Sample mnemonics are the following:

  ■ The notes on a treble staff are FACE for the space notes and Empty Garbage Before Dad Flips (EGBDF) for the line notes. The notes on the bass staff are All Cows Eat Granola Bars (ACEGB) or Grizzly Bears Don't Fly Airplanes (GBDFA).

  ■ The order of the planets from the Sun are My Very Educated Mother Just Served Us Nine Pizzas (Mercury, Venus, Earth, Mars, Jupiter, Saturn, Uranus, Neptune, and Pluto—although, in reality, Pluto and Neptune alternate in this order because of their elliptical orbits).

  ■ The names of the Great Lakes: HOMES for Huron, Ontario, Michigan, Erie, and Superior.

  ■ Visual mnemonics are useful too, such as remembering that Italy is shaped in the form of a boot.

■ *Comparing and contrasting.* Similarities and differences between items are found and recorded.

■ *Visual tools.* A variety of terms describing the visual tools useful for learning have been invented terms (some of which are synonymous), such as brainstorming web, mind-mapping web, spider map, cluster, concept map, cognitive map, semantic map, Venn diagram, visual scaffold, and graphic organizer. Visual tools are separated into three categories, according to purpose: (a) *brainstorming tools* (such as mind mapping, webbing, and clustering) for developing one's knowledge and creativity; (b) *task-specific organizers* (such as life cycle diagrams used in biology, decision trees used in mathematics, and text structures used in reading); and (c) *thinking process maps* (such as concept mapping) for encouraging cognitive development across disciplines.[27] It is the latter about which we are interested here.

Based on Ausubel's theory of meaningful learning,[28] thinking process mapping has been found useful for helping students change their prior notions—their misconceptions, sometimes referred to as *naïve views.* It can help students in their ability to organize and represent their thoughts as well as to connect new knowledge to their past experiences and precepts.[29] Simply put, *concepts* can be thought of as classifications that attempt to organize the world of objects and events into a smaller number of categories. In everyday usage, the term *concept* means "idea," as when someone says, "My concept of love is not the same as yours." Concepts embody a meaning that develops in complexity with experience and learning over time. For example, the concept of love that is held by a second grader is unlikely to be as complex as that held by a ninth grader. Thinking process mapping is a graphical way of demonstrating the relationships among concepts.

Typically, a thinking process map refers to a visual or graphic representation of concepts with bridges (connections) that show relationships. Figure 8.9 shows a partially complete thinking process map in social studies, where students have made connections of concept relationships related to fruit farming and marketing. The general procedure for thinking process mapping is to have the students (a) identify important concepts in materials being studied, often by circling them; (b) rank order the concepts from the most general to the most specific; and (c) arrange the concepts on a sheet of paper, connect related ideas with lines, and define the connections between the related ideas.

Other activities include the following:

■ *Inferring.* For instance, students assume the roles of people (real or fictional) and infer their motives, personalities, and thoughts.

■ *Outlining.* Each group completes an outline that contains some of the main ideas but with subtopics omitted.

■ *Paraphrasing.* In a brief summary, each student restates a short selection of what was read or heard.

■ *Reciprocal teaching.* In classroom dialogue, students take turns generating questions, summarizing, clarifying, and predicting.[30]

■ *Study strategies.* Important strategies that should be taught explicitly include vocabulary expansion, reading and interpreting graphic information, locating resources, using advance organizers, adjusting one's reading rate, and skimming, scanning, and study reading.[31]

■ *Textbook study strategies.* Students use the SQ4R or related study strategies (see Chapter 5).

■ *Vee mapping.* This road map is completed by students as they learn, showing the route they follow from prior knowledge to new and future knowledge.

■ *Venn diagramming.* This is a technique for comparing two concepts or, for example, two stories to show similarities and differences. Using stories as an example, a student is asked to draw two circles that intersect and to mark the circles 1 and 2 and the area where they intersect 3. In circle 1, the student lists characteristics of one story, and in circle 2 he or she lists the characteristics of the

Figure 8.9   **Sample of a Partially Completed Thinking Process Map**

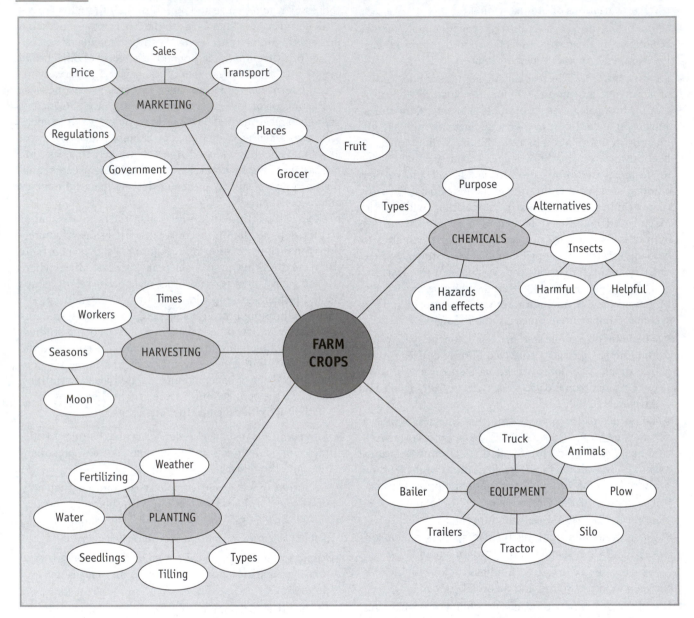

second story. In the area of the intersection, marked 3, the student lists characteristics common to both stories.

■ *Visual learning log (VLL).* This is another kind of road map completed by students showing the route they follow from prior knowledge to new and future knowledge, except that the VLL consists of pictograms (free-form drawings) that each student makes and that are maintained in a journal. Now, to further explore inquiry teaching and integrated learning, do Exercise 8.5.

Summary

You have learned about the importance of learning modalities, active learning, and instructional modes as well as about the importance of creating an accepting and

supportive learning environment. You have learned important principles of teaching and learning.

This chapter has initiated the development of a repertoire of teaching strategies necessary for you to become an effective teacher. As you know, many students can be quite peer conscious, have relatively short attention spans, and prefer active learning experiences that engage many of their senses. Most are intensely curious about things of interest to them. Cooperative learning, independent study, and teaching strategies that emphasize shared inquiry and discovery within a psychologically safe environment encourage the most positive aspects of thinking and learning. Central to your strategy selection should be those strategies that encourage students to become independent thinkers and skilled learners who can help in the planning, structuring, regulating, and assessing of their own learning and learning activities.

In this chapter, we presented and discussed a number of teaching strategies that all have two common elements: social interaction and problem solving. These teaching strategies require students to interact with one another and to draw conclusions, learn concepts, and form generalizations through induction, deduction, and observation or through application of principles. The premises underlying these methods are (a) that a person learns to think by thinking and sharing his or her thoughts with others, thereby obtaining feedback and doing further thinking, and (b) that knowledge gained through active learning and self-discovery is more meaningful, permanent, and transferable than knowledge obtained through expository techniques.

The strategies that have been presented in this chapter are not easy to implement. Using them effectively and without classroom control problems requires conviction and careful preparation. Even then, there may need to be a period of trial and error before you perfect your skills in their implementation. Yet techniques that use cooperative learning, problem solving, and discovery are important teaching tools. They are absolutely worth the effort, time, and potential frustrations that can occur for the beginning teacher who deviates from the traditional, teacher-centered strategies. Such expository methods of instruction are presented in Chapter 9.

Exercise
8.1

Meaningful Direct Experiences

Instructions: The purpose of this exercise is for you to reflect on your past direct experiences. Recall a lesson from your middle or secondary schooling when you learned by doing something. Include the following details: grade, course, lesson duration, and disciplines integrated. Then answer the following questions and share your responses with your classmates.

1. Why do you remember this particular direct experience?
2. What did you experience?
3. How could the experience have been better?
4. Which learning modalities were embedded in the direct experience? Explain how the various sensory preferences were addressed.

Exercise
8.2

A Reflection on My Past Involvement with Student-Centered Instructional Activities

Instructions: The purpose of this exercise is for you to reflect on your past involvement in participatory activities and then to share those thoughts with your classmates. To that end, this exercise contains a list of such activities.

1. For each activity, write *F* if you are familiar with it, *E* if you have observed it effectively used by a teacher, and *L* if as a student it was an activity that you liked. You may use any one, two, or all three of the letter codes in your response to each activity.

_____ Brainstorming	_____ Discovery	_____ Jury trial	_____ Roundtable discussion
_____ Buzz session	_____ Discussion, whole class	_____ Learning activity center	_____ Simulation
_____ Case study	_____ Field trip	_____ Panel discussion	_____ Sociodrama
_____ Committee	_____ Fishbowl	_____ Project or independent study	_____ Symposium
_____ Cooperative learning	_____ Forum		
_____ Debate	_____ Inquiry	_____ Role playing	

2. Share your marks and experiences with your classmates in small groups of three or four per group.
3. As you study this chapter, try to engage in various group activities with your classmates. Assume the various roles discussed. Keep records of involvement and interaction. Perhaps ask someone to serve each time as observer to help you analyze the process and its effectiveness. As you gain knowledge and experience about these various student-centered activities, consider how you might use them in your own teaching.

Exercise
8.3
Recalling My Own Learning Experiences in College

Instructions: The purpose of this exercise is to recall and share learning experiences from your own college days. Reflect on those with respect to their relationship to the Learning Experiences Ladder and the discussion of the access and delivery modes of instruction.

1. Recall one vivid learning experience from each level of your college schooling and identify its position on the Learning Experiences Ladder (Figure 8.2).

   College experience:

   Position on ladder:

2. Was the access or delivery mode used?

3. List the weaknesses and the strengths of the mode used.

4. Share with classmates in small groups. After sharing your experiences with others of your group, what, if anything, can your group conclude? Write down those conclusions and then share them with the entire class.

Exercise
8.4
Cooperative Learning Groups

Instructions: The purpose of this exercise is for you to reflect on a positive experience working in a cooperative learning group. Reflect back on your participation in a cooperative learning group during your middle or secondary schooling. Then answer the following questions and share your responses with your classmates.

1. What roles were included in the cooperative learning group you participated in? What was the task at hand? How long did you work in the group? What was the culminating product the cooperative learning group was expected to produce? How were you graded?

2. One common complaint about cooperative learning groups is that everyone does not pull his or her weight. Students often say that they feel they do most of the work while other members are off-task or uninvolved. How can you address these concerns if you ask your students to participate in cooperative learning groups?

3. Identify the advantages and disadvantages of cooperative learning groups. Brainstorm the advantages and disadvantages from the students' and the teacher's perspective.

Exercise
8.5
A Study of Inquiry and Strategy Integration

Instructions: The purpose of this exercise is for you to experience a Level II inquiry, to analyze the Locating a Colony inquiry (Figure 8.7) and the preceding discussion about integrating strategies, and to synthesize that information for use in your own teaching. We suggest that you first answer the questions of this exercise and then share your answers with others in your discipline (in groups of about four). Finally, share your group's collective responses with the entire class.

1. My subject field:

2. a. How I could use the Locating a Colony inquiry in my subject field (for what purpose, goals, or objectives):

   b. Content in my subject field that students might be expected to learn from doing the Locating a Colony inquiry:

3. How I could involve my students in cooperative learning while doing the Locating a Colony inquiry:

4. How brainstorming could be used while doing the Locating a Colony inquiry:

5. How clustering could be used while doing the Locating a Colony inquiry:

6. How thinking process mapping could be used while doing the Locating a Colony inquiry:

7. How comparing and contrasting could be used while doing the Locating a Colony inquiry:

8. How outlining could be used while doing the Locating a Colony inquiry:

9. How paraphrasing could be used while doing the Locating a Colony inquiry:

10. How summarizing could be used while doing the Locating a Colony inquiry:

11. How memory strategies could be used while doing the Locating a Colony inquiry:

12. How inferring could be used while doing the Locating a Colony inquiry:

13. What other skills could be taught while doing the Locating a Colony inquiry? For each, briefly describe how.

Chapter 8   POSTTEST

Short Explanation

1. Explain when and why vicarious student learning experiences are appropriate.

2. Describe the steps to critical thinking and problem solving. Describe a situation in your own teaching where you would engage your students in critical thinking and problem solving.

3. Explain the concept of hands-on, minds-on learning.

4. Explain the advantages and disadvantages of project-centered teaching and learning in your subject field.

5. Explain the rationale for using cooperative learning groups in teaching. Do you believe that the use of cooperative learning groups enhances or impedes the learning of students who are identified as being academically gifted and talented? Explain your answer and reason for it.

Essay

1. Explain why you agree or disagree with the statement: Every teacher should emphasize skill development in reading, writing, thinking, and studying.

2. Do you accept the view that achievement in school learning is the product of creative inquiry through social interaction with the students as active participants in that inquiry? Explain why you do or do not agree.

3. From your current observations and fieldwork related to this teacher preparation program, clearly identify one specific example of educational practice that seems contradictory to exemplary practice or theory presented in this chapter. Present your explanation for the discrepancy.

4. Is problem solving a teaching strategy or a way of thinking? Explain.

5. Describe any prior concepts you held that changed as a result of the experiences of this chapter. Describe the changes.

Teacher-Centered Instructional Strategies

Alamy Images

Creating hope in oneself as a teacher and nourishing or rekindling it in one's students is the central issue educators face these days. After 30 years of teaching and trying to reform public schools while continuing to work in the framework of hope, I have had to examine the sources of my hope as well as my struggles with the temptation to despair and quit. This examination has taken me on a personal journey that has led to some ideas about how hope can be instilled and nurtured in young people. One of the most powerful of those ideas concerns the value of imagination in creating hope. The first step in gaining that value is to create an environment in which the imagination can thrive.[1]

—HERBERT KOHL

Specific Objectives

At the completion of this chapter, you will be able to:

▸ Demonstrate your knowledge and skill in using teacher talk and questioning as instructional strategies.

▸ Describe techniques for using student recitations and classroom demonstrations effectively.

▸ Explain your understanding of using homework and assignments for meaningful learning.

▸ Confirm your awareness of the importance of equality in the classroom and ways of ensuring it.

▸ Evidence your awareness of the importance of student questioning, memorizing, and reviewing to learning.

Chapter 9 Overview

In this chapter, we consider teaching methods that are basically expository in nature, such as lecturing, whole-class discussion and recitation, questioning, and demonstrating. All of these methods are largely or usually teacher centered; their basic purpose is to deliver information to students. Although strategies presented in this chapter are somewhat easier to implement than the student-centered strategies covered in Chapter 8 because classroom control is more easily managed, they are no less difficult to master. As a consequence, there are, perhaps, more boring classes taught by ineffective teachers using teacher-centered approaches than there are by ineffective teachers using student-centered approaches.

Therefore, to use teacher-centered instructional strategies effectively, you need to become skilled in their use and either mix them with strategies that are more student centered or make the strategies themselves more student centered. In this chapter, we discuss the importance of ensuring equality in the classroom, present guidelines for the use of assignments and homework, and discuss the significance of students memorizing and reviewing material that is being studied.

Introduction

Consider again the potential strengths and weaknesses of teacher-centered instruction, as presented in Figure 8.1 in Chapter 8. The strengths include (a) much content can be covered within a short span of time, (b) the teacher has great control over the content covered and the time allotted, and (c) student achievement of specific content is predictable and manageable.

The weaknesses include (a) the sources of student motivation are mostly extrinsic, (b) students have little control over pacing and make few important decisions about their learning, (c) opportunity for divergent or creative thinking is lacking, and (d) student self-esteem may be inadequately served. Here we will cover teacher talk, demonstrations, recitations, questioning, leading classroom discussions, and using homework and assignments in depth.

Teacher Talk: Formal and Informal

Teacher talk encompasses both lecturing *to* students and talking *with* students. A lecture is considered formal teacher talk, whereas a discussion with students is considered informal teacher talk.

Cautions in Using Teacher Talk

Whether your talk is formal or informal, there are certain cautions that you need to keep in mind. Perhaps the most important is that of *talking too much*. If a teacher talks too much, the significance of the teacher's words may be lost because some students will tune the teacher out.

Another caution is to avoid *talking too fast*. Remember, the material you are covering is probably new to students, and they are hearing it for the first time. Besides, students can hear faster than they can understand what they hear. It is a good idea to remind yourself to talk slowly and to check frequently for student comprehension of what you are talking about. By *frequent checks for comprehension*, we mean, on the average, at least one check per minute. Checks for comprehension can be in the form of questions you ask and those the students ask during the lesson as well as various kinds of checklists.

It is also important to remember that students respond to sensory input (auditory in this instance) at different rates. Because of this, you will need to pause to let words sink in, and you will need to pause during transitions from one point or activity to the next.

A third caution is to be sure you are *being heard and understood*. Sometimes teachers talk in too low a pitch or use words that are not understood by many of the students or both. You should vary the pitch of your voice, and you should stop and help students with their understanding of vocabulary that may be new to them. Remember, as discussed in Part 1, if you have students in your class who are English Language Learners, then you need to help them learn what is essentially two new vocabularies—the vocabulary of the English language in general and the vocabulary that is unique to the subject you teach.

A fourth caution is to *remember* that *just because students have heard something before does not necessarily mean that they understand it or have learned it*. From our earlier discussions of learning experiences (such as the Learning Experiences Ladder in Figure 8.3 in Chapter 8), remember that although verbal communication is an important form of communication, because of its reliance on the use of abstract symbolization it is not a very *reliable* form of communication. Teacher talk relies on words and on skill in listening, a skill that is not mastered by many adolescents (or, for that matter, even many adults). Therefore, to ensure student understanding, it is good to reinforce your teacher talk with either direct or simulated learning experiences.

Related to that is yet another caution—*to resist believing that students have attained a skill or have learned something that was taught previously by you or by another teacher*. During any discussion (formal or informal), rather than assuming that your students know something, you should ensure they know it. For example, if the discussion and a student activity involve a particular thinking skill, then you will want to make sure that students know how to use that skill (thinking skills are discussed later in this chapter).

Still another problem is *talking in a humdrum monotone*. Students need teachers whose voices exude enthusiasm and excitement (although not to be overdone) about the subject and about teaching and learning. Such enthusiasm and excitement for learning are infectious. A voice that demonstrates enthusiasm for teaching and learning is more likely to motivate students to learn.

Keep these cautions in mind as you study the general principles and specific guidelines for the productive and effective use of teacher talk.

Teacher Talk: General Guidelines

Certain general guidelines should be followed whether your talk is formal or informal. First, *begin the talk with an advance organizer*. **Advance organizers** are introductions that mentally prepare students for a study by helping them make connections with material already learned or experienced—a *comparative organizer*—or by providing students with a conceptual arrangement of what is to be learned—an *expository organizer*.[2] The value of using advance organizers is well documented by research.[3] An advance organizer can be a brief introduction or statement about the main idea you intend to convey and how it is related to other aspects of the students' learning (an expository organizer), or it can be a presentation of a discrepancy to arouse curiosity (a comparative organizer, in this instance causing students to compare what they have observed with what they already knew or thought they knew). Preparing an organizer helps you plan and organize the sequence of ideas, and its presentation helps students organize their own learning and become motivated about it. An advance organizer can also make their learning meaningful by providing important connections between what they already know and what is being learned.

Second, *your talk should be planned so that it has a beginning and an end, with a logical order between*. During your talk, you should reinforce your words with visuals (discussed in the specific guidelines that follow). These visuals may include writing unfamiliar terms on the board (helping students learn new vocabulary), visual organizers, and prepared graphs, charts, photographs, and various audiovisuals.

Third, *pacing is important*. Your talk should move briskly but not too fast. The ability to pace the instruction is a difficult skill for many beginning teachers (the tendency among many beginning teachers is to talk too fast and too much) but one that will improve with experience. Until you have honed your skill in pacing lessons, you probably will need to constantly remind yourself during lessons to slow down and provide silent pauses (allowing for **think-time**) and frequent checks for student comprehension. Specifically, your talk should be as follows:

- Be brisk though not too fast, with occasional slowdowns to change the pace and to check for student comprehension. Allow students time to think, ask questions, and make notes.
- Have a time plan. A talk planned for 10 minutes, if interesting to students, will probably take longer. If not interesting to them, it will probably take less time.
- Always plan with careful consideration of the characteristics of the students. For example, if you have a fairly high percentage of English Language Learners or students with special needs, then your teacher talk may be less brisk, sprinkled with even more visuals and repeated statements and frequent checks for student comprehension.

Fourth, *encourage student participation*. Their active participation enhances their learning. This encouragement can be planned as questions that you ask, time allowed for students to comment and ask questions, or some sort of a visual and conceptual outline that students complete during the talk.

Fifth, *plan a clear ending (closure)*. Be sure your talk has a clear ending, followed by another activity (during the same or next class period) that will help secure the learning. As for all lessons, you want to strive for planning a clear and mesmerizing beginning, an involving lesson body, and a firm and meaningful ending.

Teacher Talk: Specific Guidelines

Specific guidelines for using teacher talk are presented in the following paragraphs.

UNDERSTAND THE VARIOUS PURPOSES FOR USING TEACHER TALK Teacher talk, formal or informal, can be useful to discuss the progress of a unit of study, explain an inquiry, introduce a unit of study, present a problem, promote student inquiry or critical thinking, provide a transition from one unit of study to the next, provide information otherwise unobtainable by students, share the teacher's experiences, share the teacher's thinking, summarize a problem, summarize a unit of study, and teach a thinking skill by modeling that skill.

CLARIFY THE OBJECTIVES OF THE TALK Your talk should center around one idea. The learning objectives, which should not be too numerous for one talk, should be clearly understood by the students.

CHOOSE BETWEEN INFORMAL AND FORMAL TALK Although an occasional formal cutting-edge lecture may be appropriate for some classes, spontaneous interactive informal talks of 5 to 12 minutes are preferred. You should never give long lectures with no teacher-student interaction. Remember, a formal period-long noninteractive lecture, common in some college teaching, is developmentally inappropriate when teaching most groups of young adolescent learners. (Some experts believe that its appropriateness is questionable for most learning even at the college level.)

Remember also, today's youth are of the "media," or "light," generation; they are accustomed to video interactions and "commercial breaks." For many lessons, especially those that are teacher centered, after about 10 minutes student attention is likely to begin to stray. For that eventuality, you need elements planned to recapture student attention. These planned elements can include (a) analogies to help connect the topic to students' experiences; (b) verbal cues, such as voice inflections; (c) pauses to allow information to sink in; (d) humor; (e) visual cues, such as the use of slides, overhead transparencies, charts, board drawings, excerpts from videos, DVDs or YouTube, real objects (realia), or body gestures; and (f) sensory cues, such as eye contact and proximity.

VARY STRATEGIES AND ACTIVITIES FREQUENTLY Perhaps the most useful strategy for recapturing student attention is changing to an entirely different strategy or learning modality. For example, from teacher talk (a teacher-centered strategy) you would change to a student activity (a student-centered strategy). Notice that changing from a lecture (mostly teacher talk) to a teacher-led discussion (mostly more teacher talk) would not be changing to an entirely different modality. Figures 9.1A and 9.1B provide a comparison of different changes.

As a generalization, when using teacher-centered instruction, with most classes you will want to change the learning activities about every 10 to 15 minutes. (That is one reason that in the sample preferred lesson plan format shown in Figure 7.2 in Chapter 7, you find space for at least four activities, including the introduction and closure.) This means that in a 60-minute time block, for example, you should probably plan three or four *sequenced* learning activities, with some that are teacher centered and many others that are more student centered. In a 90-minute block, plan five or six learning activities. In exemplary classrooms, teachers often have several activities concurrently being performed by individuals, dyads, and small groups of students (i.e., using multitasking or multilevel instruction).

PREPARE AND USE NOTES AS A GUIDE FOR YOUR TALK Planning your talk and preparing notes to be used during formal and informal teacher talk is important—just as important as implementing the talk with visuals. There is absolutely nothing wrong with using notes during your teaching. As you move around the room, your notes can be

Figure 9.1A **Comparison of Recapturing Student Attention by Changing the Instructional Strategy**

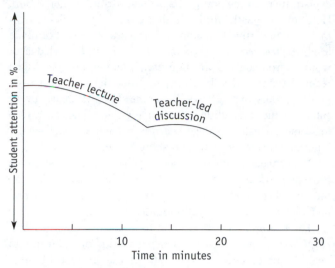

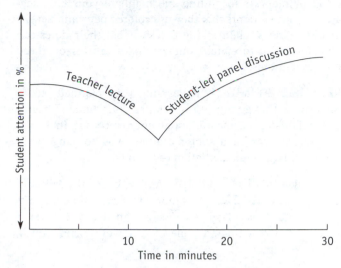

Example 1: Changing from teacher talk (lecture) to more teacher talk (e, g., teacher-led discussion).

Example 2: Changing from teacher talk (teacher-centered activity) to student-led panel discussion (student-centered activity).

Figure 9.1B **Comparison of Recapturing Student Attention by Changing the Instructional Strategy**

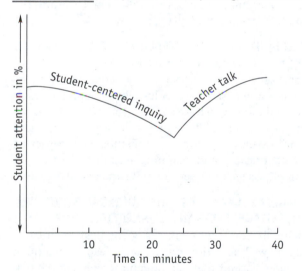

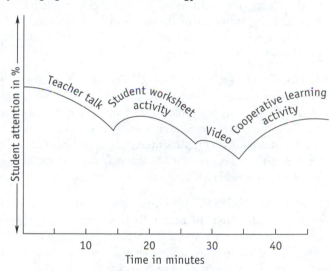

Example 3: Changing from inquiry (student-centered) to teacher talk fueled by student questions from inquiry.

Example 4: Changing from teacher talk (teacher-centered activity) to cooperative learning activity (student-centered activity).

carried on a clipboard, perhaps a brightly colored one that gives students a visual focus. Your notes for a formal talk can first be prepared in narrative form; for class use, though, they should be reduced to an outline form. *Talks to students should always be from an outline, never read from prose.*

In your outline, use color coding with abbreviated visual cues to yourself. You will eventually develop your own coding system; whatever coding system you use, keep it simple so you do not forget what the codes are for. Consider these examples of coding: where transition of ideas occurs and you want to allow silent moments for ideas to sink in, mark *P* for *pause*, *T* for a *transition*, and *S* for moments of *silence*;

where a slide or other visual aid will be used, mark *AV* for *audiovisual*; where you intend to stop and ask a question, mark *TQ* for *teacher question* and mark *SQ* or *?* where you want to stop and allow time for *student questions*; where you plan to have a discussion, mark *D*; mark *SG* where you plan *small-group* work and *L* where you plan to switch to a *laboratory investigation*; and for *reviews* and *comprehension checks*, mark *R* and *CS*.

Share your note organization with your students. Prepare a guided lecture and provide students with a skeletal outline so that they can add information as you lecture. This will help the students take notes and decide what kinds of things they should write down. Use colored chalk or markers to outline and highlight your talk; suggest to your students that they use colored pens and pencils or highlighters when taking notes so that their notes can be color coded to match your writing board (or overhead projector) notes.

REHEARSE YOUR TALK Rehearsing your planned talk is important. Using your lesson plan as your guide, rehearse your talk using a camcorder or an audio recorder. Including a time plan for each subtopic allows you to gauge your timing during implementation of the talk.

AVOID RACING THROUGH THE TALK SOLELY TO COMPLETE IT BY A CERTAIN TIME It is more important that students understand some of what you say than that you cover it all and they understand none of it. If you do not finish, continue it later.

AUGMENT YOUR TALK WITH MULTISENSORY STIMULATION AND ALLOW FOR THINK-TIME Your presentation should not overly rely on verbal communication. When using visuals, such as video excerpts or overhead transparencies, do not think that you must be constantly talking; after clearly explaining the purpose of a visual, give students time to look at it, think about it, and ask questions about it. The visual is new to the students, so give them sufficient time to take it in.

CAREFULLY PLAN THE CONTENT OF YOUR TALK The content of your talk should supplement and enhance what is found in the student textbook rather than simply rehash content from the textbook. Students may never read their book, so if you can tell them in an interesting and condensed fashion everything that they need to know from it, perhaps they will learn the material.

MONITOR YOUR DELIVERY Your voice should be pleasant and interesting to listen to rather than a steady, boring monotone or a constantly shrieking, irritating, high pitch. However, it is good to show enthusiasm for what you are talking about while teaching and learning. Occasionally, you should use dramatic voice inflections to emphasize important points and meaningful body language to give students a visual focus.

As is always the case when teaching, *avoid standing in the same spot for long periods of time.* Even during direct instruction, you need to monitor student behavior. Use proximity as a means of keeping students on task.

VIEW THE VOCABULARY OF THE TALK AS AN OPPORTUNITY TO HELP STUDENTS WITH THEIR WORD MORPHOLOGY The students should easily understand words you use, though you should still model professionalism and help students develop their vocabulary—both the special vocabulary of your subject area and the more general vocabulary of the English language. During your lesson planning, predict when you are likely to use a word that is new to most students and plan to stop to ask a student to help explain its meaning and perhaps demonstrate its derivation. Help students with word meaning. This helps students with their remembering. Remember, regardless of subject or grade level, *all teachers are language-arts teachers.* Knowledge of word morphology is an important component of skilled reading and includes the ability to generate new words from prefixes, roots, and suffixes. For some students, nearly every subject in the curriculum is challenging. That is certainly true for some English Language Learners for whom teacher talk, especially formal teacher talk, should be used sparingly if at all. Every teacher has the responsibility of helping students learn how to learn, and that includes helping students develop their word comprehension skills, reading skills, thinking and memory skills, and motivation for learning.

For example, if introducing to students the word *hermaphrodite*, the science teacher has the opportunity to teach a bit of Greek mythology in the process of helping the students understand that important biology term through showing students the origin of the word's two roots (Hermes, or Mercury, the messenger of the gods, and Aphrodite, or Venus, goddess of love and beauty). Taking time to teach a bit of Greek mythology affords the science teacher an opportunity to cross disciplines and captures the interest of a few more students.

GIVE THOUGHTFUL AND INTELLIGENT CONSIDERATION TO STUDENT DIVERSITY During the preactive phase of planning, while preparing your talk, consider students in your classroom who are culturally and linguistically different and those who have special needs. Personalize the talk for them by choosing your vocabulary carefully and appropriately, speaking slowly and methodically, repeating often, paraphrasing, and planning meaningful analogies and examples as well as relevant audio and visual displays.

USE FAMILIAR EXAMPLES AND ANALOGIES TO HELP STUDENTS MAKE RELEVANT CONNECTIONS (BRIDGES) Although this sometimes takes a great deal of creative thinking as well as action during the preactive planning phase, it is important that you attempt to connect the talk with ideas and events with which the students are already familiar. The most effective talk is one that makes frequent and meaningful connections between what students already know and what they are learning, bridging what they are learning with what they have experienced in their lives. Of course, this means you need to "know" your students. (See the section "Get to Know Your Students as People" in Chapter 4.)

ESTABLISH EYE CONTACT FREQUENTLY Your primary eye contact should be with your students—always. That important point cannot be overemphasized. Only momentarily should you look at your notes, your visuals, the projection screen, the writing board, and other adults or objects in the classroom. You can learn to establish eye contact with each student about once a minute. To

Teaching Scenario — Teacher Expectations

Anna is a 28-year-old mother of three who is currently studying to become a teacher. Anna is of Mexican descent; she was born in southern California and grew up in East Los Angeles. Anna and her sister were raised by their maternal grandparents, who were monolingual Spanish speakers. Even though Anna's mother would occasionally speak English with her and her sister, she says that it wasn't until she entered kindergarten that she was formally introduced to English. Anna wants to teach at the secondary level but has not yet decided whether she should pursue a Spanish middle and high school license exclusively or concentrate at the high school level and get an English as-a-second-language endorsement on her Spanish license.

Anna wants to be a teacher and serve as a role model for Latino/Latina and other minority students because she was often misunderstood as a student and felt that many of her

teachers and guidance counselors did not expect much from her. Reflecting back on her secondary school experience, Anna had this to share: "I was good in math. I took algebra I in junior high. In high school they wanted me to take intermediate algebra. I said, why? I already got an A in real algebra. My counselor said my grades might not reflect what I can do. I was really ticked off because I wanted to take geometry. My eighth-grade math teacher recommended higher math for me, but the school didn't try to further people.... I took geometry and did well, but my teacher had a complicated pregnancy and she left. We had a substitute for three weeks. Then my counselor wanted me to retake geometry because my teacher missed three weeks! I said, no way. I was mad that they kept wanting me to prove myself. I asked to change counselors but that was something you didn't do in my school."

"establish" eye contact means that you hold the eye contact with that particular person for several seconds; the student is aware that you are looking at him or her.

Frequent eye contact can have two major benefits. First, as you read a student's body posture and facial expressions, you gain clues about that student's attentiveness and comprehension. Second, eye contact helps to establish rapport between you and a student. Be alert, though, for students who are from cultures where eye contact is infrequent or unwanted and could have negative consequences. In other words, be culturally sensitive.

Frequent eye contact is easier when using an overhead projector than when using the writing board. When using a writing board, you have to turn at least partially away from your audience, and you may also have to pace back and forth from the board to the students in order to retain that important proximity to them. Remember our discussions about "overlapping" (Chapter 4) as an important teaching skill? This is one of those times when its importance really comes into play. While lecturing on a topic, you must remain aware and attentive to everything that is happening in the classroom (i.e., to student behavior as well as to the content of your lecture).

Demonstration

Most students like demonstrations because the demonstrator is actively engaged in a learning activity rather than merely verbalizing about it. Demonstrations can be used by any teacher in any subject and for a variety of purposes. The teacher demonstrates role playing in preparation for a social studies simulation. A teacher demonstrates the steps in solving a mathematics problem. A language-arts/English teacher demonstrates clustering to students ready for a creative writing assignment. A science teacher demonstrates the effect of combining an acid and a base to form

salt water. The physical education teacher demonstrates the proper way to serve in volleyball.

Purposes of Demonstrations

A demonstration can be designed to serve any of the following purposes: to assist in recognizing a solution to an existing problem, to bring an unusual closure to a lesson or unit of study, to demonstrate a thinking skill, to model a skill used in conflict resolution, to establish problem recognition, to give students an opportunity for vicarious participation in active learning, to illustrate a particular point of content, to introduce a lesson or unit of study in a way that grabs the students' attention, to reduce potential safety hazards (where the teacher demonstrates with materials that are too dangerous for students to handle), to review, to save time and resources (as opposed to the entire class doing that which is being demonstrated), and to set up a discrepancy recognition.

Guidelines for Using Demonstrations

When planning a demonstration, consider the following guidelines: decide what is the most effective way to conduct the demonstration, such as a verbal or a silent demonstration; by a student or by the teacher; by the teacher with a student helper; to the entire class or to small groups; or by some combination of these, such as first by the teacher, followed by a repeat of the demonstration by a student or a succession of students.

Be sure that the demonstration is visible to all students. Practice with the materials and procedure before demonstrating to the students. During your practice, try to prepare for anything that could go wrong during the real demonstration; if you don't, as Murphy's Law says, anything that can go wrong probably will. Then, if something does go wrong during the live demonstration, use that as an opportunity for a teachable moment—engage the students in trying to understand what went wrong or, if that isn't feasible, go to Plan B (see Chapter 10).

Teaching Scenario	The Abacus Tour: Cross-Cultural Math Lessons for Middle School Students

Filbert College in Oregon has a long history of welcoming faculty from Wenzhou Normal College in China for scholarly exchanges. During her year in the U.S., Professor Yang had the opportunity to share an aspect of her Chinese culture by teaching seventh and eighth graders about the abacus. Her mentor set up several visits to math classes in middle schools throughout Montana and Colorado. Professor Yang went on a monthlong tour. She shared the abacus's history and taught students how to make their own abacus out of pipe cleaners and colored Cheerios. Students enjoyed doing simple calculations on their abaci, but what excited them the most were the competitions. Yes, Professor Yang would do multiplication and division problems on the abacus while students computed the answers on their calculators. Professor Yang was unbeatable. She always finished first. Students loved her lessons.

When she returned to Ashford, OR, she was asked to share her legendary abacus lessons with several math classes at the two local middle schools. Once again, the students were excited to make their own abaci and were very impressed with Professor Yang's mastery of the abacus. Then she was invited to share her lesson with non-native English-speaking students at the high school. Because Professor Yang taught English in China, she was excited to meet the English Language Learners (ELLs).

At Dunn High, there were several packed classrooms along the English as-a-Second-Language Hall when Professor Yang visited. In the ELL Algebra II class she was invited to, there were students ranging in age from 16 to 20. Some sat with their arms folded tightly across their chests; others chatted with their peers in their native Spanish during her lesson. To her dismay, all ignored her when she demonstrated how to make an abacus.

In the ELL program at the high school, the overwhelming majority, approximately 95%, of the students spoke Spanish as their first language; their families come from Michoacán, Mexico. These non-native English speakers were disengaged, frustrated, and marginalized. The older adolescents were insulted by the abacus lesson. Many of the students recalled making an abacus in their math classes in their primary school in Mexico. In their high school courses in America, they were often presented with curriculum that was neither challenging nor appropriate. They were also often isolated physically and socially from their English-speaking peers. Spanish was spoken almost exclusively in their English as-a-second-language beginning classes as well as in their advanced content courses. These students had little opportunity to practice their English-language skills, master core curriculum content in English, or prepare for postsecondary educational pursuits. Professor Yang's experience reminded her that lack of language proficiency does not warrant a "dumbing down" of the curriculum so that students are asked to perform a task that is inappropriate for their age or grade level.

Think About It

If you are interested in finding out more about the history and use of the abacus, peruse the following websites:

http://www.joernluetjens.de/sammlungen/abakus/abakus-en.htm
http://mysite.du.edu/~jcalvert/math/chinum.htm
http://www.answers.com/topic/abacus
http://www.themathlab.com/alltreasure/chinesecalculation/elecabacus.htm
http://www.educalc.net/144267.page
http://www.twinpinefarm.com/abacus

Consider your pacing of the demonstration, allowing for enough student wait-see and think-time. At the start of the demonstration, explain its purpose and the learning objectives. Remember this adage: tell them what you are going to do, show them, and then tell them what they saw. As with any lesson, plan your closure and allow time for questions and discussion. During the demonstration, as in other types of teacher talk, use frequent stops to check for student understanding.

Safety is key, so be sure that the demonstration table and area are free of unnecessary objects that could distract, be in the way, or pose a safety hazard. With potentially hazardous demonstrations, such as might occur in physical education, science, or vocational classes, you should first decide whether the demonstration is really that important and necessary. If your answer is "yes," then be sure to *model* proper safety precautions: wear safety goggles, have fire-safety equipment at hand, and position a protective shield between the demonstration table and nearby students. To review the components of the lecture, do Exercises 9.1A and 9.1B.

Questioning

A strategy of fundamental importance to any mode of instruction is questioning. You will use questioning for so many purposes that you must be skilled in its use to teach effectively.

Purposes for Using Questioning

You will adapt the type and form of each question to the purpose for which it is asked. The purposes that questions can serve can be separated into five broad categories, as follows:

1. *To make polite requests.* An example is "José, would you please turn out the lights so we can show the slides?" Although they probably should avoid doing so, teachers sometimes also use rhetorical questions for the purpose of regaining student attention and maintaining classroom control, like "José, would you please attend to your work?" Rhetorical questions can sometimes backfire on the teacher. In this case, for example, José might say

"No"; then the teacher would have a problem that could perhaps have been avoided had the teacher at first been more direct and simply told José to attend to his work rather than asking him if he would.

2. *To review and remind students of classroom procedures.* For example, if students continue to talk when they shouldn't, you can stop the lesson and ask, "Class, I think we need to review the procedure for listening when someone else is talking. Who can tell me, what is the procedure that we agreed on?"

3. *To gather information.* Examples are "How many of you have finished the assignment?" or, to find out whether a student knows something, "Louise, can you please tell us the difference between a synonym and an antonym?"

4. *To discover student knowledge, interests, or experiences.* Examples might be "How many of you think you know the process by which water in our city is made potable?" or "How many of you have visited the local water treatment plant?"

5. *To guide student thinking and learning.* It is this category of questioning that is the focus here. In teaching, questions in this category are used to do the following:

   - *Develop appreciation.* For example, "Do you now understand the ecological relationship among that particular root fungus, voles, and the survival of the large conifers of the forests of the Pacific Northwest?"

   - *Develop student thinking.* For example, "What do you suppose the effects on the ecology are when standing water is sprayed with an insecticide that is designed to kill all mosquito larvae?"

   - *Diagnose learning difficulty.* For example, "What part of the formula don't you understand, Sarah?"

   - *Emphasize major points.* For example, "If humans have never been to the sun, how do we know what it is made of?"

   - *Encourage students.* For example, "Okay, so you didn't remember the formula for glucose. What really impressed me in your essay is what you did understand about photosynthesis."

   - *Establish rapport.* For example, "We have a problem here, but I think we can solve it if we put our heads together. What do you think ought to be our first step?"

   - *Evaluate learning.* For example, "John, what is the effect when two rough surfaces are rubbed together?"

   - *Give practice in expression.* For example, "Yvonne, would you please share with us the examples of impressionism that you found?"

   - *Help students in their own metacognition.* For example, "Yes, something did go wrong in the experiment. Do you still think your original hypothesis is correct? If not, then where was the error in your thinking? Or if you still think your hypothesis is correct, then where might the error have been in the design of your experiment? How might we find out?"

   - *Help students interpret materials.* For example, "Something seems to be wrong with this compass. How do you suppose we can find out what is wrong with it?"

   - *Help students organize materials.* For example, "If you really want to carry out your proposed experiment, then we are going to need certain materials. We are going to have to deal with some strategic questions here, such as what do you think we will need, where can we find those things, who will be responsible for getting them, and how will we store and arrange them once we are ready to start the investigation?"

   - *Provide drill and practice.* For example, "Team A has prepared some questions that they would like to use as practice questions for our unit exam, and they are suggesting that we use them to play the game of Jeopardy on Friday. Is everyone in agreement with their idea?"

   - *Provide review.* For example, "Today, in your groups, you are going to study the unit review questions I have prepared. After each group has studied and prepared its answers to these written questions, your group will pick another group and ask them your set of review questions. Each group has a different set of questions. Members of team A will keep score, and the group that has the highest score from this review session will receive free pizza at tomorrow's lunch. Ready?"

   - *Show agreement or disagreement.* For example, "Some scientists fear that the Antarctic ice shelf is breaking up and melting and that this will cause worldwide flooding. With evidence that you have collected from recent articles and what you have found searching the Internet, do you agree with this conclusion? Explain why or why not."

   - *Show relationships such as cause and effect.* For example, "What do you suppose would be the global effect if just one inch of the total Antarctic ice shelf were to suddenly melt?"

   - *Build the curriculum.* It is the students' questions that provide the basis for the learning that occurs in an effective program that is inquiry based and project centered, as discussed in Chapter 8. We return to this category of students' questions later in this discussion of questioning.

Questions to Avoid Asking

Although it is important to avoid asking rhetorical questions, that is, questions for which you do not want a response, you should also avoid asking questions that call for little or no student thinking, such as those that can be answered with a simple yes or no or some other sort of alternative response. Unless followed up with questions calling for clarification, questions that call for simple responses such as yes or no have little or no diagnostic value; they encourage guessing and inappropriate student responses that can cause classroom control problems for the teacher.

It is even more important to avoid using questions that embarrass a student, punish a student, or in any way deny the student's dignity. Questions that embarrass or punish tend to damage the student's developing self-esteem and serve no meaningful academic or instructional purpose. Questioning is an important instructional tool that should be used by the teacher only for academic reasons. Although it is not always possible to predict when a student might be embarrassed by a question, a teacher should *never* deliberately ask questions for the purpose of embarrassment or punishment. In other words, avoid asking a student a content question when you know full well that the student was not paying attention and/or does not know the answer.

Types of Questions: A Glossary

Let us now define, describe, and provide examples for each of the kinds of questions that you will use in teaching. This will be followed by a discussion about a special technique called **Socratic questioning**. Following that, your attention is focused on the *levels* of questions.

CLARIFYING QUESTION The **clarifying question** is used to gain more information from a student to help the teacher better understand a student's ideas, feelings, and thought processes. Often, asking a student to elaborate on an initial response will lead the student to think more deeply, restructure his or her thinking, and, while doing so, discover a fallacy in the original response. Examples of clarifying questions are "What I hear you saying is that you would rather work alone than in your group. Is that correct?" and "So, Patrick, you think the poem is a sad one, is that right?" Research has shown a strong positive correlation between student learning and development of metacognitive skills (i.e., their thinking about thinking) and the teacher's use of questions that ask for clarification.[4] In addition, by seeking clarification, you are likely to be demonstrating an interest in the student and his or her thinking.

CONVERGENT-THINKING QUESTION **Convergent-thinking questions**, also called *narrow questions*, are low-order thinking questions that have a single correct answer (such as recall questions, discussed further in the next section). Examples of convergent questions are "How would you classify the word spelled *c-l-o-s-e*, as a homophone or homograph?," "If the radius of a circle is 20 meters, what is its circumference?," and "What is the name of what is considered to be the first battle of the Civil War?" When using questions of this type, try to come back with follow-up questions when possible so the student answering can demonstrate thinking beyond rote memory.

CUEING QUESTION If you ask a question to which, after sufficient **wait time**, no students respond or to which their inadequate responses indicate they need more information, then you can ask a **cueing question** that cues the answer

or response you are seeking.[5] In essence, you are going backward in your questioning sequence to cue the students. For example, to introduce a lesson on the study of prefixes, a teacher asks her students, "How many legs each do crayfish, lobsters, and shrimp have?" If no one accurately responds, she might then cue the answer with the following information and question: "The class to which those animals belong is class Decapoda. Does that give you a clue about the number of legs they have?" If that clue is not enough and after allowing sufficient time for students to think (longer than two seconds), she might ask, "What is a decathlon?," "What is the decimal system?," "What is a decimeter?," "What is a decibel?," "What is a decade?," "What is the Decalogue?," and so on.

DIVERGENT-THINKING QUESTION **Divergent-thinking questions** (also known as *broad*, *reflective*, or *thought questions*) are *open-ended* (i.e., usually having no singularly correct answer), higher-order thinking questions (requiring analysis, synthesis, or evaluation) that require students to think creatively—to leave the comfortable confines of the known and reach out into the unknown. Examples of questions that require divergent thinking are "What measures could be taken to reduce crime in our neighborhood?" and "What measures could be taken to improve the post-lunchtime trash problem on our campus?"

EVALUATIVE QUESTION Whether convergent or divergent, some questions require students to place a value on something or to take a stance on some issue; these are referred to as **evaluative questions**. If the teacher and the students all agree on certain premises, then the evaluative question would also be a convergent question. If original assumptions differ, then the response to the evaluative question would be more subjective, and therefore that evaluative question would be divergent. Examples of evaluative questions are "Should the United States allow clear-cutting in its national forests?," "Should women have the right as individuals to choose whether to have abortions?," and "Is it an impeachable offense?"

FOCUS QUESTION This category includes any question that is designed to focus student thinking. For example, the first question of the preceding paragraph is a **focus question** when the teacher asking it is attempting to focus student attention on the economic issues involved in clear-cutting.

PROBING QUESTION Similar to a clarifying question, the **probing question** requires student thinking to go beyond superficial first-answer or single-word responses. An example of a probing question is "Why, Antoine, do you think that every citizen should have the right to have a gun?"

So far in this chapter, we have reviewed the purposes behind how teachers use questions to obtain information from students, and we have defined, described, and provided examples for seven different types of questions you

Activity
9.1

Developing Your Questioning Technique

It is important for you to become skilled at asking thought-provoking, stimulating questions to engage your students in critical thinking and problem solving. There are numerous types of questions. In the Questioning Toolkit mentioned below, there are 17 question types included. These different types of questions allow teachers to accomplish a variety of tasks. A detailed description of each questioning category, a selection of cluster diagrams, quotes, charts, advance organizers, and numerous examples of questions under each category are provided. In fact, this comprehensive collection of different types of questioning descriptions and techniques can help you develop questions to use with your students.

Apply Your Knowledge

Peruse the Questioning Toolkit website at **http://fno.org/ nov97/toolkit.html** and then write questions with a particular grade level in mind or for a specific course or unit. Design one to three sample questions in several of the 17 questioning categories: essential, subsidiary, hypothetical, telling, planning, organizing, probing, sorting and sifting, clarification, strategic, elaborating, unanswerable, inventive, provocative, irrelevant, divergent, and irreverent. Then share your questions with your classmates.

---

are likely to use in your interactions with your students. They included the following seven question types: clarifying questions, convergent-thinking questions, cueing questions, divergent-thinking questions, evaluative questions, focus questions, and probing questions. Complete Exercise 9.2A to practice creating questions for each of the question types described above. In addition to covering the seven different types of questions included here, before you read the explanation of the Socratic Method, we would like to introduce you to another schema for categorizing question types that you may find helpful.

There are various ways to categorize question types; to explore an alternative questioning categorization to the one presented here, complete Activity 9.1. Dr. Jamie McKenzie of *From Now On* has compiled a comprehensive list of question types. At his website, you can review a detailed description of the numerous types of questions you can use when interacting with your students, regardless of the grade level and/or subject you teach, that will promote critical thinking and problem solving. The different categories include essential, subsidiary, hypothetical, telling, planning, organizing, probing, sorting and sifting, clarification, strategic, elaborating, unanswerable, inventive, provocative, irrelevant, divergent, and irreverent question.

Socratic Questioning

In the fifth century b.c.e., Socrates, the great Athenian teacher, used the art of questioning so successfully that to this day we still hear of the Socratic method.[6] What, exactly, is the Socratic method? Socrates' strategy was to ask his students a series of leading questions that gradually snarled them up to the point where they had to look carefully at their own ideas and think rigorously for themselves. Today that strategy is referred to as the Socratic approach or Socratic method.

Socratic discussions were informal dialogues. Socrates sometimes had to go to considerable lengths to ignite his students' intrinsic interest; their response was natural and spontaneous. In his dialogues, Socrates tried to aid students

in developing ideas. He did not impose his own notions on the students. Rather, he encouraged them to develop their own conclusions and draw their own inferences. Of course, Socrates may have had preconceived notions about what the final learning should be and carefully aimed his questions so that the students would arrive at the desired conclusions. Still, his questions were open ended, causing divergent rather than convergent thinking. The students were free to go mentally wherever the facts and their thinking led them.

Throughout history, teachers have tried to adapt the Socratic method to the classroom. In some situations, they have been quite successful in using it as a major mode of instruction. However, we must remember that Socrates used this method in the context of a one-to-one relationship between the student and himself. Some teachers have adapted it for whole-class direct instruction by asking questions first of one student and then of another, moving slowly about the class. This technique may work, but it is difficult because the essence of the Socratic technique is to build question on question in a logical fashion so that each question leads the student a step closer toward the understanding sought. When you spread the questions around the classroom, you may find it difficult to build up the desired sequence and to keep all the students involved in the discussion. Sometimes you may be able to use the Socratic method by directing all the questions to one student—at least for several minutes— while the other students look on and listen in. That is how Socrates did it. When the topic is interesting enough, this technique can be quite successful and even exciting, but in the long run, the Socratic method works best when the teacher is working in one-on-one coaching situations or with small groups of students rather than in whole-class direct instruction.

In using Socratic questioning, the focus is on the questions, not answers, and thinking is valued as the quintessential activity.[7] In essence, to conduct Socratic questioning with the student or class, identify a problem (either student or teacher posed) and then ask the students a series

---

Teaching Scenario   **By Sharing Her Passion, She Created Page Turners**

Ms. Miller is a 34-year-old middle school science teacher who is a devoted Harry Potter fan. To say that she likes Harry Potter would be an understatement. She has made midnight runs to her nearby Barnes & Noble to stand in line to buy each novel the evening it was released. She plowed through every book and saw every movie as soon as it came out. Every inch of wall space in her classroom and home office is decorated with Harry Potter paraphernalia. Often Miller can be seen wearing round glasses, a shaggy dark wig, and her long black Hogwarts robe. She also carries a wand. According to her students, Miller has a remarkable resemblance to the young wizard. According to Miller, a little Harry Potter integrated in her science curriculum goes a long way.

Over the past decade, the Harry Potter phenomenon has captivated the imaginations of many 5- to 17-year-olds. The seven-novel fantasy series written by English author J. K. Rowling has been a publishing sensation and resulted in a merchandise frenzy. In Miller's classroom, the adventures of this adolescent boy and his friends at Hogwarts School of Witchcraft and Wizardry were often the topic of discussion. Although it is debated whether the books have really managed to turn youngsters into lifelong readers or not, Harry Potter's immense popularity, critical acclaim, and marketing success are undeniable.

Miller believes that her passion for reading in general and her love for Harry Potter in particular have allowed her to strengthen her rapport with and influence on her students. "What great modeling. I've been able to instill a love of reading in my kids,

even the ones who have never read a book before. The students see me reading at lunchtime, before and after class, and during our 20-minute silent reading time and usually join in. So many of them are following the series," Miller explains. In fact, it has been so popular among children worldwide that it has been translated into more than 64 languages. In addition, an unprecedented first run of 12 million copies of the seventh novel was printed for sale in the U.S. alone.

Miller asserts, "Teachers should read Harry Potter because that is what their students are reading." According to Miller, at first critics said kids would never read a book that was 300, let alone 700 pages. But, she argues, "kids are reading. Kids are reading in the summer. Parents are reading with their children. The book is crossing over at home and school. Both girls and boys like it. The series is really ideal for middle school students. Its sophisticated vocabulary and concepts engage students. They are motivated to read."

Since *Harry Potter and the Sorcerer's Stone* was published over a decade ago, more than 325 million copies of the series have been sold worldwide. In addition to the novels, all the movies have also been made. Miller has read and seen them all. Now the series has come to an end. No more books, no more blockbusters on the big screen, no more fanfare. Miller peacefully sighed when Harry broke the world's most powerful wand because she knows in her heart that she has been part of an amazing journey. After all, she saw millions of children around the world engrossed in reading, devouring Harry Potter.

---

of probing questions designed to cause them to examine critically the problem and potential solutions to it. The main thrust of the questioning and the key questions must be planned in advance so that the questioning will proceed logically. You will use the Socratic method in a *micro* peer-teaching exercise later in this chapter (Exercise 9.7).

Levels of Cognitive Questions and Student Thinking

The questions you pose are cues to your students to the level of thinking expected of them, ranging from the lowest level of mental operation, requiring simple recall of knowledge (convergent thinking), to the highest, requiring divergent thought and application of that thought. It is important that you are aware of the levels of thinking and that you understand the importance of attending to student thinking from lower to higher levels of operation. What one student may view as a matter of simple recall of information for another student may *require* a higher-order mental activity, such as figuring something out by deduction.

You should structure and sequence your questions (and assist students in developing their own skill in structuring and sequencing their questions) in a way that is designed to guide students to higher levels of thinking. For example, when students respond to questions in complete sentences

that provide supportive evidence for their ideas, it is fairly safe to assume that their thinking is at a higher level unlike when the response is an imprecise and nondescriptive single-word answer.

To help your understanding, three levels of questioning and thinking are described next.[8] You may recognize the similarity between these three levels of questions and the six levels of thinking from Bloom's Taxonomy of cognitive objectives (Chapter 5). For your daily use of questioning, though, it is just as useful but more practical to think and behave in terms of these three levels rather than Bloom's six.

1. *Lowest level (the data input phase): Gathering and recalling information.* At this level, questions are designed to solicit from students concepts, information, feelings, or experiences that were gained in the past and stored in memory. Sample key words and desired behaviors are *complete, count, define, describe, identify, list, match, name, observe, recall, recite,* and *select.*

   Thinking involves receiving data through the senses, followed by the processing of those data. Inputting without processing is brain dysfunctional. Information that is not processed is stored only in short-term memory.

2. *Intermediate level (the data processing phase): Processing information.* At this level, questions are designed to draw relationships of cause and effect to synthesize, analyze, summarize, compare, contrast, or classify data. Sample key words and desired behaviors are *analyze, classify, compare, contrast, distinguish, explain, group, infer, make an analogy, organize, plan,* and *synthesize.*

Thinking and questioning that involve processing of information can be conscious or unconscious. When students observe the teacher thinking aloud and when they are urged to think aloud, to think about their thinking, and to analyze it as it occurs, they are in the process of developing their intellectual skills.

At the processing level, this internal analysis of new data may challenge a learner's preconceptions (and misconceptions) about a phenomenon. The learner's brain will naturally resist this challenge to existing beliefs. The greater the mental challenge, the greater will be the brain's effort to draw on data already in storage. With increasing data, the mind will gradually examine existing concepts and ultimately, as necessary, develop new mental concepts.

If there is a match between new input and existing mental concepts, no problem exists. Piaget called this process *assimilation*.[9] If, however, in processing new data there is no match with existing mental concepts, then the situation is what Piaget called **cognitive disequilibrium**. The brain does not like this disequilibrium and will drive the learner to search for an explanation for the discrepancy. Piaget called this process *accommodation*. However, although learning is enhanced by challenge, in situations that are threatening the brain is less flexible in accommodating new ideas. As discussed in Chapter 4, that is why each student must feel welcomed in the classroom and why the classroom environment must be perceived by the learner as challenging but nonthreatening—what is referred to as an environment of *relaxed alertness*.[10]

3. *Highest level (the data output phase): Applying and evaluating in new situations.* Questions at the highest level encourage learners to think intuitively, creatively, and hypothetically; to use their imagination; to expose a value system; or to make a judgment. Sample key words and desired behaviors are *apply a principle, build a model, evaluate, extrapolate, forecast, generalize, hypothesize, imagine, judge, predict,* and *speculate.*

You must use questions at the level best suited for the purpose, use questions of a variety of different levels, and structure questions in a way intended to move student thinking to higher levels. When teachers use higher-level questions, their students tend to score higher on tests of critical thinking and on standardized tests of achievement.[11]

When questioning students about reading material in particular, consider using the **question-answer relationship (QAR) strategy**. QAR involves asking a question and, if a student is unable to respond, providing one of three types of cues. The cues are related to the level of thinking required. "Right there" is used for questions for the lowest level, that is, in which the answer can be found explicitly stated in the sentence or paragraph. "Search and think" means the answer is not directly stated and therefore must be inferred. "On your own" is used for highest-level critical thinking questions for which the answers are neither explicit nor inferred in the text.[12]

With the use of questions as a strategy to move student thinking to higher levels, the teacher is facilitating the students' intellectual development. Developing your skill in using questioning requires attention to detail and practice. The following guidelines will provide that detail and some practice. But first, do Exercise 9.2B to check your understanding of the levels of questions.

Guidelines for Using Questioning

As emphasized many times in several ways throughout this book, your goals are to help your students learn how to solve problems, to make decisions and value judgments, to think creatively and critically, and to feel good about themselves, their schools, and their learning—rather than simply to fill their minds with bits and pieces of information that will likely last only a brief time in the students' short-term memory. How you construe your questions and how you carry out your questioning strategy are important to the realization of these goals.

PREPARING QUESTIONS When preparing questions, consider the following guidelines:

Key cognitive questions should be planned, thoughtfully worded, and written into your lesson plan. Thoughtful preparation helps to ensure that questions are clear and specific, not ambiguous; that the vocabulary is appropriate; and that each question matches its purpose. Incorporate questions into your lessons as instructional devices, welcomed pauses, attention grabbers, and as checks for student comprehension. Thoughtful teachers even plan questions that they intend to ask specific students, targeting questions to the readiness level, interest, or learning profile of a student.

Match questions with their target purposes. Carefully planned questions allow them to be sequenced and worded to match the levels of cognitive thinking expected of students. To help students in developing their thinking skills, you need to demonstrate how to do this by using terminology that is specific and that provides students with examples of experiences supporting the meanings of the cognitive words. You should demonstrate this every day so students learn the cognitive terminology. As stated by Brooks and Brooks, "Framing tasks around cognitive activities such as analysis, interpretation, and prediction—and explicitly using those terms with students—fosters the construction of new understandings."[13] See the three examples in Figure 9.2.

Figure 9.2 **Examples of Questions Converted to Appropriate Cognitive Terminology**

Instead of	Say
"How else might it be done?"	"How could you *apply*... ? "
"Are you going to get quiet?"	"If we are going to hear what Joan has to say, what do you need to do?"
"How do you know that is so?"	"What evidence do you have?"

IMPLEMENTING QUESTIONING Careful preparation of questions is one part of the skill of questioning. Implementation is the other part. Here are guidelines for effective implementation:

Ask your well-worded question before calling on a student for a response. A common error made is when the teacher first calls on a student and then asks a question, such as "Sean, would you please tell us what you believe the author meant by the title 'We Are One'?" Although probably not intended by the teacher, as soon as the teacher called on Sean, that signaled to the rest of the class that they were released from having to think about the question. The preferred strategy is to phrase the question, allow time for all students to think, and then call on Sean and other students for their interpretations of the author's meaning of the title.

Avoid bombarding students with too much teacher talk. Sometimes teachers talk too much. This could be especially true for teachers who are nervous, as might be the case for many during their initial weeks of student teaching. Knowing the guidelines presented here will help you avoid that syndrome. Remind yourself to be quiet after you ask a question that you have carefully formulated. Sometimes, because of a lack of confidence and especially when a question hasn't been carefully thought out during the preactive phase of instruction, the teacher asks the question and then, with a slight change in wording, asks it again or asks several questions one after another. This is called "shotgun questioning," and it only confuses students, allowing too little time for them to think.

After asking a question, provide students with adequate time to think. The pause after asking a question is called wait time (or think time). Because they know the subject better than the students know it and have given prior thought to the subject, too many teachers, after asking a question, fail to allow students sufficient time to think, especially for questions that require processing of information and higher-order thinking. In addition, by the time they have reached the middle school grades, students have learned pretty well how to play the "game"—that is, they know that if they remain silent long enough, the teacher will probably answer his or her own question. After asking a well-worded question, you

should remain quiet for a while, allowing students time to think and to respond. If you wait long enough, they usually will.

As researchers have verified since the original and now classic wait-time studies of M. B. Rowe in 1974, increasing wait time to at least two seconds often leads to longer and higher-quality student responses and participation by a greater number of students.[14] After asking a question, how long should you wait before you do something? You should wait at least two seconds and as many as five seconds. Stop reading now and look at your watch or a clock to get a feeling for how long two seconds is. Then observe how long five seconds is. Because most of us are not used to silence in the classroom, two seconds of silence can seem quite long, while five seconds may seem eternal. If, for some reason, students have not responded after a period of two to five seconds of wait time, then you can ask the question again (but don't reword an already carefully worded question, or else students are likely to think it is a new question). Pause for several seconds, and then, if you still haven't received a response, you can call on a student, then another, if necessary, after sufficient wait time. Soon you will get a response that can be built on. Avoid answering your own question.

Now do Activity 9.2 to further your understanding about the art of questioning and the importance of student think-time.

Practice gender equity. To practice gender equity while using questioning, here are four rules to follow: (1) avoid going to a boy to bail out a girl who fails to answer a question and (2) avoid going to a boy to improve on a girl's answer. For the first, without seeming to badger, try to give the female student clues until she can answer with success. For the second, hold and demonstrate high expectations for all students. For the third, (3) allow equal wait time regardless of student gender and finally (4) call on males and females equally.

Practice calling on all students. Related to rule (4) of the preceding paragraph, you must call on not just the bright or the slow, not just the boys or the girls, not only those in the front or middle of the room, but all the students. To do these things takes concentrated effort on your part, but it is important. To ensure that students are called on equally, some teachers hold in hand laminated copies of their seating charts, perhaps on bright neon-colored clipboards (gives students a visual focus), and, with a wax pencil or water-soluble marker, make a mark next to the name of the student each time he or she is called on. With the seating chart laminated and using erasable markers, the marks can be erased later and the seating chart used over and over. Additional suggestions for practicing equity follow later in this chapter.

Give the same minimum amount of wait time (think-time) to all students. This, too, will require concentrated

Activity
9.2

Think Time and the Art of Questioning—An In-Class Role Play

Instructions: The purpose of this exercise is to further your understanding of the art and power of questioning, of the importance of well-worded questions with well-prepared and clear instructions, and of allowing students time to think.

1. Role-play simulation: From your class ask for three volunteers. One volunteer will read the lines of Estella, a second will read the one line of the student, while the third volunteer uses a stopwatch to direct Estella and the student to speak their lines at the designated times. The rest of your class can pretend to be students in Estella's English class.

   1:00: Estella: "Think of a man whom you admire, perhaps a father figure, and write a three-sentence paragraph describing that person." Students begin their writing.

   1:00:05: Estella: "Only three sentences about someone you look up to. It might be your father, uncle, anyone."

   1:00:07: Student: "Does it have to be about a man?" *Estella:* "No, it can be a man or a woman, but someone you truly admire."

   1:01: Estella works the rows, seeing that students are on task.

   1:01:10: Estella: "Three sentences are all you need to write."

   1:01:15: Estella: "Think of someone you really look up to and write three sentences in a paragraph that describes that person."

   1:01:30: Estella: "Someone you would like to be like."

   1:02: Estella continues walking around helping students who are having difficulty. All students are on task.

   1:04: Estella: "Now I want you to exchange papers with the person behind or beside you, read that person's description of the person they admire and describe a setting that you see their person in. Write a paragraph that describes that setting."

   1:04:–1:05: Students exchange papers; teacher walks around seeing that everyone has received another student's paper.

   1:05: Estella: "Where do you see that person being? Below the paragraph I want you to write a new paragraph describing where you see this person, perhaps in an easy chair watching a ball game or on a porch, in a car, or in the kitchen cooking."

   1:05:10: Estella: "Describe a scene you see this person in."

   1:05:15: Estella: "After you read the description, I want you to create a setting for the person described."

   1:05:18: Students seem confused either about what they are reading (e.g., asking the writer what a word is or means) or what they are supposed to do.

   1:05:19: Estella: "Anything is fine. Use your imagination to describe the setting."

   1:05:22: Estella: "Describe a setting for this person."

   1:09: Estella: "Now I want you to exchange papers with yet someone else and, after reading the previous two paragraphs written by two other students, write a third paragraph describing a problem you think this admired person has."

2. After the role-play simulation, hold a whole-class or small-group discussion and use the following as a springboard for your discussion: Describe what you believe are the good points and weak points of this portion of Estella's lesson and her implementation of it.

effort on your part, but it is important to do. A teacher who waits for less time when calling on a slow student or students of one gender is showing bias toward or lack of confidence in certain students, both of which are detrimental when a teacher is striving to establish for all students a positive, equal, and safe environment for classroom learning. Show confidence in all students and never discriminate by expecting less or more from some than from others. Although some students may take longer to respond, it is not necessarily because they are not thinking or have less ability. There may be cultural differences to think about in that some cultures simply allow more wait time than others do. The important point here is to individualize to allow students who need more time to have it. Variation in wait time should be used not to single out some students and to lead to lower expectations but rather to allow for higher expectations for all students.

Require students to raise their hands and be called on. When you ask questions, instead of allowing students to randomly shout out their answers, require students to raise their hands and to be called on before responding. Establish that procedure at the beginning of the school year and stick with it. This helps to ensure that you call on all students equally, fairly distributing your interactions with the students, and that girls are not interacted with less because boys tend to be more boisterous. Even in same-gender classrooms, some students tend to be more vocal while others are less so and, when allowed by the instructor, tend to monopolize and control the flow of the verbal interactions. Every teacher has the responsibility to guarantee a nonbiased classroom and an equal distribution of interaction time in the classroom. Another important reason for this advice is to aid students in learning to control their impulsivity. Controlling one's impulsivity is one of the characteristics of intelligent behavior presented in the previous chapter.

Actively involve as many students as possible in the questioning-answering discussion session. The traditional method of the teacher asking a question and then calling on a student to respond is essentially a one-on-one interaction. Many students, those not called on, are likely to view that as their opportunity to disengage in the lesson at hand. Even though you call on one student, you want the other students not to mentally disengage.

There are many effective ways to keep all engaged. Consider the following.

To keep all students mentally engaged, before calling on anyone you can have all students write their answers to the question. You will want to call on students who are sitting quietly and have not raised their hands as well as those who have, but avoid badgering or humiliating an unwilling participant. When a student has no response, you might suggest he or she think about it. Then come back to the student to ensure that he or she eventually understands or has an answer to the original question.

By dividing a single question into several parts, the number of students involved can be increased. For example, "What are the causes of the Civil War? Who can give one reason?," followed then by "Who can give another?" Or you can involve several students in answering a single question. For example, ask one student for an answer to a question such as "What was the first battle of the Civil War?," a second to read the text aloud to verify the student's answer, and sometimes a third to explore the reason or thinking that makes it the accepted answer.

Carefully gauge your responses to students' responses to your questions. The way you respond to students' answers influences their subsequent participation. Responses by the teacher that encourage student participation include probing for elaboration, discussing student answers, requesting justification, asking how answers were arrived at, and providing positive reinforcement.[15]

Use strong praise sparingly. If you want students to think divergently and creatively, you should be stingy with the use of strong praise to student responses. Strong praise from a teacher tends to terminate divergent and creative thinking.

One of your goals is to help students find **intrinsic** sources for **motivation**, that is, an inner drive of intent or desire that causes them to want to learn. Use of strong praise tends to build conformity, causing students to depend on outside forces—that is, the giver of praise— for their worth rather than on themselves. An example of a strong praise response is "That's right! Very good." In brainstorming sessions, the teacher could generate a great deal of expression of high-level thought.

Questions from Students: The Question-Driven Classroom

Student questions can and should be used as springboards for further questioning, discussions, and investigations. Indeed, in a constructivist learning environment, student questions often drive content. Students should be encouraged to ask questions that challenge the textbook, the process, or other persons' statements, and they should be encouraged to seek the supporting evidence behind a statement.

Being able to ask questions may be more important than having right answers. Knowledge is derived from asking questions. Being able to recognize problems and to formulate questions is a skill and the key to problem solving and critical thinking skill development. You have a responsibility to encourage students to formulate questions and to help them word their questions in such a way that tentative answers can be sought. That is the process necessary to build a base of knowledge that can be drawn on whenever necessary to link, interpret, and explain new information in new situations.

QUESTIONING: THE CORNERSTONE OF CRITICAL THINKING, REAL-WORLD PROBLEM SOLVING, AND MEANINGFUL LEARNING With real-world problem solving, there are usually no absolute right answers. Rather than answers being correct, some are better than others. The student needs to learn how to (a) recognize the problem, (b) formulate a question about that problem (e.g., Should I date this person or not? Should I take this job or not? To which colleges should I apply? Should I study Spanish or not?), (c) collect data, and (d) arrive at a temporarily acceptable answer to the problem while realizing that at some later time new data may dictate a review of the former conclusion. For example, if an astronomer believes that she has discovered a new planetary system, there is no textbook or teacher or any other outside authoritative source to which she may refer in order to inquire if she is correct. Rather, on the basis of her self-confidence in identifying problems, asking questions, collecting enough data, and arriving at a tentative conclusion based on those data, she assumes that for now her conclusion is safe.

Encourage students to ask questions about content and process. As emphasized in the book *Tried and True*, question asking often indicates that the inquirer is curious, puzzled, and uncertain; it is a sign of being engaged in thinking about a topic. Yet in too many classrooms, too few students ask questions.[16] Students should be encouraged to ask questions. From students, there is no such thing as a dumb question. Sometimes students, like everyone else, ask questions that could just as easily have been looked up or are irrelevant or show lack of thought or sensitivity. Those questions can consume precious class time. For a teacher, they can be frustrating. A teacher may too quickly and mistakenly brush off that type of question with sarcasm while assuming that the student is too lazy to look up an answer. In such instances, you are advised to think before responding and to respond kindly and professionally, although in the busy life of a classroom teacher that may not always be so easy to remember to do. However, be assured that there is a reason for a student's question. Perhaps the student is signaling a need for recognition or simply demanding attention.

As mentioned in Chapter 1, in large schools it is sometimes easy for a student to feel alone and insignificant (although this seems less the case with schools

Activity
9.3

Whole-Class Discussion as a Teaching Strategy

Instructions: Answer the following questions, then share your responses with your class, perhaps in discussion groups organized by subject area or grade level.

1. Your grade-level interest or subject area:
2. For what reasons would you hold a whole-class discussion?
3. Assuming that your classroom has movable seats, how would you arrange them?
4. What would you do if the seats were not movable?
5. What rules would you establish before starting the discussion?
6. Should student participation be forced? Why or why not? If so, how?
7. How would you discourage a few students from dominating the discussion?
8. What preparation should the students and the teacher be expected to make before beginning the discussion?
9. How would you handle digression from the topic?
10. Should students be discussion leaders? Why or why not? If so, what training, if any, should they receive and how?
11. What teacher roles are options during a class discussion?
12. When is each of these roles most appropriate?
13. When, if ever, is it appropriate to hold a class meeting for discussing class procedures, not subject matter?
14. Can brainstorming be a form of whole-class discussion? Why or why not?
15. What follow-up activities would be appropriate after a whole-class discussion? On what basis would you decide to use each?
16. What sorts of activities should precede a class discussion?
17. Should a discussion be given a set length? Why or why not? If so, how long? How is the length to be decided?
18. Should students be graded for their participation in class discussion? Why or why not? If so, how? On what basis? By whom?
19. For effective discussions, 10 to 12 feet is the maximum recommended distance between participants. During a teacher-led discussion, what can a teacher do to keep within this limit?
20. Are there any pitfalls or other points of importance that a teacher should be aware of when planning and implementing a whole-class discussion? If so, explain them and how to guard against them.

---

that use a "house" plan or where one cadre of teachers remains with the same cohort of students for two or more years[17]). When a student makes an effort to interact with you, that can be a positive sign, so gauge carefully your responses to those efforts. If a student's question is really off track, off the wall, out of order, and out of context with the content of the lesson, consider using this response: "That is an interesting question, and I would very much like to talk with you more about it. Could we meet at lunchtime or before or after school or at some other time that is mutually convenient?"

Avoid bluffing an answer to a question for which you do not have an answer. Nothing will cause you to lose credibility with students faster than faking an answer. There is nothing wrong with admitting that you do not know. It helps students realize that you are human. It helps them maintain an adequate self-esteem, realizing that they are okay. What is important is that you know where and how to find possible answers and that you help students develop that same knowledge and those same skills. Now, to reinforce your comprehension, do Exercises 9.3, 9.4, and 9.5.

Whole-Class Discussion

Whole-class discussion, usually directed by the teacher, is a frequently used teaching technique. On this topic, you should consider yourself an expert. Having been a student in formal learning for at least 15 years, you are undoubtedly knowledgeable about the advantages and disadvantages of whole-class discussions. Therefore, explore your knowledge and experiences by responding to Activity 9.3. Then

Activity
9.4

Generating Guidelines for Using Whole-Class Discussions

Instructions: Share your responses to Activity 9.3 with your classmates. Then individually answer the first two questions below. Next, as a group, use all three questions to guide you as you generate a list of five general guidelines for the use of whole-class discussion as a strategy in teaching. Share your group's guidelines with the entire class. Then, as a class, derive a final list of general guidelines.

1. How effective was your small-group discussion in sharing Activity 9.3?
2. What allowed for or inhibited the effectiveness of that small-group discussion?
3. How effective is this small-group discussion? Why?

List five general guidelines generated from small-group discussion:
General guidelines: final list derived from whole-class discussion:

do Activity 9.4, where guidelines for the use of the whole-class discussion will be generated.

Recitation

The old-fashioned recitation method continues to be used, although it is perhaps less in vogue today. Theoretically, it should be one of the easiest to conduct, for essentially it consists of only three steps: (1) the teacher assigns students something to study, (2) the students study it, and (3) the teacher asks the students (in a whole-class situation ordinarily) about what they have studied to see if they have understood it.

This method has merit. Because of its long history, it is reasonably well understood and accepted by students.

The question-and-answer technique both provides reinforcement for what has been learned and gives students feedback about accuracy. The expectation of having to face questions in class has motivational value as well. Finally, recitation provides opportunities for students to learn from each other.

If practiced too frequently, though, the recitation method has more faults than merits. Too much of the questioning, for example, is of simple recall. When poorly used, the method tends to yield only superficial understanding and may even discourage the development of higher mental processes, including attitudes, appreciations, ideals, and skills. When used by an unskilled teacher, recitation tends to be boring and to create an unfriendly, anti-intellectual class atmosphere. To liven recitations up, focus them on interesting and thought-provoking questions.

OPEN-TEXT RECITATION The open-textbook recitation is a discussion in which the students may consult their books and other materials to back up their arguments and justify their opinions. The procedure for conducting an open-text recitation is basically the same as that outlined in the previous section. The teacher first makes a study assignment that includes suggestions and questions designed to encourage students to think and draw inferences about what they are to read and study. Then the recitation is focused on open-ended, thought-provoking questions of the Socratic, divergent, or evaluative type. Lower-order recall and convergent questions should be used as well, but ordinarily they do not play as important a role as do broader, open-ended questions. As the recitation proceeds, the teacher encourages students both to challenge and respond to others' statements and to express their own interpretations, inferences, and conclusions. At any time, the students are free to consult their texts, notes, or other materials to support their arguments. Finally, someone—the teacher or a student—provides a summary. In many instances, no final decisions or arguments are necessary or desirable—the summary simply cites the positions and arguments taken. At other times, the facts of the case and the nature of the subject matter may require a definite conclusion.

This technique has many advantages. It frees the class from overemphasis on simple recall of facts and opens it up to higher levels of thinking. It helps students realize that facts are means to ends, such as concepts, ideas, understandings, and the ability to think critically. It gives students practice in checking and documenting. In the best of circumstances, it shows them the importance of getting the facts straight, of listening to and respecting the opinions of others, and of suspending judgments until sufficient data are in. All in all, this is an excellent means of helping students to use and develop their higher mental faculties because the basic technique is to use broad divergent and evaluative questions and to bounce follow-up questions around the class until the group begins to discuss the questions freely.

Equality in the Classroom

Especially when conducting direct whole-group discussions, it is easy for a teacher to fall into the trap of interacting with only "the stars," only those in the front of the room or on one side, or only the loudest and most assertive. You must exercise caution and avoid falling into that trap. To ensure a psychologically safe and effective environment for learning for every student in your classroom, you must attend to all students and try to involve all of them equally in all class activities. You must avoid any biased expectations about certain students, and you must avoid discriminating against students according to their gender or some other personal characteristic.

Title IX: Student Rights

As a result of federal legislation passed more than a quarter century ago—Title IX of the Education Amendments of 1972, Public Law 92-318—a teacher is prohibited from discriminating against students on the basis of their gender. In all aspects of school, male and female students must be treated the same. This means, for example, that a teacher must not pit males against females in a quiz game—or for any other activity or reason. Further, no teacher, student, administrator, or other school employee should make sexual advances toward a student (i.e., touching or speaking in a sexual manner). Students should be informed by their schools of their rights under Title IX, and they should be encouraged to report any suspected violations of their rights to the school principal, Title IX officer, or other designated person. Many schools provide students with a publication of their rights as students. Each school or district should have a clearly delineated statement of steps to follow in the process of protecting students' rights.

Still, today, research identifies the unintentional tendency of teachers of *both* sexes to discriminate on the basis of gender. For example, teachers, along with the rest of society, tend to have lower expectations for girls than for boys in mathematics and science. They tend to call on and encourage boys more than girls. They often let boys interrupt girls but praise girls for being polite and waiting their turn. Avoiding such discrimination may take special effort on your part, no matter how aware of the problem you may be. Some researchers believe that the problem is so insidious that separate courses about it are needed in teacher training.[18]

You must not discriminate against students on any basis for any reason. To guarantee equity in interaction with students, many teachers have found it helpful to ask someone secretly to tally classroom interactions between the teacher and students during a class discussion. After an analysis of the results, the teacher arrives at decisions about his or her own attending and facilitating behaviors. Such an analysis is the purpose of Exercise 9.6. You are welcome to make blank copies and share them with your teaching colleagues.

Ensuring Equity

In addition to the advice given earlier about using questioning (e.g., practice gender equity or call on all students), there are many other ways of ensuring that students are treated fairly in the classroom, including the following:

- Encourage students to demonstrate an appreciation for one another by applauding all individual and group presentations.

- Have and maintain high expectations, although not necessarily identical expectations, for all students.

- Insist on politeness in the classroom. For example, a student can be shown appreciation—such as with a sincere "thank you" or "I appreciate your contribution" or with a genuine smile—for his or her contribution to the learning process.

- Insist that students be allowed to finish what they are saying, without being interrupted by others. Be certain that you model this behavior yourself.

- During whole-class instruction, insist that students raise their hands and be called on by you before they are allowed to speak.

- Keep a stopwatch handy to unobtrusively control the wait time given for each student. Although at first this idea may sound impractical, it works.

- Use a seating chart attached to a clipboard. Next to each student's name, make a tally for each interaction you have with that student. This is a good way to maintain records to reward students for their contributions to class discussion. Again, it is workable at any grade level. The seating chart can be laminated so that it can be used day after day simply by erasing the marks of the previous day.

If you haven't already, do Exercise 9.6, through which you will examine a teacher's behavior with students according to gender or other personal characteristics.

Learning from Assignments and Homework

An assignment is a statement of *what* the student is to accomplish or do and is tied to a specific instructional objective. Assignments, whether completed at home or at school, can ease student learning in many ways, but when poorly planned, they can be discouraging to the student. *Homework* is any out-of-class task that a student is assigned as an extension of classroom learning. Like all else that you do as a professional teacher, it is your professional responsibility to think about and plan carefully any and all homework assignments that you give to students, including thinking about how you would feel were you given the assignment and how much out-of-class time you expect the assignment to take.

Purposes and Guidelines for Using Assignments and Homework

Purposes for giving homework assignments can be any of the following: to constructively extend the time that students are engaged in learning, to help students develop personal learning, to help students develop their research skills, to help students develop their study skills, to help students organize their learning, to individualize the learning, to involve parents and guardians in their children's learning, to provide a mechanism by which students receive constructive feedback, to provide students with an opportunity to review and practice what has been learned, to reinforce classroom experiences, and to teach new content. As a general rule, homework assignments should stimulate thinking by arousing a student's curiosity, raising questions for further study, and encouraging and supporting the self-discipline required for independent study.

Plan early and thoughtfully the types of assignments you will give (e.g., daily and long range; minor and major; in class, at home, or both; or individual, paired, or group)[19] and prepare assignment specifications. Assignments must correlate with specific instructional objectives and should never be given as busywork or as punishment. For each assignment, let students know what the objectives are, for example, whether the assignment is to prepare the student for what is to come in class, to practice what has been learned in class, or to extend the learning of class activities.

Use caution in giving assignments that could be controversial or that could pose a hazard to the safety of students. In such cases (especially if you are new to the community), before giving the assignment it is probably a good idea to talk it over with your colleagues, the departmental chair, or an administrator. Also, for a particular assignment, you may need to have parental or guardian permission and even support for students to do it or be prepared to give an alternate assignment for some students.

Provide differentiated, tiered, or optional assignments—assignment variations given to students or selected by them on the basis of their interests, cultural backgrounds, and learning capacities.[20] Students can select or be assigned different activities to accomplish the same objective, such as read and discuss, or they can participate with others in a more direct learning experience. After their study, as a portion of the assignment, students share what they have learned. This is an example of using multilevel teaching.

Teachers have found it beneficial to prepare individualized study guides with questions to be answered and activities to be done by the student while reading textbook chapters as homework. One advantage of a study guide is that it can make the reading more than a visual experience. A study guide can help to organize student learning by accenting instructional objectives, emphasizing important points to be learned, providing a guide for studying for tests, and encouraging the student to read the homework assignment.

Determine the resources that students will need to complete assignments and check the availability of these resources. This is important; students can't be expected to use that which is unavailable to them. Many will not use that which is not readily available.

Avoid yelling out assignments as students are leaving your classroom. When giving assignments in class, you should write them on a special place on the writing board or give a copy to each student or require that each student write the assignment into his or her assignment folder, taking extra care to be sure that assignment specifications are clear to students and that you allow time for students to ask questions about an assignment. In some schools, especially middle schools, it is policy that students use a daily assignment book to record homework and additional reminders. In some cases, the teachers initial the page, and parents are to sign it daily or weekly. The belief is that this policy helps students to become organized and responsible for their own learning. Using a daily assignment book also reduces or eliminates the "I didn't know it was due today" excuse. Whatever procedure you use for giving and collecting assignments, it's important that it is consistent throughout the school year.

Students should be given sufficient time to complete their assignments. In other words, avoid announcing an assignment that is due the very next day. As a general rule, all assignments should be given earlier than the day before they are due. Try to avoid changing assignment specifications after they are given. Especially avoid changing them at the last minute. Changing specifications at the last minute can be very frustrating to conscientious students who have already completed the assignment, and it shows little respect for those students.

Allow time in class for students to begin work on homework assignments so that you can give them individual attention (guided or coached practice). The opportunity to coach students is the reason for scheduling in-class time for working on assignments. As you have learned, many schools have extended the length of class periods. Extended periods allow more in-class time for teacher guidance on assignments. As said earlier, the benefits of this coached practice include (a) monitoring student work so that a student does not go too far in a wrong direction, (b) helping students reflect on their thinking, (c) assessing the progress of individual students, and (d) discovering or creating a "teachable moment." For example, while monitoring students doing their work, you might discover a commonly shared student misconception. Then, taking advantage of this teachable moment, you may stop and talk about it and attempt to clarify the misconception.

Timely, constructive, and corrective feedback from the teacher on the homework—and grading of homework—increases its positive contributions.[21] If the assignment is important for students to do, then you must give your full and immediate attention to the product of their efforts. Although with varying degrees of scrutiny, read everything that students write. Students are much more willing to do homework when they believe it is useful; when it is treated as an integral part of instruction; when it is read, commented on, and evaluated by the teacher; and when it counts as part of the grade. See the section "How to Avoid Having So Many Papers to Grade that Time for Effective Planning Is Restricted" later in this chapter.

Provide feedback about each student's work and be positive and constructive in your comments. Always think

---

Teaching Scenario | **Late Homework Paper from a Student At Risk**

Tabby, an 11th-grade student at Centaurus High School, in Omaha, NE, was considered a fun-loving, hardworking, mature adolescent. She had a good attendance record, handed in her work on time, and participated in class activities. She was performing well in most of her classes her junior year, and her semester grades reflected her efforts. She had lots of friends, sang in the choir, and was a reporter for the school newspaper. Tabby was excited about applying to colleges in the spring and was looking forward to a fun senior year. Just after the winter break during her junior year, there was a dramatic change in her demeanor. Tabby appeared to be depressed, preoccupied, and disinterested in her school work. In mid-February, she turned in an English class assignment, an essay on *When I Was Puerto Rican* by Esmeralda Santiago, to Mr. Laferty several days late.

Laferty accepted her essay without penalty, although his policy was that late papers would be severely penalized. The week before the assignment was due, Tabby had suffered a miscarriage. In this instance, her teacher accepted the paper late sans penalty because Tabby was under a lot of stress. Because of the situation she found herself in, she was emotionally drained. It was obvious to Tabby's friends, classmates, and teachers that she was doing the best she could and struggling to hold it together. Consequently, Laferty felt that turning in the paper at all was a positive act; if the paper had not been accepted or had been accepted only with severe penalty to her grade, then, in his opinion, Tabby would have simply quit trying and probably dropped out of school altogether.

Think About It

Only 72% of high school students actually graduate in the U.S. In fact, every school day approximately 7,200 students drop out. That works out to one young person leaving school every 26 seconds. Although all high school dropouts do not face a bleak future, many of them have limited employment possibilities. Many students make the decision to drop out as early as middle school. The most alarming stories are when students have been successful and circumstances derail them. Students who are "overwhelmed" with what life throws their way are particularly vulnerable.

1. Why is it important for teachers to bend the rules sometimes?
2. What can teachers do to help students who are facing challenging circumstances from dropping out of school?

about the written comments that you make to be relatively certain that they will convey your intended message to the student. When writing comments on student papers, consider using a color other than red, such as green or blue. Although to you this may sound unimportant, to many people red carries a host of negative connotations (e.g., blood, hurt, danger, and stop), and students often perceive its use as punitive.

Giving Students a Second Chance

Although it is important to encourage high-quality initial efforts by students, sometimes, for a multitude of reasons, a student's first effort is inadequate or is lacking entirely. Perhaps the student is absent from school without legitimate excuse or the student does poorly on an assignment or fails to turn in an assignment on time or at all. Although accepting late work from students is extra work for the teacher and although allowing the resubmission of a marked or tentative-graded paper increases the amount of paperwork, we agree with teachers and administrators who believe that it is worthwhile to give students a second chance, that is, who believe in giving students an opportunity for recovery and limited time to make corrections and resubmit an assignment for an improved score.[22] However, out of regard for students who do well from the start and meet due dates, it is probably ill advised to allow a resubmitted paper or a late paper to receive an A grade.

Students sometimes have legitimate reasons for not completing an assignment by the due date. (Consider the Teaching Scenario "Late Homework Paper from a Student At Risk.") It is our opinion that the teacher should listen and exercise professional judgment in each instance. As someone once said, there is nothing democratic about treating unequals as equals. The provision of recovery options seems a sensible and scholastic tactic.

How to Avoid Having So Many Papers to Grade That Time for Effective Planning Is Restricted

A downfall for some beginning teachers or teachers of certain subjects (language arts and social studies) is that of being buried under mounds of student papers to be read and graded, leaving less and less time for effective planning. To keep this from happening to you, consider the following suggestions. Although we believe in providing second-opportunity options and that the teacher should read almost everything that students write, papers can be read with varying degrees of intensity and scrutiny, depending on the purpose of the assignment. For assignments that are designed for learning, understanding, and practice, you can allow students to check them themselves using either self-checking or peer checking. During the self- or peer checking, you can walk around the room, monitor the activity, and record whether a student did the assignment, or, after

the checking, you can collect the papers and do a quick read and your recording. Besides reducing the amount of paperwork for you, student self- or peer checking provides other advantages: (a) it allows students to see and understand their errors, (b) it encourages productive peer dialogue, and (c) it helps them develop self-assessment techniques and standards. If the purpose of the assignment is to assess mastery competence, then the papers should be read, marked, and graded only by you.

WARNING ABOUT USING PEER CHECKING Peer checking can, however, be a problem. During peer checking of student work, students may spend more time watching the person checking their paper than accurately checking the one given to them. In addition, this strategy does not necessarily allow the student to see or understand his or her mistakes.

The issue of privacy is perhaps an even greater concern. When student A becomes knowledgeable of the academic success or failure of student B, student A, the "checker," could cause emotional or social embarrassment to student B. Peer checking of papers perhaps should be done only for editing classmates' drafts of stories or research projects or for making suggestions about content and grammar but not for assigning a grade or marking answers right or wrong. To protect students' privacy rights, like the public posting of grades, the use of peer grading for papers also should be avoided. Students may feel harassed and embarrassed, which does not provide a positive and safe learning environment.

Memorizing and Reviewing: Unavoidable Learning Strategies

Sometimes students must memorize things. There is even a time for memorization without much understanding. For example, to learn a language, you must first memorize the alphabet. To learn to play the trumpet, you must memorize the fingering. To learn mathematics, you must first learn the numbering system. In the study of chemistry, you should know the symbols for the common elements. The alphabet, the fingering on the trumpet, numbers, and symbols are all kinds of tools. In mathematics, certain assumptions must be memorized before other concepts can be developed. In fact, in all the disciplines, there are basic points that must be memorized before a learner can understand the major concepts.

When teaching through memorizing, the following guidelines will be helpful:

- *Avoid overuse of memorizing.* Be sure there is a purpose for the memorizing and that the students see what that purpose is. Have students memorize only those things that are absolutely essential to memorize.
- *If possible, have students study for meaning before memorizing.* Some things must be memorized, meaningful or

not, such as German word order or Greek letters, whose shapes seem arbitrary. These are tools of the trade, and they must be mastered to move on. But it is much easier to memorize those things that have meaning if you understand the meaning. For instance, for someone who does not know Latin, it is probably much easier to remember "There is no accounting for taste" than to remember "*De gustibus non est disputandum.*"

■ *Use the recall method, where students study and then try to recall without prompting.*

■ *Encourage the use of mnemonics to aid students in their memorization.* Mnemonics are devices students invent or ones supplied by you. Examples of common mnemonic devices were shown in the section "Integrating Strategies for Integrated Learning," in Chapter 8.

In any class, frequent reviews are necessary because memory is aided by use and because understanding is improved by review. In the sciences, for instance, many concepts cannot be fully understood in isolation. Neither can all the scientific terms be fully appreciated until they are seen in the context of later topics. Frequently, notions that were understood only dimly the first time they were studied become much clearer when revisited later while studying other topics.

In conducting reviews, the teacher must be aware both of the character of the students and of the discipline being pursued. In mathematics and in foreign languages, where so much depends on every link in the great chain, frequent reviews are often necessary. It is profitable to recall almost daily some principles that were previously studied. In disciplines where the parts have less direct connection, such as geography, the reviews may be given at larger intervals, though daily review helps to keep students on their toes.

Here again the techniques of questioning come into play. As far as possible, the review should connect facts to concepts to principles to life's applications, whether in that order or in reverse order or some other combination. Experience in thinking is often more profitable than the knowledge itself.

It is always advantageous to have a general review at the close of any particular study, such as at the end of a unit or of a semester of study. This again enables you to detect any false notions that the students entertained during the study. You now can present the subject as a whole and view one part in the light of another. In human physiology, for instance, much more understanding is gained about the process of growth after a person has studied absorption and secretion. Similarly, the economy of respiration is much clearer when viewed in connection with the circulation of the blood.

A general review can be an enlightening process and is always profitable with perhaps one exception: when the review is instituted solely as preparation for a written examination. Then review may degenerate merely into a device for passing the exam. The purpose of reviewing should be to master the subject for its own sake—to unify concepts—but not to be able to talk about it on one special occasion.

In summary, a review is an opportunity for the students to look at a topic again. It is a "review," a repeat look. It is not the same as drill or practice, though sometimes a teacher can use the same methodology. Review is useful every day as a means for tying the day's lesson to preceding lessons. At this time, you can summarize points that should have been made and establish relationships with past and future lessons. End-of-unit and end-of-term reviews are useful, but it is important that reviewing be more frequent than only at the end of a unit or term because frequent reviews are more effective. Besides, end-of-unit and end-of-term reviews tend to become preparations for examinations.

Almost any technique can be used in review sessions, although the common oral quiz in which the teacher goes around the room asking one fact question after another can become pretty boring. If you do use this type of review, use some scheme to mix up the questions to keep students alert. Tactics that you might want to consider are student summaries, quiz games (classroom Jeopardy seems well liked by students and teachers), dramatizations, student-provided test questions, discussion, broad questioning, and application problems. Techniques that require students to use what they should have learned are good because those techniques may not only serve as review but also provide motivation by opening new vistas for students. Now do Exercise 9.7.

Summary

In this chapter, you learned guidelines for the use of a number of traditional teaching methods that generally are centered on the teacher and involve a lot of teacher talk. Lectures, questioning, discussions, recitations, and so on have all stood the test of time, but unless modified to be more student-centered, they are less useful today than in the past, because of (a) the diversity of students in our schools and classrooms, (b) what has been learned about how young people learn and construct their knowledge, and (c) rapid technological developments for the enhancement of learning and instruction. The latter is the topic of Chapter 10.

You are advised to learn well how to use the strategies discussed in this chapter, however, and to continue to expand your repertoire of methods by developing your understanding and skills in the use of strategies of both modes of acquiring knowledge and skills: the access, or student-centered, mode and the delivery, or teacher-centered, mode. Remember, you should strive to be eclectic in your teaching style—use the best of each mode to make the learning personal, interesting, meaningful, and lasting for your students.

To help make the learning personal, interesting, meaningful, and lasting, there are many instructional aids and materials from which you may choose. That is the topic of the next and final chapter of Part 3.

Exercise 9.1A — The Lecture—Summary Review and Practice

Instructions: The purpose of this exercise is to provide a summary review to check your comprehension of this important, often used, and frequently misused teaching strategy. Answer each of the following questions and then share your responses with your classmates.

1. How does the lecture differ from informal teacher talk?

2. Although sometimes a useful technique, lecturing should be used sparingly in high school classes and even less in junior high and middle school classes. Why is it not as useful as some other strategies?

3. Specifically, when might you use a formal lecture?

4. What can a lecturer do to arouse and maintain interest in the lecture?

5. While planning a lecture, what principles should be kept in mind?

6. Identify at least five things you can do to make a lecture successful.

7. Thinking back to the classes given by the best lecturer in your college experience, what did that professor do that made his or her lectures better than average?

8. Thinking of a lecture or informal talk given by one of your current professors or colleagues, what aids did the lecturer use to spice up the lecture? What devices might have been used that were not? If you were the lecturer, would you have done it differently? If so, explain how.

9. For a specific grade level, prepare a major behavioral objective for a topic in your field. Identify the major points that you would try to make and how you would try to get those points across in a lecture designed to support that major objective.
   Field: Grade level: Topic:
   Major objective:
   Major points:
   Method of achieving:
   Estimate of amount of time needed to present this lecture:

10. Now implement the lecture of item 9 to a group of your peers and obtain their feedback, using the criteria of item 7 for that feedback. If the equipment is available, you may wish to videotape your lecture so you can watch it and evaluate it yourself. On completion of implementing the lecture and obtaining evaluative feedback about it, prepare a self-evaluation of the lecture, again using the criteria of item 8. Share this self-evaluation with your course instructor.

Exercise 9.1B — Prepare a Mini-Lecture

Instructions: The purpose of this exercise is to have you expand on your responses to item 9 from Exercise 9.1A and prepare and deliver a 15-minute mini-lecture. Prepare and use note cards and an outline as guides for your talk. See the guidelines listed in the beginning of this chapter under "Teacher Talk: Formal and Informal." Then share your lecture with your classmates, answer the following questions, and complete and review the suggestions in item 10 in Exercise 9.1A.

1. What color-coding scheme or hierarchy labels did you use to highlight information on your note cards?

2. What advance organizer did you use to hook your audience?

3. What examples and analogies did you use to make your mini-lecture relevant to your audience?

4. What multisenory aspects did you take into consideration?

5. What did you learn from this experience? What would you do differently next time?

Exercise 9.2A — Asking Discipline-Specific Questions

Instructions: There are seven types of questions listed in the section "Types of Questions: A Glossary." Select a topic you are likely to teach in your discipline and prepare an example for each of the following types of questions: clarifying, convergent thinking, cueing, divergent thinking, evaluative, focus, and probing. Then share your responses with your classmates.

Exercise
9.2B

Identifying the Cognitive Levels of Questions—A Self-Check Exercise

Instructions: The purpose of this exercise is to test your understanding and recognition of the levels of questions. Mark each of these questions with the following:

- *1* if it is at the lowest level—gathering and recalling data
- *2* if it requires the student to process data
- *3* if it is at the highest level of mental operation, requiring the student to apply or to evaluate data in a new situation

Check your answers against the answer key found on page 360. Resolve problems by discussing them with your instructor and classmates.

_____ **1.** John, do you agree with Maria?

_____ **2.** How does the repetition in *Bolero* affect you?

_____ **3.** Do you believe that argument will hold up in the case of Swaziland?

_____ **4.** What must I multiply by in order to clear the fractions in this equation?

_____ **5.** Did O. Henry's trick ending make the story more interesting?

_____ **6.** How would you end the story?

_____ **7.** Who came out of the door, the lady or the tiger?

_____ **8.** How do the natural resources of the United States compare with those of China?

_____ **9.** If you were setting up the defense of the colonies, where would you put the forts?

_____ **10.** In view of all the information we have, do you believe the union's sending out 70,000 letters asking voters to defeat the six assemblymen was justified?

_____ **11.** What difference has an equal rights amendment made?

_____ **12.** Who was Otto Jespersen?

_____ **13.** Should a teacher be entitled to unemployment benefits during the summer months when school is not in session?

_____ **14.** What would you do in this situation if you were governor?

_____ **15.** What would have happened if Washington had decided to attack New Brunswick rather than Quebec?

_____ **16.** What would happen if you used H_2SO_4 instead of HCl?

_____ **17.** How would you set up the equation?

_____ **18.** Why did you like this poem better than the previous one?

_____ **19.** Which type of cell, animal or plant, has a cell wall?

_____ **20.** When $2N - 10 = 0$, what does N equal?

Exercise
9.3

An Analysis of the Quality of Questions—A Self-Check Exercise

Instructions: The purpose of this exercise is to practice your skill in analyzing questions. Evaluate the following questions by checking the Poor, Fair, or Good column for each question. Use the following code in the right column to indicate your reasons why.

A = Calls for no answer and is a pseudoquestion

B = Asks for recall but little or no thinking

C = Challenging, stimulating, or discussion-provoking type of question that calls for high-level thinking, including reasoning and problem solving

On completion, check your responses against the answer key found on page 360 and discuss any problems with your classmates and instructor.

Questions	Poor	Fair	Good	Why?
1. In what region are major earthquakes located?				
2. According to the theory of isostasy, how would you describe our mountainous regions?				
3. What mineral will react with HCl to produce CO_2?				
4. What kind of rock is highly resistant to weathering?				
5. Will the continents look different in the future? Why?				
6. Who can describe what a continental shelf is?				
7. What caused the industrial revolution?				

Exercise 9.3   **An Analysis of the Quality of Questions—A Self-Check Exercise** *continued*

Questions	Poor	Fair	Good	Why?
8. What political scandal involved President Harding?				
9. This is a parallelogram, isn't it?				
10. Wouldn't you agree that the base angles of an isosceles triangle are congruent?				
11. In trying to determine the proof of this exercise, what would you suggest we examine at the outset?				
12. What conclusion can be drawn concerning the points of intersection of two graphs?				
13. Why is pure water a poor conductor of electricity?				
14. How do fossils help explain the theory of plate tectonics?				
15. If Macbeth had told you about his encounter with the apparitions, what advice would you have offered?				
16. Who said, "If it were done when 'tis done, then 'twere well it were done quickly"?				
17. In the poem "The Sick Rose," what do you think Blake means by "the invisible worm"?				
18. Should teachers censor the books that students read?				
19. Explain the phrase "ontogeny recapitulates phylogeny."				
20. Name the 10 life functions.				
21. What living thing can live without air?				
22. What is chlorophyll?				
23. Explain the difference between RNA and DNA.				
24. Who developed the periodic table based on the fact that elements are functions of their atomic weight?				
25. Johnny, why aren't you in your seat?				

Exercise
9.4
Observing the Cognitive Levels of Classroom Verbal Interaction

Instructions: The purpose of this exercise is to develop your skill in recognizing the levels of classroom questions. Arrange to visit a middle school or secondary school classroom. Tally each time you hear a question (or statement) from the teacher that causes students to gather or recall information, to process information, or to apply or evaluate data. In the left-hand column, you may want to write in additional key words to assist your memory. After your observation, compare and discuss the results of this exercise with your classmates.

School and class visited: _____

Date of observation: _____

Level	Tallies of Level of Question or Statement
1. Recall level (key words: *complete, count, define, describe,* and so on)	1.
2. Processing level (key words: *analyze, classify, compare,* and so on)	2.
3. Application level (key words: *apply, build, evaluate,* and so on)	3.

Exercise
9.5
A Cooperative Learning Exercise in the Use of Questioning—Micro Peer-Teaching—MPT II

Instructions: The purpose of this exercise is to practice preparing and asking questions that are designed to lead student thinking from the lowest level to the highest. Before class, prepare a five-minute lesson for posing questions that will guide the learner from lowest to highest levels of thinking. Teaching will be one-on-one, in groups of four, with each member of the group assuming a particular role—teacher, student, judge, or recorder. Each of the four members of your group will assume each of those roles once for five minutes. (If there are only three members in a group, the roles of judge and recorder can be combined during each five-minute lesson; if there are five members in the group, one member can sit out each round or two can work together as judges.) Each member of the group should have his or her own tally sheet.

(continued)

Exercise 9.5 **A Cooperative Learning Exercise in the Use of Questioning—Micro Peer-Teaching—MPT II** *continued*

Suggested Lesson Topics
- Teaching styles
- Characteristics of youngsters of a particular age
- Learning styles of students
- Evaluation of learning achievement
- A skill or hobby
- Teaching competencies
- A particular teaching strategy
- Student teaching and what it will really be like

Each of your group members should keep the following role descriptions in mind:
- *Teacher (sender)*. Pose recall (input), processing, and application (output) questions related to one of the topics above or to any topic you choose.
- *Student (receiver)*. Respond to the questions of the teacher.
- *Judge*. Identify the level of each question or statement used by the teacher *and* the level of the student's response.
- *Recorder*. Tally the number of questions or statements used by the teacher (S = sender) at each level, as indicated by the judge; also tally the level of student responses (R = receiver). Record any problems encountered by your group.

Exercise 9.6 **Teacher Interaction with Students According to Student Gender or Other Personal Characteristics**

Instructions: The purpose of this exercise is to provide a tool for your analysis of your own interactions with students according to gender. (*Note:* In addition to the gender variable, the exercise can be modified to include responses and their frequencies according to other teacher-student interactions, such as calling on all students equally for responses to your questions, calling on students equally to assist you with classroom helping jobs, chastising students for their inappropriate behavior, or asking questions to assume classroom leadership roles.) To become accustomed to the exercise, you should do a trial run in one of your university classes, then use it during your student teaching and again during your first years of teaching. The exercise can be modified to include (a) the amount of time given for each interaction, (b) the response time given by the teacher according to student gender, and (c) other student characteristics, such as race.

Prior to class, select a student (this will be you during the trial run recommended above) or an outside observer, such as a colleague, to do the tallying and calculations as follows. Ask the person to tally secretly the interactions between you and the students by placing a mark after the name of each student (or on the student's position on a seating chart) with whom you have verbal interaction. If a student does the tallying, he or she should not be counted in any of the calculations.

Exact time at start _____

Exact time at end _____

Total time in minutes _____

Calculations before Tallying

a. Total number of students _____

b. Number of female students _____

c. Number of male students _____

d. Percentage of students who are female _____ (= b divided by a)

e. Percentage of students who are male _____ (= c divided by a) (Check: d + e should = 100%)

Calculations after Tallying

f. Total females interacting _____

g. Total males interacting _____

h. Percentage of students interacting _____ (f + g divided by a)

i. Total female tallies _____

j. Total male tallies _____

k. Total of all tallies (i + j) _____

l. Percentage of interactions with students who are female _____ (i divided by k)

m. Percentage of interactions with students who are male _____ (j divided by k)

n. Most tallies for any one male _____

o. Percentage of class interactions directed to most frequently addressed male _____ (n divided by k)

p. Most tallies for any one female _____

q. Percentage of class interactions directed to most frequently addressed female _____ (p divided by k)

Teacher Conclusions:

Exercise
9.7

Developing a Lesson Using Inquiry Level II, Thinking Skill Development, a Demonstration, or an Interactive Lecture—Micro Peer-Teaching—MPT III

Instructions: The purpose of this exercise is to provide the opportunity for you to create a brief lesson (about 20 minutes of instructional time but to be specified by your instructor) designed for a specific grade level and subject and to try it out on your peers for their feedback in an informal (i.e., nongraded) micro peer-teaching demonstration.

Divide your class into four groups. The task of each group's members is to prepare lessons (individually) that fall into one of the four categories: Level II inquiry, thinking level, demonstration, or interactive lecture. Schedule class presentations so that each class member has the opportunity to present his or her lesson and to obtain feedback from class members about it. For feedback, class members who are the "teacher's" audience can complete the assessment rubric shown after this exercise and give their completed form to the teacher for use in self-assessment. Before your class starts this exercise, you may want to review the scoring rubric and make modifications to it that the class agrees on.

To structure your lesson plan, use one of the sample lesson plan formats presented in Chapter 7; however, each lesson should be centered around one major theme or concept and be planned for about 20 minutes of instructional time.

Group 1: Develop a Level II inquiry lesson.

Group 2: Develop a lesson designed to raise the level of student thinking.

Group 3: Develop a lesson that involves a demonstration.

Group 4: Develop a lesson that is an interactive lecture.

Chapter 9 POSTTEST

Short Explanation

1. Identify and describe five cautions when using teacher talk.

2. Identify ways you can recapture student attention during your use of direct instruction.

3. Explain precautions a teacher needs to consider when going from a student-centered activity to a teacher-centered activity during the same class period.

4. Is hands-on learning necessarily minds-on learning as well? Explain.

5. Identify some of the specific strategies you can use to help students develop their critical thinking and problem-solving skills in your subject area.

6. Explain the meaning of "establishing eye contact" as it is discussed in this chapter.

7. Distinguish between role play and simulation as instructional activities.

8. Give an example of a mnemonic and explain why your example is a mnemonic.

9. Give an example of a demonstration that you would be likely to use for a specific grade level/course (identify) in your subject area. Explain why you would use the demonstration for teaching this content rather than some other strategy.

10. Explain the meaning of metacognition. How would you use metacognition in your teaching?

Essay

1. Which category of instructional strategies—student centered or teacher centered—do you believe contributes more to a student's developing self-esteem? Explain why.

2. Describe when, if ever, students should be expected to memorize material in your subject area.

3. Describe specific strategies that you would use to exercise equality in your classroom.

4. From your current observations and fieldwork related to this teacher preparation program, clearly identify one specific example of educational practice that seems contradictory to exemplary practice or theory presented in this chapter. Present your explanation for the discrepancy.

5. Describe any prior concepts you held that changed as a result of your experiences with this chapter. Describe the changes.

Newscom

Educational Technology, Media, Computer-Based Instructional Tools, and Other Resources

The most extraordinary thing about a really good teacher is that he or she transcends accepted educational methods. Such methods are designed to help average teachers approximate the performance of good teachers.[1]

—MARGARET MEAD

Specific Objectives

At the completion of this chapter, you will be able to:

▸ Demonstrate an awareness of and competency in using a variety of materials, tools, and resources in your teaching.

▸ Develop a philosophy for integrating technology in your teaching.

▸ Explain copyright laws and fair use guidelines for using printed and media materials for teaching.

▸ Illustrate an understanding about using community resources, speakers, and field trips.

▸ Demonstrate an awareness of electronic media available for teaching in your subject field, how they can be used, and how and where they can be obtained.

Chapter 10 Overview

It is important to note that there is a vast variety of useful materials and effective tools that can complement your instructional strategies and help you to engage your students. We are sure you are familiar with some of them that are highlighted here; many may be new to you. Although there are numerous textbooks, manuals, ebooks, and professional development workshops designed specifically to acquaint you with the National Education Technology Standards and new and emerging technologies, in this chapter we cover how best to take advantage of a variety of overlooked but enduring resources and suggest how you can transform your learning environment and the teaching and learning process by infusing technology to improve your classroom instruction. In addition to reviewing the resources in this chapter, see the lesson and unit plans included in Chapter 7 for effective use of a variety of the materials and tools covered here.

Because we have already covered textbooks (in Chapter 5), we begin this chapter with a discussion of other printed resources and visual displays that can supplement textbooks in addition to covering visual displays like the writing board and bulletin board. We also discuss resources available through connections in the local community, potential guest speakers, and possible field trips. Networks and educational technology like the Internet, World Wide Web, search engines, Wikipedia, virtual field trips, communication tools, and other tools are also covered. In this chapter, we also mention media tools in addition to the wealth of computer software, programmed instructional systems, and digital technologies from which you can draw as you plan your instructional strategies.

Since you could become easily overwhelmed by the sheer quantity of different materials and tools available for classroom use, we have described the most accessible and practical ones available here to heighten your awareness and highlight their application in the field of education. You could spend a lot of time reviewing, sorting, selecting, and practicing with these materials and tools. Although nobody can make the job easier for you, information in this chapter may expedite the process or get you thinking about how best to use different materials and tools in addition to how best to integrate technology across your curriculum. This chapter also provides suggestions about where to procure resources for instruction—after all, if you do not have them, you cannot use them. What you need to know in order to abide by copyright laws and apply fair use guidelines is also addressed. As you peruse this chapter, we remind you again about starting a professional resources file (see Figure 1.4 in Chapter 1).

Introduction

Long ago, before writing as we know it today was invented, men and women taught their children by means of very simple and practical tools. Oral tradition, where adults passed down important information to children, was a preferred teaching technique, but there were other teaching and learning methods, too. Children, through play, learned to hunt by practicing with spears, by throwing sticks, and by simulating animal hunts. Parents taught geography by maps drawn in the sand and religion by pictures drawn on the walls of caves. Dance and drama portrayed the history, customs, and lore of a group. From the very earliest times, teachers have depended on diverse teaching tools to make their teaching interesting and effective.

Today, teachers still depend on a variety of teaching tools. In some respects, modern teaching tools are much more sophisticated than those of earlier times. Yet we use our new tools for the same purposes and in much the same ways that our ancestors used theirs: to make things clear, to make instruction real, to spice up the learning process, and to make it possible for students to teach themselves. Teaching would be impossible without some instructional aids. Here we will review a variety of tools and materials that are available to teachers today. Although what is covered in this chapter is not meant to be exhaustive, we will highlight numerous tools and possibilities for their application.

Printed Materials and Visual Displays

Historically, of all the materials available for instruction, the printed textbook has had and still has the most influence on teaching and learning (discussed in Chapter 5). Besides the student textbook and perhaps an accompanying workbook, there is a vast array of other printed materials available for use in teaching, many of which are available for free. (See the section "Sources of Free and Inexpensive Printed Materials" that follows.) Printed materials include books, workbooks, pamphlets, magazines, brochures, newspapers, professional journals, periodicals, and copied materials, including those from Internet sources (which will be covered later in this chapter).

As mentioned in Chapter 5, when selecting textbooks, you need to consider the appropriateness of the material in both content and reading level. Other printed materials you may decide to use in your lessons include (a) current articles from newspapers, magazines, and periodicals related to the content that your students will be studying or to the skills they will be learning; (b) workbooks available from trade book publishers that emphasize thinking and problem solving rather than rote memorization (with an assortment of workbooks, you can have students working on similar but different assignments, depending on their interests and abilities—an example of multilevel teaching); (c) various pamphlets, brochures, and other printed materials that students can read for specific information and viewpoints about particular topics; and (d) inexpensive paperbacks that would provide multiple book readings for your students. To use these supplemental materials, you need to consult copyright laws (see Figure 10.3).

Sources of Free and Inexpensive Printed Materials

For free and inexpensive printed materials, look for sources at your college or university, the public library, the curriculum library in your education department, or the resource center at a local school district, such as those listed in Figure 5.2 in Chapter 5. Additionally, teachers can obtain free and inexpensive teaching materials through connections on the Internet. When considering using materials that you have obtained for free or inexpensively, you will want to ensure that the materials are appropriate for use with the age-group with which you work and that they are free of bias or an unwanted message. The **National Education Association (NEA)** has published guidelines for teachers to consider before purchasing or using commercial materials; for a free copy, contact NEA Communications, 1201 16th St. NW, Washington, DC 20036; phone: 202-822-7200.

Professional Journals and Periodicals

Figure 10.1 lists examples of the many professional periodicals and journals that can provide useful teaching ideas and website information and that carry information about instructional materials and how to get them. Some of these may be in your university or college library, and others may be accessible through your library's interlibrary loan agreement. Still, other full-text journal articles are accessible through Internet sources. Check around for these and other titles of interest to you.

The ERIC Information Network

The Educational Resources Information Center (ERIC) system, established by the Institute of Education Sciences of the U.S. Department of Education, is a widely used network providing access to information and research in education. In fact, ERIC is the largest digital library of educational literature in the world. It is searchable and easy to use. In addition to the comprehensive bibliography, journal lists, and nonjournal sources, including books, conference papers, conference proceedings, and policy papers, ERIC catalogs many full-text articles. Selected ERIC clearinghouses and their addresses are shown in Figure 10.2.

Figure 10.1 Selected Professional Journals and Periodicals of Interest to Middle School and Secondary School Teachers

The American Biology Teacher	*Journal of Physical Education and Recreation*	*Praxis*
American Educational Research Quarterly	*Journal of Reading*	*The Reading Teacher*
The American Music Teacher	*Journal of Teaching in Physical Education*	*Reading Today*
American Teacher	*Language Arts*	*School Arts*
The Art Teacher	*Language Learning*	*School Library Journal*
Classroom Connect	*Learning*	*The School Musician*
The Computing Teacher	*The Mathematics Teacher*	*School Science and Mathematics*
The Earth Scientist	*Mathematics Teaching in the Middle School*	*School Shop*
Educational Leadership		*Science*
English Journal	*The Middle School Journal*	*Science Activities*
English Language Teaching Journal	*Modern Language Journal*	*Science Scope*
Hispania	*Music Educator's Journal*	*The Science Teacher*
The History Teacher	*NEA Today*	*Social Education*
Journal of Business Education	*The Negro Educational Review*	*The Social Studies*
Journal of Chemical Education	*The New Advocate*	*Social Studies Review*
Journal of Economic Education	*Nexus: A Journal for Teachers in Development*	*Teacher Magazine*
Journal of Geography		*Teaching Tolerance*
Journal of Home Economics	*OAH Magazine of History*	*TESOL Quarterly*
Journal of Learning Disabilities	*Phi Delta Kappan*	*Theory and Research in Social Education*
Journal of the National Association of Bilingual Educators	*Physical Education*	*Voices from the Middle*
	The Physics Teacher	

Figure 10.2 Selected ERIC Addresses

- **Assessment and Evaluation.** http://ericae.net
- **Disabilities and Gifted Children.** Council for Exceptional Children (CEC), 1920 Association Drive, Reston, VA 22191-1589. http://www.sedoparking.com/ericec.org
- **ERIC.** http://www.ed.gov
  Links to:
  - American Indian and Alaska Native Education
  - Mexican American Education
  - Migrant Education
  - Outdoor Education
  - Rural Education
  - Small Schools

- **Information and Technology.** Center for Science and Technology, Syracuse University, Syracuse, NY 13244-4100. http://ericit.org/
- **Languages and Linguistics.** Center for Applied Linguistics. http://www.cal.org/resources/archive/eric/index.html
- **Practical Assessment, Research and Evaluation** (formerly ericae). http://pareonline.net/
- **Social Studies/Social Science Education.** http://teacherpathfinder.org/school/subjects/socstud/gensoc.html
- **Center for Applied Linguistics (CAL).** http://www.cal.org

Copying Printed and Other Materials

Remember that, although on many printed materials and on Web pages there are no specific notices indicating that the material is covered under copyright, the material is still copyrighted. Original material is protected by copyright law; that is just as true for the intellectual property created by a minor as it is for that created by an adult.

Although space here prohibits full inclusion of the U.S. legal guidelines, your local school district should be able to provide a copy of current district policies for compliance with copyright laws. District policies should include guidelines for teachers and students in publishing materials on

the Internet. If no district guidelines are available, adhere to the guidelines shown in Figure 10.3 when using printed materials.[2] Also, complete Activity 10.1 to better understand **fair use guidelines.**

When preparing to make a copy, you must find out whether the law permits the copying under the category of "permitted use." If not allowed under "permitted use," then you must get written permission to reproduce the material from the holder of the copyright. If the address of the source is not given on the material, addresses may be obtained from various references, such as *Literary Marketplace*, *Audio-Visual Marketplace*, and *Ulrich's International Periodicals Directory*.

Figure 10.3   **Guidelines for Copying Printed Materials That Are Copyrighted**

Permitted uses—you may make:

1. Single copies of a(n):
   - chapter of a book.
   - article from a periodical, magazine, or newspaper.
   - short story, short essay, or short poem whether or not from a collected work.
   - chart, graph, diagram, drawing, or cartoon.
   - illustration from a book, magazine, or newspaper.

2. Multiple copies for classroom use (not to exceed one copy per student in a course) of a(n):
   - complete poem if less than 250 words.
   - excerpt from a longer poem, but not to exceed 250 words.
   - complete article, story, or essay of less than 2,500 words.
   - excerpt from a larger printed work not to exceed 10 percent of the whole or 1,000 words.
   - chart, graph, diagram, cartoon, or picture per book or magazine issue.

Prohibited uses—you may *not*:

1. Copy more than one work or two excerpts from a single author during one class term (semester or year).
2. Copy more than three works from a collective work or periodical volume during one class term.
3. Reproduce more than nine sets of multiple copies for distribution to students in one class term.
4. Copy to create or replace or substitute for anthologies or collective works.
5. Copy "consumable" works (e.g., workbooks, standardized tests, or answer sheets).
6. Copy the same work year after year.

SOURCE: Section 107 of the 1976 Federal Omnibus Copyright Revision Act.

The Classroom Writing Board

As is true for an auto mechanic, a brain surgeon, or any other professional, a teacher needs to know when and how to use the tools of the trade. One of the tools available to almost every classroom teacher is the **writing board**. In this section, you will find guidelines for using this important tool.

Writing boards used to be—and in some schools still are—slate blackboards (slate is a type of metamorphic rock). In today's classroom, however, the writing board is more likely to be either a board made of painted plywood (chalkboard), which, like the blackboard, is also quickly becoming obsolete to some extent because of the concern about the dust created from using chalk,[3] or a white or colored (light green and light blue are common) multipurpose dry-erase board, on which you write with special nonpermanent marking pens and erase with a soft cloth. In addition to providing a surface on which you can write and draw, the multipurpose board can be used as a projection screen and as a surface to which figures cut from colored transparency film will stick. It may also have a magnetic backing.

Use colored chalk or marking pens to highlight your board talk. This is especially helpful for students with learning challenges. Beginning at the top left of the board, print neatly and clearly, with the writing intentionally positioned to indicate content relationships (e.g., causal, oppositional, numerical, comparative, categorical, and so on). Use the writing board to acknowledge acceptance and to record student contributions.

Print instructions for an activity on the board in addition to giving them orally. Learn to use the board without having to turn your back entirely on students and without blocking their view of the board. When you have a lot of material to put on the board, do it before class and then cover it. Better yet, put the material on transparencies and use the overhead projector rather than the board or use both.

The Classroom Bulletin Board

Bulletin boards also are found in nearly every classroom, although they are sometimes poorly used or not used at all. However, they can be relatively inexpensively transformed

Activity 10.1   **Fair Use Guidelines**

Deciding what materials you can copy from a book and distribute to your students, what documentaries you can tape on PBS and show in class, what images found online you can integrate into your PowerPoint or Prezi presentations, or what you can post on the Internet without infringing copyright law can be a daunting task. To help educators "do the right thing," several different groups have attempted to interpret copyright law and establish fair use guidelines. Although the earliest guidelines appeared in 1976, more recent ones came from the Conference on Fair Use in the 1990s. To find out what fair use is, when to apply it, and what four factors are covered under the limits of fair use, check out the website of the Copyright Management Center at **http://www.copyright .iupui.edu/index.htm.**

You can also review a summary of key court cases, common classroom scenarios, and guidelines on the following: photocopying; taping television broadcasts; using software, music, and digital images; delivering distance learning and transmitting materials; showing videos and movies; and obtaining copyright permissions.

Apply Your Knowledge

After perusing the various information on fair use guidelines presented on the Copyright Management Center website listed above, take the Copyright Quiz at **http://www.csus.edu/indiv/p/ peachj/edte230/copyright/quiz.htm** to test your knowledge of common copyright questions that arise in educational settings.

into attractive and valuable instructional tools. Among other uses, the bulletin board is a convenient location to post reminders, assignments and schedules, and commercially produced materials and to celebrate and display model student work and anchor papers.

To plan, design, and prepare bulletin board displays, some teachers use student assistants or committees, giving those students guidance and responsibility for planning, preparing, and maintaining bulletin board displays. When preparing a bulletin board display, keep these guidelines in mind: the display should be simple—emphasizing one main idea, concept, topic, or theme—and captions should be short and concise; illustrations can accent learning topics; verbs can vitalize the captions; phrases can punctuate a student's thoughts; and alliteration can announce anything you wish on the board. Finally, as in all other aspects of the classroom learning environment, remember to ensure that the bulletin board display reflects gender, racial, and ethnic equity.

Resources

There are many ways to make your lessons relevant to your students' lives by leveraging connections between school and the real world. Accessing resources that are available in your community, inviting guest speakers into your classroom, and taking your students on educational field trips are all ways to create a supportive environment where all students can grow.

The Community as a Resource

One of the richest resources for learning is the local community and the people and places in it. You will want to build your own file of community resources—speakers, sources for free materials, and field trip locations. Your school may already have a community resource file available for your use. However, it may need updating. A community resource file (see Figure 10.4) should contain information about (a) possible field trip locations, (b) community resource people who could serve as guest speakers or mentors, and (c) local agencies that can provide information and instructional materials.

There are many ways of using community resources, and several have been demonstrated by the schools specifically mentioned throughout this book (see *Schools* in the index). Here the discussion is limited to two often used although sometimes abused instructional tools: (1) guest speakers and (2) out-of-classroom and off-campus excursions, commonly called *field trips*.

Guest Speakers

Bringing outside speakers into your classroom can be a valuable educational experience for students but not automatically so. In essence, guest speakers can be classified within a spectrum of four types, two of which should not be considered. First, ideally, a speaker is both informative and inspiring. Second, a speaker may be inspiring but with nothing substantive to offer, except for the possible diversion the talk might offer from the usual rigors

Figure 10.4 **Community Resource for Speakers, Materials, and Field Trips**

Airport	Farm	Newspaper plant
Apiary	Fire department	Observatory
Aquarium	Fish hatchery	Oil refinery
Archaeological site	Flea market	Park
Art gallery	Foreign embassy	Poetry reading
Assembly plant	Forest and forest preserve	Police station
Bakery	Freeway under construction	Post office and package delivery company
Bird and wildlife sanctuary	Gas company	Recycling center
Book publisher	Geological site	Retail store
Bookstore	Health department and hospital	Sanitation department
Broadcasting and TV station	Highway construction site	Sawmill or lumber company
Building being razed	Highway patrol station	Shopping mall
Building under construction	Historical sites and monuments	Shoreline (stream, lake, wetland, ocean)
Canal lock	Industrial plant	Telecommunications center
Cemetery	Legislature session	Town meeting
Chemical plant	Levee and water reservoir	Universities and colleges
City or county planning commission	Library and archive	Utility company
Courthouse	Mass transit authority	Warehouse
Dairy	Military installation	Water reservoir and treatment plant
Dam and floodplain	Mine	Weather bureau and storm center
Dock and harbor	Museum	Wildlife park and preserve
Factory	Native American Indian reservation	Zoo

of classroom work. Third, the speaker might be informative but boring to students. Finally, at the worst end of this spectrum is the guest speaker who is both boring and uninformative. So, just like any other instructional experience, making a guest speaker effective takes careful planning on your part. To make sure that the experience is beneficial to student learning, consider the following guidelines:

- If at all possible, meet and talk with the guest speaker in advance to inform him or her about your students and your expectations for the presentation as well as to gauge how motivational and informative he or she might be. If you believe the speaker might be informative but boring, then perhaps you can help structure the presentation in some way to make it a bit more inspiring. For example, stop the speaker every few minutes and involve the students in questions and discussions of points made.

- Prepare students in advance with key points of information that you expect them to obtain.

- Guide students in preparing questions to ask the speaker. Focus on things the students want to find out and information you want them to inquire about.

- Follow up the presentation with a thank-you letter to the guest speaker and perhaps further questions that developed during class discussions subsequent to the speaker's presentation.

Field Trips

What is the most memorable field trip that you were ever on as a student? What made it memorable? You may want to discuss these questions and others like them with your students.

Today's schools often have very limited funds for the transportation and liability costs of field trips. In some cases, there are no funds at all. At times, parent-teacher groups, businesses, and civic organizations help by providing financial resources so that students get valuable firsthand experiences that field trips so often can offer.

To prepare for and implement a successful field trip, there are three important stages of planning—before, during, and after—and critical decisions to be made at each stage. Consider the following guidelines.

BEFORE THE FIELD TRIP When the field trip is your idea (and not the students'), discuss the idea with your teaching team, principal, or department chair (especially when transportation will be needed) *before* mentioning the idea to your students. There is no cause served by getting students excited about a trip before you know if it is feasible.

Once you have obtained the necessary but tentative approval from school officials, take the trip yourself (or with team members), if possible. A previsit allows you to determine how to make the field trip most productive. For this previsit, you might consider taking a couple of your students along for their ideas and help. If a previsit is not

possible, you still will need to arrange for travel directions; arrival and departure times; parking; briefing by the host, if there is one; storage of students' personal items, such as coats and lunches; provisions for eating and restrooms; and fees, if any.

If there are fees involved, inquire about reduced costs for large groups or possible grants to waive admissions fees for school groups. Arrange for the collection of money that is needed for fees. If there are out-of-pocket costs to be paid by students, this information needs to be included on the permission form. No students should ever be excluded from the field trip because of a lack of money. If you need to pay the admissions fees, you need to talk with your administration about who will cover the fees. If the trip is worth taking, the school should cover the costs. If that is not possible, perhaps students can plan a fund-raising activity or financial assistance can be obtained from some other source. If this does not work, you might consider an alternative that does not involve costs.

Arrange for official permission from the school administration. This usually requires a form for requesting, planning, and reporting field trips. After permission has been obtained, you can discuss the field trip with your students and arrange for permissions from their parents or guardians. Although the permission form should include a statement that the parent or guardian absolves the teacher and the school from liability should an accident occur, it *does not* lessen the teacher's and the school's responsibilities should there be negligence by a teacher, driver, or chaperone.

Arrange for students to be excused from their other classes while on the field trip. Using an information form prepared and signed by you and perhaps by the principal, the students should then assume responsibility for notifying their other teachers of the planned absence from classes and for assuring them that whatever work is missed will be made up. In addition, you will need to make arrangements for your own teaching duties to be covered. In some schools, teachers cooperate by filling in for those who will be gone. In other schools, substitute teachers are hired. Sometimes teachers have to hire their own substitute.

Arrange for whatever transportation is needed. Your principal or the principal's designee will help you with the details. In many schools, someone else is responsible for arranging transportation. In any case, the use of private automobiles is ill advised because you and the school could be liable for the acts of the drivers.

Plan details for student safety and the monitoring of their safety from departure to return. A first-aid kit and a system of student control, such as a buddy system whereby students must remain paired throughout the trip, should be in place. The pairs sometimes are given numbers that are recorded and kept by the teacher and the chaperones and then checked at departure time, periodically during the trip, at the time of return, and again on return. Use adult chaperones. As a very general rule, there should be one adult chaperone for every 10 students. Some districts have a policy regarding this. While on a field trip, at all times all students should be under the direct supervision of an adult.

Establish and discuss, to the extent you believe necessary, the rules of behavior your students should follow, including details of the trip, its purpose, directions, what they should wear and bring, academic expectations of them (e.g., consider giving each student a study guide), and follow-up activities. In addition, cover information about what to do if anything should go awry, for example, if a student is late for the departure or return, loses a personal possession along the way, gets lost, is injured, becomes sick, or misbehaves.

Because a field trip is supposed to promote learning, the learning expectations need to be clearly defined and the students given an explanation of how and where they may encounter the learning experience. Before the field trip, students should be asked questions such as "What do we already know about _____?," "What do we want to find out about _____?," and "How can we find out _____?," and then, with their assistance, an appropriate guide can be prepared for the students to use during the field trip. To further ensure learning and individual student responsibility for that learning, you may want to assign different roles and responsibilities to students, just as would be done in cooperative learning, ensuring that each student has a role with responsibility. One role you may assign would be to record the field trip experience.

DURING THE FIELD TRIP If your field trip has been carefully planned according to the preceding guidelines, it should be a valuable and safe experience for all. En route, while at the trip location, and on the return to school, you and the adult chaperones should monitor student behavior and learning just as you do in the classroom.

AFTER THE FIELD TRIP Plan the follow-up activities. As with any other lesson plan, the field trip lesson is complete only when there is both a proper introduction and a well-planned closure. All sorts of follow-up activities can be planned as an educational wrap-up to this educational experience. For example, a bulletin board committee can plan and prepare an attractive display summarizing the trip. Students can write about their experiences in their journals or as papers. Small groups can give oral reports to the class about what they did and learned. Their reports can then serve as springboards for further class discussion and perhaps further investigations. Finally, for future planning, all who were involved should contribute to an assessment of the experience.

Networks and Educational Technology

We are preparing students for jobs that do not exist right now. This is a daunting task. How do we know what our students will need? Although we cannot predict the specifics surrounding the knowledge, skills, and abilities the future will demand, what educators do know is that our students will need what is summarized by the four Cs of 21st Century Skills: (1) critical thinking and problem solving, (2) communication, (3) collaboration, and (4) creativity and innovation (as described in Chapter 2).

Technology is a gateway to engaging students in the classroom and guiding them to develop the skills mentioned here. Students are invested in learning when they see relevance and applicability to their world. Since students are using technology every day inside and outside the classroom, it is important for teachers to recognize its powerful potential. Using technologies that students already love helps motivate them and sparks interest in the topic presented. Students learn in a variety of ways, and technology, when used well, can incorporate several of Gardner's Multiple Intelligences (discussed in Chapter 3) in a short amount of time. For example, students who are shy will write, students who are creative will publish, and problem solvers will research.

Technology motivates, plain and simple. The seven-year-old child who can operate an iPad, download his own flash cards to learn his multiplication tables, search the World Wide Web to find out why spiders have eight legs, and create a slide show of his family vacation and set it to music, all with very little instruction or support from his parents, is a member of the technology revolution. It is important that we keep in mind that as digital learners, our students are motivated to use technology for learning and sharing information at home and in the classroom. They have grown up with video games, cell phones, televisions, home computers, screen media, text messaging, and a plethora of other technology tools. Technology motivates students because it allows them to be in control of their own learning, provides them with the opportunity to be creative, and allows them to teach each other.

The Internet

Accessing information on the World Wide Web has changed how middle- and secondary-level teachers plan, design their lessons, and assess their students. Today, many students and teachers in the United States have access to the Internet and its many resources. In fact, the Internet is considered a powerful tool in the teaching-learning process. For many students who have grown up in the digital age, the Internet is ubiquitous, yet many do not know the origins of this global system of connected networks representing millions of private, public, academic, business, and government interests. Here we will provide a brief overview of how the Internet came to be.

Originating from a Department of Defense project (called ARPAnet, named after the federal government's Advanced Research Projects Agency) at the University of California, Los Angeles, computer science department in 1969, designed to establish a computer network of military researchers, the federally funded Internet has become an enormous, steadily expanding, worldwide system of connected computer networks. The Internet (also known as the "Information Superhighway," "cyberspace," or simply the "Net") provides literally millions of resources to explore, with thousands more added nearly every day. In 1998, when the sixth edition of this book was published, it was difficult to find published information about the Internet. Today, you can surf the Internet and find many sources about how to use it. You can even search the Internet to find numerous ways that educators at all levels and across all disciplines are using the Internet with their students. In Chapter 7, we highlighted ways that teachers designed their lesson and unit plans for their middle- and secondary-level students to access and use the Internet and its vast resources.

However, new technologies are steadily emerging, and the Internet changes every day; some sites and resources disappear or are not kept current, others change their location and undergo reconstruction, and still other new ones appear. Therefore, it would be superfluous for us in this book, which will be around for several years, to get *too* enthused about sites that we personally have viewed and can recommend as teacher resources. Nevertheless, Figure 8.8 in Chapter 8 and Figure 10.5 list available Internet resources that we found and liked. Other sites have been mentioned throughout this book and are highlighted in this chapter; every effort has been made to verify that the websites included here are active links. Perhaps you have found others that you can share with your classmates (and with us). To that end, now do Exercise 10.1.

Cautions and Guidelines for Using the Internet

If you have not yet learned to use the Internet, there are many resources available to you, including the experts that can be found among your peers, on your college or university staff, and among members of any public school faculty. It is important that you become familiar with the Internet and all the information you can glean through its resources because many of your future middle and secondary students access the Internet several times a day for varied purposes: entertainment, recreation, and communication. Even if they access the Internet regularly, your students may be less familiar with the many ways the information found on the Internet can be used for educational purposes. If students have been already using the Internet for research purposes, they may not know how to evaluate resources to determine if they are reliable, accurate, current, appropriate, or unbiased.

There is a proliferation of information today on the Internet. You may wonder, except for the obvious reliable sites such as the *New York Times* and the Library of Congress, how a person can determine the validity and currency of a particular piece of information. When searching for useful and reliable information on a particular topic, how can one be protected from wasting valuable time sifting

Figure 10.5 Internet Sites: Materials and Technology Use

- **California Learning Resource Network** http://www.clrn.org/home/?CFID=61266341&CFTOKEN=60303725&jsessionid=f030c87f268faf81600c405f4f403e5e4667
- **Education World** http://www.education-world.com/
- **Educator's Reference Desk** http://www.eduref.org/
- **Electronic Reference Formats** http://www.apastyle.org/elecref.html
- **Enhance Learning with Technology** http://members.shaw.ca/priscillatheroux/differentiating.html
- **Epicenter** http://www.epicent.com
- **ERIC** http://www.eric.ed.gov
- **Interactive Frog Dissection** http://frog.edschool.virginia.edu/
- **International Tele Mentor Program** http://www.telementor.org
- **Learn the 'Net** http://www.learnthenet.com
- **Map Resources** http://www.mapresources.com/
- **Mathematics Archives** http://archives.math.utk.edu/
- **Middlebury College: Center for Educational Technology** http://w99.middlebury.edu/ID013A/CEThowto.html
- **MLA-Style Citations of Electronic Sources** http://www.greekforme.com/mla-citations.html
- **National Archives** http://www.archives.gov/index.html
- **National Education Association (NEA)** http://www.nea.org/index.html
- **National Endowment for the Arts** http://www.nea.gov/
- **National Geographic** http://www.nationalgeographic.com
- **School Match** http://schoolmatch.com
- **School Page** http://www.eyesoftime.com/teacher/index.html
- **School World** http://schoolworld.edline.com
- **Science Stuff** http://www.sciencestuff.com
- **Teacher's Network** A teacher's exchange http://teachersnetwork.org/
- **Telementoring Young Women in Science, Engineering, and Computing** http://www.edc.org/CCT/telementoring
- **The 21st Century Teacher's Network** http://www.21ct.org
- **United States Copyright Office** http://www.copyright.gov
- **WWW4 Teachers** http://www.4teachers.org/

through all the information? Just because information is found on a printed page or is published on the Internet does not necessarily mean that the information is accurate, free of bias, or current. You can prepare your students to read and review information with a critical eye by helping them develop skills in locating and assessing materials and information found on the Internet. This can be done by reviewing pertinent criteria with them and directing them to sites that can walk them through the evaluation process. Using a checklist, such as the ones found at Evaluating Information at **http://webliminal.com/search/search-web12.html**, is a good place to start. This website answers the question, "Why evaluate resources?" and provides examples of materials that do and do not meet the criteria of the included checklists, in addition to providing guidelines for carrying out an evaluation, activities to practice evaluating resources, and a variety of other helpful links. Another resource you could use and introduce your students to that can help them evaluate websites is Kathy Schrock's *Critical Evaluation Survey: Teacher Sites* found at **http://school.discoveryeducation.com/schrockguide/pdf/ evalteacher.pdf**.

Search Engines

No matter what subject or grade level you teach, instructing your students about the benefits and limitations to searching and critically analyzing the information available on the World Wide Web will serve them well in their academic pursuits and future careers. Internet **search engines** are invaluable in the research process. Since there are hundreds of millions of pages available on the Internet, search engines, special sites on the World Wide Web, are designed to help you find and select information. Search engines perform three basic tasks: they search the Internet by looking for key words or phrases, they keep an index of the words they find, and they allow users to search for words in those indexes. This is no small feat since search engines may index hundreds of millions of pages, documents, and other resources and respond to tens of millions of queries a day.

There are numerous search engines available. You are probably familiar with the most popular ones: Google, Yahoo!, Bing, and Altavista. Dogpile is an example of a metasearch engine that allows you to search the World Wide Web, images, audio, video, news, and much more on Google, Yahoo!, and Bing in a single search. Although each of the search engines listed here has its merits, Google is a teacher's best friend. It strives to be the largest library in the world. In fact, 2.7 billion searches are conducted on Google each month. Google has created a specific education site that will help you in the classroom: **http://www.google .com/educators/index.html**. Google is also developing ways to make searching and filtering through the growing accumulation of information more efficient. When you are at the search bar in Google, type in the words "Google Squared," and you can access, collect, and categorize your information in a table. Another great search tool for educators can be found at Google Scholar. This site will allow you to do a scholarly search across many disciplines by gathering information from research articles, books, theses, and other sources on a specific topic you want to know more about so that you can complement or update your knowledge and cover the topic in your curriculum. Google has many other specialized sites that support teaching and learning and even offers professional development opportunities to help you bring innovative technology into your classroom. Be sure to explore all the Google sites and applications that are available.

Wikipedia

Of particular concern is the students' overreliance on **Wikipedia** in their investigative research process. In fact, Wikipedia, the free online encyclopedia, is a favorite research destination for students. It was started in 2001 and is written in English, but it is also available in 25 additional languages. Currently, there are nearly 4 million articles available at Wikipedia. Wikipedia has information grouped in numerous categories in addition to General References, including "culture and the arts, geography and places, health and fitness, history and events, mathematics and logic, natural and physical sciences, people and self, philosophy and thinking, religion and belief systems, society and social sciences, and technology and applied sciences." There are also many subcategories covering myriad topics. It is important to caution students about relying on Wikipedia to consistently provide accurate, reliable information since Wikipedia is a wiki. By definition, that means that Wikipedia is a live document and is always evolving. Anyone can access the information on Wikipedia, edit it, and save the revised version. Yes, Wikipedia, like other wikis, is a place where people can collaborate and change a body of work. Therefore, if students use information found on Wikipedia as a primary source or as their sole source for their research, they could be reporting inaccurate, altered, manipulated information unless the page they access is authentic and reliable or the students engage in a more exhaustive research process. Wikis have their place in the world and are discussed later in this chapter, but accepting information from Wikipedia without scrutiny or further investigation would be a careless mistake.

Virtual Field Trips

Virtual field trips are a great way to visit the world without leaving the classroom. If you are talking about financial literacy, why not take a virtual field trip to the New York Stock Exchange (NYSE)? At the NYSE, middle and secondary students can learn the basics about stock ownership, trading publicly, and financial responsibility. Students can see what the floor looks like, learn what each person does, and peruse the 8,000 issues from 55 different countries. If you are studying the Mona Lisa, why not take a virtual tour of the Musée du Louvre in Paris, which houses the masterpiece? This way, students can walk through the gallery and read about the artist Leonardo da Vinci and his paintings. If you are studying Canadian culture, why not chat with Pierre Faucher, the owner of the Sucrerie de la Montagne (Sugar Shack) in Rigaud, Quebec, to learn how maple syrup is produced the old-fashioned way? A virtual field trip allows you to do all this and so much more. You can take your class on a field trip via technology to a special museum, exhibit, or business. You can do this with students at individual computers, or you can use an interactive or electronic whiteboard (described in the next section of this chapter) or individual computer to transport students wherever they desire. Some virtual field trips can even be set up as "live" events where the students can ask questions online during class and the presenter will answer them in real time.

Communication Tools

Earlier in the chapter, we talked about Wikipedia, the most famous wiki. Here, we will describe wikis as communication tools that support and facilitate collaboration. A wiki is a website where students can expand on ideas across several interlinked pages as they are jointly created. The creation is a living document and is always evolving. Wikis have their place in the world of technology since group collaboration is a wonderful way to make and nurture connections. To get a visual of what wikis are and how they work, check out Wikis in Plain English at **http://www.commoncraft.com/video/wikis**. Students can create a free Wiki account at Web 2.0: Cool Tools for School at **http://cooltoolsforschools.wikispaces.com**, which includes a wealth of tools and examples of amazing things students have done with wikis. In addition to collaborative tools, this award-winning website also has extensive collections of presentation, research, video, slide show, graphing, quiz and poll, drawing, writing, and organizing tools.

WRITEBOARDS Web-based documents that allow contributors to "write, share, revise, and compare" ongoing changes to a sharable real-time document are called Writeboards. Writeboard is a free collaborative site the students can use to work on an assignment together; it can be accessed at **http://123.writeboard.com**. Writeboard is simple and easy to use for any student who has a school account. Writeboard is a free, Web-based tool that allows multiple students to easily collaborate on a single document online. Different versions of the document are automatically tracked and saved so that old ideas are never lost and contributions can be easily monitored by teachers. Students can access their documents through any computer in the world. Sharing Writeboards with other students is easy; students need to enter a classmate's email address, and an invitation with a link to view and edit the Writeboard will be sent automatically.

BLOGS A blog is a type of website where students can create, write, and share their stories. The idea of using a computer as a personal online diary to post commentary, news, information on certain subjects, or day-to-day happenings and allow access to a select few or to everyone worldwide has become quite popular. Famous people, professionals, students, and educators alike maintain **blogs**. You can check out 10 Popular Technology Blogs at **http://www.blogs.com/topten/10-popular-technology-in-education-blogs**, the Top 100 Education Blogs at **http://oedb.org/library/features/top-100-education-blogs**, or Celebrating Blogging and Social Media in Education at **http://edublogawards.com**. Blogs allow students to upload and share photos, text, videos, and other media; they help bring writing alive in the classroom. There are numerous applications for using blogs with your students. Ms. Sunday, at Estes Park Middle School in Estes Park, CO, has her sixth-grade geography students learn about Canadian politics by accessing a blog.

David Jacobson, the U.S. ambassador to Canada, maintains a blog at **http://blogs.ottawa.usembassy.gov/ambassador**. On his blog, Ambassador Jacobson writes about the daily activities of serving as the head of the embassy of the U.S. in Ottawa. He recently blogged about Prince William and Kate Middleton's royal visit to Canada's capital.

PODCASTS Podcasts can be an audio stream or an audiovisual stream archived on the Internet that can be accessed from any computer or downloaded and transferred to a student's MP3 player. To learn how to create, publish, and publicize a podcast, visit PodBean's free publishing tools at **http://www.podbean.com**. PodBean's tools work especially well for classrooms. There is no technology to learn; podcast episodes can be uploaded and published in a matter of minutes. All you need is a Web camera, a microphone, and software to record your sound file. If you do not want to create and publicize your own podcasts, you may enjoy accessing published podcasts. Many organizations, such as ABC and NASA, have created many podcasts that are appropriate for use with middle and secondary students.

TWITTER AND SOCIAL NETWORKING TOOLS Twitter is a **social networking** site similar to Facebook. Both sites allow students to post pictures and video clips and to collect friends on their sites. For students, going to these sites is comparable to attending a party where the guest list includes everyone from their contact list. There are numerous ways that teachers can use Twitter and social networking tools. For instance, teachers can create fake Facebook pages as a teaching lesson. Teachers can also tweet tips, links, and resources for current service learning projects in the community. To explore a variety of uses for Twitter in the classroom, check out 50 Ideas on Using Twitter in Education at **http://cooper-taylor.com/2008/08/50-ideas-on-using-twitter-for-education**.

It is important for teachers to talk to students about the dangers of social networking utilities and to warn students about the consequences of their digital footprint. To learn more about Twitter, MySpace, Facebook and other social networks and how students are using them to communicate, complete Activity 10.2.

SKYPE Every day, millions of people around the world use **Skype** to stay in touch with family and friends for free. Skype is a software application that allows users to talk over the Internet by voice and video as well as chat over the Internet. There are many classroom applications for Skype. Skype is helpful when talking to a guest speaker from another country or talking to someone from a local or remote business or for students across the U.S. to communicate with each other. The possibilities are endless. Check out 50 Awesome Ways to Use Skype in the Classroom at **http://www.teachingdegree.org/2009/06/30/50-awesome-ways-to-use-skype-in-the-classroom** for more ideas. Most laptops have built-in microphones and webcams, and if they

Activity
10.2

Making Connections: MySpace, Facebook, Twitter, and Other Social Networking Tools

Students everywhere are participating in social interaction via the Internet. MySpace, the 159th most visited English-language website worldwide, is a mainstay of popular culture. Founded in August 2003 and made popular by Internet entrepreneur Brad Greenspan, this networking tool permits its users to submit their individual network of friends and decide with whom they wish to share their personal profiles, photos, videos, music, and so much more. Users usually provide information in two standard categories: "About Me" and "Who I'd Like to Meet" as well as providing "Interests." Adolescents age 14 and older can register an account on MySpace.

Facebook, a social networking website, has become a popular way for students to keep in touch. In February 2004, founder Mark Zuckerberg, a 20-year-old student at Harvard, created Facebook. The website caught on regionally, spreading from Harvard to other universities and colleges on the East Coast and across the U.S. In September 2005, Zuckerberg took what he referred to as "the next logical step" and launched the high school version of Facebook. Since September 2006, Facebook can be joined by anyone with a valid email address. Currently, this international website boasts college and high school communities worldwide; it is the second most frequently visited website. On Facebook, you can create your own profile, upload photos or post videos on your profile, publish notes, share news with your friends, or join a network.

Jack Dorsey, Biz Stone, and Evan Williams created and launched Twitter in 2006. It has gained immense popularity worldwide. Twitter is an online social networking service that also supports microblogging. Users can send messages, or "tweets," of up to 140 characters. Twitter allows users to connect to friends, experts in a variety of fields, and popular celebrities as well as follow breaking news. Many teachers have explored various creative ways to use Twitter in the classroom.

Apply Your Knowledge

Check out the following articles to learn more about MySpace, Facebook, and Twitter.

New Teen Addictions: Facebook and MySpace
http://www.insidebayarea.com/bayarealiving/ci_6977277

Facebook Gets in MySpace's Face: Targets High Schools
http://www.siliconbeat.com/entries/2005/09/02/facebook_gets_in_myspaces_face_targets_high_schools.html

Facebook Open to High School Students
http://mycollegeguide.org/Article.php?ArticleID=25

Taking MySpace: Facebook Launches at High Schools Nationwide
http://www.minorityrapport.com/2005/09/taking_myspace_.html

New Facebook Feature Could Out Students: Undergrads May Wish to Conceal Sexual Orientation from High School Site Users
http://www.thecrimson.com/article/2006/3/2/new-facebook-feature-could-out-students

6 Examples of Using Twitter in the Classroom
http://www.emergingedtech.com/2009/06/6-examples-of-using-twitter-in-the-classroom

Information for the description of MySpace and Facebook adapted from MySpace (retrieved September 20, 2007, from http://en.wikipedia.org/wiki/MySpace) and Facebook (retrieved from http://en.wikipedia.org/wiki/Facebook).

do not, all you need is a computer, a microphone, and a webcam to speak to anyone around the world. Software is free, as are calls.

Copyright and the Internet

The remaining paragraphs of this section address the "how" of using the Internet from an academic perspective. Let's begin with the fictitious although feasible Teaching Scenario "Natural Disasters." In the scenario, there is both a desirable aspect and a not-so-desirable aspect. On the positive side, the students used a good technological tool (the Internet) to research a variety of sources, including many primary ones. But when they published their document on the Internet and when they made copies of their guide to be sold, they did so without permission from the original copyright holders, and they were thus infringing copyright law. Although it would take an attorney to say for sure, with this scenario it is probable that the students, teacher, school, and school district would be liable. As is true for other documents (such as published photos, graphics, and text), unless there is an explicit statement that materials taken from the Internet are public domain,

it is best to assume that they are copyrighted and should not be republished without permission from the original source.

As emphasized in this chapter, teaching all students how to access, assess, and critically evaluate the resources available on the World Wide Web adds to their repertoire of skills for lifelong learning. Consider allowing each student or teams of students to become experts on specific websites during particular units of study. It might be useful to start a chronicle of student-recorded log entries about particular websites to provide comprehensive long-term data about those resources. When students use information from the Internet, require that they print copies of sources of citations and materials so that you can check for accuracy. These copies may be maintained in their portfolios.

Student work published on the Internet should be considered intellectual material and, as such, is protected from plagiarism by others. Most school districts now post a copyright notice on their home page. Someone at the school usually is assigned to supervise the school website to see that district and school policy and legal requirements are observed.

Teaching
Scenario **Natural Disasters**

Let us suppose that the students in your class have been working nearly all year on an interdisciplinary thematic unit titled "Surviving Natural Disasters." As culmination to their study, they "published" a document titled *Natural Disaster Preparation and Survival Guide for [name of their community]* and proudly distributed the guide to their parents and members of the community.

Long before preparing the guide, however, the students had to do research. To learn about the history of various kinds of natural disasters that had occurred or that might occur locally and about the sorts of preparations a community should take for each kind of disaster, students searched sources on the Internet, such as federal documents, scientific articles, and articles from newspapers from around the world where natural disasters had occurred. They also searched in the local library and the local newspaper's archives to learn about floods, tornadoes, and fires that had occurred during the past 200 years. Much to their surprise, they also learned that their community is located very near the New Madrid Fault, which did, in fact, experience a serious earthquake in 1811 although none since. As a result of that earthquake, two nearby towns completely disappeared, while the Mississippi River flowed in reverse, changing its course and causing the formation of a new lake in Tennessee.

From published and copyrighted sources, including websites, the students found many useful photographs, graphics, and articles, and they included those in whole or in part in their survival guide. They did so without obtaining permission from the original copyright holders or even citing those sources.

You, the other members of your teaching team, and other people were so impressed with the students' work that students were encouraged to offer the document for publication on the school's website. In addition, the document was received with so much acclaim that the students decided to sell it in local stores. This would help defray the original cost of duplication and enable them to continue to supply guides.

Media Tools

Media tools are teaching tools that depend on electricity to project light and sound and to focus images on screens, including projectors of various sorts, computers, digital videodiscs (DVDs), sound recorders, and video recorders. The aim here is *not* to provide specific instruction on how to operate equipment but to help you develop a philosophy for using it and to provide strategies for using media tools in your teaching. Consequently, to conserve space in this book, we devote no attention to traditional audiovisual equipment, such as 16-mm film, opaque projectors, and slide projectors, but we do cover overhead projectors, document cameras, interactive writing boards, and **classroom response systems**.

It is important to remember that the role of media tools is to aid student learning, not to teach for you. You must still select the objectives, orchestrate the instructional plan, assess the results, and follow up the lessons, just as you have learned to do with various other instructional strategies. If you use media tools prudently, your teaching and students' learning will benefit.

The Overhead Projector

In addition to a writing board and a bulletin board, nearly every classroom is equipped with an overhead projector. The overhead projector is a versatile, effective, and reliable teaching tool. Except for the bulb burning out, not much else can go wrong with an overhead projector. The overhead projector projects light through transparent objects. A properly functioning overhead projector usually works quite well in a fully lit room. Truly portable overhead projectors are available that can be carried easily from place to place in their compact cases.

In some respects, the overhead projector is more practical than the writing board, particularly for a beginning teacher who is nervous. Using the overhead projector rather than the writing board can help avoid tension by decreasing the need to pace back and forth to the board. And by using an overhead projector rather than a writing board, you can maintain both eye contact and physical proximity with students, both of which are important for maintaining classroom control.

GUIDELINES FOR USING THE OVERHEAD PROJECTOR As with any projector, find the best place in your classroom to put it. If there is no classroom projection screen, you can hang white paper or a sheet, use a white multipurpose board, or use a white or near-white wall.

Although it seems like using the overhead projector should be straightforward, proper use is not necessarily intuitive and therefore warrants an explanation of effective use. Have you ever attended a presentation by someone who was not using an overhead projector properly? It can be frustrating to members of an audience when the image is too small, out of focus, partially off the screen, or partially blocked from view by the presenter. To use this teaching tool in a professional manner, do the following:

- *Turn on the projector (the switch is probably on the front), and place it so that the projected white light covers the entire screen and hits the screen at a 90-degree angle; then focus the image to be projected.*

- *Face the students while using the projector.* The fact that you do not lose eye contact with your students is a major advantage of using the overhead projector rather than a writing board.

- *Lay the pencil directly on the transparency with the tip of the pencil pointing to the detail being emphasized* rather than using your finger to point to the detail or pointing to the screen, thereby turning away from your students.

- *To lessen distraction, turn the overhead projector off during long pauses or group discussions or when you want the students to shift attention back to you.*

For writing on overhead projector transparencies, ordinary felt-tip pens are not satisfactory; instead, select a transparency-marking pen. The ink of these pens is water soluble, so keep the palm of your hand from resting on the transparency, or you will have ink smudges on your transparency and on your hand. To highlight the writing on a transparency and to organize student learning, use pens in a variety of colors. Practice writing on a transparency and also practice making overlays. You can use an acetate transparency roll or single sheets of flat transparencies. Flat sheets of transparency come in different colors—clear, red, blue, yellow, and green—which can be useful in making overlays.

Some teachers prepare lesson outlines in advance on transparencies, allowing more careful preparation of the transparencies and making them ready for use at another time. For preparation of permanent transparencies, you will probably want to use permanent marker pens rather than those that are water soluble and easily smudged.

There are certain guidelines you should keep in mind when preparing text transparencies in your word processing program. First, select an easy-to-read font (Helvetica or other sans serif typefaces work best). Do not use type smaller than you can comfortably read by placing your transparency on the floor and reading it from a standing position (approximately 18 point). Do not overcrowd the page; instead, select key points to highlight.

Other transparent objects can be shown on an overhead projector, such as transparent rulers, protractors, and Petri dishes for science activities. Even opaque objects can be used if you simply want to show silhouette, as you might in math and art activities. Calculators, too, are available specifically for use on the overhead projector, as is a screen that fits onto the platform and is circuited to a computer so that whatever is displayed on the computer monitor is also projected onto the classroom screen. The overhead projector can also be used for tracing transparent charts or drawings into larger drawings on paper or on the writing board. The image projected onto the screen can be made smaller or larger by moving the projector closer or farther away, respectively, and then traced when you have the size you want.

Commercial transparencies are available from a variety of school supply houses. For sources, check the catalogs available in your school office or at the audiovisual and resources centers in your school district. Publishers also often supply supplemental transparencies with the teacher's edition of the textbook.

The Document Camera

Although much more expensive than overhead projectors, the prices on document cameras have come down, and they are becoming affordable, popular tools in classrooms across the country. In fact, document cameras are versatile classroom presentation tools. They are portable, lightweight, and easy to use. When used in conjunction with a projection system, you can project three-dimensional as well as two-dimensional objects, slides, and other microscopic objects in addition to displaying text on the document camera. You can also zoom in on objects. You can even use a classroom document camera connected to a computer as a scanner by saving images of objects placed on the document camera to share with students in PowerPoint presentations or on websites. Whether you want to do a live dissection of a frog in front of your students in your biology course, show the texture of rocks in a geology lab, model how to use a calculator, highlight a passage from your literature textbook, or simply share a student's essay, the document camera allows you to integrate technology, display student work, and decrease the number of copies you need to make and distribute to students. Check out Your Classroom and the Document Camera at **http://www.camcor.com/guides/ Classroom_DocumentCameras.html** or 50 Plus Ideas for Using a Document Camera in Class at **http://www.edtechnetwork .com/document_cameras.html** to explore other creative ways to use a document camera in your subject area and at various grade levels.

The Interactive or Electronic Whiteboard

Extending the purposes of the multipurpose board and correlated with modern technology is an *interactive or electronic whiteboard* that can transfer information written on it to a connected computer monitor, which in turn can save the material as a computer file. Interactive or electronic whiteboards have replaced traditional chalkboards, dry-erase boards, or flip charts in many schools. A projector is used to display a computer's video output on the interactive or electronic whiteboard, which then acts as a large touch screen. Since they use touch recognition and are intuitive, students can easily input, access, or save data on the interactive whiteboard. Students get to come up to the board and move information, change it, and make the presentation and notes come alive. The electronic whiteboard uses dry-erase markers and special erasers that have optically encoded sleeves that enable the device to track their position on the board. Interactive whiteboards usually come with these special colored pens, which use digital ink and replace traditional whiteboard markers, but students can also use their fingers to write or their palms to erase as well. Once created, the data are converted into a display for the computer monitor, which may then be printed, cut and pasted into other applications, sent as an email or fax message, or networked to other sites.[4]

If you happen to teach in a school with limited computer access, having a computer, a projector, and an interactive whiteboard in your classroom provides computer access to the whole class. With an interactive electronic whiteboard, you can accommodate different learning styles, encourage your students to become actively involved in learning, provide repetition of material presented for students who are absent from school or for struggling learners, and help students review for examinations. Interactive or electronic whiteboards allow a teacher to write in color, save and print the notes they are writing for students, show videos, and create and use interactive lessons. In fact, there are numerous YouTube instructional video clips that can help a new teacher begin to use this tool in creative ways. We will highlight a few uses here.

The interactive nature of electronic whiteboards provides many practical uses for the classroom because it allows students to manipulate information and work collaboratively. Interactive whiteboards can be used for presentations created by students or the teacher. Teachers can use whiteboards as timers, to create classroom competitions and races, as interactive graphic organizers, for brainstorming, as interactive maps, and so much more. They can be used for digital storytelling, teaching students how to conduct research on the Internet, showing streamed or downloaded videos, taking students on a virtual field trip, reinforcing skills, having students work collaboratively on a variety of writing projects, and having students create and edit multimedia presentations.

Classroom Response Systems

Wireless systems that allow a teacher to ask questions and receive and tally responses from students are quite popular. More commonly known as "clickers," classroom response systems use both hardware and software to collect students' answers to teachers' questions. The process is really quite simple. A teacher can use clickers to ask a multiple-choice or true-or-false question to students by putting the question on an overhead transparency or on the computer projector or by delivering the question orally. Students then respond to the question using their handheld clickers. The clicker transmits a radio-frequency signal to the receiver, which is attached to the teacher's computer. The software on the teacher's computer compiles the students' responses and creates a graphic display of the results instantly. This technology allows the teacher to poll the class and share the results. Clickers are a great way to engage learners, get student feedback immediately so that you can address or reteach difficult concepts that students failed to grasp, clarify misunderstandings, reinforce key concepts, conduct formative assessments, encourage students to share opinions on controversial issues, introduce real-world scenarios and obtain feedback, and monitor effectiveness of various instructional strategies.

Recording Pens

Another tool that many students find very helpful is a **recording pen** with an embedded computer and digital audio recorder in it. There are numerous manufacturers of these pens; some of the pens are more sophisticated and offer large memory capacity and more features than others, but even the most affordable models can record what is said by the teacher as well as take what is written down or drawn by the student and convert handwritten notes to text. The audio fidelity is surprisingly good; the pens clearly record all audio contributions. In fact, the pens can be used to record a teacher's lecture and small-group conversations, as well as whole-class discussions. By using one of these pens, students never miss a word. When used with special paper, the pen records what it writes for later uploading to a computer and synchronizes those notes with any audio it has recorded. This allows a student to be selective and to replay specific portions of a recording by tapping on the notes he or she was taking at the time the recording was made. It is also possible to search for key terms and select which portion of a recording to replay. These pens make note taking less troublesome for students who may not write quickly or for students who have physical or hearing impairments.

Recording pens can also be used by students for studying. Students can review for the test, go back and listen to the lectures, and replay the part of the lecture they did not fully follow or understand over and over again. There are other great ways that students can use recording pens. Even if a student does not have computer access, with a recording pen, he or she can replay the teacher's explanation as often as needed, anywhere and anytime. Recording pens can also be used for testing accommodations. If a student has an Individualized Education Program (IEP) that requires that test directions be read out loud, a recording pen can be used. If a student needs to respond to test questions orally, a recording pen can record the student's responses and/or answers can be recorded by a scribe.

Students can even create a pencast, a digital version of his or her notes and audio. Pencasts are interactive documents that allow you to hear, see, and relive notes exactly as they were captured. With pencasts, students could use their recording pens to complete an assignment, pencast it, and then send it to their teacher. Students could even pencast their homework to their teacher. Students could use their pens to do an assignment and then pencast it and send the link to their teacher. Teachers could listen to a student's problem-solving process as he or she "thinks aloud" from anywhere and then discuss the student's process with him or her.

Television, Videos, and DVDs

Television, videos, and DVDs represent a powerful medium. Their use as teaching aids, however, may present scheduling, curriculum, and physical problems that some school systems are yet unable to handle adequately.

TELEVISION   For purposes of professional discussion, television programming can be divided into three categories: instructional television, educational television, and general commercial television. Instructional television refers to programs specifically designed as classroom instruction. Educational television refers to programs of cable television and of public broadcasting designed to educate in general but not aimed at classroom instruction. Commercial television programs include the entertainment and public service programs of the television networks and local stations.

Watch for announcements for special educational programs in professional journals. And, of course, television program listings can be obtained from your local commercial, educational, or cable companies or by writing directly to network stations. Some networks sponsor Internet websites. For example, peruse **http://www.pbs.org/sitesa2z** to see PBS educational programs.

VIDEOS/DVDS Combined with a television monitor, the VCR (videocassette recorder) and DVD player are popular and frequently used tools in today's classrooms. In addition, the VCR, combined with a video camera, makes it possible to record students during activities, practice, projects, and demonstrations as well as yourself when teaching. It gives students a marvelous opportunity to self-assess as they see and hear themselves in action.

Entire course packages, as well as supplements, are now available on videocassettes and DVDs. The schools where you student teach and where you eventually are employed may have a collection of such programs. Some teachers make their own. You can also look for resources in the curriculum library in your education department, at your college or university library, or at the school district's resource center.

Carefully selected programs, tapes, discs, films, and slides enhance student learning. For example, DVDs offer quick and efficient accessibility of thousands of visuals, thus providing an appreciated boost to teachers of students with limited language proficiency. With the use of frame control, students can observe phenomena, in detail, that previous students only read about. Figure 10.6 provides sample addresses from which you may obtain catalogs of information.

When Equipment Malfunctions: Troubleshooting

When using media equipment, it is nearly always best to set up the equipment and have it ready to go before students arrive, thereby avoiding problems in classroom management that can occur when there is a delay because the equipment is not ready. Like any other well-prepared professional, a competent teacher is ready when the work is to begin. Of course, delays may be unavoidable when equipment breaks down or malfunctions. Remember Murphy's Law, which says that if anything can go wrong, it will? It is particularly relevant when using audiovisual equipment. You want to be prepared for such emergencies. Effectively planning for and responding to this eventuality are a part of your system of movement management and take place during the preactive stage of your planning. That preparation includes consideration of a number of factors.

When equipment malfunctions, three principles should be kept in mind: (1) you want to avoid dead time in the classroom, (2) you want to avoid causing permanent damage to equipment, and (3) you want to avoid losing the content continuity of a lesson. So, what do you do when equipment breaks down? Again, the answer is to be prepared for the eventuality.

If a projector bulb goes out, quickly insert another. That means you should have an extra bulb on hand. If, while teaching, a computer program freezes or aborts on the screen or if a fuse blows or for some other reason you lose power and you feel that there is going to be too much dead time before the equipment is working again, that is the time to go to an alternate lesson plan. You have probably heard

Figure 10.6 Selected Resources for Videotapes, Computer Software, and Interactive Multimedia

- **Agency for Instructional Technology,** Box A, Bloomington, IN 47402-0120, 800-457-4509. http://www.ait.net
- **Broderbund Software,** 500 Redwood Boulevard, Novato, CA 94948, 800-474-8840. http://www.broderbund.com
- **CLEARVUE/eav,** 6465 N. Avondale Avenue, Chicago, IL 60631, 800-253-2788. http://store.discoveryeducations.com
- **DK Publishing & Multimedia,** 95 Madison Avenue, New York, NY 10016, 212-213-4800. http://www.dk.com
- **Educational Activities, Inc.,** 1937 Grand Avenue, Baldwin, NY 11510, 800-645-3739. http://www.edact.com
- **EME Corp.,** 10 Central Parkway, Station 312, Stuart, FL 34995, 800-848-2050. http://www.emescience.com/index.html
- **Environmental Media Corp.,** 1102 11th Street, Port Royal, SC 29935, 800-368-3382. http://www.envmedia.com
- **Harcourt School Publishers,** 6277 Sea Harbor Drive, Orlando, FL 32887, 800-346-8648. http://www.hmhco.com
- **Higher-Order Thinking Co.,** 1733 N.E. Patterson Drive, Lee's Summit, MO 64086, 816-524-2701.
- **IBM Global Education,** 4111 Northside Parkway, Atlanta, GA 30301-2150, 800-426-4968. http://www.ibm.com/solutions/us/en
- **Mindscape,** 88 Rowland Way, Novato, CA 94945, 800-231-3088. http://www.mindscape.com
- **Modern School Supplies,** P.O. Box 958, Hartford, CT 06143, 800-243-2329. http://www.modernss.com/home.asp
- **NASCO-Modesto,** 4825 Stoddard Road, P.O. Box 3837, Modesto, CA 95352-3827, 800-558-9595. http://enasco.com
- **Pitsco, Inc.,** 915 East Jefferson Street, Pittsburg, KS 66762, 800-835-0686. http://www.pitsco.com
- **Sargent, Welch/VWR Scientific Products,** P.O. Box 5229, Buffalo Grove, IL 60089-5229, 800-SAR-GENT. http://www.SargentWelch.com
- **Schoolmasters Science,** 745 State Circle, P.O. Box 1941, Ann Arbor, MI 48106, 800-521-2832. http://www.schoolmasters.com
- **Science Kit and Boreal Laboratories,** 777 East Park Drive, Tonawanda, NY 14150, 800-828-7777. http://www.sciencekit.com
- **Tom Snyder Productions,** 80 Coolidge Hill Road, Watertown, MA 02472-5003, 800-342-0236. http://www.tomsnyder.com
- **Troll School & Library L.L.C.,** 100 Corporate Drive, Mahwah, NJ 07430, 800-979-8765. http://teacher.scholastic.com/clubs/routing.asp

the expression "go to Plan B." It is a useful phrase; what it means is that without missing a beat in the lesson, to accomplish the same instructional objective or another objective, you immediately and smoothly switch to an alternate learning activity. For you, the beginning teacher, it does not mean that you must plan two lessons for every one but that when planning a lesson that uses media equipment, you should plan an alternative activity in your lesson, just in case. Then, you move your students into the planned alternative activity quickly and smoothly.

Computer-Based Instructional Tools

As a middle school or secondary school classroom teacher, you must be **computer literate**—you must understand and be able to use computers as well as you can read and write. The computer can be valuable to you in several ways. For example, the computer can help you manage instruction by obtaining information, storing and preparing test materials, maintaining attendance and grade records, and preparing programs to aid in the academic development of individual students. This category of computer uses is referred to as **computer-managed instruction (CMI)**.

The computer can also be used for instruction by employing various instructional software programs, and it can be used to teach about computers and to help students develop their metacognitive skills as well as their skills in computer use.[5] When the computer is used to assist students in

their learning, it is called **computer-assisted instruction** or *computer-assisted learning*.

There are several computer programs to help English Language Learners improve their written and communication skills as well as comprehensive core curriculum packages to provide self-paced alternatives for students with special needs. There are programs that allow middle school students who struggle with reading to improve their reading comprehension, programs with the "drill and kill" substitution exercises of the past that help students master key concepts, and programs with eclectic activities that help students improve their academic skills.

WebQuests, which are student-centered and inquiry-based instructional tools, also provide a structure to assist students in their learning. Now read about how WebQuests can be used by completing Activity 10.3. Be sure to revisit Lesson Plan 7.5A and 7.5B in Chapter 7, titled "Plains Indians' Dependence on the Bison and Other Natural Resources," as a good example of a WebQuest. Also, complete Activity 10.4 to learn how you can create a website in order to communicate with your students and their parents, your colleagues, and others as well as promote student learning.

The Placement and Use of Computers: The Online Classroom

How you use the computer for instruction and learning is determined by several factors, including your knowledge of

---

Activity 10.3   **WebQuests**

WebQuests were developed by Bernie Dodge at San Diego State University in 1995. Since then, numerous teachers have adapted the WebQuest model to meet the needs of their students, their content area, and their learning context. WebQuests are inquiry-based lessons set up so that the majority, if not all, of the information and resources the students need to access can be located on the Web. The task, which provides a goal and a focus, is what guides learners through the WebQuest project. If the task is designed well, then learners will be engaged and their problem-solving and higher-order thinking skills tapped. There are common WebQuest formats; templates and online authoring systems are available to novices wanting to see how the Internet can be used as an important educational tool. To develop effective WebQuests, peruse and critically evaluate numerous examples. At "WebQuest Taskonomy: A Taxonomy of Tasks" (see URL below), a dozen task types are described in detail, and many K–12 samples are provided. The WebQuest formats focus on the following tasks: retelling, compilation, mystery, journalistic, design, creative products, consensus building, persuasion, self-knowledge, analytical, judgment, and scientific.

Apply Your Knowledge

To develop great Web-based lessons, you need to explore the possibilities. Before you start to create your own WebQuests,

review the information, guidelines, and examples on the following websites. Once you have done that, go to "A WebQuest about WebQuests" developed by Bernie Dodge (see URL listed below). Select middle school and/or middle/high school and complete the lesson in small groups. Share what you learned with your peers.

1. What criteria/features make a WebQuest good or not in your opinion?
2. Which task types might be most appropriate for the subject area, grade level, and particular content you may cover?
3. What sample WebQuests did you find most effective? Why?

WebQuest Taskonomy: A Taxonomy of Tasks
http://webquest.sdsu.edu/taskonomy.html

The Amistad Case: A Mock Trial—Persuasion Task
http://projects.edtech.sandi.net/hoover/amistad

WebQuest.org
http://webquest.org/index.php

A WebQuest about WebQuests
http://webquest.sdsu.edu/webquestwebquest.html

Activity
10.4 **Create a Website**

As a teacher, creating a personal website can be a fun, practical way to communicate with your students and their parents, record your school year, keep track of events, post lesson plans, and capture memories. There are a variety of resources and features that you may decide to include on your personal website. For instance, you may decide to add the following to your website: an audio greeting, videos, animation, online lesson plans, your classroom management plan, your teacher resource library, student projects, class newsletters, clip art, and so on.

Apply Your Knowledge

Peruse the websites listed below to determine which of the available features you would like to include. Check out these great free resources to build your educational website.

How to Create a Web Page: HTML Commands Explained with Numerous Examples
http://www.make-a-web-site.com

Create a Website
http://www.quackit.com/create-a-website

The Teachers.Net Homepage Maker
http://teachers.net/sampler

Teachnology: The Online Teacher Resource
http://www.teach-nology.com/web_tools/web_site

Edutopia: Information and Inspiration for Innovative Teaching in K–12 Schools: How to Create a Web Site That's a Learning Community
http://www.edutopia.org/how-to-create-learning-community

Thirteen Ed Online: How to Create a Web Site for Your Class
http://www.thirteen.org/edonline/primer/create.html

and skills in its use, the number of computers that you have available for instructional use, where computers are placed in the school, the software that is available, printer availability, and the telecommunications capabilities (i.e., wiring and phone lines, modems, Ethernet, DSL, wireless capabilities, and servers).

Schools continue to purchase or to lease computers and to upgrade their telecommunications capabilities. Regarding computer placement and equipment and technological support available, here are some possible scenarios and how classroom teachers work within each.

SCENARIO 1 With the assistance of a computer lab and the lab technician, computers are integrated into the whole curriculum. In collaboration with members of interdisciplinary teaching teams, in a computer lab students use computers, software, and Internet sources as tools to build their knowledge, to write stories with word processors, to illustrate diagrams with paint utilities, to create interactive reports with hypermedia, and to graph data they have gathered using spreadsheets.

SCENARIO 2 In some schools, students take a computer class as an elective or exploratory course. Students in your classes who are simultaneously enrolled in such a course may be given special computer assignments by you that they can then share with the rest of the class.

SCENARIO 3 Some classrooms have a computer connected to a large-screen video monitor. The teacher or a student works the computer, and the entire class can see the monitor screen. As they view the screen, students can verbally respond to and interact with what is happening on the computer.

SCENARIO 4 You may be fortunate to have one or more computers in your classroom for all or a part of the school year, especially ones with Internet connections and DVD playing capabilities; an overhead projector; and an LCD (liquid crystal display) projection system. Coupled with the overhead projector, the LCD projection system allows you to project onto your large wall screen (and television monitor at the same time) any image from computer software or a videodisc. With this system, all students can see and verbally interact with the multimedia instruction.

SCENARIO 5 Many classrooms have at least one computer with telecommunications capability, and some have many. When this is the case in your classroom, you most likely will have one or two students working at the computer station while others are doing other learning activities (**multilevel teaching**). Computers can be an integral part of a learning center and an important aid in your overall effort to personalize the instruction within your classroom.

Multimedia Tools

Multimedia tools include computers, DVDs, and projectors. A classroom may vary in regard to the computers that are available for student and teacher use, from Macs to PCs; some schools may have both platforms in the district or building. A great site to visit that has many ideas for multimedia tools in the classroom is The Innovative Educator: Way Out of the Box, which you can access at **http://theinnovativeeducator.blogspot.com/2008/08/instructional-technology-tips-for-new.html**. At this website, you will find a wealth of technology and tools and information about integrating technology in innovative ways that every new teacher should learn.

Selecting Computer Software

When selecting software programs, you and your colleagues need, of course, to choose those that are compatible with your brand of computer(s) and with your instructional objectives. Programs are continually being developed and enhanced to make use of the new and more powerful computers being made available. For evaluating computer software programs and testing them for their compatibility with your instructional objectives, there are usually forms available from the local school district or from the state department of education as well as from professional associations.

Multimedia Software

A **multimedia program** is a collection of teaching and learning materials involving more than one type of medium and organized around a single theme or topic. The types of media involved vary from rather simple kits—perhaps including videotapes, games, activity cards, student worksheets, and manuals of instructions for the teacher—to sophisticated packages involving building-level site-licensed computer software, student handbooks, reproducible activity worksheets, classroom wall hangings, and online subscriptions to telecommunication networks. Some kits are designed for teacher use and others for individuals or small groups of students; many more are designed for the collaborative use of students and teachers. Teachers sometimes incorporate multimedia programs with learning activity centers.

Many multimedia programs are available on DVDs; they are designed principally as reference resources for students and teachers but include other aspects as well. One example is National Geographic's *Mammals: A Multimedia Encyclopedia*, which provides a lesson-planning guide, facts on more than 200 animals, 700 still-color photos, range maps, animal vocalizations, full-motion movie clips, an animal classification game, a glossary, and a printing capability.

Global Positioning System

Have you ever wished you could find your car in a crowded parking garage without wandering from level to level or locate a business in an unfamiliar city without using a map? The Global Positioning System (GPS) allows just that; it is a space-based navigation system. The U.S. government maintains this satellite network. Anyone who owns a **GPS** receiver can use the device to pinpoint locations. How can this technology be helpful in the classroom? GPS is relatively inexpensive to purchase. The device costs approximately $100. With GPS, students can create an accurate representation of an area. They can find the location of their school and plot an area around their school and upload the coordinates to Geographic Information Systems software and plot out this information on **Google Earth**. GPS can be used to reinforce scientific inquiry, engage students in problem-based learning, help students develop analytical skills, and reinforce collaboration. GPS can easily be integrated into geography, mathematics, physical education, language-arts,

and social studies curricula. Check out GPS Resources at **http://www.gis2gps.com/GPS/gps.html** to read about how classroom teachers are using GPS to create meaningful learning experiences for their students.

Google Earth

Every once in a while, an amazing technology comes along that changes the way people think about and perceive the world around them. Google Earth is such a technology. It is a free download that can be added to a PC or Mac computer that allows students to tour the Earth through pictures and landscapes at a street level or through space. In fact, through Google Earth students can view satellite imagery, three-dimensional maps, and so much more, giving students the sensation that they are traveling the world, flying to local as well as remote locations. Google Earth allows you to enter your own address where you will most likely see a picture of your house; you can even choose a view that emulates driving down your street. This technology has made the world seem smaller and people and places more accessible. Check out an innovative curriculum designed by Michael Munson, a Salish descendant, for her sixth-grade class in Missoula, Montana, that uses Google Earth to help students explore their "sense of place" and learn about the relationship of the Salish and Pend d'Oreille with the land and its plants and animals. You can read about The Place Names Project at **http://www.spatialsci.com/PlaceNames/index.php/fuseaction/about.main.htm**.

Presentation Software

Presentation software makes it easy to create and modify presentations; there are even already-made presentations on numerous topics available for download that you could modify for your purposes. A very popular commercial presentation software is PowerPoint by Microsoft. PowerPoint presentations can be designed by teachers and students alike. PowerPoint presentations are a great way to bring information into the classroom, but you have to make sure you do not create boring presentations that will put your students to sleep. To make your presentation more appealing, you can include text, graphics, charts, maps, sound, movies, and other objects in the individual pages or slides. Animation and multimedia possibilities, as well as templates, exist to help you use visuals to enhance what you say. There are numerous ways to highlight certain text, main ideas, or quotations to teach new ideas or concepts; to practice and drill; and to engage students in games for review. The presentation can easily be assembled as a handout and printed, displayed live on a computer, or navigated through by the presenter. PowerPoint presentations can also have live links or video clips included within the slides that become interactive. Several of the presentation guidelines detailed in this chapter about overhead projector transparency use are applicable to creating presentation slides. There are many free presentation programs that have already been created; you can view them at **http://www.pppst.com**.

PREZI An alternative to presentation software like PowerPoint, Prezi is an online "slideless" presentation tool that allows educators to create a presentation on a single page. The major difference is in the way the presentation unfolds. PowerPoint creates slides that transition from slide to slide. With Prezi, educators can create interactive presentations and zoom in and out and wander all over the presentation. Another advantage of Prezi is the fact that videos can be embedded in the project (PowerPoint creates a link and will use an Internet browser to open the video), but Prezi accesses the link directly. Prezi acts like a giant map full of information where the creator can control how much information is seen at once and in which direction the creator wants the viewer to see the information. See Lesson Plan 7.15A and 7.15B in Chapter 7, titled "The Blackfeet Confederacy Timeline," for an example of a Prezi presentation, a detailed comparison of PowerPoint and Prezi, and guidelines for creating a Prezi presentation.

Screen Recording and Video Editing Software

Screencasting or lecture capture is a digital recording with visuals from computer screen output that can be supplemented with audio. Screen recording and video editing software allows teachers to record, edit, and share their screencasts with their students. With screen recording and video editing software, you can record anything that you can view on your computer screen, such as Web pages, software applications, PowerPoint or Prezi presentations, and much more. You can also record your lectures with a webcam, a video camera that feeds its images in real time to your computer. You can add audio to your presentations by talking into a microphone or your computer's audio or by including music tracks. Once you have done your recording, you can edit your screencast and add graphics, titles, links to Web pages, and transitions to add emphasis to certain points as well as guide your students through your presentation. You can even create quizzes so that students can make sure they got the key concepts from your screencast. By using screencasts, you can supplement visuals with your narration. Screencasts are high quality and relatively low cost. They are an efficient way to provide material for students who are absent when you deliver your presentation and/or demonstration because of illness, an athletic event, or another reason. They also work well for capturing challenging concepts that students would benefit from reviewing. If you teach multiple preps of the same course during a semester or teach the same course over and over again each semester or year or find yourself reteaching key concepts repeatedly, using screencasts can allow you to save and edit your presentations efficiently.

Sources of Free and Inexpensive Audiovisual Materials

For free and inexpensive audiovisual materials, check Internet sources as well as your college or university library for sources. It is also fun to attend estate sales, garage sales, library book sales, and flea markets to search for audiovisual materials. Discount stores, pawn shops, and secondhand stores also have VHS tapes, DVDs, and other audiovisual resources that may be appropriate for classroom use at very reasonable prices. Sometimes you are lucky and can find real treasures.

Using Copyrighted Video, Computer, and Multimedia Programs

You must be knowledgeable about the laws on the use of copyrighted videos and computer software materials. Although space here prohibits full inclusion of U.S. legal guidelines, your local school district undoubtedly can provide you with a copy of current district policies to ensure your compliance with all copyright laws. As was discussed earlier in this chapter in regard to the use of printed materials that are copyrighted, when preparing to make any copy, you must find out whether the copying is permitted by law under the category of "permitted use." If not allowed under "permitted use," then you must get written permission to reproduce the material from the holder of the copyright. Figures 10.7 and 10.8 present guidelines for the copying of videotapes and of computer software.

Usually, when purchasing DVDs and other multimedia software packages intended for school use, you are also paying for a license to modify and use its contents for

Figure 10.7   Copyright Law for Off-Air Videotaping

Permitted uses—you may:

1. Request your media center or audiovisual coordinator to record a program for you if you cannot or if you lack the equipment.
2. Keep a video-recorded copy of a broadcast (including cable transmission) for 45 calendar days, after which the program must be erased.
3. Use the program in class once during the first 10 school days of the 45 calendar days, and a second time if instruction needs to be reinforced.
4. Have professional staff view the program several times for evaluation purposes during the full 45-day period.
5. Make a few copies to meet legitimate needs, but these copies must be erased when the original video recording is erased.
6. Use only a part of the program if instructional needs warrant.
7. Enter into a licensing agreement with the copyright holder to continue use of the program.

Prohibited uses—you may *not*:

1. Video record premium cable services such as HBO without expressed permission.
2. Alter the original content of the program.
3. Exclude the copyright notice on the program.
4. Video record before a request for use is granted—the request to record must come from an instructor.
5. Keep the program, and any copies, after 45 days.

SOURCE: From Instructional Media and Technologies for Learning (6th ed., p. 389), by Robert Heinich, Michael Molenda, James D. Russell, and Sharon E. Smaldino, 1999, by Merrill/Prentice Hall. Upper Saddle River, NJ: Merrill/Prentice Hall. Reprinted with permission.

Figure 10.8 **Copyright Law for Use of Computer Software**

Figure 10.8 **Copyright Law for Use of Computer Software**

Permitted uses—you may:

1. Make a single backup or archival copy of the computer program.
2. Adapt the computer program to another language if the program is unavailable in the target language.
3. Add features to make better use of the computer program.

Prohibited uses—you may *not*:

1. Make multiple copies.
2. Make replacement copies from an archival or backup copy.
3. Make copies of copyrighted programs to be sold, leased, loaned, transmitted, or given away.

instructional purposes. However, not all DVDs include copyright permission, so always check the copyright notice on any disc you purchase and use. Whenever in doubt, do not use it until you have asked your district media specialists about copyrights or have obtained necessary permissions from the original source.

As yet, there are no guidelines for fair use of films, filmstrips, slides, and multimedia programs. A general rule of thumb for use of any copyrighted material is to treat the work of others as you would want your own material treated were it protected by a copyright (see Figures 10.7, 10.8, and 10.9).

Distance Learning

Distance learning (or distance education) is the popular term for describing any instructional situation in which the learner is separated in time or space from the point of instruction. Although telecommunications technologies have provided courses (e.g., by mail correspondence) and workshops (e.g., by video) for industry training, medical organizations, and higher education for many years, recent developments have created a renewed interest in distance learning. In fact, Roger Schank at Northwestern University's Institute for the Learning Sciences predicts that learning and instruction over the Internet will be the driving force for educational changes in the 21st century, with an accompanying change in the role of the classroom teacher from less of a deliverer of instruction to more of a facilitator of learning both by

providing individual tutoring and by helping students work together in groups.[6]

With the technology of distance learning, students in small rural schools can receive instruction in courses that, because of limited local resources, might otherwise have been unavailable to them; via the Internet, all students can interact in real time with people from around the world.

The National Distance Learning Center is a centralized electronic information source for distance learning programs and resources for K–12 education as well as for adult learning and higher education. Access to the database is via the Internet at **telnet://ndlc@ndlc.occ.uky.edu**. Additional resources on distance learning may be found at **http://ericec.org/faq/disted-x.htm**.

Summary

You have learned about the variety of materials and tools available to supplement your instruction. When used wisely, these resources will help you reach more of your students more of the time. As you know, teachers must meet the needs of diverse students, including many who are linguistically and culturally different. The material selected and presented in this chapter should be of help in doing that. The future will undoubtedly continue to bring technological innovations that will be even more helpful—DVDs, computers, and telecommunications equipment have marked only the beginning of a revolution for teaching. New instructional delivery systems made possible by microcomputers and multimedia workstations will likely fundamentally alter what had become the traditional role of the classroom teacher during the 20th century.

You should remain alert to current and developing technologies for your teaching. DVDs, multimedia, and telecommunications offer exciting technologies for learning. New instructional technologies are advancing at an increasingly rapid rate. You and your colleagues must maintain vigilance over new developments by constantly looking for those that not only will help make student learning meaningful and interesting and your teaching effective but that are cost effective as well.

Figure 10.9 **Fair Use Guidelines for Using Multimedia Programs**

1. For portions of copyrighted works used in your own multimedia production for use in teaching, follow normal copyright guidelines (e.g., the limitations on the amount of material used, whether it be motion media, text, music, illustrations, photographs, or computer software).
2. You may display your own multimedia work, using copyrighted works, to other teachers, such as in workshops. However, you may *not* make copies to give to colleagues without obtaining permission from copyright holders.
3. You may use your own multimedia production for instruction over an electronic network (e.g., distance learning) provided there are limits to access and to the number of students enrolled. You may *not* distribute such work over any electronic network without expressed permission from copyright holders.
4. You must obtain permissions from copyright holders before using any copyrighted materials in educational multimedia productions for commercial reproduction and distribution or before replicating more than one copy, distributing copies to others, or using copies outside your own classroom.

Exercise
10.1

Internet Sites of Use to Teachers

Instructions: The purpose of this exercise is to search the Internet for sites that you find interesting and useful (or useless) for teaching and to share those sites with your classmates (and, if you want, with the authors of this book). Make copies of this page for each site visited; then share your results with your classmates.

Website I investigated: http:// _____

I consider the site *highly useful, moderately useful, of no use*

Specifically for teachers of (grade level and/or subject field):

Sponsor of site:
Features of interest and usefulness to teachers:

Chapter 10   POSTTEST

Short Explanation

1. Describe how the use of audiovisual materials helps to reinforce student learning.

2. It has been said that the overhead projector can be one of the teacher's best friends. Explain what this means.

3. Explain how your effective use of the writing board can help students see relationships among verbal concepts or information.

4. Describe what you should look for when deciding whether material that you have obtained free or inexpensively is suitable for use in your teaching.

5. Explain why you agree or disagree that any material obtained free is okay to use in teaching.

Essay

1. Describe your knowledge, observations, and feelings about the use of multimedia and telecommunications for teaching. What more would you like to know about the use of multimedia and telecommunications for teaching? Describe how you might learn more about these things.

2. The local school board is concerned about copyright law and how it relates to instruction. You have been asked to make a presentation on the topic to the board. Prepare a summary of your presentation.

3. What do you predict will be the nature of the student textbook in the year 2025?

4. From your current observations and fieldwork related to this teacher preparation program, clearly identify one specific example of educational practice that seems contradictory to exemplary practice or theory presented in this chapter. Present your explanation for the discrepancy.

5. Describe any prior concepts you held that changed as a result of the experiences of this chapter. Describe the changes.

CHAPTER **ELEVEN**

Pearson

Assessing and Reporting Student Achievement

Making students accountable for test scores works well on a bumper sticker and it allows many politicians to look good by saying that they will not tolerate failure. But it represents a hollow promise. Far from improving education, high-stakes testing marks a major retreat from fairness, from accuracy, from quality, and from equity.[1]

—**SENATOR PAUL WELLSTONE**

Specific Objectives

At the completion of this chapter, you will be able to:

▸ Demonstrate an understanding of the importance of assessment in teaching and learning and explain the value of and give an example of a performance assessment that could be used in a particular grade level and discipline.

▸ Explain how rubrics, checklists, portfolios, and journals are used in the assessment of student learning.

▸ Differentiate among diagnostic assessment, authentic assessment, summative assessment, and formative assessment, with examples of when and how each can be used.

▸ Describe the importance of self-assessment in teaching and learning.

▸ Describe the importance of and manner by which parents can be involved in the education of their children.

Chapter 11 Overview

This chapter discusses grading and reporting of student achievement, two responsibilities that can consume much of a teacher's valuable time. Grading is time consuming and frustrating for many teachers. What should be graded? Should grades represent student growth, level of achievement in a group, effort, attitude, general behavior, or a combination of these? What should determine grades—homework, tests, projects, class participation and group work, or some combination of these? And what should be their relative weights? These are just a few of the questions that burden teachers, parents, and, indeed, the profession. When teachers are aware of alternative systems, they may be able to develop assessment and reporting processes that are fair and effective for all students in a variety of situations. After beginning with assessment, the final focus in this chapter considers today's principles and practices in grading and reporting student achievement.

Introduction

The importance of continuous assessment mandates that you know various principles and techniques of assessment. Here we explain and demonstrate how to construct and use assessment instruments. We will define terms related to assessment, suggest procedures to use in the construction of assessment items, point out the advantages and disadvantages of different types of assessment items and procedures, and explain the construction and use of alternative assessment devices.

Still today, in too many schools, the grade progress report and final report card are about the only communication between the school and the student's home. Unless the teacher and the school have clearly determined what grades represent and unless such understanding is periodically reviewed with each set of new parents or guardians, these reports may create unrest and dissatisfaction on the parts of parents, guardians, and students and thereby prove to be alienating devices. The grading system and reporting scheme, then, instead of informing parents and guardians, may separate even further the home and the school, which do have a common concern—the intellectual, physical, social, and psychological development of the student.

Purposes and Principles of Assessment

The development of the student encompasses growth in the cognitive, affective, and psychomotor domains. Traditional objective paper-and-pencil tests provide only a portion of the data needed to indicate student progress in those domains. As experts have done in the past, many experts today also question the traditional sources of data and encourage the search for, development of, and use of alternative means to assess more authentically the students' development of thinking and higher-level learning. Although best practices in assessment continue to evolve, one point that is clear is that various techniques of assessment must be used to determine how the student works, what the student is learning, and what the student can produce as a result of that learning. As a teacher, you must develop a repertoire of means of assessing learner behavior and academic progress.

Although grades have been a part of school for over 100 years, it is clear to many experts that the conventional report card with grades falls short of being a developmentally appropriate procedure for reporting the academic performance or progress of learners. Some schools are experimenting with other ways of reporting student achievement in learning, but the use of letter grades in middle schools and secondary schools is still firmly entrenched. Parents, students, colleges, and employers have come to expect grades as evaluations. Some critics suggest that the emphasis in schools is on scoring high on standardized tests or getting a good grade in a class rather than on learning, arguing that, as traditionally measured, the two do not necessarily go hand-in-hand. Today's interest is (or should be) more on what the student can do (performance testing) as a result of learning than merely on what the student can recall (memory testing) from the experience.

In addition, there have been complaints about subjectivity and unfair practices in testing. As a result of these concerns, a variety of systems of assessment and reporting have evolved, are still evolving, and will likely continue to evolve throughout your professional career. We will define key terms and discuss different types of assessment, designing test items, and reporting grades.

Assessment of achievement in student learning is designed to serve the following purposes:

1. *To assist in student learning.* This is the purpose usually first thought of when speaking of assessment, and it is

the principal topic of this chapter. For the classroom teacher, it is (or should be) the most important purpose.

2. *To identify students' strengths and weaknesses.* Identification and assessment of students' strengths and weaknesses are necessary for two reasons: to structure and restructure the learning activities and to restructure the curriculum. Concerning the first step, for example, gathering data on student strengths and weaknesses in content and process skills is important in planning activities appropriate for both skill development and intellectual development. This is **diagnostic assessment** (known also as *preassessment*). For the second step, analyzing data on student strengths and weaknesses in content and skills is useful for making appropriate modifications to the curriculum.

3. *To assess the effectiveness of a particular instructional strategy.* It is important for you to know how well a particular strategy helped accomplish a particular goal or objective. Competent teachers continually reflect on and evaluate their strategy choices, using a number of sources, including student achievement as measured by assessment instruments, their own intuition, informal feedback given by the students, and, sometimes, informal feedback given by colleagues, such as members of a teaching team or mentor teachers. (Mentor teachers are discussed in Chapter 12.)

4. *To assess and improve the effectiveness of curriculum programs.* Components of the curriculum are continually assessed by committees composed of teachers and administrators and sometimes parents, students, and other members of the school and community. The assessment is done while students are learning (i.e., formative assessment) and after the learning has taken place (summative assessment).

5. *To assess and improve teaching effectiveness.* To improve student learning, teachers are periodically evaluated on the basis of (a) their commitment to working with students at a particular level; (b) their ability to cope with students at a particular age, developmental, or grade level; and (c) their mastery of appropriate instructional techniques articulated throughout this book.

6. *To provide data that assist in decision making about a student's future.* Assessment of student achievement is important in guiding decision making about course and program placement, promotion, school transfer, class standing, eligibility for honors and scholarships, and career planning.

7. *To provide data in order to communicate with parents and guardians and to involve them in their children's learning.* Parents, communities, and school boards all share in accountability for the effectiveness of children's learning. Today's schools are reaching out more than ever before and engaging parents, guardians, and the community in their children's education. All teachers play an important role in the process of communicating with, reaching out to, and involving parents and the community.

Because the welfare and, indeed, the future of so many people depend on the outcomes of assessment, it is impossible to overemphasize its importance. For a learning endeavor to be successful, the learner must have answers to basic questions: Where am I going? Where am I now? How do I get where I am going? How will I know when I get there? Am I on the right track for getting there? These questions are integral to a good program of assessment. Of course, in the process of teaching and learning, the answers may be ever changing, and the teacher and students continue to assess and adjust plans as appropriate and necessary. The **exemplary school** is in a mode of continual change and progress.

The following principles, based on the preceding questions, guide the assessment program and are reflected in the discussions in this chapter:

- Teachers need to know if *they* are meeting their instructional objectives.
- Students need to know how well they are doing.
- Assessment is a reciprocal process, which includes assessment of teacher performance as well as student achievement.
- The program of assessment should aid teaching effectiveness and contribute to the intellectual and psychological growth of children.
- Evidence and input data for knowing how well the teacher and students are doing should come from a variety of sources and types of data-collecting devices.
- Assessment is a continuous process. The selection and implementation of plans and activities require continual monitoring and assessment to check on progress and to change or adopt strategies to promote desired behavior.
- **Reflection** and self-assessment are important components of any successful assessment program. Reflection and self-assessment are important if students are to develop the skills necessary for them to assume increasingly greater ownership of their own learning.
- A teacher's responsibility is to facilitate student learning and to assess student progress in that learning, and for that, the teacher is or should be held accountable.

Terms Used in Assessment

When discussing the assessment component of teaching and learning, it is easy to be confused by the terminology. The following clarification of terms is offered to aid your reading and comprehension.

Assessment and Evaluation

Assessment is the process of finding out what students are learning, and it is a relatively neutral process. In contrast, **evaluation** is making sense of what was uncovered, a subjective process.

Measurement and Assessment

Measurement refers to quantifiable data about specific behaviors. Tests and the statistical procedures used to analyze the results are examples. Measurement is a descriptive and objective process; that is, it is relatively free from human value judgments.

Assessment includes objective data from measurement but also other types of information, some of which are more subjective, such as information from anecdotal records and teacher observations and ratings of student performance. In addition to the use of objective data (data from measurement), assessment also includes arriving at value judgments made on the basis of subjective information.

An example of the use of these terms is as follows. A teacher may share the information that Jerilee Jackson received a score in the 90th percentile on the eighth-grade statewide achievement test in reading (a statement of measurement) but may add that "according to my assessment of her work in my language-arts class, she has not performed to her potential" (a statement of assessment).

Validity and Reliability

The degree to which a measuring instrument actually measures that which it is intended to measure is the instrument's **validity**. For example, when we ask if an instrument (such as a performance assessment instrument) has validity, key questions concerning that instrument are the following:

- Does the instrument adequately sample the intended content?
- Does it measure the cognitive, affective, and psychomotor knowledge and skills that are important to the unit of content being tested?
- Does it sample all the instructional objectives of that unit?

The accuracy with which a technique consistently measures that which it does measure is its **reliability**. If, for example, you know that you weigh 125 pounds and a scale consistently records 125 pounds when you stand on it, then that scale has reliability. However, if the same scale consistently records 120 pounds when you stand on it, we can still say the scale has reliability. By this example, then, it should be clear to you that an instrument could be reliable (it produces similar results when used again and again) although not necessarily valid. In this second instance, the scale is not measuring what it is supposed to measure, so, although it is reliable, it is not valid. Although a technique might be reliable but not valid, a technique must have reliability before it can have validity. The greater the number of test items or situations on a particular content objective, the higher the reliability. The higher the reliability, the more consistency there will be in students' scores measuring their understanding of that particular objective.

Authentic Assessment: Advantages and Disadvantages

When assessing for student achievement, it is important that you use procedures that are compatible with the instructional objectives. This is referred to as **authentic assessment**. Other terms used for *authentic* assessment are *accurate, active, aligned, alternative,* and *direct*. Although the term performance assessment is sometimes used, **performance assessment** refers to the type of student response being assessed, whereas *authentic* assessment refers to the assessment situation. Although not all performance assessments are authentic, assessments that are authentic are most assuredly performance assessments.

Consider this example: "If students have been actively involved in classifying objects using multiple characteristics, it sends them a confusing message if they are then required to take a paper-and-pencil test that asks them to 'define classification' or recite a memorized list of characteristics of good classifications schemes."[2] An authentic assessment technique would be a performance item that actually involves the students in classifying objects. In other words, to obtain an accurate assessment of a student's learning, the teacher uses a performance-based assessment procedure, that is, a procedure that requires students to produce rather than to select a response.

Advantages claimed for the use of authentic assessment include (a) the direct (also known as performance-based,

criterion-referenced, or outcome-based) measurement of what students should know and can do and (b) an emphasis on higher-order thinking. However, disadvantages of authentic assessment include a higher cost, difficulty in making results consistent and usable, and problems with validity, reliability, and comparability.

Unfortunately, a teacher may never see a particular student again after a given school semester or year is over, and the effects that teacher has had on a student's values and attitudes may never be observed by that teacher at all. In schools where groups or teams of teachers remain with the same cohort of students—as in the house concept and looping programs discussed in Chapter 1—those teachers often do have the opportunity to observe the positive changes in their students' values and attitudes.

Diagnostic, Formative, and Summative Assessment

Assessing a student's achievement is a three-stage process involving the following:

1. *Diagnostic assessment (sometimes called* preassessment). The assessment of the student's knowledge and skills before the new instruction
2. *Formative assessment.* The assessment of learning during the instruction
3. *Summative assessment.* The assessment of learning after the instruction, ultimately represented by the student's final term, semester, or year's achievement grade

Grades or marks shown on unit tests, progress reports, deficiency notices, and interim reports are examples of formative evaluation reports. However, an end-of-chapter test or a unit test is summative when the test represents the absolute end of the student's learning of material for that instructional unit.

Assessing Student Learning: Three Avenues

Three general avenues are available for assessing a student's achievement in learning. You can assess the following:

1. What the student *says*—for example, the quantity and quality of a student's contributions to class discussions
2. What the student *does*—for example, a student's performance (e.g., the amount and quality of a student's participation in the learning activities)
3. What the student *writes*—for example, as shown by items in the student's portfolio (e.g., homework assignments, checklists, project work, and written tests)

In a diverse classroom, an eclectic approach to assessment that includes the different stages and avenues highlighted here will allow students to demonstrate their comprehension of covered material and to improve in areas they find challenging.

Importance and Weight of Each Avenue

Although your own situation and personal philosophy will dictate the levels of importance and weight you give to each avenue of assessment, you should have a strong rationale if you value and weigh the three avenues for assessment differently than one-third each.

Assessing What a Student Says and Does

When evaluating what a student says, you should listen to the student's oral reports, questions, responses, and interactions with others and observe the student's attentiveness, involvement in class activities, creativeness, and responses to challenges. Notice that we say you should *listen* and *observe*. While listening to what the student is saying, you should also be observing the student's nonverbal behaviors. For this, you can use narrative observation forms (see Figure 11.1), observations with checklists and scoring rubrics (see sample checklists in Figures 11.2, 11.4, and 11.5 and sample scoring rubrics in Figures 11.2, 11.3, and 11.10 through 11.14), and periodic conferences with the student.

With each technique used, you must proceed from your awareness of anticipated learning outcomes (the instructional objectives), and you must assess a student's progress toward meeting those objectives, referred to as **criterion-referenced assessment**.

OBSERVATION FORM Figure 11.1 illustrates a sample generic form for recording and evaluating teacher observations of a student's verbal and nonverbal behaviors. With modern technology, for example, using the software program Learner Profile™ or personal digital assistants, a teacher can record observations electronically anywhere at any time.[3]

CHECKLIST VERSUS SCORING RUBRIC As you can see from the sample rubric and sample checklist shown in Figure 11.2, there is little difference between what a checklist is and what a rubric is. The difference is that rubrics show the degrees for the desired characteristics, while checklists usually show only the desired characteristics. The checklist could easily be made into a scoring rubric, and the rubric could easily be made into a checklist. See Activity 11.1 for detailed explanations and several examples of rubrics.

Figure 11.1 Evaluating and Recording Student Verbal and Nonverbal Behaviors: Sample Form

Student _____	Course _____	School _____
Observer _____	Date _____	Period _____
Objective for Time Period	Desired Behavior	What Student Did, Said, or Wrote

Teacher's (Observer's) Comments:

Figure 11.2 Checklist and Rubric Compared

Sample rubric for assessing a student's skill in listening:

Score Point 3—Strong listener
- responds immediately to oral directions
- focuses on speaker
- maintains appropriate attention span
- listens to what others are saying
- is interactive

Score Point 2—Capable listener
- follows oral directions
- usually attentive to speaker and to discussions
- listens to others without interrupting

Score Point 1—Developing listener
- has difficulty following directions
- relies on repetition
- often inattentive
- has short attention span
- often interrupts the speaker

Sample checklist for assessing a student's skill in map work:

Check each item if the map comes up to standard in this particular category.

_____ 1. Accuracy

_____ 2. Neatness

_____ 3. Attention to details

Activity
11.1   **Using Rubrics as an Assessment Tool**

Rubrics can be very helpful in assessing student performance. Rubrics are authentic assessment tools that help teachers evaluate complex and subjective criteria. Using rubrics can help clarify goals, expectations, and focus. Teachers can involve students in the teaching-learning process by empowering them to help align instructional objectives and assessment.

TeacherVision: Creating Rubrics
This is a collection of five articles covering what a rubric is, why you should use rubrics, how to create rubrics, the similarities and differences between analytic and holistic rubrics, using weighted rubrics, and student-generated rubrics.
http://www.teachervision.fen.com/teaching-methods-and
-management/rubrics/4521.html?for_printing=1&detoured=1

Guidelines for Rubric Development
Includes steps in rubric development, terms to use in measuring range/scoring levels, and concept words that convey various degrees of performance.
http://edweb.sdsu.edu/triton/july/rubrics/Rubric_Guidelines
.html

Rubrics for Web Lessons
This site includes several resources: articles on authentic assessment, guidelines for creating a rubric for a specific task, sample rubrics, a rubric template, additional links, and software and books available on designing and using rubrics.
http://webquest.sdsu.edu/rubrics/weblessons.htm

A Rubric for Evaluating WebQuests
This rubric covers overall aesthetics, the introduction, the task, the process, resources, and evaluation. This rubric design can be used in a variety of situations.
http://webquest.sdsu.edu/webquestrubric.html

Teachers.org Teach with Technology: Assessment
This website contains links to some great resources on assessment. They are grouped in the following categories: using learning indicators, using rubrics, special needs assessment, using portfolios, and management and assessment.
http://www.4teachers.org/profdev/index.php?profdevid
=as&PHPSESSID=b5b8a04801eac36a88578076cdc10885

GUIDELINES FOR ASSESSING WHAT A STUDENT SAYS AND DOES When assessing a student's verbal and nonverbal behaviors, you should do the following:

1. Maintain an anecdotal record (teacher's log) book or folder with a separate section in it for your records of each student.

2. List the desirable behaviors for a specific activity.

3. Check the list against the specific instructional objectives.

4. Record your observations as quickly as possible following your observation. Audio or video recordings and, of course, computer software programs can help you maintain records and check the accuracy of your memory, but if this is inconvenient, you should spend time during school, immediately after school, or later that evening recording your observations while they are still fresh in your memory.

5. Record your professional judgment about the student's progress toward the desired behavior but think it through before transferring it to a permanent record.

6. Write comments that are reminders to yourself, such as "Discuss observation with the student," "Check validity of observation by further testing," "Discuss observations with student's mentor" (e.g., an adult representative from the community), and "Discuss observations with other teachers on the teaching team."

Assessing What a Student Writes

When assessing what a student writes, you can use worksheets, written homework and papers, student journal writing, student writing projects, student portfolios, and tests (all discussed later in this chapter). In many schools, portfolios, worksheets, and homework assignments are the tools

usually used for the formative evaluation of each student's achievement. Tests, too, should be a part of this assessment, but tests are also used for summative evaluation at the end of a unit and for diagnostic purposes.

Your summative evaluation of a student's achievement and any other final judgment made by you about a student can have an impact on the psychological and intellectual development of that student. Non-native English speakers may be sensitive to criticism of their language progress. You want to help these students improve, but you do not want them to feel that anything short of a native-like command of the English language is acceptable. Focus on the message and avoid correcting every grammatical, pronunciation, or vocabulary error he or she makes while participating in class discussions or doing a formal presentation. Later in the section, we will pay special attention to this matter in "Recording Teacher Observations and Judgments."

GUIDELINES FOR ASSESSING STUDENT WRITING Use the following guidelines when assessing what a student writes. *Student writing assignments, test items, and scoring rubrics* (see Figure 11.3) *should be criterion referenced*; that is, they should correlate and be compatible with specific instructional objectives. Regardless of the avenue chosen and their relative weights given by you, you must evaluate against the instructional objectives. Any given objective may be checked by using more than one method and by using more than one instrument. Subjectivity, inherent in the assessment process, may be reduced as you check for validity, comparing results of one measuring strategy against those of another.

Read nearly everything a student writes (except, of course, for personal writing in a student's journal). If it is

Figure 11.3 **Sample Scoring Rubric for Assessing Student Writing**

Score Point 4—correct purpose, mode, audience; effective elaboration; consistent organization; clear sense of order and completeness; fluent

Score Point 3—correct purpose, mode, audience; moderately well elaborated; organized but possible brief digressions; clear, effective language

Score Point 2—correct purpose, mode, audience; some elaboration; some specific details; gaps in organization; limited language control

Score Point 1—attempts to address audience; brief, vague, unelaborated; wanders off topic; lack of language control; little or no organization; wrong purpose and mode

important for the student to do the work, then it is equally important that you give your professional attention to the product of the student's efforts. Of course, papers can be read with varying degrees of intensity and scrutiny, depending on the purpose of the assignment.

Provide written or verbal comments about the student's work and be positive in those comments. Rather than just writing "good" on a student's paper, briefly state what it was about it that made it good. Rather than simply saying or pointing out that the student didn't do it right, tell or show the student what is acceptable and how to achieve it. For reinforcement, use positive comments and encouragement as frequently as possible. Think before writing a comment on a student's paper, asking yourself how you think the student (or a parent or guardian) will interpret and react to the comment and if that is a correct interpretation or reaction to your intended meaning.

When assessing written work completed by English Language Learners, provide separate feedback on the mechanics (spelling, punctuation, and grammar) of the paper and the content. Avoid writing evaluative comments or grades in student journals.[4] Student journals are for encouraging students to write, to think about their thinking, and to record their creative thoughts. In journal writing, students should be encouraged to write about their experiences in and out of school and especially about their experiences related to what is being learned. They should be encouraged to write their feelings about what is being learned and about how they are learning it. Writing in journals gives them practice in expressing themselves in written form and in connecting their learning; you should provide nonthreatening freedom to do it. Avoid correcting spelling or grammar or making value statements. Comments and evaluations from teachers might discourage creative and spontaneous expression. You can write simple empathic comments such as "Thank you for sharing your thoughts" or "I think I understand what makes you feel that way."

When reading student journals, talk individually with students to seek clarification about their expressions. Student journals are useful to the teacher (of any subject)

in understanding the student's thought processes and writing skills (diagnostic assessment) and should not be graded. For grading purposes, teachers may simply record whether the student is maintaining a journal and, perhaps, an assessment regarding the quantity of writing in it, but no judgment should be made about the quality.

When reviewing student portfolios, discuss with students individually the progress in their learning as shown by the materials in their portfolios. As with student journals, the portfolio should not be graded or compared in any way with those of other students. Its purpose is for student self-assessment and to show progress in learning. For this to happen, students should keep in their portfolios all or major samples of papers related to the course. (Student portfolios are discussed later.)

Assessment for Affective and Psychomotor Domain Learning

Whereas assessment of cognitive domain learning lends itself to traditional written tests of achievement, learning within the affective and psychomotor domains is best assessed by the use of performance checklists where student behaviors can be observed in action. However, many educators today are encouraging the use of alternative assessment procedures (i.e., alternatives to traditional paper-and-pencil written testing). After all, in learning that is most important and that has the most meaning to students, the domains are inextricably interconnected. Learning that is meaningful to students is not as easily compartmentalized as the taxonomies of educational objectives would imply. Alternative assessment strategies include the use of projects, portfolios, skits, papers, and oral presentations in addition to performance tests.

Student Involvement in Assessment

Students' continuous self-assessment should be planned as an important component of the assessment program. If students are to progress in their understanding of their own thinking (**metacognition**) and in their intellectual development, then they must receive instruction and guidance in how to become more responsible for their own learning. During that empowerment process, they learn to think better of themselves and of their individual capabilities. Achieving this self-understanding and improved self-esteem requires the experiences afforded by successes, along with guidance in self-understanding and self-assessment.

To meet these goals, teachers provide opportunities for students to think about what they are learning, about how they are learning it, and about how far they have progressed. Specifically, to engage students in the assessment process, you can provide opportunities for the students to identify learning targets that are especially valued by the students, to help in the design of assessment devices for the units of study, to evaluate the tests that are furnished by the textbook publisher in terms of how well they match learning targets identified by you and the students, and to help interpret assessment results. To aid in the interpretation of results, students can maintain portfolios of their work, using rating scales or checklists periodically to self-assess their progress.

Using Student Portfolios

Portfolios are used by teachers as a means of instruction and by teachers and students as one means of assessing student learning. Although there is little research evidence to support or to refute the claim, educators believe that the instructional value comes from the process of the student's assembling and maintaining a personal portfolio. During that creative process, the student is expected to self-reflect and to think critically about what has and is being learned and assume some responsibility for his or her own learning.

Student portfolios fall into three general categories, and the purpose in a given situation may transcend some combination of all three. The categories are (1) *selected works portfolio*, in which students maintain samples of their work as prompted by the teacher; (2) *longitudinal or growth portfolio*, which is oriented toward outcome-driven goals and includes samples of student work from the beginning and end of the school term (or thematic unit of study) to exemplify achievement toward the goals; and (3) *passport or career portfolio*, which contains samples of student work that will enable the student to transition, such as from one school grade level to the next.

Student portfolios should be well organized and, depending on the purpose (or category), should contain assignment sheets, class worksheets, the results of homework, project binders, forms for student self-assessment and reflection on their work, and other class materials thought important by the students and teacher.[5] As a model of a real-life portfolio, you can share your personal career portfolio with your students (see Chapter 12).

PORTFOLIO ASSESSMENT: KNOWING AND DEALING WITH ITS LIMITATIONS Although **portfolio assessment** has gained momentum in recent years as an alternative to traditional methods of evaluating student progress, establishing standards has been difficult. Research on the use of portfolios for assessment indicates that validity and reliability of teacher evaluation are often quite low. In addition, portfolio assessment is not always practical for use by every teacher. For example, if you are the sole art teacher at a middle school and are responsible for teaching art to every one of the 700 students in the school, you are unlikely to have the time or storage capacity for 700 portfolios. For your assessment of student learning, the use of checklists, rubrics, and student self-assessment may be more practical.

Before using portfolios as an alternative to traditional testing, you are advised to carefully consider and clearly understand the reasons for doing it and its practicality in your situation. Then carefully decide portfolio content, establish rubrics or expectation standards, anticipate grading problems, and consider and prepare for parent reactions.

While emphasizing the criteria for assessment, rating scales and checklists provide students with means of expressing their feelings and give the teacher still another source of input data for use in assessment. To provide students with reinforcement and guidance to improve their learning and development, teachers can meet with individual students to discuss their self-assessments. Such conferences should provide students with understandable and achievable short-term goals as well as help them develop and maintain an adequate self-esteem.[6]

Although almost any instrument used for assessing student work can be used for student self-assessment, in some cases it might be better to construct specific instruments with the student's understanding of the instrument in mind. Student self-assessment and self-reflection should be done on a regular and continuing basis so that periodic comparisons can be made by the student. You will need to help students learn how to analyze these comparisons. Comparisons should provide a student with information previously not recognized about his or her own progress and growth.

Using Checklists

One of the items that can be maintained by students in their portfolios is a series of checklists. Checklist items can be used easily by a student to compare with previous self-assessments. Items on the checklist will vary depending on your purpose, subject, and grade level. (See sample forms in Figures 11.4 and 11.5.) Open-ended questions allow the student to provide additional information as well as to do some expressive writing. After a student has demonstrated each of the skills satisfactorily, a check is made next to the student's name either by the teacher alone or in conference with the student.

GUIDELINES FOR USING PORTFOLIOS FOR ASSESSMENT Here are general guidelines for using student portfolios in the assessment of learning:

- Contents of the portfolio should reflect course aims and objectives.
- Students should date everything that goes into their portfolios.
- Determine what materials should be kept in the portfolio and announce clearly (post schedule in room) when, how, and by what criteria portfolios will be reviewed by you.
- Give responsibility for maintenance of the portfolios to the students.
- Portfolios should be kept in the classroom.
- The portfolio should not be graded or compared in any way with those of other students. Its purpose is for student self-assessment and for showing progress in learning. For this to happen, students should keep in their portfolio all papers (or major papers) related to the course. For grading purposes, you can simply record whether the portfolio was maintained and, by checklist, whether all materials are in the portfolio that are supposed to be.

Figure 11.4 **Sample Checklist: Assessing a Student's Oral Report**

Checklist: Oral Report Assessment

Student _____   Date _____

Teacher _____   Time _____

Did the student:	Yes	No	Comments
1. Speak so that everyone could hear?			
2. Finish sentences?			
3. Seem comfortable in front of the group?			
4. Give a good introduction?			
5. Seem well informed about the topic?			
6. Explain ideas clearly?			
7. Stay on the topic?			
8. Give a good conclusion?			
9. Use effective visuals to make the presentation interesting?			
10. Give good answers to questions from the audience?			

Maintaining Records of Student Achievement

You must maintain well-organized and complete records of student achievement. You may do this on an electronic record book or in a written record book. At the very least, the record book should include attendance records and all records of scores on tests, homework, projects, and other assignments.

Daily interactions and events occur in the classroom that may provide informative data about a student's intellectual and psychological development. Maintaining a dated log of your observations of these interactions and events can provide important information that might otherwise be forgotten. At the end of a unit and again at the conclusion of a grading term, you will want to review your records. During the course of the school year, your anecdotal records (and those of other members of your teaching team) will provide important information about the development of each student and ideas for attention to be given to individual students.

Recording Teacher Observations and Judgments

You must think carefully about any written comments that you intend to make about a student. Teenagers can be quite sensitive to what others say about them, especially to comments made about them by a teacher.

Additionally, we have seen anecdotal comments in students' permanent records that said more about the teachers who made the comments than about the recipient students. Comments that have been carelessly, hurriedly, and thoughtlessly made can be detrimental to a student's welfare and progress in school. Teacher comments must be professional; that is, they must be diagnostically useful to the continued intellectual and psychological development

of the student. This is true for any comment you make or write, whether on a student's paper, on the student's permanent school record, or on a message sent to the student's home.

As an example, consider the following unprofessional comment observed in one student's permanent record. A teacher wrote, "John is lazy." Describing John as *lazy* could be done by anyone; it is nonproductive, and it is certainly not a professional diagnosis. How many times do you suppose John needs to receive such negative descriptions of his behavior before he begins to believe that he is just that—lazy—and, as a result, to act that way even more often? Written comments like that can also be damaging because they may be read by the teacher who next has John in class and may lead that teacher to simply perpetuate the same expectation of John. To say that John is lazy merely describes behavior as judged by the teacher who wrote the comment. More important and more professional would be for the teacher to try to analyze *why* John is behaving that way and then to *prescribe* activities that are likely to motivate John to assume more constructive charge of his own learning behavior.

For students' continued intellectual and psychological development, your comments should be useful, productive, analytical, diagnostic, and prescriptive. The professional teacher makes diagnoses and prepares descriptions; a professional teacher does not label students as *lazy*, *vulgar*, *slow*, *stupid*, *difficult*, or *dumb*. The professional teacher sees the behavior of a student as being goal directed. Perhaps *lazy* John found that particular behavioral pattern won him attention. John's goal, then, was attention (don't we all need attention?), and John assumed negative, perhaps even self-destructive, behavioral patterns to reach that goal. The professional task of any teacher is to facilitate the learner's understanding (perception) of a goal and help the student identify acceptable behaviors positively designed to reach that goal.

Figure 11.5 Sample Checklist: Student Learning Assessment for Use with Interdisciplinary Thematic Instruction

Checklist: Interdisciplinary Thematic Unit Learning			
Student _____		Date _____	
Teacher _____		Time _____	
Did the student:	Yes	No	*Comments/Evidence*
1. Identify theme, topic, main idea of the unit			
2. Identify contributions of others to the theme			
3. Identify problems related to the unit of study			
4. Develop skill in:			
Applying knowledge			
Assuming responsibility			
Categorizing			
Classifying			
Decision making			
Discussing			
Gathering resources			
Impulse control			
Inquiry			
Justifying choices			
Listening to others			
Locating information			
Metacognition			
Ordering			
Organizing information			
Problem recognition/identification			
Problem solving			
Reading maps and globes			
Reading text			
Reasoning			
Reflecting			
Reporting to others			
Self-assessing			
Sharing			
Studying			
Summarizing			
Thinking			
Using resources			
Working independently			
Working with others			
(Others unique to the unit)			
Additional teacher and student comments:			

Grading and Marking Student Achievement

If conditions were ideal (which they are not) and if teachers did their job perfectly well (which many of us do not) and if students all worked up to their academic potential, then all students would receive top marks (the ultimate in mastery or quality learning), and there would be less of a need here to talk about grading and marking. Mastery learning implies that some end point of learning is attainable; however, there

probably isn't an end point. In any case, because conditions for teaching are never ideal and we teachers are mere humans, let us continue with the topic of grading, which is undoubtedly of special interest to you; your students, their parents, or their guardians; school counselors, administrators and school boards; potential employers; providers of scholarships; and college admissions officers.

The term *achievement*, used frequently throughout this book, means accomplishment, but is it accomplishment of the instructional objectives against preset standards, or is it simply accomplishment? Most teachers probably choose the former, where the teacher subjectively establishes a standard that must be met in order for a student to receive a certain grade for an assignment, project, test, quarter, semester, or course. Achievement, then, is decided by degrees of accomplishment.

Preset **standards** are usually expressed in percentages (degrees of accomplishment) needed for marks or ABC grades. If no student achieves the standard required for an A grade, for example, then no student receives an A. However, if all students meet the preset standard for the A grade, then all receive As. Determining student grades on the basis of preset standards is referred to as *criterion-referenced grading*.

Criterion-Referenced versus Norm-Referenced Grading

While criterion-referenced (or competency-based) grading is based on preset standards, **norm-referenced** grading measures the relative accomplishment of individuals in the group (e.g., one classroom of high school chemistry students) or in a larger group (e.g., all students enrolled in high school chemistry) by comparing and ranking students and is commonly known as *grading on a curve*. Because it encourages competition and discourages cooperative learning, *norm-referenced grading is not recommended* for the determination of student grades. Norm-referenced grading is educationally dysfunctional. For your personal interest, after several years of teaching, you can produce frequency-distribution studies of grades you have given over a period of time, but *do not* give students grades that are based on a curve. The idea that grading and reporting should always be done in reference to learning criteria and never on a curve is well supported by research studies and authorities on the matter.[7] Grades for student achievement should be tied to performance levels and determined on the basis of each student's achievement toward preset standards.

In criterion-referenced grading, the aim is to communicate information about an individual student's progress in knowledge and work skills in comparison to that student's previous attainment or in the pursuit of an absolute, such as content mastery. Criterion-referenced grading is featured in programs that focus on personalized (individualized) education.

Criterion-referenced grading is based on the level at which each student meets the specified objectives (standards) for the course or grade level. The objectives must be clearly stated to represent important student learning outcomes. This approach implies that effective teaching and learning result in high grades (As) or marks for most students. In fact, when a mastery concept is used, the student must accomplish the objectives before being allowed to proceed to the next learning task. The philosophy of teachers who favor criterion-referenced procedures recognizes individual potential. Such teachers accept the challenge of finding teaching strategies to help students progress from

where they are to the next designated level. Instead of wondering how Juanita compares with Sally, the comparison is between what Juanita could do yesterday and what she can do today and how well these performances compare to the preset standard.

Most school systems use some sort of combination of both norm-referenced and criterion-referenced data usage. Sometimes both kinds of information are useful. For example, a report card for a student in the eighth grade might indicate how that student is meeting certain criteria, such as an A grade for addition of fractions. Another entry might show that this mastery is expected, however, in the sixth grade. Both criterion- and norm-referenced data may be communicated to the parents or guardians and the student. Appropriate procedures should be used: a criterion-referenced approach to show whether the student can accomplish the task and, if so, to what degree and a norm-referenced approach to show how well that student performs compared to the larger group to which the student belongs. The latter is important information for college admissions officers and for committees that award academic scholarships.

Determining Grades

Final grades have significant impacts on the futures of students. When determining achievement grades for student performance, you must make several important and professional decisions. Although in a few schools and for certain classes or assignments only marks such as *E*, *S*, and *I* or "pass/no pass" are used, percentages of accomplishment and letter grades are used for most courses taught in middle and secondary schools.[8]

GUIDELINES FOR DETERMINING GRADES For determining student grades, consider the guidelines presented in the following paragraphs.

At the start of the school term, explain your grading policies *first to yourself* and then to your students and to their parents or guardians at back-to-school night, by a written explanation that is sent home, or both. Share sample scoring and grading rubrics with students and parents. In fact, engaging students with you in the collaborative development of rubrics can be a potent benefit to *instruction*.[9] In addition, include your grading policy when you cover your course syllabus.

When converting your interpretation of a student's accomplishments to a letter grade, be as objective as possible. For the selection of criteria for ABC grades, select a percentage standard, such as 92% for an A, 85% for a B, 75% for a C, and 65% for a D. Cutoff percentages used are your decision, although the district, school, program area, or department may have established guidelines that you are expected to follow.

For the determination of students' final grades, many teachers use a point system, where things that students write, say, and do are given points (but not journals or portfolios, except perhaps simply for whether the student does one); then the possible point total is the factor for determining grades. For example, if 92% is the cutoff for an A and 500 points are possible, then any student with 460 points or more (500 × .92) has achieved an A. Likewise, for a test or any other assignment, if the value is 100 points, the cutoff for an A is 92 (100 × .92). With a point system and preset standards, the teacher and students, at any time during the grading period, always know the current points possible and can easily calculate a student's current grade standing. Report grades frequently to students—weekly if possible but no fewer than two times during a given semester. Then, as far as a current grade is concerned, students always know where they stand in the course.

It is important to remember that a grade of zero has a negative effect on student effort, motivation, and grade averages, especially when using a point system for grading. These negative effects caused by a zero grade can be offset by providing options such as the elimination of one low grade, second-effort rewards, and recovery (see Chapter 9).

Build your grading policy around degrees of accomplishment rather than failure and when students proceed from one accomplishment to the next. This *continuous promotion* is not necessarily the promotion of the student from one grade level to the next but rather promotion within the classroom.

Remember that *assessment* and *grading* are not synonymous. As you learned earlier, assessment implies the collection of information from a variety of sources, including measurement techniques and subjective observations. These data, then, become the basis for arriving at a final grade, which in effect is a final value judgment. Grades are one aspect of evaluation and are intended to communicate educational progress to students and to their parents or guardians. To be valid as an indicator of that progress, data for determining a student's final grade must come from a variety of sources.

Decide beforehand your policy about makeup work. Students will be absent and will miss assignments and tests, so it is best that your policies about late assignments and missed tests be clearly communicated to students and to their parents or guardians. For makeup work, consider the following.

HOMEWORK ASSIGNMENTS As discussed earlier (in Chapter 9), we recommend that after due dates have been negotiated or set for assignments, no credit or reduced credit be given for work that is turned in late. Sometimes, however, a student has legitimate reasons why he or she could not get an assignment done by the due date, and the teacher must exercise a professional judgment in each instance. Although it is important that teachers have rules and procedures— and that they consistently apply those—the teacher is a professional who must consider all aspects of a student's situation and, after doing so, show compassion, caring, and understanding of the human situation. (Refer to the section "Giving Students a Second Chance" in Chapter 9.)

TESTS If students are absent when tests are given, you have several options. Some teachers allow students to miss or discount one test per grading period. Another technique is to allow each student to substitute a written homework assignment or project for one missed test. Still another option is to give the absent student the choice of either taking a makeup test or having the next test count double. When makeup tests are given, they should be taken within a week of the regular test unless there is a compelling reason (e.g., medical or family problem) why this cannot happen.

Sometimes students miss a testing period not because of being absent from school but because of involvement in other school activities. In those instances, the student may be able to arrange to come and take the test during another of your class periods or your prep period on that day or the next. If a student is absent during performance testing, the logistics and possible diminished reliability of having to readminister the test for one student may necessitate giving the student an alternate paper-and-pencil test or some other option.

QUIZZES Many teachers give frequent and brief quizzes as often as every day. As opposed to tests (see the next section), quizzes are usually brief (perhaps taking only five minutes of class time) and intended to reinforce the importance of frequent study and review. (However, quizzes should be prepared using the same care and precision as presented in the guidelines that follow in the sections for testing and preparation of assessment items.) When quizzes are given at frequent intervals, no single quiz should count very much toward the student's final grade. Therefore, you will probably want to avoid having to schedule and give makeup quizzes for students who were absent during a quiz period. The following are reasonable options for administering makeup quizzes and are presented here in order of our preference, the first item being our first choice. (a) Give a certain number of quizzes during a grading period, say 10, but allow a student to discount a few quiz scores, say 2 of the 10, thereby allowing the student to discount a low score, a missed quiz, or both because of absence. (b) Count the next quiz double for a student who missed one because of absence. About the only problem with this option is when a student misses several quizzes. If that happens, (c) count the unit test a certain and relative percentage greater for any student who missed a quiz during that unit. By the way, we see absolutely no educational value in giving "pop" or unannounced quizzes that are graded and recorded.

Testing for Achievement

One source of information used for determining grades is data obtained from testing for student achievement. There are two kinds of tests: those that are standardized and those that are not.

Standardized and Nonstandardized Tests

Standardized tests are those that have been constructed and published by commercial testing bureaus and used by states and districts to determine and compare student achievement, principally in the core subjects. Standardized norm-referenced tests are best for diagnostic purposes and should not be used for determining student grades. There is not enough space in this book to include a detailed description of standardized achievement testing. Instead, our focus is on nonstandardized tests that are designed by you, the classroom teacher, for your own unique group of students.

Textbook publishers' tests, test item pools, and standardized tests are available from a variety of sources. As discussed in Chapter 2, the testing craze and pressure for students to achieve well on standardized tests nationwide have caused many teachers to "teach to the test." However, these publishers' materials and standardized texts were not prepared specifically for your students. Because schools, teachers, and students are different, most of the time you will be designing or collaboratively participating in designing and preparing tests for your own purposes for your distinct group of students.

Competent planning, preparing, administering, and scoring of tests is an important professional skill. You may want to refer to the guidelines that follow while you are student-teaching and again occasionally during your initial years as an employed teacher.

Purposes for Testing

Tests can be designed for several purposes, and several types of tests and alternate test items will keep your testing program interesting, useful, and reliable. As a college student, you are probably most experienced with testing that measures achievement, but as a teacher you will use tests for other reasons as well. Tests are also used to assess and aid in curriculum development; help determine teaching effectiveness; help students develop positive attitudes, appreciations, and values; help students increase their understanding and retention of facts, principles, skills, and concepts; motivate students; provide diagnostic information for planning for individualization of the instruction; provide review and drill to enhance teaching and learning; and serve as informational data for students and parents.

Frequency of Testing

First of all, assessment for student learning should be continuous; that is, it should be going on every minute of every class day. For grading or marking purposes, it is difficult to generalize about how often to formally test for student achievement, but we believe that testing should be cumulative and frequent. By *cumulative*, we mean that each assessment should assess the student's understanding of previously learned material as well as for the current unit of study—that is, it should assess connected learning whenever possible and appropriate. By *frequent*, we mean as often as once a week for classes that meet for an hour or so each

day. Advantages of assessment that is cumulative include the review, reinforcement, and articulation of old material with the most recent. Advantages of frequent assessment include a reduction in student anxiety over tests and an increase in the validity of the summative assessment.

Test Construction

After determining the reasons for which you are designing and administering a test, you need to identify the specific instructional objectives the test is being designed to measure. (As you learned in Chapter 5, your written instructional objectives are specific so that you can write assessment items to measure against those objectives, and that is criterion-referenced assessment.) So, the first step in test construction is identification of the purpose(s) for the test. The second step is to identify the objectives to be measured, and the third step is to prepare the test items. The best time to prepare draft items is after you have prepared your instructional objectives—while the objectives are fresh in your mind, meaning before the lessons are taught. After a lesson is taught, you will want to rework your first draft of the test items to make any modifications based on the instruction that occurred.

Administering Tests

For many students, test taking can be a time of high anxiety. Middle school and secondary school students demonstrate test anxiety in various ways. Just before and during testing some are quiet and thoughtful, while others are noisy and disruptive. To more accurately measure student achievement, you will want to take steps to reduce their anxiety. To control or reduce student anxieties, consider the following discussion as guidelines for administering tests.

Since many people respond best to a familiar routine, plan your formative assessment program so that tests are given at regular intervals and administered at the same time and in the same way. In some secondary schools in particular, days of the week are assigned to departments for administering major tests. For example, Tuesdays might be assigned for language arts and mathematics testing, while Wednesday is the day for social studies and science testing.

Avoid tests that are too long and that will take too much time. Sometimes beginning teachers have unreasonable expectations of young people about their attention spans during testing. Frequent testing with frequent sampling of student knowledge is preferred over infrequent and long tests that attempt to cover everything.

Make the classroom environment as comfortable as possible. Try to arrange the classroom so it is well ventilated, the temperature is comfortable, and, when giving paper-and-pencil tests individually, the seats are well spaced. If spacing is a problem, then consider group testing or using alternate forms of the test, where students seated adjacent to one another have different forms of the same test (e.g., multiple-choice answer alternatives are arranged in different order).

Teaching Scenario	¡Ya lo creo!

Señora Campos had been teaching Spanish for seven years at Merion High School when she met Paco (the name he selected for class). She had had the gamut of students: students who were enrolled in Spanish to meet the language requirement, students who thought Spanish was an easy A and would boost their grade-point average (GPA), the football players who couldn't seem to pass any other language course, students who had heard of her legendary fiestas with homemade tamales and flan, and the occasional student who was genuinely interested in the language and culture. Some were gifted linguists, some worked hard, some never really applied themselves, and still others would enroll in Spanish I multiple times and never seem to get it. Still, with all her experience, Campos had never met a student like Paco. He exasperated her. He always asked detailed grammatical questions, challenged her explanations, and sidetracked his classmates whenever possible.

Although Paco irritated her on so many levels, he did make her a better teacher—well, at least a better test preparer. It was the fifth week of the term, and Campos gave the students the first test reviewing the simple present tense and basic vocabulary—the same test she had administered every semester since she started teaching. The directions were simple: answer the following questions; do not respond with a one-word answer. So, "sí" and "no" were not considered appropriate responses.

On the weekend, Campos sat down to start her grading marathon. All her students this time, like the many before them, answered the test questions similarly. They started by saying "sí" or "no" and then conjugated the verb and regurgitated the sentence. For example, ¿Hablas español? (Do you speak Spanish?) was often answered with Sí, hablo español un poquito (Yes, I speak a little Spanish).

When she got to Paco's paper, she was dumbfounded, but she understood why he finished the test way before his classmates. Every question had the same response: ¡Ya lo creo! The translation may vary, but the general meaning of ¡Ya lo creo! is, Yes indeed! Certainly! It goes without saying! At first she was outraged and decided to flunk him. But then she calmed down, mulled it over, reread her directions, and decided he could use the idiomatic expression ¡Ya lo creo! for each question on the test.

Read through the sample test questions listed below and respond ¡Ya lo creo! (yes indeed). It works, doesn't it? So, when Campos handed back the tests on Monday morning, Paco received an A, and she never wrote another test without very specific explanations about what constituted an appropriate response.

Sample Questions from Señora Campos's First Test Reviewing the Present Tense

¿Hablas español? (Do you speak Spanish?)
¿Te gusta la clase de español? (Do you like Spanish class?)
¿Estudias mucho? (Do you study a lot?)
¿La comida está deliciosa? (Is the meal good?)
¿Tienes hambre? (Are you hungry?)
¿Bailas bien? (Do you dance well?)
¿Cantas en el baño? (Do you sing in the bathroom?)

Before distributing the test, explain to students what they are to do when finished, such as quietly beginning an assignment or an anchor activity (see Chapter 6), because not all the students will finish at the same time. It is unreasonable to expect most students to just sit quietly after finishing a test; they need something to do.

When ready to test, don't drag it out. Distribute tests quickly and efficiently. Once testing has begun, avoid interrupting the students. Items or announcements of important information can be written on the board or, if unrelated to the test, held until all students are finished with the test. Stay in the room and visually monitor the students. If the test is not going to take an entire class period (for class periods of 50 or more minutes, and most shouldn't) and it's a major test, then administer it at the beginning of the period, if possible, unless you are planning a test review just prior to it (although that seems rather late to conduct a meaningful review).

Controlling Cheating

Cheating does occur. In a recent national survey of teachers, 90% of the teachers claimed that cheating by students was a problem.[10] There are steps you can take to discourage cheating in your classroom or to reduce the opportunity and pressure that cause students to cheat on tests. Consider the following.

PREVENTING CHEATING Space students or, as mentioned before, use alternate forms of the test. Another technique used by some teachers, especially those in middle schools and where students sit at tables rather than at individual desks, is to use space dividers. Space dividers can be made by attaching three approximately 8- by 10-inch rectangular sections of cardboard. The divider is placed in front of the student, making it impossible for neighboring students to see over. Dividers can be made from cardboard boxes or heavy folders of various sorts. It could be a project at the beginning of the year for each student to design and make his or her own space divider, which is then stored in the classroom for use on test days. Students enjoy being allowed to personalize their dividers.

Frequent testing and not allowing a single test to count too much toward a term grade reduce test anxiety and the pressure that can cause cheating as well as increase student learning by "stimulating greater effort and providing intermittent feedback" to the student.[11] Prepare test questions that are clear and not ambiguous, thereby reducing student frustration that is caused by a question or instructions that students do not understand. Avoid giving tests that will take too much time. During long tests, some students get discouraged and restless; that is a time when classroom management problems can occur.

Creative Cheating

Many educational critics have commented that we seem to care more about the grades that students earn on tests than we do about whether students are learning the material. Peer pressure, laziness, difficulty learning content, and lack of time or interest are often blamed for the rise in cheating. Whatever the cause, cheating is rampant in our middle and secondary schools. A top researcher and founder of the Center for Academic Integrity, Don McCabe, says that students today have a cavalier attitude where cheating is concerned. During the 2000–2001 academic year, McCabe interviewed 4,500 students from 25 different high schools and reported that as many as 75% of the participants admitted to cheating on tests. In another recent survey, 64% of seventh graders said that they collaborated with classmates when they were expected to work individually, 48% said that they copied a classmate's homework, and 87% said that they let another student copy their work.

Cheating in the 21st century has gone high-tech. The old standbys of peeking at a classmate's paper, whispering answers, or writing answers on the tops of books placed on the floor, on the teacher's desk, on cheat sheets in backpacks, on the inside labels of water bottles, on the thighs of short-skirted girls, or in baggy or multiple-pocket pants have evolved with the advent of information technology.

On May 30, 2007, Discover Inspiring Technology posted "7 Hi-Tech Gadgets That Can Help You Cheat at Exams" on the Internet at **http://discoverx.wordpress.com/2007/05/30/ 7-hi-tech-gadgets-that-can-help-you-cheat-at-exams**. Here is a summary of the list of some of the high-tech cheating techniques and devices they claim students are likely to use: (a) text messaging answers to classmates on their cell phone; (b) snapping a photograph of test questions with the built-in digital camera on their cell phone and sending them to classmates for the answers via instant messaging; (c) recording notes and transferring them to their MP3 player to play back during the test; (d) entering lists on their iPod that imitate song titles or displaying images, videos, graphs, and so on; (e) using an audio gadget and an earphone or SoundBug to transmit accompanying audio or sticking wireless earphones into their ears and small microphones up their sleeves to communicate answers with classmates; (f) using a programmable calculator like a TI-83 Plus, which allows them to increase the memory and load software so they can use their calculator like a pocket notebook; and (g) using PocketPC, Palm, and other personal digital assistants to make a wireless connection to the Internet.

Think About It

In fact, even good students are tempted to cheat. It is our job as educators to teach our students about academic honesty and ethical behavior.

1. What other creative ways to cheat are you familiar with?
2. What can you do to deter student cheating?
3. How will you handle students who cheat on quizzes/tests in your classes?

By their sheer nature, performance tests can cause pressure on students and can also provide greater opportunity for cheating. When administering performance tests to an entire class, it is best to have several monitors, such as members of your teaching team. If that isn't possible, consider testing groups of students, such as cooperative learning groups, rather than individuals. Evaluation of test performance, then, would be based on group rather than individual achievement.

Consider using open-text and open-notebook tests or allowing each student to prepare a page of notes to use during the test. Allowing students to use their books and notes not only reduces anxiety but also helps them with the organization of information and the retention of what has been learned.

STOPPING CHEATING The preceding paragraphs provide hints to prevent student cheating. If you suspect that cheating is occurring, move and stand in the area of the suspected student. That will usually stop it. Now read about a cheating misunderstanding by completing Activity 11.2.

DEALING WITH CHEATING When you suspect cheating has occurred, you are faced with a dilemma. Unless your suspicion is backed by solid proof, you are advised to forget it but to keep a close watch on the student the next time to prevent cheating from happening. Your job is not to catch students being dishonest but to discourage dishonesty. If you have absolute proof that a student has cheated, then you are obligated to proceed with school policy on student cheating, which may call for a session with the counselor or the student and the student's parent or guardian, perhaps an automatic F grade on the test, and even a temporary suspension from class.

Determining the Time Needed to Take a Test

Again, avoid giving tests that are too long and that will take too much time. Preparing and administering good tests is a skill that you will develop over time. In the meantime, it is best to test frequently and to use tests that sample student achievement rather than try for a comprehensive measure of that achievement.

Some students take more time on the same test than do others. You want to avoid giving too much time, or problems in classroom management will result. However, you don't want to cut short the time needed by students who can do well but need more time to think and to write. As a very general guide, use the table of time needed for different types of test items (Table 11.1). This is only a guide for determining the approximate amount of time to allow students to complete a test. For example, for a test made up of 10 multiple-choice items, five arrangement items, and two

Activity 11.2　| **Cheating Confessions**

Cheating has been around as long as students have been. High school students have often felt pressure to perform well on assessments in order to get good grades in their high school courses and to be accepted into the college of their choice. During the 1961–1962 academic year, Sam Sloan was a senior at E. C. High School in Lynchburg, VA. Go to the following website to read about how Sloan and his classmates wrongfully accused fellow classmate Charles Pryor of cheating on his physics exams and how Mr. A. J. Fielder, their teacher, handled the situation.

Sloan's account of what happened in his high school physics course can be found at A Story about High School Cheating at **http://www.samsloan.com/pryor.htm.**

Apply Your Knowledge

1. What cheating schemes did you observe, participate in, or hear about during middle or secondary school?
2. Were you or a classmate ever accused of cheating on a quiz or test? If so, how did the teacher handle it?
3. Think of a time when you jumped to conclusions about the academic dishonesty of a classmate. What happened?

Table 11.1　| Approximate Time to Allow for Testing as Determined by the Types of Items*

Type of Test Item	Time Needed Per Item
Matching	1 minute per matching item
Multiple choice	1 minute
Completion	1 minute
Completion drawing	2–3 minutes
Arrangement	2–3 minutes
Identification	2–3 minutes
Short explanation	2–3 minutes
Essay and performance	10 or more minutes

NOTE: *Students with special needs and English Language Learners may need more time per item.

short-explanation items, you would want to plan for about 30 minutes for students to complete the test.

Preparing Assessment Items

Preparing and writing good assessment items is yet another professional skill, and becoming proficient at it takes study, time, practice, and reflection. Because of the importance of an assessment program, assume this professional charge seriously and responsibly. Although poorly prepared items take no time at all to construct, they will cause you more trouble than you can ever imagine. As a professional, you should take time to study different types of assessment items that can be used and how best to write them and then practice writing them. Remember, when preparing assessment items, ensure that they match and sufficiently cover the instructional objectives. In addition, you should prepare each item carefully enough to be reasonably confident that each item will be understood by the students in the manner that you anticipate its being understood. With the diversity of students in today's classrooms, especially with respect to their proficiency in oral and written English and/or their special needs, this is an important point. Finally, after administering a test, you must take time to analyze the results and reflect on the value of each item before ever using that item again.

General Guidelines for Preparing for Assessment

Consider the following six general guidelines when preparing for assessment: (1) include several kinds of items and assessment instruments (see 12 types that follow); (2) ensure that content coverage is complete (i.e., that all objectives are being measured); (3) ensure that each item is reliable—that is, that it measures the intended objective (one way to check item reliability is to have more than one item measuring the same objective); (4) ensure that each item is clear and unambiguous to all students; (5) plan each item to be difficult enough for the poorly prepared student but easy enough for the student who is well prepared; and (6) because it is time consuming to write good assessment items, you are advised to maintain a bank of items, with each item coded according to its matching instructional objective, its domain of learning (cognitive, affective, or psychomotor), perhaps its level within the hierarchy of a particular domain, and whether it requires thinking that is recall, processing, or application. Computer software programs are available for this. Ready-made electronic test item banks are available and accompany many programs or textbooks. If you use them, be certain that the items were well written and match your course objectives. When preparing items for your test bank, use your creative thinking and best writing skills—prepare items that match your objectives, put them aside, think about them, and then work them over again.

Every test that you administer to your students should represent your best professional effort—void of spelling and grammar errors. A quickly and poorly prepared test can cause you more grief than you can imagine. One that is obviously hurriedly prepared and wrought with spelling and grammar errors will quickly be frowned on by discerning parents or guardians.

Classification of Assessment Items

Assessment items and assessment instruments (such as entire tests) can be classified as verbal (oral or written words), visual (pictures and diagrams), and manipulative or performance (handling of materials and equipment or performing). Written verbal items are the ones that have traditionally been most frequently used in testing. However, visual items and visual tests are useful, for example, when working with students who lack fluency with the written word or when testing students who are English Language Learners.

Performance items and tests are useful when measuring psychomotor skill development. Common examples are performance testing of a student's ability to carry a microscope or hold a jumping rope in place (gross motor skill) or to focus a microscope or to jump rope (fine motor skill). Performance testing also can and should be a part of a wider testing program that includes testing for higher-level thinking skills and knowledge, as, for example, when a student or small group of students is given the problem of creating from discarded materials a habitat for an imaginary animal and then display, write about, and orally present their product to the rest of the class.

For the past decade or so, and as noted often throughout this book, educators have taken a rekindled interest in this last described form of performance testing as a means of assessing learning that is closer to measuring for the real thing—that is, authentic. In a program for teacher preparation, **micro peer teaching** and the **student-teaching** experience are examples of performance assessment, that is, assessment practices used to assess the teacher candidate's ability to teach (to perform). It seems axiomatic that assessment of student teaching is a more authentic assessment of a candidate's ability to teach than would be a written (paper-and-pencil test) or verbal (oral test) form of assessment. Although less direct and perhaps less reliable than a checklist observation and analysis of a student teacher actually teaching, an observation of a student teacher's analysis of a video-recorded episode (i.e., with pictures) of another teacher's performance would be another way of more authentically assessing a teacher's ability to teach than would be a paper-and-pencil response item test.

Performance Testing Can Be Expensive and Time Intensive

Performance testing is usually more expensive and time consuming than is verbal testing, which in turn is more time demanding and expensive than is written testing. However, a good program of assessment will use alternate forms of assessment and not rely solely on one form (such as written) and one type of written item (such as multiple choice) so that all students have ample opportunities to demonstrate their learning.

The type of test and the items that you use depend on your purpose and objectives. Carefully consider the alternatives within that framework. To provide validity checks and to account for the individual differences of students, a good assessment program should include items from all three types. That is what writers of articles in professional journals are referring to when they talk about **alternative assessment**. They are encouraging the use of multiple assessment items as opposed to the traditional heavy reliance on objective items, such as multiple-choice questions.

Attaining Content Validity

To ensure that your test measures what is supposed to be measured, you can construct a table of specifications. A two-way grid indicates behavior in one dimension and content in the other (see Figures 11.6 and 11.7).

In this grid, behavior relates to the three domains: cognitive, affective, and psychomotor. In Figure 11.6, the cognitive domain is divided, according to Bloom's Taxonomy (Chapter 5), into six categories: knowledge or simple recall, comprehension, application, analysis, synthesis (often involving an original product in oral or written form), and evaluation. The specifications table in Figure 11.6 does not specify levels within the affective and psychomotor domains.

To use a table of specifications, the teacher examining objectives for the unit decides what emphasis should be given to the behavior and to the content. For instance, if

Figure 11.6 **Table of Specifications I**

CONTENT	BEHAVIORS								
Social Studies Grade 8	Cognitive						Affective	Psychomotor	TOTAL
Ancient Greece	Knowledge	Comprehension	Application	Analysis	Synthesis	Evaluation			
I. Vocabulary Development		2 (1,2)	1 (2)						3
II. Concepts		2	2(3,4)						4
III. Applications	1	1(5)	1 (5)	1 (5)	1 (5)	1 (5)			6
IV. Problem-solving			1 (6)		1 (6)				2
TOTAL	1	5	5	1	2	1			15

Figure 11.7 **Table of Specifications II**

CONTENT	BEHAVIORS							TOTAL
	Cognitive			Affective		Psychomotor		
	Input	Processing	Application	Low	High	Low	High	
I.								
II.								
III.								
IV.								
TOTAL								

vocabulary development is a concern for this eighth-grade study of ancient Greece, then probably 20 % of the test on vocabulary would be appropriate, but 50 % would be unsuitable. This planning enables the teacher to design a test to fit the situation rather than a haphazard test that does not correspond to the objectives either in content or in behavior emphasis. Since knowledge questions are easy to write, tests often fail to go beyond that level even though the objectives state that the student will analyze and evaluate. The sample table of specifications for an eighth-grade social studies unit on ancient Greece indicates a distribution of questions on a test. Since this test is to be an objective test and it is so difficult to write objective items to test affective and psychomotor behaviors, this table of specifications calls for no test items in these areas. If these categories are included in the unit objectives, some other assessment devices must be used to test learning in these domains. The teacher could also show the objectives tested, as indicated within parentheses in Figure 11.6. Then, checking later for inclusion of all objectives is easy.

Some teachers prefer the alternative table shown in Figure 11.7. Rather than differentiating among all six of Bloom's cognitive levels, this table separates cognitive objectives into just three levels: those that require simple low-level recall of knowledge, those that require information processing, and those that require application of the new knowledge (refer to the section "Levels of Cognitive Questions and Student Thinking" in Chapter 9). In addition, the affective and psychomotor domains each are divided into low- and high-level behaviors. A third alternative, not illustrated here, is a table of specifications that shows all levels of each of the three domains.

Types of Assessment Items: Descriptions, Examples, and Guidelines for Preparing and Using Them

This section presents descriptions, advantages and disadvantages, and guidelines for preparing and using 12 types of assessment items. When reading about the advantages and

disadvantages of each, you will notice that some types are appropriate for use in direct or performance assessment, while others are not.

Arrangement

DESCRIPTION Terms or real objects (**realia**) are to be arranged in a specified order.

Example 1 Arrange the following list of events on a timeline in the order of their occurrence: Maximilian I elected King of Germany; Maximilian I becomes Holy Roman Emperor; Diet of Augsburg establishes Council of Regency, divides Germany into six regions; Charles I of Spain becomes Holy Roman Emperor; Ferdinand I assumes the title of Holy Roman Emperor.

Example 2 The assortment of balls on the table represents the planets in our solar system. (*Note:* The balls are of various sizes, such as marbles, tennis balls, basketballs, and so on, each labeled with a planetary name, with a large sphere in the center labeled the Sun.) Arrange the balls in their proper order around the Sun.

ADVANTAGES This type of item tests for knowledge of sequence and order and is good for review, for starting discussions, and for performance assessment. Example 2 is also an example of a performance test item.

DISADVANTAGES Scoring could be difficult, so be cautious and meticulous when using this type of item for grading purposes.

GUIDELINES FOR USE To enhance reliability, you may need to include instructions asking students to include the rationale for their arrangement, making it a combined arrangement and short-explanation type of assessment and allowing space for explanations on an answer sheet. This item is useful for small, heterogeneous group assessment to allow students to share and learn from their collaborative thinking and reasoning.

Completion Drawing

DESCRIPTION An incomplete drawing is presented and the student is to complete it.

Example 1 Connect the following items with arrow lines to show the stages from introduction of a new bill to it becoming law (items not included here).

Example 2 In the following food web (not included here), draw arrow lines indicating which organisms are consumers and which are producers.

ADVANTAGES This type requires less time than would a complete drawing that might be required in an essay item. Scoring is relatively easy.

DISADVANTAGES Care needs to be exercised in the instructions so students do not misinterpret the expectation.

GUIDELINES FOR USE Use occasionally for diversion, but take care in preparing. This type can be instructive when assessing for student thinking and reasoning, as it can measure conceptual knowledge. Consider making the item a combined completion-drawing, short-explanation type by having students include their rationales for the thinking behind their completion drawing. Be sure to allow space for their explanations. This assessment item is useful for small, heterogeneous group assessment to allow students to share and learn from their collaborative thinking and reasoning.

Completion Statement
DESCRIPTION
Sometimes called a fill-in-the-blank item, an incomplete sentence is presented and the student is to complete it by filling in the blank space(s).

Example 1 A group of words that have a special meaning, such as "a skeleton in the closet," is called a(n) _____.

Example 2 To test their hypotheses, scientists and social scientists conduct _____.

ADVANTAGES This type is easy to devise, take, and score.

DISADVANTAGES When using this type, there is a tendency to emphasize rote memory and measure procedural knowledge only. Provision of a word bank of possible answers is sometimes useful, especially with English Language Learners, to reduce dependency on rote memory. It is difficult to write this type of item to measure for conceptual knowledge and higher levels of cognition. You must not overlook a correct response that is different from what you expected. For example, in example 2, although the teacher's key has *experiments* as the correct answer, a student might answer the question with *investigations* or *tests* or some other response that is equally valid.

GUIDELINES FOR USE Use occasionally for review or for preassessment of student knowledge. Avoid using this type of item for grading unless you can write quality items that extend student thinking beyond mere recall. In all instances, avoid copying items verbatim from the student book. As with all types, be sure to provide adequate space for students'

answers and large spaces for students with motor control difficulties. Try to use only one blank per item.

Correction
DESCRIPTION This is similar to the completion type except that sentences or paragraphs are complete but with italicized or underlined words that can be changed to make the sentences correct.

Example 1 The work of the Tennessee Valley Authority was started by building *sandcastles*. A *sandcastle* is a wall built across a *kid* to stop its flow. The *sandcastle* holds back the *football* so the *kids* do not overflow their *backpacks* and cause *tears*.

Example 2 1, 1, 2, 3, 5, 8, *12*, 21, 34, *87*, 89.

ADVANTAGES Writing this type of assessment item can be fun for the teacher for the purpose of preassessment of student knowledge or for review. Students may enjoy this type, especially when used only occasionally, for the tension relief afforded by the incorrect absurdities. This type can be useful for introducing words with multiple meanings.

DISADVANTAGES As with the completion type, the correction type tends to measure for low-level recall and rote memory (although this is not necessarily the case in Example 2; if a student is unfamiliar with the Fibonacci number series in mathematics, it would be a relatively high-level question). The underlined incorrect items could be so whimsical that they might cause more classroom disturbance than you want.

GUIDELINES FOR USE Use occasionally for diversion and discussion. Try to write items that measure for higher-level cognition. Consider making it a combined correction, short-explanation type. Be sure to allow space for student explanations.

Essay
DESCRIPTION A question or problem is presented, and the student is to compose a response in the form of sustained prose, using the student's own words, phrases, and ideas within the limits of the question or problem.

Example 1 In the story just read, does the author elaborate the setting in great detail or barely sketch it? Explain your response.

Example 2 A healthy green coleus plant sitting in front of you has been planted in fertile soil and sealed in a glass jar. If we place the jar on the windowsill where it will receive strong sunlight and the temperature inside the jar is maintained between 60 and 80° F, how long do you predict the plant will live? Justify your prediction.

ADVANTAGES This type measures conceptual knowledge and higher mental processes, such as the ability to synthesize material and express ideas in clear and precise

Activity
11.3

Detecting Plagiarism

Internet cheating is prolific. As teachers, it is important to teach students what plagiarism consists of in the age of technology and to promote academic honesty. Students are required to write essays in many courses and often resort to creative cutting and pasting, fraudulent citation, copying papers from friends/siblings/classmates, and other dishonest practices. Another common activity is paper purchasing. "Paper mills" sell essays and term papers at bargain rates on a variety of subjects for all grade levels.

Apply Your Knowledge

Review the following websites on academic honesty and plagiarism, websites students use to purchase papers, and detection tools from a teacher's and a student's perspective.

Information on Academic Honesty and Plagiarism
http://www.academicintegrity.org
http://www.web-miner.com/plagiarism
Web Sites Students Used to Buy Papers
http://custom-writing.org/buy-essay
http://www.myessays.com/buy.php
http://www.4freeessays.com
http://www.masterpapers.com/high_school_essay.htm
Detection Tools
http://www.ncusd203.org/central/html/where/
    plagiarism_stoppers.html
http://www.plagiarism.org
http://www.turnitin.com

---

written language. It is especially useful in integrated thematic teaching. It provides practice in written expression and can be used in performance assessment, as is the case for Example 2.

DISADVANTAGES Essay items require a good deal of time to read and score. They tend to provide an unreliable sampling of achievement and are vulnerable to teacher subjectivity and unreliable scoring. Furthermore, they tend to punish the student who writes slowly and laboriously, one who has limited proficiency in the written language but who may have achieved as well as a student who writes faster and is more proficient in the language. Essay items tend to favor students who have fluency with words but whose achievement may not necessarily be better. In addition, unless the students have been given instruction in the meaning of key directive verbs and in how to respond to them, the teacher should not assume that all students understand such verbs (such as *explain* in the first example and *justify* in the second). Now read about how to promote academic honesty and curtail plagiarism by reviewing the websites listed in Activity 11.3.

GUIDELINES FOR USING AN ESSAY ITEM

1. When preparing an essay-only test, many questions, each requiring a relatively short prose response (see the short-explanation type), are preferable to fewer questions requiring long prose responses. Briefer answers tend to be more precise, and the use of many items provides a more reliable sampling of student achievement. When preparing short prose response questions, be sure to avoid using words verbatim from the student textbook.

2. Allow students adequate test time for a full response.

3. Different qualities of achievement are more likely comparable when all students must answer the same questions as opposed to providing a list of essay items from which students may select those they answer.

4. After preparing essay items, make a tentative scoring key and determine the key ideas you expect students to identify and how many points will be allotted to each.

5. Students should be informed about the relative test value for each item. Point values, if different for each item, can be listed in the margin of the test next to each item.

6. Inform students of the role of spelling, grammar, and sentence structure in your scoring of their essay items.

7. When reading student essay responses, read all student papers for one item at a time in one sitting and, while doing that, make notes to yourself; then repeat and, while reading that item again, score each student's paper for that item. Repeat the process for the next item but alter the order of the papers so you are not reading them in the same order by student. While scoring essay responses, keep in mind the nature of the objective being measured, which may or may not include the qualities of handwriting, grammar, spelling, punctuation, and neatness.

8. To nullify the "halo effect" that can occur when you know whose paper you are reading, have students put their name on the back of the paper or use a number code rather than having students put their names on essay papers so that while reading the papers, you are unaware of whose paper you are reading.

9. While having some understanding of a concept, many students may not have perfected their written expression, so you must remember to be patient, tolerant, positive, and prescriptive. Mark papers with positive and constructive comments, showing students how they could have explained or responded better.

10. Prior to using an essay question test item, give instruction and practice to students in responding to key directive verbs that will be used (see Figure 11.8).

Figure 11.8   Meaning of Key Directive Verbs for Essay Item Responses

Compare asks for an analysis of similarity and difference, but with a greater emphasis on similarities or likenesses.

Contrast asks more for differences than for similarities.

Criticize asks for the good and bad of an idea or situation.

Define means to express clearly and concisely the meaning of a term, as from a dictionary or in the student's own words.

Diagram means to put quantities or numerical values into the form of a chart, graph, or drawing.

Discuss means to explain or argue, presenting various sides of events, ideas, or situations.

Enumerate means to name or list one after another, which is different from "explain briefly" or "tell in a few words."

Evaluate means to express worth, value, and judgment.

Explain means to describe, with emphasis on cause and effect.

Generalize means to arrive at a valid generalization from provided specific information.

Identify means to state recognizable or identifiable characteristics.

Illustrate means to describe by means of examples, figures, pictures, or diagrams.

Infer means to forecast what is likely to happen as a result of information provided.

Interpret means to describe or explain a given fact, theory, principle, or doctrine within a specific context.

Justify means to show reasons, with an emphasis on correct, positive, and advantageous.

List means just that, to simply name items in a category or to include them in a list, without much description.

Outline means to give a short summary with headings and subheadings.

Prove means to present materials as witnesses, proof, and evidence.

Relate means to tell how specified things are connected or brought into some kind of relationship.

Summarize means to recapitulate the main points without examples or illustrations.

Trace means to follow a history or series of events, step by step, by going backward over the evidence.

Grouping

DESCRIPTION Several items are presented, and the student is to select and group those that are in some way related.

Example 1 Separate the following words into two groups (words are not included here); those that are homonyms place in group A, and those that are not homonyms place in group B.

Example 2 Circle the figure that is least like the others (showing a wrench, screwdriver, saw, and swing).

ADVANTAGES This type of item tests knowledge of grouping and can be used to measure conceptual knowledge, to gain higher levels of cognition, and to stimulate discussion. As Example 2 shows, it can be similar to a multiple-choice item.

DISADVANTAGES Remain alert for the student who has an alternative but valid rationale for his or her grouping.

GUIDELINES FOR USE To allow for an alternative correct response, consider making the item a combination grouping, short-explanation type, being certain to allow adequate space to encourage student explanations.

Identification

DESCRIPTION Unknown "specimens" are to be identified by name or some other criterion.

Example 1 Identify each of the plant specimens on the table by its common name.

Example 2 Identify by style each of the three poems shown on the screen.

ADVANTAGES Verbalization (i.e., the use of abstract symbolization) is less significant, as the student is working with real materials; identification should be measuring for higher-level learning rather than simple recall. The item can also be written to measure for procedural understanding, such as for the identification of steps for booting up a computer program. This is another useful type of item for authentic and performance assessments.

DISADVANTAGES Because of a special familiarity with the material, some students may have an advantage over others; to be fair, specimens used should be equally familiar or unfamiliar to all students. This type takes more time than many of the other item types both for the teacher to prepare and for students to do.

GUIDELINES FOR USE Whatever specimens are used, they must be familiar to all or to none of the students, and they must be clear, not confusing (e.g., fuzzy photographs or unclear photocopies, dried and incomplete plant specimens, and garbled music recordings can be confusing and frustrating to try to discern). Consider using dyad or team rather than individual testing.

Matching

DESCRIPTION Students are to match related items from a list of numbered items to a list of lettered choices or in some way to connect those items that are the same or are related. Or, to eliminate paper-and-pencil and make the item more direct, use an item such as "Of the materials on the table, pair up those that are most alike."

Example 1 In the blank space next to each description in column A (stem or premises column), put the letter of the correct answer from column B (answer or response column).

A (stem column)	B (answer column)
____1. Current president of the United States	A. George W. Bush
____2. Most recent past president of the United States	B. Barack Obama
	C. Thomas Jefferson
____3. U.S. president during the Persian Gulf War	D. George Washington
____4. First president of the United States	E. etc.

Example 2 Match items in column A (stem column) to those in column B (answer column) by drawing lines connecting the matched pairs.

Column A	Column B
ann/enn	conquer
auto	large
min	self
vic/vinc	small
(etc.)	year

ADVANTAGES Matching items can measure for ability to judge relationships and to differentiate between similar facts, ideas, definitions, and concepts. They are easy to score and can test a broad range of content. They reduce guessing, especially if one group (e.g., answer column) contains more items than the other and they are interesting to students and adaptable for performance assessment.

DISADVANTAGES Although the matching item is adaptable for performance assessment, items are not easily adapted to measuring for higher cognition. Because all parts must be homogeneous, it is possible that clues will be given, thus reducing item validity.

GUIDELINES FOR USE The number of items in the response or answer column should exceed the number in the stem column. The number of items in the stem column to be matched should not exceed 10. Less is better. Matching sets should have high homogeneity (i.e., items in both columns or groups should be of the same general category; avoid, for example, mixing dates, events, and names). Answers in the response column should be kept short, to one or two words each, and should be ordered logically, such as alphabetically. If answers from the response column can be used more than once—and that is advised to avoid guessing by elimination—the directions should state so. Be prepared for the student who can legitimately defend an incorrect response.

Multiple Choice

DESCRIPTION This type is similar to the completion item in that statements are presented (the stem), sometimes in incomplete form, but with several options or alternatives requiring recognition or even higher cognitive processes rather than mere recall.

Example 1 Of four cylinders with the following dimensions, the one that would cause the highest-pitched sound would be

a. 4 inches long and 3 inches in diameter.

b. 4 inches long and 1 inch in diameter.

c. 8 inches long and 3 inches in diameter.

d. 8 inches long and 1 inch in diameter.

Example 2 Which one of the following is a pair of antonyms?

a. loud—soft

b. halt—finish

c. absolve—vindicate

d. procure—purchase

ADVANTAGES Items can be answered and scored quickly. A wide range of content and higher levels of cognition can be tested in a relatively short time. This type is excellent for all testing purposes—motivation, review, and assessment of learning.

DISADVANTAGES Unfortunately, because multiple-choice items are relatively easy to write, there is a tendency to write items measuring only for low levels of cognition. Multiple-choice items are excellent for major testing, but it takes care and time to write quality questions that measure higher levels of thinking and learning.

GUIDELINES FOR USING MULTIPLE-CHOICE ITEMS

1. If the item is in the form of an incomplete statement, it should be meaningful in itself and imply a direct question rather than merely lead in to a collection of unrelated true and false statements.

2. Use a level of language that is easy enough for even the poorest readers and those who are English Language Learners to understand; avoid unnecessary wordiness.

3. If there is much variation in the length of alternatives, arrange the alternatives in order from shortest to longest (i.e., first alternative is the shortest, last alternative is the longest). For single-word alternatives, consistent use of arrangement of alternatives is recommended, such as by length of answer or alphabetically.

4. Arrangement of alternatives should be uniform throughout the test and listed in vertical (column) form rather than in horizontal (paragraph) form.

5. Incorrect responses (distracters) should be plausible and related to the same concept as the correct alternative. Although an occasional humorous distracter may help relieve test anxiety, along with absurd distracters they should generally be avoided. They offer no measuring value and increase the likelihood of the student *guessing* the correct response.

6. It is not necessary to maintain a fixed number of alternatives for every item, but the use of fewer than three is not recommended. Although it is not always possible to

come up with four or five plausible responses, the use of four or five reduces chance responses and guessing, thereby increasing reliability for the item. If you cannot think of enough plausible distracters, include the item on a test the first time as a completion item. As students respond, wrong answers will provide you with a number of plausible distracters that you can use the next time to make the item a multiple-choice type of item.

7. Some students (with special needs) may work better when allowed to circle their selected response rather than writing its letter or number in a blank space.

8. Responses such as "all of these" or "none of these" should be used only when they will contribute more than another plausible distracter. Care must be taken that such responses answer or complete the item. "All of the above" is a poorer alternative than "none of the above" because items that use it as a correct response need to have four or five correct answers; also, if it is the right answer, knowledge of any two of the distracters will cue it.

9. Every item should be grammatically consistent. For example, if the stem is in the form of an incomplete sentence, it should be possible to complete the sentence by attaching any of the alternatives to it.

10. The stem should state a single and specific point.

11. The stem must mean the same thing to every student.

12. The item should be expressed in positive form. A negative form can present a psychological disadvantage to students. Negative items are those that ask what is not characteristic of something or what is the least useful. Discard the item if you cannot express it in positive terminology.

13. The stem must not include clues to the correct alternative. For example, "A four-sided figure whose opposite sides are *parallel* is called _____."

   a. an octagon

   b. a parallelogram

   c. a trapezoid

   d. a triangle

   Use of the word *parallel* clues the answer.

14. There must be only one correct or best response. However, this is easier said than done (refer to guideline 19).

15. Measuring for understanding of definitions is better tested by furnishing the name or word and requiring choice between alternative definitions than by presenting the definition and requiring choice between alternative words.

16. Avoid using alternatives that include absolute terms such as *never* and *always*.

17. Multiple-choice items need not be entirely verbal. Consider the use of realia, charts, diagrams, videos, and other visuals. This will make the test more interesting, especially to students with low verbal abilities or those who are English Language Learners. Consequently, it will make the assessment more direct.

18. Once you have composed a series of multiple-choice items or a test comprised completely of this item type, tally the position of answers to be sure they are evenly distributed to avoid the common psychological habit (when there are four alternatives) of having the correct alternative in the third position. In other words, when alternative choices are A, B, C, and D or 1, 2, 3, and 4, unless the test designer is aware and avoids it, more correct answers will be in the "C" or "3" position than in any other.

19. Consider providing space between test items for students to include their rationales for their response selections, thus making the test a combination multiple-choice and short-explanation item type. This provides for the measurement of higher levels of cognition and encourages writing. It provides for the student who can rationalize an alternative that you had not considered plausible, which is especially possible today with the diversity of cultural experiences represented by students. For example, we recall the story of the math question on a test that asked if a farmer saw eight crows sitting on a fence and shot three of them, how many would be left? Of course, the "correct" response on the answer key was five. One critical thinking student chose *none* as his response, an answer that was marked "wrong" by the teacher. However, the student was thinking that those crows that weren't shot would be frightened and would all fly away; thus, he selected *none* as his answer.

20. While scoring, on a blank copy of the test, for each item tally the incorrect responses. Analyze incorrect responses for each item to discover potential errors in your scoring key. If, for example, many students select B for an item for which your key says the correct answer is A, you may have made a mistake on your scoring key or in teaching the lesson.

21. Sometimes teachers attempt to discourage cheating by preparing several versions of the multiple-choice exam with the questions in different order. This could be giving one group of students an unfair advantage if the order of their questions is in the same sequence in which the information was originally presented and learned and, for another group of students, the questions are in a random order. To avoid this, questions should be in random order on every version of the exam.

Performance

DESCRIPTION Provided with certain conditions or materials, the student solves a problem or accomplishes some other action.

Example 1 Write a retelling of your favorite fable and create a diorama to go along with it.

Example 2 (As a culminating project for a unit on sound, groups of students were challenged to design and make their own musical instruments.) The performance assessment included the following:

1. Play your instrument for the class.
2. Show us the part of the instrument that makes the sound.
3. Describe the function of other parts of your instrument.
4. Demonstrate how you change the pitch of the sound.
5. Share with us how you made your instrument.

Example 3 Demonstrate your understanding of diffusion by designing and completing an experiment using only those chemicals and materials located at this learning station.

Example 4 Measure and calculate the square footage of our gymnasium playing floor to the nearest centimeter.

ADVANTAGES Performance test item types come closer to direct measurement (authentic assessment) of certain expected outcomes than do most other types. As has been indicated in discussions of the preceding question types, other types of questions can actually be prepared as performance-type items, that is, where the student actually does what he or she is being tested for.

DISADVANTAGES This type can be difficult and time consuming to administer to a group of students. Maintaining an adequate supply of materials could be a problem. Scoring may tend to be subjective. It could be difficult to give makeup tests to students who were absent.

GUIDELINES FOR USE Use your creativity to design and use performance tests, as they tend to measure well the important objectives. To set up a performance assessment situation, see instructions in Figure 11.9. To reduce subjectivity in scoring, prepare distinct scoring guidelines (rubrics), as was discussed in scoring essay-type items and as shown, for example, in Figures 11.10 through 11.14.

Figure 11.9 **Procedure for Setting Up a Performance Assessment Situation**

1. Specify the performance objective.
2. Specify the test conditions.
3. Establish the standards or criteria (scoring rubric) for judging the quality of the process and/or product.
4. Prepare directions in writing, outlining the situation, with instructions that the students are to follow.
5. Share the procedure with a colleague for feedback before using it with students.

Figure 11.10 **Grading Rubric for Sixth-Grade Geography, South America Unit PowerPoint Project**

Criteria	Advanced	Proficient	Partially Proficient	Unsatisfactory	Points Earned
Possible Points	3	2	1	0	
Organization x 5 pts.	The sequence of information is logical and intuitive. Paths are clear and purposeful.	The sequence of information is logical. Most paths are clear and purposeful.	The sequence of information is somewhat logical. The paths are confusing.	Not logical. Paths are not evident.	
Originality x 5 pts.	The project shows significant evidence of originality and inventiveness, used drawings. and created images and effects.	Some evidence of originality and inventiveness uses some new and Internet produced images.	Only used clip art, no real changes and originality.	The work is minimal and uses other people's ideas and words.	
Subject Knowledge x 10 pts.	Answer questions completely with good details and information. How, what, when, where, why, so what.	Some information and some criteria missing.	Some information. Some inaccurate information	Copied information. Some inaccurate information.	
Slides x 3 pts.	8 or more slides and title page and titles	7 slides	6 slides	5 or less	
Graphics x 5 pts.	Includes 4 pictures from clip art, Internet, and created your own 2 different backgrounds	Includes 3 images from 2 sources 1 background	Includes 2 from one source No background	Includes 1 graphic from one source	
Animations x 5 pts.	Creates many transition and animate slides and text and pictures Adds sounds from Internet or CD and animation	Creates few animations Adds one sound from animation	Creates one animation No sounds	No animation No sounds	
Total Points Possible (99)					

SOURCE: Contributed by Anastasia Sunday, 6th Grade Geography Teacher, Estes Park Middle School, Estes Park, Colorado. Used with Permission.

Figure 11.11 **Grades 9 through 12 Language Arts Five-Paragraph Essay Rubric**

Category	Advanced 50–40	Proficient 39–30	Partially Proficient 29–20	Unsatisfactory 19–0	Score
Introduction: Thesis, Road Map, and Background Information	First paragraph is catchy. Thesis is evident and point to be argued well stated. Background information and road map are clearly stated.	First paragraph has a weak "grabber." Thesis is mixed among many sentences and hard to piece together. Background info. and road map evident.	A catchy beginning was attempted but was confusing rather than catchy. Thesis is not entirely apparent although topic is evident.	No attempt was made to catch the reader's attention in the first paragraph. Thesis is not apparent nor is the topic of the essay.	_____
Accuracy of Facts, Examples, and Details	All facts, examples, and details presented in the essay are accurate and relate back to the thesis.	Almost all facts, examples, and details presented in the essay are accurate and occasionally relate back to the thesis.	Most facts presented in the story are accurate (at least 70%). Evidence is scattered about rather than used to prove the thesis.	There are several factual errors in the essay. There is no real effort to make the piece cohesive.	_____
Organization	The essay is very well organized. Five-paragraph format is evident. One idea or scene follows another in a logical sequence with clear transitions.	The essay is pretty well organized. Five-paragraph format is evident. One idea may seem out of place. Clear transitions are used.	The essay is a little hard to follow. Paragraphs are unclear. The transitions are sometimes not clear.	Ideas seem to be randomly arranged. Minimal effort at paragraph organization.	_____
Content/Focus on Assigned Topic	The entire essay is related to the assigned topic and allows the reader to understand much more about the topic.	Most of the essay is related to the assigned topic. The essay wanders off at one point, but the reader can still learn something about the topic.	Some of the essay is related to the assigned topic, but a reader does not learn much about the topic.	No attempt has been made to relate the essay to the assigned topic.	_____
Mechanics	The essay has few, if any, mechanics errors: spelling, punctuation, capitalization, grammar, or usage errors.	The essay has two or three mechanics errors: spelling, punctuation, capitalization, grammar, or usage errors.	The essay has four or five mechanics errors: spelling, punctuation, capitalization, grammar, or usage errors.	The essay has more than five mechanics errors: spelling, punctuation, capitalization, grammar, or usage errors.	_____

TOTAL POINTS: _____

Figure 11.12 **Grade 12 Language Arts Indian Education for All (IEFA) Group Presentations**

Categories	Advanced	Proficient	Developing	Your Points
Critical Evaluations of Websites **(20 possible points)**	1) Each group member selected a different website from those suggested and each completed the *Critical Evaluation of a Web Site: Web Sites for Use by Educators*. The following were addressed: technical and visual aspects, content authenticity, bias, pedagogical significance, and the narrative evaluation of the websites are detailed. 2) Thorough recommendations for why or why not these sites are (or are not) valid for your purpose are provided. **20–15 points**	1) Group members selected some different websites from those suggested and completed the *Critical Evaluation of a Web Site: Web Sites for Use by Educators*. Some of the following were addressed: technical and visual aspects, content authenticity, bias, pedagogical significance, and the narrative evaluation of the websites are detailed. 2) Some recommendations for why or why not these sites are (or are not) valid for your purpose are provided. **14–9 points**	1) Group members selected few different websites from those suggested and completed the *Critical Evaluation of a Web Site: Web Sites for Use by Educators*. Few of the following were addressed: Technical and visual aspects, content authenticity, bias, pedagogical significance, and the narrative evaluation of the web sites are missing or not thorough. 2) Few or no recommendations for why or why not these sites are (or are not) valid for your purpose are provided. **8–0 points**	_____
Description of an IEFA Resource **(20 possible points)**	A thorough description of the resource your group selected that relates directly to your project and a detailed summary of what knowledge you acquired that you used in your IEFA presentations is included. **20–15 points**	A basic description of the resource your group selected that relates somewhat to your project and a basic summary of what knowledge you acquired you used in your IEFA presentations is included. **14–9 points**	A minimal description of the resource your group selected that relates minimally or not at all to your project and an inadequate summary of what knowledge you acquired that you used in your IEFA presentations is included. **8–0 points**	_____

(*continued*)

Figure 11.12　**Grade 12 Language Arts Indian Education for All (IEFA) Group Presentations**　*continued*

Categories	Advanced	Proficient	Developing	Your Points
Seven Essential Understandings (7 EUs) **(15 possible points)**	A clear understanding of several of the 7 EUs is demonstrated. The presentations are designed to address: EU 1 Reservations: Tribal Groups; EU 2 Diversity of the American Indian; EU 3 Ideologies of Native Traditional Beliefs and Spirituality and Oral Histories; EU4 Lands Reserved by the Tribes; EU 5 Federal Policy Periods; EU 6 Indigenous Perspectives of History; and EU 7 Tribal Sovereignty **15–11 points**	A basic understanding of some of the 7 EUs is demonstrated. The presentations are designed to address: EU 1 Reservations: Tribal Groups; EU 2 Diversity of the American Indian; EU 3 Ideologies of Native Traditional Beliefs and Spirituality and Oral Histories; EU4 Lands Reserved by the Tribes; EU 5 Federal Policy Periods; EU 6 Indigenous Perspectives of History; and EU 7 Tribal Sovereignty **10–6 points**	An inadequate understanding of the 7 EUs is demonstrated. The presentations are not designed to address: EU 1 Reservations: Tribal Groups; EU 2 Diversity of the American Indian; EU 3 Ideologies of Native Traditional Beliefs and Spirituality and Oral Histories; EU4 Lands Reserved by the Tribes; EU 5 Federal Policy Periods; EU 6 Indigenous Perspectives of History; and EU 7 Tribal Sovereignty **5–0 points**	_____
Tribal Specific **(15 possible points)**	Lesson plans avoid pan-Indianism, and lessons focus on one or more of the 12 Montana tribes: Crow, Northern Cheyenne, Assiniboine, Sioux, Gros Ventre, Chippewa, Cree, Blackfeet, Salish, Kootenai, Peine d'Oreille, Little Shell. **15–11 points**	Lesson plans avoid pan-Indianism, but lessons do not focus on one or more of the 12 Montana tribes: Crow, Northern Cheyenne, Assiniboine, Sioux, Gros Ventre, Chippewa, Cree, Blackfeet, Salish, Kootenai, Peine d'Oreille, Little Shell. **10–6 points**	Lesson plans do not avoid pan-Indianism, nor do the lessons focus on one or more of the 12 Montana tribes: Crow, Northern Cheyenne, Assiniboine, Sioux, Gros Ventre, Chippewa, Cree, Blackfeet, Salish, Kootenai, Peine d'Oreille, Little Shell. **5–0 points**	_____
IEFA Group Presentation **(20 possible points)**	Group members met the majority of the following expectations: honored the time, reviewed standards, reviewed EUs, reviewed instructional objectives, divided the presentation among all group members, differentiated instruction, addressed learning modalities, included a preassessment, distributed a handout, involved the audience. **20–15 points**	Group members met some of the following expectations: honored the time, reviewed standards, reviewed EUs, reviewed instructional objectives, divided the presentation among all group members, differentiated instruction, addressed learning modalities, included a preassessment, distributed a handout, involved the audience. **14–9 points**	Group members met few of the following expectations: honored the time, reviewed standards, reviewed EUs, reviewed instructional objectives, divided the presentation among all group members, differentiated instruction, addressed learning modalities, included a preassessment, distributed a handout, involved the audience. **8–0 points**	_____
Self/Peer Evaluations (Forms provided by instructor) **(5 possible points)**	1) All group members evaluated their involvement, attendance, collaboration skills, and knowledge. 2) The following questions were answered by group members: We decided on dividing the work by … . How did your group work together? Did everything go as you planned? Explain. My greatest strengths as a group member are (list three). What I have learned about our topic is … . **5–4 points**	1) Some group members evaluated their involvement, attendance, collaboration skills, and knowledge. 2) Some of the following questions were answered by group members: We decided on dividing the work by … . How did your group work together? Did everything go as you planned? Explain. My greatest strengths as a group member are (list three). What I have learned about our topic is … . **3–2 points**	1) Few of the group members evaluated their involvement, attendance, collaboration skills, and knowledge. 2) A few of the following questions were answered by group members: We decided on dividing the work by … . How did your group work together? Did everything go as you planned? Explain. My greatest strengths as a group member are (list three). What I have learned about our topic is … . **1–0 points**	_____
Reflection Based on Feedback from Peers/Classmates **(5 possible points)**	1) All group members reviewed the feedback sheets their classmates completed on their presentation. Ideas for project presentation improvement, based on comments from classmates, are summarized and included with the final project description. 2) Feedback sheets were turned in with the final project. **5–4 points**	1) Some group members reviewed the feedback sheets their classmates completed on their presentation. Some ideas for project presentation improvement, based on comments from classmates, are summarized and included with the final project description. 2) Feedback sheets were turned in with the final project. **3–2 points**	1) Few or no group members reviewed the feedback sheets their classmates completed on their presentation. Few or no ideas for project presentation improvement, based on comments from classmates, are summarized and included with the final project description. 2) Feedback sheets were not turned in with the final project. **1–0 points**	_____
100 Total Possible Points			**Your Total Score**	_____

Figure 11.13 **Advanced Placement Psychology Research Paper Presentation Rubric**

Name_____

Topic_____

Poster

Research   6   12   18   24   30
Minimum number of sources used
Information carefully reported
Comments:

Graphics/ Pictures   4   8   12   16   20
Graphs, charts, or pictures used to present information clearly
Attractively presented on poster board
Comments:

Presentation

Presentation   6   12   18   24   30
Student appears to have practiced presentation
Information is clearly presented, and summaries are spoken to class members or read from note cards, not read directly from poster
Information on graphs and charts is explained
Student shares excitement and interest with the class
Questions are answered thoughtfully
Comments:

Questions

Written Questions   4   8   12   16   20
Student submitted five open-ended questions that fairly and clearly reflected information presented
Comments:
Score _____/100

SOURCE: Contributed by Joyce Jarosz Hannula, Advanced Placement Psychology Instructor, Bozeman High School, Bozeman, Montana. Used with permission.

Figure 11.14 **Advanced Placement Psychology Research Project Evaluation Rubric**

Topic   2   4   6   8   10
  Valid research idea; formed and presented a hypothesis

Design   4   8   12   16   18   20
  Designed project thoughtfully; sampled carefully

Results   4   6   8   10   12   15
  Explained results clearly

Conclusion   2   4   6   8   10
  Conclusion appears justified by research

Observation   4   6   8   10   12   15
  Good observations about what variables might have affected study

Presentation   2   4   6   8   10
  Planning and preparation of presentation obvious; group members participated equally

Total Possible = 80   Score_____

SOURCE: Contributed by Joyce Jarosz Hannula, Advanced Placement Psychology Instructor, Bozeman High School, Bozeman, MT. Used with permission.

Short Explanation

DESCRIPTION The short explanation question is like the essay type but requires a shorter answer.

Example 1 Briefly explain in a paragraph how you would end the story.

Example 2 Briefly explain why organ pipes are made to vary in length.

ADVANTAGES As with the essay type, student understanding is assessed, but this type takes less time for the teacher to read and to score. By using several questions of this type, a greater amount of content can be covered than with a fewer number of essay questions. This type of question is good practice for students to learn to express themselves succinctly in writing.

DISADVANTAGES Some students will have difficulty expressing themselves in a limited fashion or in writing. They need practice, coaching, and time.

GUIDELINES FOR USE This type is useful for occasional reviews and quizzes and as an alternative to other types of questions. For scoring, establish a scoring rubric and follow the same guidelines as for the essay-type item.

True or False

DESCRIPTION A statement is presented that students are to judge as being accurate or not.

Example 1 A suffix is any bound morpheme added to the end of a root word. T or F?

Example 2 Christopher Columbus discovered America in 1492. T or F?

ADVANTAGES Many items can be answered in a relatively short time, making broad content coverage possible. Scoring is quick and simple. True-or-false items are good as discussion starters, for review, and for diagnostic evaluation (preassessment) of what students already know or think they know.

DISADVANTAGES It is sometimes difficult to write true-or-false items that are purely true or false or without qualifying them in such a way that clues the answer. In the second sample question, for example, the student may question whether Columbus really did discover America or misunderstand the meaning of *discovering America*. Weren't there people already there when he landed? Where, in fact, did he land? What is meant by *America*? Example 2 is poor also because it tests for more than one idea—Columbus, America, and 1492. Much of the content that most easily lends itself to the true-or-false type of test item is trivial. Students have a 50% chance of guessing the correct answer, thus giving this item type both *poor validity and poor reliability*. Scoring and grading give no clue about why the student missed an item. Finally, for students who tend to think abstractly, true-or-false items cause unwanted stress because those students tend to analyze every word, reading much more into the questions than necessary. Consequently, the disadvantages of true-or-false items far outweigh the advantages. *Pure true-false items should not be used for arriving at grades.*

GUIDELINES FOR PREPARING TRUE-OR-FALSE ITEMS

1. For preparing a false statement, first write the statement as a true statement; then make it false by changing a word or phrase.

2. Try to avoid using negative statements because they tend to confuse students.

3. A true-or-false statement should include only one idea.

4. Use close to an equal number of true and false items.

5. Try to avoid using specific determiners (e.g., *always*, *all*, or *none*) because they usually clue that the statement is false. Avoid also words that may clue that the statement is true (e.g., *often*, *probably*, and *sometimes*).

6. Avoid words that may have different meanings for different students.

7. Avoid using verbatim language from the student textbook.

8. Avoid trick items, such as a slight reversal of numbers in a date.

9. Rather than using symbols for the words *true* and *false* (sometimes teachers use symbols such as 1 and 2), which might be confusing, or having students write the letters *T* and *F* (sometimes a student does not write the letters clearly enough for the teacher to be able to distinguish which it is), either have students write out the words *true* and *false* or, better yet, have students simply circle *T* and *F* in the left margin of each item.

10. Proofread your items (or have a friend do it) to be sure that sentences are well constructed and free from typographical errors.

11. To avoid "wrong" answers caused by variations in thinking and to make the item more valid and reliable, students should be encouraged to write in their rationale for selecting *true* or *false*, making the item a *modified true-or-false* item. For example: When a farmer saw eight crows sitting on the fence surrounding his corn field, he shot three of them. Five were left on the fence. T or F? _____

Explanation:_____

Now do Exercise 11.1 to start the development of your skill in writing assessment items. As you work on Exercise 11.1, you may want to correlate it with your previous work on Exercise 4.5 in Chapter 4 and Exercise 5.11 in Chapter 5.

Reporting Student Achievement

One of your responsibilities as a classroom teacher is to report student progress in achievement to parents or guardians as well as to the school administration for record keeping. In some instances, the reporting is of student progress and effort as well as achievement. As described in the discussions that follow, reporting is done in at least two and sometimes more than two ways.

The Grade Report

Periodically, a grade report (report card) is issued (generally from three to six times a year, depending on the school, its purpose, and its type of scheduling). Grade reports may be distributed during an advisory period, or they may be mailed to the student's home. This grade report represents an achievement grade (formative evaluation). The final report of the semester is the semester grade, and for courses that are only one semester long, it also is the final grade (summative evaluation). In essence, the first and sometimes second reports are progress notices, with the semester grade being the one that is transferred to the student's transcript of records.

In addition to the student's academic achievement, you must report the student's social behaviors (classroom conduct) while in your classroom. Whichever reporting form is used, you must separate your assessments of a student's social behaviors from the student's academic achievement. Academic achievement (or accomplishment) is represented by a letter (sometimes a number) grade (A through E or F; E, S, and U; P or F; 1 to 5; and sometimes with minuses and pluses), and the social behavior by a *satisfactory* or an *unsatisfactory*, by more specific items, or supplemented by teacher-written or computer-generated comments.

In addition to grading and reporting on subject matter knowledge, some secondary schools are including a broader set of *workplace or life skills* that transcend particular subject areas. For example, Academy High School (Fort Myers, FL) uses a *work ethic checklist* that is part of the senior portfolio in the school's internship preparation program.

In some instances, especially at the middle school level, there may be a location on the reporting form for the teacher to check whether basic grade-level standards have been met in the core subjects.

More about Parental Involvement and Home-School Connections

Study after study shows that when parents get involved in their child's school and school work, students learn better and earn better grades, and teachers experience more positive feelings about teaching. As a result, many schools increasingly are searching for new and better ways to involve parents. What follows are additional suggestions and resources.

Contacting Parents

Although it is not always obligatory, some teachers make a point to contact parents or guardians by telephone or by email, especially when a student has shown a sudden turn for either the worse or the better in academic achievement or in classroom behavior. That initiative and contact by the teacher are usually welcomed by parents and can lead to productive conferences with the teacher. By being proactive and making the first contact, you show concern and you may gain an ally.

Another way of contacting parents is by letter. You may ask for help in translating your letter for culturally and linguistically diverse parents. Contacting a parent by letter gives you time to think and to make clear your thoughts and concerns to that parent and to invite the parent to respond at his or her convenience by letter, by phone, or by arranging to have a conference with you.

Also, most schools have either a computer-link assignment/progress report hotline for parent use or a progress report form that, on request by a parent, can be obtained as often as weekly.

Meeting Parents

You will meet some of the parents or guardians early in the school year during fall "back-to-school," "meet-the-teacher," or "curriculum" night; throughout the year in individual parent conferences; and later in the year during spring open house. For the beginning teacher, these meetings with parents can be anxious times. But, in fact, it is a time to celebrate your work and to solicit parental support. The following paragraphs provide guidelines to help you with those experiences.[12]

Back-to-school night is the evening early in the school year when parents (and guardians) come to the school and meet their children's teachers. After arriving at the school at a designated time, the parents proceed through a simulation of their child's school day; as a group, they meet each class and each teacher for a few minutes. Later, in the spring, there is an open house where parents may have more time to talk individually with teachers, although the major purpose of the open house is for the school and teachers to celebrate and display the work and progress of the students for that year. Throughout the school year, there will be opportunities for you and parents to meet and talk about their child.

At back-to-school night, parents are anxious to learn as much as they can about their children's teachers. You will meet each group of parents for a brief time, perhaps about 10 minutes. During that meeting, you will provide them with a copy of the course syllabus, make some straightforward remarks about yourself, and talk about the course, its requirements, your expectations of the students, and how the parents can support their children's learning.

Although there will be precious little time for questions from the parents, during your introduction the parents will be delighted to learn that you have your program well planned, appreciate their interest and welcome their support, and will communicate with them. The parents and guardians will be pleased to know that you are "from the school of the three Fs"—that is, that you are firm, friendly, and fair.

Specifically, parents will expect to learn about your curriculum—goals and objectives, any long-term projects, class size, when tests will be given and whether given on a regular basis, and your grading procedures. They will want to know what you expect of them: Will there be homework, and if so, should they help their children with it? How can they contact you? Try to anticipate other questions. Your principal, department chair, or colleagues can be of aid in helping you anticipate and prepare for these questions. Of course, you can never prepare for the question that comes from left field. Just remain calm and avoid being flustered (or at least appear so). Ten minutes will fly by quickly, and parents will be reassured to know you are an in-control person.

Parent Conferences

When meeting parents for conferences, you should be as specific as possible when explaining to a parent the

---

Teaching Scenario   Building Partnerships with Parents from Our Diverse Cultures

As a future teacher, you will be interacting with your students' parents. Although this can be a challenging task, establishing strong parent-school partnerships is important. Strong family involvement in a child's education and school environment is essential to the success of the child and the school. Yet many well-meaning teachers and principals find they are not able to connect with parents in our increasingly diverse schools. Many traditional parent involvement strategies are designed for middle-class American-born parents who speak English, and thus they often do not reach parents from immigrant or minority cultures. New strategies designed to meet the specific needs of our diverse communities are required.

Annandale High—a school with students from some 90 nations and wide-ranging economic levels in the Washington, D.C., suburb of Fairfax County, VA—recognized that traditional parent engagement strategies were meeting the needs of fewer and fewer families. School leadership, including parent leaders, undertook an Immigrant Parent Leadership Initiative, comprised of leadership classes for immigrant parents in English and Spanish; parent programs geared to specific ethnic groups, held in Spanish, Korean, and Vietnamese; faculty action research; and a new Parent Resource Center. These substantive efforts to develop partnerships with immigrant parents resulted in direct evidence that parents who are engaged in the school have a stronger, positive hand in guiding their children's education.

The school undertook the work to develop an outreach program that honors diverse parents' life experiences and culture. With multiple cultures within a school community, this can seem overwhelming. However, the reward of gaining support from individual parents and entire communities was well worth the effort. When teachers and administrators develop partnerships with parents, both sides gain. Among the lessons learned were the following:

- Building personal relationships is at the core of reaching parents who are disconnected from school.
- Multiple contacts are essential, including personal phone calls from school personnel as well as other parents from that culture.
- Members of the various communities should be involved in developing programming and carrying out publicity.

The details of the Annandale High effort were published in Andrea Sobel and Eileen Gale Kugler, "Building Partnerships with Immigrant Parents," *Educational Leadership* 64, no. 6 (March 2007): 62–66, and can be found under "Resources" at **http://www.EmbraceDiverseSchools.com**.

SOURCE: Contributed by Eileen Kugler, Embrace Diverse Schools, EKugler@ EmbraceDiverseSchools.com. Author of *Debunking the Middle-Class Myth: Why Diverse Schools Are Good for All Kids* (Lanham, MD: Rowman & Littlefield Education, 2002).

---

progress of that parent's child in your class. Again, express your appreciation for the parent's interest. Be helpful to his or her understanding and avoid overwhelming the parent with more information than he or she needs. Resist any tendency to talk too much. Allow time for the parent to ask questions. Keep your answers succinct. Never compare one student with another or with the rest of the class. If the parent asks a question for which you do not have an answer, tell the parent you will try to find an answer and will phone the parent as quickly as you can. Then do it. Have students' portfolios and other work with you during the parent conference so that you can show examples of what is being discussed. Also, have your grade book on hand or a computer printout of it but be prepared to protect from parents the names and records of other students.

Sometimes it is helpful to have a three-way conference—a conference with the parent, the student, and you—or a conference with the parent, the principal or counselor, and several or all of the student's teachers. If, especially as a beginning teacher, you would like the presence of an administrator at a parent-teacher conference as backup, don't hesitate to arrange that.

Some educators prefer a student-led conference, arguing that "placing students in charge of the conference makes them individually accountable, encourages them to take pride in their work, and encourages student-parent communication about school performance."[13] However, like most innovations in education, the concept of student-led conferences has its limitations—the most important of which perhaps is the matter of time.[14]

When a parent asks how he or she may help in the student's learning, the paragraphs that follow offer suggestions for your consideration. Many schools have made special and successful efforts to link home and school. At some schools, through homework hotlines, parents have phone access to their children's assignment specifications and to their progress in their schoolwork, and parents with a personal computer and a modem have access to tutorial services to assist their children with assignments.

Helping students become critical thinkers is one of the aims of education and one that parents can help with by reinforcing the strategies being used in the classroom. Ways to do this are to ask "what if" questions; think aloud as a model for the student's thinking development; encourage the student's own metacognition by asking questions

---

Teaching Scenario   ## Communicating with Parents Using Infinite Campus

Anastasia Sunday is a master teacher with 15 years of teaching experience under her belt. She is certified to teach social studies, science, and technology at the secondary level and has held teaching positions where she has taught those subjects at all middle and secondary school grade levels. Currently, she is a sixth-grade geography teacher at Estes Park Middle School in Estes Park, CO. In her tenure as a classroom teacher, Sunday has seen a lot of changes in the field of education. Most notable is the infusion of technology in her day-to-day operations allowing her to communicate with everyone throughout her day. To Sunday, "Teaching is another word for communicating." In fact, she thinks that the success she experiences in her job is dependent on effective, consistent communication with a variety of stakeholders.

According to Sunday, "In a given day, I communicate with many people. My principal may request a write up on the day's lesson, the students want a description of what is being covered in class, the school secretary needs to know if the students arrived to class on time, and parents ask to know how their children/adolescents did on the recent test as well as what homework they are expected to complete that evening." Everyone wants to be kept in the loop. Everyone wants to have access to timely, pertinent information. But how are teachers able to communicate effectively with parents when they are expected to meet the needs of more than 120 middle school students day in and day out?

Fortunately, school districts around the country are adding software programs to help simplify teachers' communication. One such program, Infinite Campus, is the program used by educators in the Estes Park School District. The program serves numerous functions. Infinite Campus allows teachers to create seating charts, arrange and label photographs of their students, post test scores, view students' home contact information, review students' schedules, calculate grades, and track absences in addition to sending out messages.

The Teacher Messenger function is a very valuable feature that allows teachers to create listservs and then send email messages to all their students or all the parents or to address a certain subgroup and so on instantaneously. Sunday has used Teacher Messenger to remind her students of homework assignments that are due the next day or in the near future. She has also sent email messages to update individual parents on their child's grade and to notify them of their child's eligibility for sports that week in addition to sharing upcoming assignments with parents. Sunday's principal, like other administrators, can also log in to the portal to view how Sunday is using Teacher Messenger to facilitate communication with parents.

Parents can also log in to the portal on Infinite Campus at any time to find out a lot of important information. They can check what their child's grade is in a class, what assignment their child is missing, or to see if their child arrived to class on time that day. Parents can also check cumulative standardized tests scores. Most parents have access to email, and they appreciate hearing from their child's teachers frequently about their child and his or her progress. Here is a recent posting that Sunday made to update the parents of her sixth-grade geography students on a current project.

Good morning,

I wanted to let you know that your student is working on a written report and a project about Latin America in 6th grade Geography. The rough draft and outline is due Wednesday, January 27th and the final report is due February 1st. The students are expected to work on their project at home. I gave each student a green and a yellow sheet with choices for possible projects and a blue sheet that is a calendar to help them use their time wisely. They also have the rubrics on how I will grade them. We will have an Inca archeological activity in class on Thursday and a guest speaker on Friday from Paraguay. Next week we will have a test on the countries and capitals of South America. Thank you for your time, Anastasia Sunday, 6th grade Geography

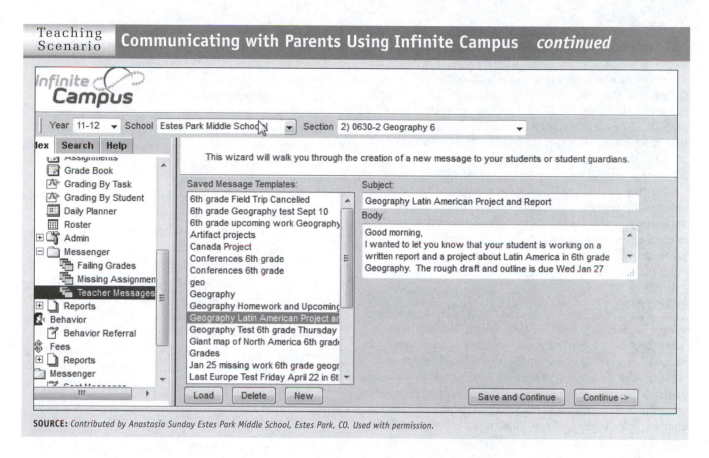

SOURCE: *Contributed by Anastasia Sunday Estes Park Middle School, Estes Park, CO. Used with permission.*

Figure 11.15 **Resources for Developing Home-School Partnerships**

Alliance for Parental Involvement in Education, P.O. Box 59, East Chatham, NY 12060-0059; 518-392-6900.

Center on Families, Communities, Schools & Children's Learning, 3505 N. Charles St., Baltimore, MD 21218; 410-516-8800.

National Coalition for Parent Involvement in Education, Box 39, 1201 16th St. NW, Washington, DC 20036.

National Community Education Association, 3929 Old Lee Highway, Suite 91A, Fairfax, VA 22030-2401; 703-359-8973.

National PTA, 330 North Wabash Ave., Ste. 2100, Chicago, IL 60611-3690; 312-670-6782.

Parents for Public Schools, P.O. Box 12807, Jackson, MS 39236-2807; 800-880-1222.

such as "How did you arrive at that conclusion?" or "How do you feel about your conclusion now?" and asking these questions about the student's everyday social interactions, topics that are important to the student; ask the student to elaborate on his or her ideas; and accept the fact that the young person may make mistakes but encourage the student to learn from them.

Many resources are available for parents to use at home. The U.S. government, for example, has a variety of free or low-cost booklets available. For information, contact the Federal Citizen Information Center, Department BEST, Pueblo, CO 81009, or call 1-888-8PUEBLO (1-888-878-3256). Figure 11.15 presents addresses for additional ideas and resources for home-school partnerships.

Dealing with an Irate Parent or Guardian

If a parent or guardian is angry or hostile toward you and the school, the paragraphs that follow offer guidelines for dealing with that hostility.

Remain calm in your discussion with the parent, allowing the parent to talk out his or her hostility while you say very little; usually, the less you say, the better off you will be. Staying calm shows strength. It is hard to scream at someone who is acting concerned, collected, and reasonable. By controlling your emotions, you will help deescalate the situation. What you do say must be objective and to the point of the student's work in your classroom. The parent may just need to vent frustrations that might have very little to do with you, the school, or even the student.

Do not allow yourself to be intimidated, put on the defensive, or backed into a verbal corner. If the parent tries to do so by attacking you personally, do not press your defense at this point. Perhaps the parent has made a point that you should take time to consider, and now is a good time to arrange for another conference with the parent for about a week later. In a follow-up conference, if the parent agrees, you may want to consider bringing in a mediator, such as another member of your teaching team, an administrator, or a school counselor.

You must *not* talk about other students; keep the conversation focused on this parent's child's progress. The parent is *not* your rival; at least, he or she should not be. You both share a concern for the intellectual and psychological well-being of the student. Use your best skills in critical thinking and problem solving by trying to focus the discussion on identifying the problem, defining it, and then arriving at some decision about how mutually to go about solving it. To this end, you may need to ask for help from a third party, such as the student's school counselor. If agreed to by the parent, take that step.

Parents do *not* need to hear about how busy you are, about your personal problems, or about how many other students you are dealing with on a daily basis unless, of course, a parent asks. Parents expect you to be the capable professional who knows what to do and is doing it.

Summary

Whereas preceding parts of this book addressed the *why*, *what*, and *how* components of teaching, this chapter has focused your attention on the fourth and final component— the *how well* component—and on the first of two aspects of that component. Assessment is an integral and ongoing factor in the teaching-learning process; consequently, this chapter has emphasized the importance of your including the following in your teaching performance:

- Collect a body of evidence, using a variety of instruments to reliably assess students' learning, that focuses on their individual development.

- Involve students in the assessment process; keep students informed of their progress. Return tests promptly, review answers to all questions, and respond to inquiries about marks given.

- Consider your assessment and grading procedures carefully, plan them, and explain your policies to the students and to their parents when and where appropriate.

- Make sure to explain any ambiguities that result from the terminology used and base your assessments on the material that has been taught.

- Strive for objective and impartial assessment as you put your assessment plan into operation.

- Try to minimize arguments about grades, cheating, and teacher subjectivity by involving students in planning, in reinforcing individual student development, and in providing an accepting, stimulating learning environment.

- Maintain accurate and clear records of assessment results so that you will have an adequate supply of data on which to base your judgmental decisions about achievement.

Because teaching and learning work hand-in-hand and because they are reciprocal processes in that one depends on and affects the other, the *how well* component deals with the assessment of both how well the students are learning and how well the teacher is teaching. This chapter has dealt with the former. In the next and final chapter of this book, your attention is directed to techniques designed to help you develop your teaching skills and assess that development, a process that will continue throughout your teaching career.

Exercise
11.1
Preparing Assessment Items

Instructions: The purpose of this exercise is for you to practice your skill in preparing the different types of assessment items discussed here. For use in your own teaching, select one specific instructional objective and write assessment items for it. When it is completed, share this exercise with your classmates for their feedback.

Objective: _____ Grade and subject: _____

1. Arrangement item
2. Completion drawing item
3. Completion statement item
4. Correction item
5. Essay item
6. Grouping item
7. Identification item
8. Matching item
9. Multiple-choice item
10. Performance item
11. Short-explanation item
12. *Modified* true-or-false item

Chapter 11   POSTTEST

Short Explanation

1. Other than a paper-and-pencil test, identify three alternative techniques for assessing student learning during or at completion of an instructional unit.

2. When using a point system for determining student grades for a course, is it educationally defensible to give a student a higher grade than that student's points call for? A lower grade? Give a rationale for your answers.

3. Explain the dangers in using true-or-false and completion-type items to assess student learning and in using the results for grade determination.

4. Explain the concept of authentic assessment. Is it the same as performance assessment? Explain why or why not.

5. Describe any student learning activities or situations that should not be graded but should or could be used for assessment of student learning.

Essay

1. For a course and grade level that you intend to teach, describe the items and their relative weights that you would use for determining course grades. Explain your rationale for the percentage weight distribution.

2. Explain the value and give a specific example of a performance test item that you would use in teaching your subject to middle school or secondary school students.

3. Do you believe that a student's self-esteem is bolstered from a "feel-good" grade inflation system where no students get less than a C and where those who do not excel are still given As? Explain why you agree or disagree with the idea that being generous to students on their report cards is a way to spur them toward higher achievement.

4. From your current observations and fieldwork related to this teacher preparation program, clearly identify one specific example of educational practice that seems contradictory to exemplary practice or theory presented in this chapter. Present your explanation for the discrepancy.

5. Describe any prior concepts you held that changed as a result of the experiences of this chapter. Describe the changes.

Jioanna Carjuzaa

Reflecting on Teaching Practices and Engaging in Professional Development

They have shown that excellent teachers don't develop full-blown at graduation from professional development programs; nor are they just "born teachers." Instead, teachers are always in the process of "becoming." Given the dynamics of their work, teachers need to continually rediscover who they are and what they stand for through their dialogue and collaboration with peers, through ongoing and consistent study, and through deep reflection about their craft.[1]

—SONIA NIETO

Specific Objectives

At the completion of this chapter, you will be able to:

▶ Demonstrate your growing teacher competencies.

▶ Describe the various ways to gain from practical field experiences.

▶ Share your awareness of the scope and importance of the student-teaching experience.

▶ Develop your awareness of ways to find a teaching job.

▶ Demonstrate knowledge of how to remain an alert and effective classroom teacher throughout your teaching career.

Chapter 12 Overview

Although most of us are not born with innate teaching skills, teaching skills can be learned. Teachers who wish to improve their teaching can do so, and (in addition to this book) there are many resources that can help prepare you. This chapter addresses the evaluation and development of your effectiveness as a classroom teacher, a process that continues throughout your professional career. Teaching is such an electrifying profession that it is not easy to remain energetic and to stay abreast of changes and trends that result from research and practice. You will need to make a continuous and determined effort to remain an alert and effective teacher.

One way to collect data and to improve your effectiveness is through periodic assessment of your teaching performance either by an evaluation of your teaching in the real classroom or, if you are enrolled in a teacher preparation program, by a technique called *micro peer teaching*. The latter is the focus of the final section of this chapter and is an example of a type of final performance (authentic) assessment for this textbook. Two terms used throughout this chapter are **pre-service** and **in-service**. By pre-service, we are referring to the teacher in training/teacher candidate, that is, to all the professional experiences prior to credentialing (or licensing) and employment as a teacher. In-service refers to the experiences of the credentialed (or licensed) and employed teacher.

Introduction

In order to prepare you to teach in today's middle and secondary school classrooms, most teacher education programs integrate classroom experience with coursework. It is important that you have ample opportunities to work with middle and secondary students during your teacher preparation program. Classroom observation, aiding, one-on-one or small-group tutoring, team teaching, and/or solo teaching a lesson or two may all be required components of your professional field experiences. These hands-on classroom experiences will help you to be ready for the demands of student teaching. Practical field experiences can also help undecided students discover if they want to pursue a career in teaching or help students wavering among grade levels or content areas commit to an age-group and/or subject they really want to teach. Here we will describe various practical field experiences you may participate in, tips for finding a teaching position, advice on building a career portfolio, and opportunities for continued professional development.

Professional Development through Field Experiences

Professional field experiences include the portions of your college or university program in which you observe classroom teachers in the act of teaching, participate in conducting classes, teach simulated classes and mini-lessons, microteach, and work with curricula as well as teach real classes in the student-teaching or internship experience. Field experiences prior to student teaching are called *early field experiences* or practica and can be included as early as the junior year of your undergraduate preparation program or even earlier. Student-teaching and internship experiences generally come toward the end of the program. Evidence indicates that more and earlier field experiences result in better-prepared teachers.[2]

Internship can sometimes refer simply to student teaching, or it can sometimes refer to a longer or more independent and paid apprenticeship period. In this chapter, the term *student teaching* refers to both concepts. This chapter considers observation, participation, and student-teaching experiences that occur in middle and secondary schools.

Unless you are different from the majority of pre-service teachers, your professional field experiences will have the greatest impact of all your college or university experiences. These experiences are real, often exciting, and full of opportunities for creative learning and application of what you have learned and are learning. They provide a milieu in which you can experiment with different styles and strategies and develop skills in a variety of instructional strategies.

Classroom Observation

Most teacher preparation programs provide early field experience opportunities so that you can observe teachers and students in the public schools. Often, a portion of the observation will occur in a middle school, then in a junior or senior high school, and then sometimes in alternative schools. Your program may also allow you to observe how other students teach as well as provide demonstration lessons. This variety of observation can give you insights into the interactions between students and teachers, the various backgrounds of students you will teach, and the effects of different teaching strategies, different instructional

materials, and different styles of teaching. The greater number of styles you observe and analyze, the better your understanding of the potentials of the various approaches will be. To get the most out of your observations, consider the following suggestions:

- *Concentrate on watching the students in the classrooms.* Note the range of differences in appearance, abilities, and interests in a single class. Note how students react to different teaching approaches. Which teaching techniques and materials excite their interest and which engender boredom? Follow a student's schedule all day long—this is called *shadowing* a student. How does it feel to go through the routine of being a middle or secondary school student today? (It may be quite different from what you remember.) Try to think of ways that you as a teacher could make the classes more enjoyable and profitable.

- *Observe the classroom management techniques the teacher uses.* How does the teacher have the classroom arranged? Are the classroom guidelines or rules posted? What are the expectations of the students? How does the teacher deal with students who are off task? Is the student morale high or low, and what seems to be the cause for the state of the morale?

- *Observe the ways different teachers handle their classes.* How do they get their classes started? How do they bring their classes to a conclusion? How do they develop the important points? How do they create interest? How do they get students involved in their own learning? How do they provide for differences in students? What techniques for motivation, probing, discovery, inquiry, closure, and reinforcement are used? How do students respond to the various tactics? What procedures are used to establish and maintain classroom control?

- *Give particular attention to the manner in which the teachers implement various instructional strategies and the students' responses to each of the strategies.* Does the teacher use an eclectic approach including both teacher-directed and student-centered techniques? Are all learning modalities addressed? How is technology integrated into the instruction?

- *Observe the ways teachers promote equal educational opportunity.* How are the needs of English Language Learners; students with learning disabilities; students with mental, emotional, or physical challenges; gifted and talented students; and so forth addressed? Do you notice any gender differences? Are students treated equally? What lesson accommodations does the teacher make?

Student Teaching

During your student-teaching assignment, you will have a period of observation and participation, followed by the gradual takeover of some of the classes and other duties that make up a teacher's load, under the supervision of one or more cooperating teachers as well as a college or university supervisor. The experience is expected to develop into a genuine simulation of teaching reality. The cooperating teacher, the professional of record, always retains ultimate responsibility for what happens in the classroom, but the intent is for the student teacher to assume as much responsibility as possible—as though the class were fully his or hers to lead. The legal, instructional, and pedagogical ramifications of this activity are such that only a simulation of reality is possible. However, the greater the effort to approximate the real thing and the greater the sensitivity to the goals of the activity on the part of everyone concerned, the more rewarding the student-teaching experience will be. For most teacher candidates, student teaching is the capstone of their teacher preparation program. It can be both exciting and rewarding. It can also be both difficult and trying.

Perhaps the first thing to remember about student teaching is that, like observation and participation, it is intended to be a learning experience. It is during student teaching that you will have the opportunity to apply the theories and techniques learned in college classes to real teaching situations. Here you will have an opportunity to try out various strategies and techniques to begin to build a wide repertoire of teaching skills and to develop an effective, comfortable teaching style. From the beginning, it is important that the students identify you as a teacher. Your dress and professional demeanor will help you to establish your position.

Student teaching is also a time of trial and error. Do not be discouraged if you make mistakes or your lessons do not go well at first. If you were already a skilled teacher, you would not need the practice. Making mistakes is part of the learning process. Use them as a means for improvement. With the help of your cooperating teacher and supervisor, try to analyze your teaching to find what steps to take to do better next time. Perhaps your execution of the strategies and techniques was faulty; perhaps you used a strategy or technique inappropriate for the particular situation. Such errors can be quite easily remedied as you gain experience. Failure to devote enough time to planning adequately, neglect of previewing audiovisual equipment and/or other technology, lack of research on the topic of presentation, and overusing a limited repertoire of instructional strategies are common errors new teachers make and should be avoided.

As you become more skilled in using various strategies and techniques, you will find that all have their uses. Do not be quick to reject a teaching strategy or technique that fails for you. Do not allow yourself to become one of those boring teachers who can teach in only one way. Instead, if a strategy or technique does not work for you, examine the situation to see what went wrong. Then try it again in a new situation after brushing up your technique and correcting your faults.

During your student-teaching assignment, you may have multiple sections of the same course (prep), and a lesson may go very differently in one class than it does with another group of students. Teaching multiple sections of the same course provides you with the opportunity to compare and contrast your interactions with your students and reflect on what went well and what you could have done better. By isolating variables and examining the dynamics of the classroom, you may uncover interesting information about your teaching style and your students.

Since student teaching is a time for learning and for getting the mistakes out of your system, it is important not to become discouraged. Many student teachers who do miserably for the first weeks blossom into excellent teachers by the end of the student-teaching period. However, if things seem to go well at first, do not become overconfident. Many beginners who are quickly satisfied with their early success become complacent and doom themselves to mediocrity. In any case, examine your classes to see what went well and what went wrong. Then try to correct your faults and capitalize on your strengths.

After your initial anxiety and nervousness wear off, use your student teaching as an opportunity to try out new strategies and techniques. Avoid becoming a clone of the cooperating teacher or a replica of the old-time teacher who gave lectures, heard recitations, and sometimes did very little else. But work out the new approaches and techniques you wish to try with your cooperating teacher before you use them. Usually, the cooperating teacher can show you how to get the most out of your new ventures and warn you of pitfalls you might encounter. Things will go more smoothly if you continue with the same strategies and tactics to which the class is accustomed. Students used to a particular style may not readily adapt to innovations. This reluctance is especially bad when the teacher confronts students with quick changes in the length and difficulty of homework assignments or an abrupt switch from prescriptive, didactic methods to discovery and inquiry approaches.

Sometimes the cooperating teacher may think it necessary to veto what seems to you to be your best ideas. Usually, there is a sound basis for the veto. It may be, in the cooperating teacher's view, that these ideas will not serve the objectives well, or they may require time, money, or equipment not available to you; violate school policy; or seem unsuited to the age and abilities of the students. Sometimes your ideas may be rejected because they conflict with the cooperating teacher's pedagogical and philosophical beliefs or biases. Whatever the objection, you should accept the decision gracefully and concentrate on procedures that the cooperating teacher finds acceptable. After all, you are a temporary guest in the classroom, and ultimately the classes and the instruction are the cooperating teacher's responsibility.

Furthermore, you need to become a master of many techniques. If you master the techniques and style that your cooperating teacher recommends now, you will have begun to assemble a suitable repertoire of teaching skills. Later, when you are teaching your own classes, you can expand your repertoire by trying out other strategies and styles you find appealing.

Success in student teaching requires more study and preparation than most teacher candidates think possible. To do the job, you must know what you are doing, so pay particular attention to your planning. Carefully review the content of your lessons and units and lay them out step-by-step. Leave nothing to chance. Check and double-check to be sure you have your facts straight, that your teaching strategies and tactics will yield your objectives, that you have the necessary teaching materials on hand, that you know how to use them, and so on. It is most embarrassing when you find you cannot solve the problems you have given to the students, cannot answer the students' questions, and cannot find the equipment you need or cannot operate the technology. As a rule, you should ask your cooperating teacher to approve your plan before you become committed to it. If the cooperating teacher suggests changes, incorporate them into the plan and try to carry them out.

Often you will be required to design and produce a unit plan during your student-teaching assignment. Planning lessons and units for student teaching is no easy task. Becoming really sure of your subject matter and thinking out how to teach it in the short time available during your student teaching are a lot to ask. Therefore, prepare as much as you can before the student-teaching period begins. Try to find out what topics you will be expected to teach and master the content before you report for your student teaching. Then when you start student teaching, you can concentrate on planning and teaching, confident that you have a firm understanding of the content. Many students have botched their student teaching because they had to spend so much time learning the content that they never had time to learn how to teach. Remember that middle and secondary school classes are not replicas of college classes.

Because student teaching is difficult and time demanding, most teacher education institutions strongly recommend or require that student teachers not combine student teaching with other courses or outside work. If you have to work to eat, you must, but very few people are able to both hold down a job and perform successfully in their student teaching. Outside jobs, additional courses, trying to master inadequately learned subject content, and preparing classes are just too much for one ordinary person to do well at the same time. It is true that many successful teachers have moonlighted on outside jobs or on coursework for advanced degrees. It is also true that many undergraduate students have maintained high grades with a full load of college courses and have simultaneously worked full-time in the evenings. But the student-teaching experience is so unique and intense in the many demands that it makes on a student teacher's time that it is virtually impossible for you to perform in a superior fashion if you bog yourself down with outside responsibilities during this crucial early part of your career.

Usually, student teaching starts with a few days of observing. This gives you a few days to get ready for teaching. Use this time to become familiar with the classroom situation. Get to know the students. Learn their names. Borrow the teacher's seating chart and study it and the students as the class proceeds. In this way, you will learn to associate names with faces and get to know your students. Learn the classroom routines and other details of classroom management. Familiarize yourself with the types of teaching, activities, and assignments that the class is used to so that you can gradually assume the classroom teaching responsibility without too much disruption. Remember, at first students are likely to resent too much deviation from what they have come to expect.

In your observation of the efforts of your cooperating teacher in the act of teaching, keep in mind the following topics and questions:

- *Objectives.* What were the objectives of the lesson? How did the teacher make the students aware of them? Were the objectives achieved?

- *Administrative duties.* How did the teacher handle taking the roll and reporting attendance? How were tardies handled? How were announcements made? How did the teacher handle other serendipitous events?

- *Homework.* Did the teacher make a homework assignment? At what point in the lesson was the assignment made? How did the assignment relate to the day's work? How was the assignment from the previous day handled? How did the teacher deal with students who failed to submit completed work? How much time did the teacher spend on the assignment for the next day? Did the students appear to understand the assignment?

- *Review.* How much of the period was devoted to review of the previous lesson? Did the teacher make any effort to fit the review into the day's lesson? How did the teacher conduct the review—question and answer or student summarization of important points?

- *Methods.* What various methods did the teacher use in the day's lesson? Was multilevel instruction used? Did the teacher lecture? For what length of time? How did the teacher shift from one method to the next (**transitions**)? How did the teacher motivate the students to attend? Was any provision made for individual differences and learning styles among the students? Was any provision made for student participation in the lesson? How did the teacher engage students who were not involved? Were the students kept busy during the entire period? Did any classroom management problems arise? How did the teacher handle them?

- *Accommodations.* How did the teacher modify the lesson to address the needs of all of the students?

- *Miscellaneous.* Was the teacher's voice pleasant enough to listen to? Did the teacher have any distracting idiosyncratic habits? Were lighting and ventilation adequate? What system did the teacher use for checking attendance?

- *Evaluation.* How might this lesson have been improved? What went well?

Guidelines for Behaving Professionally during Field Experiences

When you participate in professional field experiences, you are in a rather delicate position. In a sense, you are neither teacher nor student; yet, in another sense, you are both teacher and student. Many teacher candidates have found this position trying. Therefore, included here are a number of suggestions that may help you to be successful during your field experiences. Although these suggestions apply to observation, participation, and student teaching, they are somewhat geared toward student teaching. These suggestions are conclusions drawn from years of observing and mentoring student teachers.

In professional field experiences, your relationship with your cooperating teacher is critical. You should concentrate on keeping these relationships friendly and professional. Whether you like it or not, student teaching—and, to a lesser degree, observation and participation—is a job as well as a learning experience, and the cooperating teacher and college or university supervisor are your bosses. Ordinarily, you can expect them to be nice bosses who will not only strive to help you in every way they can but also be tolerant of your mistakes. They are bosses, however, and must be perceived as such.

They will—or should—have pretty high expectations of you. Not only will they expect you to have an adequate command of the subject to be taught, but they will also expect you to have (a) an ability to work with other adults, (b) an ability to reflect on your work and to listen to and accept suggestions, (c) a current understanding of the nature of middle and secondary school learners and learning, (d) a repertoire of teaching skills and a developing competence in using them, and (e) a functional understanding of the purposes and processes of assessment. Do not disappoint them. You should check yourself in each of these areas. If you believe yourself deficient in any of them, now is the time to bring yourself up to par. Student teaching is too hectic to take time out for learning and collecting what you already should have learned and collected.

Your colleagues in the school will also expect you to be a professional—a beginning professional but a professional just the same. You will be expected to do your job carefully without fussing, criticizing, or complaining. Carry out instructions carefully. Keep to the routines of the school. If next week's lesson plans are due at the department head's office before the beginning of school Friday morning, make sure that they are there. Be prompt with all assignments. Never be late or absent unless previous arrangements have been made. If an emergency arises, phone in. Pay attention to details. Fill out reports, requisitions, and so on, accurately and on time. Be meticulous in the preparation of your unit and lesson plans. Never approach a class unprepared. Be sure you know your content and exactly how you plan to teach it. *Nothing upsets cooperating teachers and college or university supervisors more than classes that do not go well because the student teacher was not sufficiently prepared.*

Build a reputation for being responsible and dependable by carrying out your assignments faithfully and accurately. Sometimes student teachers fail because they do not fully understand what their responsibilities are or how to carry them out. Study the student teacher's handbook, observe the cooperating teacher, and follow the cooperating teacher's instructions so that you will know just what to do and when and how. If you are uncertain about what to do or how to do it, ask even though it may embarrass you to admit ignorance. It is much better to admit you do not understand than to keep quiet and reveal it.

Be proactive. Evidence of initiative impresses teachers, principals, and college supervisors. Volunteer to do things before you have to be asked. Willingly take on such tasks as reading papers and correcting tests. Take part in cafeteria supervision, extracurricular activities, attendance at PTO meetings, and the like. Participating in such activities will give you experience and expertise in these areas of the teacher's job and will also indicate to your colleagues that you are a professionally minded person who does not shun the nitty-gritty. Develop a close relationship with your college or university supervisor. Keep in frequent (weekly if not daily) contact with him or her. Once you have started your student teaching, it can be helpful toward establishing a feeling of community, reducing your sense of isolation, and encouraging reflection if you and your college or university supervisor can communicate by email.[3]

During your professional field experiences, you are a guest of the school in which you are observing, participating, or student teaching. Your place in the school is not a right but a privilege. Behave in a way that will make you and future student teachers welcome. As quickly as you can, adapt yourself to the culture of the school and conform to the mores of the school as they apply to teachers. Do not stand on your rights—as a guest of the school, you may not have many—but concentrate on your responsibilities. Try as soon as possible to become a member of the school staff and to set up pleasant relationships with your cooperating teacher and other colleagues. As a student teacher, it helps if you have your own mailbox and your own desk or workspace, too.

Be sure to protect student confidentiality and refrain from criticizing the school, its administration, or its teachers. Be particularly careful about what you say to teachers and other student teachers. If some things in a situation bother you, seek the advice of your university supervisor before you do anything drastic. If there is to be any friction, let the supervisor absorb the sparks. It is your university supervisor's job to see that your experience runs smoothly and that you get the best practical learning experience possible.

Do not under any circumstances discuss school personnel with the students. Often students tell student teachers how much better they are than their regular teachers. Regardless of how much your ego loves to hear it, do not respond to such bait. Allowing yourself to discuss a teacher's performance and personality with a student is unprofessional and can only lead to trouble.

Professional field experiences, particularly student teaching, throw students and cooperating teachers into a closeness that can be richly rewarding and also extremely difficult. From the point of view of the cooperating teacher, the student-teaching period presents a threat in several ways. Allowing a newcomer to interfere in the smooth running of the class is risky. More than one teacher has had to work extra long hours to repair the damage done to a class by an incompetent student teacher. Teachers who are insecure may find the presence of any other adult in their classes threatening; the presence of a student teacher critically observing the teacher's work can be particularly disturbing. So, avoid any appearance of opposing or competing with the cooperating teacher. Consult with him or her before you undertake anything and follow his or her advice and instructions carefully. If you believe the instructions or advice is wrong, your only recourse is to consult with your university supervisor.

Above all, listen to what the cooperating teacher tells you. Teachers (and college supervisors as well) sometimes complain that student teachers do not listen to what they are told. If a student teacher does not listen, it is probably because the student teacher is so caught up in his or her personal problems that the student teacher finds it difficult to concentrate on anything else. The student teacher may be too busy justifying his or her own behavior or explaining away what has gone amiss in class to hear someone else's criticism. Although it may require some effort, try to hear what the cooperating teacher has to say and follow through on the suggestions. Teachers and supervisors find it exasperating when student teachers carry on in unwanted ways in spite of the teacher's long and detailed instructions or explanations of what should be done.

As with any public figure in the community, you can expect that students as well as parents in the community will discuss you and your performance. Know that student teachers are held to the same high standards expected of all school personnel. Before being placed for your student-teaching assignment, you will probably be asked to complete a character questionnaire or sign a professional conduct document prepared by your state department of education or your teacher education program stating that you will uphold high professional standards for ethical behavior. You most likely will also need to be fingerprinted and have a criminal background check run on you before you ever enter the classroom.

Once placed in the school, you may hear all sorts of comments from students. Sometimes you hear chance remarks as you walk through the halls or as students are leaving the room. Let them not turn your head because often these remarks are quite flattering. At the same time, guard against that feeling of depression that usually follows derogatory statements about your efforts or intentions. Whether you are praised or denounced, try to assume an objective attitude and use the comments for the inherent value they may possess. Remind yourself that you cannot always be all things to all people, nor should you even try to be. Your personality, the school regulations, and the classroom procedures will not let you be equally appealing to or effective with all of your students. You must expect that in the process of upholding your standards, you will leave an occasional student dissatisfied. Only by keeping your reactions under control will you be able to preserve a positive feeling for your job.

CO-TEACHING   Classroom teachers in middle and secondary schools are under a lot of pressure these days. The No Child Left Behind Act and subsequent reform efforts, in addition to the reauthorization of federal special education legislation, have increased the pressure that educators feel to make sure all their students meet the high standards established under these policies. This expectation is especially daunting since an increasing number of adolescent students come to school with a variety of challenges that render them at risk.

Consequently, this accountability dilemma has made some educators reluctant to agree to host a student teacher and turn the responsibility for their students' academic achievement over to an individual who is an inexperienced novice. Many alternatives to providing soon-to-be classroom teachers with an opportunity to teach in a real classroom setting and still guarantee that middle and secondary classroom students are receiving the excellent instruction necessary to help them succeed academically have been explored.

Co-teaching, an innovative approach to the traditional student-teaching placement, is a popular model designed to meet the needs of diverse learners and promote student success while providing pre-service teachers with a venue and students where they can hone their craft. In the co-teaching model, the cooperating teacher and the student teacher share the classroom and the students as well as the instruction. In fact, the two teachers work together and share in the planning, organization, delivery, and assessment of their students.

In essence, the middle and high school students are more successful because they have the benefit of two collaborating teachers. Although co-teaching is not a new concept among certified classroom teachers, pairing a cooperating teacher and student teacher in this way has been fairly uncharted territory until recently. The co-teaching model has been piloted for the past five years with teacher candidates enrolled in the teacher preparation program at St. Cloud State University in Minnesota.[4] The educators there found that when student teachers are placed with cooperating teachers and both are trained in the **co-teaching** model, there is an increase in the academic achievement of the students they share. Other schools of education and their local school district partners across the country are adopting the co-teaching model. This win-win proposition might be a possibility for your capstone practical experience in your teacher preparation program.

| Teaching Scenario | Some Advice from Daniel Blanchard, Author of *Feeling Lucky?* |

Hello future teachers. I have been doing your soon-to-be job of teaching tomorrow's leaders for over two decades. I started my career off as a special education teacher and a wrestling coach. I eventually became a middle school teacher and the football coach. Presently, I am teaching social studies in Connecticut's largest inner-city high school, New Britain High. Every day is an adventure for me. I can't remember the last time I was bored teaching in such a diverse environment surrounded by so many intriguing kids from all corners of the globe. Every year I get the privilege of learning new names that I have never seen or heard before. Teaching in such a mixed milieu has been very rewarding for me in terms of professional accomplishments as well as positive, interesting student interaction, and special recognition from my students. Over the years, my students have awarded me with plaques to hang on my wall that they spent their own money and time to get. Furthermore, upon graduation, several of my students have chosen me to be the recipient of their winner-awards, essays highlighting how I inspired them. In the end, I am blessed with more life-long relationships than I can keep track of. Teaching certainly has been worth it, as well as quite an adventure for me!

Speaking of an adventure, I believe Helen Keller once said, "Life is to be lived as an adventure or nothing at all." Well the advice I'm about to give all you aspiring teachers also comes from Helen Keller. You ready? Here is comes! Helen Keller once said, "Security is mostly a superstition. It does not exist." And I believe she may be right. However, if security does exist then I think it would exist in the form of C.A.N.D.I. This is something that we all strive for everyday with our students and we shouldn't forget to live what we teach and preach. As a matter of fact, we have to live what we teach and preach or our students will see right through us and will refuse to live up to the miracle that they truly are!

Through living a life of C.A.N.D.I. our students will always be watching us, as adolescents tend to do, but our students will be watching us with smiles on their faces, inspiration in their eyes, and hearts pounding in their chests, revving to go.

If we live a life of C.A.N.D.I., all of our futures will be brighter and sweeter.

You're probably asking what C.A.N.D.I. is by now? It's **C**onstant **A**nd **N**ever-ending **D**eliberate **I**mprovement! By improving a little tiny bit every day of our lives we will be able to soar to heights we had not even dared to dream of before. And even better, many of our students are going to notice our success and want to go along for the ride. In short, our C.A.N.D.I. will inspire our students to give more and work harder for us than they ever thought they could for themselves! Like corks rising together in the ocean during high tide, as we teachers rise in our level of skills, knowledge, and abilities, so will our students!

Dare to be great and improve a little bit every day. If you do, you'll truly be leaders and your students will follow in your footsteps. In addition, they may even create a few footsteps of their own for the next generation to follow! How sweet is success and C.A.N.D.I.!

In conclusion, not only will your motivation and personal success positively influence your students, but in return, their motivation and personal success will also positively influence you. This creates a better world for us all to live in. It's like one hand washing the other and then both cleaning the face. Working together, we all win. Over the years I have learned from my students and athletes that you have to teach to truly learn and you have to give to truly get. The only reason that my teen leadership book, *Feeling Lucky?*, with its message of not making excuses and working hard to create your own luck, even exists is because my students for the past decade kept encouraging me to write a book about what I know so that other students from around the world could also learn from me. For their encouragement, I am forever grateful! I believe that if you read my book, you too will be feeling lucky and ready to create your own success as a teacher and person! Good luck and enjoy the wonderful world of teaching!

Note: Check out a book review on *Feeling Lucky?* at **http://bestfeaturedarticles.com/arts-and-entertainment/book-review-feeling-lucky-gettingbookreviews-com.html**

SOURCE: Contributed by Daniel Blanchard. Used with permission.

Relationships with Students

Your relationships with students may make or break you in your practical field experience, so try to make them as friendly and purposeful as possible. Students like teachers who treat them with respect and whom they can respect. Therefore, treat your students courteously and tactfully but at the same time require standards of behavior and academic productivity reasonably close to those established by the regular teacher. Show that you have confidence in them and expect them to do well. Let them know you are interested in them and in their activities.

The best way to earn the students' respect is to do a good job of teaching and to treat all students fairly and cordially. Do not, however, become overly friendly. Be friendly, not chummy. Your role is not to be a buddy but to be a teacher. The students will respect and like you more if you act your age and assume your proper professional role. Seek respect rather than popularity and above all avoid personal fraternization and inappropriate contact with students. Remember that you are an adult, not a kid.

In her report *Educator Sexual Misconduct: A Synthesis of Existing Literature*, Dr. Charol Shakesaft of Hofstra University claims that the incidence of illegal sexual misconduct in our schools is greater than we are led to believe. Shakesaft conducted a comprehensive literature review that describes educator sexual misconduct in our schools, the common characteristics of offenders, and suggestions for addressing this problem. According to Shakesaft, 9.6% of students in our public school system are victimized by teachers during their school careers.[5] Fortunately, most schools adhere to a no-tolerance policy where sexual misconduct is concerned. Under no circumstances should you ever engage in inappropriate sexual relationships with your students. Now read about educational tours in Activity 12.1.

A c t i v i t y
12.1   **Educational Tours**

Do you want to have a lasting impact on your students? Consider a travel program, an excellent way to bring the real world into the classroom. Several companies design customized tours for educational groups that emphasize student learning. Travel opportunities are available for a variety of middle and high school classes and clubs, including special groups, organizations, music performance troupes, graduation trips, day trips, weekend getaways, spring break tours, summer travel, and more. In some cases, students can earn academic credit, gain valuable experience, and have fun while learning.

Apply Your Knowledge

Check out possible destinations, teacher testimonials, resources, lesson plans, educational curriculum, sample itineraries, photos and videos, and so on by perusing the following websites.

People to People Student Ambassador Programs

http://www.peopletopeople.com/OurPrograms/Pages/default
    .aspx

Smithsonian Student Travel

http://www.smithsonianstudenttravel.com/error404.aspx?item
    =%2fteachersinterior%2fsmithsonianmaterial&user=extranet
    \Anonymous&site=website

Education First: Educational Tours

http://www.eftours.com

Suburban Tours: Student Travel and Educational Tours

http://www.suburbantours.com

Educational Travel Adventures

http://www.educationaltraveladventures.com/?gclid
    =CI3Uz7rxOI4CFSCTWAod815sAg

ASD Cultural Exchange

http://asdculturalexchange.com

Contemporary Tours

http://www.contemporarytours.com

1. What travel opportunities did you have in middle and/or secondary school?
2. What was your key takeaway from the travel experience?
3. What travel courses or tours do you think you would like to lead your students on?

Finding a Teaching Position

As your successful student-teaching experience draws to a close, you will embark on finding your first paid teaching position. You should be encouraged in your goal of finding that first job by the fact that the projected need for new teachers for the next several years is great. The guidelines that follow should help you accomplish your goal.

Guidelines for Locating a Teaching Position

To prepare for finding the position you want, you should focus on (a) letters of recommendation from your cooperating teacher(s), your college or university supervisor, and, in some instances, the school principal; (b) your professional preparation as evidenced by your letters of recommendation and other items in your professional portfolio (discussed next); and (c) your job-interviewing skills.

First, consider the recommendations about your teaching. Most colleges and universities have a career center, usually called a *job (or career) placement center*, where there is probably a counselor or adviser who can advise you how to open the job placement file that will hold your professional recommendations. This enables prospective personnel directors or district personnel who are expecting to employ new teachers to review your recommendations. Sometimes there are special forms for writing these recommendations. It is your responsibility to request letters of recommendation and, when appropriate, to supply the person writing the recommendation with the blank form and an appropriately addressed stamped envelope. Sometimes the job

placement files are confidential, so your recommendations will be mailed directly to the placement office. The confidentiality of recommendations may be optional, and, when possible, you may want to maintain your own copies of letters of recommendation and include them in your professional portfolio.

The letters of recommendation from educators at the school(s) where you did your student teaching should include the following information: the name of the school and district where you did your student teaching, the grade levels and subjects you taught, your proven skills in meeting the needs of diverse students in the classroom, your content mastery, your skills in assessing student learning and in reflecting on your teaching performance and learning from that reflection, and your skills in communicating and interacting with students and adults. If you choose to ask your former university faculty members to write recommendation letters for you, provide them with a current copy of your résumé and, perhaps, a list of your accomplishments in the courses you took with them as well as other pertinent information. That way, they can write a comprehensive recommendation highlighting your academic achievements.

Second, consider your preparation as a teacher. Teachers, as you have learned, represent myriad specialties. Hiring personnel will want to know how you see yourself—for example, as a specialist in middle school core or as a high school music teacher. You may indicate a special interest or skill, such as competency in teaching English as a second language. Or, perhaps, although your teaching field is mathematics, you also are bilingual and have had rich and varied cross-cultural experiences. The hiring personnel who consider your application will be interested in your sincerity and will want to see that you are academically and socially impressive.

Finally, consider your in-person interview with a district official. Sometimes, you will have several interviews, or you will be interviewed simultaneously with other candidates. There may be an initial screening interview by an administrative panel from the district, followed by an interview by a department chairperson, a school principal, or a school team composed of one or more teachers and administrators from the interested school or district. In all interviews, your verbal and nonverbal behaviors will be observed as you respond to various questions, including (a) factual questions about your student teaching or about particular curriculum programs with which you would be expected to work and (b) hypothetical questions, such as "What would you do if … ?" Often these are questions that relate to your philosophy of education, your reasons for wanting to be a teacher, your approach to handling a particular classroom situation, and perhaps specifically your reasons for wanting to teach at this particular school and in this district. Interview guidelines follow later in this section.

The Professional Career Portfolio

A way to be proactive in your job search is to create a professional portfolio to be shared with persons who are considering your application for employment. That is the objective of Exercise 12.1. The professional career portfolio is organized to provide clear evidence of your teaching skills and to make you professionally desirable to a hiring committee. A professional portfolio is not simply a collection of your accomplishments randomly tossed into a folder. It is a deliberate, current, and organized collection of your skills, attributes, experiences, and accomplishments. Exercise 12.1 suggests categories and subcategories of items to include in your portfolio, listed in the order that they may be best presented in portfolios A and B.[6]

Resources for Locating Teaching Vacancies

To locate teaching vacancies, you can establish contact with any of the following resources:

1. *Academic employment network.* A network employment page is available at **http://www.academploy.com**. Contact AEN, 2665 Gray Rd., Windham, ME 04062 (phone: 800-890-8283; email: infoacademploy.com).
2. *College or university placement office.* Establishing a career placement file with your local college or university placement service is an excellent way to begin the process of locating teaching vacancies.
3. *Local school or district personnel office.* You can contact school personnel offices to obtain information about teaching vacancies and sometimes about open job interviews.
4. *County educational agency.* Contact local county offices of education about job openings.
5. *State departments of education.* Some state departments of education maintain information about job openings

statewide. Peruse state department of education Internet addresses for current openings.
6. *Independent schools.* You can contact non–public-supported schools that interest you either directly or through educational placement services such as IES (Independent Educational Services), 20 Nassau St., Princeton, NJ 08540 (phone: 800-257-5102), and the European Council of Independent Schools, 21B Lavant St., Petersfield, Hampshire, GU32 3EL, England.
7. *Commercial placement agencies.* Nationwide job listings and placement services are available from such agencies as Carney, Sandoe & Associates, 136 Boylston Street, Boston, MA 02116 (phone: 800-225-7986); National Education Service Center, PO Box 1279, Department NS, Riverton, WY 82501-1279 (phone: 307-856-0170); and National Teachers Clearinghouse SE, PO Box 267, Boston, MA 02118-0267 (phone: 617-267-3204).
8. *Out-of-country teaching opportunities.* Information regarding teaching positions outside the United States can be obtained from American Field Services Intercultural Programs, 313 East 43rd St., New York, NY 10017; Department of Defense Dependent Schools, 4040 N. Fairfax Dr., Arlington, VA 22203-1634; European Council of Independent Schools, 21B Lavant St., Petersfield, Hampshire, GU32 3EL, England; International Schools Services, PO Box 5910, Princeton, NJ 08543; Peace Corps, Recruitment Office, 806 Connecticut Ave. NW, Washington, DC 20526; Teachers Overseas Recruitment Centers, National Teacher Placement Bureaus of America, Inc., PO Box 09027, 4190 Pearl Rd., Cleveland, OH 44109; and YMCA of the USA, Attn: Teaching in Japan and Taiwan, 101 N. Wacker Dr., Chicago, IL 60606.
9. *Professional educational journals and other publications.* Professional teaching journals (as found in Figure 8.9 in Chapter 8) often run advertisements of teaching vacancies, as do education newspapers such as *Education Week*. These can be found in your college or university library. See also *Education Week*'s site on the Internet at **http://www.topschooljobs.org/?intc=thed**.

State (and Territorial) Sources for Information about Credential Requirements

If you are interested in the credential requirements for other states and U.S. territories, check at the appropriate office of your own college or university teacher preparation program to see what information is available about requirements for states of interest to you and whether the credential that you are about to receive has reciprocity with other states. Addresses and contact numbers for information about state credentials are available on the Internet at **http://wdcrobcolp01.ed.gov/Programs/EROD/org_list.cfm?category_ID=SEA**.

The Professional Résumé

Résumé preparation is the subject of how-to books, computer programs, and commercial services, but a teacher's résumé is specific. Although no one can tell you exactly what résumé will work best for you, a few basic guidelines are especially helpful for the preparation for a teacher's résumé (see Figure 12.1).

Figure 12.1 **Sample Teaching Résumé**

Richard Da Teacher
1993 Schoolhouse Drive
Dewey, CA 95818

OBJECTIVE: Secondary school teaching position in English/language arts

EDUCATION: California Single Subject Teaching Credential
                     California State University, Sacramento—2004
                     Bachelor of Arts Degree in English
                     California State University, Chico—2004

RELATED EXPERIENCES:

2/04–6/04   *Student Teaching.* Valley High School, Elk Grove Unified School District, Elk Grove, CA

                     Taught one 10th-grade English class and two classes of junior literature, each class of 30–34 ethnically diverse students. Advised school German club. Coached girl's volleyball team.

9/03–12/03   *Student Teaching.* Eddy Middle School, Elk Grove Unified School District, Elk Grove, CA

                     Planned, developed, and implemented interdisciplinary thematic lessons for 7th- and 8th-grade students in 2-hour humanities blocks. Year-round scheduling of students was experienced. Planned and taught a literature unit on *The Courage of Sarah Noble* with a multicultural emphasis. Paid assistant in after-school tutoring program.

9/02–2/03   *Teacher Aide.* Premier Day Care Center, Dewey, CA. Worked in teaching and supervisory positions with ethnically diverse children from kindergarten through grade 6. Planned weekly thematic activities for all children.

OTHER EXPERIENCES AND ABILITIES:

- Volunteer at California Reading Association Conference, Fall 2002.
- Paid editor of MA theses, Department of English, California State University, Sacramento, academic year 2002–2003.
- Musical ability—Have played saxophone and other reed instruments for more than 14 years; can read any type of music. Six years of professional work experience in the music recording industry.
- Travel experiences to Austria, Denmark, Germany, Holland, Sweden, and Switzerland.
- Speaking and writing ability in English, German, and Spanish. Speaking ability also in American Sign.

REFERENCES:

- Dr. Patricia Englisia, University Supervisor of Student Teaching, California State University, Sacramento (916) 278-7020.
- Mr. Ray Combs, Cooperating Teacher at Valley High School, Elk Grove, CA (916) 778-8900.
- Ms. Gloria Evans, Cooperating Teacher at Eddy Middle School, Elk Grove, CA (916) 777-2496.

- The résumé should be no more than *two pages* in length. If it is any longer, it becomes a life history rather than a professional résumé. If you feel it is necessary to include more information, you may consider printing your résumé back-to-back or on an 11- by 17-inch sheet that you can fold to the 8½ by 11-inch format. On the extra space you gain, you may decide to include an inspirational quote, a photograph of you teaching, or a photo of your students' work.

- The presentation should be neat and uncluttered.

- Page size should be standard 8½ by 11 inches. Oversized and undersized pages can get lost.

- The paper stock should be white or off-white.

- Do *not* give information such as your age, height, weight, marital status, or the number or names of your children. Including personal data may make it appear that you are trying to prejudice members of the hiring committee, which is simply unprofessional.

- Sentences should be clear and concise; avoid educational jargon, awkward phrases, abbreviations, or unfamiliar words. No personal pronouns should be included, and verbs should be in the past tense.

- Organize the information carefully in this order: your name, address, telephone number, and email address, followed by your education, professional experience, credential status, location of placement file, professional affiliations, honors, and special skills, abilities, and knowledge.

- When identifying your experiences—academic, teaching, and life—do so in *reverse chronological order*, listing your most recent degree or your current position first.

- Be absolutely truthful; avoid any distortions of facts about your degrees, experiences, or any other information that you provide on your résumé.

- Take time to develop your résumé and then keep it current. Do not duplicate hundreds of copies; produce a new copy each time you apply for a job. If you maintain an electronic copy of your résumé, then it is easy to make modifications and print a current copy each time one is needed.

- Prepare a cover letter to accompany your résumé that is written specifically for the position for which you are applying. Address the letter personally but formally to the personnel director. Limit the cover letter to one page and emphasize who you are, your teaching experiences and interests, and reasons that you are best qualified for the position. Show a familiarity with the particular school or district. Again, if you maintain an electronic copy of a generic application letter, you can easily modify it to make it specific for each position.

- Have your résumé and cover letter edited by someone familiar with résumé writing and editing, perhaps an English-teaching friend. A poorly written, poorly typed, or poorly copied résumé fraught with spelling and grammar errors will guarantee that you will not be considered for the job. In addition to avoiding misspellings, check for inaccuracies and omissions. Keep a consistent format. Leave some white space; do not overcrowd the page.

- Be sure that your application reaches the personnel director by the announced deadline. If for some reason it will be late, then telephone the director, explain the circumstances, and request permission to submit your application late.

The In-Person Interview

If your application and résumé are attractive to the personnel director, you will be notified and scheduled for a personal or small-group interview, although in some instances the hiring interview may precede the request for your personal papers. Whichever the case, during the interview you should be honest, and you should be yourself. Practice an interview, perhaps with aid of a video camera. Ask someone to role-play an interview with you and ask you some tough questions. Plan your interview wardrobe and get it ready the night before. Leave early for your interview so that you arrive in plenty of time. If possible, long before your scheduled interview, locate someone who works in the school district and discuss curriculum, classroom management policies, popular programs, and district demographics with that person. If you anticipate a professionally embarrassing question during the interview, think of diplomatic ways to respond. This means that you should think of ways to turn your weaknesses into strengths. For instance, if your cooperating teacher has mentioned that you need to continue to develop your room environment skills (meaning that you were sloppy), admit that you realize that you

need to be more conscientious about keeping supplies and materials neat and tidy but mention your concern about the students and the learning and that you realize you have a tendency to interact with students more than with objects. Assure someone that you will work on this skill, and then do it.

The paragraphs that follow offer additional specific guidelines for preparing for and handling the in-person interview. As you peruse these guidelines, know that what may seem trite and obvious to one reader is not necessarily obvious to another.

You will be given a specific time, date, and place for the interview. Regardless of your other activities, accept the time, date, and location suggested rather than trying to manipulate the interviewer around a schedule more convenient for you.

As a part of the interview you may be expected to do a formal but abbreviated (10 to 15 minutes) teaching demonstration. You may or may not be told in advance of this expectation. So, it is a good idea to thoughtfully develop and rehearse a model one that you could perform on immediate request. Just in case it might be useful, some candidates carry to the interview a videotape of one of their best real-teaching episodes, such as one that was made during student teaching.

Dress for success. Regardless of what else you may be doing for a living, take the time necessary to make a professional and proud appearance.

Avoid coming to the interview with small children. If necessary, arrange to have them taken care of by someone. Arrive promptly, shake your dry hands firmly with members of the committee, and initiate conversation with a friendly comment, based on your personal knowledge, about the school or district.

Be prepared to answer standard interview questions. Sometimes school districts will send candidates the questions that will be asked during the interview; at other times, these questions are handed to the candidate on arrival at the interview. The questions that are likely to be asked will cover the following topics:

- *Your experiences with students of the relevant age.* The committee wants to be reasonably certain that you can effectively manage and teach at this level. You should answer this question by sharing specific successes that demonstrate that you are a decisive and competent teacher.

- *Hobbies and travels.* The committee wants to know more about you as a person to ensure that you will be an interesting and energetic teacher to the students as well as a congenial member of the faculty.

- *Extracurricular interests and experiences.* The committee wants to know about all the ways in which you might be helpful in the school and to know that you will promote the interests and cocurricular activities of students and the school community. Be sure to include any relevant coaching experience or interests.

- *Classroom management techniques.* You must convince the committee that you can effectively manage a classroom of diverse learners in a manner that will help the students to develop their self-esteem.

- *Knowledge of the curriculum standards and the subject taught at the grade for which you are being considered.* The committee needs to be reasonably certain that you have command of the subject and its place within the developmental stages of students at this level. This is where you should show your knowledge of national standards and of state and local curriculum documents.

- *Commitment to embracing diversity.* The committee needs to know that you will value your students' cultural heritages and validate their life experiences. They want to hear about how you are actively working on your journey to cultural competence. You need to share that you hold high expectations for *all* students and that you will be employing differentiated instruction to help your students be successful and reach their academic, emotional, and social potential.

- *Knowledge of assessment strategies relevant for use in teaching at this level.* This is your place to shine with your professional knowledge about using rubrics and performance assessment.

- *Commitment to teaching at this level.* The committee wants to be assured that you are knowledgeable about and committed to teaching and learning at this level as opposed to just seeking this job until something better comes along.

- *Your ability to reflect on experience and to grow from that reflection.* Demonstrate that you are a reflective decision maker and a lifelong learner. If you are asked about your weaknesses, you have an opportunity to show that you can effectively reflect and self-assess, that you can think reflectively and critically, and that you know the value of learning from your own errors and how to do so. Be prepared for this question by identifying a specific error that you have made, perhaps while student-teaching, and explain how you turned that error into a profitable learning experience.

Throughout the interview you should maintain eye contact with the interviewer, demonstrating interest, enthusiasm, and self-confidence. It is very important that you research the school, district, and position and prepare questions for your interviewer(s). When an opportunity arises, ask one or two planned questions that demonstrate your knowledge of and interest in the position and the community and school or district.

When the interview has obviously been brought to a close by the interviewer, that is your signal to leave. Do not hang around, which is a sign of lacking confidence. Follow the interview with a thank-you letter addressed to the personnel director or interviewer; even if you do not get the job, you will be better remembered for future reference.[7]

Once you are employed as a teacher, your professional development continues. The sections that follow demonstrate ways in which that can happen.

What to Expect at Your First Teaching Job

It is an unfortunate reality that many teachers leave the education profession in their first few years of teaching. It is estimated that over 1,000 teachers nationwide leave their teaching positions each school day. Teacher attrition is costly on many levels. Local districts and states invest a lot to recruit and train their teachers in an effort to keep experienced instructors in their classrooms working with their students. Since student achievement is being closely tied to teacher quality in our current education debates, it is of the utmost importance for schools to be able to retain high-quality teachers.

Numerous research studies have been conducted to determine the relationship between the quality of teacher induction programs and beginning-teacher job satisfaction. Consequently, many school districts strive to support new teachers in becoming the very best educators that they can be. Growing evidence suggests that new teachers are more likely to remain in the teaching profession and continue to develop deeper pedagogical content knowledge and stronger abilities to implement standards-based instruction if they participate in comprehensive induction programs.

Once you are hired, you will need to do a lot of investigation; you will watch, you will listen, and you will ask lots of questions of your colleagues. In addition to your informal information gathering, you will most likely be asked to participate in a formal orientation. Most school districts have induction programs in place for new teachers and incoming veteran teachers to introduce you to the school culture and to support you through your first years of teaching. You most likely will be expected to participate in an induction program. The goal of most comprehensive teacher induction programs is to provide meaningful learning experiences for new teachers that will improve achievement for *all* students, promote the school district's goals and expectations, and increase the professional competencies of participants. You will also most likely be assigned a mentor. Mentors are usually veteran teachers. You will meet with your mentor regularly to discuss a structured list of things such as school rules, classroom management, teaching strategies, and professional development. Providing a collaborative support system is paramount if we expect new teachers to be able to walk into the classroom the first day with confidence and to make the job more effective, less anxiety producing, and more rewarding.

In induction programs, new teachers are introduced to the district's rules and policies. You most likely will tour the school, meet your mentor, and go through a simulated day. You will also learn about the school's services and record keeping. As a new hire, you will also be asked to review and sign a memorandum of understanding that serves as your master contract. You will also be provided with a copy of the faculty handbook.

Most middle and secondary schools have detailed **faculty handbooks** that will help to acquaint you with the practices, policies, and procedures of your school and district that you are expected to know and abide by. It is important to familiarize yourself with them so that you can act appropriately. Be sure to read your faculty handbook thoroughly and

---

Reflections of a First-Year Teacher Abroad

Many teachers would categorize their first year of teaching as daunting, frustrating, and somewhat overwhelming but in a way that experience will help shape them into the amazing educators they aspire to become. I decided that if I were going to endure this trial, I wanted to place myself in an environment that was just as unique of an experience as teaching was going to be. I am a Montanan and received my B. A. in English and my secondary teaching certification from Montana State University, Bozeman. Coming from a small rural town, I jumped at every chance to travel in the United States since traveling has always been an educational experience for me.

Leafing through eerily similar job announcements across the U.S. presented me with the idea of broadening my horizons elsewhere or, more simply, "going abroad." This commitment to expand my teaching experience would find me in a small city in the center of Thailand. After getting through the initial hardships and shock of transitioning into a new culture, I began to come to terms with the task of teaching in a foreign country. I was hired as an English lecturer at a government university called Rajabhat University in Nakhon Sawan, Thailand. This university caters to students from rural areas and schools. The students had the curious and innocent nature of secondary students back home. I fell in love with them immediately. As a secondary teacher by training, I felt I hadn't stepped too far out of the high school environment. I was given a broad range of English courses to teach varying from listening and speaking to English writing to drama. These classes were designed to strengthen the Thai students' ability to communicate in English.

Working in a developing country presents obstacles commonplace in most classrooms in addition to other unique challenges. Conflicts with administration, overcrowding, and time restraints make the task of teaching all the more taxing. The standard classrooms in Thailand I experienced consist of desks and a chalkboard (chalk included!). Subject-specific curriculum and materials are limited. Technology is sparse and usually occupied. In fact, Thailand lacks many of the amenities that my university professors taught me to utilize in the classroom. But the absence of these elements began to benefit me in many ways. It has greatly diversified my lesson planning, instructional approach, and supplementary activities. Classes are held for three hours at a time, doubling the need for motivation. This has driven me to create more stimulating and engaging lessons. In my school setting, teachers are often asked to come up with lessons and activities on the spot, which has considerably strengthened my

preparation and sharpened my wit. Moving from a high school language-arts curriculum to an English-as-a-foreign-language context presented a challenging switch as well. Being presented with these obstacles has helped me to expand my methods.

The most rewarding and vexing part of the job is the Thai students themselves. You won't meet a friendlier, more lighthearted group anywhere else in the world. But, at the same time, they can be somewhat lackadaisical and inattentive as students. In my opinion, the Thai students lack some of the academic drive and competitive spirit that is commonplace in the West. In this regard, my Thai students have been very beneficial to my professional development. Their educational outlook has forced me to meticulously dissect my lessons, creating the simplest possible steps and tasks ensuring that the students understand and are engaged with the lesson. Like little supervillains, they are effective at finding the tiniest loopholes in my exercises foiling my plans over and over again. They have compelled me to create stronger and more student-centered activities that stimulate their interest and provide active student participation.

The Thais' desire to learn the English language has summoned teachers from all over the English-speaking world. I have had the privilege to meet classroom teachers and other educators from across the globe who have shared their educational perspectives and mentored me as a first-year teacher. Chinese students and teachers are also a common sight at the university, and befriending them has added to my multicultural experience. The collaboration with these teachers brings energy for new ideas to a profession where teachers can often feel isolated. Their guidance has shown me the need for support and encouragement in this profession.

My Thai teaching experience has opened a refreshing doorway giving me the opportunity to discover new and exciting teaching methods as well as providing me with the opportunity to examine the traditional concepts of Western education. I have gained the ability to adapt and respond to different ideologies and teaching situations. The hurdles I have faced here have prepared me for the teaching profession with a positive attitude and the confidence to teach anywhere. Experiencing this new culture has encouraged me to stay and teach in Thailand another year. I hope to continue exploring Asia and teach in Singapore and China in the future. Understanding and working with different cultures has been the most beneficial aspect of my development as a teacher.

SOURCE: Contributed by Kris Wootan Rajabhat University, Nakhon Sawan, Thailand. Used with Permission.

---

refer to it often. A well-put-together faculty handbook will help prepare you to be successful at your new job.

Faculty handbooks often start with the school's mission and/or vision statements. They may also include the words to the alma mater, a description of the school colors, and pictures of the school mascot. They might also include a building schematic labeling the location of all the classrooms, facilities, and common areas in the school with room assignments, important phone numbers, and other contact information. Beyond this basic information, faculty handbooks vary tremendously in content, layout and design, and function. Activity 12.2 provides you with the opportunity to examine a variety of faculty handbooks to identify common features.

In addition to addressing guidelines for staff development and participation in an induction program, your faculty handbook may include some or all of the following: contact information, workday logistical information, day-to-day operations, safety, schedules, other duties, instruction, classroom management, deciphering data, equipment and supplies, professional development, student evaluation, employee policies, and staff conduct.

The following is meant not to serve as an exhaustive list but rather to highlight some of the information you are likely to have included in your faculty handbook. Supporting student well-being and promoting student achievement are top priorities. Student evaluation, the standard letter-grading system, grade books, progress reports, honor roll, and

Activity
12.2
Faculty Handbooks

There are a plethora of faculty handbooks available on the Internet. Peruse a middle school and high school sample faculty handbook from the list below and then search for additional examples on the Internet. Then answer the questions that appear at the end of this activity.

Nauset Regional High School, North Eastham, MA
http://www.nausetschools.org/nrhs/faculty_handbook.pdf

Sparkman High School, Harvest, AL
http://www.madison.k12.al.us/shs/Teachers/Faculty%20Handbook%202007-2008%5B3%5D.pdf

Southside High School, Greenville, SC
http://www.greenville.k12.sc.us/Southside/SHS_Teachers_HB_01-02.pdf

Jonesboro-HodgeMiddle School, Jonesboro, LA
http://www.jpsb.us/JHMSteacherhandbook.pdf

Plantation Middle School, Plantation, FL
http://www.broward.k12.fl.us/plantationmiddle/Faculty/Teacher%20Handbook%202007-08%20rev8-15-07.pdf

C. J. Hooker Middle School, Goshen, NY
http://www.gcsny.org/District/StaffDevelopment/0910/FacultyHndbk0910.pdf

Apply Your Knowledge

Compare and contrast the information you find in faculty handbooks from a variety of middle and secondary schools and then answer the following questions.

1. Who are the authors of the handbook?
2. Who is the intended audience? Was this handbook created to be used by faculty, staff, students, administrators, or parents?
3. What information do you think was most important?
4. What information do you think a teacher would reference often?
5. What can you tell about the school context from what they include or leave out of their handbook?

---

awards are often included, as are detailed procedures on how to report child abuse, alcohol and drug abuse, and sexual harassment. Guidelines for how best to establish open lines of communication with parents, including parent conferences, parent participation, and parent volunteering, are also usually available in your faculty handbook.

Your faculty handbook may include a layout of the school's master schedule, important/necessary forms, a schedule of faculty and team meetings, a list of special education and Section 504 meetings, state and local standards, an introduction to the software packages used for taking attendance and grading, classroom management tips and strategies to use in the classroom, and committee assignments. There may be an explanation of what duties other staff at the school perform, including paraprofessionals, the counselor, media personnel, the school nurse, library/media personnel, and cafeteria and custodial services.

Under the section on safety in your faculty handbook, you might find information on safety and first aid, fire drill procedures, emergency lockdown procedures, and crisis response codes. Logistics may include obtaining keys, how to work the security system, ID badges, parking, mailboxes, telephone usage, visitors, snow days, and early dismissal and delayed start. In the section on day-to-day operations, the following may be included: attendance policy, hall passes, tardies, referrals, truancy, suspension, patriotism/Pledge of Allegiance, announcements, assemblies, and lockers. A chart of duties, including a detailed duty schedule outlining expected coverage in common areas, at the area where the buses load and unload, hall duty, cafeteria duty, and so on, may be included. Detailed instructions on equipment usage, copy machines, supplies and materials, purchases, and requisitions may also be available in your faculty handbook.

Some faculty handbooks include overall schoolwide guidelines all students are expected to abide by; for instance, no hats/hoods are to be worn inside during school hours, no personal electronics (including cell phones, iPods, and personal games) are to be used in classes, no gum chewing, and so on.

Often handbooks include detailed sections covering your responsibilities and duties as an employee. Substituting for other teachers, dress code, annual leave, sick leave, personal leave and substitute procedures, your evaluation cycle, the appeal process and details on the employee evaluation process, a pay scale chart, and a description of teacher salaries and benefits may also be included. Professional ethics, staff conduct, use of the Internet, and electronic communications are also usually addressed.

As you can see, starting your new job will be an exciting adventure. Your professional journey will consist of ongoing learning. Know that other professionals will be there to guide you.

Professional Development through Reflection and Self-Assessment

Beginning now and continuing throughout your career, you will reflect on your teaching, and you will want to continue to grow as a professional as a result of those reflections (growth is not so likely unless self-initiated and systematically planned). The most competent professional is one who is proactive, that is, who takes charge and initiates his or her own continuing professional development. One useful way of continuing to reflect, self-assess, and grow professionally is by maintaining a *professional journal*, much as your students do when they maintain journals reflecting on what they are learning. Another is by continuing to maintain the professional career portfolio that you began assembling early in your pre-service program and finalized for your job search (as discussed earlier in this chapter). Some teachers maintain *professional logbooks*, which serve not only as documentation of their specific professional contributions and activities but also as documentation of the breadth of their professional involvement. Some teachers maintain research logs as a way of recording questions that come up during the busy teaching day and as a way of establishing a plan for finding answers. The *research log* strategy can be of tremendous benefit to you in actively researching and improving your classroom work, but also it can be of interest to colleagues. Finally, working in teams and sharing your work with team members is still another way of continuing to reflect, self-assess, and grow as a teacher. Check out the available online resources for new teachers highlighted in Activity 12.3 and read about the support you can have from colleagues by participating in **learning communities** by reading Activity 12.4.

Professional Development through Mentoring

Mentoring, one teacher facilitating the learning of another teacher, can aid in professional development.[8] In what is sometimes called *peer coaching*, a mentor teacher volunteers, is selected by the teacher who wishes to improve, or is selected by a school administrator, formally or informally. The mentor observes and coaches the teacher to help him or her improve in teaching. Sometimes the teacher being coached simply wants to learn a new skill. In other instances, the teacher remains with the mentor teacher for an entire school year, developing and improving old and new skills or learning how to teach with a new program. In many districts, teachers are automatically assigned to mentor new teachers for their first and, sometimes, second year in an induction program.

Professional Development through In-Service and Advanced Study

In-service workshops and programs are offered for teachers by the school, by the district, and by other agencies, such as a county office of education or a nearby college or university. In-service workshops and programs are usually designed for specific purposes, such as to train teachers in new teaching skills, to update their knowledge in content, and to introduce them to new teaching materials or programs. For example, Baltimore City Public Schools (MD) provides a systemwide professional development program for teachers of grades 6 through 8, administrators, and staff at its Lombard Learning Academy Demonstration Center. The Lombard Learning Academy is a school within a school located at Lombard Middle School. Cohorts of 5 to 10 teachers from other schools in the district visit the academy for five-day periods to observe instruction, practice strategies, and hone their skills in the use of technology.

University graduate study is yet another way of continuing your professional development. Some teachers pursue master's degrees in academic teaching fields; many pursue master's degrees in curriculum and methods of instruction or in educational administration or counseling. Some universities offer a master of arts in teaching, a program of courses in specific academic fields that are especially designed for teachers.

Activity 12.3 **Resources for New Teachers**

New teachers often feel overwhelmed. On the Educator's Reference Desks, Jeff Zachwieja, reference and electronic services librarian at Marygrove College Library, has compiled and maintains an extensive list of useful websites for new teachers on a variety of topics related to teacher induction, mentoring, leadership, and retention.

Apply Your Knowledge

Check out some of the websites and the descriptions of their contents listed here; then go to **http://www.eduref.org/cgi-bin/print.cgi/Resources/Teaching/Beginning_Teachers.html** to explore other resources.

Internet sites as they appear on Jeff Zachwieja's website:

Survival Guide for New Teachers
Presents advice from award-winning first-year teachers on how to work with veteran teachers, parents, principals, and teacher educators.
http://www.ed.gov/teachers/become/about/survivalguide/index.html

What to Expect Your First Year of Teaching (September 1998)
Based on discussions among winners of the 1996 First Class

Teacher Awards, this document contains advice for new teachers, those who educate teachers, and others who are interested. Questions asked of the participants included the following: What was it like the first year? What were your toughest challenges, your greatest rewards? Did you get the right preparation? Do you have any insights you could offer new teachers?
http://www.ed.gov/pubs/FirstYear

USC Clearinghouse of Resources for Beginning Teacher Support and Assessment
A collection of online resources for new teachers and those involved with supporting them.
http://www.usc.edu/dept/education/CMMR/CMMR_BTSA_home.html

New Teachers OnLine
An excellent resource for new teachers and their mentors and supporters from the Teachers Network.
http://teachersnetwork.org/ntol

Activity 12.4   Learning Communities

Learning communities have been in existence for decades in higher education. Recently, the learning community concept has been implemented in many middle and secondary schools where reform efforts have promoted smaller groups of students. Larger schools are being restructured to personalize the learning experience. Freshman academies, "schools-within-a-school," and student advisories group students by grade, career interests, or theme. Benefits for students and faculty alike have been reported. Learning communities boast an increase in academic achievement, student involvement, and motivation as well as a higher retention rate. Students who participate in learning communities are often empowered and more intellectually mature. Faculty members who participate in these learning communities have the opportunity to share their instructional strategies, collaborate with colleagues across disciplines, and develop their mentoring skills.

Apply Your Knowledge

Peruse the following websites to learn about learning communities.

NSDC (National Staff Development Council) Learning Communities

**http://www.learningforward.org/standards/
learningcommunities.cfm**

SEDL (Southwest Educational Development Laboratory) Professional Learning Communities: What Are They and Why Are They Important?
http://www.sedl.org/change/issues/issues61.html

New Small High Schools and Small Learning Communities
http://www.bobpearlman.org/BestPractices/
    NewSmallSchools.htm

National Middle School Association: Small Schools and Small Learning Communities
http://www.nmsa.org/AboutNMSA/PositionStatements/
    SmallSchools/tabid/293/Default.aspx

Organizing Schools into Small Learning Communities
http://www.nassp.org/portals/0/content/48670.pdf

1. What are the benefits students and faculty identified for participating in learning communities?
2. What learning communities did your middle and/or secondary school have?
3. What could you contribute to a learning community?

Teaching Scenario   Online Professional Development

Steve grew up in Chicago and attended Illinois State University, where he enrolled in courses in the College of Education. Steve always wanted to teach and assumed that he would take a job as an English teacher in a large inner-city public high school when he graduated. As fate would have it, during his junior year, Steve met Cassie, an elementary education major, while he was pursuing his dream. Cassie was from Libby, a small town in the northwestern corner of Montana. She was hoping to return to Montana after graduation and teach in a rural one-room schoolhouse.

Neither Steve nor Cassie ended up where they thought they would, but both agreed that they were happy with how their job search worked out. When they finished their studies, the couple attended a teaching fair and accepted teaching positions in Homer, AK. Moving out of the lower 48 and leaving family, friends, and classmates behind was difficult, but the couple was up for the adventure. It took some adjusting, but both came to appreciate the quiet and loved life in their small Alaskan town. Steve taught language arts at Homer High School, and Cassie was a third-grade teacher at Voznesenka Elementary. They loved their jobs, and both became very involved in their community. They knew all their students and their families quite well.

Although they loved to hike, to explore, to crab, and to take photographs, they sometimes missed the days when they were able to hop the train downtown to attend the various lectures, special events, and myriad performances on their campus and in downtown Chicago. Most important, they missed the opportunity to attend lectures and workshops focusing on teaching and learning.

Discovering the plethora of webinars, virtual symposiums, workshops, audio courses, podcasts, digitally delivered programs, and so forth that are available for educators made all

the difference for these novice teachers. Both Steve and Cassie were able to continue their professional development by participating in a variety of online activities. It helped them to grow professionally and to feel connected to other classroom teachers worldwide.

Apply Your Knowledge

No matter where you end up living and teaching, it is important to remember that the world is interconnected and that through the wonders of technology you can participate in online learning. If you are interested in knowing what webinars, virtual symposiums, workshops, audio courses, podcasts, and digitally delivered programs are available for teachers, peruse the websites listed below.

National Teachers Enhancement Network
http://www.scienceteacher.org

Heritage Online
http://www.hol.edu

PBS Teacher Line
http://teacherline.pbs.org/teacherline

PAEC-Learning Workshops
http://www.paec.org/teacher2teacher

ASCD: For the Success of Every Learner
**http://www.ascd.org/portal/site/ascd/
    menuitem.3e48d6b1bb1a4846111d0a10e3108a0c**

National Staff Development Council
http://www.nsdc.org

Today's Middle Level Educator
http://www.nmsa.org/Publications

<table><tr><td>Teaching Scenario</td><td>**Science Horizons Initiative**</td></tr></table>

Faculty at institutes of higher education often host professional development workshops, conferences, and meetings for K–12 classroom teachers. A few years ago, Dr. C. W. (Bill) McLaughlin fulfilled one of his dreams and established the Science Horizons Initiative at Montana State University, Bozeman (MSU), to support the professional development of middle and high school science teachers working in schools on or near American Indian reservations across Montana. He created the Science Horizons Initiative to provide classroom teachers with the opportunity to improve their teaching skills, collaborate with university faculty and teaching peers, design an innovative project to introduce a scientific concept to their middle and secondary school students, integrate Montana's Indian Education for All mandate in their curriculum, and gain support for the implementation of innovative science lessons.

McLaughlin explained his reasoning behind the name of the project this way: "The horizon appears as a boundary, or limit, to some. To others the horizon offers a calling to seek the challenges found there, then to see what lies beyond. This initiative is designed for those individuals that see horizons in science education and have the initiative and creativity to strive toward that horizon; then go beyond that to develop other 'horizons of opportunity.'"

His promotional materials question, "Do you see a horizon in your science teaching environment? Do you have a creative plan to expand that horizon into interesting challenges for your students? The Science Horizons Initiative seeks to support the horizon-expanding science curriculum ideas for selected individuals involved in middle and/or high school teaching on reservations and/or in schools with significant American Indian student populations."

To apply for the opportunity to participate in this professional development endeavor, teachers are asked to follow a simple four-step application process that requires them to provide a brief professional biography, write an outline or narrative that describes their proposal for improving science learning in their current teaching position, obtain a letter of support from their direct administrative supervisor indicating approval and ensuring that the proposal will have support in the district, and include a letter from a teaching colleague who can describe their teaching style.

In the summer, the Science Horizon Initiative has funded the expenses (travel, meals, and accommodations) for the participants to come to MSU's campus for five exciting packed days of planning, interacting, sharing, and developing individual science education improvement proposals. Participants even have the option to register for one to two hours of graduate credit at MSU. The Initiative has also provided the participants with an unrestricted Horizon Grant up to $500 for related supplies to implement their plan. Additionally, each participant has received a $250 personal stipend for his or her participation.

The intense, weeklong schedule ends with formal presentations of the projects. Under the guidance of McLaughlin, the participants created innovative lessons that will most definitely engage their students. The diverse, impressive collection of topics addressed include Fire on the Land, Using Flip Cameras in High School Physics, Human Organ Systems, Gel Electrophoresis, Developing Science Observation Skills, Martin Tap Water Toxicity, Hydrogen and Oxygen and Their OH Properties, and Engineering an Economical and Ecological Outdoor Classrooms. You can check out the participants' presentations at **http://www.sciencehorizonsinitiative.com/prev/prev.html**.

McLaughlin has taught chemistry for 42 years. In addition to serving as the director of the Science Horizons Initiative for improving science education for Native Americans, he is currently an adjunct professor at Montana State University in the Department of Chemistry and Biochemistry. In 2009, he received the MSU President's Award for Outstanding Teaching. He is the coauthor of the *Physical Science* textbook with Glencoe/McGraw-Hill and author of the teacher ancillary materials for Prentice Hall's *Analytical Chemistry* textbook. Annually, he presents science curriculum workshops and outreach activities for students.

Professional Development through Participation in Professional Organizations

There are many professional organizations: local, statewide, national, and international. The organizations are usually discipline specific, such as the National Council of Teachers of English, the International Reading Association, the National Council of Teachers of Mathematics, the National Council for the Social Studies, and the National Science Teachers Association. In most states, there is a statewide organization, probably affiliated with a national organization. In addition, there are the National Education Association, the Association of American Educators, and the **American Federation of Teachers.**

Local, district, state, and national organizations have meetings that include guest speakers, workshops, and publishers' displays. Professional meetings of teachers are educational, enriching, and fulfilling for those who attend. In addition, many other professional associations, such as those for reading teachers, supply speakers and publish articles in their journals that are often of interest to teachers other than the target audience.

Professional organizations publish newsletters and journals for their members, and these will likely be found in your college or university library. Sample periodicals are listed in Figure 10.1 in Chapter 10. Many professional organizations have special membership prices for teachers who are still college or university students, a courtesy that allows for an inexpensive beginning affiliation with a professional association. For information on special membership prices and association services, contact those of interest to you. See listings in Chapter 10. Also, check out what becoming National Board Certified entails by doing Activity 12.5.

Activity 12.5 — National Board Certification

The National Board for Professional Teaching Standards (NBPTS) was created in 1987 after *A Nation Prepared: Teachers for the 21st Century* was released. Since then, more than 55,000 teachers have achieved the coveted distinction of National Board Certification. The NBPTS describes the knowledge, skills, and dispositions of accomplished teachers and awards certificates in 24 subject areas and developmental levels.

The NBPTS philosophy is described in five key propositions:

1. Teachers are committed to students and learning.
2. Teachers know the subjects they teach and how to teach those subjects to students.
3. Teachers are responsible for managing and monitoring student learning.
4. Teachers think systematically about their practice and learn from experience.
5. Teachers are members of learning communities.

To be eligible, potential candidates have to have a bachelor's degree, hold a valid teaching license, and teach for a minimum of three years in an early childhood, elementary, middle, or secondary school(s). Teachers are expected to prepare a portfolio that includes the following evidence: a classroom-based entry with student work, two video recordings of student classroom interactions, and documentation of accomplishments outside the classroom that affect student learning, along with a narrative explanation describing, analyzing, and reflecting on its importance.

Seeking National Board Certification can be a costly endeavor; however, many school districts encourage their teachers to pursue certification and cover the costs associated with the process.

Apply Your Knowledge

If you are interested in learning more about National Board Certification, check out the following website: **http://www.nbpts.org**.

Professional Development through Communications with Other Teachers

Visiting teachers at other schools; attending in-service workshops, graduate seminars, and programs; participating in teacher study groups[9] and meetings of professional organizations; participating in teacher networks;[10] and sharing with teachers by means of electronic bulletin boards are all valuable experiences, if for no other reason than talking and sharing with teachers not only across this country but around the world. These discussions include sharing not only "war stories" but also ideas and descriptions of new programs, books, materials, and techniques that work.

Teachers need to practice and model their communication skills both in and out of the classroom. This includes communicating with other teachers to improve one's own repertoire of strategies and knowledge about teaching as well as sharing one's experiences with others. Teaching other teachers about your own special skills and sharing your experiences are important components of the communication and professional development processes.

Professional Development through Summer and Off-Teaching Work Experience

In many areas of the U.S., there are special programs of short-term employment available to interested teachers. These are available especially although not exclusively to teachers of physical education, mathematics, science, and social studies and are offered by public agencies, private industry, foundations, and research institutes. These institutions are interested in disseminating information and providing opportunities for teachers to update their skills and knowledge, with an ultimate hope that the teachers will stimulate in more students a desire to develop their physical fitness, to understand civic responsibilities, and to consider careers in science and technology. Participating industries, foundations, governments, and institutes provide on-the-job training with salaries or stipends to teachers who are selected to participate. During the program of employment and depending on the nature of that work, a variety of people (e.g., scientists, technicians, politicians, businesspersons, social workers, and sometimes university educators) meet with teachers to share experiences and discuss what is being learned and its implications for teaching and curriculum development.

Some of the programs for teachers are government sponsored, field centered, and content specific. For example, a program may concentrate on geology, anthropology, mathematics, or reading. At another location, a program may concentrate on teaching, using a specific new or experimental curriculum. These programs, located around the country, may have university affiliation, which means that university credit may be available. Room and board, travel, and a stipend are sometimes granted to participating teachers.

Sources of information about the availability of programs include publications and Web pages of professional organizations, the local chamber of commerce, and meetings of the local or regional teacher's organization. In areas where there are no organized programs of part-time work experience for teachers, some teachers have successfully initiated their own by establishing contact with management personnel of local businesses or companies.

Teaching Scenario　STUDY CANADA Summer Institute for K–12 Educators

"This program has connected me to places, people and geography in a way that could never be taught in a textbook. The professional connections are priceless. I understand our neighbor and partner to the north in ways I never imagined."

I know the expression "three times is a charm" is the adage, but I can assure you that the STUDY CANADA Summer Institute for K–12 Educators is an exception to the rule. Participating in the program the first time served as a great introduction to teaching about our northern neighbor and being able to participate two summers in a row was pure delight. Having a chance to attend a third time would be extraordinary!

If you cover Canada in your curriculum [and we can all better integrate information about Canada into our respective content areas], I highly recommend participating in the STUDY CANADA Summer Institute for K–12 Educators offered by Western Washington University. This program has provided American educators with a strong foundation for teaching about Canada for the past 33 years and is a perfect professional development opportunity for middle and high school educators.

I have participated in numerous intensive professional development programs throughout my career but none can compare to the STUDY CANADA Summer Institutes I attended in 2010, "Experience B.C. from the 5 Themes of Geography to the 2010 Olympics," and in 2011 (which relocated from British Columbia to Ontario and Québec), "A Capital View of Canada: Nations within a Nation."

My Canadian adventures all started back in the fall of 2009 when I attended my local regional social studies conference, hosted by the Colorado Council for Social Studies. I discovered a new session being offered on how to teach about Canada. Why did the Canada session catch my eye? Well, I teach sixth-grade geography and the Western Hemisphere, and Canada is included in my curriculum.

During the session, I met Karen Palmarini, a representative of the Consulate General of Canada in Denver who was highlighting how important it is for students and teachers in the United States to learn more about Canada. She distributed posters, books, and other literature about Canada to each attendee. In the materials she gave us, I saw a pamphlet on the STUDY CANADA program and resources offered by "K–12 STUDY CANADA," the outreach arm of a U.S. Department of Education National Resource Center on Canada at Western Washington University and the University of Washington. I perused **http://www.k12studycanada.org**, read about the program, and made a bold decision. I would apply for the grant they were offering to help attendees participate in the six-day summer course. Receiving enough financial support to cover the program's costs allowed me to attend the best professional development workshop I had ever experienced.

This opportunity benefited me both professionally and personally. When I arrived in British Columbia, I met Tina Storer and Don Alper, who coordinate and direct this program. They introduced us to professors and community leaders in Vancouver and Whistler and guided our learning about Canada's diverse peoples and regions. In fact, I learned a great deal about how a city hosts the Olympics and the significance this event has to the locals. I learned that Canada is our biggest trading partner, not China. I returned home with a better understanding of the similarities and differences between our countries. I received a wealth of resources to take back into my classroom and felt a new connection to our neighbors to the north. How did I use these resources? In

November, I received a resource trunk from Western Washington University filled with videos, books, software, activities, and stuff for my bulletin boards to use for two weeks with my students. The loan kit was wonderful and one of several that can be booked online. So, in a way, my students participated in STUDY CANADA as well.

I quickly decided to attend STUDY CANADA the following year as well since the program was moving to a new location in Ottawa and Montreal and would offer a new focus on multiculturalism as well as its core social studies topics (geography, history, government, etc.) and new enrichment activities. I didn't think it was possible to top the experience in B.C., but to my amazement, the second year was even better. I knew more about Canada than I had a year earlier, and with confidence I could focus on the particulars I wanted to bring back and introduce in my classroom. I was surprised by how deeply I felt about seeing a few others I had met the year before. This year, I made even more connections including educators who worked at higher levels of education and can help change social studies at the state level as well as a state geography bee coordinator. I had the opportunity to learn from the U.S. ambassador to Canada, a member of Parliament, a separatist former premier of Quebec, and outstanding professors, among others. I even met Pierre Faucher, the owner of *Sucrerie de la Montagne*, and learned about harvesting maple syrup and Québécois folklore among other traditions. It was a special treat since I had been showing a video to students in my classes for the past four years on northern Canada that featured Pierre.

What I have learned in these summer institutes has been priceless; it has broadened my world and provided me with opportunities to network with teaching peers around Colorado and across the United States; share resources and lesson ideas; meet and connect with local experts, educators, and politicians; experience cultural traditions firsthand; reenergize my spirit and delight in what I do; learn about current events; enrich my curriculum; and present at professional conferences. The close connections I made with the STUDY CANADA organizers and K–12 STUDY CANADA outreach staff are ongoing. Unlike other one-shot deals, I know this is an everlasting friendship, as continuous as the 4,500-mile border that connects us.

SOURCE: *Anastasia Sunday, sixth-grade geography teacher, Estes Park Middle School, Estes Park, CO. Used with permission.*

It's hard to select lessons to highlight because there are so many excellent choices, but here are a few you can start with:

http://www.k12studycanada.org/files/SCSI_2007/Lesson _Plans/J_Spano-Comparing_Foundations_of_Democracy.pdf
(Comparing Foundations of Democracy, grades 11–12)

http://www.k12studycanada.org/files/lesson_plans/Canada _General/CanadaGeneralLibraryInternetResearchProject.pdf
(Internet Research Project, grade 10, adaptable for middle/high school)

http://www.k12studycanada.org/files/lesson_plans/ Canada_US_Relations_Current_Affairs/Intro_to_Canada _US_Borders.pdf
(Do You Have Anything to Declare? An Introduction to the Canada-US Border, grades 6–12)

http://www.k12studycanada.org/files/lesson_plans/History/ SCSI2003_Irisjones.pdf

(Canada: Terminus of the Underground Railway, grades 9–12)
http://www.k12studycanada.org/files/lesson_plans/2010SCSI
    _CarjuzaaJ_CriticallyAnalyzingReviewing
    PictureBooksAboriginalCanada_Gr11_12.pdf

(Critically Examining, Analyzing and Evaluating Picture Books on Aboriginal Canada, adaptable for grades 11–12)

    To peruse the impressive collection of curricula provided by K–12 STUDY CANADA outreach, go to

http://www.k12studycanada.org/resources_teacher
    _resources.html

There you'll find all kinds of materials for teaching, not only teacher-developed lesson plans created

as part of the summer institute but also loan kits, PowerPoint presentations, and so on.

SOURCE: Kudos and special thanks to Tina Storer, education and curriculum specialist at the Center for Canadian-American Studies; Dr. Don Alper, director of Canadian-American studies and the Border Policy Research Institute; and Dr. Paul Storer, professor and chair of the Department of Economics, all at Western Washington University; to Nadine Fabbi, associate director, Canadian Studies Center, Henry M. Jackson School of International Studies, University of Washington; and to all others who annually contribute to this outstanding program of study. See Figure 12.2 for more details on the STUDY CANADA Summer Institute for K–12 Educators.

Professional Development through Micro Peer-Teaching

Micro peer-teaching (MPT) is a skill development strategy used for professional development by both pre-service and in-service teachers. MPT is a scaled-down teaching experience involving the following:

- A limited objective
- A brief interval for teaching a lesson
- A lesson taught to a few (8 to 10) peers (as your students)
- A lesson that focuses on the use of one or several instructional strategies

MPT can be a predictor of later teaching effectiveness in a regular classroom. More important, it can provide an opportunity to develop and improve specific teaching behaviors. A videotaped MPT allows you to see yourself in action for self-evaluation and diagnosis. Evaluation of an MPT session is based on the following:

- The quality of the teacher's preparation and lesson implementation
- The quality of the planned and implemented student involvement
- Whether the instructional objective(s) was reached
- The appropriateness of the cognitive level of the lesson

Whether a pre-service or in-service teacher, you are urged to participate in one or more MPT experiences. Formatted differently from previous exercises in this book, Exercise 12.2 can represent a summative performance assessment for the course for which this book is being used.

Points to Ponder

1. Do you believe that teachers' salaries should be tied to student achievement?

2. In 1998, young teachers (ages 22 to 28) earned an average of nearly $8,000 less per year than did other college-educated people of the same age cohort. Further, for teachers in the age range of 44 to 50, the gap was three times greater than for their counterparts in other occupations. Worse yet, teachers of that age range (44 to 50) who had master's degrees earned an average of more than $32,000 less than did their nonteacher counterparts with master's degrees.[11]

3. If offered by a district or requested by your school principal, would you accept a job teaching a subject that is out of your field of training?

4. Would you be willing to have your surgical operation performed by an unlicensed surgeon? Would you be willing to be defended in trial by an unlicensed attorney? Would you be willing to insure your automobile with an unlicensed insurance agent? Would you be willing to leave your child each day in the care of an unlicensed teacher?

5. Some teachers become disenchanted working in a profession where they see no opportunity to improve their salary through merit. They argue that in most other careers there is at least the option of requesting a raise and that if you perform well you can get a bonus or promotion. That just isn't the case in teaching.

Figure 12.2   The STUDY CANADA Summer Institute for K–12 Educators

The Center for Canadian-American Studies at Western Washington University
Annually presents:

The STUDY CANADA Summer Institute for K-12 Educators
A CAPITAL VIEW OF CANADA: NATIONS WITHIN A NATION
(5 nights at the Westin Ottawa with a daytrip to Montréal QC)

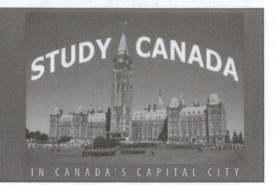

What did 2011 participants think about "STUDY CANADA"?

"This was the best teacher workshop ever! The mixture of in-class lectures to hands-on learning and tours was amazing...true engagement learning. History came alive this week for me."   - M.S. Thornton (Orangeburg, SC)

Information about the STUDY CANADA Summer Institute [Also visit www.k12studycanada.org/scsi.html]

"STUDY CANADA" (C/AM 410) is a 3 university quarter credit or 40 clock hour professional development course that provides teachers with an excellent foundation for teaching about their northern neighbor. Teachers from across the country attend this renowned program to develop a better understanding of Canada, gain global perspectives of civic issues, and receive numerous resources for curriculum development. The course includes core topics such as geography, history and economics and goes beyond the classroom to include a series of unique learning experiences that simply are not available through regular tourism.

* Earn 3 university quarter credits (C/AM 410 - WWU) *or* 40 clock hours as you learn about Canada, its capital, and the distinct cultures that have formed the second largest nation in the world — all within comfortable and unique classroom settings and sessions offered by university faculty, government officials and tribal leaders.

* Banish stereotypes and meet real Canadians while exploring Ottawa and Montréal, two of Canada's most historically important cities.

* Witness parliamentary democracy with special sessions in the Parliament Buildings and learn about the importance of Canada-US relations at the US Embassy. Canada's history will come alive with customized tours of Ottawa, Old Montréal and the Canadian Museum of Civilization.

* Develop a lesson plan on Canada that meets NCSS/state standards, gain tools to create a PowerPoint presentation on Canada suitable for your students/colleagues and perhaps even become a K-12 STUDY CANADA Teacher Associate with NRC support in offering presentations about Canada in your region.

* Receive multiple classroom materials at a Resource Fair to improve curriculum connections to Canada for your students.

* Scholarships and Travel Award opportunities are available to eligible participants (more details offered online).

Registration Information [Contact tina.storer@wwu.edu or call 360-650-7370 with program inquiries.]

Registration: Forms available online at www.k12studycanada.org/scsi.html. Registration opens November 1 and closes May 1 annually (unless the 20 person maximum is reached earlier). The program's location/thematic beyond 2014 is subject to change.
Registration Cost: Expected to be $600 [NB: Full payment due with registration. This includes course fees, hotel lodging, most activity fees and RT Ottawa-Montréal transportation. Travel to Ottawa (or other future location) is **not** included.]
Accommodations: Hotel rooms [www.thewestinottawa.com] have 2 double beds shared by 2 same-gendered participants.
Supplemental Fees: If a private room is preferred, a $400 supplemental fee is required. If a non-registered companion joins you, a supplemental fee of $450 is required for shared accommodation and RT Ottawa-Montréal transportation.

Download registration forms/other information posted online:

* SCSI Handout (PDF)
* Registration Form
* SCSI Draft Agenda
* SCSI Detailed Info
* SCSI Funding Rationale
* Scholarship & Travel Award Information

Primary Sponsors: The Pacific Northwest National Resource Center for Canada (Western Washington University and the University of Washington) with funding from the US Department of Education (Title VI Grant) and the Embassy of Canada (Outreach Grant).

Additional support is provided by the Department of Foreign Affairs and International Trade Canada, the U.S. Embassy in Ottawa, the U.S. Consulate General in Montréal, the Government of Québec, *l'Observatoire sur les États-Unis de la Chaire Raoul-Dandurand* (Université du Québec à Montreal), and the Canada-America Society of Washington (Seattle, WA).

SOURCE: Center for Canadian-American Studies at Western Washington University. Used with Permission.

Summary

Because teaching and learning go hand-in-hand and the effectiveness of one affects that of the other, the final two chapters of this book have dealt with both aspects of the "how well" component of teacher preparation—how well the students are learning and how well the teacher is teaching. In addition, you have been presented with guidelines about how to obtain your first teaching job and how to continue your professional development. Although you have not been told everything you will ever need to know about the assessment of teaching and learning, about other aspects of public middle school and secondary school teaching, about finding a job, or about continuing your professional development, we have addressed the essentials. Throughout your teaching career, you will continue improving your knowledge and skills in all aspects of teaching and learning.

We began this book by providing input data about schools and teaching and then proceeded to guide you through additional ways to collect and share data as well as ways to process those data into your own plans for teaching. Now you are ready for the highest application of your knowledge and skills—a full-time teaching position where you are paid for teaching.

You have arrived at the end of this text. We thank you for allowing us to be a part of your journey to become a competent, culturally sensitive, inspirational teacher. We hope your quest has been and will continue to be enjoyable and profitable, and we wish you the very best in your new career. Teaching is a profession to be proud of. We welcome you to it.

Exercise 12.1   Development of My Professional Portfolio

Instructions: The purpose of this exercise is to guide you in the creation of a professional portfolio that will be shared with persons who are considering your application for employment as a credentialed teacher. Because it would be impractical to send a complete portfolio with every application you submit, it is suggested that you have a minimum portfolio (portfolio B) that could be sent with each application in addition to a complete portfolio (portfolio A) that you could make available on request or that you would take with you to an interview. However it is done, the actual contents of the portfolio will vary depending on the specific job being sought; you will continually add to and delete materials from your portfolio. Suggested categories and subcategories of items to include in your portfolio, listed in the order that they may be best presented in portfolios A and B, are as follows.

1. Table of contents of portfolio (not too lengthy)—portfolio A only.

2. Your professional résumé—both portfolios.

3. Evidence of your language and communication skills (evidence of your use of English and of other languages, including American Sign Language)— portfolio A. (Also state this information briefly in your letter of application. See the résumé section.)
   a. Your teaching philosophy.
   b. Other evidence to support this category.

4. Evidence of teaching skills—portfolio A.
   a. For planning skills, include instructional objectives, a syllabus, and a unit plan. (See Exercises 5.5, 6.2, and 7.3.)
   b. For teaching skills, include a sample lesson plan and a video of your actual teaching.
   c. For assessment skills, include a sample personal assessment and samples of student assessment.

5. Letters of recommendation and other documentation to support your teaching skills—both portfolios.

6. Other (e.g., personal interests related to the position for which you are applying)—portfolio A.

Exercise 12.2   Pulling It All Together—Micro Peer-Teaching—MPT IV

Instructions: The purpose of this exercise is to learn how to further develop your own micro peer-teaching (MPT) experiences. You will prepare and teach a lesson that is prepared as a lesson presentation for your peers, at their level of intellectual maturity and understanding (i.e., as opposed to teaching the lesson to peers pretending that they are public school students). Forms A, B, and C appear on pages 349–350.

This experience has two components:

1. Your preparation and implementation of a demonstration lesson

2. Your completion of an analysis of the summative peer assessment and the self-assessment, with statements of how you would change the lesson and your teaching of it were you to repeat the lesson

You should prepare and carry out a 15- to 20-minute lesson to a group of peers. The exact time limit for the lesson should be set by your group, based on the size of the group and the amount of time available. When the time limit has been set, complete the time-allowed entry (item 1) on Form A of this exercise. Some of your peers will serve as your students; others will be evaluating your teaching. (The process works best when "students" do not evaluate while being students.) Your teaching should be videotaped for self-evaluation.

Exercise 12.2 **Pulling It All Together—Micro Peer-Teaching—MPT IV** Continued
_____

For your lesson, identify one concept and develop your lesson to teach toward an understanding of that concept. Within the time allowed, your lesson should include both teacher talk and a hands-on activity for the students. Use Form A for the initial planning of your lesson. Then complete a lesson plan, selecting a lesson plan format as discussed in Chapter 7. Present the lesson to the "students." The peers who are evaluating your presentation should use Form B of this exercise.

After your presentation, collect your peer evaluations (the Form B copies that you gave to the evaluators). Then review your presentation by viewing the videotape. After viewing the tape, prepare the following:

- A tabulation and statistical analysis of peer evaluations of your lesson
- A self-evaluation based on your analysis of the peer evaluations, your feelings having taught the lesson, and your thoughts after viewing the videotape
- A summary analysis that includes your selection and description of your teaching strengths and weaknesses as indicated by this peer-teaching experience and how you would improve were you to repeat the lesson

Tabulation of Peer Evaluations

The procedure for tabulating the completed evaluations received from your peers is as follows:

1. *Use a blank copy of Form B for tabulating.* In the left margin of that copy, place the letters *N* (number) and σ (total) to prepare for two columns of numbers that will fall below each of those letters. In the far right margin, place the word *Score*.
2. *For each item (a through y) on the peer evaluation form, count the number of evaluators who gave a rating (from 1 to 5) on the item.* Sometimes an evaluator may not rate a particular item, so although there may have been 10 peers evaluating your MPT, the number of evaluators giving you a rating on any one particular item could be less than 10. For each item, the number of evaluators rating that item we call *N*. Place this number in the *N* column at the far left margin on your blank copy of Form B, next to the relevant item.
3. *Using a calculator, obtain the sum of the peer ratings for each item.* For example, for item a, *lesson preparation evident*, you add the numbers given by each evaluator for that item. If there were 10 evaluators who gave you a number rating on that item, then your sum on that item will not be more than 50 (5 × 10). Because individual evaluators will make their *X* marks differently, you sometimes must estimate an individual evaluator's number rating—that is, rather than a clear rating of 3 or 3.5 on an item, you may have to estimate it as a 3.2 or a 3.9. In the left-hand margin of your blank copy of Form B, in the σ column, place the sum for each item.
4. *Now obtain a score for each item, a through y.* The score for each item is obtained by dividing σ by *N*. Your score for each item will range between 1 and 5. Write this result in the column in the right-hand margin under the word *Score* parallel to the relevant item. This is the number you will use in the analysis phase.

Procedure for Analyzing the Tabulations

Having completed the tabulation of the peer evaluations of your teaching, you are ready to proceed with your analysis of those tabulations.

1. To proceed, you need a blank copy of Form C of this exercise, your self-analysis form.
2. On the blank copy of Form C, there are five items: Implementation, Personal, Voice, Materials, and Strategies.
3. In the far left margin of Form C, place the letter σ for the sum. To its right, and parallel with it, place the word *Average*. You now have arranged for two columns of five numbers each—a σ column and an *Average* column.
4. For each of the five items, get the total score for that item, as follows:
   a. *Implementation.* Add all scores (from the right-hand margin of blank Form B) for the four items a, c, x, and y. The total should be 20 or less (4 × 5). Place this total in the left-hand margin under σ (to the left of *1. Implementation*).
   b. *Personal.* Add all scores (from the right-hand margin of blank Form B) for the nine items f, g, m, n, o, p, q, s, and t. The total should be 45 or less (9 × 5). Place this total in the left-hand margin under σ (to the left of *2. Personal*).
   c. *Voice.* Add all scores (from the right-hand margin of blank Form B) for the three items h, i, and j. The total should be 15 or less (3 × 5). Place this total in the left-hand margin under σ (to the left of *3. Voice*).
   d. *Materials.* Add all scores (from the right-hand margin of blank Form B) for item k. The total should be 5 or less (1 × 5). Place this total in the left-hand margin under σ (to the left of *4. Materials*).
   e. *Strategies.* Add all scores (from the right-hand margin of blank Form B) for the eight items b, d, e, l, r, u, v, and w. The total should be 40 or less (8 × 5). Place this total in the left-hand margin under σ (to the left of *5. Strategies*).
5. Now, for each of the five categories, divide the sum by the number of items in the category to get your peer evaluation average score for that category. For item 1, you will divide by 4; for item 2, by 9; for item 3, by 3; for item 4, by 1; and for item 5, by 8. For each category, you should then have a final average peer evaluation score of between 1 and 5. If correctly done, you now have average scores for each of the five categories: Implementation, Personal, Voice, Materials, and Strategies. With those scores and evaluators' comments, you can prepare your final summary analysis.

The following table includes three sample analyses of MPT lessons based *only* on the scores—that is, without reference to comments made by individual evaluators, although peer evaluators' comments are important considerations for actual analyses.

Sample Analyses of MPTs Based Only on Peer Evaluation Scores

Teacher	Category/Rating 1	2	3	4	5	Possible Strengths and Weaknesses
A	4.2	2.5	2.8	4.5	4.5	Good lesson, weakened by personal items and voice
B	4.5	4.6	5.0	5.0	5.0	Excellent teaching, perhaps needing a stronger start
C	2.5	3.0	3.5	1.0	1.5	Poor strategy choice, lack of student involvement

Exercise 12.2A — Form A

MPT Preparation

Form A is to be used for initial preparation of your MPT lesson. (For preparation of your lesson, study Form B.) After completing Form A, proceed with the preparation of your MPT lesson using a lesson plan format as discussed in Chapter 7. A copy of the final lesson plan should be presented to the evaluators at the start of your MPT presentation.

1. Time allowed:

2. Title or topic of lesson I will teach:

3. Concept:

4. Specific instructional objectives for the lesson:
Cognitive
Affective
Psychomotor

5. Strategies to be used, including approximate time plan:
Set introduction
Transitions
Closure
Others

6. Student experiences to be provided (i.e., specify for each—visual, verbal, kinesthetic, and tactile experiences):

7. Materials, equipment, and resources needed:

Exercise 12.2B — Form B

Peer Evaluation

Evaluators use Form B, making an *X* on the continuum between 5 and 1. Far left (5) is the highest rating; far right (1) is the lowest. Completed forms are collected and given to the teacher on completion of that teacher's MPT and are reviewed by the teacher prior to reviewing his or her videotaped lesson.

To evaluators: Comments as well as marks are useful to the teacher.

To teacher: Give one copy of your lesson plan to the evaluators at the start of your MPT. (*Note:* It is best if evaluators can be together at a table at the rear of the room.)

Teacher _____   Date _____

Topic _____

Concept _____

1. Organization of lesson

		5	4		3	2		1
a.	Lesson preparation evident	very		somewhat		no		
b.	Lesson beginning effective	yes		somewhat		poor		
c.	Subject matter knowledge apparent	yes		somewhat		no		
d.	Strategies selection effective	yes		somewhat		poor		
e.	Closure effective	yes		somewhat		poor		

Comments

continued

Exercise 12.2B **Form B** Continued

2. Lesson implementation

		5	4		3	2		1
f.	Eye contact	effective		okay			poor	
g.	Enthusiasm evident	yes		somewhat			no	
h.	Speech delivery	articulate		minor problems			poor	
i.	Voice inflection; cueing	effective		minor problems			poor	
j.	Vocabulary use	well chosen		minor problems			poor	
k.	Aids, props, and materials	effective		okay			none	
l.	Use of examples and analogies	effective		needs improvement			none	
m.	Student involvement	effective		okay			none	
n.	Use of overlapping skills	good		okay			poor	
o.	Nonverbal communication	effective		a bit confusing			distracting	
p.	Use of active listening	effective		okay			poor	
q.	Responses to students	personal and accepting		passive or indifferent			impersonal and antagonistic	
r.	Use of questions	effective		okay			poor	
s.	Use of student names	effective		okay			no	
t.	Use of humor	effective		okay			poor	
u.	Directions and refocusing	succinct		a bit vague			confusing	
v.	Teacher mobility	effective		okay			none	
w.	Use of transitions	smooth		a bit rough			unclear	
x.	Presentation motivating	very		somewhat			not at all	
y.	Momentum (pacing) of lesson	smooth and brisk		okay			too slow or too fast	

Comments

Exercise
12.2C   **Form C**

Teacher's Summative Peer Evaluation
See instructions within Exercise 12.2 for completing this form.

	5	4	3	2	1
1. Implementation (items a, c, x, y)	5	4	3	2	1
2. Personal (items f, g, m, n, o, p, q, s, t)	5	4	3	2	1
3. Voice (items h, i, j)	5	4	3	2	1
4. Materials (item k)	5	4	3	2	1
5. Strategies (items b, d, e, l, r, u, v, w)	5	4	3	2	1
Total =					_____

Comments

Chapter 12 POSTTEST

Short Explanation

1. During your student teaching, suppose you should try out a new teaching technique and it fails miserably for you. Describe what you should do.

2. Identify three danger signals that a cooperating teacher needs to be alert for to try to prevent a student teacher from getting into serious teaching trouble.

3. Identify and explain three ways that you can prepare yourself to be successful in your job-seeking endeavors and get hired as a classroom teacher.

4. Explain what the benefits are to joining a professional organization in your teaching field.

5. Identify five ways you plan to continue to grow professionally.

Essay

1. Explain why you agree or disagree that classroom observations and theory courses in education should precede the student-teaching experience in teacher preparation.

2. Identify and define the categories by which teacher effectiveness is determined.

3. From your current observations and fieldwork related to your teacher preparation program, clearly identify one specific example of educational practice that seems contradictory to exemplary practice or theory presented in this chapter. Present your explanation for the discrepancy.

4. Describe any prior concepts you held that changed as a result of the experiences of this chapter. Describe the changes.

5. Explain why teaching is considered to be a profession. Explain when, if ever, it is not a profession.

End Notes

Chapter 1

1 Excerpted from C. Rogers, *On Becoming a Person* (Cambridge, MA: Riverside Press, 1961).

2 See W. J. Urban and J. L. Wagoner Jr., *American Education: A History*, 2nd ed. (Boston: McGraw-Hill, 2000).

3 See K. D. Moore, *Middle and Secondary School Instructional Methods*, 2nd ed. (Boston: McGraw-Hill College, 1999).

4 See J. H. Spring, *The American School, 1642–2000*, 5th ed. (Boston: McGraw-Hill, 2001).

5 See M. P. Sadker and D. M. Sadker, *Teachers, Schools and Society*, 7th ed. (Boston: McGraw-Hill, 2005).

6 Ibid., chap. 8.

7 See Moore, *Middle and Secondary School Instructional Methods*.

8 See Sadker and Sadker, *Teachers, Schools and Society*.

9 T. M. Smith, G. T. Rogers, N. Alsalam, M. Perie, R. P. Mahoney, and V. Martin, *The Condition of Education 1994* (Washington, DC: U.S. Department of Education, Office of Educational Research and Improvement, National Center for Education Statistics, 1994).

10 J. H. Lounsbury, Perspectives on the Middle School Movement, in *Transforming Middle Level Education: Perspectives and Possibilities*, ed. J. L. Irvin (Needham Heights, MA: Allyn & Bacon, 1992), 295–313.

11 Ibid.

12 See Spring, *The American School, 1642–2000*.

13 H. Mizell, Guiding Questions for Middle School Reform (remarks made at a meeting convened by the Los Angeles Unified School District by Hayes Mizell, director of the Program for Student Achievement at the Edna McConnell Clark Foundation, January 16, 2003).

14 Moore, *Middle and Secondary School Instructional Methods*.

15 D. G. Armstrong and T. Savage, *Teaching in the Secondary Schools*, 4th ed. (Upper Saddle River, NJ: Merrill, 1998).

16 S. Ansell, *Achievement Gap*, Education Week on the Web: American Education's Online Newspaper of Record, http://edweek.org/context/topics/issuepage.cfm?id = 61 (July 16, 2004).

17 E. W. Eisner, Questionable Assumptions about Schooling, *Phi Delta Kappan* 8, no. 9 (2003): 648–57.

18 P. A. Noguera, Beyond Size: The Challenge of High School Reform, *Educational Leadership* 59, no. 5 (2002): 60–64.

19 Mizell, Guiding Questions for Middle School Reform.

20 A. C. Lewis, High Schools and Reform, *Phi Delta Kappan* 85, no. 8 (2004): 563–64.

21 K. Brooks and F. Edwards, *The Middle School in Transition: A Research Report on the Status of the Middle School Movement* (Lexington: College of Education, University of Kentucky, 1978). See also, for example, the story of Oregon City High School in C. Paglin and J. Fager, *Grade Configuration: Who Goes Where?* (Portland, OR: Northwest Regional Educational Laboratory, 1997), 29–31, and visit the West Orange High School (Orlando, Florida) Ninth Grade Center at http://www.scott.k12.hy.us/9th/8thhistory.html.

22 G. Arriaza, Making Changes That Stay Made: School Reform and Community Involvement, *High School Journal* 87, no. 4 (2004): 10–35. See, for example, M. McCord, Bursting at the Seams: Financing and Planning for Rising Enrollments, *School Business Affairs* 63, no. 6 (June 1997): 20–23; B. P. Venable, A School for All Seasons, *Executive Educator* 18, no. 7 (July 1996): 24–27; C. C. Kneese, Review of Research on Student Learning in Year-Round Education, *Journal of Research and Development in Education* 29, no. 2 (Winter 1996): 60–72; and N. R. Brekke, *Year-Round Education: Does It Cost More?* (Madison, WI: Consortium for Policy Research in Education, 1997).

23 M. Barrett, The Case for More School Days, *Atlantic Monthly* 266, no. 5 (November 1990): 78–106, http://www.theatlantic.com/politics/education/barr2f.htm.

24 W. D. Gee, The Copernican Plan and Year-Round Education: Two Ideas That Work Together, *Phi Delta Kappan* 78, no. 10 (June 1997): 795.

25 See, for example, P. L. Kubow, K. L. Wahlstrom, and A. E. Bemis, Starting Time and School Life: Reflections from Educators and Students, *Phi Delta Kappan* 80, no. 5 (January 1999): 344–47, and K. L. Wahlstrom, The Prickly Politics of School Starting Times, *Phi Delta Kappan* 80, no. 5 (January 1999): 366–71.

26 The phrases "students of their students" and "turn on learning" are borrowed from C. A. Grant and C. E. Sleeter, *Turning on Learning* (Upper Saddle River, NJ: Prentice Hall, 1989), 2.

27 See, for example, L. Kohn, Quest High School's Mission and the "Fully Functioning Person," in *Perceiving, Behaving, Becoming: Lessons Learned*, by H. J. Freiberg (Alexandria, VA: Association for Supervision and Curriculum Development, 1999), 64–67, and D. K. Schnitzer and M. J. Caprio, Academy Rewards, *Educational Leadership* 57, no. 1 (September 1999): 46–48. Celebration School is a professional development school, founded as a collaboration among the Osceola County School District, Stetson University, and the Walt Disney Company. See the school's website at http://www.cs.osceola.k12.fl.us.; more about professional development schools can be found in Holmes Group, *Tomorrow's Schools: Principles for the Design of Professional Development Schools* (East Lansing, MI: Holmes Group, 1990), and R. E. Ishler and K. M. Edens, eds., *Professional Development Schools: What Are They? What Are the Issues and Challenges? How Are They Funded? How Should They Be Evaluated?* (Kingston, RI: Association of Colleges and Schools of Education in State Universities and Land Grant Colleges, 1995).

28 See, for example, A. C. Howe and J. Bell, Factors Associated with Successful Implementation of Interdisciplinary Curriculum Units, *Research in Middle Level Education Quarterly* 21, no. 2 (Winter 1998): 39–52, and N. Flowers et al., The Impact of Teaming: Five Research-Based Outcomes, *Middle School Journal* 31, no. 2 (November 1999): 57–60.

29 See, for example, D. Barnett et al., A School Without a Principal, *Educational Leadership* 55, no. 7 (April 1998): 48–49.

30 See, for example, B. R. Cobb, S. Abate, and D. Baker, Effects on Students of a 4 × 4 Junior High School Block Scheduling Program, *Education Policy Analysis Archives* 7, no. 3 (1999).

31 See, for example, M. D. DiRocco, How an Alternating-Day Schedule Empowers Teachers, *Educational Leadership* 56, no. 4 (December 1998/January 1999): 82–84.

32 See, for example, T. L. Shortt and Y. V. Thayer, Block Scheduling Can Enhance School Climate, *Educational Leadership* 56, no. 4 (December 1998/January 1999): 76–81; W. J. Ullrich and J. T. Yeamen, Using a Modified Block Schedule to Create a Positive Learning Environment, *Middle School Journal* 31, no. 1 (September 1999): 14–20; S. Black, Learning on the Block, *American School Board Journal* 185, no. 1 (January 1998): 32–34; and Most Commonly Asked Questions About Block Scheduling, on the website of the National Association of Secondary School Principals, http://nassp.org/services/blockfaq.htm (June 8, 1998).

33 See, for example, S. L. Kramer, What We Know About Block Scheduling and Its Effects on Math Instruction, Part II, *NASSP (National Association of Secondary School Principals) Bulletin* 81, no. 587 (March 1997): 69–82.

34 D. T. Conley, Restructuring: In Search of a Definition, *Principal* 72, no. 3 (January 1993): 12–16.

35 Advanced placement courses are available online. For further information, contact APEX Online Learning, 110 110th Ave. NE, Suite 210, Bellevue, WA 98004; phone: 800-453-1454; email: inquiries@apexlearning.com.

36 Southern Regional Education Board, *Outstanding Practices* (Atlanta: Southern Regional Education Board, 1995), 3.

37 Southern Regional Education Board, *Outstanding Practices*, 9, 10.

38 Southern Regional Education Board, *Outstanding Practices* (Atlanta: Southern Regional Education Board, 1998), 20.

[39] P. I. Tiedt and I. M. Tiedt, *Multicultural Teaching: A Handbook of Activities, Information, and Resources*, 5th ed. (Boston: Allyn & Bacon, 1999), 35.

[40] R. J. Rossi and S. C. Stringfield, What We Must Do for Students Placed at Risk, *Phi Delta Kappan* 77, no. 1 (September 1995): 73–76.

[41] See, for example, T. L. Williams, *The Directory of Programs for Students at Risk* (New York: Eye on Education, 1999). Visit the home page of the National Institute on the Education of At-Risk Students at http://www.ed.gov/offices/OERI.

[42] J. A. Brown and C. A. Moffett, *The Hero's Journey: How Educators Can Transform Schools and Improve Learning* (Alexandria, VA: Association for Supervision and Curriculum Development, 1999), 24.

[43] A. L. Costa, *The School as a Home for the Mind* (Palatine, IL: Skylight Publishing, 1991), 97–106.

[44] In R. A. Villa and J. S. Thousands, eds., *Creating an Inclusive School* (Alexandria, VA: Association for Supervision and Curriculum Development, 1995), 36.

[45] See, for example, P. Wasley, Teaching Worth Celebrating, *Educational Leadership* 56, no. 8 (May 1999): 8–13.

[46] See P. Sullivan, The PTA's National Standards, *Educational Leadership* 55, no. 8 (May 1998): 43–44. For a copy of the standards, contact the National PTA, 330 N. Wabash Ave., Chicago, IL 60611-3690, phone: 312-670-6782; fax: 312-670-6783.

[47] See, for example, the Hand in Hand Web page at http://www.handinhand.org.

[48] See, for example, T. Whiteford, Math for Moms and Dads, *Educational Leadership* 55, no. 8 (May 1998): 64–66.

[49] See, for example, C. Gustafson, Phone Home, *Educational Leadership* 56, no. 2 (October 1998): 31–32.

[50] See C. Bodinger-deUriarte et al., A Guide to Promising Practices, *Educational Partnerships*, ED392980 (Washington, DC: U.S. Government Printing Office, 1996); the articles in the May 1998 theme issue, Engaging Parents and the Community in School, of *Educational Leadership* 55, no. 8; and W. C. Hope, Service Learning: A Reform Initiative for Middle Level Curriculum, *Clearing House* 72, no. 4 (March/April 1999): 236–38.

[51] See, for example, K. Kesson and C. Oyler, Integrated Curriculum and Service Learning: Linking School-Based Knowledge and Social Action, *English Education* 31, no. 2 (January 1999): 135–49; L. Cummings and M. Winston, Service-Based Solutions, *Science Teacher* 65, no. 1 (January 1998): 39–41; J. P. Cloud, School Community Partnerships That Work, *Social Studies Review* 37, no. 2 (Spring/Summer 1998): 45–48; and J. Westheimer and J. Kahne, Service Learning Required: But What Exactly Do Students Learn?, *Education Week* 19, no. 20 (January 26, 2000): 32, 52.

[52] See, for example, G. I. Maeroff, ed., *Imaging Education: The Media and School in America* (New York: Teachers College Press, 1998).

[53] For copies of the INTASC document, contact CCSSO, 1 Massachusetts Ave. NW, Suite 700, Washington, DC 20001-1431; phone: 202-408-5505; http://www.ccsso.org.

[54] Access the standards at http://www.nbpts.org/nbpts/standards/mc-gen.html. You may want to compare the 11 standards of the NBPTS document with the 22 "components of professional practice" in C. Danielson, *Enhancing Professional Practice: A Framework for Teaching* (Alexandria, VA: Association for Supervision and Curriculum Development, 1996).

Chapter 2

[1] See R. Gibson, *Rethinking the Future: Rethinking Business Principles, Competition, Control and Complexity, Leadership, Markets and the World*, foreword by Alvin and Heidi Toffler. London: N. Brealey Publishers, 1997.

[2] See A. Toffler, *Future Shock*. New York: Random House, 1970, 271.

[3] U.S. Department of Education, National Center for Educational Statistics, *Language Minority Students*. Condition of Education, June 1, 2004. Washington, DC: U.S. Department of Education, http://nces.ed.gov/programs/coe (June 8, 2004).

[4] J. Richardson, "Quality Education" Is Our Moon Shot: An Interview with Secretary of Education, *Phi Delta Kappan* 91, no. 1 (2009): 25.

[5] D. G. Armstrong and T. Savage, *Teaching in the Secondary School*, 4th ed. (Upper Saddle River, NJ: Merrill, 1998).

[6] S. Ansell, *Achievement Gap*, Education Week on the Web: American Education's Online Newspaper of Record, http://www.edweek.org/context/topics/issuepage.cfm?id=61 (July 16, 2004).

[7] L. Olson, Report Points Out Lack of Clarity for High School Reforms, *Education Week* 23, no. 37 (May 19, 2004): 18.

[8] A. C. Lewis, High Schools and Reform, *Phi Delta Kappan* 85, no. 8 (2004): 563–64.

[9] C. Hendrie, High Schools Nationwide Paring Down, *Education Week* 23, no. 40 (2004): 1, 28–30.

[10] G. Arriaza, Making Changes That Stay Made: School Reform and Community Involvement, *High School Journal* 87, no. 4 (2004): 10–35.

[11] Hendrie, High Schools Nationwide Paring Down.

[12] H. Mizell, *Guiding Questions for Middle School Reform* (remarks made at a meeting convened by the Los Angeles Unified School District by Hayes Mizell, director of the Program for Student Achievement at the Edna McConnell Clark Foundation, January 16, 2003).

[13] G. A. Donaldson Jr., Working Smarter Together, *Educational Leadership* 51, no. 2 (October 1993): 12–16.

[14] Richardson, "Quality Education" Is Our Moon Shot, 24–29.

[15] See President Discusses Proposal for ESEA, March 15, 2010, http://www.ed.gov/blog/2010/03/president-discusses-proposal-for-esea June 12, 2011).

[16] See ibid.

[17] As quoted in A. Duncan, Making the Middle Grades Matter: Secretary Arne Duncan's Remarks at the National Forum's Annual Schools to Watch Conference, June 23, 2011, http://www.ed.gov/news/speeches/making-middle-grades-matter (June 27, 2011).

[18] Mizell, *Guiding Questions for Middle School Reform*.

[19] See Secondary School Reform at http://ssr.dadeschools.net.

[20] H. Voke, Student Engagement: Motivating Students to Learn, Infobrief 28 (Alexandria, VA: Association for Supervision and Curriculum Development, 2002).

[21] See W. Jassey, *Center for Japanese Study Abroad*, Fastback 386 (Bloomington, IN: Phi Delta Kappa Educational Foundation, 1995).

[22] L. A. Mulholland and L. A. Bierlein, *Understanding Charter Schools*, Fastback 383 (Bloomington, IN: Phi Delta Kappa Educational Foundation, 1995), 7. See also the theme issue, The Charter School Movement, in the March 1998 *Phi Delta Kappan* 79, no. 7, and the several articles about charter schools in the October 1998 issue of *Educational Leadership* 56, no. 2. Connect to the charter school home pages via the United States Charter School website at http://www.uscharterschools.org. For additional information and for a copy of the *National Charter School Directory*, contact the Center for Education Reform at 800-521-2118; see the website at http://edreform.com/research/css9697.htm.

[23] Some schools belong to the National Network of Partnership 2000 Schools. For information, contact the Center on School, Family, and Community Partnerships, Johns Hopkins University, 3506 N. Charles St., Baltimore, MD 21216; phone: 410-516-8807; fax: 410-516-8890. See also M. G. Sanders, Improving School, Family, and Community Partnerships in Urban Middle Schools, *Middle School Journal* 31, no. 2 (November 1999): 35–41, and W. Johnson et al., Texas Scholars, *Phi Delta Kappan* 79, no. 10 (June 1998): 781–83.

[24] See, for example, B. L. Brown, *Tech Prep: Is It Working? Myths and Realities* (Columbus, OH: ERIC Clearinghouse on Adult, Career, and Vocational Education, 1998).

[25] See, for example, H. Raham, Full-Service Schools, *School Business Affairs* 64, no. 6 (June 1998): 24–28; D. MacKenzie and V. Rogers, The Full Service School: A Management and Organizational Structure for 21st Century Schools, *Community Education Journal* 25, no. 3–4 (Spring/Summer 1997): 9–11; and J. G. Dryfoos, Full Service Schools: Revolution or Fad?, *Journal of Research on Adolescence* 5, no. 2 (1995): 147–72.

[26] IBO offers a Primary Years Program (for children ages 3 to 12), a Middle Years Program (for students ages 11 to 16), and a Diploma

Program for students in the final two years of high school. See IBO's website at http://www.ibo.org.

27 See B. Schnur, A Newcomer's High School, *Educational Leadership* 56, no. 7 April 1999): 50–52.

28 See, for example, Alternative Schools: Caring for Kids on the Edge, *Northwest Education* 3, no. 4 (Summer 1998).

29 See J. E. Rockoff, Stuck in the Middle: How and Why Middle Schools Harm Student Achievement, *Education Next*, http://educationnext.org/stuck-in-the-middle (June 20, 2011).

30 See National Forum to Accelerate Middle-Grades Reform, *Policy Statement on Grade Configuration*, issue 5 (July 2008), http://www.mgforum.org (May 13, 2010).

31 J. E. Rockoff and B. B. Lockwood, Stuck in the Middle: How and Why Middle Schools Harm Student Achievement, *Education Next* 10, no. 4 (2010): 68–75.

32 See W. J. Popham, Transform Toxic AYP into a Beneficial Tool, *Phi Delta Kappan* 90, no. 8 (2009): 577–681, and U.S. Department of Education, National Center for Education Statistics, *The Condition of Education 2011* (NCES 2011-033), 2011, http://nces.ed.gov/fastfacts/display.asp?id=30.

33 See D. R. Walling, Ed., *Hot Buttons: Unraveling 10 Controversial Issues in Education* (Bloomington, IN: Phi Delta Kappa International, 1997).

34 See Carnegie Group of New York, *Time to Act: An Agenda for Advancing Adolescent Literacy for College and Career Success*, 2010, http://carnegie.org/fileadmin/Media/Publications/PDF/tta_Main.pdf (May 14, 2010).

35 Ibid.

36 Alliance for Excellent Education, *The High Cost of High School Dropouts: What the Nation Pays for Inadequate High Schools* (Washington, DC: Alliance for Excellent Education, 2007).

37 W. S. Grigg, M. C. Daane, Y. Jin, and J. R. Campbell, *The Nation's Report Card: Reading 2002* (Washington, DC: National Center for Education Statistics, 2003).

38 E. B. Fleishman, Adolescent Literacy: A National Reading Crisis, Scholastic Professional Paper, http://teacher.scholastic.com/products/read180/pdfs/612_Profl_Paper_Fleishman.pdf (September 17, 2007).

39 P. Grant, From Struggle to Success: One High School's Journey to Literacy Achievement, *NCREL's Learning Point* 4 (2004): 18–20.

40 Alliance for Excellent Education, *The High Cost of High School Dropouts*.

41 See J. W. Tippeconnic III, and S. C. Faircloth, The Dropout/Graduation Crisis Among American Indian and Alaska Native Students, http://civilrightsproject.ucla.edu/research/k-12-education/school-dropouts/the-dropout-graduation-crisis-among-american-indian-and-alaska-native-students-failure-to-respond-places-the-future-of-native-peoples-at-risk (June 17, 2011).

42 Alliance for Excellent Education, *The High Cost of High School Dropouts*.

43 See E. Ellis, R. A. Gable, M. Gregg, and M. L. Rock, REACH: A Framework for Differentiating Classroom Instruction, *Preventing School Failure* 52, no. 2 (2008): 32.

44 S. D. Allan and C. A. Tomlinson, *Leadership for Differentiating Schools and Classrooms* (Alexandria, VA: Association for Supervision and Curriculum Development, 2000).

45 Ibid.

46 National Center on Response to Intervention, What Is RTI?, http://www.rti4success.org/whatisrti (June 25, 2011).

47 G. Batsche, J. Elliott, J. L. Graden, J. Grimes, J. F. Kovaleski, D. Prasse, D. J. Reschly, J. Schrag, and W. D. Tilly III, *Response to Intervention: Policy Considerations and Implementation* (Alexandria, VA: National Association of State Directors of Special Education, 2005).

48 See Response to Intervention: A Tiered Approach to Instructing All Students, http://www.youtube.com/watch?v=nkK1bT8ls0M.

49 See ibid.

50 See William N. Bender's publications on Response to Intervention, including *RTI in Middle and High Schools* (Bloomington, IN: Solution Tree, 2011).

51 G. Wiggins and J. McTighe, *Understanding by Design Professional Development Workbook* (Alexandria, VA: Association for Supervision and Curriculum Development, 2004).

52 See Partnership for 21st Century Skills, *21st Century Skills FAQ*, http://www.p21.org/index2.php?option+com_content&task=view&id=... (June 25, 2011).

53 E. Silva, Measuring Skills for 21st-Century Learning, *Phi Delta Kappan* 90, no. 9 (2009): 630–34.

54 Partnership for 21st Century Skills, Results That Matter: 21st Century Skills and High School Reform, 2006, http://www.p21.org//documents/RTM2006.pdf (June 25, 2011).

55 R. J. Warren and E. Grodsky, Exit Exams Harm Students Who Fail Them—and Don't Benefit Students Who Pass Them, *Phi Delta Kappan* 90, no. 9 (2009): 645–49.

56 N. Flowers and D. M. H. Carpenter, You Don't Have to Be a Statistician to Use Data: A Process for Data-Based Decision Making in Schools, *Phi Delta Kappan* 91, no.2 (2009): 64–67.

57 Ibid.

58 A. Furco and S. Root, Research Demonstrates the Value of Service Learning, *Phi Delta Kappan* 91, no. 5 (2010): 16–20.

59 S. Martin, M. Neal, J. Kielsmeier, and A. Crossley, The Impact of Service Learning on Transitions to Adulthood, in *Growing to Greatness: The State of Service Learning Project* (St. Paul, MN: National Youth Leadership Council, 2006), 4–24.

60 J. F. Zaff and R. M. Lerner, Research Demonstrates the Value of Service Learning, *Phi Delta Kappan* 91, no. 5 (2010): 21–23.

Chapter 3

1 Excerpt from *Our Boys*, in Maya Angelou, *Wouldn't Take Nothing for My Journey Now* (New York: Random House, 1993), 124.

2 C. Stevenson, *Teaching Ten to Fourteen Year Olds*, 3rd ed. (Boston: Allyn & Bacon, 2002).

3 Ibid., 77–78.

4 D. M. Gollnick and P. C. Chinn, *Multicultural Education in a Pluralistic Society* (Upper Saddle River, NJ: Merrill/Prentice Hall, 2002).

5 Ibid., 277.

6 Ibid.

7 See U.S. Department of Education, National Center for Education Statistics, Common Core of Data., 2009, *Public Elementary/Secondary School Universe Survey*, http://nces.ed.gov/programs/digest/d09/tables/dt09_042.asp.

8 See U.S. Department of Education, National Center for Education Statistics, 2010, *The Condition of Education 2010* (NCES 2010028), http://nces.ed.gov/pubs2010/2010028.pdf.

9 J. V. Diller and J. Moule, *Cultural Competence: A Primer for Educators* (Belmont, CA: Thompson Wadsworth, 2005), 2.

10 Gollnick and Chinn, *Multicultural Education in a Pluralistic Society*,5.

11 M. Levine, Celebrating Diverse Minds, *Educational Leadership*, October 2003, 14.

12 K. Koppelman and L. Goodhart, *Understanding Human Differences: Multicultural Education for a Diverse America* (Boston: Pearson Education, 2005).

13 Gollnick and Chinn, *Multicultural Education in a Pluralistic Society*, 5.

14 Levine, Celebrating Diverse Minds, 12–18.

15 M. H. Futrell, J. Gomez, and D. Bedden, Teaching the Children of a New America: The Challenge of Diversity, *Phi Delta Kappan* 84, no. 5 (2003): 283.

16 National Center for Education Statistics, *The Condition of Education 2003* (NCES 2003-067) (Washington, DC: U.S. Department of Education, Institute of Education Sciences, 2003), http://nces.ed.gov/pubs2003/2003067.pdf.

17 B. A. Starnes, Indian Education for All: Toward an Education Worthy of American Ideals, *Phi Delta Kappan* 88, no. 3 (2006): 184–92.

18 L. M. Cleary and T. D. Peacock, *Collected Wisdom: American Indian Education* (Needham Heights, MA: Allyn & Bacon, 1998).

[19] D. Juneau, Indian Education for All, *Montana's Agenda: Issues Shaping Our State* 3, no. 2 (2006): 1–4, http://www.umt.edu/urelations/Agenda/Fall2006.pdf.

[20] Montana Office of Public Instruction, Indian Education Division, http://opi.mt.gov/programs/indianed/IEFA.html.

[21] I. Zangwill, *The Melting-Pot: Drama in Four Acts* (New York: Macmillan, 1909).

[22] J. A. Banks and C. A. McGee Banks, eds., *Multicultural Education: Issues and Perspectives* (Boston: Allyn & Bacon, 1989), 1.

[23] U.S. Census Bureau, *National Population Projections*, August 18, 2004, http://www.census.gov/population/www/projections/natsum-T3.html.

[24] L. Baines, Future Schlock, *Phi Delta Kappan* 78, no. 7 (March 1997): 497.

[25] U.S. Census Bureau, *National Population Projections*, 2000, http://www.census.gov/population/www/projections/natsum-T3.html.

[26] T. L. Good and J. E. Brophy, *Looking in Classrooms*, 8th ed. (New York: Addison Wesley Longman, 2000), 127.

[27] P. Stone, How We Turned Around a Problem School, *Principal* 72, no. 2 (November 1992): 34–36. See also B. G. Barron et al., Effects of Time of Day Instruction on Reading Achievement of Below Grade Readers, *Reading Improvement* 31, no. 1 (Spring 1994): 59–60.

[28] R. Dunn, *Strategies for Educating Diverse Learners*, Fastback 384 (Bloomington, IN: Phi Delta Kappa Educational Foundation, 1995), 9.

[29] D. A. Kolb, *Experiential Learning: Experience as the Source of Learning and Development* (Upper Saddle River, NJ: Prentice Hall, 1984).

[30] C. G. Jung, *Psychological Types* (New York: Harcourt Brace, 1923).

[31] See B. McCarthy, A Tale of Four Learners: 4MAT's Learning Styles, *Educational Leadership* 54, no. 6 (March 1997): 47–51.

[32] See R. Karplus, *Science Curriculum Improvement Study* (Berkeley: University of California, 1974).

[33] See, for example, A. Colburn and M. P. Clough, Implementing the Learning Cycle, *Science Teacher* 64, no. 5 (May 1997): 30–33; E. A. Kral, Scientific Reasoning and Achievement in a High School English Course, *Skeptical Inquirer* 21, no. 3 (May/June 1997): 34–39; A. C. Rule, *Using the Learning Cycle to Teach Acronyms, a Language Arts Lesson* (East Lansing, MI: National Center for Research on Teacher Learning, 1995) (ERIC Documentation Reproduction Service No. ED383000); J. E. Sowell, Approach to Art History in the Classroom, *Art Education*, 46, no. 2 (March 1993): and M. M. Bevevino, J. Dengel, and K. Adams, Constructivist Theory in the Classroom: Internalizing Concepts Through Inquiry Learning, *Clearing House* 72, no. 5 (May/June 1999): 275–278.

[34] The three phases of the learning cycle are comparable to the three levels of thinking, described variously by others. For example, in E. Eisner's *The Educational Imagination* (New York: Macmillan, 1979), the levels are referred to as *descriptive, interpretive,* and *evaluative.*

[35] For information about 4MAT, contact Excel, Inc., 23385 W. Old Barrington Rd., Barrington, IL 60010; phone: 847-382-7272; or 6322 Fenworth Ct., Agoura Hills, CA 91301; phone: 818-879-7442; http://www.excelcorp.com/4mataboutlong.html.

[36] B. McCarthy, Using the 4MAT System to Bring Learning Styles to Schools, *Educational Leadership* 48, no. 2 (October 1990): 33.

[37] R. DeLay, Forming Knowledge: Constructivist Learning and Experiential Education, *Journal of Experiential Education* 19, no. 2 (August/September 1996): 76–81.

[38] For Gardner's distinction between learning style and intelligences, see H. Gardner, Multiple Intelligences: Myths and Messages, *International Schools Journal* 15, no. 2 (April 1996): 8–22, and the many articles in the "Teaching for Multiple Intelligences" theme issue of *Educational Leadership* 55, no. 1 (September 1997).

[39] For example, see G. Gallagher, Multiple Intelligences, *Middle Ground* 1, no. 2 (October 1997): 10–12.

[40] See, for example, R. J. Marzano, 20th Century Advances in Instruction, in *Education in a New Era*, ed. R. S. Brandt (Alexandria, VA: Association for Supervision and Curriculum Development, 2000), 76.

[41] See P. Guild, The Culture/Learning Style Connection, *Educational Leadership* 51, no. 8 (May 1994): 16–21.

[42] Dunn, *Strategies for Educating Diverse Learners*, 30.

[43] See, for example, M. L. Yell, The Legal Basis of Inclusion, *Educational Leadership* 56, no. 2 (October 1998): 70–73. For information about education law as related to special education students, see http://www.access.digex.net/ ~edlawinc.

[44] E. Tiegerman-Farber and C. Radziewicz, *Collaborative Decision Making: The Pathway to Inclusion* (Upper Saddle River, NJ: Merrill/Prentice Hall, 1998), 12–13.

[45] Such is the case, for example, for the K–12 Celebration School (Celebration, Florida). See http://www.cs.osceola.k12.fl.us.

[46] See L. Farlow, A Quartet of Success Stories: How to Make Inclusion Work, *Educational Leadership* 53, no. 5 (April 1996): 51–55, and other articles in the "Students with Special Needs" theme issue.

[47] See J. Cummins, *Bilingualism and Special Education: Issues in Assessment and Pedagogy* (San Diego: College-Hill Press, 1984), and P. Berman et al., *School Reform and Student Diversity, Volume II: Case Studies of Exemplary Practices for LEP Students* (Berkeley, CA: National Center for Research on Cultural Diversity and Second Language Learning, 1995).

[48] D. R. Walling, *English as a Second Language: 25 Questions and Answers*, Fastback 347 (Bloomington, IN: Phi Delta Kappa Educational Foundation, 1993), 12–13.

[49] Ibid., 26.

[50] See K. M. Johns and C. Espinoza, *Mainstreaming Language Minority Children in Reading and Writing*, Fastback 340 (Bloomington, IN: Phi Delta Kappa Educational Foundation, 1992).

[51] C. Minicucci et al., School Reform and Student Diversity, *Phi Delta Kappan* 77, no. 1 (September 1995): 77–80.

[52] See the discussion in G. Clark and E. Zimmerman, Nurturing the Arts in Programs for Gifted and Talented Students, *Phi Delta Kappan* 79, no. 10 (June 1998): 747–51.

[53] See, for example, J. F. Feldhusen, Programs for the Gifted Few or Talent Development for the Many?, *Phi Delta Kappan* 79, no. 10 (June 1998): 735–38.

[54] C. Dixon, L. Mains, and M. J. Reeves, *Gifted and at Risk*, Fastback 398 (Bloomington, IN: Phi Delta Kappa Educational Foundation, 1996), 7.

[55] S. B. Rimm, Underachievement Syndrome: A National Epidemic, in *Handbook of Gifted Education*, 2nd ed., ed. N. Colangelo and G. A. Davis (Needham Heights, MA: Allyn & Bacon, 1997), 416.

[56] S. Schwartz, *Strategies for Identifying the Talents of Diverse Students*, ERIC/CUE Digest, no. 122 (ED410323) (New York: ERIC Clearinghouse on Urban Education, May 1997).

[57] Adapted from Dixon et al., *Gifted and at Risk*, 9–12 (Copyright 1996 by Phi Delta Kappa Educational Foundation. Adapted with permission). See also K. Checkley, Serving Gifted Students in the Regular Classroom, *Curriculum Update* 5 (Winter 2000).

[58] See K. Burrett and T. Rusnak, *Integrated Character Education*, Fastback 351 (Bloomington, IN: Phi Delta Kappa Educational Foundation, 1993).

[59] Ibid., 15.

[60] See D. W. Johnson and R. T. Johnson, *Reducing School Violence Through Conflict Resolution* (Alexandria, VA: Association for Supervision and Curriculum Development, 1995).

[61] Ibid., chap. 11.

[62] See J. Van Til, Facing Inequality and the End of Work, *Educational Leadership* 54, no. 6 (March 1997): 78–81.

Chapter 4

[1] H. Ginott, *Teacher and Child: A Book for Parents and Teachers* (New York: Simon & Schuster, 1994), 15–16.

[2] See B. McEwan, *The Art of Classroom Management: Effective Practices for Building Equitable Learning Communities* (Upper Saddle River, NJ: Merrill/Prentice Hall, 2000).

[3] See V. Jones and L. Jones, *Comprehensive Classroom Management: Creating Communities of Support and Solving Problems*, 7th ed. (Boston: Pearson, 2004).

[4] L.C. Rose and A. C. Gallup, The Phi Delta Kappa/Gallup Poll of the Public's Attitudes Toward the Public Schools, *Phi Delta Kappan* 88, no. 1 (2006): 45.

[5] W. J. Bushaw and J. A. McNee, Americans Speak Out. Are Educators Listening? The 41st Phi Delta Kappa/Gallup Poll of the Public's Attitudes toward the Public Schools, *Phi Delta Kappan* 91, no. 1 (2009): 10; W. J. Bushaw and S. J. Lopez, A Time for Change. The 42nd Phi Delta Kappa/Gallup Poll of the Public's Attitudes toward the Public Schools, *Phi Delta Kappan* 92, no. 1 (2010): 12.

[6] J. L. T. Jones, *Positive Classroom Discipline: Instructor's Guide* (Santa Cruz, CA: Fredric H. Jones & Associates, 1994).

[7] See Jones and Jones, *Comprehensive Classroom Management*, chap. 1.

[8] See, for example, D. E. Matus, Humanism and Effective Urban Secondary Classroom Management, *Clearing House* 72, no. 5 (May/June 1999): 305–7.

[9] I. A. Hyman and J. D'Allessandro, Oversimplifying the Discipline Problem, *Education Week* 3, no. 29 (April 11, 1984): 24.

[10] See B. F. Skinner, *The Technology of Teaching* (New York: Appleton-Century-Crofts, 1968), and *Beyond Freedom and Dignity* (New York: Knopf, 1971).

[11] See L. Canter and M. Canter, *Assertive Discipline: Positive Behavior Management for Today's Schools*, rev. ed. (Santa Monica, CA: Lee Canter & Associates, 1992).

[12] See R. Dreikurs and P. Cassel, *Discipline Without Tears* (New York: Hawthorne Books, 1972), and R. Dreikurs, B. B. Grunwald, and F. C. Pepper, *Maintaining Sanity in the Classroom: Classroom Management Techniques*, 2nd ed. (New York: Harper & Row, 1982).

[13] L. Albert, *A Teacher's Guide to Cooperative Discipline: How to Manage Your Classroom and Promote Self-Esteem* (Circle Pines, MN: American Guidance Service, 1989; revised 1996).

[14] J. Nelsen, *Positive Discipline* 2nd ed.) (New York: Ballantine Books, 1987); J. Nelsen, L. Lott, and H. S. Glenn, *Positive Discipline in the Classroom: How to Effectively Use Class Meetings and Other Positive Discipline Strategies* (Rocklin, CA: Prima Publishing, 1993).

[15] See, for example, W. Glasser, A New Look at School Failure and School Success, *Phi Delta Kappan* 78, no. 8 (April 1997): 597–602.

[16] See H. G. Ginott, *Teacher and Child* (New York: Macmillan, 1971).

[17] T. Gordon, *Discipline That Works: Promoting Self-Discipline in Children* (New York: Penguin, 1989).

[18] F. Jones, *Positive Classroom Discipline* (New York: McGraw-Hill, 1987); F. Jones, *Positive Classroom Instruction* (New York: McGraw-Hill, 1987).

[19] J. S. Kounin, *Discipline and Group Management in Classrooms* (New York: Holt, Rinehart and Winston, 1977).

[20] For guidelines for holding class meetings, see B. M. Landau and P. Gathercoal, Creating Peaceful Classrooms: Judicious Discipline and Class Meetings, *Phi Delta Kappan* 81, no. 6 (February 2000): 450–52, 454.

[21] C. Jung, *The Development of Personality* (New York: Pantheon, 1964), 144.

[22] Jones, *Positive Classroom Discipline*, chap. 1.

[23] Ibid., chap. 8.

[24] E. T. Emmer, C. M., Evertson, B. S. Clements, and M. E. Worsham, *Classroom Management for Secondary Teachers*, 4th ed. (Boston: Allyn & Bacon, 1997).

[25] Ibid., chap. 4.

[26] See J. A. Queen et al., *Responsible Classroom Management for Teachers and Students* (Upper Saddle River, NJ: Merrill/Prentice Hall, 1997), especially standards and guidelines versus rules and replacing rules with standards, pp. 110 and 111–12, respectively.

[27] D. Harrington-Lueker, Emotional Intelligence, *High Strides* 9, no. 4 (March/April 1997): 1.

[28] See, for example, T. L. Good and J. E. Brophy, *Looking in Classrooms*, 8th ed. (New York: Addison-Wesley/Longman, 2000), 165.

[29] Jones, *Positive Classroom Discipline*, 87.

[30] D. W. Johnson and R. T. Johnson, *Reducing School Violence Through Conflict Resolution* (Alexandria, VA: Association for Supervision and Curriculum Development, 1995), 1.

[31] J. Cohen, The First "R": Reflective Capacities, *Educational Leadership* 57, no. 1 (September 1999): 70–75.

[32] See examples in Southern Regional Education Board, *1995 Outstanding Practices* (Atlanta: Southern Regional Education Board, 1995).

[33] See National Schools of Character Awards, January 30, 2000, http://www.character.org/schools/index.cgi?detail:schools.

[34] See the Education Reporter, Number 207, The Newspaper of Education Rights, April 2003, http://www.eagleforum.org/educate/2003/apr03/WI-High-School.shtml.

[35] S. G. Weinberger, *How to Start a Student Mentor Program*, Fastback 333 (Bloomington, IN: Phi Delta Kappa Educational Foundation, 1992), 8.

[36] See, for example, D. K. Schnitzer and M. J. Caprio, Academy Rewards, *Educational Leadership* 57, no. 1 (September 1999): 48.

[37] Edwards, *Classroom Discipline and Management*, 71–72.

[38] For further reading about the relation between impulse control and intelligence, see D. Goleman, *Emotional Intelligence: Why It Can Matter More Than IQ* (New York: Bantam Books, 1995), and Harrington-Lueker, Emotional Intelligence, 1, 4–5.

[39] D. T. Gordon, Rising to the Discipline Challenge, *Harvard Education Letter* 15, no. 5 (September/October 1999): 3.

Chapter 5

[1] Contact American Council on the Teaching of Foreign Languages, 6 Executive Plaza, Yonkers, NY 10701-6801.

[2] Contact National Geographic Society, PO Box 1640, Washington, DC 20013-1640.

[3] Contact the American Alliance for Health, Physical Education, Recreation and Dance, 1900 Association Dr., Reston, VA 22091.

[4] Bureau of Indian Affairs, 1849 C St. NW, Washington, DC 20240-0001; phone: 202-208-3710; http://www.doi.gov/bureau-indian-affairs.html.

[5] M. P. Sadker and D. M. Sadker, *Teachers, Schools, and Society*, 7th ed. (Boston: McGraw-Hill, 2005), 260–61.

[6] J. V. D. Diller and J. Moule, *Cultural Competence: A Primer for Educators* (Belmont, CA: Thomson Wadsworth, 2005), 165–66.

[7] At least 24 states use statewide textbook adoption committees to review books and then to provide local districts with lists of recommended titles from which to choose.

[8] L. Chavkin, Readability and Reading Ease Revisited: State-Adopted Science Textbooks, *Clearing House* 70, no. 3 (January–February 1997): 151–54.

[9] Source of K-W-L: D. M. Ogle, K-W-L: A Teaching Model That Develops Active Reading of Expository Text, *Reading Teacher* 39, no. 6 (February 1986): 564–70; source of POSSE: C. S. Englert and T. V. Mariage, Making Students Partners in the Comprehension Process: Organizing the Reading "POSSE," *Learning Disability Quarterly* 14, no. 1 (September 1991): 23–138; source of PQRST: E. B. Kelly, *Memory Enhancement for Educators*, Fastback 365 (Bloomington, IN: Phi Delta Kappa Educational Foundation, 1994), 18; source of RAP: J. B. Schumaker et al., *The Paraphrasing Strategy* (Lawrence, KS: Edge Enterprises, 1984); source of SQ3R: F. P. Robinson, *Effective Study*, rev. ed. (New York: Harper & Brothers, 1961). The original source of SQ4R is unknown. For SRQ2R, see M. L. Walker, Help for the "Fourth-Grade Slum"—SRQ2R Plus Instruction in Text Structure or Main Idea, *Reading Horizons* 36, no. 1 (1995): 38–58. About reciprocal teaching, see C. J. Carter, Why Reciprocal Teaching?, *Educational Leadership* 54, no. 6 (March 1997): 64–68, and T. L. Good and J. E. Brophy, *Looking in Classrooms*, 8th ed. (New York: Addison Wesley Longman, 2000), 431–32.

[10] R. Reinhold, Class Struggle, *New York Times Magazine*, September 29, 1991, 46.

[11] The National Education Association (NEA) published guidelines for teachers to consider before using commercial materials. For a free copy of the guidelines, contact NEA Communications, 1201 16th St. NW, Washington, DC 20036; phone: 202-822-7200.

[12] See, for example, J. C. Baker and F. G. Martin, *A Neural Network Guide to Teaching*, Fastback 431 (Bloomington, IN: Phi Delta Kappa Educational Foundation, 1998), and Good and Brophy, *Looking in Classrooms*, 252–53.

13 See, for example, the many articles in "The Constructivist Classroom," the November 1999 theme issue of *Educational Leadership*, volume 57, number 3; D. R. Geelan, Epistemological Anarchy and the Many Forms of Constructivism, *Science and Education* 6, no. 1–2 (January 1997): 15–28; and R. DeLay, Forming Knowledge: Constructivist Learning and Experiential Education, *Journal of Experiential Education* 19, no. 2 (August/September 1996): 76–81.

14 B. S. Bloom, ed., *Taxonomy of Educational Objectives, Book 1, Cognitive Domain* (White Plains, NY: Longman, 1984).

15 See R. M. Gagne, L. J. Briggs, and W. W. Wager, *Principles of Instructional Design*, 4th ed. (New York: Holt, Rinehart and Winston, 1994).

16 Compare Bloom's higher-order cognitive thinking skills with R. H. Ennis's A Taxonomy of Critical Thinking Dispositions and Abilities and Qellmalz's Developing Reasoning Skills, both in *Teaching Thinking Skills: Theory and Practice*, ed. J. B. Barron and R. J. Sternberg (New York: W. H. Freeman, 1987), and with Marzano's "complex thinking strategies" in R. J. Marzano, *A Different Kind of Classroom: Teaching with Dimensions of Learning* (Alexandria, VA: Association for Supervision and Curriculum Development, 1992).

17 D. R. Krathwohl, B. S. Bloom, and B. B. Masia, *Taxonomy of Educational Goals, Handbook 2, Affective Domain* (New York: David McKay, 1964).

18 A. J. Harrow, *Taxonomy of the Psychomotor Domain* (New York: Longman, 1977). A similar taxonomy for the psychomotor domain is that of E. J. Simpson, *The Classification of Educational Objectives in the Psychomotor Domain. The Psychomotor Domain: Volume 3* (Washington, DC: Gryphon House, 1972).

19 R. N. Caine and G. Caine, *Education on the Edge of Possibility* (Alexandria, VA: Association for Supervision and Curriculum Development, 1997), 104–5.

20 E. A. Wynne and K. Ryan, *Reclaiming Our Schools: A Handbook on Teaching Character, Academics, and Discipline* (Upper Saddle River, NJ: Prentice Hall, 1993), 3.

Chapter 6

1 J. Goodlad, *A Place Called School: Prospects for the Future* (New York: McGraw-Hill, 1984), 231.

1 Southern Regional Educational Board, *1995 Outstanding Practices* (Atlanta: Southern Regional Educational Board, 1995), 8.

2 V. LaPoint et al., *Report 1: The Talent Development High School–Essential Components* http://www.csos.jhu.edu/crespar/CRESPAR%20Reports/report01entire.html (June 19, 1998), 6.

3 See *Integrating the Curriculum* with Heidi Hayes Jacobs, (1998), The Video Journal of Education, Salt Lake City, UT; 1-800-572-1153; ISBN 1-58740-016-2.

4 See, for example, the articles in the theme issue of *Educational Leadership* 49, no. 2 (October 1994).

5 The section titled "The Spectrum of Integrated Curriculum" was first developed in 1996 by Richard D. Kellough and has appeared since then in similar form in several Prentice Hall publications authored or coauthored by Kellough.

Chapter 7

1 R. Fulghum, *It Was on Fire When I Lay Down on It* (New York: Villard Books, 1989).

Chapter 8

1 C. G. Jung, *The Development of Personality* (New York: Pantheon, 1964), 144.

2 See, for example, E. Jensen, *Teaching with the Brain in Mind* (Alexandria, VA: Association for Supervision and Curriculum Development, 1998), and J. C. Baker and F. G. Martin, *A Neural Network Guide to Teaching*, Fastback 431 (Bloomington, IN: Phi Delta Kappa Educational Foundation, 1998).

3 See D. Gollnick and P. Chinn, *Multicultural Education in a Pluralistic Society* (Upper Saddle River, NJ: Merrill/Prentice Hall, 2002); M. B. Ginsberg and R. J. Wlodkowski, *Creating Highly Motivating Classrooms for All Students: A Schoolwide Approach to Powerful Teaching with Diverse Learners* (San Francisco: Jossey-Bass, 2000); J. P. Comer and N. M. Haynes, *Summary of School Development Program Effects: The Family*

Is Critical to Student Achievement (New Haven, CT: Yale Child Study Center, 1992); and G. Ladson-Billings, But That's Just Good Teaching! The Case for Culturally Relevant Pedagogy, *Theory into Practice* 34, no. 3 (1995): 159–65.

4 See, for example, E. S. Foster-Harrison, *Peer Tutoring for K–12 Success*, Fastback 415 (Bloomington, IN: Phi Delta Kappa Educational Foundation, 1997).

5 A. W. Longwill and H. L. Kleinert, The Unexpected Benefits of High School Peer Tutoring, *Teaching Exceptional Children* 30, no. 4(March/April 1998): 60–65.

6 See, for example, T. G. Jones et al., Show-and-Tell Physics, *Science Teacher* 63, no. 8 (November 1996): 24–27.

7 See, for example, C. Kaplan, Homework Partners, *Mathematics Teaching in the Middle School* 2, no. 3 (January 1997): 168–69.

8 See, for example, R. E. Slavin, Cooperative Learning in Middle and Secondary Schools, *Clearing House* 69, no. 4 (March/April 1996): 200–204.

9 For details about these CLG strategies and others, see R. E. Slavin, *Student Team Learning: A Practical Guide for Cooperative Learning*, 3rd ed. (Washington, DC: National Education Association, 1991), and E. Coelho, *Learning Together in the Multicultural Classroom* (Portsmouth, NH: Heinemann, 1994).

10 T. L. Good and J. E. Brophy, *Looking in Classrooms*, 8th ed. (New York: Addison Wesley Longman, 2000), 291.

11 See S. Kagan, Group Grades Miss the Mark, *Educational Leadership* 52, no. 8)May 1995): 68–71, and D. W. Johnson and R. T. Johnson, The Role of Cooperative Learning in Assessing and Communicating Student Learning, in *Communicating Student Learning*, ASCD Yearbook, ed. T. R. Guskey (Alexandria, VA: Association for Supervision and Curriculum Development, 1996), chap. 4.

12 See, for example, C. A. Tomlinson et al., Use of Cooperative Learning at the Middle Level: Insights from a National Survey, *Research in Middle Level Education Quarterly* 20, no. 4 (Summer 1997): 37–55.

13 B. K. Beyer, *Practical Strategies for the Teaching of Thinking* (Boston: Allyn and Bacon, 1987).

14 A. L. Costa, *The School as a Home for the Mind* (Palatine, IL: Skylight Publishing, 1991), 20–31. See also Armstrong's 12 qualities of genius—curiosity, playfulness, imagination, creativity, wonderment, wisdom, inventiveness, vitality, sensitivity, flexibility, humor, and joy—in T. Armstrong, *Awakening Genius in the Classroom* (Alexandria, VA: Association for Supervision and Curriculum Development, 1998), 2–15, and Project Zero's 7 dispositions for good thinking—the disposition (a) to be broad and adventurous; (b) toward wondering, problem finding, and investigating; (c) to build explanations and understandings; (d) to make plans and be strategic; (e) to be intellectually careful; (f) to seek and evaluate reasons; and (g) to be metacognitive.

15 See, for example, M. Goos and P. Galbraith, Do It This Way! Metacognitive Strategies in Collaborative Mathematics Problem Solving, *Educational Studies in Mathematics* 30, no. 3 (April 1996): 229–60.

16 For further reading about the relation of impulse control to intelligence, see D. Goleman, *Emotional Intelligence: Why It Can Matter More Than IQ* (New York: Bantam Books, 1995), and D. Harrington-Lueker, Emotional Intelligence, *High Strides* 9, no. 4 (March/April 1997): 1, 4–5.

17 See, for example, J. W. Astington, Theory of Mind Goes to School, *Educational Leadership* 56, no. 3 (November 1998): 46–48, and K. D. Wood and C. P. Fisher, Building Assets in the Classroom Through Creative Response, *Middle School Journal* 31, no. 4 (March 2000): 57–60.

18 J. Piaget, *The Psychology of Intelligence* (Totowa, NJ: Littlefield Adams, 1972).

19 I. Kohlberg, *The Meaning and Measurement of Moral Development* (Worcester, MA: Clark University Press, 1981).

20 See, for example, A. Whimbey, Test Results from Teaching Thinking, in *Developing Minds: A Resource Book for Teaching Thinking*, ed. A. L. Costa (Alexandria, VA: Association for Supervision and Curriculum Development, 1985), 269–71.

21 B. Z. Presseisen, Implementing Thinking in the School's Curriculum, unpublished paper presented at the third annual meeting of the

International Association for Cognitive Education, Riverside, CA, February 9, 1992.

22 Costa, *Developing Minds*, 312.

23 From P. L. Roberts and R. D. Kellough, *A Guide for Developing Thematic Units*, 2nd ed. (Upper Saddle River, NJ: Merrill/Prentice Hall, 2000), 147–48. Adapted with permission.

24 See, for example, E. L. Wright and G. Govindarajan, Discrepant Event Demonstrations, *Science Teacher* 62, no. 1 (January 1995): 24–28; T. O'Brien et al., Baker's Dozen of Discrepantly Dense Demos, *Science Scope* 18, no. 2 (October 1994): 35–38; and C. Ruck et al., Using Discrepant Events to Inspire Writing, *Science Activities* 28, no. 2 (Summer 1991): 27–30.

25 See, for example, A. O'Grady, Information Literacy Skills and the Senior Project, *Educational Leadership* 57, no. 2 (October 1999): 61–62.

26 See, for example, M. Tassinari, Hands-On Projects Take Students Beyond the Book, *Social Studies Review* 34, no. 3 (Spring 1996): 16–20.

27 D. Hyerle, *Visual Tools for Constructing Knowledge* (Alexandria, VA: Association for Supervision and Curriculum Development, 1996).

28 D. P. Ausubel, *The Psychology of Meaningful Learning* (New York: Grune and Stratton, 1963).

29 About thinking process mapping, see J. D. Novak, Concept Maps and Vee Diagrams: Two Metacognitive Tools to Facilitate Meaningful Learning, *Instructional Science* 19, no. 1 (1990): 29–52; J. D. Novak and B. D. Gowin, *Learning How to Learn* (Cambridge: Cambridge University Press, 1984); and E. Plotnick, *Concept Mapping: A Graphical System for Understanding the Relationship Between Concepts*, ED407938 (Syracuse, NY: ERIC Clearinghouse on Information and Technology, 1997).

30 See C. J. Carter, Why Reciprocal Teaching?, *Educational Leadership* 54, no. 6 (March 1997): 64–68.

31 J. S. Choate and T. A. Rakes, *Inclusive Instruction for Struggling Readers*, Fastback 434 (Bloomington, IN: Phi Delta Kappa Educational Foundation, 1998).

Chapter 9

1 H. Kohl, Hope and the Imagination, *Reading Today's Youth* 4, no. 4 (2000): 39–41.

2 D. P. Ausubel, *The Psychology of Meaningful Learning* (New York: Addison Wesley Longman, 2000), 252–53.

3 T. L. Good and J. E. Brophy, *Looking in Classrooms*, 8th ed. (New York: Addison Wesley Longman, 2000), 252–53.

4 A. L. Costa, *The School as a Home for the Mind* (Palatine, IL: Skylight Publishing, 1991), 63.

5 Studies in wait time began with the classic study of M. B. Rowe, Wait Time and Reward as Instructional Variables, Their Influence on Language, Logic and Fate Control: Part I. Wait Time, *Journal of Research in Science Teaching* 11, no. 2 (June 1974): 81–94.

6 See, for example, V. C. Polite and A. H. Adams, *Improving Critical Thinking Through Socratic Seminars*, Spotlight on Student Success, no. 110 (Philadelphia: Mid-Atlantic Laboratory for Student Success, 1996); S. Schoeman, Using the Socratic Method in Secondary Teaching, *NASSP Bulletin* 81, no. 587 (March 1997): 19–21; and M. L. Tanner and L. Casados, Promoting and Studying Discussions in Math Classes, *Journal of Adolescent and Adult Literacy* 41, no. 5 (February 1998): 342–50.

7 B. R. Brogan and W. A. Brogan, The Socratic Questioner: Teaching and Learning in the Dialogical Classroom, *Educational Forum* 59, no. 3 (Spring 1995): 288–96.

8 This three-tiered model of thinking has been described variously by others. For example, in E. Eisner's *The Educational Imagination* (Upper Saddle River, NJ: Prentice Hall, 1979), the levels are referred to as *descriptive, interpretive,* and *evaluative.* For a comparison of thinking models, see Costa, *The School as Home for the Mind*, 44.

9 See, for example, J. Piaget, *The Development of Thought: Elaboration of Cognitive Structures* (New York: Viking, 1977).

10 R. N. Caine and G. Caine, *Education on the Edge of Possibility* (Alexandria, VA: Association for Supervision and Curriculum Development, 1997), 107.

11 See, for example, B. Newton, Theoretical Basis for Higher Cognitive Questioning—An Avenue to Critical Thinking, *Education* 98, no. 3 (March–April 1978): 286–90, and D. Redfield and E. Rousseau, A Meta-Analysis of Experimental Research on Teacher Questioning Behavior, *Review of Educational Research* 51, no. 2 (Summer 1981): 237–45.

12 M. E. McIntosh and R. J. Draper, Using the Question-Answer Relationship Strategy to Improve Students' Reading of Mathematics Texts, *Clearing House* 69, no. 3 (January/February 1996): 154–62.

13 J. G. Brooks and M. G. Brooks, *In Search of Understanding: The Case for Constructivist Classrooms* (Alexandria, VA: Association for Supervision and Curriculum Development, 1993), 105.

14 See Rowe, Wait-Time and Rewards as Instructional Variables, Their Influence on Language, Logic, and Fate Control; M. B. Rowe, Wait-Time: Slowing Down May Be a Way of Speeding Up, *American Educator* 11, no. 1 (Spring 1987): 38–47; and J. Swift, C. Gooding, and P. Swift, Questions and Wait Time, in *Questioning and Discussion: A Multidisciplinary Study*, ed. J. Dillon (Norwood, NJ: Ablex, 1988), 192–212.

15 J. S. Choate and T. A. Rakes, *Inclusive Instruction for Struggling Readers*, Fastback 434 (Bloomington, IN: Phi Delta Kappa Educational Foundation, 1998), 26.

16 U.S. Department of Education, *Tried and True: Tested Ideas for Teaching and Learning from the Regional Educational Laboratories* (Washington, DC: Office of Educational Research and Improvement, U.S. Department of Education, 1997), 53.

17 See, for example, M. A. Raywid, Small Schools: A Reform That Works, *Educational Leadership* 55, no. 4 (December/January 1997–1998): 34–39, and M. A. Raywid, *Current Literature on Small Schools*, ED425049 (Charleston, WV: ERIC Clearinghouse on Rural Education and Small Schools, 1999).

18 See, for example, S. Zaher, Gender and Curriculum in the School Room, *Education Canada* 36, no. 1 (Spring 1996): 26–29, and S. M. Bailey, Shortchanging Girls and Boys, *Educational Leadership* 53, no. 8 (May 1996): 75–79. For information on how to identify equity problems and develop programs to help schools achieve academic excellence for all students, contact EQUITY 2000, 1233 20th St. NW, Washington, DC 20056-2304; phone: 202-822-5930.

19 See, for example, C. Kaplan, Homework Partners, *Mathematics Teaching in the Middle School* 2, no. 3 (January 1997): 168–69.

20 See, for example, M. H. Sullivan and P. V. Sequeira, The Impact of Purposeful Homework on Learning, *Clearing House* 69, no. 6 (July/August 1996): 346–48.

21 H. J. Walberg, Productive Teaching and Instruction: Assessing the Knowledge Base, *Phi Delta Kappan* 71, no. 6 (February 1990): 472.

22 To learn how one teacher made "rigid due dates a thing of the past," see the article by Kenan High School (Warsaw, North Carolina) teacher S. H. Benson, Make Mine an A, *Educational Leadership* 57, no. 5 (February 2000): 30–32.

Chapter 10

1 M. Mead, What Has Happened to the Generation Gap?, *Redbook* 139 (September 1972): 70.

2 See also the Copyright and Fair Use website of Stanford University at http://fairuse.stanford.edu.

3 See M. M. Mullan, Modern Classrooms See Chalkboards Left in the Dust, *Education Week* 19, no. 17 (January 12, 2000): 6.

4 Sources of electronic whiteboards include MicroTouch, Tewksbury, MA (800-642-7686); Numonics, Montgomeryville, PA (215-362-2766); Smart Technologies, Calgary, AB, Canada (403-245-0333); SoftBoard, Portland, OR (888-763-8262); and TEGRITY, San Jose, CA (408-369-5150).

5 See, for example, X. Bornas et al., Preventing Impulsivity in the Classroom: How Computers Can Help Teachers, *Computers in the Schools* 13, no. 1–2 (1997): 27–40.

6 R. C. Schank, A Vision of Education for the 21st Century, *T.H.E. Journal* 27, no. 6 (January 2000): 43–45.

Chapter 11

1 P. Wellstone, High Stakes Tests: A Harsh Agenda for America's Children, remarks by U.S. Senator Paul D. Wellstone (Minnesota) at Teacher's College, Columbia University, March 31, 2000, http://www.educationrevolution.org/paulwellstone.html.

2 S. J. Rakow, Assessment: A Driving Force, *Science Scope* 15, no. 6 (March 1992): 3.

3 For information about Learner Profile™, see Sunburst Technology at http://www.sunburst.com or phone 1-800-321-7511.

4 See, for example, A. Chandler, Is This for a Grade? A Personal Look at Journals, *English Journal* 86, no. 1 (January 1997): 45–49.

5 Software packages for the development of student electronic portfolios are available, such as Classroom Manager from CTB Macmillan/McGraw-Hill (Monterey, California), *Electronic Portfolio* from Learning Quest (Corvallis, Oregon), and Grady Profile from Aurbach and Associates (St. Louis, Missouri).

6 For a discussion of the biological importance and educational benefits of positive feedback, student portfolios, and group learning, see R. Sylwester, The Neurobiology of Self-Esteem and Aggression, *Educational Leadership* 54, no. 5 (February 1997): 75–79.

7 See, for example, T. R. Guskey, ed., *Communicating Student Learning* (Alexandria, VA: Association for Supervision and Curriculum Development, 1996), 18–19, and R. J. Stiggins, *Student-Centered Classroom Assessment*, 2nd ed. (Upper Saddle River, NJ: Prentice Hall, 1997), 436–37.

8 For other methods being used to report student achievement, see J. Bailey and J. McTighe, Reporting Achievement at the Secondary Level: What and How, in Guskey, *Communicating Student Learning*, 119–40.

9 H. G. Andrade, Using Rubrics to Promote Thinking and Learning, *Educational Leadership* 57, no. 5 (February 2000): 13–18.

10 K. Bushweller, Generation of Cheaters, *American School Board Journal* 186, no. 4 (April 1999): 24–30, 32.

11 H. J. Walberg, Productive Teaching and Instruction: Assessing the Knowledge Base, *Phi Delta Kappan* 71, no. 6 (February 1990): 472.

12 For suggestions for "delivering powerful presentations to parents" at back-to-school night, see W. B. Ribas, Tips for Reaching Parents, *Educational Leadership* 56, no. 1 (September 1998): 83–85.

13 See note 12.

14 For a discussion of the pros and cons of using the student-led conference and for a conference organizer tool, see J. Bailey and J. McTighe, Reporting Achievement at the Secondary Level, 137–39. See also L. Countryman and M. Schroeder, When Students Lead Parent-Teacher Conferences, *Educational Leadership* 53, no. 7 (April 1996): 64–68,

and D. G. Hackmann, *Student-Led Conferences at the Middle Level*, ED407171 (Champaign, IL: ERIC Clearinghouse on Elementary and Early Childhood Education, 1997).

Chapter 12

1 S. Nieto, What Keeps Teachers Going? And Other Thoughts on the Future of Public Education, *Equity and Excellence in Education* 34, no. 1 (2001): 14.

2 See, for example, P. J. Hallman, *Field-Based Teacher Education: Restructuring Texas Teacher Education Series 1* (Austin: Texas State Board for Educator Certification, 1998), and L. Huling, *Early Field Experiences in Teacher Education*, ED429054 (Washington, DC: ERIC Clearinghouse on Teaching and Teacher Education, 1998).

3 R. P. Johanson et al., Internet and List-Serves to Support the Student Teaching Semester (paper presented at the annual meeting of the American Association of Colleges for Teacher Education, Washington, DC, February 24–27, 1999).

4 N. Bacharach, T. Washut Heck, and K. Dahlberg, Changing the Face of Student Teaching Through Coteaching, *Action in Teacher Education* 32, no. 1 (2006): 3–13.

5 C. Shakesaft, *Educator Sexual Misconduct: A Synthesis of Existing Literature*, Report ED-02-PO-3281 (Washington, DC: U.S. Department of Education Office of the Under Secretary, Policy and Program Studies Service, June 2004), available at http://www.ed.gov/rschstat/research/pubs/misconductreview/report.pdf.

6 You may be interested in several articles about portfolios in the theme issue of *Teacher Education Quarterly* 25, no. 1 (Winter 1998).

7 For additional suggestions for preparing for a teaching job interview, see http://www.teachnet.com.

8 For additional information, see the International Center for Information About New Teacher Mentoring and Induction at http://www.teachermentors.com/MCenter%20Site/AdviceBegTchr.html and a description of California's Beginning Teacher Support and Assessment Program at http://www.ccoe.k12.ca.us/coe/curins.sbtsa. See also A. Gratch, Beginning Teacher and Mentor Relationships, *Journal of Teacher Education* 49, no. 3 (May/June 1998): 220–27.

9 See, for example, G. Cramer et al., *Teacher Study Groups for Professional Development*, Fastback 406 (Bloomington, IN: Phi Delta Kappa Educational Foundation, 1996).

10 See, for example, A. Lieberman and M. Grolnick, Networks, Reform, and the Professional Development of Teachers, in *Rethinking Educational Change with Heart and Mind*, ed. A. Hargreaves (Alexandria, VA: Association for Supervision and Curriculum Development, 1997), 192–215.

11 Source of the data: Quality Counts 2000, *Education Week* 19, no. 18 (January 13, 2000): 8

Answers
to Self-Correct Exercises

Exercise 5.7

1. The following verbs should be circled: 2, 3, 5, 13, 15, 16, 21, 22, 26, 30. If you missed more than a couple, then you need to read the previous sections again and discuss your errors with your classmates and instructor.

   *Words in English often have multiple meanings. For example, grasp as listed here could mean "to take hold," or it could mean "to comprehend." For the former, it would be an acceptable verb for use in overt objectives; for the latter, it would not.

Exercise 5.8

	Objective 1	Objective 2
Audience	you	the student
Behavior	will write a 500-word account of the battle between the forces of Gondor and its allies against those of Mordor and its allies	will be able to read the schedule
Conditions	completely from memory	given an interurban bus schedule
Performance level	this account will be accurate in all basic details and include all the important incidents of the battle	well enough to determine (and) with at least 90% accuracy

Exercise 5.9

1. This is a behavioral objective. Although another verb might be more appropriate (e.g., recognize), understanding is a kind of behavior. In this case, understanding that slavery was the basic issue that brought about secession is the terminal behavior the teacher expects of the students.

2. This is not a behavioral objective. Rather, it is a description of a concept and does not describe an expected terminal behavior.

3. This is not a behavioral objective. It describes teacher behavior rather than student terminal behavior. It is more a teaching procedure than an objective.

4. This is not a behavioral objective—or even an objective of any type. It is a topic or title.

5. This is a behavioral objective. It describes clearly what the students will be able to do as a result of the instruction; it describes their expected terminal behavior.

6. This is a behavioral objective. The objective is rather broad, and another verb might have been more useful. Understanding is a kind of terminal behavior, but the objective might have been more measurable had the teacher used a verb other than understanding. A better formulation would have been the following: "The students will be able to recall that . . ." or "The students will be able to demonstrate that . . ."

7. This is a behavioral objective. It is specific and very clear about the teacher's expectation of student behavior at completion of the lesson.

8. This is a clearly written behavioral objective.

9. This is a behavioral objective. Although the terminal behavior described is vague and general, it is nevertheless a terminal behavior. Perhaps a clearer formulation would have been the following: "The students will demonstrate an appreciation of the problems faced by those who have emigrated from Southeast Asia to the United States by recalling the many problems the people faced before, during, and following that emigration."

10. This is not a behavioral objective. It describes no behavior of any kind. It is the title of a topic with a mention of methods.

11. This is not a behavioral objective. It is not an objective at all but rather a description of the teaching procedure to be used.

12. This is not a behavioral objective. Again, this is a title of a topic. It describes no behavior and no objective.

Exercise 5.10

1. P	**4.** A	**7.** C	**9.** A
2. C	**5.** A	**8.** C	**10.** P
3. C	**6.** C		

Exercise 9.2

1. 2 (analyze, compare)	**11.** 3 (generalize)
2. 3 (evaluate)	**12.** 1 (recall)
3. 3 (evaluate)	**13.** 3 (judge)
4. 1 (recall)	**14.** 3 (design)
5. 3 (evaluate)	**15.** 3 (hypothesize)
6. 3 (design)	**16.** 3 (predict)
7. 1 (recall)	**17.** 2 (explain)
8. 2 (compare)	**18.** 3 (evaluate)
9. 3 (hypothesize)	**19.** 1 (recall)
10. 3 (evaluate)	**20.** 2 (apply)

Exercise 9.3

1. F, B	**8.** F, B	**14.** G, C	**20.** F, B
2. G, C	**9.** P, A	**15.** G, C	**21.** F, B
3. F, B	**10.** P, A	**16.** F, B	**22.** F, B
4. F, B	**11.** G, C	**17.** G, C	**23.** G, C
5. G, C	**12.** G, C	**18.** G, C	**24.** F, B
6. P, A	**13.** F, B	**19.** G, C	**25.** P, A
7. G, C			

Glossary

A

Ability grouping The assignment of students to separate classrooms or to separate activities within a classroom according to their perceived academic abilities. *Homogeneous grouping* is the grouping of students of similar abilities; *heterogeneous grouping* is the grouping of students of mixed abilities.

Academies Private secondary schools that prepared students for a number of fields. The first academy was founded in Philadelphia by Benjamin Franklin in 1751.

Accommodation The cognitive process of modifying a schema or creating new schemata.

Accountability Reference to the concept that an individual is responsible for his or her behaviors and should be able to demonstrate publicly the worth of the activities carried out.

Adolescence The period of life from the onset of puberty to maturity, terminating legally at the age of majority, generally the ages of 12 to 20, although young or early adolescence may start as soon as age 9.

Advance organizer Preinstructional cues that encourage a mental set; used to enhance retention of content to be studied.

Advisor-advisee Common to many middle schools and increasingly in high schools, the program (sometimes referred to as *home base* or *advisory* program) that provides each student the opportunity to interact with peers about school and personal concerns and to develop a meaningful relationship with at least one adult.

Affective domain The area of learning related to interests, attitudes, feelings, values, and personal adjustment.

Aims The most general educational objectives.

Alternative assessment Assessment of learning in ways that are different from traditional paper-and-pencil objective testing, such as a portfolio, project, or self-assessment. See *authentic assessment.*

American Federation of Teachers (AFT) A national professional organization of teachers founded in 1916, currently affiliated with the American Federation of Labor and Congress of Industrial Organizations (AFL-CIO). It was recently merged in at least two states with the National Education Association.

Anticipatory set See *advance organizer.*

Articulation Term used when referring to the connectedness of the various components of the formal curriculum—*vertical articulation* refers to the connectedness of the K–12 curriculum, and *horizontal articulation* refers to the connectedness across a grade level.

Assessment The relatively neutral process of finding out what students will or have learned as a result of instruction.

At-risk General term given to a student who shows a high potential for not completing school.

Authentic assessment The use of assessment procedures (usually portfolios and projects) that are highly compatible with the instructional objectives. Also referred to as *accurate, active, aligned, alternative, direct,* and *performance assessment.*

B

Behavioral objective A statement of expectation describing what the learner should be able to do on completion of the instruction.

Behaviorism A theory that equates learning with changes in observable behavior.

Block scheduling The school programming procedure that provides large blocks of time (e.g., 90 minutes or 2 hours) in which individual teachers or teacher teams can organize and arrange groupings of students for varied periods of time, thereby more effectively individualizing the instruction for students with various needs and abilities.

Blogs A special type of website where students can create, write, and share their stories, opinions, and thoughts by posting commentary, news, and other information.

Brainstorming An instructional strategy used to create a flow of new ideas, during which judgments of the ideas of others are forbidden.

Brown v. Board of Education In 1954, this landmark decision of the U.S. Supreme Court declared that it is unconstitutional for states to establish separate public schools for black and white students.

C

CD-ROM (compact disc—read-only memory) Digitally encoded information (up to 650 MB of data that can include animation, audio, graphics, text, and video) permanently recorded on a compact (4.72-inch [12-cm diameter]) disc.

Character education A program that focuses on the development of the values of honesty, kindness, respect, and responsibility.

Charter school A school that is "an autonomous educational entity operating under a charter, or contract, that has been negotiated between the organizers, who create and operate the school, and a sponsor, who oversees the provisions of the charter."

Classroom Response Systems Commonly called "clickers," these are wireless devices that allow teachers to ask questions and receive and tally responses from students instantaneously.

Clarifying question A question used to gain more information from a student to help the teacher better understand a student's ideas, feelings, and thought processes.

Classroom control The process of influencing student behavior in the classroom.

Classroom management The teacher's system of establishing a climate for learning, including techniques for preventing and handling student misbehavior.

Closure The means by which a teacher brings the lesson to an end.

Coaching See *mentoring.*

Cognition The process of thinking.

Cognitive disequilibrium The mental state of not yet having made sense out of a perplexing (discrepant) situation.

Cognitive domain The area of learning related to intellectual skills, such as retention and assimilation of knowledge.

Cognitive psychology A branch of psychology devoted to the study of how individuals acquire, process, and use information.

Cognitivism A theory that holds that learning entails the construction or reshaping of mental schemata and that mental processes mediate learning. Also known as *constructivism.*

Common Core State Standards In March 2010, in an effort to define the skills and knowledge all students should obtain during their K–12 education regardless of where they live and attend school and to guarantee that students are ready for college courses or entry into the job market when they graduate high school, the Common Core State Standards were released for public comment.

Common planning time A regularly scheduled time during the school day when teachers who teach the same students meet for joint planning, parent conferences, materials preparation, and student evaluation.

Compact disc (CD) A 4.72-inch disc on which a laser has recorded digital information.

Comprehension A level of cognition that refers to the skill of understanding.

Comprehensive high school School that offers college preparatory, general, and vocational tracks.

Computer literacy The ability, at some level on a continuum, to understand and use computers.

Computer-assisted instruction (CAI) Instruction received by a student when interacting with lessons programmed into a computer system. Also known as *computer-assisted learning (CAL)*

Computer-managed instruction (CMI) The use of a computer system to manage information about learner performance and learning-resources options in order to prescribe and control individual lessons.

Concept map A visual or graphic representation of concepts and their relationships; words related to a key word are written in categories around the key word, and the categories are labeled.

Constructivism See *cognitivism.*

Co-teaching This innovative approach to the traditional student teaching placement is a popular model where the cooperating teacher and the student teacher share the classroom and the students and work together and share in the planning, organization, delivery, and assessment of their students.

Continuous progress An instructional procedure that allows students to progress at their own pace through a sequenced curriculum.

Convergent thinking Thinking that is directed to a preset conclusion.

Convergent thinking question A low-order thinking question that has a single correct answer such as a recall question.

Cooperative learning A genre of instructional strategies that use small groups of students working together and helping each other on learning tasks, stressing support for one another rather than competition.

Core curriculum Subject or discipline components of the curriculum considered as being absolutely necessary. Traditionally these are English/language arts, mathematics, science, and social studies/history.

Course A complete sequence of instruction that presents a major division of a subject matter or discipline. Courses are laid out for a year, semester, quarter, or, in the case of minicourses or intensive courses, a few weeks.

Covert behavior A learner behavior that is not outwardly observable.

Criterion A standard by which behavioral performance is judged.

Criterion-referenced assessment Assessment in which standards are established and behaviors are judged against the present guideline rather than against the behaviors of others.

Critical literacy An instructional approach that provides students with strategies to actively analyze the texts they are assigned to read and increase their comprehension.

Critical thinking The ability to recognize and identify problems, to propose and to test solutions, and to arrive at tentative conclusions based on the data collected.

Cueing question When a teacher goes backward in a questioning sequence to cue students.

Cultural competence As defined by Diller and Moule, cultural competence "is the ability to successfully teach students who come from cultures other than your own. It entails mastering complex awareness and sensitivities, various bodies of knowledge, and a set of skills that, taken together, underlie effective cross-cultural teaching."

Cultural literacy This concept highlights that in addition to basic literacy skills, citizens in the United States should share a common body of knowledge in order to be considered educated/literate and fully participate in society.

Culturally sensitive pedagogy A student-centered approach that integrates the students' cultural beliefs, traditions, and values into the teaching/learning process while emphasizing integration, critical thinking, and community involvement.

Culture Simply stated, culture is shared, learned behavior. It shapes values, beliefs, traditions and mores. Our cultural heritage determines who we are and helps us to make sense of the world.

Curriculum Originally derived from a Latin term referring to a race course for the chariots, the term still has no widely accepted definition. As used in this text, curriculum is that which is planned and encouraged for teaching and learning. This includes both school and nonschool environments, overt (formal) and hidden (informal) curriculums, and broad as well as narrow notions of content—its development, acquisition, and consequences.

Curriculum mapping The initial step in the process of designing integrated curriculum where middle and high school teachers list what they each teach in their disciplines in a calendar year.

Curriculum standards Statements of the essential knowledge, skills, and attitudes to be learned.

Cyberbullying A form of bullying where aggressors use email, instant messaging, chat room exchanges, website posts, or digital messages or images sent via a cellular phone or personal digital assistant to intimidate and terrorize victims.

D

Dame school The first schools, run by women in their homes during the colonial era. Reading, writing, and basic math skills were taught.

Deductive learning Learning that proceeds from the general to the specific. See also *expository learning.*

Detracking An effort to minimize or eliminate separate classes or programs for students who are of differing abilities.

Developmental characteristics A set of common intellectual, psychological, physical, and social characteristics that, when considered as a whole, indicate an individual's development relative to others during a particular age span.

Developmental needs A set of needs unique and appropriate to the developmental characteristics of a particular age span.

Diagnostic assessment See *preassessment.*

Didactic teaching See *direct instruction.*

Differentiated instruction Varying the methods and content of instruction according to individual student differences and needs.

Direct experience Learning by doing (applying) that which is being learned.

Direct instruction Teacher-centered expository instruction, such as lecturing or a teacher-guided group discussion.

Direct intervention Teacher use of verbal reminders or verbal commands to redirect student behavior, as opposed to nonverbal gestures or cues.

Direct teaching See *direct instruction.*

Discipline The process of controlling student behavior in the classroom. The term has been largely replaced by the terms *classroom control* or *classroom management.* It is also used in reference to the subject taught (e.g., language arts, science, mathematics, and so forth).

Discovery learning Learning that proceeds from identification of a problem, through the development of hypotheses, the testing of the hypotheses, and the arrival at a conclusion. See also *critical thinking.*

Divergent thinking Thinking that expands beyond original thought.

Divergent thinking question Open-ended (i.e., usually having no single correct answer) higher-order thinking questions (requiring analysis, synthesis, or evaluation) that require students to think creatively, to leave the comfortable confines of the known and reach out into the unknown.

Downshifting Reverting to earlier learned, lower-cognitive-level behaviors.

DVD (digital versatile disc or digital video disc) Media storage device like a CD-ROM but with a much greater storage capacity.

E

Early adolescence The developmental stage of young people as they approach and begin to experience puberty. This stage usually occurs between 10 and 14 years of age and deals with the successful attainment of the appropriate developmental characteristics for this age span.

Eclectic Utilizing the best from a variety of sources.

Effective school A school where students master basic skills, seek academic excellence in all subjects, demonstrate achievement, and display good behavior and attendance. Also known as an *exemplary school.*

Elective High-interest or special needs courses that are based on student selection from various options.

Elementary school Any school that has been planned and organized especially for children of some combination of grades kindergarten through 6. There are many variations, though; for example, a school might house children of preschool through grade 7 or 8 and still be called an elementary school.

Empathy The ability to understand the feelings of another person.

English classical school These schools provided a free public education for all students. They first opened in Boston in 1821 and offered a practical curriculum.

English Language Learners (ELLs) Students whose first language is other than English who are in the process of developing English-language proficiency.

Equality Considered to be the same in status or competency level.

Equity Fairness and justice, that is, impartiality.

Evaluation Like assessment but includes making sense out of the assessment results, usually based on criteria or a rubric. Evaluation is more subjective than is assessment.

Evaluative question A question that requires students to take a stance on some issue.

Exceptional learner A child who deviates from the average in any of the following ways: mental characteristics, sensory ability, neuromotor or physical characteristics, social behavior, communication ability, or multiple handicaps. Also known as a child with special needs.

Exemplary school See *effective school.*

Exploratory course A course designed to help students explore curriculum experiences based on their felt needs, interests, and abilities.

Expository learning The traditional classroom instructional approach that proceeds as follows: presentation of information to the learners, reference to particular examples, and application of the information to the learner's experiences.

Extended-year school Schools that have extended the school-year calendar from the traditional 180 days to a longer period, such as 200 days.

Extrinsic motivators Motivation of learning by rewards outside of the learner, such as parent and teacher expectations, gifts, certificates, stamps, and grades.

F

Facilitating behavior Teacher behavior that makes it possible for students to learn.

Facilitative teaching See *indirect instruction.*

Fair Use Guidelines Although the earliest guidelines appeared in 1976, more recently several organizations have tried to interpret copyright law and inform teachers of what they may do under the law when using printed materials, illustrations, videos, computer software, resources on the Internet, television programming, and so on in their teaching.

Faculty handbooks These manuals usually contain clear descriptions of the expectations for faculty to help to acquaint them with the practices, policies, and procedures of a school and district.

Family See *school-within-a-school.*

Feedback Information sent from the receiver to the originator that provides disclosure about the reception of the intended message.

Flexible scheduling Organization of classes and activities in a way that allows for variation from day to day as opposed to the traditional, fixed schedule that does not vary from day to day.

Focus question A question that is designed to focus student thinking.

Formative assessment Evaluation of learning in progress.

For-profit school A public school that is operated by a for-profit company.

Full-service school A school that serves as a hub for quality education and comprehensive social services.

Fundamental school A school that specializes in teaching basic skills.

G

Generalizations General statements that can help explain commonalities shared to some degree with individuals who belong to various microcultures.

Goal An idea an individual intends to reach or hopes to accomplish.

Goal, course A broad generalized statement about the expected outcomes of a course.

Goal, educational A desired instructional outcome that is broad in scope.

Goal, student A statement about what the student hopes to accomplish.

Goal, teacher A statement about what the teacher hopes to accomplish.

Goals 2000 A reform initiative started in 1989 when then President George H. W. Bush convened all the governors to discuss the state of education. The resulting six national education goals were modified and became know as Goals 2000 under President Clinton.

Google Earth A free download that allows students to tour the earth through pictures and landscapes at a street level or through space.

GPS Global Positioning System is a navigation system that is a space-based satellite network maintained by the U.S. government.

H

Hands-on learning Learning by actively doing.

Heterogeneous grouping A grouping pattern that does not separate students into groups based on their intelligence, learning achievement, or physical characteristics.

High school A school that houses students in any combination of grades 9–12.

High-stakes assessment An assessment is called high stakes if use of the assessment's results carry serious consequences, such as if a student's grade promotion rests on the student's performance on one test or the student's graduation from high school rests on the student's performance on a single test.

Holistic learning Learning that incorporates emotions with thinking.

Homogeneous grouping A grouping pattern that separates students into groups based on common characteristics, such as intelligence, achievement, or physical characteristics.

House See *school-within-a-school.*

I

Illiteracy The condition when students are unable to read or write or who are not proficient in comprehending the meaning of their grade-appropriate textbooks.

Inclusion The commitment to the education of each student with special needs, to the maximum extent appropriate, in the school and classroom the student would otherwise attend.

Independent study An instructional strategy that allows a student to select a topic, set the goals, and work alone to attain them.

Indian Boarding Schools Federal Indian policies in the late 1800s and early 1900s sought to civilize Indian children by removing them from their homes and teaching them rudimentary English and basic industrial trades and exposing them to religious indoctrination in boarding schools.

Indian Education for All Landmark legislation that amended the Montana Constitution in 1972 to incorporate the teaching of American Indian cultures and histories in the statutory definition of a quality education. This model exemplifies culturally responsive pedagogy in practice.

Indirect instruction Student-centered teaching using discovery and inquiry as learning strategies.

Individualized instruction The self-paced process whereby individual students assume responsibility for learning through study, practice, feedback, and reinforcement with appropriately designed instructional modules.

Individualized learning Self-paced instruction which is modified to meet the needs of individual students. Accommodating students with special needs can be accomplished by modifying lessons.

Inductive learning Learning that proceeds from specifics to the general. See also *discovery learning*.

Inquiry teaching Like discovery learning, except the learner designs the processes to be used in resolving the problem.

In-service teacher Term used when referring to credentialed and employed teachers.

Instruction Planned arrangement of experiences to help a learner develop understanding and achieve a desirable change in behavior.

Instructional module Any freestanding instructional unit that includes these components: rationale, objectives, pretest, learning activities, comprehension checks with instructive feedback, and posttest.

INTASC standards The Interstate New Teacher Assessment and Support Consortium has articulated standards that highlight what all beginning teachers should know and what they should be able to do.

Integrated curriculum Curriculum organization that combines subject matter traditionally taught independently.

Interdisciplinary instruction Instruction that combines subject matter disciplines traditionally taught independently.

Interdisciplinary team An organizational pattern of two or more teachers representing different subject areas. The team shares the same students, schedule, areas of the school, and the opportunity for teaching more than one subject. Also called *interdisciplinary teaching teams*.

Interdisciplinary thematic unit (ITU) A thematic unit that crosses boundaries of two or more disciplines.

Interdisciplinary thematic unit (integrated unit) A team representative of several disciplines—English/language arts, mathematics, science, social studies/history, and so forth—that plans collaboratively and creates unit plans that integrate their content areas by making relevant, meaningful connections across the curriculum.

Intermediate grades Term sometimes used to refer to grades 4 through 6.

Internalization The extent to which an attitude or value becomes a part of the learner. That is, without having to think about it, the learner's behavior reflects the attitude or value.

International Baccalaureate School A school with a curriculum approved by the International Baccalaureate Organization (IBO), a worldwide nonprofit educational foundation founded in the 1960s and based in Switzerland.

Interscholastic sports Athletic competition between teams from two or more schools.

Intervention A teacher's interruption to redirect a student's behavior, either by direct intervention (e.g., by a verbal command) or by indirect intervention (e.g., by eye contact or physical proximity).

Intramural program Organized activity program that features events between individuals or teams from within the school.

Intrinsic motivation Motivation of learning through the student's internal sense of accomplishment.

Intuition Knowing without conscious reasoning.

J

Junior high school A school that houses grades 7 through 9 or 7 through 8 and that has a schedule and curriculum that resemble those of the senior high school (grades 9–12 or 10–12) more than they do those of the elementary school.

K

K–8 Schools A reorganization alternative designed to better address the developmental needs of their preadolescents and early adolescents.

K An instructional technique developed by Donna Ogle in 1986 where students record what they know about a subject/issue/topic (K), what students want to learn (W), and what students have learned (L) after an intervention in a graphic organizer designed to help them construct meaning.

L

Latin grammar school In 1635 the first secondary schools were founded in Boston. In the Latin grammar schools, young boys between 7 and 14 years of age received an education focusing on the classics.

Lau v. Nichols In 1974, the U.S. Supreme Court ruled in favor of Chinese students in San Francisco, expanding the rights of all limited English Proficient students across the United States.

Lead teacher The member of a teaching team who is designated to facilitate the work and planning of that team.

Leadership team A group of teachers and administrators, and sometimes students, designated by the principal or elected by the faculty (and student body) to assist in the leadership of the school.

Learning The development of understandings and the change in behavior resulting from experiences. For different interpretations of learning, see *behaviorism* and *cognitivism*.

Learning center (LC) An instructional strategy that utilizes activities and materials located at a special place in the classroom and is designed to allow a student to work independently at his or her own pace to learn one area of content. See also *learning station*.

Learning communities A group of teachers and students who are actively engaged in learning together. Students who participate in learning communities are often empowered and more intellectually mature. Faculty members who participate in learning communities can share their instructional strategies, collaborate with colleagues across disciplines, and develop their mentoring skills.

Learning modality The way a person receives information. Four modalities are recognized: visual, auditory, tactile (touch), and kinesthetic (movement).

Learning resource center The central location in the school where instructional materials and media are stored, organized, and accessed by students and staff.

Learning station (LS) Like a learning center, except that where each learning center is distinct and unrelated to others, learning stations are sequenced or in some way linked to one another.

Learning style The way a person learns best in a given situation.

Least restrictive environment (LRE) Under Public Law 94-142, the Education for All Handicapped Children Act—IDEA emphasized the normalization of the educational environment for students with disabilities. The legislation requires provision of an environment that is as normal as possible.

Lesson A subdivision of a unit, usually taught in a single class period or, on occasion, for two or three successive periods.

Looping An arrangement in which the cohort of students and teachers remain together as a group for several or for all the years a child is at a particular school. Also referred to as *multiyear grouping*, *multiyear instruction*, *multiyear placement*, and *teacher-student progression*.

M

Magnet school A school that specializes in a particular academic area, such as science, mathematics and technology, the arts, or international relations. Also referred to as a *theme school*.

Mainstreaming Placing an exceptional child in regular education classrooms for all or part of the school day.

Mandala A diagram, usually circular, with spiritual and ritual significance.

Mastery learning The concept that a student should master the content of one lesson before moving on to the content of the next.

Measurement The process of collecting and interpreting data.

Mentoring One-on-one coaching, tutoring, or guidance to facilitate learning.

Metacognition Planning, monitoring, and evaluating one's own thinking. Also known as *reflective abstraction*.

Micro peer-teaching (MPT) Teaching a limited objective for a brief period to a small group of peers for the purpose of evaluation and improvement of particular teaching skills.

Microcultures Also referred to as microcultural groups, subcultures, or subsocieties. Groups whose members share certain cultural patterns. Individuals' cultural identities are based on their identity with or membership in a variety of microcultures including race, ethnicity, religion, gender, age, socioeconomic status, ability, and language.

Middle grades Grades 5 through 8.

Middle-level education Any school unit between elementary and high school.

Middle school A school that has been planned and organized especially for students of ages 10 to 14.

Minds-on learning Learning in which the learner is intellectually active, thinking about what is being learned.

Misconception Faulty understanding of a major idea or concept. Also known as a *naïve theory* and *conceptual misunderstanding*.

Modeling The teacher's direct and indirect demonstration, by actions and by words, of the behaviors expected of students.

Multicultural education A deliberate attempt to help students understand facts, generalizations, attitudes, and behaviors derived from their own ethnic roots as well as others. In this process, students unlearn racism and biases and recognize the interdependent fabric of society, giving due acknowledgment for contributions made by its members.

Multilevel instruction See *multitasking*.

Multilevel teaching See *multitasking*.

Multimedia program The combined use of sound, video, and graphics for instruction.

Multiple intelligences A theory of several different intelligences, as opposed to just one general intelligence; intelligences that have been described are verbal/linguistic, musical, logical/mathematical, naturalist, visual/spatial, bodily/kinesthetic, interpersonal, and intrapersonal.

Multipurpose board A writing board with a smooth plastic surface used with special marking pens rather than chalk. Sometimes called a visual aid panel, the board may have a steel backing and then can be used as a magnetic board as well as a screen for projecting visuals.

Multitasking The simultaneous use of several levels of teaching and learning in the same classroom, with students working on different objectives or different tasks leading to the same objective. Also called *multilevel teaching*.

N

Naïve theory See *misconception.*

National Education Association (NEA) The nation's oldest professional organization of teachers, founded in 1857 as the National Teachers Association and changed in 1879 to its present name. Recently merged in at least two states (Montana and Minnesota) with the American Federation of Teachers.

No Child Left Behind (NCLB) Landmark legislation that promises to improve student achievement and change the culture of America's schools while providing equal educational opportunity for all students. It became law on January 8, 2002.

Normal school The first teacher education programs designed to prepare teachers to teach.

Norm-referenced Individual performance is judged relative to overall performance of the group (e.g., grading on a curve), as opposed to being criterion-referenced.

O

Objectives Instructional objectives are statements describing what the student will be able to do upon completion of the instructional experience.

Orientation set See *advance organizer.*

Overhead projector A teaching tool that projects light through objects that are transparent.

Overlapping A teacher behavior where the teacher is able to attend to more than one matter at once.

Overt behavior A behavior that is outwardly observable.

P

Partnership school A school that has entered into a partnership agreement with community business and industry to link school studies with the workplace.

Peer-tutoring An instructional strategy that places students in a tutorial role in which one student helps another learn.

Performance assessment See *authentic assessment.*

Performance-based instruction Instruction designed around the instruction and assessment of student achievement against specified and predetermined objectives.

Performance objective See *behavioral objective.*

Phonics The application of sound-symbol relationships to the teaching of reading.

Podcasts Audio or audiovisual streams archived on the Internet that can be accessed from any computer or downloaded and transferred to an MP3.

Portfolio assessment An alternative approach to evaluation that assembles representative samples of a student's work over time as a basis for assessment.

Positive reinforcer A means of encouraging desired student behaviors by rewarding those behaviors when they occur.

Preassessment Diagnostic assessment of what students know or think they know prior to the instruction.

Pre-service teacher Term used when referring to teachers in training, as opposed to in-service teachers; teachers who are employed.

Primary sources Materials, information, and accounts provided by witnesses or recorders that are firsthand accounts of events, practices, or conditions. They may include diaries, letters, reports, photographs, creative works, newspaper articles, and so on.

Probationary teacher An untenured teacher. After a designated number of years in the same district, usually three, on rehire the probationary teacher receives a tenure contract.

Probing question Similar to a clarifying question, the probing question requires student thinking to go beyond superficial first-answer or single-word responses.

Procedure A statement telling the student how to accomplish a task.

Psychomotor domain The domain of learning that involves locomotor behaviors.

Q

Question-answer relationship (QAR) A strategy used to question students about reading material that involves asking questions and providing one of three types of cues: "right there," "search and think," or "on your own."

R

Race to the Top Under President Obama, states participated in a competitive grant program to support innovation and reform in an effort to improve student achievement.

Realia Real objects used as visual props during instruction, such as political campaign buttons, plants, memorabilia, art, balls, and so forth.

Reciprocal teaching A form of collaborative teaching in which the teacher and the students share the teaching responsibility and all are involved in asking questions, clarifying, predicting, and summarizing.

Recording Pens These sophisticated pens have an embedded computer and digital recorder that allow students to record what the teacher or classmates say and convert drawings and handwritten notes to text.

Reflection The conscious process of mentally replaying experiences.

Reflective abstraction See *metacognition.*

Relational Aggression A type of covert aggression or bullying often used by female adolescents to hurt an individual's social status and/or control her relationships.

Reliability In measurement, the consistency with which an item or instrument is measured over time.

Response to Intervention (RTI) A method of intervention designed to provide early, systematic assistance to students experiencing academic difficulty.

Rubric An outline of the criteria used to assess a student's work.

Rules In classroom management, rules are the standards of expectation for classroom behavior.

S

Schema (plural: schemata) A mental construct by which the learner organizes his or her perceptions of situations and knowledge.

School-within-a-school Sometimes referred to as a *house*, *cluster*, *village*, *pod*, or *family*, it is a teaching arrangement in which one team of teachers is assigned to work with the same group of about 125 students for a common block of time, for the entire school day, or, in some instances, for all the years those students are at that school.

Search engines These special websites on the World Wide Web compile like websites to aid users to find and select information.

Secondary school Traditionally, any school housing students for any combination of grades 7 through 12.

Self-contained classroom Commonly used in the primary grades, it is a grouping pattern in which one teacher teaches all or most all subjects to one group of children.

Self-paced learning See *individualized learning.*

Senior high school Usually a high school that houses only students in grades 9 through12 or 10 through 12.

Sequencing Arranging ideas in logical order.

Service learning A method of teaching, learning, and reflecting that combines academic classroom curriculum with meaningful community service.

Sheltered Instruction Observation Protocol (SIOP) A research-based model of sheltered instruction that promotes the teaching of content to English Language Learners in strategic ways that make subject matter concepts comprehensible while promoting the students' English language development.

Simulation An abstraction or simplification of a real-life situation.

Skype A software application that allows users to talk over the Internet by voice and video as well as chat over the Internet.

Social networking Sites like Twitter and Facebook allow users to post pictures, video clips, and collect friends on their sites.

Socratic questioning Named for the Athenian teacher, Socrates, a questioning strategy in which a teacher asks students a series of questions and encourages students to develop their own conclusions and draw their own inferences.

Special needs student See *exceptional child.*

Special transitional school A one-year school designed to help recent immigrant students feel welcome and self-assured and to succeed in learning to read and write in English.

SQ3R A study strategy; students survey the reading, create questions, read to answer the questions, recite the answers, and review the original material.

SQ4R Similar to SQ3R but with the addition of recording; the students survey the reading, ask questions about what was read, read to answer the questions, recite the answers, record important items in their notebooks, and then review it all.

Standards See *curriculum standards.*

Stereotypes Absolute and inflexible descriptions of groups of individuals that ignore individual differences.

Student teaching A field experience component of teacher preparation, traditionally the culminating experience, where the teacher candidate practices teaching children while under the supervision of a credentialed teacher and a university supervisor.

Summative assessment Assessment of learning after instruction is completed.

T

Teacher leader See *lead teacher.*

Teaching See *instruction.*

Teaching style The way teachers teach; their distinctive mannerisms complemented by their choices of teaching behaviors and strategies.

Teaching team A team of two or more teachers who work together to provide instruction to the same group of students, either by alternating the instruction or by team teaching simultaneously.

Team teaching Two or more teachers working together to provide instruction to a group of students.

Tech prep high school A school that has a 4–2 coordinated curriculum that is articulated from grades 9 through 12 to the first two years of college, leading to an associate of applied science degree.

Tenured teacher After serving a designated number of years in the same school district (usually three) as a probationary teacher, on rehire the teacher receives a tenure contract, which means that the teacher is automatically rehired each year thereafter unless the contract is revoked by either the district or the teacher and for specific and legal reasons.

Terminal behavior That which has been learned as a direct result of instruction.

Thematic unit A unit of instruction built on a central theme or concept.

Theme school See *magnet school.*

Think-time Providing students with sufficient time to take things in and think about them before expecting them to react to them. See also *wait time.*

This We Believe: Keys to Educating Young Adolescents A position paper where the Association for Middle Level Education highlights the 16 characteristics of successful schools for adolescents ages 10 to 15.

Tiered Assignments Allow classroom teachers to teach concepts, skills, or ideas to a class of diverse learners by differentiating instruction to meet their individual needs.

Tracking The practice of voluntary or involuntary placement of students in different programs or courses according to their ability and prior academic performance. See also *ability grouping.*

Traditional teaching Teacher-centered direct instruction, typically using lectures, discussions, textbooks, and worksheets.

Transition In a lesson, the planned procedures that move student thinking from one idea to the next or that move their actions from one activity to the next. With reference to schooling, transitions are the times when a student moves from one level of school to the next.

21st Century Skills There are multiple descriptions of this term, but most include some of the following skills: life skills, workforce skills, technological skills, interpersonal skills, applied skills, and noncognitive skills.

U

Understanding by Design (backwards design) Invented by Grant Wiggins and Jay McTighe, this instructional method has teachers start with the end in mind and focus on the enduring understandings they want their students to develop.

Unit A major subdivision of a course, comprising planned instruction about some central theme, topic, issue, or problem for a period of several days to several weeks.

Untracking See *detracking.*

V

Validity In measurement, the degree to which an item or instrument measures that which is intended to measure.

Village See *school-within-a-school.*

W

Wait time In the use of questioning, the period of silence between the time a question is asked and the inquirer (teacher) does something, such as repeats the question, rephrases the question, calls on a particular student, answers the question him- or herself, or asks another question. Also referred to as *think-time.*

Web Quests Designed by Bernie Dodge in 1995, these inquiry-based lessons are set up so that the majority if not all of the information and resources that the students need to access can be located on the Web.

Whole-language learning A point of view with a focus on seeking or creating meaning that encourages language production, risk taking, independence in producing language, and the use of a wide variety of print materials in authentic reading and writing situations.

Wikipedia Started in 2001, this is s free online encyclopedia that groups information in numerous categories on myriad topics.

Withitness The teacher's timely ability to intervene and redirect a student's inappropriate behavior.

Writeboard A Web-based free tool that allows multiple students to all be working on a document at the same time and share and revise their collaborative creation.

Y

Year-round school A school that operates as is traditional, that is, with 180 school days, but the days are spread over 12 months rather than the usual 10. Most common is the 9-weeks-on, 3-weeks-off format.

Young adolescent The 10- to 14-year-old experiencing the developmental stage of early adolescence.

Name/Author Index

Subject Index